LEGACY

of ASHES

ALSO BY TIM WEINER

Blank Check: The Pentagon's Black Budget

Betrayal: The Story of Aldrich Ames, an American Spy
(with David Johnston and Neil A. Lewis)

LEGACY
of ASHES

The History of the

CIA

TIM WEINER

ALLEN LANE
an imprint of
PENGUIN BOOKS

For Kate, Emma, and Ruby

ALLEN LANE

Published by the Penguin Group
Penguin Books Ltd, 80 Strand, London WC2R 0RL, England
Penguin Group (USA) Inc., 375 Hudson Street, New York, New York 10014, USA
Penguin Group (Canada), 90 Eglinton Avenue East, Suite 700, Toronto, Ontario, Canada M4P 2Y3
(a division of Pearson Penguin Canada Inc.)
Penguin Ireland, 25 St Stephen's Green, Dublin 2, Ireland (a division of Penguin Books Ltd)
Penguin Group (Australia), 250 Camberwell Road, Camberwell,
Victoria 3124, Australia (a division of Pearson Australia Group Pty Ltd)
Penguin Books India Pvt Ltd, 11 Community Centre,
Panchsheel Park, New Delhi – 110 017, India
Penguin Group (NZ), 67 Apollo Drive, Rosedale, North Shore 0632, New Zealand
(a division of Pearson New Zealand Ltd)
Penguin Books (South Africa) (Pty) Ltd, 24 Sturdee Avenue,
Rosebank, Johannesburg 2196, South Africa

Penguin Books Ltd, Registered Offices: 80 Strand, London WC2R 0RL, England

www.penguin.com

First published in the United States by Doubleday, a division of
Random House, Inc., New York 2007
First published in Great Britain with a Foreword by Allen Lane 2007
2

Copyright © Tim Weiner, 2007

The moral right of the author has been asserted

Printed in Great Britain by Clays Ltd, St Ives plc

A CIP catalogue record for this book is available from the British Library

HARDBACK
978–1–846–14046–4

TRADE PAPERBACK
978–1–846–14064–8

www.greenpenguin.co.uk

CONTENTS

There are no secrets that time does not reveal.

—Jean Racine, *Britannicus* (1669)

Legacy of Ashes is the record of the first sixty years of the Central Intelligence Agency. It describes how the most powerful country in the history of Western civilization has failed to create a first-rate spy service. That failure constitutes a danger to the national security of the United States.

Intelligence is secret action aimed at understanding or changing what goes on abroad. President Dwight D. Eisenhower called it "a distasteful but vital necessity." A nation that wants to project its power beyond its borders needs to see over the horizon, to know what is coming, to prevent attacks against its people. It must anticipate surprise. Without a strong, smart, sharp intelligence service, presidents and generals alike can become blind and crippled. But throughout its history as a superpower, the United States has not had such a service.

History, Edward Gibbon wrote in *The Decline and Fall of the Roman Empire,* is "little more than the register of crimes, follies, and misfortunes of mankind." The annals of the Central Intelligence Agency are filled with folly and misfortune, along with acts of bravery and cunning. They are replete with fleeting successes and long-lasting failures abroad. They are marked by political battles and power struggles at home. The agency's triumphs have saved some blood and treasure. Its mistakes have squandered both. They have proved fatal for legions of American soldiers and foreign agents; some three thousand Americans who died in New York, Washington, and Pennsylvania on September 11, 2001; and three thousand more who have died since then in Iraq and Afghanistan. The one crime of lasting consequence has been the CIA's inability to carry out its central mission: informing the president of what is happening in the world.

The United States had no intelligence to speak of when World War II began, and next to none a few weeks after the war ended. A mad rush to demobilize left behind a few hundred men who had a few years' experience in the world of secrets and the will to go on fighting a new enemy. "All major powers except the United States have had for a long time past permanent worldwide intelligence services, reporting directly to the highest echelons of their Government," General William J. Donovan, the commander of the wartime Office of Strategic Services, warned President Truman in August 1945. "Prior to the present war, the United States had no foreign secret intelligence service. It never has had and does not now have a coordinated intelligence system." Tragically, it still does not have one.

The CIA was supposed to become that system. But the blueprint for the agency was a hasty sketch. It was no cure for a chronic American weakness: secrecy and deception were not our strengths. The collapse of the British Empire left the United States as the sole force able to oppose Soviet communism, and America desperately needed to know those enemies, to provide foresight to presidents, and to fight fire with fire when called upon to light the fuse. The mission of the CIA, above all, was to keep the president forewarned against surprise attack, a second Pearl Harbor.

The agency's ranks were filled with thousands of patriotic Americans in the 1950s. Many were brave and battle-hardened. Some had wisdom. Few really knew the enemy. Where understanding failed, presidents ordered the CIA to change the course of history through covert action. "The conduct of political and psychological warfare in peacetime was a new art," wrote Gerald Miller, then the CIA's covert-operations chief for Western Europe. "Some of the techniques were known but doctrine and experience were lacking." The CIA's covert operations were by and large blind stabs in the dark. The agency's only course was to learn by doing— by making mistakes in battle. The CIA then concealed its failures abroad, lying to Presidents Eisenhower and Kennedy. It told those lies to preserve its standing in Washington. The truth, said Don Gregg, a skilled cold-war station chief, was that the agency at the height of its powers had a great reputation and a terrible record.

Like the American public, the agency dissented at its peril during the

Vietnam War. Like the American press, it discovered that its reporting was rejected if it did not fit the preconceptions of presidents. The CIA was rebuked and scorned by Presidents Johnson, Nixon, Ford, and Carter. None of them understood how the agency worked. They took office "with the expectation that intelligence could solve every problem, or that it could not do anything right, and then moved to the opposite view," notes a former deputy director of central intelligence, Richard J. Kerr. "Then they settled down and vacillated from one extreme to the other."

To survive as an institution in Washington, the agency above all had to have the president's ear. But it soon learned that it was dangerous to tell him what he did not want to hear. The CIA's analysts learned to march in lockstep, conforming to conventional wisdom. They misapprehended the intentions and capabilities of our enemies, miscalculated the strength of communism, and misjudged the threat of terrorism.

The supreme goal of the CIA during the cold war was to steal Soviet secrets by recruiting spies, but the CIA never possessed a single one who had deep insight into the workings of the Kremlin. The number of Soviet spies with important information to reveal—all of them volunteers, not recruits—could be counted on the fingers of two hands. And all of them died, captured and executed by Moscow. Almost all had been betrayed by officers of the CIA's Soviet division who were spying for the other side, under Presidents Reagan and George H. W. Bush. Under Reagan, the CIA set off on misconceived third-world missions, selling arms to Iran's Revolutionary Guards to finance a war in Central America, breaking the law and squandering what trust remained reposed in it. More grievously, it missed the fatal weakness of its main enemy.

It fell to machines, not men, to understand the other side. As the technology of espionage expanded its horizons, the CIA's vision grew more and more myopic. Spy satellites enabled it to count Soviet weapons. They did not deliver the crucial information that communism was crumbling. The CIA's foremost experts never saw the enemy until after the cold war was over. The agency had bled the Soviets by pouring billions of dollars of weapons into Afghanistan to help fight the Red Army's occupying forces. That was an epic success. But it failed to see that the Islamic warriors it supported would soon take aim at the United States, and when that understanding came, the agency failed to act. That was an epochal failure.

The unity of purpose that held the CIA together during the cold war came undone in the 1990s, under President Clinton. The agency still had people who strove to understand the world, but their ranks were far too thin. There were still talented officers who dedicated themselves to serving the United States abroad, but their numbers were far too few. The FBI had more agents in New York than the CIA had officers abroad. By the end of the century, the agency was no longer a fully functioning and independent intelligence service. It was becoming a second-echelon field office for the Pentagon, weighing tactics for battles that never came, not strategies for the struggle ahead. It was powerless to prevent the second Pearl Harbor.

After the attacks on New York and Washington, the agency sent a small skilled cadre of covert operators into Afghanistan and Pakistan to hunt down the leaders of al Qaeda. It then forfeited its role as a reliable source of secret information when it handed the White House false reports on the existence of weapons of mass destruction in Iraq. It had delivered a ton of reportage based on an ounce of intelligence. President George W. Bush and his administration in turn misused the agency once proudly run by his father, turning it into a paramilitary police force abroad and a paralyzed bureaucracy at headquarters. Bush casually pronounced a political death sentence upon the CIA in 2004 when he said that the agency was "just guessing" about the course of the war in Iraq. No president had ever publicly dismissed the CIA that way.

Its centrality in the American government ended with the dissolution of the office of director of central intelligence in 2005. Now the CIA must be rebuilt if it is to survive. That task will take years. The challenge of understanding the world as it is has overwhelmed three generations of CIA officers. Few among the new generation have mastered the intricacies of foreign lands, much less the political culture of Washington. In turn, almost every president, almost every Congress, and almost every director of central intelligence since the 1960s has proved incapable of grasping the mechanics of the CIA. Most have left the agency in worse shape than they found it. Their failures have handed future generations, in the words of President Eisenhower, "a legacy of ashes." We are back where we began sixty years ago, in a state of disarray.

Legacy of Ashes sets out to show how it has come to pass that the United States now lacks the intelligence it will need in the years ahead. It is drawn from the words, the ideas, and the deeds set forth in the files of the American national-security establishment. They record what our leaders really said, really wanted, and really did when they projected power abroad. This book is based on my reading of more than fifty thousand documents, primarily from the archives of the CIA, the White House, and the State Department; more than two thousand oral histories of American intelligence officers, soldiers, and diplomats; and more than three hundred interviews conducted since 1987 with CIA officers and veterans, including ten directors of central intelligence. Extensive endnotes amplify the text.

This book is on the record—no anonymous sources, no blind quotations, no hearsay. It is the first history of the CIA compiled entirely from firsthand reporting and primary documents. It is, by its nature, incomplete: no president, no director of central intelligence, and certainly no outsider can know everything about the agency. What I have written here is not the whole truth, but to the best of my ability, it is nothing but the truth.

I hope it may serve as a warning. No republic in history has lasted longer than three hundred years, and this nation may not long endure as a great power unless it finds the eyes to see things as they are in the world. That once was the mission of the Central Intelligence Agency.

FOREWORD TO THE BRITISH EDITION

We Americans inherited from the British our language, our laws, our high culture, and our drive for empire. Whether this last legacy will long endure is now an open question. An Englishwoman I know, born in India, was the seventh generation in her family to come into the world as a child of British foreign intelligence. Her forebears and their countrymen did something the Americans have never accomplished: they lived in the nations they presumed to control. They learned to speak in foreign tongues, and they became part of the landscape on the peripheries of their power. They did not rule merely by fear and force. They were fascinated by the people they sought to control. Their empire was sustained through an intertwining of intelligence, diplomacy, military technology and economic power that first took root in the realm of Elizabeth I and flourished until the reign of Elizabeth II.

America had no such tradition. When the United States was attacked at Pearl Harbor, the nation had no intelligence service. We were unprepared to conduct a global war, and unable to gather insight on our enemies. "The U.S. fought the first year of the war in Europe entirely on the basis of British intelligence," said President Dwight D. Eisenhower, the Supreme Allied Commander. British special operations soldiers schooled the Americans in the arts of secret warfare; British spies taught Yank tyros their tradecraft. We were eager students. The roots of the Central Intelligence Agency were nurtured in British soil. And when the sun began setting on the British empire in 1947, the CIA took shape as a force to bear the burden slipping from English hands. "America bestrides the world like a colossus," the Labour politician Harold Laski wrote that year, and "neither Rome at the height of its power nor Great Britain in the period of economic supremacy enjoyed an influence so direct, so profound, or so pervasive."

With that passing came a new American responsibility for anti-communist aspirations from the Baltic to the Balkans. The American intelligence officer Jim McCargar put it well: "The British had taken the position that they had lodged and supported the governments-in-exile in London during the Second World War. 'Your turn,' they said to us. 'We're not going to do it again. All yours.'" Exiles from Eastern Europe—former prime ministers, former foreign ministers, former finance ministers—came seeking secret support from the CIA. It was the first duty of the new clandestine American service to try to turn these émigrés into a fighting force. Many of the important American covert operations of the early cold war depended on the remaining possessions of the British Empire—a safe house in Malta, an underground in Iran. "Whenever we're in trouble," said the first chief of the CIA's clandestine service, Frank Wisner, "the British always have a little piece of territory that's very useful."

As the cold war became a global battle, with spies and soldiers skirmishing from the Mediterranean to the South China Sea, the Anglo–American alliance became strained. In 1953, their joint operation to overthrow the government of Iran began as a gleam in Winston Churchill's eye and came perilously close to ending in a fiasco. In 1956, Her Majesty's government thought it best not to tell Washington about the coming attack on the Suez Canal and the government of Egypt. (Nor did the CIA see it coming.) By the late 1950s, the imperial dreams of re-establishing British power under American guidance in the Middle East came undone in a series of failed plots.

Anglo–American covert action in the cold war reached a nadir in the muddy streets of British Guiana, one of the last outposts of British imperialism in the western hemisphere. Together we subverted the elected leader and installed a corrupt puppet leader in 1964. Few Americans could have found that godforsaken country on a map, much less grasped the crucial importance that London and Washington ascribed to it. By then, American ambitions in south-east Asia were diverging from British aspirations; London's refusal to support the American adventure in Vietnam with combat troops put an end to joint covert operations for years to come. Penny-pinching Labour and Tory leaders alike cut back British intelligence; from the early 1970s onward, SIS suffered a steady deterioration in its abilities to conduct espionage, assay secret intelligence, and validate the work of their spies.

American intelligence suffered much the same in the seventies, though the proximate causes were quite different. The Agency had been spying on American citizens in contravention of its charter as a foreign intelligence service. It had plotted operations that, in the tenor of the times, seemed to violate both the law and common sense. The United States Congress tried to investigate, and for a few months the CIA's files were ransacked as if its headquarters were a conquered city. The Agency was diminished and its role as a purely secret Presidential power was forever altered. Allied services such as the SIS prudently kept their distance during these years.

While the special relationship took other forms, notably in intelligence-sharing from a growing global electronic-eavesdropping aegis, the operational relationship did not revive until Ronald Reagan and Margaret Thatcher teamed up to bleed the Russian bear by shipping weapons to Afghanistan in 1981. Theirs was a marriage of true minds, and with the notable exception of the Falklands, for a few years in the mid-1980s CIA and SIS were partners on more than a few of the front lines of the cold war. But with the end of that struggle came a further diminishing in the ambitions and the skills of American and British intelligence. In the 1990s, CIA and SIS both lost a quarter of their payrolls, experienced a sharp decrease in expertise and institutional knowledge and failed to assess the impact of these losses on secret intelligence in the information age.

The abridgement of intelligence on both sides of the Atlantic made it possible for both services to conclude that Saddam Hussein had a formidable arsenal that justified a war in 2002. As Lord Butler's 2004 inquiry concluded, this farce was in part the result of a British secret service whose reporting powers were placed in the hands of feckless youngsters while more experienced officers were assigned to sharpen the Service's operational teeth. "Their ability to challenge the validity of cases and their reporting was correspondingly reduced," the report concluded. SIS and CIA produced deeply flawed reporting—and their respective leaders lacked the authority to prevent those reports from being further distorted to make their government's case for war. Both services violated the fundamental requirement to speak truth to power. The CIA's performance resulted in the abolition of the post of Director of Central Intelligence in 2005, a decision so hastily implemented that it will be years before its consequences are clear.

While the goals of American and British intelligence may be similar, the differences are fundamental. In the United States, the legislature theoretically has far more power to control the CIA than the British parliament holds over the SIS. But for much of the past sixty years Congress has overlooked, rather than overseen, the Agency. In the United States, there is nothing—so far—resembling an Official Secrets Act. Instead, the CIA continually fights rearguard battles against the declassification of documents dating back to the 1940s. In theory, the United States has a thirty-year statute of limitations on secrets. In reality, it is observed in the breach, while the British have successfully imposed a fifty-year limit.

In theory, Americans live under laws demanding freedom of information. In reality, our secrets often scare us. This book is in part the annals of the official secrets of the CIA, and it may serve to explain why our history appalls us.

Churchill once said that the imperial goal of Great Britain was to give peace to warring tribes, to administer justice, and to increase peoples' capacities for pleasure while diminishing their chances of pain. The history of the CIA reflects how distant such aims appear to Americans. We have yet to come to terms with the operations of secret intelligence in our open democracy. We have been unable to create a well-run clandestine service. We seem to lack the ability to build one. Without trustworthy intelligence, we cannot run a global empire. *Legacy of Ashes* sets out to explain how that has come to pass.

PART ONE

"In the Beginning, We Knew Nothing"

The CIA Under Truman

1945 to 1953

---

1. "INTELLIGENCE MUST BE GLOBAL AND TOTALITARIAN"

All Harry Truman wanted was a newspaper.

Catapulted into the White House by the death of President Franklin D. Roosevelt on April 12, 1945, Truman knew nothing about the development of the atomic bomb or the intentions of his Soviet allies. He needed information to use his power.

"When I took over," he wrote in a letter to a friend years later, "the President had no means of coordinating the intelligence from around the world." Roosevelt had created the Office of Strategic Services, under the command of General William J. Donovan, as America's wartime intelligence agency. But Donovan's OSS was never built to last. When the new Central Intelligence Agency arose from its ashes, Truman wanted it to serve him solely as a global news service, delivering daily bulletins. "It was not intended as a 'Cloak & Dagger Outfit'!" he wrote. "It was intended merely as a center for keeping the President informed on what was going on in the world." He insisted that he never wanted the CIA "to act as a spy organization. That was never the intention when it was organized."

His vision was subverted from the start.

———

"In a global and totalitarian war," General Donovan believed, "intelligence must be global and totalitarian." On November 18, 1944, he had written to President Roosevelt proposing that the United States create a peacetime "Central Intelligence Service." He had started sketching his plan the year before, at the behest of Lieutenant General Walter Bedell Smith, chief of staff to General Dwight D. Eisenhower, who wanted to know how the OSS would become part of the military establishment of the United States. Donovan told the president that he could learn the "capabilities, intentions and activities of foreign nations" while running "subversive operations abroad" against America's enemies. The OSS had never been stronger than thirteen thousand members, smaller than a single army division. But the service Donovan envisioned would be its own army, a force skillfully combating communism, defending America from attack, and serving up secrets for the White House. He urged the president to "lay the keel of the ship at once," and he aimed to be its captain.

Nicknamed "Wild Bill" after a fast but errant pitcher who managed the New York Yankees from 1915 to 1917, Donovan was a brave old soldier—he had won the Congressional Medal of Honor for heroism in the trenches of France during World War I—but a poor politician. Very few generals and admirals trusted him. They were appalled by his idea of making a spy service out of a scattershot collection of Wall Street brokers, Ivy League eggheads, soldiers of fortune, ad men, news men, stunt men, second-story men, and con men.

The OSS had developed a uniquely American cadre of intelligence analysts, but Donovan and his star officer, Allen W. Dulles, were enthralled by espionage and sabotage, skills at which Americans were amateurs. Donovan depended on British intelligence to school his men in the dark arts. The bravest of the OSS, the ones who inspired legends, were the men who jumped behind enemy lines, running guns, blowing up bridges, plotting against the Nazis with the French and the Balkan resistance movements. In the last year of the war, with his forces spread throughout Europe, North Africa, and Asia, Donovan wanted to drop his agents directly into Germany. He did, and they died. Of the twenty-one two-man teams that went in, only one was ever heard from again. These were the kinds of missions General Donovan dreamed up daily—some daring, some deluded.

"His imagination was unlimited," said his right-hand man, David K. E. Bruce, later the American ambassador to France, Germany, and England. "Ideas were his plaything. Excitement made him snort like a racehorse. Woe to the officer who turned down a project, because, on its face, it seemed ridiculous, or at least unusual. For painful weeks under his command I tested the possibility of using bats taken from concentrations in Western caves to destroy Tokyo"—dropping them into the sky with incendiary bombs strapped to their backs. That was the spirit of the OSS.

President Roosevelt always had his doubts about Donovan. Early in 1945, he had ordered his chief White House military aide, Colonel Richard Park, Jr., to conduct a secret investigation into the wartime operations of the OSS. As Park began his work, leaks from the White House created headlines in New York, Chicago, and Washington, warning that Donovan wanted to create an "American Gestapo." When the stories broke, the president urged Donovan to shove his plans under the rug. On March 6, 1945, the Joint Chiefs of Staff formally shelved them.

They wanted a new spy service to serve the Pentagon, not the president. What they had in mind was a clearinghouse staffed by colonels and clerks, distilling information gathered by attachés and diplomats and spies, for the benefit of four-star commanders. Thus began a battle for control of American intelligence that went on for three generations.

"AN EXTREMELY DANGEROUS THING"

The OSS had little standing at home, and less inside the Pentagon. The organization was barred from seeing the most important intercepted communications from Japan and Germany. Senior American military officers thought an independent civilian intelligence service run by Donovan, with direct access to the president, would be "an extremely dangerous thing in a democracy," in the words of Major General Clayton Bissell, the assistant chief of staff for military intelligence.

These were many of the same men who had slept through Pearl Harbor. Well before dawn on December 7, 1941, the American military had broken some of Japan's codes. It knew an attack might be coming, but it never imagined Japan would take so desperate a gamble. The broken code was too secret to share with commanders in the field. Rivalries within the military meant that information was divided, hoarded, and scattered. Because no one possessed all the pieces of the puzzle, no one

saw the big picture. Not until after the war was over did Congress investigate how the nation had been taken by surprise, and not until then was
it clear that the country needed a new way to defend itself.

Before Pearl Harbor, American intelligence covering great swaths of
the globe could be found in a short row of wooden filing cabinets at the
State Department. A few dozen ambassadors and military attachés were
its sole sources of information. In the spring of 1945, the United States
knew next to nothing about the Soviet Union, and little more about the
rest of the world.

Franklin Roosevelt was the only man who could revive Donovan's
dream of a far-seeing, all-powerful American intelligence service. When
Roosevelt died on April 12, Donovan despaired for the future. After sitting up half the night grieving, he came downstairs at the Ritz Hotel, his
favorite haunt in liberated Paris, and had a gloomy breakfast with
William J. Casey, an OSS officer and a future director of central intelligence.

"What do you think it means for the organization?" Casey asked.

"I'm afraid it's probably the end," Donovan said.

That same day, Colonel Park submitted his top secret report on the
OSS to the new president. The report, fully declassified only after the
cold war ended, was a political murder weapon, honed by the military
and sharpened by J. Edgar Hoover, the FBI director since 1924; Hoover
despised Donovan and harbored his own ambitions to run a worldwide
intelligence service. Park's work destroyed the possibility of the OSS continuing as part of the American government, punctured the romantic
myths that Donovan created to protect his spies, and instilled in Harry
Truman a deep and abiding distrust of secret intelligence operations. The
OSS had done "serious harm to the citizens, business interests, and national interests of the United States," the report said.

Park admitted no important instance in which the OSS had helped to
win the war, only mercilessly listing the ways in which it had failed. The
training of its officers had been "crude and loosely organized." British
intelligence commanders regarded American spies as "putty in their
hands." In China, the nationalist leader Chiang Kai-shek had manipulated the OSS to his own ends. Germany's spies had penetrated OSS operations all over Europe and North Africa. The Japanese embassy in
Lisbon had discovered the plans of OSS officers to steal its code books—
and as a consequence the Japanese changed their codes, which "resulted

in a complete blackout of vital military information" in the summer of 1943. One of Park's informants said, "How many American lives in the Pacific represent the cost of this stupidity on the part of OSS is unknown." Faulty intelligence provided by the OSS after the fall of Rome in June 1944 led thousands of French troops into a Nazi trap on the island of Elba, Park wrote, and "as a result of these errors and miscalculations of the enemy forces by OSS, some 1,100 French troops were killed."

The report personally attacked Donovan. It said the general had lost a briefcase at a cocktail party in Bucharest that was "turned over to the Gestapo by a Rumanian dancer." His hiring and promotion of senior officers rested not on merit but on an old-boy network of connections from Wall Street and the Social Register. He had sent detachments of men to lonely outposts such as Liberia and forgotten about them. He had mistakenly dropped commandos into neutral Sweden. He had sent guards to protect a captured German ammunition dump in France and then blown them up.

Colonel Park acknowledged that Donovan's men had conducted some successful sabotage missions and rescues of downed American pilots. He said the deskbound research and analysis branch of OSS had done "an outstanding job," and he concluded that the analysts might find a place at the State Department after the war. But the rest of the OSS would have to go. "The almost hopeless compromise of OSS personnel," he warned, "makes their use as a secret intelligence agency in the postwar world inconceivable."

After V-E Day, Donovan went back to Washington to try to save his spy service. A month of mourning for President Roosevelt was giving way to a mad scramble for power in Washington. In the Oval Office on May 14, Harry Truman listened for less than fifteen minutes as Donovan made his proposal to hold communism in check by undermining the Kremlin. The president summarily dismissed him.

All summer long, Donovan fought back in Congress and in the press. Finally, on August 25, he told Truman that he had to choose between knowledge and ignorance. The United States "does not now have a coordinated intelligence system," he warned. "The defects and the dangers of this situation have been generally recognized."

Donovan had hoped that he could sweet-talk Truman, a man he had always treated with cavalier disdain, into creating the CIA. But he had misread his own president. Truman had decided that Donovan's plan had the earmarks of a Gestapo. On September 20, 1945, six weeks after he dropped America's atomic bombs on Japan, the president of the United States fired Donovan and ordered the OSS to disband in ten days. America's spy service was abolished.

2. "THE LOGIC OF FORCE"

In the rubble of Berlin, Allen Dulles, the ranking OSS officer in Germany, had found a splendid and well-staffed mansion for his new headquarters in the summer of 1945. His favorite lieutenant, Richard Helms, began trying to spy on the Soviets.

"What you have to remember," Helms said half a century later, "is that in the beginning, we knew nothing. Our knowledge of what the other side was up to, their intentions, their capabilities, was nil, or next to it. If you came up with a telephone book or a map of an airfield, that was pretty hot stuff. We were in the dark about a lot of the world."

Helms had been happy to return to Berlin, where he had made his name as a twenty-three-year-old wire service reporter by interviewing Hitler at the 1936 Olympics. He was dumbstruck by the abolition of the OSS. At the outfit's operations center in Berlin, a commandeered sparkling-wine factory, the anger and alcohol flowed freely on the night the order from the president arrived. There would be no central headquarters for American intelligence as Dulles had envisioned. Only a skeleton crew would stay on overseas. Helms simply could not believe the mission could come to an end. He was encouraged a few days later when a message arrived from OSS headquarters in Washington, telling him to hold the fort.

"THE HOLY CAUSE OF CENTRAL INTELLIGENCE"

The message came from Donovan's deputy, Brigadier General John Magruder, a gentleman soldier who had been in the army since 1910. He adamantly believed that without an intelligence service, America's new supremacy in the world would be left to blind chance, or beholden to the British. On September 26, 1945, six days after President Truman signed away the OSS, General Magruder stalked down the endless corridors of the Pentagon. The moment was opportune: the secretary of war, Henry Stimson, had resigned that week, and Stimson had been dead-set against the idea of a CIA. "Seems to me most inadvisable," he had told Donovan a few months earlier. Now General Magruder seized the opening left by Stimson's departure.

He sat down with an old friend of Donovan's, the assistant secretary of war, John McCloy, one of the great movers and shakers of Washington. Together, the two men countermanded the president.

Magruder walked out of the Pentagon that day with an order from McCloy that said, "the continuing operations of OSS must be performed in order to preserve them." That piece of paper kept the hope for a Central Intelligence Agency alive. The spies would stay on duty, under a new name, the Strategic Services Unit, the SSU. McCloy then asked his good friend Robert A. Lovett, the assistant secretary for air war and a future secretary of defense, to set up a secret commission to plot the course for American intelligence—and to tell Harry Truman what had to be done. Magruder confidently informed his men that "the holy cause of central intelligence" would prevail.

Emboldened by the reprieve, Helms set to work in Berlin. He purged officers who had plunged into Berlin's black market, where everything and everyone was for sale—two dozen cartons of Camels, purchased for $12 at the American military PX, bought a 1939 Mercedes-Benz. He searched for German scientists and spies to ferret out to the West, with the aim of denying their skills to the Soviets and putting them to work for the United States. But these tasks soon took second place to the struggle to see the new enemy. By October, "it was very clear our primary target was going to be what the Russians were up to," remembered Tom Polgar, then a twenty-three-year-old officer at the Berlin base. The Soviets were seizing the railroads and co-opting the political parties of eastern Germany. At first the best the American spies could do was to try to track the movement of Soviet military transports to Berlin, giving the Pentagon a sense that someone was trying to keep an eye on the Red Army. Furious at Washington's retreat in the face of the Soviet advance, working against the resistance from the ranking American military men in Berlin, Helms and his men began trying to recruit German police and politicians to establish spy networks in the east. By November, "we were seeing the total takeover by the Russians of the East German system," said Peter Sichel, another twenty-three-year-old SSU officer in Berlin.

The Joint Chiefs of Staff and the forceful secretary of the navy, James V. Forrestal, now began to fear that the Soviets, like the Nazis before them, would move to seize all of Europe—and then push on to the eastern Mediterranean, the Persian Gulf, northern China, and Korea. One false move could lead to a confrontation no one could contain. And as the fear of a new war increased, the future leaders of American intelligence split into two rival camps.

One believed in the slow and patient gathering of secret intelligence through espionage. The other believed in secret warfare—taking the battle to the enemy through covert action. Espionage seeks to know the world. That was Richard Helms. Covert action seeks to change the world. That would be Frank Wisner.

Wisner was the charming son of land-rich Mississippi gentry, a dashing corporate lawyer in a tailored military uniform. In September 1944 he had flown into Bucharest, Romania, as the new OSS station chief. The Red Army and a small American military mission had seized control in the capital, and Wisner's orders were to keep an eye on the Russians. He was in his glory, conspiring with the young King Michael, plotting the rescue of downed Allied airmen, and requisitioning the thirty-room mansion of a Bucharest beer baron. Under its sparkling chandeliers, Russian officers mingled with the Americans, toasting one another with Champagne. Wisner was thrilled—he was one of the first OSS men to bend an elbow with the Russians—and he proudly reported to headquarters that he had made a successful liaison with the Soviet intelligence service.

He had been an American spy for less than a year. The Russians had been at the game for more than two centuries. They already had well-placed agents within the OSS and they quickly infiltrated Wisner's inner circle of Romanian allies and agents. By midwinter, they took control of the capital, herded tens of thousands of Romanians who had German bloodlines into railroad cars, and shipped them eastward to enslavement or death. Wisner watched twenty-seven boxcars filled with human cargo rolling out of Romania. The memory haunted him all his life.

He was a deeply shaken man when he arrived at OSS headquarters in Germany, where he and Helms became uneasy allies. They flew to Washington together in December 1945, and as they talked during the eighteen-hour journey, they realized they had no idea whether the United States would have a clandestine service after they landed.

"AN APPARENTLY BASTARD ORGANIZATION"

In Washington, the battle over the future of American intelligence was growing fierce. The Joint Chiefs of Staff fought for a service firmly under their control. The army and the navy demanded their own. J. Edgar Hoover wanted the FBI to conduct worldwide espionage. The State Department sought dominion. Even the postmaster general weighed in.

General Magruder defined the problem: "Clandestine intelligence operations involve a constant breaking of all the rules," he wrote. "To put it baldly, such operations are necessarily extra-legal and sometimes illegal." He argued, convincingly, that the Pentagon and the State Department could not risk running those missions. A new clandestine service would have to take charge.

But almost no one was left to fill its ranks. "The intelligence collection effort more or less came to a standstill," said Colonel Bill Quinn, General Magruder's executive officer at the Strategic Services Unit. Five of every six OSS veterans had gone back to their old lives. They saw what was left of American intelligence as "transparently jerry-built and transient," Helms said, "an apparently bastard organization with an unpredictable life expectancy." Their number fell by nearly 10,000 in three months, down to 1,967 by the end of 1945. The London, Paris, Rome, Vienna, Madrid, Lisbon, and Stockholm stations lost almost all their officers. Fifteen out of twenty-three Asian outposts closed. On the fourth anniversary of Pearl Harbor, convinced that Truman had run American intelligence off the rails, Allen Dulles returned to his desk at Sullivan and

Cromwell, the New York law firm where his brother John Foster Dulles was a partner. Frank Wisner followed his lead and went back to his own New York law firm, Carter, Ledyard.

The remaining intelligence analysts were dispatched to form a new research bureau at the State Department. They were treated like displaced persons. "I don't suppose there had ever been or could ever be a sadder or more tormented period of my life," wrote Sherman Kent, later a founding father of CIA's directorate of intelligence. The most talented soon left in despair, back to their universities and newspapers. No replacements appeared. There would be no coherent intelligence reporting in the American government for many years to come.

President Truman had relied on his budget director, Harold D. Smith, to oversee the orderly dismantling of the American war machine. But demobilization was turning into disintegration. Smith warned the president on the day he dismembered the OSS that the United States was at risk of returning to the state of innocence that had prevailed before Pearl Harbor. He feared that American intelligence had become "royally bitched up." At a hastily convened White House meeting on January 9, 1946, Admiral William D. Leahy, Truman's crusty military chief of staff, bluntly told the president that "intelligence had been handled in a disgraceful way."

Truman saw he had created a snafu and decided to set it straight. He summoned the deputy director of naval intelligence, Rear Admiral Sidney W. Souers. A reservist, Souers was a Democratic Party stalwart from Missouri, a wealthy businessman who made his money in life insurance and Piggly Wiggly shops, the nation's first self-service supermarkets. He had served on a postwar commission studying the future of intelligence created by Secretary of the Navy James Forrestal, but his sights were set on nothing grander than a swift return to Saint Louis.

Souers discovered to his dismay that the president was going to make him the first director of central intelligence. Admiral Leahy recorded the moment of the investiture in his office diary for January 24, 1946: "At lunch today in the White House, with only members of the Staff present, RAdm Sidney Souers and I were presented with black cloaks, black hats, and wooden daggers" by Truman. The president then knighted Souers as chief of the "Cloak and Dagger Group of Snoopers" and "Director of Centralized Snooping." This vaudeville act placed the flabbergasted reservist in command of the misbegotten and short-lived organization called the Central Intelligence Group. Souers was now in charge of nearly two thousand intelligence officers and support staff who controlled files and dossiers on some 400,000 individuals. Many of them had no idea what they were doing, or what they were supposed to do. Someone asked Souers after his swearing-in what *he* wanted to do. "I want to go home," he said.

Like every director of central intelligence who followed him, he was given great responsibility without equivalent authority. He had no direction from the White House. The trouble was that no one really knew what the president wanted—least of all the president himself. Truman said he only needed a daily intelligence digest, to keep from having to read a two-foot stack of cables every morning. It seemed to the charter members of the Central Intelligence Group that it was the only aspect of their work he ever considered.

Others saw the mission very differently. General Magruder maintained that there was a tacit understanding at the White House that the Central Intelligence Group would operate a clandestine service. If so, not a word of it appeared on paper. The president never spoke of it, so almost no one else in the government recognized the new group's legitimacy. The Pentagon and the State Department refused to talk to Souers and his people. The army, the navy, and the FBI treated them with the deepest disdain. Souers lasted barely a hundred days as director, though he stayed on to serve the president as an adviser. He left behind only one note of consequence, a top secret memo with the following plea: "There is an urgent need to develop the highest possible quality of intelligence on the USSR in the shortest possible time."

The only American insights on the Kremlin in those days came from the newly appointed American ambassador in Moscow, the future director of central intelligence, General Walter Bedell Smith, and his ranking Russia hand, George Kennan.

"WHAT DOES THE SOVIET UNION WANT?"

Bedell Smith was a shopkeeper's son from Indiana who rose from buck private to general without the polish of West Point or a college degree.

As Eisenhower's chief of staff in World War II, he had thought through every battle in North Africa and Europe. His fellow officers respected and feared him; he was Ike's unsmiling hatchet man. He worked himself beyond exhaustion. After receiving blood transfusions for a bleeding ulcer when he collapsed at the end of a late dinner with Eisenhower and Winston Churchill, he argued his way out of a British hospital and back to his commander's tent. He had broken bread with Russian military officers, sitting down for awkward dinners at Allied headquarters in Algiers to plan joint operations against the Nazis. He had personally accepted the Nazi surrender that ended the war in Europe, staring down with contempt at the German command in the battered little red schoolhouse in Rheims, France, that served as the American military's forward headquarters. On V-E Day, May 8, 1945, he had met for a few fleeting minutes in Rheims with Allen Dulles and Richard Helms. Dulles, cursed by gout, hobbling on a crutch, had come to see Eisenhower and win his approval for the creation of an all-powerful American intelligence center in Berlin. Ike had no time for Dulles that morning—a bad omen.

Bedell Smith arrived in Moscow in March 1946 to be schooled by George Kennan, the chargé d'affaires at the American embassy. Kennan had spent many years in Russia, many dark hours trying to decipher Joseph Stalin. The Red Army had seized almost half of Europe in the war, a prize taken at the terrible price of twenty million Russian dead. Its forces had liberated nations from the Nazis, but now the shadow of the Kremlin was falling over more than 100 million people beyond Russia's borders. Kennan foresaw that the Soviets would hold their conquests by brute strength. He had warned the White House to prepare for a showdown.

A few days before Bedell Smith landed in Moscow, Kennan unleashed the most famous cable in the history of American diplomacy, the "long telegram," an eight-thousand-word portrait of Soviet paranoia. Kennan's readers—at first a few, in time millions—all seemed to seize on a single line: the Soviets were impervious to the logic of reason but highly sensitive to "the logic of force." In short order, Kennan would gain fame as the greatest Kremlinologist in the American government. "We had accustomed ourselves, through our wartime experience, to having a great enemy before us," Kennan reflected many years later. "The enemy must always be a center. He must be totally evil."

Bedell Smith called Kennan "the best possible tutor a newly arrived chief of mission could have had."

On a cold, starry night in April 1946, Bedell Smith rode a limousine flying the American flag into the fortress of the Kremlin. At the gates, Soviet intelligence officers checked his identity. His car passed the ancient Russian cathedrals and the huge broken bell at the foot of a tall tower within the Kremlin's walls. Saluting soldiers in high black leather boots and red-striped breeches ushered him inside. He had come alone. They took him down a long corridor, through tall double doors padded with dark green quilted leather. Finally, in a high-ceilinged conference room, the general met the generalissimo.

Bedell Smith had a double-barreled question for Stalin: "What does the Soviet Union want, and how far is Russia going to go?"

Stalin stared into the distance, puffing on a cigarette and doodling lopsided hearts and question marks with a red pencil. He denied designs on any other nation. He denounced Winston Churchill's warning, delivered in a speech a few weeks earlier in Missouri, about the iron curtain that had fallen across Europe.

Stalin said Russia knew its enemies.

"Is it possible that you really believe that the United States and Great Britain are united in an alliance to thwart Russia?" Bedell Smith asked.

"*Da,*" said Stalin.

The general repeated: "How far is Russia going to go?"

Stalin looked right at him and said: "We're not going to go much further."

How much further? No one knew. What was the mission of American intelligence in the face of the new Soviet threat? No one was sure.

"AN APPRENTICE JUGGLER"

On June 10, 1946, General Hoyt Vandenberg became the second director of central intelligence. A handsome pilot who had led Eisenhower's tactical air war in Europe, he now ran a fly-by-night outfit based in a cluster of undistinguished masonry buildings at the far end of Foggy Bottom, atop a small bluff overlooking the Potomac. His command post stood at 2430 E Street, the old headquarters of the OSS, surrounded by an abandoned gasworks, a turreted brewery, and a roller-skating rink.

Vandenberg lacked three essential tools: money, power, and people. The Central Intelligence Group stood outside the law, in the judgment of Lawrence Houston, general counsel for Central Intelligence from 1946 to 1972. The president could not legally create a federal agency out of thin air. Without the consent of Congress, Central Intelligence could not legally spend money. No money meant no power.

Vandenberg set out to get the United States back into the intelligence business. He created a new Office of Special Operations to conduct spying and subversion overseas and wrangled $15 million under the table from a handful of congressmen to carry out those missions. He wanted to know everything about the Soviet forces in Eastern and Central Europe—their movements, their capabilities, their intentions—and he ordered Richard Helms to deliver in a hurry. Helms, in charge of espionage in Germany, Austria, Switzerland, Poland, Czechoslovakia, and Hungary, with 228 overseas personnel on his roster, said he felt like "an apprentice juggler trying to keep an inflated beach ball, an open milk bottle and a loaded machine gun in the air." All over Europe, "a legion of political exiles, former intelligence officers, ex-agents and sundry entrepreneurs were turning themselves into intelligence moguls, brokering the sale of fabricated-to-order information." The more his spies spent buying intelligence, the less valuable it became. "If there are more graphic illustrations of throwing money at a problem that hasn't been thought through, none comes to mind," he wrote. What passed for intelligence on the Soviets and their satellites was a patchwork of frauds produced by talented liars.

Helms later determined that at least half the information on the Soviet Union and Eastern Europe in the CIA's files was pure falsehood. His stations in Berlin and Vienna had become factories of fake intelligence. Few of his officers or analysts could sift fact from fiction. It was an ever present problem: more than half a century later, the CIA confronted the same sort of fabrication as it sought to uncover Iraq's weapons of mass destruction.

From the first day Vandenberg took office, he was shaken by terrifying reports from overseas. His daily bulletins generated heat but little light. It was impossible to determine whether the warnings were true, but they went up the chain of command regardless. Flash: a drunken Soviet officer boasted that Russia would strike without warning. Flash: the commander of Soviet forces in the Balkans was toasting the coming fall of Istanbul. Flash: Stalin was prepared to invade Turkey, encircle the Black Sea, and take the Mediterranean and the Middle East. The Pentagon determined that the best way to blunt a Soviet advance was to cut the Red Army's supply lines in Romania. Senior staff members under the Joint Chiefs started drawing up battle plans.

They told Vandenberg to prepare the first covert operation of the cold war. In an attempt to carry out that order, Vandenberg changed the mission of the Central Intelligence Group. On July 17, 1946, he sent two of his aides to see Truman's White House counsel, Clark Clifford. They argued that "the original concept of the Central Intelligence Group should now be altered" to make it an "operating agency." Without any legal authority, it became one. On that same day, Vandenberg personally asked Secretary of War Robert Patterson and Secretary of State James Byrnes to slip him an additional $10 million in secret funds to finance the work of "intelligence agents all over the world." They did.

Vandenberg's Office of Special Operations set out to create an underground resistance force in Romania. Frank Wisner had left behind a network of agents in Bucharest desperate to work with Americans but deeply infiltrated by Soviet intelligence. Charles W. Hostler, the first station chief in Bucharest for the Office of Special Operations, found himself surrounded by "conspiracy, intrigue, nastiness, double-dealing, dishonesty, occasional murder and assassination" among fascists, communists, monarchists, industrialists, anarchists, moderates, intellectuals, and idealists—"a social and political environment for which young American officers were poorly prepared."

Vandenberg ordered Lieutenant Ira C. Hamilton and Major Thomas R. Hall, based at the tiny American military mission in Bucharest, to organize Romania's National Peasant Party into a resistance force. Major Hall, who had been an OSS officer in the Balkans, spoke some Romanian. Lieutenant Hamilton spoke none. His guide was the one important agent Wisner had recruited two years before: Theodore Manacatide, who had been a sergeant on the intelligence staff of the Romanian army and now worked at the American military mission, translator by day and spy by night. Manacatide took Hamilton and Hall to meet the National Peasant Party leaders. The Americans offered the clandestine support of the United States—guns, money, and intelligence. On October 5, working with the new Central Intelligence station in occupied Vienna, the Americans smuggled the former foreign minister of Romania and five other members of the would-be liberation army into Austria, sedating them, stuffing them in mail sacks, and flying them to safe harbor.

It took Soviet intelligence and the Romanian secret police only a few weeks to sniff out the spies. The Americans and their chief agent ran for their lives as communist security forces crushed the mainstream Romanian resistance. The Peasant Party's leaders were charged with treason and imprisoned. Manacatide, Hamilton, and Hall were convicted in absentia at a public trial after witnesses swore that they had represented themselves as agents of a new American intelligence service.

Frank Wisner opened *The New York Times* on November 20, 1946, and read a short article on page ten reporting that his old agent Manacatide, "formerly employed by the United States Mission," had been sentenced to life imprisonment, "on the grounds that he accompanied a Lieutenant Hamilton of the American Military Mission to a National Peasant congress." By winter's end, nearly every one of the Romanians who had worked for Wisner during the war was jailed or killed; his personal secretary had committed suicide. A brutal dictatorship took control of Romania, its rise to power hastened by the failure of American covert action.

Wisner left his law firm and went to Washington, securing a post at the State Department, where he oversaw the occupied zones of Berlin, Vienna, Tokyo, Seoul, and Trieste. He had greater ambitions. He was convinced that the United States had to learn to fight in a new way, with the same skills and the same secrecy as its enemy.

3. "FIGHT FIRE WITH FIRE"

Washington was a small town run by people who believed that they lived in the center of the universe. Their city within the city was Georgetown, a square-mile enclave of cobblestone streets lush with magnolias. In its heart, at 3327 P Street, stood a fine four-story house built in 1820, with an English garden out back and a formal dining room with high windows. Frank and Polly Wisner made it their home. On Sunday evenings in 1947, it became the seat of the emerging American national-security establishment. The foreign policy of the United States took shape at the Wisners' table.

They started a Georgetown tradition, a Sunday night potluck supper. The main dish was liquor, all hands having sailed out of the Second World War on a tide of alcohol. The Wisners' eldest son, Frank's namesake, who in time rose to the heights of American diplomacy, saw the Sunday night suppers as "extraordinarily important events. They were not just trifling social affairs. They became the very lifeblood of the way the government thought, fought, worked, compared notes, made up its mind, and reached consensus." After dinner, in the British tradition, the ladies retired, the gentlemen remained, and the bold ideas and boozy banter went late into the night. On any given evening the guests might include Wisner's close friend David Bruce, the OSS veteran en route to becoming the American ambassador in Paris; Chip Bohlen, counsel to the secretary of state and a future ambassador to Moscow; Undersecretary of State Robert Lovett and the future secretary of state Dean Acheson; and the newly eminent Kremlinologist George Kennan. These men believed it was in their power to change the course of human events, and their great debate was how to stop a Soviet takeover of Europe. Stalin was consolidating his control of the Balkans. Leftist guerrillas battled a right-wing monarchy in the mountains of Greece. Food riots broke out in Italy and France, where communist politicians called for general strikes. British soldiers and spies were pulling out of their posts all over the world, leaving wide swaths of the map open for the communists. The sun was setting on the British Empire; the exchequer could not sustain it. The United States was going to have to lead the free world alone.

Wisner and his guests listened closely to Kennan. They had absorbed his "long telegram" from Moscow and they shared his view of the Soviet threat. So did Navy Secretary James Forrestal, soon to be the first secretary of defense, a Wall Street wonder boy who saw communism as a fanatical faith to be fought with a still-deeper conviction. Forrestal had become Kennan's political patron, installing him in a general's mansion at the National War College and making his work required reading for thousands of military officers. Director of Central Intelligence Vandenberg brainstormed with Kennan about how to spy on Moscow's atomic weapons work. The new secretary of state, George C. Marshall, the chief of the U.S. Army in World War II, determined that the nation needed to reshape its foreign policy, and in the spring he put Kennan in charge of the State Department's new Policy Planning Staff.

Kennan was drawing up a battle plan for the newly named cold war. Within the course of six months, the ideas of this obscure diplomat gave rise to three forces that shaped the world: the Truman Doctrine, a political warning to Moscow to halt its subversion of foreign nations; the Marshall Plan, a global bastion for American influence against communism; and the clandestine service of the Central Intelligence Agency.

"THE GREATEST INTELLIGENCE SERVICE IN THE WORLD"

In February 1947, the British ambassador had warned acting secretary of state Dean Acheson that England's military and economic aid to Greece and Turkey would have to cease in six weeks. The Greeks would need something on the order of a billion dollars over the next four years to fight the threat of communism. From Moscow, Walter Bedell Smith sent his assessment that British troops were the only force keeping Greece from falling into the Soviet orbit.

At home, the red scare was rising. For the first time since before the Great Depression, the Republicans now controlled both houses of Congress, with men like Senator Joseph McCarthy of Wisconsin and Congressman Richard Nixon of California gaining power. Truman's popularity was plunging; his approval rating in public opinion polls had fallen 50 points since the end of the war. He had changed his mind about Stalin and the Soviets. He was now convinced that they were an evil abroad in the world.

Truman and Acheson summoned Senator Arthur Vandenberg, the Republican chairman of the Committee on Foreign Relations. (The newspapers that day noted that the senator's nephew Hoyt soon would be relieved as director of central intelligence, after only eight months in power.) Acheson explained that a communist beachhead in Greece would threaten all of Western Europe. The United States was going to have to find a way to save the free world—and Congress was going to have to pay the bill. Senator Vandenberg cleared his throat and turned to Truman. "Mr. President," he said, "the only way you are ever going to get this is to make a speech and scare the hell out of the country."

On March 12, 1947, Truman made that speech, warning a joint session of Congress that the world would face disaster unless the United States fought communism abroad. Hundreds of millions of dollars had to be sent to shore up Greece, now "threatened by the terrorist activities of several thousand armed men," the president said. Without American aid, "disorder might spread throughout the Middle East," despair would deepen in the nations of Europe, and darkness could descend on the free world. His credo was something new: "I believe that it must be the policy of the United States to support free peoples who are resisting attempted subjugation by armed minorities or by outside pressures." Any attack launched by an American enemy in any nation of the world was an attack on the United States. This was the Truman Doctrine. Congress rose for a standing ovation.

Millions of dollars started flowing to Greece—along with warships, soldiers, guns, ammunition, napalm, and spies. Soon Athens became one of the biggest American intelligence posts in the world. Truman's decision to fight communism overseas was the first clear direction that

American spies received from the White House. They still lacked a strong commander. General Vandenberg was counting the days until he could take over the new air force, but he delivered secret testimony to a handful of members of Congress in his last days as director of central intelligence, saying that the nation faced foreign threats as never before. "The oceans have shrunk, until today both Europe and Asia border the United States almost as do Canada and Mexico," he said, in a turn of phrase repeated, eerily, by President Bush after 9/11.

In World War II, Vandenberg said, "we had to rely blindly and trustingly on the superior intelligence system of the British"—but "the United States should never have to go hat in hand, begging any foreign government for the eyes—the foreign intelligence—with which to see." Yet the CIA would always depend on foreign intelligence services for insight into lands and languages it did not understand. Vandenberg ended by saying it would take at least five more years to build a professional cadre of American spies. The warning was repeated word for word half a century later, in 1997, by Director of Central Intelligence George J. Tenet, and Tenet said it again upon resigning in 2004. A great spy service was always five years over the horizon.

Vandenberg's successor, the third man to hold the post in fifteen months, was Rear Admiral Roscoe Hillenkoetter, sworn in on May Day 1947. Hilly, as everyone called him, was a miscast man. He exuded insignificance. Like his predecessors, he never wanted to be director of central intelligence—"and probably never should have been," says a CIA history of the era.

On June 27, 1947, a congressional committee held secret hearings that led to the formal creation of the CIA at summer's end. It spoke volumes that not Hillenkoetter but Allen Dulles—a lawyer in private practice—was selected to conduct a secret intelligence seminar for a few select members of Congress.

Allen Dulles had an "Onward, Christian Soldiers" sense of patriotic duty. He was born into the best family of Watertown, New York, in 1893. His father was the town's Presbyterian pastor; his grandfather and his uncle both had served as secretary of state. The president of his college, Princeton, was Woodrow Wilson, later to be president of the United States. Dulles had been a junior diplomat after World War I and a white-shoe Wall Street lawyer in the Depression. By virtue of his carefully cultivated reputation as an American master spy, built as the OSS chief in Switzerland, he was regarded by the Republican leadership as the director of central intelligence in exile, in the way that his brother John Foster Dulles, the party's principal foreign policy spokesman, was seen as a shadow secretary of state. Allen was genial in the extreme, with twinkling eyes, a belly laugh, and an almost impish deviousness. But he was also a duplicitous man, a chronic adulterer, ruthlessly ambitious. He was not above misleading Congress or his colleagues or even his commander in chief.

Room 1501 of the Longworth Office Building was sealed off by armed guards; everyone inside was sworn to secrecy. Puffing away on his pipe, a tweedy headmaster instructing unruly schoolboys, Allen Dulles described a CIA that would be "directed by a relatively small but elite corps of men with a passion for anonymity." Its director would require "judicial temperament in high degree," with "long experience and profound knowledge"—a man not unlike Allen Dulles. His top aides, if they were military men, would "divest themselves of their rank as soldiers, sailors or airmen and, as it were, 'take the cloth' of the intelligence service."

Americans had "the raw material for building the greatest intelligence service in the world," Dulles said. "The personnel need not be very numerous"—a few hundred good men would do the trick. "The operation of the service must neither be flamboyant nor over-shrouded in the mystery and abracadabra which the amateur detective likes to assume," he reassured the members of Congress. "All that is required for success is hard work, discriminating judgment, and common sense."

He never said what he really wanted: to resurrect the wartime covert operations of the OSS.

The creation of a new American clandestine service was at hand. President Truman unveiled the new architecture for the cold war by signing the National Security Act of 1947 on July 26. The act created the air force as a separate service, led by General Vandenberg, and a new National Security Council was to be the White House switchboard for presidential decisions. The act also created the office of secretary of defense; its first occupant, James Forrestal, was ordered to unify the American military. ("This office," Forrestal wrote a few days later, "will probably be the greatest cemetery for dead cats in history.")

And, in six short and sketchy paragraphs, the act gave birth to the Central Intelligence Agency on September 18.

The CIA was born with crippling defects. From the outset, it faced fierce and relentless opponents within the Pentagon and the State Department—the agencies whose reports it was supposed to coordinate. The agency was not their overseer, but their stepchild. Its powers were poorly defined. No formal charter or congressionally appropriated funds would come for nearly two more years. The CIA's headquarters would survive until then on a subsistence fund maintained by a few members of Congress.

And its secrecy would always conflict with the openness of American democracy. "I had the gravest forebodings about this organization," wrote Dean Acheson, soon to be secretary of state, "and warned the President that as set up neither he, the National Security Council, nor anyone else would be in a position to know what it was doing or to control it."

The National Security Act said nothing about secret operations overseas. It instructed the CIA to correlate, evaluate, and disseminate intelligence— and to perform "other functions and duties related to intelligence affecting the national security." Embedded in those eleven words were the powers that General Magruder had preserved in his end run around the president two years before. In time, hundreds of major covert actions—eighty-one of them during Truman's second term—would be driven through this loophole.

The conduct of covert action required the direct or implied authority of the National Security Council. The NSC in those days was President Truman, the secretary of defense, the secretary of state, and the military chiefs. But it was an evanescent body. It seldom convened, and when it did, Truman was rarely at the table.

He came to the first meeting on September 26, as did a very wary Roscoe Hillenkoetter. The CIA's counsel, Lawrence Houston, had warned the director against the growing calls for covert action. He said the agency had no legal authority to conduct them without the express consent of Congress. Hilly sought to limit the CIA's overseas missions to the gathering of intelligence. He failed. Momentous decisions were being made in secret, often over breakfast on Wednesdays at Secretary of Defense Forrestal's house.

On September 27, Kennan sent Forrestal a detailed paper calling for the establishment of a "guerrilla warfare corps." Kennan thought that although the American people might never approve of such methods, "it might be essential to our security to fight fire with fire." Forrestal fervently agreed. Together, they set the American clandestine service in motion.

"THE INAUGURATION OF ORGANIZED POLITICAL WARFARE"

Forrestal called Hillenkoetter into the Pentagon to discuss "the present widespread belief that our Intelligence Group is entirely inept." He had good reason. The mismatch between the CIA's capabilities and the missions it was called upon to carry out was staggering.

The new commander of the CIA's Office of Special Operations, Colonel Donald "Wrong-Way" Galloway, was a strutting martinet who had reached the apex of his talent as a West Point cavalry officer teaching equestrian etiquette to cadets. His deputy, Stephen Penrose, who had run the Middle East division of the OSS, resigned in frustration. In a bitter memo to Forrestal, Penrose warned that "CIA is losing its professionals, and is not acquiring competent new personnel," at the very time "when, as almost never before, the government needs an effective, expanding, professional intelligence service."

Nevertheless, on December 14, 1947, the National Security Council issued its first top secret orders to the CIA. The agency was to execute "covert psychological operations designed to counter Soviet and Soviet-inspired activities." With this martial drum roll, the CIA set out to beat the Reds in the Italian elections, set for April 1948.

The CIA told the White House that Italy could become a totalitarian police state. If the communists won at the ballot box, they would seize "the most ancient seat of Western Culture. In particular, devout Catholics everywhere would be gravely concerned regarding the safety of the Holy See." The prospect of a godless government surrounding the pope at gunpoint was too awful to contemplate. Kennan thought that a shooting war would be better than letting the communists take power legally—but covert action modeled on communist techniques of subversion was the next best choice.

The CIA's F. Mark Wyatt, who cut his teeth on this operation, remembered that it began weeks before the National Security Council formally authorized it. Congress, of course, never gave a go-ahead. The mission was illegal from the start. "In CIA, at headquarters, we were absolutely terrified, we were scared to death," Wyatt said, and with good reason. "We were going beyond our charter."

Cash, lots of it, would be needed to help defeat the communists. The best guess from the CIA's Rome station chief, James J. Angleton, was $10 million. Angleton, partly reared in Italy, had served there with the OSS and stayed on; he told headquarters that he had penetrated the Italian secret service so deeply that he practically ran it. He would use its members as a bucket brigade to distribute the cash. But where would the money come from? The CIA still had no independent budget and no contingency fund for covert operations.

James Forrestal and his good friend Allen Dulles solicited their friends and colleagues from Wall Street and Washington—businesspeople, bankers, and politicians—but it was never enough. Forrestal then went to an old chum, John W. Snyder, the secretary of the treasury and one of Harry Truman's closest allies. He convinced Snyder to tap into the Exchange Stabilization Fund set up in the Depression to shore up the value of the dollar overseas through short-term currency trading, and converted during World War II as a depository for captured Axis loot. The fund held $200 million earmarked for the reconstruction of Europe. It delivered millions into the bank accounts of wealthy American citizens, many of them Italian Americans, who then sent the money to newly formed political fronts created by the CIA. Donors were instructed to place a special code on their income tax forms alongside their "charitable donation." The millions were delivered to Italian politicians and the priests of Catholic Action, a political arm of the Vatican. Suitcases filled with cash changed hands in the four-star Hassler Hotel. "We would have liked to have done this in a more sophisticated manner," Wyatt said. "Passing black bags to affect a political election is not really a terribly attractive thing." But it worked: Italy's Christian Democrats won by a comfortable margin and formed a government that excluded communists. A long romance between the party and the agency began. The CIA's practice of purchasing elections and politicians with bags of cash was repeated in Italy—and in many other nations—for the next twenty-five years.

But in the weeks before the election, the communists scored another victory. They seized Czechoslovakia, beginning a brutal series of arrests and executions that lasted for nearly five years. The CIA station chief in Prague, Charles Katek, worked to deliver about thirty Czechs—his agents and their families—over the border to Munich. Chief among them was the head of Czech intelligence. Katek arranged to have him smuggled out of the country, stuffed between the radiator and the grille of a roadster.

On March 5, 1948, while the Czech crisis was exploding, a terrifying cable came to the Pentagon from General Lucius D. Clay, chief of American occupation forces in Berlin. The general said he had a gut feeling that a Soviet attack could come at any minute. The Pentagon leaked the cable and Washington was swamped by fear. Though the CIA's Berlin base sent a report reassuring the president that there was no sign of any impending attack, no one listened. Truman went before a joint session of Congress the next day warning that the Soviet Union and its agents threatened a cataclysm. He demanded and won immediate approval of the great undertaking that became known as the Marshall Plan.

The plan offered billions of dollars to the free world to repair the damage done by the war and to create an American economic and political barricade against the Soviets. In nineteen capitals—sixteen in Europe, three in Asia—the United States would help rebuild civilization, with an American blueprint. George Kennan and James Forrestal were among the plan's principal authors. Allen Dulles served as a consultant.

They helped devise a secret codicil that gave the CIA the capability to conduct political warfare. It let the agency skim uncounted millions of dollars from the plan.

The mechanics were surprisingly simple. After Congress approved the Marshall Plan, it appropriated about $13.7 billion over five years. A nation that received aid from the plan had to set aside an equivalent sum in its own currency. Five percent of those funds—$685 million all told—was made available to the CIA through the plan's overseas offices.

It was a global money-laundering scheme that stayed secret until well after the cold war ended. Where the plan flourished in Europe and in Asia, so would American spies. "We'd look the other way and give them a little help," said Colonel R. Allen Griffin, who ran the Marshall Plan's Far East division. "Tell them to stick their hand in our pocket."

Secret funds were the heart of secret operations. The CIA now had an unfailing source of untraceable cash.

In a top secret paper sent to perhaps two dozen people at the State De-

partment, the White House, and the Pentagon on May 4, 1948, Kennan
proclaimed "the inauguration of organized political warfare" and called
for the creation of a new clandestine service to conduct covert operations worldwide. He stated clearly that the Marshall Plan, the Truman
Doctrine, and the CIA's covert operations were all interlocking parts of a
grand strategy against Stalin.

The money that the CIA siphoned from the Marshall Plan would finance a network of false fronts—a façade of public committees and
councils headed by distinguished citizens. The communists had front organizations all over Europe: publishing houses, newspapers, student
groups, labor unions. Now the CIA would set up its own. Those fronts
would recruit foreign agents—the émigrés of Eastern Europe, refugees
from Russia. These foreigners, under CIA control, would create underground political groups in the free nations of Europe. And the underground would pass the flame to "all-out liberation movements" behind
the iron curtain. If the cold war turned hot, the United States would
have a fighting force on the front lines.

Kennan's ideas caught on quickly. His plans were approved in a secret
order from the National Security Council on June 18, 1948. NSC directive 10/2 called for covert operations to attack the Soviets around the
world.

The strike force Kennan conceived to carry out that secret war received
the blandest name imaginable—the Office of Policy Coordination (OPC).
It was a cover, serving to veil the group's work. It was placed inside the
CIA, but its chief would report to the secretaries of defense and state, because the director of central intelligence was so weak. The State Department wanted it to carry out "rumor-spreading, bribery, the organization
of non-communist fronts," according to a National Security Council report declassified in 2003. Forrestal and the Pentagon wanted "guerrilla
movements . . . underground armies . . . sabotage and assassination."

"ONE MAN MUST BE BOSS"

The biggest battleground was Berlin. Frank Wisner worked ceaselessly to
shape American policy in the occupied city. He urged his superiors at the

State Department to undertake a stratagem aimed at subverting the Soviets by introducing a new German currency. Moscow was sure to reject the idea, so the postwar power-sharing agreements in Berlin would collapse. A new political dynamic would push the Russians back.

On June 23, the Western powers instituted the new currency. In immediate response, the Soviets blockaded Berlin. As the United States mounted an airlift to beat the blockade, Kennan spent long hours in the crisis room, the double-locked overseas communications center on the fifth floor of the State Department, agonizing as cables and telexes flashed in from Berlin.

The CIA's Berlin base had been trying unsuccessfully for more than a year to obtain intelligence on the Red Army in occupied Germany and Russia, to track Moscow's progress in nuclear weapons, fighter jets, missiles, and biological warfare. Still, its officers had agents among Berlin's police and politicians—and most important, a line into the Soviet intelligence headquarters at Karlshorst in East Berlin. It came from Tom Polgar, the Hungarian refugee who was proving himself one of the CIA's best officers. Polgar had a butler, and his butler had a brother working for a Soviet army officer in Karlshorst. Creature comforts such as salted peanuts flowed from Polgar to Karlshorst. Information flowed back. Polgar had a second agent, a teletypist in the Soviet liaison section at the Berlin police headquarters. Her sister was the mistress of a police lieutenant who was close to the Russians. The lovers met in Polgar's apartment. "That brought me fame and glory," he remembered. Polgar delivered crucial intelligence that reached the White House. "I was completely certain, in the Berlin blockade, that the Soviets would not move," he said. The CIA's reports never wavered from that assessment: neither the Soviet military nor their newly created East German allies were readying for battle. The Berlin base did its part to keep the cold war cold in those months.

Wisner was ready for a hot war. He argued that the United States should battle its way into Berlin with tanks and artillery. His ideas were rejected, but his fighting spirit was embraced.

Kennan had insisted that covert operations could not be run by committee. They needed a top commander with the full backing of the Pentagon and the State Department. "One man must be boss," he wrote. Forrestal, Marshall, and Kennan all agreed that Wisner was the man.

He was just shy of forty, deceptively courtly in appearance. He had been a handsome man in his youth, but his hair was starting to thin and his face and torso were starting to swell from his thirst for alcohol. He had less than three years' experience as a wartime spy and crypto-diplomat under his belt. Now he had to create a clandestine service from scratch.

Richard Helms observed that Wisner burned with "a zeal and intensity which imposed, unquestionably, an abnormal strain" on him. His passion for covert action would forever alter America's place in the world.

4. "THE *MOST* SECRET THING"

Frank Wisner took charge of American covert action on September 1, 1948. His mission: to roll the Soviets back to Russia's old boundaries and free Europe from communist control. His command post was a crumbling tin-roofed shanty, one of a long row of temporary War Department buildings flanking the reflecting pool between the Lincoln Memorial and the Washington Monument. Vermin scuttled down the corridors. His men called the place the Rat Palace.

He worked himself into a controlled frenzy, twelve hours or more a day, six days a week, and he demanded the same of his officers. He rarely told the director of central intelligence what he was doing. He alone would decide whether his secret missions conformed to American foreign policy.

His organization soon grew bigger than the rest of the agency combined. Covert operations became the agency's dominant force, with the most people, the most money, the most power, and so they remained for more than twenty years. The CIA's stated mission had been to provide the president with secret information essential to the national security of the United States. But Wisner had no patience for espionage, no time for sifting and weighing secrets. Far easier to plot a coup or pay off a politician than to penetrate the Politburo—and for Wisner, far more urgent.

Within a month, Wisner had drawn up battle plans for the next five years. He set out to create a multinational media conglomerate for propaganda. He sought to wage economic warfare against the Soviets by

counterfeiting money and manipulating markets. He spent millions trying to tip the political scales in capitals across the world. He wanted to
recruit legions of exiles—Russians, Albanians, Ukrainians, Poles, Hungarians, Czechs, Romanians—for armed resistance groups to penetrate
the iron curtain. Wisner believed there were 700,000 Russians adrift in
Germany who could join the cause. He wanted to transform one thousand of them into political shock troops. He found seventeen.

On Forrestal's orders, Wisner created networks of stay-behind agents—
foreigners who would fight the Soviets on the opening days of World
War III. The goal was to slow the advance of hundreds of thousands of
the Red Army's troops in Western Europe. He wanted arms, ammunition, and explosives stockpiled in secret caches all over Europe and the
Middle East, to blow up bridges, depots, and Arab oil fields in the face of
a Soviet advance. General Curtis LeMay, the new chief of the Strategic
Air Command and the controller of American nuclear weapons, knew
that his bombers would run out of fuel after dropping their weapons on
Moscow, and on their return flights his pilots and crews would have to
bail out somewhere east of the iron curtain. LeMay told Wisner's right-
hand man Franklin Lindsay to build a ratline inside the Soviet Union—
an evacuation route for his men to escape overland. Air force colonels
barked commands at their CIA counterparts: steal a Soviet fighter-
bomber, preferably with its pilot stuffed in a gunnysack; infiltrate agents
with radios onto every airfield between Berlin and the Urals; sabotage
every military runway in the Soviet Union at the first warning of war.
These were not requests. They were orders.

Above all, Wisner needed thousands of American spies. The hunt for
talent, then as now, was a constant crisis. He set out on a recruiting drive
that ran from the Pentagon to Park Avenue to Yale and Harvard and
Princeton, where professors and coaches were paid to spot talent. He
hired lawyers, bankers, college kids, old school friends, veterans at loose
ends. "They would pull people off the streets, anybody with warm blood
who could say yes or no or move arms and legs," said the CIA's Sam
Halpern. Wisner aimed to open at least thirty-six stations overseas within
six months; he managed forty-seven in three years. Almost every city
where he set up shop had two CIA station chiefs—one working on covert
action for Wisner, the other working on espionage for CIA's Office of Special Operations. Inevitably they double-crossed one another, stole each
other's agents, fought for the upper hand. Wisner poached hundreds of

officers from the Office of Special Operations, offering higher salaries and the promise of greater glories.

He commandeered aircraft, arms, ammunition, parachutes, and surplus uniforms from the Pentagon and its bases in the occupied zones of Europe and Asia. He soon controlled a military stockpile worth a quarter of a billion dollars. "Wisner could call on any agency of the Government for personnel and such support as he may require," said James McCargar, one of the first men Wisner hired at the Office of Policy Coordination. "The CIA was, of course, a publicly known agency whose operations were secret. OPC's operations were not only secret, the existence of the organization itself was also secret. It was, in fact, for its first years, and this must be emphasized, since few people now seem aware of it, the *most* secret thing in the U.S. Government after nuclear weapons." And like the first nuclear weapons, whose test blasts were more powerful than their designers anticipated, Wisner's covert action shop grew faster and spread farther than anyone imagined.

McCargar had toiled for the State Department in the Soviet Union during World War II, where he learned quickly that "the only methods which would help you get your work done were clandestine." He had single-handedly evacuated Hungarian political leaders from Budapest, delivering them to a safe house in Vienna set up by Al Ulmer, the first CIA station chief in that occupied capital. The two became friends, and when they found themselves in Washington in the summer of 1948, Ulmer invited McCargar to meet his new boss. Wisner took them both to breakfast at the Hay-Adams Hotel, the fanciest in Washington, just across Lafayette Park from the White House. McCargar was hired on the spot as a headquarters man and placed in charge of seven nations— Greece, Turkey, Albania, Hungary, Romania, Bulgaria, and Yugoslavia. When he reported for work in October 1948, "there were only ten of us, including Wisner, a couple of officers, the secretaries, and myself—ten people," McCargar said. "Within a year, we were 450, and a few years after that there were so many thousands."

"WE WERE SEEN AS KINGS"

Wisner sent Al Ulmer to Athens, where he set out to cover ten nations, across the Mediterranean, the Adriatic, and the Black Sea. The new station chief bought a mansion on a hilltop overlooking the city, a walled compound with a sixty-foot-long dining room and top-drawer diplomats for neighbors. "We were in charge," Ulmer said many years later. "We ran things. We were seen as kings."

The CIA began channeling clandestine political and financial support to Greece's most ambitious military and intelligence officers, recruiting promising young men who might someday lead the nation. The connections they cultivated could pay great dividends later on. First in Athens and Rome, then across Europe, politicians, generals, spy chiefs, newspaper publishers, union bosses, cultural organizations, and religious associations began looking to the agency for cash and for counsel. "Individuals, groups, and intelligence services quickly came to see that there was a force abroad in the world around which they could rally," said a secret CIA chronicle of Wisner's first years in power.

Wisner's station chiefs needed cash. Wisner flew to Paris in mid-November 1948 to talk that problem over with Averell Harriman, the Marshall Plan's director. They met in a gilded suite at the Hotel Talleyrand, once the home of Napoleon's foreign minister. Under the gaze of a marble bust of Benjamin Franklin, Harriman told Wisner to dip as deeply as he needed into the plan's grab bag of dollars. Armed with that authority, Wisner returned to Washington to meet Richard Bissell, the Marshall Plan's chief administrator. "I had met him socially and knew and trusted him," Bissell remembered. "He was very much part of our inner circle of people." Wisner came right to the point. Bissell was baffled at first, but "Wisner took the time to assuage at least some of my concerns by assuring me that Harriman had approved the action. When I began to press him about how the money would be used, he explained that I could not be told." Bissell would learn soon enough. A decade later he took Wisner's job.

Wisner proposed to break communist influence over the largest trade federations in France and Italy with cash from the plan; Kennan personally authorized these operations. Wisner chose two talented labor leaders to run the first of those operations in late 1948: Jay Lovestone, a former chairman of the American Communist Party, and Irving Brown, his devoted follower; both men were dedicated anticommunists, transformed by the bitter ideological battles of the 1930s. Lovestone served as executive secretary of the Free Trade Union Committee, a spin-off of the American Federation of Labor; Brown was his chief representative in Europe. They delivered small fortunes from the CIA to labor groups backed by Christian Democrats and the Catholic Church. Payoffs in the gritty ports of Marseilles and Naples guaranteed that American arms and military materiel would be off-loaded by friendly longshoremen. The CIA's money and power flowed into the well-greased palms of Corsican gangsters who knew how to break a strike with bare knuckles.

One of Wisner's more genteel tasks was underwriting an arcane association that became an influential CIA front for twenty years: the Congress for Cultural Freedom. He envisioned "a vast project targeted on the intellectuals—'the battle for Picasso's mind,' if you will," in the elegant phrase of the CIA's Tom Braden, an OSS veteran and Sunday-night-supper regular. This was a war of words, fought with little magazines, paperback books, and high-minded conferences. "I think the budget for the Congress for Cultural Freedom one year that I had charge of it was about $800,000, $900,000," Braden said. That included the start-up funds for the high-minded monthly called *Encounter,* which created a swirl of influence in the 1950s without selling more than forty thousand copies an issue. That was a kind of missionary work that appealed to the liberal-arts majors newly arrived at the agency. It was a good life, running a little paper or a publishing house in Paris or Rome—the junior year abroad of American intelligence.

Wisner, Kennan, and Allen Dulles saw a far better way to harness the political fervor and intellectual energies of Eastern European exiles and channel them back behind the iron curtain—Radio Free Europe. The planning began in late 1948 and early 1949, but it took more than two years to get the radios on the air. Dulles became the founder of a National Committee for a Free Europe, one of many front organizations financed by the CIA in the United States. The Free Europe board included General Eisenhower; Henry Luce, the chairman of *Time, Life,* and *Fortune;* and Cecil B. DeMille, the Hollywood producer—all recruited by Dulles and Wisner as a cover for the true management. The radios would become a powerful weapon for political warfare.

"THE HEAT OF CONFUSION"

Wisner had high hopes that Allen Dulles would be the next director of central intelligence. So did Dulles.

In early 1948, Forrestal had asked Dulles to run a top secret investigation into the structural weaknesses of the CIA. As election day approached, Dulles was putting his final touches on the report that was to serve as his own inaugural address at the agency. He was confident that Truman would be defeated by the Republican Thomas Dewey, and that the new president would elevate him to his rightful place.

The report, which remained classified for fifty years, was a detailed and brutal indictment. Count One: the CIA was churning out reams of paper containing few if any facts on the communist threat. Count Two: the agency had no spies among the Soviets and their satellites. Count Three: Roscoe Hillenkoetter was a failure as director. The CIA was not yet "an adequate intelligence service," the report said, and it would take "years of patient work to do the job" of transforming it. What was needed now was a bold new leader—and his identity was no secret. Hillenkoetter noted bitterly that Allen Dulles had all but engraved his name on the director's door. But by the time the report landed in January 1949, Truman had been re-elected, and Dulles was so closely associated with the Republican Party that his appointment was politically inconceivable. Hillenkoetter stayed on, leaving the agency effectively leaderless. The National Security Council ordered Hillenkoetter to implement the report, but he never did.

Dulles began telling his friends in Washington that unless something drastic was done at the CIA, the president faced disaster abroad. A chorus of voices joined him. Dean Acheson, now secretary of state, heard that the CIA was "melting away in the heat of confusion and resentment." His informant was Kermit "Kim" Roosevelt, President Theodore Roosevelt's grandson, FDR's cousin, and the future chief of the CIA's Near East and South Asia division. Forrestal's intelligence aide, John Ohly, warned his boss: "The greatest weakness of CIA stems from the type and quality of its personnel and the methods through which it is recruited." He noted "a complete deterioration of morale among some of the better qualified civilians who would like to make CIA a career and the loss of many able individuals who simply could not stand the situation." Worse yet, "most

of the able people left in the Agency have decided that unless changes occur within the next several months, they will definitely leave. With this
cadre of quality lost, the Agency will sink into a mire from which it will
be difficult, if not impossible, to extract it." The CIA would then become
"a poor to mediocre intelligence operation virtually in perpetuity." These
messages could have been written half a century later. They would accurately describe the agency's woes in the decade after the fall of Soviet
communism. The ranks of skilled American spies were thin, the number
of talented foreign agents next to none.

The capabilities of the CIA were not the only problem. The pressures
of the cold war were fracturing the new leaders of the national-security
establishment.

James Forrestal and George Kennan had been the creators and commanders of the CIA's covert operations. But they proved unable to control the machine they had set in motion. Kennan was becoming a
burnt-out case, seeking seclusion in his hideaway at the Library of Congress. Forrestal was beyond the edge. He resigned as secretary of defense
on March 28, 1949. During his last day in office, he broke down, moan-
ing that he had not slept in months. Dr. William C. Menninger, the most
prominent psychiatrist in the United States, found Forrestal in the midst
of a psychotic episode and committed him to a psychiatric ward at
Bethesda Naval Hospital.

After fifty haunted nights, in the final hours of his life, Forrestal was
copying out a Greek poem, "The Chorus from Ajax," and he stopped in
the middle of the word *nightingale*. He wrote "night," and then he fell to
his death from his sixteenth-floor window. *Nightingale* was the code
name of a Ukrainian resistance force Forrestal had authorized to carry
out a secret war against Stalin. Its leaders included Nazi collaborators
who had murdered thousands of people behind the German lines during World War II. Its members were set to parachute behind the iron curtain for the CIA.

5. "A RICH BLIND MAN"

In World War II, the United States made common cause with communists to fight fascists. In the cold war, the CIA used fascists to combat communists. Patriotic Americans undertook these missions in the name of the United States. "You can't run the railroads," Allen Dulles said, in an unfortunate turn of phrase, "without taking in some Nazi Party members."

More than two million people were adrift in American-occupied Germany. Many among them were desperate refugees from the spreading shadow of Soviet rule. Frank Wisner sent his officers directly into the displaced-persons camps to recruit them for a mission he defined as "encouraging resistance movements into the Soviet World and providing contacts with an underground." He made the case that the CIA had to "utilize refugees from the Soviet World in the national interests of the U.S."

Over the objections of the director of central intelligence, he wanted to send guns and money to these men. The Soviet exiles were very much in demand "as a reserve for a possible war emergency," the agency recorded, though they were "hopelessly split between groups with opposing aims, philosophies and ethnic composition."

Wisner's orders gave rise to the first of the agency's paramilitary missions—the first of many that sent thousands of foreign agents to their deaths. The full story began to reveal itself in a CIA history that first came to light in 2005.

"THE LESS WE SAY ABOUT THIS BILL, THE BETTER"

Wisner's ambitions faced a huge hurdle at the start of 1949. The agency lacked the legal authority to carry out covert action against any nation. It had no constitutional charter from Congress and no legally authorized funds for those missions. It still operated outside the laws of the United States.

In early February 1949, the director of central intelligence went to have a private chat with Carl Vinson, a Georgia Democrat and the chair of the House Armed Services Committee. Hillenkoetter warned that Congress had to pass formal legislation blessing the CIA and granting it a budget as soon as possible. The agency was up to its neck in operations, and it needed legal cover. After confiding his concerns to a few other members of the House and Senate, Hillenkoetter submitted the Central Intelligence Agency Act of 1949 for their consideration. They met for about half an hour in secret to weigh it.

"We will just have to tell the House they will have to accept our judgment and we cannot answer a great many questions that might be asked," Vinson told his colleagues. Dewey Short of Missouri, the ranking Republican on the House Armed Services Committee, agreed that it would be "supreme folly" to debate the act in public: "The less we say about this bill, the better off all of us will be."

The CIA Act was rammed through Congress on May 27, 1949. With its passage, Congress gave the agency the widest conceivable powers. It became fashionable a generation thereafter to condemn America's spies for crimes against the Constitution. But in the twenty-five years between the passage of the CIA Act and the awakening of a watchdog spirit in Congress, the CIA was barred only from behaving like a secret police force inside the United States. The act gave the agency the ability to do almost anything it wanted, as long as Congress provided the money in an annual package. Approval of the secret budget by a small armed services subcommittee was understood by those in the know to constitute a legal authorization for all secret operations. One of the congressmen voting "aye" summed up this tacit understanding many years later, when he was the president of the United States. If it's secret, it's legal, Richard M. Nixon said.

The CIA now had free rein: unvouchered funds—untraceable money buried under falsified items in the Pentagon's budget—meant unlimited license.

A key clause of the 1949 act allowed the CIA to let one hundred foreigners a year into the United States in the name of national security, granting them "permanent residence without regard to their inadmissibility under the immigration or any other laws." On the same day that President Truman signed the CIA Act of 1949 into law, Willard G. Wyman, the two-star general now running the agency's Office of Special Operations, told American immigration officials that a Ukrainian named Mikola Lebed was "rendering valuable assistance to this Agency in Europe." Under the newly approved law, the CIA smuggled Lebed into the United States.

The agency's own files described the Ukrainian faction led by Lebed as "a terrorist organization." Lebed himself had gone to prison for the murder of the Polish interior minister in 1936, and he escaped when Germany attacked Poland three years later. He saw the Nazis as natural allies. The Germans recruited his men into two battalions, including the one named Nightingale, which fought in the Carpathian Mountains, survived past the end of the war, and remained in the forests of Ukraine to haunt Secretary of Defense Forrestal. Lebed had set himself up as a self-proclaimed foreign minister in Munich and offered his Ukrainian partisans to the CIA for missions against Moscow.

The Justice Department determined that he was a war criminal who had slaughtered Ukrainians, Poles, and Jews. But all attempts to deport him ceased after Allen Dulles himself wrote to the federal immigration commissioner, saying Lebed was "of inestimable value to this Agency" and was assisting in "operations of the first importance."

The CIA "had few methods of collecting intelligence on the Soviet Union and felt compelled to exploit every opportunity, however slim the possibility of success or unsavory the agent," the secret agency history of the Ukrainian operation notes. "Émigré groups, even those with dubious pasts, were often the only alternative to doing nothing." So "the sometimes brutal war record of many émigré groups became blurred as they became more critical to the CIA." By 1949, the United States was ready to work with almost any son of a bitch against Stalin. Lebed fit that bill.

"WE DID NOT WANT TO TOUCH IT"

So did General Reinhard Gehlen.

During World War II, General Gehlen had tried to spy on the Soviets from the eastern front as a leader of the Abwehr, Hitler's military intelligence service. He was an imperious and cagey man who swore he had a network of "good Germans" to spy behind Russian lines for the United States.

"From the beginning," Gehlen said, "I was motivated by the following convictions: A showdown between East and West is unavoidable. Every German is under the obligation of contributing his share, so that Germany is in a position to fulfill the missions incumbent on her for the common defense of Western Christian Civilization." The United States needed "the best German men as co-workers . . . if Western Culture is to be safeguarded." The intelligence network he offered to the Americans was a group of "outstanding German nationals who are good Germans but also ideologically on the side of the Western democracies."

The army, unable to control the Gehlen organization, despite lavishly financing its operations, repeatedly tried to hand it off to the CIA. Many of Richard Helms's officers were dead-set against it. One recorded his revulsion at working with a network of "SS personnel with known Nazi records." Another warned that "American Intelligence is a rich blind man using the Abwehr as a seeing-eye dog. The only trouble is—the leash is much too long." Helms himself expressed a well-founded fear that "there is no question the Russians know this operation is going on."

"We did not want to touch it," said Peter Sichel, then chief of German operations at CIA headquarters. "It had nothing to do with morals or ethics, and everything to do with security."

But in July 1949, under relentless pressure from the army, the CIA took over the Gehlen group. Housed in a former Nazi headquarters outside Munich, Gehlen welcomed dozens of prominent war criminals into his circle. As Helms and Sichel feared, the East German and Soviet intelligence services penetrated the Gehlen group at the highest levels. The worst of the moles surfaced long after the Gehlen group had transformed itself into the national intelligence service of West Germany. Gehlen's longtime chief of counterintelligence had been working for Moscow all along.

Steve Tanner, a young CIA officer based in Munich, said Gehlen had convinced American intelligence officers that he could run missions aimed at the heart of Soviet power. "And, given how hard it was for us," Tanner reflected, "it seemed idiotic not to try it."

"WE WEREN'T GOING TO SIT STILL"

Tanner was an army intelligence veteran fresh out of Yale, hired by Richard Helms in 1947, one of the first two hundred CIA officers sworn into service. In Munich, his assignment was to recruit agents to gather intelligence for the United States from behind the iron curtain.

Almost every major nationality from the Soviet Union and Eastern Europe had at least one self-important émigré group seeking help from the CIA in Munich and Frankfurt. Some of the men Tanner vetted as potential spies were Eastern Europeans who had sided with Germany against Russia. They included "people with fascist backgrounds trying to save their careers by becoming useful to the Americans," Tanner said, and he was wary of them. The non-Russians "hated the Russians violently," Tanner said, "and they were automatically on our side." Others who had fled the outlying republics of the Soviet Union exaggerated their power and influence. "These émigré groups, their main goal was to convince the U.S. government of their importance, and their ability to help the U.S. government, so that they would get support in one form or another," he said.

Lacking guidelines from Washington, Tanner wrote his own: to receive the CIA's support, the émigré groups had to be founded on native soil, not in a Munich coffeehouse. They had to have contact with anti-Soviet groups in their home country. They should not be compromised by close collaboration with the Nazis. In December 1948, after a long and careful assessment, Tanner believed he had found a band of Ukrainians who deserved the CIA's backing. The group called itself the Supreme Council for the Liberation of the Ukraine. Its members in Munich served as political representatives of the fighters back home. The Supreme Council, Tanner reported to headquarters, was morally and politically sound.

Tanner spent the spring and summer of 1949 preparing to infiltrate his Ukrainians behind the iron curtain. The men had come out of the Carpathian Mountains as couriers months before, carrying messages from the Ukrainian underground written on thin sheets of paper folded into wads and sewn together. These scraps were seen as signs of a stalwart resistance movement that could provide intelligence on events in Ukraine and warning of a Soviet attack on Western Europe. Hopes were even higher at headquarters. The CIA believed that "the existence of this movement could have bearing on the course of an open conflict between the United States and the USSR."

Tanner hired a daredevil Hungarian air crew who had hijacked a Hungarian commercial airliner and flown it to Munich a few months earlier. General Wyman, the CIA's special-operations chief, formally approved the mission on July 26. Tanner supervised their training in Morse code and weaponry, planning to drop two of them back into their homeland so that the CIA could communicate with the partisans. But the CIA had no one in Munich with experience in parachuting agents behind enemy lines. Tanner finally found someone. "A Serbo-American colleague who had parachuted into Yugoslavia in World War Two taught my guys how to jump and land. And it was crazy! How can you do a backward somersault on impact with a carbine strapped to your side?" But that was the kind of operation that had made the OSS famous.

Tanner cautioned against great expectations. "We realized that in the woods of western Ukraine, they weren't liable to know what was on Stalin's mind, the big political issues," he said. "At least they could get documents, they could get pocket litter, clothing, shoes." To create a real network of spies inside the Soviet Union, the CIA would have to provide them with elements of disguise—the daily detritus of Soviet life. Even if the missions never produced much important intelligence, Tanner said, they would have strong symbolic value: "They showed Stalin that we weren't going to sit still. And that was important, because up 'til then we had done zilch as far as operations into his country."

On September 5, 1949, Tanner's men took off in a C-47 flown by the Hungarians who had hijacked their way into Munich. Singing a martial strain, they jumped into the darkness of the Carpathian night, landing near the city of Lvov. American intelligence had penetrated the Soviet Union.

The CIA history declassified in 2005 offers a terse summary of what happened next: "The Soviets quickly eliminated the agents."

"WHAT HAD WE DONE WRONG?"

The operation nevertheless set off a huge wave of enthusiasm at CIA headquarters. Wisner began drawing up plans to send more men to recruit networks of dissidents, create American-backed resistance forces, and send the White House early warning of a Soviet military attack. The CIA dispatched dozens of Ukrainian agents by air and by land. Almost every one was captured. Soviet intelligence officers used the prisoners to feed back disinformation—all's well, send more guns, more money, more men. Then they killed them. After five years of "abortive missions," the agency's history states, "CIA discontinued this approach."

"In the long run," it concludes, "the Agency's effort to penetrate the Iron Curtain using Ukrainian agents was ill-fated and tragic."

Wisner was undaunted. He started new paramilitary adventures all over Europe.

In October 1949, four weeks after the first flight into the Ukraine, Wisner teamed up with the British to run rebels into communist Albania, the poorest and most isolated nation in Europe. He saw this barren Balkan outcrop as fertile ground for a resistance army formed from exiled royalists and ragtag loyalists in Rome and Athens. A ship launched from Malta carried nine Albanians on the first commando mission. Three men were killed immediately and the secret police chased down the rest. Wisner had neither the time nor the inclination for introspection. He flew more Albanian recruits to Munich for parachute training, then turned them over to the Athens station, which had its own airport, a fleet of planes, and some tough Polish pilots.

They jumped into Albania and landed in the arms of the secret police. With each failed mission, the plans became more frantic, the training more slipshod, the Albanians more desperate, their capture more certain. The agents who survived were taken prisoner, their messages back to the Athens station controlled by their captors.

"What had we done wrong?" wondered the CIA's John Limond Hart, who was handling the Albanians in Rome. It took years before the CIA understood that the Soviets had known every aspect of the operation from the start. The training camps in Germany were infiltrated. The Albanian exile communities in Rome, Athens, and London were shot through with traitors. And James J. Angleton—the headquarters man responsible for the security of secret operations, the CIA's guardian against double agents—had coordinated the operation with his best friend in British intelligence: the Soviet spy Kim Philby, London's liaison with the agency.

Philby worked for Moscow out of a secure room in the Pentagon, adjacent to the Joint Chiefs of Staff. His friendship with Angleton was sealed with the cold kiss of gin and the warm embrace of whisky. He was an extraordinary drinker, knocking back a fifth a day, and Angleton was on his way to becoming one of the CIA's champion alcoholics, a title held against stiff competition. For more than a year, before and after many a liquid lunch, Angleton gave Philby the precise coordinates for the drop zones for every agent the CIA parachuted into Albania. Though failure followed failure, death upon death, the flights went on for four years. Roughly two hundred of the CIA's foreign agents died. Almost no one in the American government knew. It was a most secret thing.

Angleton was promoted to chief of counterintelligence when it was over. He held the job for twenty years. Drunk after lunch, his mind an impenetrable maze, his in-box a black hole, he passed judgment on every operation and every officer that the CIA aimed against the Soviets. He came to believe that a Soviet master plot controlled American perceptions of the world, and that he and he alone understood the depths of the deception. He took the CIA's missions against Moscow down into a dark labyrinth.

"A FUNDAMENTALLY BAD IDEA"

In early 1950, Wisner ordered up a new assault on the iron curtain. The job went to another Yale man in Munich, by the name of Bill Coffin, a new recruit with the special anticommunist fervor of an ardent socialist.

"The ends don't always justify the means," Coffin said of his years in the CIA. "But they are the only thing that can."

Coffin came to the CIA through a family connection, recruited by his brother-in-law, Frank Lindsay, Wisner's Eastern Europe operations officer. "I said to them, when I went into CIA, 'I don't want to do spy work, I want to do underground political work,'" he remembered in 2005. "The question was: can Russians operate underground? And that seemed to me quite morally acceptable at the time." Coffin had spent the last two years of World War II as a U.S. Army liaison with Soviet commanders. He had been part of the heartless postwar process by which Soviet soldiers were forcibly repatriated. He had been left with a great burden of guilt, which influenced his decision to join the CIA.

"I had seen that Stalin could occasionally make Hitler look like a Boy Scout," Coffin said. "I was very anti-Soviet but very pro-Russian."

Wisner placed his money on the Solidarists, a Russian group that stood as far to the right as possible in Europe after Hitler. Only the handful of CIA officers who spoke Russian, like Bill Coffin, could work with them. The CIA and the Solidarists first smuggled leaflets into Soviet barracks in East Germany. Then they launched balloons bearing thousands of pamphlets. Then they sent four-man parachute missions in unmarked airplanes flying as far east as the outskirts of Moscow. One by one the Solidarist agents floated down to Russia; one by one, they were hunted down, captured, and killed. Once again the CIA delivered its agents to the secret police.

"It was a fundamentally bad idea," Coffin said long after he quit the CIA and became known as the Reverend William Sloane Coffin, the chaplain of Yale and one of the most passionate antiwar voices in America during the 1960s. "We were quite naïve about the use of American power." Almost a decade passed before the agency admitted, in its own words, that "assistance to the émigrés for the eventuality of war with or revolution within the USSR was unrealistic."

All told, hundreds of the CIA's foreign agents were sent to their deaths in Russia, Poland, Romania, Ukraine, and the Baltic States during the 1950s. Their fates were unrecorded; no accounts were kept and no penalty assessed for failure. Their missions were seen as a matter of national survival for the United States. For only hours before Tanner's men took off on their first flight in September 1949, an air force crew flying out of Alaska had detected traces of radioactivity in the atmosphere.

While the results were being analyzed, on September 20, the CIA confidently declared that the Soviet Union would not produce an atomic weapon for at least another four years.

Three days later, Truman told the world that Stalin had the bomb.

On September 29, the CIA's chief of scientific intelligence reported that his office was unable to accomplish its mission. It lacked the talent to track Moscow's efforts to build weapons of mass destruction. The agency's work on Soviet atomic weapons had been an "almost total failure" at every level, he reported; its spies had no scientific or technical data on the Soviet bomb, and its analysts had resorted to guesstimates. He warned that "catastrophic consequences" faced the United States as a result of this failure.

The Pentagon frantically commanded the CIA to place its agents in Moscow in order to steal the Red Army's military plans. "At the time," Richard Helms reflected, "the possibility of recruiting and running any such sources was as improbable as placing resident spies on the planet Mars."

Then, without warning, on July 25, 1950, the United States faced a surprise attack that looked like the start of World War III.

6. "THEY WERE SUICIDE MISSIONS"

The Korean War was the first great test for the CIA. It gave the agency its first real leader: General Walter Bedell Smith. President Truman had called on him to save the CIA before the war broke out. But after serving as the American ambassador in Moscow, the general had come home with an ulcer that almost killed him. When the news of the Korean invasion arrived, he was at Walter Reed Army Hospital, where two-thirds of his stomach was removed. Truman implored him, but he begged off for a month to see if he would survive. Then that call became an order, and Bedell Smith became the fourth director of central intelligence in four years.

The general's task was to learn the secrets of the Kremlin, and he had a good idea of his chances. "There are only two personalities that I know of who might do it," he told the five senators who confirmed him at an August 24 hearing where he wore a newly acquired fourth star, a prize from the president. "One is God, and the other is Stalin, and I do not know that even God can do it because I do not know whether he is close enough in touch with Uncle Joe to know what he is talking about." As for what awaited him at the CIA, he said: "I expect the worst, and I am sure I won't be disappointed." Immediately upon taking office in October, he discovered that he had inherited an unholy mess. "It's interesting to see all you fellows here," he said as he looked around the table at his first staff meeting. "It'll be even more interesting to see how many of you are here a few months from now."

Bedell Smith was fiercely authoritarian, devastatingly sarcastic, and intolerant of imperfection. Wisner's sprawling operations left him sput-tering with rage. "It was the place where all the money was spent," he said, and "all the rest of the Agency was suspicious of it." In his first week in office, he discovered that Wisner reported to the State Department and the Pentagon, not to the director of central intelligence. In a towering fury, he informed the chief of covert operations that his free-booting days were over.

"AN IMPOSSIBLE TASK"

To serve the president, the general tried to salvage the analytical side of the house, which he called "the heart and soul of CIA." He overhauled the agency's procedures for writing intelligence reports, and he ultimately persuaded Sherman Kent, who had fled Washington in the dismal first days of the Central Intelligence Group, to return from Yale to create a system of national estimates, pulling together the best available information from across the government. Kent called the job "an impossible task." After all, he said, "estimating is what you do when you do not know."

Days after Bedell Smith took over, Truman was preparing to meet with General Douglas MacArthur on Wake Island in the Pacific. The president wanted the CIA's best intelligence on Korea. Above all, he wanted to know whether the communist Chinese would enter the war. MacArthur, driving his troops deep into North Korea, had insisted that China would never attack.

The CIA knew almost nothing about what went on in China. In October 1949, by the time Mao Tse-tung drove out the Nationalist forces of Chiang Kai-shek and proclaimed the People's Republic, all but a handful of the American spies in China had fled to Hong Kong or Taiwan. Already hobbled by Mao, the CIA was crippled by MacArthur, who hated the agency and did his best to ban its officers from the Far East. Though the CIA worked frantically to keep an eye on China, the chains of foreign agents it had inherited from the OSS were far too weak. So was the agency's research and reporting. Four hundred CIA analysts worked on daily intelligence bulletins for President Truman at the start of the Korean War, but 90 percent of their reporting was rewritten State Department files; most of the rest was weightless commentary.

The CIA's allies in the theater of war were the intelligence services of two corrupt and unreliable leaders: South Korea's president, Syngman Rhee, and the Chinese Nationalist chief, Chiang Kai-shek. The strongest first impression of the CIA officers upon arriving in their capitals of Seoul and Taipei was the stench of human feces fertilizing the surrounding fields. Reliable information was as scarce as electricity and running water. The CIA found itself manipulated by crooked friends, duped by communist foes, and at the mercy of money-hungry exiles fabricating intelligence. Fred Schultheis, the Hong Kong station chief in 1950, spent the next six years sorting through the trash that Chinese refugees sold the agency during the Korean War. The CIA was supporting a free market of paper mills run by con artists.

The one true source of intelligence on the Far East from the final days of World War II until the end of 1949 had been the wizards of American signals intelligence. They had been able to intercept and decrypt passages from communist cables and communiqués sent between Moscow and the Far East. Then silence fell at the very hour that the North Korean leader Kim Il-sung was consulting with Stalin and Mao on his intent to attack. America's ability to listen in on Soviet, Chinese, and North Korean military plans suddenly vanished.

On the eve of the Korean War, a Soviet spy had penetrated the codebreakers' nerve center, Arlington Hall, a converted girls' school a stone's throw from the Pentagon. He was William Wolf Weisband, a linguist who translated broken messages from Russian into English. Weisband, recruited as a spy by Moscow in the 1930s, single-handedly shattered the ability of the United States to read the Soviets' secret dispatches. Bedell Smith recognized that something terrible had happened to American signals intelligence, and he alerted the White House. The result was the creation of the National Security Agency, the signals-intelligence service that grew to dwarf the CIA in its size and power. Half a century later, the National Security Agency called the Weisband case "perhaps the most significant intelligence loss in U.S. history."

"NO CONVINCING INDICATIONS"

The president left for Wake Island on October 11, 1950. The CIA assured him that it saw "no convincing indications of an actual Chinese Communist intention to resort to full-scale intervention in Korea . . . barring a Soviet decision for global war." The agency reached that judgment despite two alarms from its three-man Tokyo station. First the station chief, George Aurell, reported that a Chinese Nationalist officer in Manchuria was warning that Mao had amassed 300,000 troops near the Korean border. Headquarters paid little heed. Then Bill Duggan, later chief of station in Taiwan, insisted that the Chicoms soon would cross into North Korea. General MacArthur responded by threatening to have Duggan arrested. The warnings never reached Wake Island.

At headquarters, the agency kept advising Truman that China would not enter the war on any significant scale. On October 18, as MacArthur's troops surged north toward the Yalu River and the Chinese border, the CIA reported that "the Soviet Korean venture has ended in failure." On October 20, the CIA said that Chinese forces detected at the Yalu were there to protect hydroelectric power plants. On October 28, it told the White House that those Chinese troops were scattered volunteers. On October 30, after American troops had been attacked, taking heavy casualties, the CIA reaffirmed that a major Chinese intervention was unlikely. A few days later, Chinese-speaking CIA officers interrogated several prisoners taken during the encounter and determined that they were Mao's soldiers. Yet CIA headquarters asserted one last time that China would not invade in force. Two days later 300,000 Chinese troops struck with an attack so brutal that it nearly pushed the Americans into the sea.

Bedell Smith was aghast. He believed that the business of the CIA was to guard the nation against military surprise. But the agency had misread every global crisis of the past year: the Soviet atom bomb, the Korean War, the Chinese invasion. In December 1950, as President Truman declared a national emergency and recalled General Eisenhower to active duty, Bedell Smith stepped up his own war to turn the CIA into a professional intelligence service. He looked first for someone to control Frank Wisner.

"A DISTINCT DANGER"

Only one name presented itself.

On January 4, 1951, Bedell Smith bowed to the inevitable and appointed Allen Dulles as the CIA's deputy director of plans (the title was a cover; the job was chief of covert operations). The two men quickly proved to be a bad match, as the CIA's Tom Polgar saw when he observed them together at headquarters: "Bedell clearly doesn't like Dulles, and it's easy to see why," he recounted. "An Army officer gets an order and he carries it out. A lawyer finds a way to weasel. In CIA, as it developed, an order is a departure point for a discussion."

Wisner's operations had multiplied fivefold since the start of the war. Bedell Smith saw that the United States had no strategy for conducting this kind of struggle. He appealed to President Truman and the National Security Council. Was the agency really supposed to support armed revolution in Eastern Europe? In China? In Russia? The Pentagon and the State Department replied: yes, all that, and more. The director wondered how. Wisner was hiring hundreds of college kids every month, running them through a few weeks of commando school, sending them overseas for half a year, rotating them out, and sending more raw recruits to replace them. He was trying to build a worldwide military machine without a semblance of professional training, logistics, or communications. Bedell Smith sat at his desk, nibbling the crackers and warm mush on which he survived after his stomach surgery, and his anger mingled with despair.

His second-in-command, the deputy director of central intelligence, Bill Jackson, resigned in frustration, saying that the CIA's operations were an impossible tangle. Bedell Smith had no choice but to promote Dulles to deputy director and Wisner to chief of covert operations. When he saw the first CIA budget the two men proposed, he exploded. It was $587 million, an elevenfold increase from 1948. More than $400 million was for Wisner's covert operations—three times the cost of espionage and analysis combined.

This posed "a distinct danger to CIA as an intelligence agency," Bedell Smith fumed. "The operational tail will wag the intelligence dog," he warned. "The top people will be forced to take up all their time in the direction of operations and will necessarily neglect intelligence." It was then that the general began to suspect that Dulles and Wisner were hiding something from him. At his daily meetings with the CIA's deputy directors and staff, recorded in documents declassified after 2002, he constantly cross-examined them about what was going on overseas. But his direct questions received unaccountably vague responses—or none at all. He warned them not "to withhold" or "to whitewash unfortunate incidents or serious errors." He ordered them to create a detailed accounting of their paramilitary missions—code names, descriptions, objectives, costs. They never complied. "In exasperation, he visited upon them more violent manifestations of his wrath than he did upon anybody else," wrote his personal representative on the NSC staff, Ludwell Lee Montague. Bedell Smith was not afraid of much. But he was angry and frightened by the thought that Dulles and Wisner were leading the CIA to "some ill-conceived and disastrous misadventure," Montague wrote. "He feared that some blunder overseas might become public knowledge."

"WE DIDN'T KNOW WHAT WE WERE DOING"

The classified CIA histories of the Korean War reveal what Bedell Smith feared.

They say the agency's paramilitary operations were "not only ineffective but probably morally reprehensible in the number of lives lost." Thousands of recruited Korean and Chinese agents were dropped into North Korea during the war, never to return. "The amount of time and treasure expended was enormously disproportionate to attainments," the agency concluded. Nothing was gained from "the substantial sums spent and the numerous Koreans sacrificed." Hundreds more Chinese agents died after they were launched onto the mainland in misconceived land, air, and sea operations.

"Most of these missions weren't sent for intelligence. They were sent to supply nonexistent or fictitious resistance groups," said Peter Sichel, who saw the string of failures play out after he became station chief in Hong Kong. "They were suicide missions. They were suicidal and irresponsible." They continued into the 1960s, legions of agents sent to their deaths chasing shadows.

In the early days of the war, Wisner assigned a thousand officers to Korea and three hundred to Taiwan, with orders to penetrate Mao's walled fortress and Kim Il-sung's military dictatorship. These men were thrown into battle with little preparation or training. One among them was Donald Gregg, fresh out of Williams College. His first thought when the war broke out was: "Where the hell is Korea?" After a crash course in paramilitary operations, he was dispatched to a new CIA outpost in the middle of the Pacific. Wisner was building a covert-operations base on the island of Saipan at a cost of $28 million. Saipan, still riddled with the bones of World War II dead, became a training camp for the CIA's paramilitary missions into Korea, China, Tibet, and Vietnam. Gregg took tough Korean farm boys plucked from refugee camps, brave but undisciplined men who spoke no English, and tried to turn them into instant American intelligence agents. The CIA sent them on crudely conceived missions that produced little save a lengthening roster of lost lives. The memory stayed with Gregg as he rose through the ranks of the Far East Division to become the CIA's station chief in Seoul, then the U.S. ambassador to South Korea, and finally the chief national-security aide to Vice President George H. W. Bush.

"We were following in the footsteps of the OSS," Gregg said. "But the people we were going up against had complete control. We didn't know what we were doing. I asked my superiors what the mission was and they wouldn't tell me. They didn't know what the mission was. It was swashbuckling of the worst kind. We were training Koreans and Chinese and a lot of other strange people, dropping Koreans into North Korea, dropping Chinese into China just north of the Korean border, and we'd drop these people in and we'd never hear from them again."

"The record in Europe was bad," he said. "The record in Asia was bad. The agency had a terrible record in its early days—a great reputation and a terrible record."

"CIA WAS BEING DUPED"

Bedell Smith repeatedly warned Wisner to watch out for false intelligence fabricated by the enemy. But some of Wisner's officers were fabricators themselves—including the station chief and the chief of operations he sent to Korea.

In February, March, and April 1951, more than 1,200 North Korean exiles were gathered on Yong-do Island, in Pusan Harbor, under the command of the operations chief, Hans Tofte, an OSS veteran with a greater talent for deceiving his superiors than his enemies. Tofte formed three brigades—White Tiger, Yellow Dragon, and Blue Dragon—with forty-four guerrilla teams. Their missions were threefold: to serve as intelligence-gathering infiltrators, as guerrilla-warfare squads, and as escape-and-evasion crews to rescue downed American pilots and crews.

White Tiger went ashore in North Korea at the end of April 1951 with 104 men, reinforced by 36 more agents dropped by parachute. Before leaving Korea four months later, Tofte sent back glowing reports on his accomplishments. But by November, most of the White Tiger guerrillas were killed, captured, or missing. Blue Dragon and Yellow Dragon met similar fates. The few infiltration teams that survived were captured and forced on pain of death to deceive their American case officers with phony radio messages. None of the guerrillas made it out alive. Most of the escape-and-evasion teams were lost or slaughtered.

In the spring and summer of 1952, Wisner's officers dropped more than 1,500 Korean agents into the North. They sent back a flood of detailed radio reports on North Korean and Chinese communist military movements. They were heralded by the CIA station chief in Seoul, Albert R. Haney, a garrulous and ambitious army colonel who boasted openly that he had thousands of men working for him on guerrilla operations and intelligence missions. Haney said he personally had overseen the recruitment and training of hundreds of Koreans. Some of his fellow Americans thought Haney was a dangerous fool. William W. Thomas, Jr., a State Department political intelligence officer in Seoul, suspected the station chief had a payroll filled with people who were "controlled by the other side."

So did John Limond Hart, who replaced Haney as the Seoul chief of station in September 1952. After a series of stinging experiences with intelligence fabricators in Europe during his first four years at the CIA, and his stint running Albanian exiles out of Rome, Hart was intensely aware of the problems of deception and disinformation, and he decided to take "a hard look at the miraculous achievements claimed by my predecessors."

Haney had presided over two hundred CIA officers in Seoul, not one of whom spoke Korean. The station depended on recruited Korean agents who supervised the CIA's guerrilla operations and intelligence-gathering missions in the North. After three months of digging, Hart determined that nearly every Korean agent he had inherited had either invented his reports or worked in secret for the communists. Every dispatch the station had sent to CIA headquarters from the front for the past eighteen months was a calculated deception.

"One particular report lives in my memory," Hart recounted. "It purported to be a recapitulation of all Chinese and North Korean units along the battle line, citing each unit's strength and numerical designation." American military commanders had hailed it as "one of the outstanding intelligence reports of the war." Hart determined that it was a complete fabrication.

He went on to discover that all of the important Korean agents Haney had recruited—not some, but all—were "con men who had for some time been living happily on generous CIA payments supposedly being sent to 'assets' in North Korea. Almost every report we had received from their notional agents came from our enemies."

Long after the Korean War was over, the CIA concluded that Hart was correct: almost all the secret information the agency gathered during the war had been manufactured by the North Korean and Chinese security services. The fictional intelligence was passed on to the Pentagon and the White House. The agency's paramilitary operations in Korea had been infiltrated and betrayed before they began.

Hart told headquarters that the station should cease operations until the ledger was cleared and the damage undone. An intelligence service penetrated by the enemy was worse than no service at all. Instead, Bedell Smith sent an emissary to Seoul to tell Hart that "the CIA, being a new organization whose reputation had not yet been established, simply could not admit to other branches of Government—least of all to the highly competitive U.S. military intelligence services—its inability to collect intelligence on North Korea." The messenger was the deputy director of intelligence, Loftus Becker. After Bedell Smith sent him on an inspection tour of all the CIA's Asian stations in November 1952, Becker came home and turned in his resignation. He had concluded that the situation was hopeless: the CIA's ability to gather intelligence in the Far East was "almost negligible." Before resigning, he confronted Frank Wisner: "Blown operations indicate a lack of success," he told him, "and there have been a number of these lately."

Hart's reports and Haney's frauds were buried. The agency had walked into an ambush and represented it as a strategic maneuver. Dulles told members of Congress that "CIA was controlling considerable resistance elements in North Korea," said air force colonel James G. L. Kellis, who had served as Wisner's paramilitary operations director. At the time, Dulles had been warned that " 'CIA's guerrillas' in North Korea were under the control of the enemy"; in truth "CIA had no such assets" and "CIA was being duped," Kellis reported in a whistle-blowing letter he sent to the White House after the war was over.

The ability to represent failure as success was becoming a CIA tradition. The agency's unwillingness to learn from its mistakes became a permanent part of its culture. The CIA's covert operators never wrote "lessons-learned" studies. Even today there are few if any rules or procedures for producing them.

"We are all aware that our operations in the Far East are far from what we would like," Wisner admitted in a headquarters meeting. "We simply have not had the time to develop the quantity and kind of people we must have if we are to successfully carry out the heavy burdens which have been placed on us." The inability to penetrate North Korea remains the longest-running intelligence failure in the CIA's history.

"SOME PEOPLE HAVE TO GET KILLED"

The agency opened a second front in the Korean War in 1951. The officers on the agency's China operations desk, frantic at Mao's entry into the war, convinced themselves that as many as one million Kuomintang Nationalist guerrillas were waiting inside Red China for the CIA's help.

Were these reports fabricated by paper mills in Hong Kong, produced by political conniving in Taiwan, or conjured up by wishful thinking in Washington? Was it wise for the CIA to make war against Mao? There was no time to think that through. "You do not have in government a basic approved strategy for this kind of war," Bedell Smith told Dulles and Wisner. "We haven't even a policy on Chiang Kai-shek."

Dulles and Wisner made their own. First they tried to enlist Americans to parachute into communist China. One potential recruit, Paul Kreisberg, was eager to join the CIA until "they tested me on my loyalty and my commitment by asking whether I would be willing to be dropped by parachute into Szechuan. My target would be to organize a group of anti-communist Kuomintang soldiers who remained up in the hills in Szechuan and work with them in a number of operations and then exfiltrate myself, if necessary, out through Burma. They looked at me, and they said, 'Would you be willing to do that?' " Kreisberg thought it over and joined the State Department. Lacking American volunteers, the CIA dropped hundreds of recruited Chinese agents into the mainland, often dropping them blindly, with orders to find their way to a village. When they went missing, they were written off as a cost of covert warfare.

The CIA also thought it could undermine Mao with Muslim horsemen, the Hui clans of China's far northwest, commanded by Ma Pu-fang, a tribal leader who had political connections with the Chinese Nationalists. The CIA dropped tons of weapons and ammunition and radios and scores of Chinese agents into western China, then tried to find Americans to follow them. Among the men they tried to recruit was Michael D. Coe, later one of the twentieth century's greatest archaeologists, the man who broke the code of Mayan hieroglyphics. Coe was a twenty-two-year-old Harvard graduate student in the fall of 1950 when a professor took him out to lunch and asked the question thousands of Ivy Leaguers would hear over the next decade: "How would you like to work for the government in a really interesting capacity?" He went to Washington and received a pseudonym selected at random out of a London telephone directory. He was told he would become a case officer in one of two clandestine operations. Either he would be dropped by parachute deep into far western China to support the Muslim fighters, or he would be sent to an island off the China coast to run raids.

"Luckily for me," Coe said, "it was the latter option." He became part of Western Enterprises, a CIA front in Taiwan created to subvert Mao's China. He spent eight months on a tiny island called White Dog. The only intelligence operation of consequence on the island was the discovery that the Nationalist commander's chief of staff was a communist spy. Back in Taipei, in the closing months of the Korean War, he saw that Western Enterprises was no more clandestine than the Chinese whorehouses his colleagues frequented. "They built a whole gated community with its own PX and officers' club," he said. "The esprit that had been there had changed. It was an incredible waste of money." Coe concluded that the CIA "had been sold a bill of goods by the Nationalists—that there was a huge force of resistance inside of China. We were barking up the wrong tree. The whole operation was a waste of time."

Hedging its bets on the Nationalist Chinese, the CIA decided that there had to be a "Third Force" in China. From April 1951 until the end of 1952, the agency spent roughly $100 million, buying enough arms and ammunition for 200,000 guerrillas, without finding the elusive Third Force. About half the money and guns went to a group of Chinese refugees based on Okinawa, who sold the CIA on the idea that a huge cadre of anticommunist troops on the mainland supported them. It was a scam. Ray Peers, the OSS veteran who ran Western Enterprises, said that if he ever found a real live soldier of the Third Force, he would kill him, stuff him, and ship him to the Smithsonian Institution.

The CIA was still searching for the elusive resistance forces when it dropped a four-man Chinese guerrilla team into Manchuria in July 1952. Four months later, the team radioed for help. It was a trap: they had been captured and turned against the CIA by the Chinese. The agency authorized a rescue mission using a newly devised sling designed to scoop up the stranded men. Two young CIA officers on their first operation, Dick Fecteau and Jack Downey, were sent into a shooting gallery. Their plane went down in a storm of Chinese machine-gun fire. The pilots died. Fecteau did nineteen years in a Chinese prison and Downey, fresh out of Yale, did more than twenty. Beijing later broadcast a scorecard for Manchuria: the CIA had dropped 212 foreign agents in; 101 were killed and 111 captured.

The final theater for the CIA in the Korean War lay in Burma. In early 1951, as the Chinese communists chased General MacArthur's troops south, the Pentagon thought the Chinese Nationalists could take some pressure off MacArthur by opening a second front. About 1,500 followers of Li Mi, a Nationalist general, were stranded in northern Burma, near the Chinese border. Li Mi asked for American guns and American gold. The CIA began flying Chinese Nationalist soldiers into Thailand, training them, equipping them, and dropping them along with pallets of guns and ammunition into northern Burma. Desmond FitzGerald, newly arrived at the agency with glittering legal and social credentials, had fought in Burma during World War II. He took over the Li Mi operation. It quickly became a farce, then a tragedy.

When Li Mi's soldiers crossed over into China, Mao's forces shot them to pieces. The CIA's espionage officers discovered that Li Mi's radioman in Bangkok was a Chinese communist agent. But Wisner's men pressed on. Li Mi's soldiers retreated and regrouped. When FitzGerald dropped more guns and ammunition into Burma, Li Mi's men would not fight. They settled into the mountains known as the Golden Triangle, harvested opium poppies, and married the local women. Twenty years later, the CIA would have to start another small war in Burma to wipe out the heroin labs that were the basis of Li Mi's global drug empire.

"There is no point in bemoaning opportunities lost . . . nor attempting to alibi past failures," Bedell Smith wrote in a letter to General Matthew B. Ridgway, MacArthur's successor as chief of the Far East Command. "I have found, through painful experience, that secret operations are a job for the professional and not for the amateur."

A postscript to the CIA's Korean calamities came soon after the armistice of July 1953. The agency saw President Syngman Rhee of South Korea as a hopeless case, and for years it sought ways to replace him. It almost killed him by mistake.

One cloudless afternoon in late summer, a yacht sailed slowly past the shoreline of Yong-do, the island encampment where the CIA trained its Korean commandos. President Rhee was on board having a party with his friends. The officers and guards in charge of the training site had not been informed that President Rhee would be passing by. They opened fire. Miraculously, no one was hurt, but the president was displeased. He called in the American ambassador and informed him that the CIA's paramilitary group had seventy-two hours to leave the country. Soon thereafter the luckless station chief, John Hart, had to start all over again, recruiting, training, and parachuting agents into North Korea from 1953 until 1955. All of them, to the best of his knowledge, were captured and executed.

The agency failed on all fronts in Korea. It failed in providing warning, in providing analysis, and in its headlong deployment of recruited agents. Thousands of deaths of Americans and their Asian allies were the consequence.

A generation later, American military veterans called Korea "the forgotten war." At the agency, it was deliberate amnesia. The waste of $152 million on weapons for phantom guerrillas was adjusted on the balance sheets. The fact that a great deal of Korean War intelligence was false or fabricated was kept secret. The question of what it had cost in lost lives was unasked and unanswered.

But the assistant secretary of state for the Far East, Dean Rusk, sniffed out a whiff of decay. He called on John Melby, a skilled State Department China hand, to investigate. Melby had worked side by side with the first American spies in Asia from the mid-1940s onward and knew the cast of characters. He went out to the region and took a long, hard look. "Our intelligence is so bad that it approaches malfeasance in office," he told Rusk in an eyes-only report that somehow wound up on the desk of the director of central intelligence. Melby was summoned to CIA headquarters for a classic chewing-out by Bedell Smith, as Deputy Director Allen Dulles sat by in silence.

For Dulles, Asia was always a sideshow. He believed that the real war for Western civilization was in Europe. That fight called for "people who are ready and willing to stand up and take the consequences," he told a few of his closest friends and colleagues at a secret conference held at the Princeton Inn in May 1952. "After all, we have had a hundred thousand casualties in Korea," he said, according to a transcript declassified in 2003. "If we have been willing to accept those casualties, I wouldn't worry if there were a few casualties or a few martyrs behind the iron curtain. . . . I don't think you can wait until you have all your troops and are sure you are going to win. You have got to start and go ahead.

"You have got to have a few martyrs," Dulles said. "Some people have to get killed."

7. "A VAST FIELD OF ILLUSION"

Allen Dulles asked his colleagues at the Princeton Inn to consider how best to destroy Stalin's ability to control his satellite states. He believed that communism could be undone by covert action. The CIA was ready to roll back Russia to its old borders.

"If we are going to move in and take the offensive, Eastern Europe presents the best place to start," he said. "I don't want a bloody battle," he said, "but I would like to see things started."

Chip Bohlen spoke up. Soon to be named the American ambassador to Moscow, Bohlen had been in on the game from the start. The seeds of the CIA's political-warfare program were first planted at the Sunday night suppers he had attended five years before. "Are we waging political warfare?" he asked Dulles rhetorically. "We have been waging it since 1946. A lot has been going on. Whether it has been effective, or done in the best way, is another question.

"When you ask, 'Shall we go on the offensive?' I see a vast field of illusion," Bohlen said.

While the war in Korea still raged, the Joint Chiefs commanded Frank Wisner and the CIA to conduct "a major covert offensive against the Soviet Union," aimed at "the heartland of the communist control system." Wisner tried. The Marshall Plan was being transformed into pacts providing America's allies with weapons, and Wisner saw this as a chance to arm secret stay-behind forces to fight the Soviets in the event of war. He was seeding the ground all over Europe. Throughout the mountains and forests of Scandinavia, France, Germany, Italy, and Greece, his men were dropping gold ingots into lakes and burying caches of weapons for the coming battle. In the marshes and foothills of Ukraine and the Baltics, his pilots were dropping agents to their deaths.

In Germany, more than a thousand of his officers were slipping leaflets into East Berlin, forging postal stamps carrying a portrait of the East German leader Walter Ulbricht with a hangman's noose around his neck, and plotting out paramilitary missions in Poland. None of this provided insight into the nature of the Soviet threat. Operations to sabotage the Soviet empire kept overwhelming plans to spy on it.

"YOU OWN HIM BODY AND SOUL"

Deeply wary, Walter Bedell Smith dispatched a trusted three-star general, Lucian K. Truscott, an officer with impeccable connections and a distinguished war record, to take over the CIA's operations in Germany and to find out what Wisner's men were doing. General Truscott's orders were to suspend every scheme he deemed dubious. Upon his arrival, he chose Tom Polgar of the CIA's Berlin base as his chief aide.

They found several ticking time bombs. Among them was one very dark secret, described in CIA documents of the day as a program of "overseas interrogations."

The agency had set up clandestine prisons to wring confessions out of suspected double agents. One was in Germany, another in Japan. The third, and the biggest, was in the Panama Canal Zone. "Like Guantánamo," Polgar said in 2005. "It was anything goes."

The zone was its own world, seized by the United States at the turn of the century, bulldozed out of the jungles that surrounded the Panama Canal. On a naval base in the zone, the CIA's office of security had refitted a complex of cinder-block prison cells inside a navy brig normally used to house drunk and disorderly sailors. In those cells, the agency was conducting secret experiments in harsh interrogation, using techniques on the edge of torture, drug-induced mind control, and brainwashing.

The project dated back to 1948, when Richard Helms and his officers in Germany realized they were being defrauded by double agents. The effort began as a crash program in 1950, when the Korean War erupted and a sense of emergency seized the CIA. Late that summer, as the temperature approached a hundred degrees in Panama, two Russian émigrés who had been delivered to the Canal Zone from Germany were injected with drugs and brutally interrogated. Along with four suspected North Korean double agents subjected to the same treatment at a military base commandeered by the CIA in Japan, they were among the first known human guinea pigs under a program code-named Project Artichoke, a small but significant part of a fifteen-year search by the CIA for ways to control the human mind.

Many of the Russians and East Germans whom the agency had recruited as agents and informers in Germany had gone sour. After they had given up what little knowledge they had, they resorted to deception or blackmail to extend their short careers. More than a few of them were suspected of working in secret for the Soviets. The issue became urgent when CIA officers came to realize that the communist intelligence and security services were far bigger and significantly more sophisticated than the agency.

Richard Helms once said that American intelligence officers were trained to believe that they could not count on a foreign agent "unless you own him body and soul." The need for a way to own a man's soul led to the search for mind-control drugs and secret prisons in which to test them. Dulles, Wisner, and Helms were personally responsible for these endeavors.

On May 15, 1952, Dulles and Wisner received a report on Project Artichoke, spelling out the agency's four-year effort to test heroin, amphetamines, sleeping pills, the newly discovered LSD, and other "special techniques in CIA interrogations." Part of the project sought to find an interrogation technique so strong that "the individual under its influence will find it difficult to maintain a fabrication under questioning." A few months later, Dulles approved an ambitious new program code-named Ultra. Under its auspices, seven prisoners at a federal penitentiary in Kentucky were kept high on LSD for seventy-seven consecutive days. When the CIA slipped the same drug to an army civilian employee, Frank Olson, he leaped out of the window of a New York hotel. Like the suspected double agents sent to the secret brig in Panama, these men were expendable conscripts in the battle to defeat the Soviets.

Senior CIA officers, including Helms, destroyed almost all the records of these programs in fear that they might become public. The evidence that remains is fragmentary, but it strongly suggests that use of secret prisons for the forcible drug-induced questioning of suspect agents went on throughout the 1950s. Members of the clandestine service, the agency's security office, and the CIA's scientists and doctors met monthly to discuss the progress of Project Artichoke until 1956. "These discussions included the planning of overseas interrogations," the agency's files show, and the use of "special interrogation" techniques continued for several years thereafter.

The drive to penetrate the iron curtain had led the CIA to adopt the tactics of its enemies.

"A WELL THOUGHT-OUT PLAN, EXCEPT . . ."

Among the CIA operations that General Truscott killed off was a project to support a group called the Young Germans. Many of its leaders were aging Hitler Youth. The membership rolls had grown to more than twenty thousand in 1952. They enthusiastically took the CIA's weapons, radios, cameras, and money and buried them all over the country. They also began drawing up their own extensive hit list of mainstream democratic West German politicians to be assassinated when the hour was at hand. The Young Germans became so blatant that their existence and their enemies list blew up into a public scandal.

"That became cause for a great deal of concern and a major flap when the secrecy was broken," said John McMahon, a future deputy director of central intelligence, then a young CIA officer on Truscott's staff.

On the same day that Dulles was speaking at the Princeton Inn, Henry Hecksher was writing a heartfelt plea to CIA headquarters. For years, Hecksher, soon to become chief of the Berlin base, had cultivated a unique agent inside East Germany, Horst Erdmann, who ran an impressive organization called the Free Jurists' Committee. The Free Jurists were an underground group of young lawyers and paralegals challenging the communist regime in East Berlin. They compiled dossiers on the crimes committed by the state. An International Congress of Jurists was set to convene in West Berlin in July 1952, and the Free Jurists could play an important political part on a world stage.

Wisner wanted to take control of the Free Jurists and turn them into an armed underground. Hecksher protested. These men were sources of intelligence, he argued, and if they were forced into a paramilitary role, they would become cannon fodder. He was overruled. Wisner's officers in Berlin selected one of General Reinhard Gehlen's officers to transform the group into a fighting force made up of three-man cells. But every member of every cell they created knew the identity of every other member of every other cell—a classic lapse in security. After Soviet soldiers kidnapped and tortured one of their leaders on the eve of the international conference, every one of the CIA's Free Jurists was arrested.

Toward the end of 1952, in the last months of Smith's tenure as director of central intelligence, more of Wisner's hastily improvised operations began coming apart. The fallout left a lasting impression on a newly anointed CIA officer named Ted Shackley, who started a supercharged career at the agency as a second lieutenant shanghaied from his job training military police in West Virginia. His first assignment was to make himself familiar with a major Wisner operation to support a Polish liberation army, the Freedom and Independence Movement, known as WIN.

Wisner and his men had dropped roughly $5 million worth of gold bars, submachine guns, rifles, ammunition, and two-way radios into Poland. They had established trusted contacts with "WIN outside," a handful of émigrés in Germany and London. They believed that "WIN inside" was a powerful force—five hundred soldiers in Poland, twenty thousand armed partisans, and a hundred thousand sympathizers—all prepared to fight the Red Army.

It was an illusion. The Polish secret police, backed by the Soviets, had wiped out WIN back in 1947. "WIN inside" was a phantom, a communist trick. In 1950, a clueless courier was sent to alert the Polish émigrés in London. His message was that WIN lived and thrived in Warsaw. The émigrés contacted Wisner's men, who leaped at the chance to build a resistance group behind enemy lines, and parachuted as many patriots as possible back into Poland. At headquarters, the CIA's leaders thought they had finally beaten the communists at their own game. "Poland represents one of the most promising areas for the development of underground resistance," Bedell Smith said at a meeting of his deputies in August 1952. Wisner told him that "WIN is now riding high."

The Soviet and Polish intelligence services had spent years setting their traps. "They were well aware of our air operations. When we would drop these agents in," McMahon said, "they would go out and make contact with people we knew would be helpful to us. And the Poles and the KGB were right in back of them and would mop them up. So it was a well thought-out plan, except we were recruiting agents of the Soviet Union. It turned out to be a monumental disaster. People died." Perhaps thirty, maybe more, were lost.

Shackley said he never forgot the sight of his fellow officers realizing that five years of planning and millions of dollars had gone down the drain. The unkindest cut might have been their discovery that the Poles had sent a chunk of the CIA's money to the Communist Party of Italy.

"CIA had clearly thought they could operate in Eastern Europe the way the OSS had operated in occupied Western Europe during the war," said the CIA's Henry Loomis, a future chief of the Voice of America. "That was clearly impossible."

In Washington, Frank Lindsay, who had run operations in Eastern Europe from headquarters, resigned in anguish. He told Dulles and Wisner that scientific and technical means of spying on the Soviets would have to replace covert action as the CIA's strategy against communism. Quixotic paramilitary missions to support imaginary resistance movements could not push the Russians out of Europe.

In Germany, McMahon had spent months reading all the cable traffic coming in to the station. He came to a stark conclusion. "We had no capability there," he said years later. "Our insight into the Soviet Union was zero."

"THE *AGENCY'S* FUTURE"

The CIA was now a worldwide force with fifteen thousand people, half a billion dollars in secret funds to spend each year, and more than fifty overseas stations. By sheer willpower, Bedell Smith had shaped it into an organization that looked much the way it would for the next fifty years. He had forged the Office of Policy Coordination and the Office of Special Operations into a single clandestine service to serve abroad, created a unified system for analysis at home, and achieved a measure of respect for the CIA at the White House.

But he had never made it a professional intelligence service. "We can't get qualified people," he lamented in his last days as director of central intelligence. "They just simply don't exist." And he had never made Allen Dulles and Frank Wisner bend to his authority. A week before the 1952 presidential election, Bedell Smith tried one last time to bring them under control.

On October 27, he convened a conference of the CIA's twenty-six most senior officers and proclaimed that "until CIA could build a reserve of well-trained people, it would have to hold its activities to the limited number of operations that it could do well, rather than attempt to cover a broad field with poor performance" from "improperly trained or inferior personnel." Galvanized by Truscott's investigations in Germany, the general ordered the convening of a "Murder Board"—a jury that could kill off the worst of the CIA's covert operations. Wisner immediately fought back. He said that shutting down dubious operations would be a long and painful process, and it would take many, many months—well into the next administration—for Bedell Smith's order to be carried out. The general was defeated and the Murder Board defused.

Dwight D. Eisenhower won the presidency on a national-security platform that called for the free world to liberate the Soviet satellites, a script written by his closest foreign-policy adviser, John Foster Dulles. Their victory plans called for a new director of central intelligence. Chosen over Bedell Smith's protests, confirmed without opposition in the Senate, and cheered on by the press, Allen Dulles finally won the job he coveted.

Richard Helms had known Dulles well for eight years, ever since they traveled together to the little red schoolhouse in France where Bedell Smith had accepted the unconditional surrender of the Third Reich. Helms was forty now, a tightly wired man, not a slicked-back hair out of place nor a stray paper on his desk when the lights went out at night. Dulles was sixty, shuffling in the carpet slippers he wore in private to ease his gout, ever the absentminded professor. Not long after Eisenhower's election, Dulles buzzed Helms into the director's chambers, and the two men sat down for a chat.

"A word about the future," Dulles said, filling the air with great clouds of pipe smoke. "The *Agency's* future."

"You remember the conniving and blood-spilling that went on when we were trying to sort things out in 1946? What would Central Intelligence be responsible for? Would there even be a service?" Dulles wanted Helms to understand that as long as he was the director of central intelligence, there was damned well going to be a service devoted to daring, difficult, dangerous missions.

"I want to be absolutely sure you understand how important covert action operations are right now," Dulles said. "The White House and this administration have an *intense interest* in every aspect of *covert action.*"

Over the next eight years, through his devotion to covert action, his disdain for the details of analysis, and his dangerous practice of deceiving the president of the United States, Allen Dulles did untold damage to the agency he had helped to create.

PART
TWO

———

"A Strange Kind of Genius"

The CIA Under Eisenhower

1953 to 1961

———

8. "WE HAVE NO PLAN"

Allen Dulles had been director of central intelligence for one week when, on March 5, 1953, Joseph Stalin died. "We have no reliable inside intelligence on thinking inside the Kremlin," the agency lamented a few days later. "Our estimates of Soviet long-range plans and intentions are speculations drawn from inadequate evidence." The new president of the United States was not pleased. "Ever since 1946," Eisenhower fumed, "all the so-called experts have been yapping about what would happen when Stalin dies and what we as a nation should do about it. Well, he's dead. And you can turn the files of our government inside out—in vain—looking for any plans laid. We have no plan. We are not even sure what difference his death makes."

Stalin's death intensified American fears about Soviet intentions. The question for the CIA was whether Stalin's successors—whoever they might be—would launch a preemptive war. But the agency's speculations about the Soviets were reflections in a funhouse mirror. Stalin never had a master plan for world domination, nor the means to pursue it. The man who eventually took control of the Soviet Union after his death, Nikita Khrushchev, recalled that Stalin "trembled" and "quivered" at the prospect of a global combat with America. "He was afraid of war," Khrushchev said. "Stalin never did anything to provoke a war with the United States. He knew his weakness."

One of the fundamental failings of the Soviet state was that every facet of daily life was subordinated to national security. Stalin and his successors were pathological about their frontiers. Napoleon had invaded from Paris, and then Hitler from Berlin. Stalin's only coherent postwar foreign policy had been to turn Eastern Europe into an enormous human shield. While he devoted his energies to murdering his internal enemies, the Soviet people stood in endless lines waiting to buy a sack of potatoes. Americans were about to enjoy eight years of peace and prosperity under Eisenhower. But that peace came at the cost of a skyrocketing arms race, political witch hunts, and a permanent war economy.

Eisenhower's challenge was to confront the Soviet Union without starting World War III or subverting American democracy. He feared that the costs of the cold war could cripple the United States; if his generals and admirals had their way, they would consume the treasury. He decided to base his strategy on secret weapons: nuclear bombs and covert action. They were far cheaper than multibillion-dollar fleets of fighter jets and flotillas of aircraft carriers. With enough nuclear firepower, the United States could deter the Soviets from starting a new world war—or win the war if it came. With a global campaign of covert action, the United States could stop the spread of communism—or, as was Eisenhower's publicly proclaimed policy, roll back the Russians.

Ike bet the fate of the nation on his nuclear arsenal and his spy service. Questions about their best use arose at almost every meeting of the National Security Council early in his presidency. The NSC, created in 1947 to govern the use of American power abroad, had been rarely convened under Truman. Eisenhower revived it and ran it as a good general runs his staff. Every week, Allen Dulles left the slightly shabby confines of his offices and stepped into his black limousine; drove past the crumbling Temporaries, where Wisner and his covert operators worked; and entered the gates of the White House. He took his seat at the great oval desk in the Cabinet Room, facing his brother Foster, the secretary of state, along with the secretary of defense, the chairman of the Joint Chiefs of Staff, Vice President Richard M. Nixon, and the president. Allen typically opened each meeting with a tour of the world's hot spots. Then the talk turned to the strategies of secret war.

"WE COULD LICK THE WHOLE WORLD"

Eisenhower worried endlessly about a nuclear Pearl Harbor, and the CIA could not ease his mind. At the June 5, 1953, meeting of the National Security Council, Allen Dulles told him that the agency could not give him "any prior warning through intelligence channels of a Soviet sneak attack." A few months later, the CIA ventured a guess that the Soviets would be incapable of launching an intercontinental ballistic missile at the United States before 1969. The estimate proved to be off by a dozen years.

In August 1953, when the Soviet Union tested its first weapon of mass destruction—not quite a thermonuclear bomb, but near enough—the agency had no clue and gave no warning. Six weeks later, when Allen Dulles briefed the president on the Soviet test, Eisenhower wondered whether he should launch an all-out nuclear strike on Moscow before it was too late. He said it looked "as though the hour of decision were at hand, and that we should presently have to really face the question of whether or not we would have to throw everything at once against the enemy," say the NSC's declassified minutes. "He had raised this terrible question because there was no sense in our now merely shuddering at the enemy's capability," especially when the United States could not know if Moscow had one nuclear weapon or one thousand. "We were engaged in the defense of a way of life, and the great danger was that in defending this way of life we would find ourselves resorting to methods that endangered this way of life. The real problem, as the President saw it, was to devise methods of meeting the Soviet threat and of adopting controls, if necessary, that would not result in our transformation into a garrison state. The whole thing, said the President, was a paradox."

When Dulles warned the president that "the Russians could launch an atomic attack on the United States tomorrow," Eisenhower replied that "he didn't think anyone here thought the cost of winning a global war against the Soviet Union was a cost too high to pay." But the price of victory might be the destruction of American democracy. The president noted that the Joint Chiefs of Staff had told him, "we should do what was necessary even if the result was to change the American way of life. We could lick the whole world . . . if we were willing to adopt the system of Adolph Hitler."

Eisenhower had thought he could confront the paradox with covert action. But a bitter battle in East Berlin had revealed the CIA's inability to confront communism head-on. On June 16 and 17, 1953, nearly 370,000 East Germans took to the streets. Thousands of students and workers struck violently at their oppressors, burning Soviet and East German Communist Party buildings, trashing police cars, and trying to stop the Soviet tanks that crushed their spirits. The uprising was far larger than the CIA first realized, but the agency could do nothing to save the rebels. Though Frank Wisner weighed the risks of trying to arm the East Berliners, he balked. His liberation armies proved worthless. On June 18, he said that the CIA "should do nothing at this time to incite East Germans to further actions." The uprising was crushed.

The next week, Eisenhower ordered the CIA to "train and equip underground organizations capable of launching large-scale raids or sustained warfare" in East Germany and the other Soviet satellites. The order also called upon the CIA to "encourage elimination of key puppet officials" in the captive states. Elimination meant what it said. But the order was an empty gesture. The president was learning the limits of the CIA's abilities. That summer, in the White House Solarium, Eisenhower convened the men he trusted most in the realm of national security—among them Walter Bedell Smith, George Kennan, Foster Dulles, and retired air force lieutenant general James R. Doolittle, the pilot who had led the bombing of Tokyo in 1942—and asked them to redefine American national strategy toward the Soviets. By the end of the Solarium project, the idea of rolling back Russia through covert action was pronounced dead at age five.

The president began trying to redirect the agency. The CIA would fight the enemy in Asia, the Middle East, Africa, and Latin America—and wherever colonial empires crumbled. Under Eisenhower, the agency undertook 170 new major covert actions in 48 nations—political, psychological, and paramilitary warfare missions in countries where American spies knew little of the culture or the language or the history of the people.

Eisenhower often made his initial decisions on covert action in private conversations with the Dulles brothers. Typically, Allen spoke to Foster with a proposal for an operation, and Foster spoke to the president over a cocktail in the Oval Office. Foster went back to Allen with the president's approval and an admonition: don't get caught. The brothers steered the course of covert action in private conversations at their respective headquarters, on the telephone, or on Sundays by the swimming pool with their sister, Eleanor, a State Department officer herself. Foster firmly believed that the United States should do everything in its power to alter or abolish any regime not openly allied with America. Allen wholeheartedly agreed. With Eisenhower's blessings, they set out to remake the map of the world.

"A RAPIDLY DETERIORATING SITUATION"

From his first days in power, Allen Dulles polished the public image of the CIA, cultivating America's most powerful publishers and broadcasters, charming senators and congressmen, courting newspaper columnists. He found dignified publicity far more suitable than discreet silence.

Dulles kept in close touch with the men who ran *The New York Times*, *The Washington Post*, and the nation's leading weekly magazines. He could pick up the phone and edit a breaking story, make sure an irritating foreign correspondent was yanked from the field, or hire the services of men such as *Time*'s Berlin bureau chief and *Newsweek*'s man in Tokyo. It was second nature for Dulles to plant stories in the press. American newsrooms were dominated by veterans of the government's wartime propaganda branch, the Office of War Information, once part of Wild Bill Donovan's domain. The men who responded to the CIA's call included Henry Luce and his editors at *Time, Look,* and *Fortune;* popular magazines such as *Parade,* the *Saturday Review,* and *Reader's Digest;* and the most powerful executives at CBS News. Dulles built a public-relations and propaganda machine that came to include more than fifty news organizations, a dozen publishing houses, and personal pledges of support from men such as Axel Springer, West Germany's most powerful press baron.

Dulles wanted to be seen as the subtle master of a professional spy service. The press dutifully reflected that image. But the archives of the CIA tell a different story.

The minutes of the daily meetings of Dulles and his deputies depict an agency lurching from international crisis to internal calamities—rampant alcoholism, financial malfeasance, mass resignations. What should be done about a CIA officer who had killed a British colleague and faced trial for manslaughter? Why had the former station chief in Switzerland committed suicide? What could be done about the lack of talent in the clandestine service? The agency's new inspector general, Lyman Kirkpatrick, became a constant bearer of bad tidings about the caliber of the CIA's personnel, training, and performance. He warned Dulles that hundreds of the skilled military officers that the CIA had hired during the Korean War were quitting, and "it was most evident that a too-high percentage were leaving with an unfriendly attitude toward the CIA."

At the end of the war, a group of junior and midlevel CIA officers, appalled at the poor morale at headquarters, demanded and received permission to conduct an internal poll of their peers. They interviewed 115 CIA personnel and wrote a long, detailed report, completed at the end of Dulles's first year as director. They described "a rapidly deteriorating situation": widespread frustration, confusion, and purposelessness. Bright and patriotic people had been recruited with promises of exciting overseas service—"a completely false impression"—and then stuck in dead-end posts as typists and messengers. Hundreds of officers returned from foreign assignments to wander through headquarters for months, looking for new assignments without success. "The harm accruing to the Agency from inert personnel practices mounts in geometric, not arithmetic progression," they reported. "For every capable officer that the Agency loses through discontent or frustration, there may well be two or three more competent men (sharing the same educational, professional or social background) that the Agency will never have the opportunity to employ. . . . The harm done may be irreparable."

The CIA's young officers worked for "too many people in responsible positions who apparently don't know what they're doing." They watched "a shocking amount of money" going to waste on failed missions overseas. One of Frank Wisner's case officers wrote that the operations he worked on were "largely ineffectual and quite expensive. Some are directed at targets that are hardly logical—let alone legitimate. Thus, to protect jobs and prestige, both here and in the field, Headquarters' mission is to whitewash operational budget and programming justifications with, to say the least, exaggerated statements." They concluded that "the Agency is shot through with mediocrity and less."

These young officers had seen an intelligence service that was lying to itself. They described a CIA in which incompetent people were given great power and capable recruits were stacked like cordwood in the corridors.

Allen Dulles suppressed their report. Nothing changed. Forty-three years later, in 1996, a congressional investigation concluded that the CIA "continues to face a major personnel crisis that it has, thus far, not addressed in any coherent way. . . . Today the CIA still does not have enough qualified case officers to staff many of its stations around the world."

"SOMEBODY TO DO THE DIRTY WORK"

Eisenhower wanted to shape the CIA into an efficient instrument of presidential power. He tried to impose a command structure on the agency through Walter Bedell Smith. In the days after Eisenhower's election, the general had expected to be named chairman of the Joint Chiefs of Staff. He was devastated by Eisenhower's decision to make him the undersecretary of state. Bedell Smith did not want to be second-in-command to Foster Dulles, a man he regarded as a pompous blowhard. But Ike wanted him—and needed him—to serve as an honest broker between himself and the Dulles brothers.

Bedell Smith vented his anger to Vice President Nixon, his neighbor in Washington. From time to time the general would drop in for a visit, Nixon remembered, and "a couple of drinks would loosen his tongue a bit in an uncharacteristic way. . . . And I remember one night we were sitting having scotch and soda, and Bedell got very emotional, and he said, 'I want to tell you something about Ike. . . . I was just Ike's prat boy. . . . Ike has to have somebody to do the dirty work that he doesn't want to do so that he can look like the good guy.' "

Bedell Smith did that work as Ike's overseer of covert action. He served as the crucial link between the White House and the CIA's secret operations. As the driving force of the newly created Operations Coordinating Board, he carried out the secret directives from the president and the National Security Council, and he oversaw the CIA's execution of those orders. His handpicked ambassadors played central roles in carrying out these missions.

   During the nineteen months that Bedell Smith served as the president's proconsul for covert action, the agency carried out the only two victorious coups in its history. The declassified records of those coups show that they succeeded by bribery and coercion and brute force, not secrecy and stealth and cunning. But they created the legend that the CIA was a silver bullet in the arsenal of democracy. They gave the agency the aura that Dulles coveted.

9. "CIA'S GREATEST SINGLE TRIUMPH"

In January 1953, a few days before Eisenhower's inauguration, Walter Bedell Smith called Kim Roosevelt in at CIA headquarters and asked: "When is our goddamn operation going to get underway?"

Two months before, in early November 1952, Roosevelt, the CIA's Near East operations chief, had gone to Tehran to clean up a mess for his friends in British intelligence. Iran's prime minister, Mohammad Mossadeq, had caught the British trying to topple him. He had expelled everyone in their embassy, including the spies. Roosevelt had arrived to preserve and pay off a network of Iranian agents who had worked for the British but were happy to accept American largesse. On the way home, he stopped in London to report to his British colleagues.

He learned that Prime Minister Winston Churchill wanted the CIA to help overthrow Iran. Iran's oil had propelled Churchill to power and glory forty years before. Now Sir Winston wanted it back.

On the eve of World War I, Churchill, as first lord of the British Admiralty, had converted the Royal Navy from coal-burning to oil-burning ships. He championed the British purchase of 51 percent of the new Anglo-Persian Oil Company, which had struck the first of Iran's oil five years before. The British took a lion's share. Not only did Iranian oil fuel Churchill's new armada, but the revenues paid for it. The oil became the lifeblood of the British exchequer. While Britannia ruled the waves, British, Russian, and Turkish troops trampled northern Iran, destroying much of the nation's agriculture and sparking a famine that killed perhaps two million people. Out of this chaos arose a Cossack commander,

Reza Khan, who seized power with guile and force. In 1925, he was proclaimed the shah of Iran. A nationalist politician named Mohammad Mossadeq was one of the four members of the Iranian parliament, the Majlis, who opposed him.

The Majlis soon discovered that the British oil giant, now the Anglo-Iranian Oil Company, systematically cheated their government of billions. Hatred of the British and fear of the Soviets ran so high in Iran in the 1930s that the Nazis made deep inroads there—so deep that Churchill and Stalin invaded Iran in August 1941. They exiled Reza Khan and installed his pliant, dewy-eyed twenty-one-year-old son, Mohammad Reza Shah Pahlavi.

While Soviet and British armies occupied Iran, American forces used its airports and roads to transport roughly $18 billion worth of military aid to Stalin. The only American of consequence in Iran during World War II was General Norman Schwarzkopf, who organized Iran's Gendarmerie, the rural police (his son and namesake was the commander of the 1991 war on Iraq, Operation Desert Storm). Roosevelt, Churchill, and Stalin held a war conference in Tehran in December 1943, but the allies left behind a starving nation where oil workers made fifty cents a day and the young shah held power through electoral fraud. After the war, Mossadeq called upon the Majlis to renegotiate the British oil concession. Anglo-Iranian Oil controlled the world's largest known reserves. Its offshore refinery at Abadan was the biggest on earth. While British oil executives and technicians played in private clubs and swimming pools, Iranian oil workers lived in shanties without running water, electricity, or sewers; the injustice bred support for the communist Tudeh Party of Iran, which claimed about 2,500 members at the time. The British took twice as much income from the oil as the Iranians. Now Iran demanded a fifty-fifty split. The British refused. They tried to sway opinion by paying off politicians, newspaper editors, and the state radio director, among others.

The British intelligence chief in Tehran, Christopher Montague Woodhouse, warned his compatriots that they were courting disaster. It came in April 1951, when the Majlis voted to nationalize Iran's oil production. A few days later, Mohammad Mossadeq became Iran's prime minister. By the end of June, British warships were off the coast of Iran. In July, the American ambassador, Henry Grady, reported that the British, in an act of "utter folly," were trying to overthrow Mossadeq. In September, the British solidified an international boycott of Iran's oil, an act of economic warfare intended to destroy Mossadeq. Then Churchill returned to power as prime minister. He was seventy-six; Mossadeq was sixty-nine. Both were stubborn old men who conducted affairs of state in their pajamas. British commanders drew up plans for seventy thousand troops to seize Iran's oil fields and the Abadan refinery. Mossadeq took his case to the United Nations and the White House, laying on the charm in public while warning Truman in private that a British attack could set off World War III. Truman told Churchill flatly that the United States would never back such an invasion. Churchill countered that the price for British military support in the Korean War was American political support for his position in Iran. They reached an impasse in the summer of 1952.

"CIA MAKES POLICY BY DEFAULT"

The British spy Monty Woodhouse flew to Washington to meet with Walter Bedell Smith and Frank Wisner. On November 26, 1952, they discussed how to "unseat Mossadeq." Their plot began in the twilight of a presidential transition—as Truman's power faded, the coup plans grew. As Wisner said when the plot was in full cry, there were times when "CIA makes policy by default." The stated foreign policy of the United States was to support Mossadeq. But the CIA was setting out to depose him without the imprimatur of the White House.

On February 18, 1953, the newly installed chief of the British Secret Intelligence Service arrived in Washington. Sir John Sinclair, a soft-spoken Scotsman known to the public as "C" and to his friends as "Sinbad," met with Allen Dulles and proposed Kim Roosevelt as field commander for a coup. The British gave their plan the prosaic title of Operation Boot. Roosevelt had a grander name: Operation Ajax, after the mythical hero of the Trojan War (a strange choice, as legend has it that Ajax went mad, slew a flock of sheep thinking they were warriors, and killed himself in shame after he came to his senses).

Roosevelt ran the show with flair. He had been working for two years on political, propaganda, and paramilitary operations to fight off a feared

Soviet invasion in Iran. CIA officers already had enough cash and guns
stashed away to support ten thousand tribal warriors for six months. He
had the authority to attack the Tudeh, the small, influential, outlawed
Communist party of Iran. Now he shifted his target, aiming to undermine support for Mossadeq inside Iran's mainstream political and religious parties.

Roosevelt started stepping up a campaign of bribery and subversion.
The agency's officers and their Iranian agents rented the allegiances of
political hacks, holy men, and thugs. They bought the services of street
gangs who broke up Tudeh rallies with their bare knuckles and mullahs
who denounced Mossadeq from the mosques. The CIA did not have
Britain's decades of experience in Iran, nor nearly as many recruited
Iranian agents. But it had more money to hand out: at least $1 million a
year, a great fortune in one of the world's poorer nations.

The CIA took its cues from the influence-buying network controlled
by British intelligence. It was run by the Rashidian brothers, three sons
of an Iranian Anglophile who controlled ships, banks, and real estate.
The Rashidians had clout with members of the Iranian parliament. They
held sway among the leading merchants of the bazaar, the unacknowledged legislators of Tehran. They bribed senators, senior military officers,
editors and publishers, goon squads, and at least one member of
Mossadeq's cabinet. They bought information with cookie tins filled with
cash. Their circle even included the shah's chief manservant. It would
prove a catalyst in the coup.

Allen Dulles walked into the March 4, 1953, National Security Council meeting with seven pages of briefing notes focused on the "consequences of Soviet take over" in Iran. The country faced "a maturing
revolutionary set-up," and if it went communist, all the dominoes of the
Middle East would fall. Sixty percent of the free world's oil would be in
Moscow's hands. This disastrous loss would "seriously deplete our re-
serves for war," Dulles warned; oil and gasoline would have to be ra-
tioned in the United States. The president did not buy a word of it. He
thought it might be better to offer Mossadeq a $100 million loan, in or-
der to stabilize his government, rather than to overthrow it.

Monty Woodhouse tactfully suggested to his American counterparts
at the CIA that they might take a different approach in presenting the
problem to Eisenhower. They could not maintain that Mossadeq was a
communist. But they could argue that the longer he remained in power,

the greater the danger that the Soviets would invade Iran. Kim Roosevelt fine-tuned this pitch for the president's ear: If Mossadeq wobbled to the left, Iran would fall to the Soviets. But if he was pushed the right way, the CIA could make sure that the government fell into American control.

Mossadeq played straight into this trap. In a miscalculated bluff, he raised the specter of the Soviet threat with the American embassy in Tehran. He expected to be "rescued by the Americans," said John H. Stutesman, an American diplomat who knew Mossadeq well and served as the State Department officer in charge of Iranian affairs in 1953. "Mossadeq felt that if he kicked out the British, and threatened the Americans with Russian hegemony, that we'd rush in. He wasn't that far wrong."

On March 18, 1953, Frank Wisner informed Roosevelt and Woodhouse that they had an initial go-ahead from Allen Dulles. On April 4, CIA headquarters sent $1 million to the Tehran station. But Eisenhower still had his doubts, as did other key players in the plan to overthrow Iran.

The president made an eloquent speech a few days later called "The Chance for Peace," in which he declared that "any nation's right to form a government and an economic system of its own choosing is inalienable," and "any nation's attempt to dictate to other nations their form of government is indefensible." These ideas struck home with the CIA's station chief in Tehran, Roger Goiran, who asked headquarters why the United States would want to ally itself with the traditions of British colonialism in the Middle East. It was a historic mistake, he argued, a long-term disaster for American interests. Allen Dulles recalled him to Washington and dismissed him as station chief. The U.S. ambassador to Iran, Loy Henderson, who had been in on the plans from the start, strongly opposed the British choice of a dissolute retired major general, Fazlollah Zahedi, as the front man for the coup. Mossadeq had told the ambassador that he knew Zahedi was a British-backed traitor.

Despite that, the British nominated and the CIA seconded Zahedi, the only man openly bidding for power who was thought to be pro-American. In late April, he went into hiding after the kidnapping and murder of Iran's national police chief—with good reason, for the suspected killers were his own supporters. He did not resurface for eleven weeks.

In May, the plot gained momentum, though it still lacked the president's approval. It was now in its final draft. Zahedi, armed with $75,000 in CIA cash, would form a military secretariat and choose colonels to mount the coup. A group of religious fanatics called the Warriors of Islam—a "terrorist gang," says a CIA history of the coup—would threaten the lives of Mossadeq's political and personal supporters inside and outside the government. They would stage violent attacks on respected religious leaders that would look as if they were the work of the communists. The CIA drew up pamphlets and posters as part of a $150,000 propaganda campaign to control Iran's press and public, proclaiming that "Mossadeq favors the Tudeh Party and the USSR. . . . Mossadeq is an enemy of Islam. . . . Mossadeq is deliberately destroying the morale of the Army. . . . Mossadeq is deliberately leading the country into economic collapse. . . . Mossadeq has been corrupted by power." On D-Day, the coup plotters led by Zahedi's military secretariat would seize the army's general staff headquarters, Radio Tehran, Mossadeq's home, the central bank, police headquarters, and the telephone and telegraph offices. They would arrest Mossadeq and his cabinet. More money, $11,000 a week, immediately went to buy off enough members of the Majlis to ensure that a majority would proclaim Zahedi as the new prime minister. This last detail had the advantage of giving the coup an appearance of legality. Zahedi, in turn, would pledge fealty to the shah and restore his monarchy to power.

Would the weak-willed shah play his role? Ambassador Henderson did not believe he had the backbone to support a coup. But Roosevelt thought it would be hopeless to go ahead without him.

On June 15, Roosevelt went to London to show the plan to the boffins of British intelligence. They met in a headquarters conference room with a sign that read, "Curb Your Guests." No objections were raised. The Americans, after all, were footing the bill. The British had conceived the coup, but their leaders could not play a commanding role in its execution. On June 23, Foreign Minister Anthony Eden had major abdominal surgery in Boston. That same day, Winston Churchill suffered a severe stroke and almost died; the news was kept so quiet that the CIA heard nothing of it.

Over the next two weeks, the agency set up a two-pronged chain of command. One would run Zahedi's military secretariat. The other would control the political warfare and propaganda campaign. Both reported directly to Frank Wisner. Kim Roosevelt set out to fly to Beirut, drive through Syria and Iraq into Iran, and link up with the Rashidian brothers. The CIA awaited a green light from the president of the United States.

It came on July 11. And from that moment on, almost everything went wrong.

"AFTER YOU, YOUR MAJESTY"

The secrecy of the mission was blown before day one. On July 7, the CIA had monitored a Tudeh Party radio broadcast. The clandestine radio warned Iranians that the American government, along with various "spies and traitors," including General Zahedi, were working "to liquidate the Mossadeq government." Mossadeq had his own military and political intelligence sources, independent of the Tudeh, and he knew what he was up against.

Then the CIA discovered that its coup had no troops. General Zahedi had not a single soldier under his control. The agency had no map of the military situation in Tehran, no roster of the Iranian army. Kim Roosevelt turned to Brigadier General Robert A. McClure, the father of U.S. special-operations forces. McClure was Eisenhower's chief intelligence officer during World War II, ran the army's Psychological Warfare Division during the Korean War, and specialized in overseeing joint operations with the CIA. He had worked side by side with Dulles and Wisner, and he trusted neither man.

General McClure had gone to Tehran to run the American military assistance advisory group, established in 1950 to provide up-and-coming Iranian officers with military support, training, and advice. As part of the CIA's war of nerves, he cut off American contact with pro-Mossadeq commanders. Roosevelt relied entirely on McClure for a picture of the Iranian military and the political loyalties of its senior officers. President Eisenhower personally insisted that McClure receive a second star after the coup, noting his "very fine relationships with the Shah and other senior people in whom we are interested." The CIA recruited a colonel who had served as the Iranian liaison to McClure's military assistance

group to help run the coup. He secretly enlisted about forty fellow officers.

Now all that was lacking was the shah.

A CIA colonel, Stephen J. Meade, flew to Paris to pick up the shah's
strong-willed and unpopular twin sister, Princess Ashraf. The CIA's script
called for her to return from exile and persuade the shah to back General Zahedi. But Princess Ashraf was nowhere to be found. The British
intelligence agent Asadollah Rashidian tracked her down on the French
Riviera. It took another ten days to coax her onto a commercial flight to
Tehran. The inducements included a large sum of cash and a mink coat
from the British intelligence service, along with a promise from Colonel
Meade that the United States would bankroll the royal family should the
coup fail. After a stormy face-to-face confrontation with her twin, she
left Tehran on July 30, wrongly convinced that she had stiffened his
spine. The CIA brought in General Norman Schwarzkopf to bolster the
shah on August 1. The shah, fearing that his palace was bugged, led the
general into the grand ballroom, pulled a small table to its center, and
whispered that he would not go along with the coup. He had no confidence that the army would back him.

Kim Roosevelt spent the next week skulking in and out of the shah's
palace, pressuring him mercilessly, warning him that his failure to follow
the CIA could lead to a communist Iran or "a second Korea"—in either
case, a death sentence for the monarch and his family. Terrified, the shah
fled to his royal resort on the Caspian Sea.

Roosevelt improvised furiously. He commissioned a royal decree dis-
missing Mossadeq and appointing General Zahedi as prime minister. He
ordered the colonel who commanded the shah's imperial guard to present a signed copy of this legally dubious document to Mossadeq at gunpoint and arrest him if he defied it. On August 12, the colonel chased
after the shah on the Caspian and returned the next night with signed
copies of the decrees. Now Roosevelt's Iranian agents cascaded into the
streets of Tehran. Newspapermen and printing presses spewed propaganda: Mossadeq was a communist, Mossadeq was a Jew. The CIA's
street thugs, posing as Tudeh Party members, attacked mullahs and
defiled a mosque. Mossadeq counterattacked by shutting down the
Majlis—under the law, only the Majlis could dismiss him, not the
shah—rendering the senators and deputies whose votes had been purchased by the CIA useless.

Roosevelt forged ahead. He cabled headquarters on August 14 with an urgent request for $5 million more to prop up General Zahedi. The coup was set for that night—and Mossadeq knew it. He mobilized the Tehran garrison of the Iranian army and surrounded his home with tanks and troops. When the shah's imperial guardsman went to arrest the prime minister, loyal officers seized him. Zahedi hid at a CIA safe house, watched over by one of Roosevelt's officers, a rookie named Rocky Stone. The CIA's hastily assembled cadre of Iranian colonels disintegrated.

Radio Tehran went on the air at 5:45 a.m. on August 16 announcing that the coup had failed. CIA headquarters had no clue what to do next. Allen Dulles had left Washington a week earlier for an extended European vacation, blithely confident that all was well. He was out of touch. Frank Wisner was out of ideas. Roosevelt, on his own, decided to try to convince the world that it was Mossadeq who had staged the failed coup. He needed the shah to sell that story, but the monarch had fled the country. The American ambassador in Iraq, Burton Berry, learned a few hours later that the shah was in Baghdad, begging for help. Roosevelt fed the outlines of a script to Berry, who advised the shah to broadcast a statement saying he had fled in the face of a left-wing uprising. He did as instructed. Then he told his pilot to file a flight plan for the world capital of exiled monarchs: Rome.

On the night of August 16, one of Roosevelt's officers handed $50,000 to the station's Iranian agents and told them to produce a crowd posing as communist goons. The next morning, hundreds of paid agitators flooded the streets of Tehran, looting, burning, and smashing the symbols of government. Actual members of the Tudeh Party joined them, but they soon realized "that a covert action was being staged," as the CIA station reported, and "tried to argue demonstrators into going home." After a second sleepless night, Roosevelt welcomed Ambassador Loy Henderson, who flew in from Beirut on August 17. On the way to meet him at the airport, members of the American embassy passed a toppled bronze statue of the shah's father, with only the boots left standing.

Henderson, Roosevelt, and General McClure held a four-hour war council inside the embassy compound. The result was a new plan to create anarchy. Thanks to McClure, Iranian military officers were dispatched to outlying garrisons to enlist soldiers to support the coup. The CIA's Iranian agents were ordered to hire more street mobs. Religious emissaries were sent to persuade the supreme Shi'ite ayatollah in Iran to declare a holy war.

But back at headquarters, Wisner despaired. He read the assessment of the CIA's best analysts that day: "The failure of the military coup in Tehran and the flight of the shah to Baghdad emphasize Prime Minister Mossadeq's continued mastery of the situation and foreshadow more drastic action on his part to eliminate all opposition." Late on the night of August 17, he sent a message to Tehran saying that, in the absence of strong recommendations to the contrary from Roosevelt and Henderson, the coup against Mossadeq should cease. A few hours later, sometime after 2 a.m., Wisner placed a frantic telephone call to John Waller, who was running the Iran desk at CIA headquarters.

The shah had flown to Rome and checked into the Excelsior Hotel, Wisner reported. And then "a terrible, terrible coincidence occurred," Wisner said. "Can you guess what it is?"

Waller could not imagine.

"Think of the worst thing you can think of," Wisner said.

"He was hit by a cab and killed," Waller replied. "No, no, no, no," Wisner responded. "John, maybe you don't know that Dulles had decided to extend his vacation by going to Rome. Now can you imagine what happened?"

Waller shot back: "Dulles hit him with his car and killed him?"

Wisner was not amused.

"They both showed up at the reception desk at the Excelsior at the very same moment," Wisner said. "And Dulles had to say, 'After you, Your Majesty.' "

"A PASSIONATE EMBRACE"

At dawn on August 19, the agency's hired mobs assembled in Tehran, ready for a riot. Buses and trucks filled with tribesmen from the south, their leaders all paid by the CIA, arrived in the capital. Ambassador Henderson's deputy chief of mission, William Rountree, described what happened next as "an almost spontaneous revolution."

"It began with a public demonstration by a health club or exercise club—lifting barbells and chains and that sort of thing," he recounted. These were weightlifters and circus strongmen recruited by the CIA for the day. "They began shouting anti-Mossadeq, pro-Shah slogans and proceeded to march through the streets. Many others joined them, and soon there was a substantial demonstration in favor of the Shah and against Mossadeq. Shouts of 'Long live the Shah!' spread throughout the city and the crowd went in the direction of the building housing the Mossadeq cabinet," where they seized ranking members of the government, burned four newspaper offices, and sacked the political headquarters of a pro-Mossadeq party. Two of the men in the crowd were religious leaders. One was the Ayatollah Ahmed Kashani. Alongside him was his fifty-one-year-old devotee, Ayatollah Ruhollah Musavi Khomeini, the future leader of Iran.

Roosevelt told his Iranian agents to hit the telegraph office, the propaganda ministry, and police and army headquarters. By afternoon, after a skirmish that killed at least three people, the CIA's agents were on the air at Radio Tehran. Roosevelt went to Zahedi's hideout, in the safe house run by the CIA's Rocky Stone, and told him to be ready to proclaim himself prime minister. Zahedi was so frightened that Stone had to button him into his military tunic. At least a hundred people died on the streets of Tehran that day.

At least two hundred more were killed after the CIA directed the shah's Imperial Guard to attack Mossadeq's heavily defended home. The prime minister escaped but surrendered the next day. He spent the next three years incarcerated and a decade more under house arrest before he died. Roosevelt handed Zahedi $1 million in cash, and the new prime minister set out to crush all opposition and jail thousands of political prisoners.

"The CIA did remarkably well in creating a situation in which, in the proper circumstances and atmosphere, a change could be effected," remembered Ambassador Rountree, later the assistant secretary of state for the Near East. "Quite clearly the matter did not work out as they had anticipated, or at least hoped, but it did work out in the end."

In his hour of glory, Kim Roosevelt flew to London. On August 26, at two in the afternoon, he was received at 10 Downing Street by the prime minister. Winston Churchill was "in bad shape," Roosevelt reported, his speech slurred, his vision occluded, his memory fleeting: "The initials CIA meant nothing to him, but he had a vague idea that Roosevelt must be connected in some way with his old friend Bedell Smith."

Roosevelt was hailed as a hero at the White House. Faith in the magic of covert action soared. "Romantic gossip about the 'coup' in Iran spread around Washington like wildfire," remembered the CIA's Ray Cline, one of the agency's star analysts. "Allen Dulles basked in the glory of the exploit." But not everyone at headquarters saw the fall of Mossadeq as a triumph. "The trouble with this seemingly brilliant success" was "the extravagant impression of CIA's power that it created," Cline wrote. "It did not prove that CIA could topple governments and place rulers in power; it was a unique case of supplying just the right amount of marginal assistance in the right way at the right time." By renting the allegiances of soldiers and street mobs, the CIA had created a degree of violence sufficient to stage a coup. Money changed hands and those hands changed a regime.

The shah returned to the throne and rigged the next parliamentary elections, using the CIA's street gangs as enforcers. He imposed three years of martial law and tightened his control over the country. He called upon the agency and the American military mission in Iran to help him secure his power by creating a new intelligence service, which became known as SAVAK. The CIA wanted SAVAK to serve as its eyes and ears against the Soviets. The shah wanted a secret police to protect his power. SAVAK, trained and equipped by the CIA, enforced his rule for more than twenty years.

The shah became the centerpiece of American foreign policy in the Islamic world. For years to come, it would be the station chief, not the American ambassador, who spoke to the shah for the United States. The CIA wove itself into Iran's political culture, locked in "a passionate embrace with the Shah," said Andrew Killgore, a State Department political officer under the American ambassador from 1972 to 1976—Richard Helms.

The coup "was regarded as CIA's greatest single triumph," Killgore said. "It was trumpeted as a great American national victory. We had changed the whole course of a country here." A generation of Iranians grew up knowing that the CIA had installed the shah. In time, the chaos that the agency had created in the streets of Tehran would return to haunt the United States.

The illusion that the CIA could overthrow a nation by sleight of hand was alluring. It led the agency into a battle in Central America that went on for the next forty years.

10. "BOMB REPEAT BOMB"

Colonel Al Haney parked his new Cadillac at the edge of a decrepit air base in Opa-Locka, Florida, a few days after Christmas in 1953, stepped out onto the tarmac, and surveyed his new domain: three two-story barracks buildings on the fringes of the Everglades. Colonel Haney had buried the human wreckage he had created as the station chief in South Korea under a top secret shroud. Then he conned his way into a new command. A handsome rogue, thirty-nine years old, newly divorced, wearing a crisp army uniform on a muscular six-foot-two frame, he was Allen Dulles's newly appointed special deputy for Operation Success, the CIA's plot to overthrow the government of Guatemala.

Plots for a coup against the president, Jacobo Arbenz, had been kicking around the agency for almost three years. They were revived the instant that Kim Roosevelt returned triumphant from Iran. An elated Allen Dulles asked him to lead the operation in Central America. Roosevelt respectfully declined. He determined after studying the matter that the agency was going in blind. It had no spies in Guatemala and no sense of the will of the army or the people. Was the military loyal to Arbenz? Could that loyalty be broken? The CIA had no idea.

Haney had orders to devise a path to power for a cashiered Guatemalan colonel selected by CIA headquarters, Carlos Castillo Armas. But his strategy was no more than an elaborate sketch. It said only that the CIA would train and equip a rebel force and point it toward the presidential palace in Guatemala City. Wisner sent the draft over to the State Department for a bolstering from General Walter Bedell Smith, who put a new team of American ambassadors in place for the operation.

"THE BIG STICK"

Pistol-packing Jack Peurifoy had made his name ridding the State Department of leftists and liberals in 1950. On his first tour abroad, as ambassador to Greece from 1951 to 1953, he worked closely with the CIA to establish covert American channels of power in Athens. Upon arriving at his new post, Peurifoy cabled Washington: "I have come to Guatemala to use the big stick." He met with President Arbenz and reported: "I am definitely convinced that if the President is not a communist, he will certainly do until one comes along."

Bedell Smith picked Whiting Willauer, a founder of Civil Air Transport, the Asian airline that Frank Wisner bought in 1949, as ambassador to Honduras. Willauer summoned pilots from CAT headquarters in Taiwan, with instructions to lie low and await orders in Miami and Havana. Ambassador Thomas Whelan went to Nicaragua to work with the dictator Anastasio Somoza, who was helping the CIA build a training base for Castillo Armas's men.

On December 9, 1953, Allen Dulles formally approved Operation Success and authorized a $3 million budget. He appointed Al Haney as field commander and named Tracy Barnes as its chief of political warfare.

Dulles believed in the romantic notion of the gentleman spy. Tracy Barnes was an exemplar. The well-bred Mr. Barnes had the classic CIA résumé of the 1950s—Groton, Yale, Harvard Law. He grew up on the Whitney estate on Long Island with his own private golf course. He was an OSS hero in World War II and won a Silver Star by capturing a German garrison. He had dash and panache and the pride that goes before a fall, and he came to represent the worst of the clandestine service. "Like those who no matter how great their effort seem doomed never to master a foreign language, Barnes proved unable to get the hang of secret operations," Richard Helms reflected. "Even worse, thanks to Allen Dulles' constant praise and pushing, Tracy apparently remained unaware of his problem." He went on to serve as chief of station in Germany and England, and then on to the Bay of Pigs.

Barnes and Castillo Armas flew to Opa-Locka on January 29, 1954, where they started hammering out their plans with Colonel Haney. They awoke the next morning to discover that their scheme had been blown sky-high. Every major newspaper in the Western Hemisphere published President Arbenz's accusations of a "counterrevolutionary plot" sponsored by a "Northern government," led by Castillo Armas, and based in a rebel training camp on Somoza's farm in Nicaragua. The leak had come from secret cables and documents that a CIA officer—Colonel Haney's liaison with Castillo Armas—had left in a Guatemala City hotel room. The hapless officer was summoned to Washington and advised to take a job as a fire watcher somewhere deep in the forests of the Pacific Northwest.

The crisis quickly revealed Al Haney as one of the loosest cannons in the CIA's arsenal. He flailed for ways to distract Guatemalans from the accounts of the plot by planting fake news in the local press. "If possible, fabricate big human interest story, like flying saucers, birth sextuplets in remote area," he cabled CIA headquarters. He dreamed up headlines: Arbenz was forcing all Catholic troops to join a new church that worshipped Stalin! A Soviet submarine was on its way to deliver arms for Guatemala! This last idea captured the imagination of Tracy Barnes. Three weeks later he had his CIA staff plant a cache of Soviet weapons on the Nicaraguan coast. They concocted stories about Soviets arming communist assassination squads in Guatemala. But few among the press and the public bought what Barnes was peddling.

The CIA's charter demanded that covert action be conducted in ways so subtle that the American hand was unseen. That mattered little to Wisner. "There is not the slightest doubt that if the operation is carried through many Latin Americans will see in it the hand of the U.S.," he told Dulles. But if Operation Success was curtailed "on the grounds that the hand of the U.S. is too clearly shown," Wisner argued, "a serious question is raised as to whether any operation of this kind can appropriately be included as one of the U.S. cold war weapons, no matter how great the provocation or how favorable the auspices." Wisner thought that an operation was clandestine so long as it was unacknowledged by the United States and kept secret from the American people.

Wisner summoned Colonel Haney to headquarters for a come-to-

Jesus meeting. "There is no operation regarded as being so important as this one and no operation on which the reputation of the Agency is more at stake," he told Haney. "The boss has to be satisfied that we have what it takes," Wisner said, but "Headquarters had never received a clear and concise statement of what the plans are with respect to what takes place on D-day." Colonel Haney's blueprint was a set of interlocking timelines scrawled on a forty-foot roll of butcher paper pinned to the wall at the Opa-Locka barracks. He explained to Wisner that you could understand the operation only by studying the scribbles on the Opa-Locka scrolls.

Wisner began "to lose confidence in Haney's judgment and restraint," Richard Bissell remembered. The fiercely cerebral Bissell, another product of Groton and Yale, the man once known as Mr. Marshall Plan, had just come aboard at the CIA. He had signed on as "Dulles's apprentice," as he put it, with promises of great responsibilities to come. The director immediately asked him to sort out the increasingly complicated logistics of Operation Success.

Bissell and Barnes represented the head and the heart of Allen Dulles's CIA. Though they had no experience in running covert action, and it was a mark of Dulles's faith that they were ordered to find out what Al Haney was up to in Opa-Locka.

Bissell said he and Barnes rather enjoyed the hyperkinetic colonel: "Barnes was very much pro-Haney and gung-ho about the operation. I believed Haney was the right man for the job because the person in charge of an operation of this kind had to be an activist and strong leader. Barnes and I both liked Haney and approved of the way he was running things. No doubt Haney's operation left a positive impression on me, because I set up a project office similar to his during the preparations for the Bay of Pigs invasion."

"WHAT WE WANTED TO DO WAS TO HAVE A TERROR CAMPAIGN"

The "bold but incompetent" Castillo Armas (to quote Barnes), along with his "extremely small and ill-trained" rebel forces (to quote Bissell), waited for a signal from the Americans to attack, under the watchful eye of Haney's man Rip Robertson, who had run some of the CIA's ill-fated guerrilla operations in Korea.

No one knew what would happen when Castillo Armas and his few hundred rebels attacked the five-thousand-man Guatemalan military. The CIA subsidized an anticommunist student movement in Guatemala City, several hundred strong. But they served mainly, in Wisner's words, as a "goon squad," not as a resistance army. So Wisner hedged his bet and opened up a second front on the war against Arbenz. He sent one of the CIA's best officers, Henry Hecksher, the chief of the Berlin base, to Guatemala City with orders to persuade senior military officers to rebel against the government. Hecksher was authorized to spend up to $10,000 a month for bribes, and he soon bought the loyalty of a minister without portfolio in Arbenz's cabinet, Colonel Elfego Monzon. The hope was that more money would drive a wedge into an officer corps already beginning to crack under the twin pressures of an arms embargo imposed by the United States and the threat of an American invasion.

But Hecksher soon became convinced that only an actual attack by the United States would embolden the Guatemalan military to overthrow Arbenz. Hecksher wrote to Haney: "The 'crucial spark' has to be generated by heat—United States heat"—in the form of bombing the capital.

CIA headquarters then sent Haney a five-page roster of fifty-eight Guatemalans marked for assassination. The targeted killing was approved by Wisner and Barnes. The list encompassed "high government and organizational leaders" suspected of communist leanings and "those few individuals in key government and military positions of tactical importance whose removal for psychological, organizational or other reasons is mandatory for the success of military action." Castillo Armas and the CIA agreed that the assassinations would take place during or immediately after his triumphant arrival in Guatemala City. They would send a message underscoring the seriousness of the rebels' intent.

One of the many myths about Operation Success, planted by Allen Dulles in the American press, was that its eventual triumph lay not in violence but in a brilliant piece of espionage. As Dulles told the story, the trick was turned by an American spy in the Polish city Stettin, on the Baltic Sea—the northern terminus of the iron curtain—posing as a bird watcher. He saw through his binoculars that a freighter called the *Alfhem* was carrying Czech arms to the Arbenz government. He then posted a letter with a microdot message—"My God, my God, why hast thou forsaken me?"—addressed to a CIA officer under deep cover in a Paris auto parts store, who relayed the coded signal by shortwave to Washington. As Dulles told the story, another CIA officer secretly inspected the hold of the ship while it docked at the Kiel Canal connecting the Baltic to the North Sea. The CIA, therefore, knew from the moment that the *Alfhem* left Europe that she was bound for Guatemala carrying guns.

A wonderful yarn, repeated in many history books, but a bald-faced lie—a cover story that disguised a serious operational mistake. In reality, the CIA missed the boat.

Arbenz was desperate to break the American weapons embargo on Guatemala. He thought he could ensure the loyalty of his officer corps by arming them. Henry Hecksher had reported that the Bank of Guatemala had transferred $4.86 million via a Swiss account to a Czech weapons depot. But the CIA lost the trail. Four weeks of frantic searching ensued before the *Alfhem* docked successfully at Puerto Barrios, Guatemala. Only after the cargo was uncrated did word reach the U.S. Embassy that a shipment of rifles, machine guns, howitzers, and other weapons had come ashore.

The arrival of the arms—many of them rusted and useless, some bearing a swastika stamp, indicating their age and origin—created a propaganda windfall for the United States. Grossly overstating the size and military significance of the cargo, Foster Dulles and the State Department announced that Guatemala was now part of a Soviet plot to subvert the Western Hemisphere. The Speaker of the House, John McCormack, called the shipment an atomic bomb planted in America's backyard.

Ambassador Peurifoy said the United States was at war. "Nothing short of direct military intervention will succeed," he cabled Wisner on May 21. Three days later, U.S. Navy warships and submarines blockaded Guatemala, in violation of international law.

On May 26, a CIA plane buzzed the presidential palace and dropped leaflets over the headquarters of the presidential guard, the most elite of the army's units in Guatemala City. "Struggle against Communist atheism!" they read. "Struggle with Castillo Armas!" It was a deft blow. "I suppose it really doesn't matter what the leaflets say," Tracy Barnes told Al Haney. He was right. What mattered was that the CIA had swooped down and dropped a weapon on a country that had never been bombed before.

"What we wanted to do was to have a terror campaign," said the CIA's E. Howard Hunt, who worked on the political-warfare portfolio for the operation—"to terrify Arbenz particularly, to terrify his troops, much as the German Stuka bombers terrified the population of Holland, Belgium and Poland at the onset of World War Two."

For four weeks, starting on May Day 1954, the CIA had been waging psychological warfare in Guatemala through a pirate radio station called the Voice of Liberation, run by a CIA contract officer, an amateur actor and skilled dramatist named David Atlee Phillips. In a tremendous stroke of luck, the Guatemalan state radio station went off the air in mid-May for a scheduled replacement of its antenna. Phillips snuggled up to its frequency, where listeners looking for the state broadcasts found Radio CIA. Unrest turned to hysteria among the populace as the rebel station sent out shortwave reports of imaginary uprisings and defections and plots to poison wells and conscript children.

On June 5, the retired chief of the Guatemalan air force flew to Somoza's farm in Nicaragua, where the broadcasts originated. Phillips's men fueled him with a bottle of whisky and induced him to talk about his reasons for fleeing Guatemala. After the tape was cut and spliced at the CIA's field studio, it sounded like a passionate call for rebellion.

"CONSIDER UPRISING A FARCE"

When Arbenz heard about the broadcast the next morning, his mind snapped. He became the dictator the CIA had depicted. He grounded his own air force for fear his fliers would defect. Then he raided the home of an anticommunist student leader who worked closely with the CIA and found evidence of the American plot. He suspended civil liberties and began arresting hundreds of people, hitting the CIA's student group the hardest. At least seventy-five of them were tortured, killed, and buried in mass graves.

"Panic spreading in government circles," the CIA station in Guatemala cabled on June 8. That was exactly what Haney wanted to hear. He sent orders to fan the flames with more falsehoods: "A group of Soviet commissars, officers and political advisers, led by a member of the Moscow Politburo, have landed. . . . In addition to military conscription, the communists will introduce labor conscription. A decree is already being printed. All boys and girls 16 years old will be called for one year of labor duty in special camps, mainly for political indoctrination and to break the influence of family and church on the young people. . . . Arbenz has already left the country. His announcements from the National Palace are actually made by a double, provided by Soviet intelligence."

Haney started flying bazookas and machine guns down south on his own initiative, issuing unauthorized orders to arm peasants and to urge them to kill Guatemalan police. "We question strongly . . . that Campesinos be enjoined kill Guardia Civil," Wisner cabled Haney. "This amounts to incitement civil war . . . discrediting movement as terrorist and irresponsible outfit willing sacrifice innocent lives."

Colonel Monzon, the CIA's agent in Arbenz's cabinet, demanded bombs and tear gas to kick off the coup. "Vitally important this be done," the CIA station told Haney. Monzon was "told he better move fast. He agreed. . . . Said Arbenz, Commies, and enemies will be executed." The CIA station in Guatemala pleaded again for an attack: "We urgently request that bomb be dropped, show strength be made, that all available planes be sent over, that army and capital be shown that time for decision is here."

On June 18, Castillo Armas launched his long-awaited assault, more than four years in the making. A force of 198 rebels attacked Puerto Barrios, on the Atlantic coast. They were defeated by policemen and dockworkers. Another 122 marched toward the Guatemalan army garrison at Zacapa. All but 30 were killed or captured. A third force of 60 rebels set out from El Salvador, only to be arrested by local police. Castillo Armas himself, clad in a leather jacket and driving a battered station wagon, led 100 men from Honduras toward three lightly defended Guatemalan villages. He camped out a few miles from the border, calling on the CIA for more food, more men, more weapons—but within seventy-two hours, more than half of his forces were killed, captured, or on the verge of defeat.

On the afternoon of June 19, Ambassador Peurifoy commandeered the CIA's secure communications line at the American embassy and wrote directly to Allen Dulles: "Bomb repeat Bomb," he pleaded. Haney weighed in less than two hours later with a blistering message to Wisner: "Are we going to stand by and see last hope of free people in Guatemala submerged to depths of Communist oppression and atrocity until we send American armed force against enemy? . . . Is not our intervention now under these circumstances far more palatable than by Marines? This is the same enemy we fought in Korea and may fight tomorrow in Indo-China."

Wisner froze. It was one thing to send legions of foreigners to their deaths. It was quite another to send American pilots to blow up a national capital.

The morning of June 20, the CIA's Guatemala City station reported that the Arbenz government was "recovering its nerve." The capital was "very still, stores shuttered. People waiting apathetically, consider uprising a farce."

The tension at CIA headquarters was almost unbearable. Wisner became fatalistic. He cabled Haney and the CIA station: "We are ready authorize use of bombs moment we are convinced would substantially increase likelihood of success without disastrous damage interests of United States. . . . We fear bombing of military installations more likely to solidify army against the rebellion than to induce defection and we are convinced attacks against civilian targets, which would shed blood of innocent people, would fit perfectly into Communist propaganda line and tend to alienate all elements of population."

Bissell told Dulles that "the outcome of the effort to overthrow the regime of President Arbenz of Guatemala remains very much in doubt." At CIA headquarters, "we were all at our wit's end as to how to proceed," Bissell wrote years later. "Grappling with continual operational snafus, we were only too aware how perilously close to failure we were." Dulles had limited Castillo Armas to three F-47 Thunderbolt fighter-bombers, in the name of deniability. Two were out of commission. Now, Bissell recorded in his memoirs, "the Agency's reputation and his own were at stake."

Dulles secretly authorized one more air strike on the capital as he prepared to meet with the president. On the morning of June 22, the single plane still flying for the CIA set a small oil tank ablaze on the outskirts of town. The fire was out in twenty minutes. "Public impression is that attacks show incredible weakness, lack of decision, and fainthearted effort," Haney raged. "Castillo Armas efforts widely described as farce.

Anti-Commie anti-government morale near vanishing point." He cabled Dulles directly, demanding more aircraft immediately.

Dulles picked up the phone and called William Pawley—one of the richest businessmen in the United States, the chairman of Democrats for Eisenhower, one of Ike's biggest benefactors in the 1952 elections, and a CIA consultant. Pawley could provide a secret air force if anyone could. Then Dulles sent Bissell to see Walter Bedell Smith, whom the CIA had consulted daily on Operation Success, and the general approved the back-channel request for aircraft. But at the last minute the assistant secretary of state for Latin America, Henry Holland, objected violently, demanding that they go to see the president.

At 2:15 p.m. on June 22, Dulles, Pawley, and Holland walked into the Oval Office. Eisenhower asked what the rebellion's chances of success were at that moment. Zero, Dulles confessed. And if the CIA had more planes and bombs? Maybe 20 percent, Dulles guessed.

The president and Pawley recorded the conversation almost identically in their memoirs—with one exception. Eisenhower erased Pawley from history, and it is clear why: he cut a secret deal with his political benefactor. "Ike turned to me," Pawley wrote, "and he said: 'Bill, go ahead and get the planes.' "

Pawley telephoned the Riggs Bank, a block away from the White House. Then he called the Nicaraguan ambassador to the United States. He drew $150,000 in cash and drove the ambassador to the Pentagon. Pawley handed over the cash to a military officer, who promptly transferred ownership of three Thunderbolts to the government of Nicaragua. The planes arrived, fully armed, in Panama from Puerto Rico that evening.

They flew into combat at dawn, unleashing a barrage against the same Guatemalan army forces whose loyalties were the linchpin of the plan to topple Arbenz. CIA pilots strafed troop trains carrying soldiers to the front. They dropped bombs, dynamite, hand grenades, and Molotov cocktails. They blew up a radio station run by American Christian missionaries and sank a British freighter docked on the Pacific coast.

On the ground, Castillo Armas failed to gain an inch. Turning back, he radioed the CIA, pleading for more air power. The Voice of Liberation, its signal relayed from a transponder atop the American embassy, broadcast craftily concocted stories that thousands of rebel troops were converging on the capital. Loudspeakers atop the embassy roof blasted the tape-recorded sounds of P-38 fighters soaring into the night. President Arbenz, drinking himself into a stupor, saw through his fog that he was under attack from the United States.

On the afternoon on June 25, the CIA bombed the parade grounds of the largest military encampment in Guatemala City. That broke the will of the officer corps. Arbenz summoned his cabinet that night and told them that elements of the army were in revolt. It was true: a handful of officers had secretly decided to side with the CIA and overthrow their president.

Ambassador Peurifoy met with the coup plotters on June 27, victory within his grasp. But then Arbenz ceded power to Colonel Carlos Enrique Diaz, who formed a junta and vowed to fight Castillo Armas. "We have been double-crossed," Peurifoy cabled. Al Haney sent a message to all CIA stations identifying Diaz as a "Commie agent." He ordered a silver-tongued CIA officer, Enno Hobbing, *Time*'s Berlin bureau chief before joining the agency, to have a little talk with Diaz at dawn the next day. Hobbing delivered the message to Diaz: "Colonel, you are not convenient for American foreign policy."

The junta vanished instantly, to be replaced in quick succession by four more, each one increasingly pro-American. Ambassador Peurifoy now demanded that the CIA stand down. Wisner cabled all hands on June 30 that it was time for "the surgeons to step back and the nurses to take over the patient." Peurifoy maneuvered for two more months before Castillo Armas assumed the presidency. He received a twenty-one-gun salute and a state dinner at the White House, where the vice president offered the following toast: "We in the United States have watched the people of Guatemala record an episode in their history deeply significant to all peoples," Richard Nixon said. "Led by the courageous soldier who is our guest this evening, the Guatemalan people revolted against communist rule, which in collapsing bore graphic witness to its own shallowness, falsity, and corruption." Guatemala was at the beginning of forty years of military rulers, death squads, and armed repression.

"INCREDIBLE"

The leaders of the CIA created a myth about Operation Success, just as they did with the coup in Iran. The company line was that the mission was a masterwork. In truth, "we really didn't think it was much of a success," said Jake Esterline, who became the new station chief in Guatemala at summer's end. The coup had succeeded largely through brute force and blind luck. But the CIA spun another story at a formal White House briefing for the president on July 29, 1954. The night before, Allen Dulles invited Frank Wisner, Tracy Barnes, Dave Phillips, Al Haney, Henry Hecksher, and Rip Robertson to his house in Georgetown for a dress rehearsal. He listened in growing horror as Haney began a rambling discourse with a long preamble about his heroic exploits in Korea.

"I've never heard such crap," said Dulles, and he ordered Phillips to rewrite the speech.

In the East Wing of the White House, in a room darkened for a slide show, the CIA sold Eisenhower a dressed-up version of Operation Success. When the lights went on, the president's first question went to the paramilitary man Rip Robertson.

"How many men did Castillo Armas lose?" Ike asked.

Only one, Robertson replied.

"Incredible," said the president.

At least forty-three of Castillo Armas's men had been killed during the invasion, but no one contradicted Robertson. It was a shameless falsehood.

This was a turning point in the history of the CIA. The cover stories required for covert action overseas were now part of the agency's political conduct in Washington. Bissell stated it plainly: "Many of us who joined the CIA did not feel bound in the actions we took as staff members to observe all the ethical rules." He and his colleagues were prepared to lie to the president to protect the agency's image. And their lies had lasting consequences.

11. "AND THEN WE'LL HAVE A STORM"

"Secrecy now beclouds everything about the CIA—its cost, its efficiency, its successes, its failures," Senator Mike Mansfield of Montana said in March 1954.

Allen Dulles answered to a very few members of Congress. They protected the CIA from public scrutiny through informal armed services and appropriations subcommittees. He regularly asked his deputies to supply him with "CIA success stories that might be used at the next budget hearing." He had none up his sleeve. On rare occasions, he was prepared to be candid. Two weeks after Mansfield's critique, Dulles faced three senators at a closed-door hearing. His briefing notes said the CIA's rapid expansion of covert operations might have been "risky or even unwise for the long pull of the Cold War." They conceded that "unplanned, urgent, one-shot operations not only usually failed, but also disrupted and even blew our careful preparations for longer-range activities."

That kind of secret could be kept safe on Capitol Hill. But one senator posed a grave and gathering threat to the CIA: the red-baiting Joseph McCarthy. McCarthy and his staff had developed an underground of informants who had quit the agency in anger toward the end of the Korean War. In the months after Eisenhower's election, McCarthy's files grew thick with allegations that "the CIA had unwittingly hired a large number of double agents—individuals who, although working for the CIA, were actually Communist agents whose mission was to plant inaccurate data," as his chief counsel, Roy Cohn, recounted. Unlike many of McCarthy's charges, this one was true. The agency could not withstand a whit of scrutiny on the issue, and Allen Dulles knew it. If the American people had learned, in the heat of the red scare, that the agency had been duped all over Europe and Asia by the Soviet and Chinese intelligence services, the CIA would be destroyed.

When McCarthy privately told Dulles face-to-face "that CIA was neither sacrosanct nor immune from investigation," the director knew its survival was at stake. Foster Dulles had opened his doors to McCarthy's bloodhounds in a public display of sanctimony that devastated the State Department for a decade. But Allen fought them off. He rebuffed the senator's attempt to subpoena the CIA's Bill Bundy, who out of old-school loyalties had contributed $400 to the defense fund of Alger Hiss, the suspected communist spy. Allen refused to let the senator scourge the CIA.

His public stance was a principled one, but he also ran a down-and-dirty covert operation on McCarthy. The clandestine campaign was outlined in a CIA officer's secret testimony before McCarthy's Senate committee and its twenty-eight-year-old minority counsel, Robert F. Kennedy, which was unsealed in 2003. It was detailed in a CIA history declassified in 2004.

After his private confrontation with McCarthy, Dulles organized a team of CIA officers to penetrate the senator's office with a spy or a bug, preferably both. The methodology was just like J. Edgar Hoover's: gather dirt, then spread it. Dulles instructed James Angleton, his counterintelligence czar, to find a way to feed disinformation to McCarthy and his staff as a means of discrediting him. Angleton convinced James McCargar—the officer who had been one of Wisner's first hires—to plant phony reports on a known member of the McCarthy underground at the CIA. McCargar succeeded: the CIA penetrated the Senate.

"You've saved the Republic," Allen Dulles told him.

"THIS FUNDAMENTALLY REPUGNANT PHILOSOPHY"

But the threat to the CIA grew as McCarthy's power began fading in 1954. Senator Mansfield and thirty-four of his colleagues were backing a bill to create an oversight committee and order the agency to keep Congress fully and currently informed about its work. (It would not pass for twenty years.) A congressional task force led by Eisenhower's trusted colleague General Mark Clark was getting ready to investigate the agency.

At the end of May 1954, the president of the United States received an extraordinary six-page letter from an air force colonel. It was an impassioned cry by the first whistle-blower from inside the CIA. Eisenhower read it and kept it.

The author, Jim Kellis, was one of the agency's founding fathers. An OSS veteran who had fought guerrilla warfare in Greece, he had gone to China and served as the first station chief in Shanghai for the Strategic Services Unit. At the CIA's birth, he was among its few experienced China hands. He went back to Greece as an investigator for Wild Bill Donovan, who as a private citizen had been asked to investigate the 1948 murder of a CBS reporter. He determined that the killing came at the hands of America's right-wing allies in Athens, not ordered by the communists, as was commonly believed. His findings were suppressed. He returned to the CIA, and during the Korean War he was in charge of the CIA's paramilitary operations and resistance forces worldwide. Walter Bedell Smith had sent him on troubleshooting investigations in Asia and Europe. He did not like what he saw. A few months after Allen Dulles took command, Kellis quit in disgust.

"The Central Intelligence Agency is in a rotten state," Colonel Kellis warned Eisenhower. "Today CIA has hardly any worthwhile operations behind the Iron Curtain. In their briefings they present a rosy picture to outsiders but the awful truth remains under the TOP SECRET label of the Agency."

The truth was that "CIA wittingly or unwittingly delivered one million dollars to a Communist security service." (This was the WIN operation in Poland; it is unlikely that Dulles told the president about the ugly details of the operation, which blew up three weeks before Eisenhower's inauguration.) "CIA unwittingly organized an intelligence network for the Communists," Kellis wrote, referring to the debacle created by the Seoul station during the Korean War. Dulles and his deputies, "fearing any aftereffects on their reputation," had lied to Congress about the agency's operations in Korea and China. Kellis had personally investigated the question on a trip to the Far East in 1952. He had determined that "CIA was being duped."

Dulles had been planting stories in the press, burnishing his image as "a scholarly affable Christian missionary, the country's outstanding intelligence expert," Kellis wrote. "For some of us who have seen the other side of Allen Dulles, we don't see too many Christian traits. I personally consider him a ruthless, ambitious and utterly incompetent government administrator." Kellis pleaded with the president to take "the drastic action needed to clean up" the CIA.

Eisenhower wanted to counter the threats to the clandestine service and clean up its problems in secret. In July 1954, shortly after the conclusion of Operation Success, the president commissioned General Jimmy Doolittle, who had worked on the Solarium project, and his good friend William Pawley, the millionaire who had provided the fighter-bombers for the Guatemala coup, to assess the CIA's capabilities for covert action.

Doolittle had ten weeks to report back. He and Pawley met with Dulles and Wisner, traveled to CIA stations in Germany and London, and interviewed senior military and diplomatic officers who worked in liaison with their CIA counterparts. They also talked to Bedell Smith, who told them that "Dulles was too emotional to be in this critical spot" and that "his emotionalism was far worse than it appeared on the surface."

On October 19, 1954, Doolittle went to see the president at the White House. He reported that the agency had "ballooned out into a vast and sprawling organization manned by a large number of people, some of whom were of doubtful competence." Dulles surrounded himself with people who were unskilled and undisciplined. The sensitive matter of "the family relationship" with Foster Dulles arose. Doolittle thought it would be better for all concerned if the personal connection were not a professional connection: "it leads to protection of one by the other or influence of one by the other." An independent committee of trusted civilians should oversee the CIA for the president.

The Doolittle report warned that Wisner's clandestine service was "filled with people having little or no training for their jobs." Within its six separate staffs, seven geographic divisions, and more than forty branches, " 'dead wood' exists at virtually all levels." The report recommended a "complete reorganization" of Wisner's empire, which had suffered from its "mushroom expansion" and "tremendous pressures to accept commitments beyond its capacity to perform." It observed that "in covert operations quality is more important than quantity. A small number of competent people can be more useful than a large number of incompetents."

Dulles was well aware that the clandestine service was out of control. The CIA's officers were running operations behind their commanders' backs. Two days after Doolittle presented his report, the director told Wisner that he was worried that "sensitive and/or delicate operations are carried out at lower levels without being brought to the attention of the appropriate Deputy, the Deputy Director of Central Intelligence or the Director of Central Intelligence."

But Dulles handled the Doolittle report the way he usually dealt with bad news, by burying it. He would not let the highest-ranking officers at the CIA see it—not even Wisner.

Though the full report remained classified until 2001, its preface was made public a quarter century before. It contained one of the grimmest passages of the cold war:

> It is now clear that we are facing an implacable enemy whose avowed objective is world domination by whatever means and at whatever cost. There are no rules in such a game. Hitherto acceptable norms of human conduct do not apply. If the United States is to survive, long-standing American concepts of "fair play" must be reconsidered. We must develop effective espionage and counterespionage services and must learn to subvert, sabotage and destroy our enemies by more clever, more sophisticated and more effective methods than those used against us. It may become necessary that the American people be made acquainted with, understand and support this fundamentally repugnant philosophy.

The report said the nation needed "an aggressive covert psychological, political and paramilitary organization more effective, more unique, and, if necessary, more ruthless than that employed by the enemy." For the CIA had never solved "the problem of infiltration by human agents," it said. "Once across borders—by parachute, or any other means—escape from detection is extremely difficult." It concluded: "The information we have obtained by this method of acquisition has been negligible and the cost in effort, dollars and human lives prohibitive."

It placed the highest priority on espionage to gain intelligence on the Soviets. It stressed that no price was too high to pay for this knowledge.

"WE DIDN'T RAISE THE RIGHT QUESTIONS"

Dulles was desperate to place an American spy inside the iron curtain.

In 1953, the first CIA officer he had dispatched to Moscow was seduced by his Russian housemaid—she was a KGB colonel—photographed in flagrante delicto, blackmailed, and fired by the agency for his indiscretions. In 1954, a second officer was caught in the act of espionage, arrested, and deported shortly after his arrival. Soon thereafter, Dulles called in one of his special assistants, John Maury, who had traveled in Russia before World War II and spent much of the war at the American embassy in Moscow representing the Office of Naval Intelligence. He asked Maury to join the clandestine service and to train for a mission to Moscow.

None of Wisner's officers had ever been to Russia, Dulles said: "They know nothing about the target."

"I don't know anything about operations," Maury responded.

"I don't think they do either," Dulles replied.

Such men could hardly provide the president with the intelligence he wanted most: strategic warning against a nuclear attack. When the National Security Council convened to talk about what to do if that attack came, the president turned to Dulles and said: "Let's not have another Pearl Harbor." That was the task the president assigned to the second secret intelligence commission he created in 1954.

Eisenhower told James R. Killian, the president of the Massachusetts Institute of Technology, to lead a group seeking ways of preventing a Soviet bolt from the blue. He pressed for techniques the Doolittle report strongly recommended: "communications and electronic surveillance" to provide "early warning of impending attack."

The CIA redoubled its own efforts to listen in on the enemy. It succeeded, in its own fashion.

Up in the attic of the Berlin base headquarters, a washed-up baseball player turned lawyer turned spy named Walter O'Brien had been photographing papers purloined from the East Berlin post office. They described the underground routes of the new telecommunications cables used by Soviet and East German officials. This espionage coup turned into the Berlin Tunnel project.

The tunnel was regarded at the time as the CIA's greatest public triumph. The idea—and its undoing—came from British intelligence. In 1951, the British had told the CIA that they had been tapping into the Soviets' telecommunications cables through a network of tunnels in the occupied zones of Vienna since shortly after the end of World War II. They suggested doing the same in Berlin. Thanks to the stolen blueprints, it became a real possibility.

A secret CIA history of the Berlin tunnel, written in August 1967 and declassified in February 2007, laid out three questions that faced William K. Harvey, a hard-drinking, gun-toting ex-FBI agent who took over as chief of the Berlin base in 1952: Could the agency dig a 1,476-foot tunnel into the Soviet zone of East Berlin and hit a target two inches in diameter—and twenty-seven inches underneath a major highway—without being caught? How could it get rid of the spoils—some three thousand tons of sandy soil—in secret? And what kind of cover story would serve to disguise the construction of an installation for the dig in a squalid district of refugees' shacks at the edge of the American zone?

Allen Dulles and his British counterpart, Sir John Sinclair, agreed in December 1953 on terms of reference for a set of conferences on the tunnel operation, which was to be code-named JOINTLY. The talks led to a plan of action the following summer. A building covering a full city block would rise amid the rubble, with antennae bristling from the roof, and the Soviets would be given to understand that it was a station for intercepting signals intelligence from the atmosphere—the magician's trick of diverting the eye. The Americans would dig the tunnel eastward, to a point beneath the cables. The British, relying on their experience in Vienna, would drive a vertical shaft from the end of the tunnel to the cables and then install the taps. A London office that grew to 317 officers would process the spoken conversations recorded by the CIA. In Washington, the agency would set 350 personnel to work transcribing teletype transmissions intercepted in the tunnel. The Army Corps of Engineers did the digging, with technical assistance from the British. The biggest problem, as ever, proved to be translating the words intercepted by the operation: "We were never successful in obtaining as many linguists as we needed," the CIA history noted, for the agency's language capabilities in Russian and even in German were sorely lacking.

The tunnel was completed at the end of February 1955, and the British began to set the taps one month later. Information began flowing in May. It came to tens of thousands of hours of conversations and teletypes, including precious details about Soviet nuclear and conventional forces in Germany and Poland, insights into the Soviet Ministry of Defense in Moscow, and the architecture of Soviet counterintelligence operations in Berlin. It provided pictures of political confusion and indecision among Soviet and East German officialdom, and the names or cover identities of several hundred Soviet intelligence officers. It delivered news—even if it took weeks or months of translation—at a cost of $6.7 million. Once it was revealed, as the CIA anticipated it would be one day, the tunnel was seen as a sign that "the U.S., almost universally regarded as a stumbling neophyte in espionage matters, was capable of a coup against the Soviet Union, which has long been the acknowledged master in such matters," the CIA history poignantly reported.

The agency had not expected the operation would be blown quite so soon. It lasted less than a year—until the following April, when the tunnel was uncovered. For the Kremlin had known about it from the start, before the first shovel of earth was turned. The plan was uncovered by a Soviet mole in British intelligence, George Blake, who had switched his allegiances while a prisoner of war in North Korea and who had let the Soviets in on the secret back in late 1953. The Soviets valued Blake so highly that Moscow let the tunnel operation run for eleven months before exposing it in a blaze of heavy-handed publicity. Years later, even after realizing that the other side had known of the tunnel from the start, the CIA still believed it had dug a gold mine. To this day, the question remains: did Moscow deliberately feed deceptive information into the tunnel? The evidence suggests that the CIA gained two invaluable and untainted kinds of knowledge from the taps. The agency learned a basic blueprint of the Soviet and East German security systems, and it never picked up a glimmer of warning that Moscow intended to go to war.

"Those of us who knew a little bit about Russia viewed it as a backward Third World country that wanted to develop along the lines of the West," said the CIA's Tom Polgar, the Berlin base veteran. But that view was rejected at the highest levels in Washington. The White House and the Pentagon presumed that the Kremlin's *intentions* were identical to theirs: to destroy their enemy on the first day of World War III. Their mission was therefore to locate Soviet military *capabilities* and destroy them first. They had no faith that American spies could do that.

But American machines might.

The Killian report was the beginning of the triumph of technology and the eclipse of old-fashioned espionage at the CIA. "We obtain little significant information from classic covert operations inside Russia," the report told Eisenhower. "But we can use the ultimate in science and technology to improve our intelligence take." It urged Eisenhower to build spy planes and space satellites to soar over the Soviet Union and photograph its arsenals.

The technology was within America's grasp. It had been for two years. Dulles and Wisner had been too busy with operational matters to pay attention to a July 1952 memo from their colleague Loftus Becker, then the deputy director for intelligence, on a proposal to develop "a satellite vehicle for reconnaissance"—a television camera launched on a rocket, to survey the Soviet Union from deep space. The key was building the camera. Edwin Land, a Nobel laureate who had invented the Polaroid, was sure that he could do it.

In November 1954, with the Berlin Tunnel under way, Land, Killian, and Dulles met with the president and won his approval to build the U-2 spy plane, a powered glider with a camera in its belly that would put American eyes behind the iron curtain. Eisenhower gave the go-ahead, along with a glum prediction. Someday, he said, "one of these machines is going to be caught, and then we'll have a storm."

Dulles gave the job of building the plane to Dick Bissell, who knew nothing about aircraft but skillfully created a secret government bureaucracy that shielded the U-2 program from scrutiny and helped speed the plane's creation. "Our Agency," he proudly told a class of CIA trainees a few years later, "is the last refuge of organizational privacy available to the U.S. government."

Bissell paced down the CIA's corridors with long strides, a gawky man with great ambitions. He believed that he someday would be the next director of central intelligence, for Dulles told him so. He became increasingly contemptuous of espionage, and disdained Richard Helms and his intelligence officers. The two men became bureaucratic rivals and then bitter enemies. They personified the battle between spies and gadgets, which began fifty years ago and continues today. Bissell saw the U-2 as a weapon—an aggressive blow against the Soviet threat. If Moscow "couldn't do a goddamn thing to prevent you" from violating Soviet airspace and spying on Soviet forces, that alone would sap Soviet pride and power. He formed a very small and secret cell of CIA officers to run the program, and he assigned the CIA's James Q. Reber, the assistant director for intelligence coordination, to decide what the plane should photograph inside the Soviet Union. Reber rose to become the longtime chairman of the committee that chose the Soviet targets for the U-2 planes and the spy satellites that succeeded them. But in the end, the Pentagon always set the requirements for reconnaissance: How many bombers did the Soviets have? How many nuclear missiles? How many tanks?

Later in life, Reber said that the cold war mentality blocked the very idea of photographing anything else.

"We didn't raise the right questions," Reber said. If the CIA had developed a bigger picture of life inside the Soviet Union, it would have learned that the Soviets were putting little money into the resources that truly made a nation strong. They were a weak enemy. If the CIA's leaders had been able to run effective intelligence operations inside the Soviet Union, they might have seen that Russians were unable to produce the necessities of life. The idea that the final battles of the cold war would be economic instead of military was beyond their imagination.

"THERE ARE SOME THINGS HE DOESN'T TELL
THE PRESIDENT"

The president's efforts to investigate the capabilities of the CIA led to a leap of technology that revolutionized the gathering of intelligence. But they never got to the root of the problem. Seven years after its creation, there was no oversight or control of the CIA. Its secrets were shared on a need-to-know basis, and Allen Dulles decided who needed to know.

No one was left to look into the agency after Walter Bedell Smith quit the government in October 1954. By sheer force of personality, Bedell Smith had tried to rein in Allen Dulles. But when he left, the ability of anyone but Eisenhower to control covert action went with him.

In 1955, the president changed the rules by creating the "Special Group"—three designated representatives of the White House, State, and Defense, charged with reviewing the secret operations of the CIA. But they had no ability to approve covert action in advance. If he chose to do so, Dulles might make passing mention of his plans at informal lunches with the Special Group—the new undersecretary of state, the deputy secretary of defense, and the president's national-security assistant. But more often he did not. A five-volume CIA history of Dulles's career as director of central intelligence noted that he believed they had no need to know about covert action. They were in no position to judge him or the agency. He felt that "no policy approval was required" for his decisions.

The director, his deputies, and his station chiefs abroad remained free to set their own policies, plot their own operations, and judge the results for themselves, in secret. Dulles advised the White House as he saw fit. "There are some things he doesn't tell the President," his sister confided to a State Department colleague. "It is better that he doesn't know."

12. "WE RAN IT IN A DIFFERENT WAY"

One weapon the CIA used with surpassing skill was cold cash. The agency excelled at buying the services of foreign politicians. The first place where it picked the future leader of a world power was Japan.

Two of the most influential agents the United States ever recruited helped carry out the CIA's mission to control the government. They had been cell mates, charged as war criminals, and imprisoned for three years in Tokyo after the end of World War II under the American occupation. They walked free at the end of 1948, the day before many of their fellow inmates were taken to the prison gallows.

With the CIA's help, Nobusuke Kishi became Japan's prime minister and the chief of its ruling party. Yoshio Kodama secured his freedom and his position as the nation's number-one gangster by helping American intelligence. Together they shaped the politics of postwar Japan. In the war against fascism, they had represented everything America hated. In the war against communism, they were just what America needed.

In the 1930s, Kodama had led a right-wing youth group that attempted to assassinate the prime minister. He was sentenced to prison, but Japan's government put him to use as a procurer of spies and strategic metals for the coming battle. After five years spent running one of the war's biggest black markets in occupied China, Kodama held the rank of rear admiral and possessed a personal fortune worth roughly $175 million. Upon his release from prison, Kodama began to pour part of his fortune into the careers of Japan's most conservative politicians, and he became a key member of a CIA operation that helped bring them to power. He worked with American businessmen, OSS veterans, and ex-diplomats to pull off an audacious covert operation, bankrolled by the CIA, during the Korean War.

The American military needed tungsten, a scarce strategic metal used for hardening missiles. Kodama's network smuggled tons of it out of Japanese military caches into the United States. The Pentagon paid $10 million for it. The CIA provided $2.8 million in financing to underwrite the operation. The tungsten-smuggling network reaped more than $2 million. But the operation left Kodama in bad odor with the CIA's Toyko station. "He is a professional liar, gangster, charlatan, and outright thief," the station reported on September 10, 1953. "Kodama is completely incapable of intelligence operations, and has no interest in anything but the profits." The relationship was severed, and the CIA turned its attention to the care and feeding of up-and-coming Japanese politicians—including Kishi—who won seats in the Diet, Japan's parliament, in the first elections after the end of the American occupation.

"WE'RE ALL DEMOCRATS NOW"

Kishi became the leader of the rising conservative movement in Japan. Within a year of his election to the Diet, using Kodama's money and his own considerable political skills, he controlled the largest faction among Japan's elected representives. Once in office, he built the ruling party that led the nation for nearly half a century.

He had signed the declaration of war against the United States in 1941 and led Japan's munitions ministry during World War II. Even while imprisoned after the war, Kishi had well-placed allies in the United States, among them Joseph Grew, the American ambassador in Tokyo when the Japanese attacked Pearl Harbor. Grew was under detention in Tokyo in 1942 when Kishi, as a member of the war cabinet, offered to let him out to play a round of golf. They became friends. Days after Kishi was freed from prison, Grew became the first chairman of the National Committee for a Free Europe, the CIA front created to support Radio Free Europe and other political-warfare programs.

Upon his release, Kishi went directly to the residence of the prime minister, where his brother, Eisaku Sato, the chief secretary of the cabinet under the occupation, handed him a business suit to replace his prisoner's uniform.

"Strange, isn't it?" Kishi said to his brother. "We're all democrats now."

Seven years of patient planning transformed Kishi from prisoner to prime minister. He took English lessons from *Newsweek*'s Tokyo bureau chief and gained introductions to American politicians from *Newsweek*'s foreign affairs editor, Harry Kern, a close friend to Allen Dulles and later in life a CIA conduit to Japan. Kishi cultivated American embassy officials like rare orchids. He moved cautiously at first. He was still a notorious man, routinely followed by the police.

In May 1954, he staged a political coming-out at the Kabuki Theater in Tokyo. He invited Bill Hutchinson, an OSS veteran who worked with the CIA in Japan as an information and propaganda officer at the American embassy, to attend the theater with him. He paraded Hutchinson around the ornate foyers of the Kabuki-za at intermission, showing him off to his friends among the Japanese elite. It was a highly unusual gesture at the time, but it was pure political theater, Kishi's way of announcing in public that he was back in the international arena—and in the good graces of the United States.

For a year, Kishi met in secret with CIA and State Department officials in Hutchinson's living room. "It was clear that he wanted at least the tacit backing of the United States government," Hutchinson remembered. The talks laid the groundwork for the next forty years of Japan's relations with the United States.

Kishi told the Americans that his strategy was to wreck the ruling Liberal Party, rename it, rebuild it, and run it. The new Liberal Democratic Party under his command would be neither liberal nor democratic, but a right-wing club of feudal leaders rising from the ashes of imperial Japan. He would first work behind the scenes while more senior statesmen preceded him as prime minister, and then take charge. He pledged to change the foreign policies of Japan to fit American desires. The United States could keep its military bases in Japan and store nuclear weapons there, a matter of some sensitivity in Japan. All he asked in return was secret political support from America.

Foster Dulles met with Kishi in August 1955, and the American secretary of state told him face-to-face that he could expect that support—if Japan's conservatives unified to help the United States fight communism.

Everyone understood what that American support would be.

Kishi told Sam Berger, the senior political officer at the American embassy, that it would be best for him to deal directly with a younger and lower-ranking man, unknown in Japan, as his primary contact with the United States. The assignment went to the CIA's Clyde McAvoy, a marine veteran who had survived the storming of Okinawa and joined the agency after a stint as a newspaper reporter. Shortly after McAvoy arrived in Japan, Sam Berger introduced him to Kishi, and one of the stronger relationships the CIA ever cultivated with a foreign political leader was born.

"A GREAT COUP"

The most crucial interaction between the CIA and the Liberal Democratic Party was the exchange of information for money. It was used to support the party and to recruit informers within it. The Americans established paid relationships with promising young men who became, a generation later, members of parliament, ministers, and elder statesmen. Together they promoted the LDP and subverted Japan's Socialist Party and labor unions. When it came to bankrolling foreign politicians, the agency had grown more sophisticated than it had been seven years earlier in Italy. Instead of passing suitcases filled with cash in four-star hotels, the CIA used trusted American businessmen as go-betweens to deliver money to benefit its allies. Among these were executives from Lockheed, the aircraft company then building the U-2 and negotiating to sell warplanes to the new Japanese defense forces Kishi aimed to build.

In November 1955, Kishi unified Japan's conservatives under the banner of the Liberal Democratic Party. As the party's leader, he allowed the CIA to recruit and run his political followers on a seat-by-seat basis in the Japanese parliament. As he maneuvered his way to the top, he pledged to work with the agency in reshaping a new security treaty between the United States and Japan. As Kishi's case officer, the CIA's Clyde McAvoy was able to report on—and influence—the emerging foreign policy of postwar Japan.

In February 1957, on the day Kishi was to be installed as prime minister, a crucial procedural vote on the security treaty was scheduled in the Diet, where the LDP held the biggest block of votes. "He and I pulled off a great coup that day," McAvoy remembered. "The United States and Japan were moving toward this agreement. The Japan Communist Party found it especially threatening. On the day of this vote, the communists planned an uprising in the Diet. I found out about this through a left-wing Socialist member of the secretariat who was my agent. Kishi was to meet the Emperor that day. I called for an urgent meeting. He made it—he showed up at the door of our safe house in top hat, striped pants and a cutaway coat—and though I had no approval to do so, I told him of the communists' plans for a riot in the Diet. Now, the custom was for members to take a break and go to the eating and drinking stalls around the Diet at 10:30 or 11 a.m. Kishi told his own party: don't take a break. And after everyone but the LDP peeled off they ran to the Diet and passed the bill."

In June 1957, barely eight years after shedding his prison uniform, Kishi traveled to the United States for a triumphal visit. He went to Yankee Stadium and threw out the ceremonial first ball. He played a round of golf at an all-white country club with the president of the United States. Vice President Nixon introduced him to the Senate as a great and loyal friend of the American people. Kishi told the new American ambassador to Japan, Douglas MacArthur II, the general's nephew, that the new security treaty would be passed and a rising left-wing tide could be stemmed if America helped him consolidate his power. Kishi wanted a permanent source of financial support from the CIA rather than a series of surreptitious payments. He convinced the American envoy that "if Japan went Communist it was difficult to see how the rest of Asia would not follow suit," Ambassador MacArthur remembered. Foster Dulles agreed. He argued that the United States had to place a big bet on Japan, and that Kishi was the best bet the United States had.

President Eisenhower himself decided that Japanese political support for the security treaty and American financial support for Kishi were one and the same. He authorized a continuing series of CIA payoffs to key members of the LDP. Politicians unwitting of the CIA's role were told that the money came from the titans of corporate America. The money flowed for at least fifteen years, under four American presidents, and it helped consolidate one-party rule in Japan for the rest of the cold war.

Others followed in Kishi's path. Okinori Kaya had been the finance minister in Japan's wartime cabinet. Convicted as a war criminal, he was sentenced to life in prison. Paroled in 1955 and pardoned in 1957, he became one of Kishi's closest advisers and a key member of the LDP's internal security committee.

Kaya became a recruited agent of the CIA either immediately before or immediately after he was elected to the Diet in 1958. After his recruitment, he wanted to travel to the United States and meet Allen Dulles in person. The CIA, skittish about the appearance of a convicted war criminal meeting with the director of central intelligence, kept the meeting secret for nearly fifty years. But on February 6, 1959, Kaya came to visit Dulles at CIA headquarters and asked the director to enter into a formal agreement to share intelligence with his internal security committee. "Everyone agreed that cooperation between CIA and the Japanese regarding countersubversion was most desirable and that the subject was one of major interest to CIA," say the minutes of their talk. Dulles regarded Kaya as his agent, and six months later he wrote him to say: "I am most interested in learning your views both in international affairs affecting relations between our countries and on the situation within Japan."

Kaya's on-and-off relationship with the CIA reached a peak in 1968, when he was the leading political adviser to Prime Minister Eisaku Sato. The biggest domestic political issue in Japan that year was the enormous American military base on Okinawa, a crucial staging ground for the bombing of Vietnam and a storehouse of American nuclear weapons. Okinawa was under American control, but regional elections were set for November 10, and opposition politicians threatened to force the United States off the island. Kaya played a key role in the CIA's covert actions aimed to swing the elections for the LDP, which narrowly failed. Okinawa itself returned to Japanese administration in 1972, but the American military remains there to this day.

The Japanese came to describe the political system created with the CIA's support as *kozo oshoku*—"structural corruption." The CIA's payoffs went on into the 1970s. The structural corruption of the political life of Japan continued long thereafter.

"We ran Japan during the occupation, and we ran it in a different way in these years after the occupation," said the CIA's Horace Feldman, who served as station chief in Tokyo. "General MacArthur had his ways. We had ours."

13. "WISHFUL BLINDNESS"

Enthralled by covert action, Allen Dulles ceased to focus on his core mission of providing intelligence to the president.

He handled most of the CIA's analysts and much of their work with studied contempt. Dulles would keep them waiting for hours when they came to prep him for the next morning's meeting at the White House. As afternoon turned to evening, he would burst out his door and blow past them, rushing to keep a dinner date.

He had fallen into "the habit of assessing briefings by weight," said Dick Lehman, a senior CIA analyst for three decades and latterly the man who prepared the president's daily briefing. "He would heft them and decide, without reading them, whether or not to accept them."

An analyst admitted to the inner sanctum in midafternoon to advise Dulles on the crisis of the moment might find the director watching a Washington Senators baseball game on the television in his office. Lounging in a reclining chair, his feet up on an ottoman, Dulles followed the game while the hapless aide faced him from the back of the TV set. As the briefer reached his crucial points, Dulles would analyze the ball game.

He became inattentive to the life-and-death questions at hand.

"INDICT THE WHOLE SOVIET SYSTEM"

Dulles and Wisner together had launched more than two hundred major covert actions overseas over the course of five years, pouring American fortunes into the politics of France, Germany, Italy, Greece, Egypt, Pakistan, Japan, Thailand, the Philippines, and Vietnam. The agency had overthrown nations. It could make or break presidents and prime ministers. But it could not get a handle on the enemy.

At the end of 1955, President Eisenhower changed the CIA's marching orders. Recognizing that covert action could not undermine the Kremlin, he revised the rules written at the start of the cold war. The new order, labeled NSC 5412/2 and dated December 28, 1955, remained in effect for fifteen years. The new goals were to "create and exploit troublesome problems for International Communism," to "counter any threat of a party or individuals directly or indirectly responsive to Communist control," and to "strengthen the orientation toward the United States of the people of the free world"—great ambitions, but more modest and nuanced than what Dulles and Wisner tried to achieve.

A few weeks later, the Soviet leader, Nikita Khrushchev, created more trouble for international communism than the CIA dreamed possible. In his February 1956 speech to the Twentieth Congress of the Communist Party of the Soviet Union, he denounced Stalin, dead less than three years, as "a supreme egotist and sadist, capable of sacrificing everything and anybody for the sake of his own power and glory." The CIA picked up rumors about the speech in March. My kingdom for a copy, Allen Dulles told his men. Could the agency finally obtain some intelligence from inside the Politburo?

Then as now, the CIA relied heavily on foreign intelligence services, paying for secrets it could not uncover on its own. In April 1956, Israel's spies delivered the text to James Angleton, who became the CIA's one-man liaison with the Jewish state. The channel produced much of the agency's intelligence on the Arab world, but at a cost—a growing American dependence on Israel to explain events in the Middle East. The Israeli perspective colored American perceptions for decades to come.

In May, after George Kennan and others judged the text as the genuine article, a great debate arose inside the CIA.

Both Wisner and Angleton wanted to keep it secret from the free

world, but leak it selectively abroad, to sow discord among the world's
communist parties. Angleton thought by tweaking the text with propaganda, "he could have used it to such advantage that he would have dis-
combobulated the Russians and their security services and perhaps used
some of these émigré groups that we still at that time hoped to activate,
and liberate the Ukraine or something," said Ray Cline, one of Dulles's
most trusted intelligence analysts at that time.

But above all, they wanted it cut for bait to lure Soviet spies, in order
to salvage one of Wisner's longest-running, least effective operations—
Red Cap.

A worldwide program that began in 1952, taking its name from the
railroad porters who helped baggage-laden travelers, Red Cap aimed to
induce Soviets to defect from their country and work for the CIA. Ide-
ally, they would serve as "defectors in place"—remaining in their government posts while spying for America. Failing that, they would flee to
the West and reveal their knowledge of the Soviet system. But the number of important Soviet sources developed under Red Cap was zero at
the time. The Soviet division of the CIA's clandestine service was run by
a narrow-minded Harvard man named Dana Durand, who held his position through a combination of accident, default, and alliance with Angleton. The division was dysfunctional, according to an inspector
general's report issued in June 1956 and declassified in 2004. The Soviet
division could not produce "an authoritative statement of its missions
and functions," much less grasp what was going on inside the Soviet
Union. The report contained a list of the CIA's twenty "controlled agents"
in Russia in 1956. One was a low-ranking naval engineering officer.
Another was the wife of a guided missile research scientist. The others
were listed as laborer, telephone repairman, garage manager, veterinar-
ian, high school teacher, locksmith, restaurant worker, and unemployed.
None of them could have had any idea what made the Kremlin tick.

On the first Saturday morning of June 1956, Dulles called Ray Cline
into the director's office. "Wisner says you think we ought to release the
secret Khrushchev speech," Dulles said.

Cline stated his case: it was a fantastic revelation of "the true feelings
of all these guys who had to work under that old bastard Stalin for many
years.

"For God's sake," he told Dulles, "let's get it out."

Dulles held his copy in trembling fingers gnarled with arthritis and gout. The old man put his carpet slippers up on the desk, leaned back, pushed his glasses up on his head, and said, "By golly, I think I'll make a policy decision!" Cline recalled. He buzzed Wisner on his intercom, "and kind of coyly talked Frank into a position where Frank could not disagree with releasing it, and using the same kind of arguments that I had, that it was a great historical chance to, as I think I told him to say, 'indict the whole Soviet system.' "

Dulles then picked up the phone and called his brother. The text was leaked through the State Department and ran three days later in *The New York Times*. The decision set events in motion that the CIA had never imagined.

"CIA REPRESENTED GREAT POWER"

For months thereafter, the secret speech was beamed behind the iron curtain by Radio Free Europe, the CIA's $100 million media machine. More than three thousand émigré broadcasters, writers, and engineers and their American overseers put the radios on the air in eight languages, filling the airwaves up to nineteen hours a day. In theory, they were supposed to play their news and propaganda straight. But Wisner wanted to use words as weapons. His interference created a split signal at Radio Free Europe.

The on-air émigrés at the radios had been begging their American bosses to give them a clear message to deliver. Here it was: the speech was recited over the air night and day.

The consequences were immediate. The CIA's best analysts had concluded a few months before that no popular uprising was likely in Eastern Europe during the 1950s. On June 28, after the speech was broadcast, Polish workers began to rise up against their communist rulers. They rioted against a reduction in wages and destroyed the beacons that jammed Radio Free Europe's transmissions. But the CIA could do nothing but feed their rage—not when a Soviet field marshal ran Poland's army and Soviet intelligence officers oversaw the secret police, who killed fifty-three Poles and imprisoned hundreds.

The Polish struggle led the National Security Council to search for a crack in the architecture of Soviet control. Vice President Nixon argued that it would serve American interests if the Soviets pounded another upstart satellite state, such as Hungary, into submission, providing a source for global anticommunist propaganda. Picking up that theme, Foster Dulles won presidential approval for new efforts to promote "spontaneous manifestations of discontent" in the captive nations. Allen Dulles promised to pump up a Radio Free Europe program that floated balloons east over the iron curtain, carrying leaflets and "Freedom Medals"—aluminum badges bearing slogans and an imprint of the Liberty Bell.

Then Dulles took off on a fifty-seven-day world tour, circling the earth in a zippered flight suit aboard a specially configured four-engine DC-6. He dropped in on the CIA stations in London and Paris, Frankfurt and Vienna, Rome and Athens, Istanbul and Tehran, Dhahran and Delhi, Bangkok and Singapore, Tokyo and Seoul, Manila and Saigon. The journey was an open secret: Dulles was received as a head of state, and he reveled in the limelight. The trip was "one of the most highly publicized clandestine tours ever made," said Ray Cline, who accompanied the director. Cloaked yet flamboyant—that was the CIA under Allen Dulles. It was a place where "truly clandestine practices were compromised" while "analysis was clothed in an atmosphere of secrecy that was unnecessary, frequently counterproductive, and in the long run damaging," Cline thought. Watching foreign leaders fawn over Dulles at state dinners, he learned another lesson: "CIA represented great power. It was a little frightening."

"WISHFUL BLINDNESS"

On October 22, 1956, shortly after Dulles returned to Washington, a deeply weary Frank Wisner flicked out the lights in his office, walked down the corridors of decaying linoleum and peeling walls in Temporary Building L, went home to his elegant house in Georgetown, and packed for his own tour of the CIA's biggest stations in Europe.

Neither he nor his boss had a clue about the two greatest events going on in the world. War plans were afoot in London and Paris, while a popular revolution was at hand in Hungary. In the course of a crucial fortnight, Dulles would misinterpret or misrepresent every aspect of these crises in his reports to the president.

Wisner sailed out over the Atlantic in darkness. After his overnight flight to London, his first order of business was a long-scheduled dinner date with Sir Patrick Dean, a senior British intelligence officer. They were to discuss their plans to topple the Egyptian leader, Gamal Abdel Nasser, who had come to power three years earlier in a military coup. The issue had been brewing for months. Sir Patrick had been in Washington a few weeks before, and the two had agreed that one way or another, their objectives required Nasser's removal from power.

The CIA had supported Nasser at first, handing him millions, building him a powerful state radio station, and promising him American military and economic aid. Yet the agency was taken by surprise by events in Egypt, despite the fact that CIA officers outnumbered State Department officials by about four to one in the American embassy in Cairo. The biggest surprise was that Nasser did not stay bought: he used part of the $3 million in bribes that the CIA had slipped him to build a minaret in Cairo on an island in front of the Nile Hilton. It was known as *el wa'ef rusfel*—Roosevelt's erection. Because Roosevelt and the CIA could not come through on their promises of American military aid, Nasser agreed to sell Egyptian cotton to the Soviet Union in exchange for arms. Then, in July 1956, Nasser challenged the legacies of colonialism by nationalizing the Suez Canal Company, the corporation created by the British and the French to run the Middle East's man-made maritime trade route. London and Paris roared with outrage.

The British proposed to assassinate Nasser and contemplated diverting the Nile River to destroy Egypt's bid for economic self-rule. Eisenhower said it would be "dead wrong" to use lethal force. The CIA favored a long, slow campaign of subversion against Egypt.

That was the issue that Wisner had to work out with Sir Patrick Dean. He was first perplexed and then furious when Sir Patrick failed to appear at their long-scheduled meeting. The British spy had another engagement: he was in a villa outside Paris, putting the final touches on a coordinated military attack on Egypt by Britain, France, and Israel. They aimed to destroy Nasser's government and take the Suez back by force. First Israel would attack Egypt, and then Britain and France would strike, posing as peacekeepers while seizing the canal.

The CIA knew none of this. Dulles assured Eisenhower that reports of a joint Israeli-UK-French military plan were absurd. He refused to heed the CIA's chief intelligence analyst and the American military attaché in Tel Aviv, both convinced that Israel was about to go to war against Egypt. Nor did he listen to an old friend, Douglas Dillon, the American ambassador in Paris, who called to warn that France was in on the plot. The director instead chose to listen to Jim Angleton and his Israeli contacts. Having won their undying gratitude for coming up with a copy of Khrushchev's secret speech, the Israelis dazzled Dulles and Angleton with disinformation, warning that there would be trouble elsewhere in the Middle East. On October 26, the director conveyed their falsehoods to the president at the National Security Council meeting: The king of Jordan has been assassinated! Egypt would soon attack Iraq!

The president pushed those headlines to the side. He declared that "the compelling news continued to be Hungary."

A great crowd had gathered at the Parliament in Budapest two days before, led by student demonstrators rising up against the communist government. The hated state security police confronted a second crowd at the government radio station, where a party functionary was denouncing the protests. Some of the students were armed. A shot rang out from the radio building, the security police opened fire, and the protestors fought the secret police all night. At the Budapest City Park, a third crowd tore a statue of Stalin from its pedestal, dragged it to the front of the National Theater, and smashed it into shards. Red Army troops and tanks entered Budapest the next morning, and the demonstrators persuaded at least a handful of the young Soviet soldiers to join their cause. Rebels rode toward the Parliament on Soviet tanks flying the Hungarian flag. Russian commanders panicked, and in a terrible moment at Kossuth Square a blinding crossfire erupted. At least a hundred people died.

Inside the White House, Allen Dulles tried to tell the president the meaning of the Hungarian uprising. "Khrushchev's days may well be numbered," he said. He was off by seven years.

Dulles contacted Wisner in London the next day, October 27. The chief of covert action wanted to do everything he could to help the uprising. He had been praying for a moment like this for eight years.

The National Security Council had commanded him to keep hope alive in Hungary. "To do less," his orders said, "would be to sacrifice the moral basis for U.S. leadership of free peoples." He had told the White House he would create a nationwide underground for political and para-military warfare through the Roman Catholic Church, peasant collectives, recruited agents, and exile groups. He had failed completely. The exiles he sent to cross the border from Austria were arrested. The men he tried to recruit were liars and thieves. His efforts to create a clandestine reporting network inside Hungary collapsed. He had buried weapons all over Europe, but when the crisis came, no one could find them.

There was no CIA station in Hungary in October 1956. There was no Hungarian operations section in the clandestine service at headquarters, and almost no one who spoke the language. Wisner had one man in Budapest when the uprising began: Geza Katona, a Hungarian American who spent 95 percent of his time doing his official work as a low-level State Department clerk, mailing letters, buying stamps and stationery, filing papers. When the uprising came, he was the only reliable set of eyes and ears the CIA had in Budapest.

During the two-week life of the Hungarian revolution, the agency knew no more than what it read in the newspapers. It had no idea that the uprising would happen, or how it flourished, or that the Soviets would crush it. Had the White House agreed to send weapons, the agency would have had no clue where to send them. A secret CIA history of the Hungarian uprising said the clandestine service was in a state of "wishful blindness."

"At no time," it said, "did we have anything that could or should have been mistaken for an intelligence operation."

"THE FEVER OF THE TIMES"

On October 28, Wisner flew to Paris and convened a few trusted members of an American delegation attending a NATO conference on the question of Eastern Europe. Its members included Bill Griffith, the senior policy adviser at Radio Free Europe's Munich headquarters. Wisner, exultant at a real revolt against communism in the making, pushed Griffith to pump up the propaganda. His exhortations produced a memo from Radio Free Europe's director in New York to the Hungarian staff in Munich: "All restraints have gone off," it read. "No holds barred. Repeat: no holds barred." Beginning that evening, Radio Free Europe urged the citizens of Hungary to sabotage railroads, tear down telephone lines, arm the partisans, blow up tanks, and fight the Soviets to the death. "This is RFE, the Voice of Free Hungary," the radio announced. "In the case of a tank attack, all the light weapons should open fire at the gun sights." Listeners were advised to throw "a Molotov cocktail . . . a wine bottle of one liter filled with gasoline . . . on the grated ventilation slit over the engine." The sign-off was "Freedom or Death!"

That night, Imre Nagy, a former prime minister who had been expelled from the Communist Party by hardliners, went on the state radio station to denounce the "terrible mistakes and crimes of these past ten years." He said that Russian troops would leave Budapest, that the old state security forces would be dissolved, and that a "new government, relying on the people's power," would fight for democratic self-rule. In seventy-two hours, Nagy would form a working coalition government, abolish one-party rule, break with Moscow, declare Hungary a neutral country, and turn to the United Nations and the United States for help. But as Nagy took power and sought to dismantle Soviet control over Hungary, Allen Dulles deemed him a failure. He told the president that the Vatican's man in Hungary, Cardinal Mindszenty, newly released from house arrest, could and should lead the nation. That became the party line on Radio Free Europe: "A reborn Hungary, and the appointed leader sent by God, have met each other in these hours."

The CIA's radios falsely accused Nagy of inviting Soviet troops into Budapest. They attacked him as a traitor, a liar, a murderer. He once had been a communist and so he was forever damned. Three new CIA frequencies were on the air at this hour. From Frankfurt, exiled Russian Solidarists said an army of freedom fighters was heading for the Hungarian border. From Vienna, the CIA amplified the low-wattage broadcasts of Hungarian partisans and beamed them back to Budapest. From Athens, the CIA's psychological warriors suggested that the Russians be sent to the gallows.

The director was ecstatic when he briefed Eisenhower on the situation in Budapest at the next National Security Council meeting on November 1. "What had occurred there was a miracle," Dulles told the president. "Because of the power of public opinion, armed force could not be effectively used. Approximately 80 percent of the Hungarian army had defected to the rebels and provided the rebels with arms."

But Dulles was dead wrong. The rebels had no guns to speak of. The Hungarian army had not switched sides. It was waiting to see which way the wind from Moscow blew. The Soviets were sending more than 200,000 troops and some 2,500 tanks and armored vehicles into the battle for Hungary.

On the morning of the Soviet invasion, Radio Free Europe's Hungarian announcer, Zoltan Thury, told his listeners that "the pressure upon the government of the U.S. to send military help to the freedom fighters will become irresistible." As tens of thousands of frantic, furious refugees poured over the border into Austria over the next few weeks, many spoke of this broadcast as "the promise that help would come." None came. Allen Dulles insisted that the CIA's radios had done nothing to encourage the Hungarians. The president believed him. It would be forty years before transcripts of the broadcasts were unearthed.

In four brutal days, Soviet troops crushed the partisans of Budapest, killing tens of thousands and hauling thousands more away to die in Siberian prison camps.

The Soviet onslaught began on November 4. That night, Hungary's refugees began besieging the American embassy in Vienna, begging America to do something. They had barbed questions, said the CIA station chief, Peer de Silva: "Why hadn't we helped? Didn't we know the Hungarians had counted on us for assistance?" He had no answers.

He was bombarded by commands from headquarters to round up nonexistent legions of Soviet soldiers who were throwing down their weapons and heading for the Austrian border. Dulles told the president about these mass defections. They were a delusion. De Silva could only guess that "headquarters was caught up in the fever of the times."

"STRANGE THINGS ARE APT TO DEVELOP"

On November 5, Wisner arrived at the CIA station in Frankfurt, commanded by Tracy Barnes, so distraught he could barely speak. As Russian tanks slaughtered teenage boys in Budapest, Wisner spent a sleepless

night at the Barnes residence playing with toy trains. He took no joy in
Eisenhower's re-election the following day. Nor did the president appreciate awakening to a fresh but false report from Allen Dulles that the Soviets were ready to send 250,000 troops to Egypt to defend the Suez
Canal from the British and French. Nor was he happy at the CIA's inability to report on the actual Soviet attack in Hungary.

On November 7, Wisner flew to the Vienna station, thirty miles from
the Hungarian border. He watched helplessly as the Hungarian partisans
sent their final messages to the free world over the wires of the Associated Press: "WE ARE UNDER HEAVY MACHINE GUN FIRE . . . GOOD-
BYE FRIENDS. GOD SAVE OUR SOULS."

He fled Vienna and flew to Rome. That night he dined with the American spies of the CIA's Rome station, among them William Colby, the future director of central intelligence. Wisner raged that people were dying
as the agency dithered. He wanted "to come to the aid of the freedom
fighters," Colby recorded. "This was exactly the end for which the
agency's paramilitary capability was designed. And a case can be made
that they could have done so without involving the United States in a
world war with the Soviet Union." But Wisner could not make a coherent case. "It was clear that he was near a nervous breakdown," Colby
recorded.

Wisner went on to Athens, where the CIA station chief, John
Richardson, saw him "revved up to an extreme velocity and intensity."
He soothed his nerves with cigarettes and alcohol. He drank whisky by
the bottle, in a swoon of misery and rage.

On December 14, he was back at headquarters, listening to Allen
Dulles assess the CIA's chances for urban warfare in Hungary. "We are
well-equipped for guerrilla fighting in the woods," Dulles said, but
"there is a serious lack of arms for street and close-in fighting and, in particular, anti-tank devices." He wanted Wisner to tell him what were "the
best weapons to put into the hands of the Hungarians" and "freedom
fighters of other iron curtain countries who might revolt against the
Communists." Wisner gave a grandiose answer. "The wounds to the
communists in Russia brought about by recent world developments are
considerable and some of them are very deep," he said. "The United
States and the free world seem to be pretty much out of the woods."
Some of his fellow officers saw a case of battle fatigue. Those closest to

Wisner saw something worse. On December 20, he lay in a hospital bed, delirious, his underlying disease misdiagnosed by his doctors.

That same day, at the White House, President Eisenhower received a formal report of a secret investigation into the clandestine service of the CIA. If it had ever become public, it would have destroyed the agency.

Ambassador David K. E. Bruce was the report's principal author, and David Bruce was one of Frank Wisner's very best friends in Washington— close enough to run over to Wisner's house for a shower and a shave one morning when the hot water in his magnificent Georgetown mansion ran out. He was an American aristocrat, Wild Bill Donovan's number-two at the OSS in London, Truman's ambassador to France, Walter Bedell Smith's predecessor as undersecretary of state, and a candidate for director of central intelligence in 1950. He knew a great deal about the CIA's operations at home and abroad. Bruce's personal journals show that he met Allen Dulles and Frank Wisner for dozens of breakfasts, lunches, dinners, drinks, and discreet chats in Paris and Washington between 1949 and 1956. He recorded his "great admiration and affection" for Dulles, who personally recommended that Bruce serve on the president's new intelligence board of consultants.

Eisenhower had wanted his own set of eyes on the agency. Back in January 1956, following the secret recommendation of the Doolittle report, he had publicly announced his creation of the president's board. He wrote in his diary that he wanted the consultants to report every six months on the value of the CIA's work.

Ambassador Bruce requested and received the president's authorization for a close look at the covert operations of the CIA—the work of Allen Dulles and Frank Wisner. His personal affection and the professional regard for them added immeasurable weight to his words. His top secret report has never been declassified—and the CIA's own in-house historians have publicly questioned whether it ever existed. But its key findings appeared in a 1961 record created by the intelligence board and obtained by the author. Some of its passages are reproduced here for the first time.

"We are sure that the supporters of the 1948 decision to launch this government on a positive psychological warfare and paramilitary program could not possibly have foreseen the ramifications of the operations which have resulted from it," the report said. "No one, other than those in the CIA immediately concerned with their day to day operation, has any detailed knowledge of what is going on."

The planning and the approval of exquisitely sensitive and extremely costly covert operations were "becoming more and more exclusively the business of the CIA—underwritten heavily by unvouchered CIA funds. . . . The CIA, busy, monied and privileged, likes its 'King-making' responsibility (the intrigue is fascinating—considerable self-satisfaction, sometimes with applause, derives from successes—no charge is made for 'failures'—and the whole business is very much simpler than collecting covert intelligence on the USSR through the usual CIA methods!)."

The report continued:

> [T]here is great concern throughout the State Department over the impacts of CIA psychological warfare and paramilitary activities on our foreign relations. The State Department people feel that perhaps the greatest contribution this board could make would be to bring to the attention of the President the significant, almost unilateral influences that CIA psychological warfare and paramilitary activities have on the actual formation of our foreign policies and our relationships with our "friends." . . .
>
> CIA support and its maneuvering of local news media, labor groups, political figures and parties and other activities which can have, at any one time, the most significant impacts on the responsibilities of the local Ambassador are sometimes completely unknown to or only hazily recognized by him. . . . Too often differences of opinion regarding the U.S. attitude toward local figures or organizations develop, especially as between the CIA and the State Department. . . . (At times, the Secretary of State–DCI brother relationship may arbitrarily set "the U.S. position.") . . .
>
> Psychological warfare and paramilitary operations (often growing out of the increased mingling in the internal affairs of other nations of bright, highly graded young men who must be doing something all the time to justify their reason for being) today are being conducted on a world-wide basis by a horde of CIA representatives [*deleted*] many of whom, by the very nature of the personnel situation [*deleted*] are politically immature. (Out of their "dealings" with shifty, changing characters their applications of "themes" suggested from headquarters or devel-

oped by them in the field—sometimes at the suggestion of local opportunists—strange things are apt to, and do, develop.)

The CIA's covert operations were conducted "on an autonomous and freewheeling basis in highly critical areas involving the conduct of foreign relations," said a follow-up report by the president's intelligence board in January 1957. "In some quarters this leads to situations which are almost unbelievable."

For his next four years in office, President Eisenhower tried to change the way the CIA was run. But he said he knew he could not change Allen Dulles. Nor could he think of anyone else to run the agency. It was "one of the most peculiar types of operation any government can have," he said, and "it probably takes a strange kind of genius to run it."

Allen had accepted no overseers. A silent nod from Foster had sufficed. There had never been a team quite like the Dulles brothers in American government, but age and exhaustion were wearing them down. Foster was seven years older than Allen, and he was dying. He knew he had a fatal cancer, and it killed him slowly over the next two years. He fought bravely, flying all over the world, rattling every saber in the American arsenal. But he dwindled, and that created a disturbing disequilibrium in the director of central intelligence. He lost a vital spark as his brother weakened. His ideas and his sense of order became as evanescent as his pipe smoke.

As Foster began to fail, Allen led the CIA into new battles across Asia and the Middle East. The cold war in Europe might be a stalemate, he told his chieftains, but the struggle had to go on with a new intensity from the Pacific to the Mediterranean.

14. "HAM-HANDED OPERATIONS OF ALL KINDS"

"If you go and live with these Arabs," President Eisenhower told Allen Dulles and the assembled members of the National Security Council, "you will find that they simply cannot understand our ideas of freedom and human dignity. They have lived so long under dictatorships of one kind or another, how can we expect them to run successfully a free government?"

The CIA set out to answer that question by trying to convert, coerce, or control governments throughout Asia and the Middle East. It saw itself wrestling with Moscow for the loyalties of millions of people, grappling to gain political and economic sway over the nations that geological accident had given billions of barrels of oil. The new battle line was a great crescent reaching from Indonesia across the Indian Ocean, through the deserts of Iran and Iraq, to the ancient capitals of the Middle East.

The agency saw every Muslim political chief who would not pledge allegiance to the United States as "a target legally authorized by statute for CIA political action," said Archie Roosevelt, the chief of station in Turkey and a cousin to Kim Roosevelt, the CIA's Near East czar. Many of the most powerful men in the Islamic world took the CIA's cash and counsel. The agency swayed them when it could. But few CIA officers spoke the language, knew the customs, or understood the people they sought to support or suborn.

The president said he wanted to promote the idea of an Islamic jihad against godless communism. "We should do everything possible to stress the 'holy war' aspect," he said at a September 1957 White House meeting attended by Frank Wisner, Foster Dulles, assistant secretary of state for the Near East William Rountree, and members of the Joint Chiefs. Foster Dulles proposed "a secret task force," under whose auspices the CIA would deliver American guns, money, and intelligence to King Saud of Saudi Arabia, King Hussein of Jordan, President Camille Chamoun of Lebanon, and President Nuri Said of Iraq.

"These four mongrels were supposed to be our defense against communism and the extremes of Arab nationalism in the Middle East," said Harrison Symmes, who worked closely with the CIA as Rountree's right-hand man and later served as ambassador in Jordan. The only lasting legacy of the "secret task force" was the fulfillment of Frank Wisner's proposal to put King Hussein of Jordan on the CIA's payroll. The agency created a Jordanian intelligence service, which lives today as its liaison to much of the Arab world. The king received a secret subsidy for the next twenty years.

If arms could not buy loyalty in the Middle East, the almighty dollar was still the CIA's secret weapon. Cash for political warfare and power plays was always welcome. If it could help create an American imperium in Arab and Asian lands, Foster was all for it. "Let's put it this way," said Ambassador Symmes. "John Foster Dulles had taken the view that anything we can do to bring down these neutralists—anti-imperialists, anti-colonialists, extreme nationalist regimes—should be done.

"He had given a mandate to Allen Dulles to do this. . . . And, of course, Allen Dulles just unleashed people." As a result, "we were caught out in attempted coups, ham-handed operations of all kinds." He and his fellow diplomats tried "to keep track of some of these dirty tricks that were being planned in the Middle East so that if they were just utterly impossible, we'd get them killed before they got any further. And we succeeded in doing that in some cases. But we couldn't get all of them killed."

"RIPE FOR A MILITARY COUP D'ETAT"

One such "dirty trick" went on for a decade: the plot to overthrow the government of Syria.

In 1949, the CIA installed a pro-American colonel, Adib Shishakli, as the Syrian leader. He won direct American military assistance along with covert financial aid. The CIA station chief in Damascus, Miles Copeland, called the colonel "a likeable rogue" who "had not, to my certain knowledge, ever bowed down to a graven image. He had, however, committed sacrilege, blasphemy, murder, adultery and theft." He lasted four years before he was overthrown by Ba'ath Party and communist politicians and military officers. In March 1955, Allen Dulles predicted that the country was "ripe for a military coup d'etat" supported by the agency. In April 1956, the CIA's Kim Roosevelt and his British Secret Intelligence Service (SIS) counterpart Sir George Young tried to mobilize right-wing Syrian army officers; the CIA delivered half a million Syrian pounds to the leaders of the plot. But the Suez fiasco poisoned the political climate in the Middle East, pushed Syria closer to the Soviets, and forced the Americans and the British to postpone their plan at the end of October 1956.

In the spring and summer of April 1957, they revived it. A document discovered in 2003 among the private papers of Duncan Sandys, Prime Minister Harold Macmillan's defense secretary, spells out their effort in detail.

Syria had to be "made to appear as the sponsor of plots, sabotage and violence directed against neighbouring governments," it said. CIA and SIS would manufacture "national conspiracies and various strong-arm activities" in Iraq, Lebanon, and Jordan, and blame them on Syria. They would create paramilitary factions and spark revolts among the Muslim Brotherhood in Damascus. The creation of the appearance of instability would destabilize the government; border clashes manufactured by American and British intelligence would serve as a pretext for the pro-Western armies of Iraq and Jordan to invade. The CIA and SIS envisioned that any new regime they installed would likely "rely first upon repressive measures and arbitrary exercise of power" to survive.

Roosevelt identified Abdul Hamid Serraj, the longtime chief of the Syrian intelligence service, as the most powerful man in Damascus. Serraj was to be assassinated, along with the chief of the Syrian general staff and the head of the Communist Party.

The CIA sent Rocky Stone, who had cut his teeth in the Iran operation, to serve as the new chief of station in Damascus. Accredited as a diplomat, a second secretary at the American embassy, he used promises of millions of dollars and unlimited political power to befriend officers in the Syrian army. He represented his recruits in reports to headquarters as a crack corps for an American-backed coup.

Abdul Hamid Serraj saw through Stone in a matter of weeks.

The Syrians set up a sting. "The officers with whom Stone was dealing took his money and then went on television and announced that they had received this money from the 'corrupt and sinister Americans' in an attempt to overthrow the legitimate government of Syria," said Curtis F. Jones, a State Department officer sent to clean up the mess Stone left behind. Serraj's forces surrounded the American embassy in Damascus, seized Stone, and interrogated him roughly. He told them everything he knew. The Syrians identified him publicly as an American spy posing as a diplomat, a veteran of the CIA's coup in Iran, and a conspirator with Syrian army officers and politicians to overthrow the government in exchange for millions of dollars in American aid.

The revelation of this "particularly clumsy CIA plot," in the words of the U.S. ambassador to Syria, Charles Yost, had consequences that reverberate today. The Syrian government formally declared Rocky Stone persona non grata. That was the first time that an American diplomat of any stripe—be he a spy working undercover or a bona fide State Department officer—had been expelled from an Arab nation. In turn, the United States expelled the Syrian ambassador to Washington, the first expulsion of any foreign diplomat from Washington since World War I. The United States denounced Syria's "fabrications" and "slanders." Stone's Syrian co-conspirators, including the former president, Adib Shishakli, were sentenced to death. A purge of every military officer who had ever been associated with the American embassy followed.

A Syrian-Egyptian alliance grew from this political turmoil: the United Arab Republic. It was the locus of anti-American sentiment in the Middle East. As America's reputation plummeted in Damascus, Soviet political and military influence grew. After the botched coup, no Americans could win the trust of the increasingly tyrannical Syrian leadership.

One trouble with blown operations such as this was that they "couldn't possibly be 'plausibly denied,' " David Bruce's report to President Eisenhower had warned. The American hand was clear to all. Was there no accounting for "the immediate costs of disappointments (Jordan, Syria, Egypt, et al.)"? asked the report. Who was "calculating the impacts on our international position"? Was the CIA "stirring up the turmoil and raising the doubts about us that exist in many countries of the world today? What of the effects on our present alliances? Where will we be tomorrow?"

"WE CAME TO POWER ON A CIA TRAIN"

On May 14, 1958, Allen Dulles convened his deputies for their regular morning meeting. He lashed out at Wisner, advising him to do "some soul-searching" about the agency's performance in the Middle East. On top of the botched coup in Syria, anti-American riots had erupted without warning in Beirut and Algiers. Was this all part of a global plot? Dulles and his aides speculated that "the Communists were in fact pulling the strings" in the Mideast and across the world. As the fear of Soviet encroachment escalated, the goal of creating a tier of pro-American nations on the Soviets' southern flank grew more urgent.

The CIA's officers in Iraq had orders to work with political leaders, military commanders, security ministers, and power brokers, offering money and guns in exchange for anticommunist alliances. But on July 14, 1958, when a gang of army officers overthrew the pro-American Iraqi monarchy of Nuri Said, the Baghdad station was sound asleep. "We were caught completely by surprise," said Ambassador Robert C. F. Gordon, then an embassy political officer.

The new regime, led by General Abdel Karim Qasim, dug into the old government's archives. They held proof that the CIA had been deeply entwined with Iraq's royalist government, paying off the leaders of the old guard. One American working under contract for the CIA, posing as a writer for an agency front, the American Friends of the Middle East, was arrested in his hotel and disappeared without a trace. The officers at the CIA station fled.

Allen Dulles began calling Iraq "the most dangerous place in the world." General Qasim began allowing Soviet political, economic, and cultural delegations into Iraq. "We have no evidence that Qasim is a communist," the CIA advised the White House, but "unless action is taken to curb Communism, or unless the Communists make a major tactical error, Iraq will probably be transformed into a Communist-controlled state." The agency's leaders acknowledged among themselves that they had no idea what to do about that threat: "The only effective and organized force in Iraq capable of countering Communism is the Army. Our basic intelligence on the present situation of the Army is very weak." The CIA, having lost one battle in Syria, and another in Iraq, agonized over what to do to stop the Middle East from turning red.

After the Iraq debacle, Kim Roosevelt, the CIA's Near East division chief since 1950, resigned to seek his fortune as a private consultant to American oil companies. He was replaced by James Critchfield, the agency's longtime liaison with General Reinhard Gehlen in Germany.

Critchfield quickly became interested in the Ba'ath Party of Iraq after its thugs tried to kill Qasim in a bungled gun battle. His officers ran another failed assassination plot, using a poisoned handkerchief, an idea that was endorsed all the way up the CIA's chain of command. It took five more years, but the agency finally backed a successful coup in Iraq in the name of American influence.

"We came to power on a CIA train," said Ali Saleh Sa'adi, the Ba'ath Party interior minister in the 1960s. One of the passengers on that train was an up-and-coming assassin named Saddam Hussein.

15. "A VERY STRANGE WAR"

The American view of the world from the Mediterranean to the Pacific was black and white: a firm American hand was needed in every capital from Damascus to Jakarta to keep the dominoes from falling. But in 1958, the CIA's effort to overthrow the government of Indonesia backfired so badly that it fueled the rise of the biggest communist party in the world outside of Russia and China. It would take a real war, in which hundreds of thousands died, to defeat that force.

Indonesia had fought for freedom from Dutch colonial rule after World War II and won it at the end of 1949. The United States supported Indonesia's independence under its new leader, President Sukarno. The nation came into the CIA's focus after the Korean War, when the agency realized that Indonesia had perhaps twenty billion barrels of untapped oil, a leader unwilling to align himself with the United States, and a rising communist movement.

The agency first raised the alarm over Indonesia in a report delivered to the National Security Council on September 9, 1953. After hearing the CIA's dire account of the situation, Harold Stassen, then director of the Mutual Security Agency, the military and economic aid organization that succeeded the Marshall Plan, told Vice President Nixon and the Dulles brothers that they "might well give thought to measures by this Government that would cause the fall of the new regime in Indonesia, since it was obviously a pretty bad one. If it is being as heavily infiltrated by Communists as CIA seemed to believe, it would be more sensible to try to get rid of it than to prop it up." But when Nixon briefed CIA officers in Washington four months later, after meeting Sukarno during a world tour, he reported that the Indonesian leader had "a tremendous hold on the people; is completely noncommunist; and there is no doubt that he is the main 'card' of the United States."

The Dulles brothers strongly doubted Nixon. Sukarno had declared himself a noncombatant in the cold war, and there were no neutrals in their eyes.

The CIA seriously considered killing Sukarno in the spring of 1955. "There was planning of such a possibility," Richard Bissell recounted. "The planning progressed as far as the identification of an asset"—an assassin—"whom it was felt might be recruited for this purpose. The plan was never reached, was never perfected to the point where it seemed feasible. The difficulty concerned the possibility of creating a situation in which the potential agent would have access to the target."

"SUBVERSION BY BALLOT"

While the agency weighed his assassination, Sukarno convened an international conference of twenty-nine Asian, African, and Arab chiefs of state in Bandung, Indonesia. They proposed a global movement of nations free to chart their own paths, aligned with neither Moscow nor Washington. Nineteen days after the Bandung conference disbanded, the CIA received a new covert-action order from the White House, numbered NSC 5518 and declassified in 2003.

It authorized the agency to use "all feasible covert means"—including payoffs to buy Indonesian voters and politicians, political warfare to win friends and subvert potential enemies, and paramilitary force—to keep Indonesia from veering to the left.

Under its provisions, the CIA pumped about $1 million into the coffers of Sukarno's strongest political opponents, the Masjumi Party, in the 1955 national parliamentary elections, the first ever held in postcolonial Indonesia. That operation fell short: Sukarno's party won, the Masjumi placed second, and the PKI—the Indonesian Communist Party—placed fourth with 16 percent of the votes. Those results alarmed Washington. The CIA continued to finance its chosen political parties and "a number of political figures" in Indonesia, as Bissell recounted in an oral history.

In 1956, the red alert was raised again when Sukarno visited Moscow and Beijing as well as Washington. The White House had listened when Sukarno said he greatly admired the American form of government. It felt betrayed when he did not embrace Western democracy as his model for governing Indonesia, an archipelago stretching more than three thousand miles, encompassing nearly one thousand inhabited islands, with thirteen major ethnic groups among a predominantly Islamic population of more than eighty million people—the world's fifth-largest nation in the 1950s.

Sukarno was a spellbinding orator who spoke in public three or four times a week, rallying his people with patriotic rants, trying to unify his nation. The few Americans in Indonesia who could understand his public speeches reported that he would quote Thomas Jefferson one day and spout communist theory the next. The CIA never quite grasped Sukarno. But the agency's authority under NSC 5518 was so broad that it could justify almost any action against him.

The CIA's new Far East division chief, Al Ulmer, liked that kind of freedom. It was why he loved the agency. "We went all over the world and we did what we wanted," he said forty years later. "God, we had fun."

By his own account, Ulmer had lived high and mighty during his long run as station chief in Athens, with a status somewhere between a Hollywood star and a head of state. He had helped Allen Dulles enjoy a romantic infatuation with Queen Frederika of Greece and the pleasures of yachting with shipping magnates. The Far East division was his reward.

Ulmer said in an interview that he knew next to nothing about Indonesia when he took over the division. But he had the full faith and trust of Allen Dulles. And he remembered vividly a conversation with Frank Wisner at the end of 1956, just before Wisner's breakdown. He recalled Wisner saying it was time to turn up the heat on Sukarno and hold his feet to the fire.

Ulmer's station chief in Jakarta told him that Indonesia was ripe for communist subversion. The chief, Val Goodell, was a rubber-industry magnate with a decidedly colonialist attitude. The essence of his firebreathing cables from Jakarta was conveyed in notes that Allen Dulles carried to his weekly White House meetings in the first four months of

1957: Situation critical. . . . Sukarno a secret communist. . . . Send weapons. Rebellious army officers on the island of Sumatra were the key to the nation's future, Goodell told headquarters. "Sumatrans prepared to fight," he cabled, "but are short of arms."

In July 1957, local election returns showed that the PKI stood to become the third most powerful political party in Indonesia, up from the fourth spot. "Sukarno insisting on Commie participation" in Indonesia's government, Goodell reported, "because of six million Indonesians who voted for Communist party." The CIA described this rise as "spectacular gains" giving the communists "enormous prestige." Would Sukarno now turn toward Moscow and Beijing? No one had the slightest notion.

The station chief strongly disagreed with the outgoing American ambassador in Indonesia, Hugh Cumming, who said Sukarno was still open to American influence. From the start, Goodell fought the new ambassador, John M. Allison, who had served as the American envoy in Japan and the assistant secretary of state for the Far East. The two quickly reached an angry impasse. Would the United States use diplomatic influence or deadly force in Indonesia?

No one seemed to know what the foreign policy of the United States was on this point. On July 19, 1957, Deputy Director of Central Intelligence Charles Pearre Cabell "recommended that the Director again attempt to find out State Department policy on Indonesia," say the minutes of the CIA chiefs' meeting. "The Director agreed to do this."

The White House and the CIA sent emissaries to Jakarta to assess the situation. Allen Dulles dispatched Al Ulmer; President Eisenhower sent F. M. Dearborn, Jr., his special assistant for security operations. Dearborn reluctantly advised Eisenhower that almost all of America's allies in the Far East were shaky. Chiang Kai-shek was leading "a dictatorship" in Taiwan. President Diem was running a "one-man show" in South Vietnam. The leaders of Laos were corrupt. South Korea's Syngman Rhee was deeply unpopular.

But the problem in Sukarno's Indonesia was different, the president's man reported: It was "subversion by ballot"—one of the dangers of participatory democracy.

Al Ulmer believed that he had to find the strongest anticommunist forces in Indonesia and support them with guns and money. He and Goodell argued furiously with Ambassador Allison over "a long and fruitless afternoon" on the veranda of the embassy residence in Jakarta.

The CIA men did not accept the fact that almost all the Indonesian army leadership remained professionally loyal to the government, personally anticommunist, and politically pro-American. They believed that CIA support for rebellious army officers could save Indonesia from a communist takeover. With the agency's support, they could create a breakaway Indonesian government on Sumatra, then seize the capital. Ulmer returned to Washington denouncing Sukarno as "beyond redemption" and Allison as "soft on communism." He swayed the Dulles brothers on both counts.

A few weeks later, at the CIA's recommendation, Ambassador Allison, one of the most experienced Asia hands remaining at the State Department, was removed from his post and reassigned on short notice to Czechoslovakia.

"I had great regard for Foster and Allen Dulles," Allison noted. "But they did not know Asians well and were always inclined to judge them by Western standards." On the question of Indonesia, "they were both activists and insisted on doing something at once." They had been convinced by the station's reporting that the communists were subverting and controlling the Indonesian army—and that the agency could thwart the threat. The CIA had engraved a self-addressed invitation to an insurrection.

"THE SONS OF EISENHOWER"

At the August 1, 1957, meeting of the National Security Council, the CIA's reporting sparked a pent-up explosion. Allen Dulles said Sukarno had "gone beyond the point of no return" and "would henceforth play the communist game." Vice President Nixon picked up the theme and proposed that "the United States should work through the Indonesia military organization to mobilize opposition to communism." Frank Wisner said the CIA could back a rebellion, but he could not guarantee "absolute control" once it started: "explosive results were always possible." The next day, he told his colleagues that "the deterioration of the situation in Indonesia is being viewed with the utmost gravity in the highest circles of the U.S. Government."

Foster Dulles threw his full weight behind a coup. He put former ambassador Hugh Cumming, five months out of Indonesia, in charge of a
committee led by officers from the CIA and the Pentagon. The group delivered its recommendations on September 13, 1957. It urged the United
States to supply covert military and economic aid to army officers seeking power.

But it also raised fundamental questions about the consequences of
American covert action. Arming the rebellious officers "could increase
the likelihood of the dismemberment of Indonesia, a country which was
created with U.S. support and assistance," members of the Cumming
group noted. "Since the U.S. played a very important role in the creation
of an independent Indonesia, doesn't it stand to lose a great deal in Asia
and the rest of the world if Indonesia breaks up, particularly if, as seems
inevitable, our hand in the breakup eventually becomes known?" The
question went unanswered.

On September 25, President Eisenhower ordered the agency to overthrow Indonesia, according to CIA records obtained by the author. He set
out three missions. First: to provide "arms and other military aid" to
"anti-Sukarno military commanders" throughout Indonesia. Second: to
"strengthen the determination, will, and cohesion" of the rebel army officers on the islands of Sumatra and Sulawesi. Third: to support and
"stimulate into action, singly or in unison, non- and anti-Communist elements" among political parties on the main island of Java.

Three days later the Indian newsweekly *Blitz*—a publication controlled by Soviet intelligence—ran a long story with a provocative headline: AMERICAN PLOT TO OVERTHROW SUKARNO. The Indonesian
press picked up the story and ran with it. The covert action had remained secret for roughly seventy-two hours.

Richard Bissell sent U-2 flights out over the archipelago and plotted
the delivery of arms and ammunition to the rebels by sea and air. He had
never run paramilitary operations or drawn up military plans. He found
it fascinating.

The operation took three months to plan. Wisner flew to the CIA station in Singapore, just across the Malacca Straits from northern Sumatra, to set up political-warfare operations. Ulmer created military
command posts at Clark Air Force Base and the Subic Bay naval station
in the Philippines, the two biggest American bases in the region. John
Mason, Ulmer's Far East operations chief, assembled a small team of

paramilitary officers in the Philippines; many were veterans of the CIA's Korean War operations. They made contact with a handful of the Indonesian army rebels on Sumatra and another contingent of commanders seeking power on the island of Sulawesi, northeast of Java. Mason worked with the Pentagon to put together a package of machine guns, carbines, rifles, rocket launchers, mortars, hand grenades, and ammunition sufficient for eight thousand soldiers, and he made plans to supply the rebels on both Sumatra and Sulawesi by sea and by air. The first arms shipment came out of Subic Bay on the USS *Thomaston,* bound for Sumatra, on January 8, 1958. Mason followed the ship in a submarine, the USS *Bluegill.* The arms arrived the following week in the northern Sumatran port of Padang, about 225 miles south of Singapore. The off-loading took place without a shred of secrecy. It drew an impressive crowd.

On February 10, the Indonesian rebels broadcast a stirring challenge to Sukarno from a newly established CIA-financed radio station at Padang. They demanded a new government and the outlawing of communism within five days. Hearing nothing from Sukarno, who was sporting in the geisha bars and bathhouses of Tokyo, they announced the establishment of a revolutionary government whose foreign minister, picked and paid by the CIA, was Colonel Maludin Simbolon, an English-speaking Christian. Reading their demands over the radio, they warned foreign powers not to interfere in Indonesia's internal affairs. Meanwhile, the CIA readied new weapons shipments from the Philippines and awaited the first signs of a nationwide popular uprising against Sukarno.

The CIA's Jakarta station told headquarters to expect a long, slow, languid period of political maneuvering, with "all factions seeking to avoid violence." Eight days later, on February 21, the Indonesian air force bombed the revolutionaries' radio stations in Central Sumatra into rubble, and the Indonesian navy blockaded rebel positions along the coast. The CIA's Indonesian agents and their American advisers retreated into the jungle.

The agency appeared unmindful that some of the most powerful commanders in the Indonesian army had been trained in the United States and referred to themselves as "the sons of Eisenhower." These were the men who were fighting the rebels. The army, led by anticommunists, was at war with the CIA.

"THE BEST CROWD WE COULD GET TOGETHER"

Hours after those first bombs fell on Sumatra, the Dulles brothers spoke by telephone. Foster said he was "in favor of doing something but it is difficult to figure out what or why." If the United States became "involved in a civil war" on the other side of the world, he said, how would it justify its case to Congress and the American people? Allen replied that the forces the CIA had assembled were "the best crowd we could get together," and he warned that "there is not too much time to consider all we have to consider."

When the National Security Council met that week, Allen Dulles told the president that "the United States faced very difficult problems" in Indonesia.

The NSC minutes say "he sketched the latest developments, most of which had been set forth in the newspapers," and then he warned: "If this dissident movement went down the drain, he felt fairly certain that Indonesia would go over to the Communists." Foster Dulles said that "we could not afford to let this happen." The president allowed that "we would have to go in if a Communist takeover really threatened." The CIA's false alarms were the basis for believing in that threat.

Allen Dulles told Eisenhower that Sukarno's forces "were not very enthusiastic about an attack on Sumatra." Hours later, reports from Indonesia came pouring in to CIA headquarters saying that those same forces had "bombed and blockaded dissident strongholds in first effort to crush rebellion by all available means" and were "planning airborne and amphibious action against central Sumatra."

American warships gathered near Singapore, ten minutes by jet from the coast of Sumatra. The USS *Ticonderoga,* an aircraft carrier with two battalions of marines aboard, dropped anchor along with two destroyers and a heavy cruiser. On March 9, as the naval battle group assembled, Foster Dulles made a public statement openly calling for a revolt against "Communist despotism" under Sukarno. General Nasution, Sukarno's army chief, responded by sending two battalions of soldiers on a fleet of eight ships, accompanied by an air force wing. They assembled off the northern coast of Sumatra, a dozen miles from Singapore's harbor.

The new U.S. ambassador to Indonesia, Howard Jones, cabled the secretary of state that General Nasution was a reliable anticommunist and the rebels had no chance of victory. He might as well have slipped the message into a bottle and tossed it into the sea.

General Nasution's chief of operations, Colonel Ahmed Yani, was one of the "sons of Eisenhower"—devotedly pro-American, a graduate of the U.S. Army's Command and General Staff course at Fort Leavenworth, and a friend to Major George Benson, the American military attaché in Jakarta. The colonel, preparing a major offensive against the rebels in Sumatra, asked Major Benson for maps to aid him in his mission. The major, unaware of the CIA's covert operation, gladly supplied them.

At Clark Air Force Base in the Philippines, the CIA's commanders had called in a twenty-two-man team of aircrews led by Polish pilots who had been flying for the agency since the ill-fated Albanian operation eight years earlier. The first of their flights carried five tons of weapons and ammunition along with bundles of cash for the rebels on Sumatra. It was detected by one of General Nasution's patrols instants after it entered Indonesian airspace. Nasution's paratroopers had the pleasure of picking up every one of the crates that the CIA's pilots dropped.

To the east, on Sulawesi, the CIA's war went just as well. U.S. Navy fliers took off on a reconnaissance mission pinpointing potential targets on Sulawesi. The American-backed rebels showed their mettle by using .50-caliber machine guns supplied by the agency to shoot up the plane. The American team barely survived a crash landing two hundred miles to the north in the Philippines. The CIA's Polish pilots received fresh targets from the reconnaissance flight. Two sets of two-man crews arrived at a Sulawesi airstrip. Their refurbished B-26 aircraft were equipped with six five-hundred-pound bombs and heavy machine guns. One of the planes successfully attacked an Indonesian military airfield. The second crashed on takeoff. Two brave Poles went home to their British wives in body bags; an elaborate cover story disguised their deaths.

The CIA's last hope lay with the rebels on Sulawesi and its outlying islands, in the far northeastern reaches of the archipelago. For in the final days of April, Sukarno's soldiers destroyed the rebels on Sumatra. The five CIA officers on the island ran for their lives. They headed south in a jeep until they ran out of fuel, then walked through the jungle to the coast, stealing food from little shops in isolated villages to sustain themselves. When they reached the ocean they commandeered a fishing boat and radioed their position to the CIA station in Singapore. A navy submarine, the USS *Tang,* came to their rescue.

The mission on Sumatra had "practically collapsed," Allen Dulles glumly reported to Eisenhower on April 25. "There seemed to be no willingness to fight on the part of the dissident forces on the island," the director told the president. "The dissident leaders had been unable to provide their soldiers with any idea of why they were fighting. It was a very strange war."

"THEY CONVICTED ME OF MURDER"

Eisenhower wanted to keep this operation deniable. He ordered that no Americans could be involved "in any operations partaking of a military character in Indonesia." Dulles disobeyed him.

The CIA's pilots had begun bombing and strafing Indonesia's outer islands on April 19, 1958. These agency air forces were described in a written CIA briefing for the White House and the president of the United States as "dissident planes"—Indonesian planes flown by Indonesians, not American aircraft flown by agency personnel. One of the Americans flying those planes was Al Pope. At age twenty-five, he was a four-year veteran of dangerous secret missions. He was distinguished by bravery and fervor.

"I enjoyed killing Communists," he said in 2005. "I liked to kill Communists any way I could get them."

He flew his first mission in Indonesia on April 27. For the next three weeks, he and his fellow CIA pilots hit military and civilian targets in the villages and harbors of northeastern Indonesia. On May Day, Allen Dulles told Eisenhower that these air strikes had been "almost too effective, since they had resulted in the sinking of a British and of a Panamanian freighter." Hundreds of civilians died, the American embassy reported. Four days later Dulles nervously recounted to the National Security Council that the bombings had "stirred great anger" among the Indonesian people, for it was charged that American pilots had been at the controls. The charges were true, but the president of the United States and the secretary of state publicly denied them.

The American embassy and Admiral Felix Stump, commander of American forces in the Pacific, alerted Washington that the CIA's operation was a transparent failure. The president asked the director of central intelligence to explain himself. A team of officers at CIA headquarters scrambled to piece together a chronology of the Indonesia operation. They noted that although the "complexity" and "sensitivity" of the operation was immense, demanding "careful coordination," it had been improvised "day-to-day." By virtue of its size and scope, "it could not be conducted as a completely covert operation." The failure of secrecy violated the agency's charter and the president's direct orders.

Al Pope spent the early hours of Sunday, May 18, over Ambon City in eastern Indonesia, sinking a navy ship, bombing a market, and destroying a church. The official death toll was six civilians and seventeen military officers. Then Pope began to pursue a seven-thousand-ton ship transporting more than a thousand Indonesian troops. But his B-26 was in the crosshairs of the ship's anti-aircraft guns. It was also being tailed by an Indonesian air force fighter. Hit from behind and below, Pope's plane burst into flames at six thousand feet. Pope ordered his Indonesian radioman to jump, jettisoned his canopy, hit the ejection seat's release, and bailed out. As he tumbled backward, his leg struck the tail of his plane. His thigh shattered at the hip. His last bomb missed the troopship by about forty feet, sparing hundreds of lives. He fell slowly back to earth, writhing in pain at the end of his parachute. In the zippered pocket of his flight suit, Pope had his personnel records, his after-action flight reports, and a membership card for the officer's club at Clark Field. The documents identified him for what he was—an American officer bombing Indonesia on orders from his government. He could have been shot on sight. But he was placed under arrest.

"They convicted me of murder and sentenced me to death," he said. "They said I wasn't a prisoner of war and was not entitled to the Geneva Convention."

The news that Pope had gone missing in battle reached CIA headquarters that same Sunday evening. The director of central intelligence conferred with his brother. They agreed they had lost this war.

On May 19, Allen Dulles sent a flash cable to his officers in Indonesia, the Philippines, Taiwan, and Singapore: stand down, cut off the money, shut down the arms pipeline, burn the evidence, and retreat.

The minutes of that morning's meeting at headquarters reflect his fury over a "glaring mix-up."

It was time for the United States to switch sides. As quickly as possible, American foreign policy reversed course. The CIA's reporting instantly reflected the change. The agency told the White House on May 21 that the Indonesian army was suppressing communism and that Sukarno was speaking and acting in ways favorable to the United States. Now it was the CIA's former friends who threatened American interests.

"The operation was, of course, a complete failure," Richard Bissell said. For the rest of his days in power, Sukarno rarely failed to mention it. He knew the CIA had tried to overthrow his government, and his army knew it, and the political establishment of Indonesia knew it too. The ultimate effect was to strengthen Indonesia's communists, whose influence and power grew for the next seven years.

"They *said* Indonesia was a failure," Al Pope reflected bitterly. "But we knocked the shit out of them. We killed thousands of Communists, even though half of them probably didn't even know what Communism meant."

The only contemporary record of Pope's service in Indonesia is one line in a CIA report to the White House, dated May 21, 1958. It is a lie, and it reads in full: "Dissident B-26 aircraft shot down during attack on Ambon on 18 May."

"OUR PROBLEMS WERE GETTING GREATER EVERY YEAR"

Indonesia was Frank Wisner's last operation as chief of the clandestine service. He came back from the Far East in June 1958 at the edge of his sanity, and at summer's end he went mad. The diagnosis was "psychotic mania." The symptoms had been there for years—the desire to change the world by force of will, the soaring speeches, the suicidal missions. Psychiatrists and primitive new psychopharmaceuticals did not help. The treatment was electroshock. For six months, his head was clamped into a vise and shot through with a current sufficient to fire a hundred-watt lightbulb. He came out less brilliant and less bold, and went off to serve as chief of station in London.

After the Indonesia operation fell apart, Dulles meandered through a series of National Security Council meetings, voicing vague and ominous warnings about the threat from Moscow. The president began wondering out loud if the CIA knew what it was doing. He once asked in astonishment: Allen, are you trying to scare me into starting a war?

At headquarters, Dulles asked his most senior officers where exactly he had to go to find intelligence on the Soviet Union. At a deputies' meeting on June 23, 1958, he said he was "at a loss as to what component of the Agency he can turn to when he desires specific information on the USSR." The agency had none to speak of. Its reporting on the Soviets was pure wind.

The CIA's Abbot Smith, one of its best analysts and later the chief of the agency's Office of National Estimates, looked back on a decade's work at the end of 1958 and wrote: "We had constructed for ourselves a picture of the USSR, and whatever happened had to be made to fit into that picture. Intelligence estimators can hardly commit a more abominable sin."

On December 16, Eisenhower received a report from his intelligence board of consultants advising him to overhaul the CIA. Its members feared that the agency was "incapable of making objective appraisals of its own intelligence information as well as of its own operations." Led by former defense secretary Robert Lovett, they pleaded with the president to take covert operations out of Allen Dulles's hands.

Dulles, as ever, fended off all efforts to change the CIA. He told the president there was nothing wrong with the agency. Back at headquarters, he told his senior staff that "our problems were getting greater every year." He promised the president that Wisner's replacement would fix the missions and organization of the clandestine service. He had just the man for the job.

16. "HE WAS LYING DOWN AND HE WAS LYING UP"

On January 1, 1959, Richard Bissell became the chief of the clandestine service. That same day, Fidel Castro came to power in Cuba. A secret CIA history unearthed in 2005 described in detail how the agency took on the threat.

The agency took a long hard look at Fidel. It did not know what to make of him. "Many serious observers feel his regime will collapse within a matter of months," predicted Jim Noel, the CIA's station chief, whose officers had spent too much time reporting from the Havana Country Club. At headquarters, some argued that Castro deserved the agency's guns and money. Al Cox, chief of the paramilitary division, proposed to "make secret contact with Castro" and offer him arms and ammunition to establish a democratic government. Cox told his superiors that the CIA could ship weapons to Castro on a vessel manned by a Cuban crew. But "the most secure means of help would be giving the money to Castro, who could then purchase his own arms," Cox wrote to his superiors. "A combination of arms and money would probably be best." Cox was an alcoholic, and his thinking might have been clouded, but more than a few of his fellow officers felt the way he did. "My staff and I were all Fidelistas" at the time, Robert Reynolds, chief of the CIA's Caribbean operations desk, said many years later.

In April and May 1959, when the newly victorious Castro visited the United States, a CIA officer briefed Castro face-to-face in Washington. He described Fidel as "a new spiritual leader of Latin American democratic and anti-dictator forces."

"OUR HAND SHOULD NOT SHOW"

The president was furious to find that the CIA had misjudged Castro. "Though our intelligence experts backed and filled for a number of months," Eisenhower wrote in his memoirs, "events were gradually driving them to the conclusion that with the coming of Castro, Communism had penetrated this hemisphere."

On December 11, 1959, having reached that conclusion, Richard Bissell sent Allen Dulles a memo suggesting that "thorough consideration be given to the *elimination* of Fidel Castro." Dulles penciled in a crucial correction to the proposal. He struck out *elimination,* a word tinged with more than a hint of murder. He substituted *removal from Cuba*—and gave the go-ahead.

On January 8, 1960, Dulles told Bissell to organize a special task force to overthrow Castro. Bissell personally selected many of the same people who had subverted the government of Guatemala six years before—and had deceived President Eisenhower face-to-face about the coup. He chose the feckless Tracy Barnes for political and psychological warfare, the talented Dave Phillips for propaganda, the gung-ho Rip Robertson for paramilitary training, and the relentlessly mediocre E. Howard Hunt to manage the political front groups.

Their chief would be Jake Esterline, who had run the Washington "war room" for Operation Success. Esterline was station chief in Venezuela when he first laid eyes on Fidel Castro in early 1959. He had watched the young *commandante* touring Caracas, fresh from his New Year's Day triumph over the dictator Fulgencio Batista, and he had heard the crowds cheering Castro as a conqueror.

"I saw—hell, anybody with eyes could see—that a new and powerful force was at work in the hemisphere," Esterline said. "It had to be dealt with."

Esterline returned to CIA headquarters in January 1960 to receive his appointment as Cuba task force chief. The group took shape as a secret cell inside the CIA. All the money, all the information, and all the decisions for the Cuban task force came through Bissell. He had little interest in the work of his spies, much less gathering intelligence from inside Cuba. He never stopped to analyze what would happen if the coup against Castro succeeded—or if it failed. "I don't think these kinds of things were ever thought about in any depth," Esterline said. "I think their first reaction was, God, we've got a possible Communist in here; we had better get him out just the way we got Arbenz out" in Guatemala.

Bissell almost never talked about Cuba with Richard Helms, his second-in-command at the clandestine service. The two men disliked and distrusted one another intensely. Helms did weigh in on one idea that filtered up from the Cuba task force. It was a propaganda ploy: a Cuban agent, trained by the CIA, would appear on the shores of Istanbul, claiming to be a political prisoner who had just jumped from a Soviet ship. He would proclaim that Castro was enslaving thousands of his people and shipping them to Siberia. The plan was known as "The Dripping Cuban." Helms killed it.

On March 2, 1960—two weeks before President Eisenhower approved a covert action against Castro—Dulles briefed Vice President Nixon on operations already under way. Reading from a seven-page paper initialed by Bissell, titled "What We Are Doing in Cuba," Dulles specified acts of economic warfare, sabotage, political propaganda and a plan to use "a drug, which if placed in Castro's food, would make him behave in such an irrational manner that a public appearance could well have very damaging results to him." Nixon was all for it.

Dulles and Bissell presented their plans to Eisenhower and Nixon at the White House in a four-man meeting at 2:30 p.m. on March 17, 1960. They did not propose to invade the island. They told Eisenhower that they could overthrow Castro by sleight of hand. They would create "a responsible, appealing and unified Cuban opposition," led by recruited agents. A clandestine radio station would beam propaganda into Havana to spark an uprising. CIA officers at the U.S. Army's jungle warfare training camp in Panama would school sixty Cubans to infiltrate the island. The CIA would drop arms and ammunition to them.

Fidel would fall six to eight months thereafter, Bissell promised. The timing was excruciatingly sensitive: election day was seven and a half months away. Senator John F. Kennedy and Vice President Nixon had won by wide margins in the New Hampshire presidential primaries the week before.

Eisenhower's staff secretary, General Andrew Goodpaster, took notes on the meeting. "The President says he knows of no better plan. . . . The great problem is leakage and security. . . . Everyone must be prepared to swear that he had not heard of it. . . . Our hand should not show in anything that is done." The agency should have needed no reminder that, under its charter, *all* covert action required secrecy so secure that no evidence would lead to the president. But Eisenhower wanted to make sure the CIA did its best to keep this one under cover.

"WE WERE GOING TO PAY FOR THAT LIE"

The president and Dick Bissell were locked in an increasingly intense struggle over the control of one of the biggest secrets of all—the U-2 spy plane. Eisenhower had not allowed any flights over Soviet terrain since his talks with Khrushchev at Camp David six months earlier. Khrushchev had returned from Washington praising the president's courage in seeking peaceful coexistence; Eisenhower wanted the "spirit of Camp David" to be his legacy.

Bissell was fighting as hard as possible to resume the secret missions. The president was torn. He truly wanted the intelligence that the U-2 gleaned.

He longed to bury the "missile gap"—the false claims by the CIA, the air force, military contractors, and politicians of both parties that the Soviets had a widening lead in nuclear weaponry. The CIA's formal estimates of Soviet military strength were not based on intelligence, but on politics and guesswork. Since 1957, the CIA had sent Eisenhower terrifying reports that the Soviet buildup of nuclear-tipped intercontinental ballistic missiles was far faster and much greater than the American arsenal. In 1960, the agency projected a mortal threat to the United States; it told the president that the Soviets would have five hundred ICBMs ready to strike by 1961. The Strategic Air Command used those estimates as the basis for a secret first-strike plan using more than three thousand nuclear warheads to destroy every city and every military outpost from Warsaw to Beijing. But Moscow did not have five hundred nuclear missiles pointed at the United States at the time. It had four.

The president had worried for five and a half years that the U-2 itself might start World War III. If the plane went down over the Soviet Union, it could take the chance for peace with it. The month after the Camp David dialogues with Khrushchev, the president had rejected a newly proposed U-2 mission over the Soviet Union; he told Allen Dulles once again, bluntly, that divining the intentions of the Soviets through espionage was more important to him than discovering details about their military capabilities. Only spies, not gadgets, could tell him about Soviet intent to attack.

Without that knowledge, the president said, the U-2 flights were "provocative pin-pricking, and it may give them the idea that we are seriously preparing plans to knock out their installations" with a sneak attack.

Eisenhower had a summit meeting with Khrushchev set for May 16, 1960, in Paris. He feared that his greatest asset—his reputation for honesty—would be squandered if a U-2 went down while the United States was, in his words, "engaged in apparently sincere deliberations" with the Soviets.

In theory, only the president had the power to order a U-2 mission. But Bissell ran the program, and he was petulant about filing his flight plans. He tried to evade presidential authority by secretly seeking to outsource flights to the British and to the Chinese Nationalists. In his memoirs, he wrote that Allen Dulles had been horrified to learn that the first U-2 flight had passed directly over Moscow and Leningrad. The director had never known; Bissell never saw fit to tell him.

He argued for weeks with the White House before Eisenhower finally gave in and agreed to an April 9, 1960, flight over the Soviet Union from Pakistan. It was, on the surface, a success. But the Soviets knew their airspace had been violated once again, and they went on high alert. Bissell fought for one more flight. The president set a deadline of April 25. The date came and went with clouds covering the Communist targets. Bissell pleaded for more time, and Eisenhower gave him six days' reprieve. The following Sunday was to be the final date for a flight before the Paris summit. Bissell then tried to circumvent the White House by going to the secretary of defense and the chairman of the Joint Chiefs of Staff to win their backing for yet *another* flight. In his zeal, he had neglected to plan for disaster.

On May Day, as the president had feared, the U-2 was shot down in central Russia. The CIA's pilot, Francis Gary Powers, was captured alive. C. Douglas Dillon was the acting secretary of state that day. "The President told me to work with Allen Dulles," Dillon recounted. "We had to put out some sort of announcement." To the shock of both men, NASA announced that a weather plane had been lost in Turkey. That was the CIA's cover story. The director of central intelligence either never knew about it or had forgotten all about it.

"We couldn't understand how this had happened," Dillon said. "But we had to get ourselves out of it."

That proved difficult. Hewing to the cover story, the White House and the State Department deceived the American people for a week about the flight. Their lies grew more and more transparent. The last one came on May 7: "There was no authorization for such a flight." That broke Eisenhower's spirit. "He couldn't allow Allen Dulles to take all the blame, because it would look like the President didn't know what was going on in the government," Dillon said.

Eisenhower walked into the Oval Office on May 9 and said out loud: "I would like to resign." For the first time in the history of the United States, millions of citizens understood that their president could deceive them in the name of national security. The doctrine of plausible deniability was dead. The summit with Khrushchev was wrecked and the brief thaw in the cold war iced over. The CIA's spy plane destroyed the idea of détente for almost a decade. Eisenhower had approved the final mission in the hope of putting the lie to the missile gap. But the cover-up of the crash made him out to be a liar. In retirement, Eisenhower said the greatest regret of his presidency was "the lie we told about the U-2. I didn't realize how high a price we were going to pay for that lie."

The president knew he would not be able to leave office in a spirit of international peace and reconciliation. He was now intent on policing as many parts of the planet as possible before leaving office.

The summer of 1960 became a season of incessant crisis for the CIA. Red arrows signifying hot spots in the Caribbean, Africa, and Asia multiplied on the maps that Allen Dulles and his men brought to the White House. The chagrin over the U-2 shootdown gave way to a murderous anger.

First Dick Bissell redoubled the CIA's plans for overthrowing Cuba. He set up a new CIA station in Coral Gables, Florida, code-named Wave. He told Vice President Nixon that he would need a force of five hundred trained Cuban exiles—up from sixty men a few weeks before—to lead the fight. But the army's jungle warfare center in Panama could not handle hundreds more raw recruits. So Bissell sent Jake Esterline down to Guatemala, where he single-handedly negotiated a secret agreement with President Manuel Ydigoras Fuentes, a retired general and a skilled wheeler-dealer. The site he secured became the main training camp for the Bay of Pigs, with its own airport, its own brothel, and its own codes of conduct. The CIA's Cubans found it "entirely unsatisfactory," reported marine colonel Jack Hawkins, Esterline's top paramilitary planner. They lived "in prison-camp conditions," which produced "political complications" that were "very difficult for C.I.A. to handle." Though the camp was isolated, the Guatemalan army was well aware of it, and the presence of a foreign force on its soil very nearly led to a military coup against their president.

Then, in mid-August, courtly, charming Dick Bissell put out a Mafia contract against Fidel Castro. He went to Colonel Sheffield Edwards, the CIA's chief of security, and asked the colonel to put him in touch with a gangster who could carry out a hit. This time he briefed Dulles, who gave his approval. An agency historian concluded: "Bissell probably believed that Castro would be dead at the hands of a CIA-sponsored assassin before the Brigade ever hit the beach" at the Bay of Pigs.

Bissell's men, knowing nothing of the Mafia plan, worked on a second murder plot. The question was how to put a trained CIA killer within shooting distance of Fidel: "Can we get a Rip Robertson close to him? Can we get a really hairy Cuban—I mean a gutsy Cuban?" said Dick Drain, the Cuba task force's chief of operations. The answer was always no. Miami was crawling with thousands of Cuban exiles ready to join the CIA's increasingly well-known covert operation, but Castro's spies were rife among them, and Fidel learned a fair amount about the CIA's plans. An FBI agent named George Davis, after spending a few months listening to loose-lipped Cubans in Miami coffee shops and bars, gave a CIA officer at the Wave station some friendly advice: it would be impossible to overthrow Castro with these chatty Cuban exiles. The only hope was to send in the marines. His CIA colleague relayed the message to headquarters. It was ignored.

On August 18, 1960, Dulles and Bissell discussed the Cuba task force in private with President Eisenhower for less than twenty minutes. Bissell asked for another $10.75 million to begin the paramilitary training of the five hundred Cubans in Guatemala. Eisenhower said yes, on one condition: "So long as the Joint Chiefs, Defense, State and CIA think we have a good chance of being successful" in "freeing the Cubans from this incubus." When Bissell tried to raise the idea of creating an American military force to lead the Cubans in battle, Dulles twice cut him off, evading debate and dissent.

The president—the man who had led the biggest secret invasion in American history—warned the CIA's leaders against "the danger of making false moves" or "starting something before we were ready."

"TO AVOID ANOTHER CUBA"

Later that same day, at a meeting of the National Security Council, the president ordered the director of central intelligence to eliminate the man the CIA saw as the Castro of Africa—Patrice Lumumba, the prime minister of the Congo.

Lumumba had been freely elected, and he appealed to the United States for assistance as his nation shook off Belgium's brutal colonial rule and declared its independence in the summer of 1960. American help never came, for the CIA regarded Lumumba as a dope-addled communist dupe. So when Belgian paratroopers flew in to reassert control in the capital, Lumumba accepted Soviet planes, trucks, and "technicians" to bolster his barely functioning government.

The week that the Belgian soldiers arrived, Dulles sent Larry Devlin, the station chief in Brussels, to take charge of the CIA post in the capital of the Congo and assess Lumumba as a target for covert action. On August 18, after six weeks in the country, Devlin cabled CIA headquarters: "CONGO EXPERIENCING CLASSIC COMMUNIST EFFORT TAKEOVER. . . . WHETHER OR NOT LUMUMBA ACTUAL COMMIE OR PLAYING COMMIE GAME. . . . THERE MAY BE LITTLE TIME LEFT IN WHICH TO TAKE ACTION TO AVOID ANOTHER CUBA." Allen Dulles delivered the gist of this message at the NSC meeting that same day. According to secret Senate testimony delivered years later by the NSC's notetaker, Robert Johnson, President Eisenhower then turned to Dulles and said flatly that Lumumba should be eliminated. After a dead silence of fifteen seconds or so, the meeting went on. Dulles cabled Devlin eight days later: "IN HIGH QUARTERS HERE IT IS THE CLEAR-CUT CONCLUSION THAT IF LLL CONTINUES TO HOLD HIGH OFFICE, THE

INEVITABLE RESULT WILL AT BEST BE CHAOS AND AT WORST PAVE THE WAY TO COMMUNIST TAKEOVER OF THE CONGO. . . . WE CONCLUDE THAT HIS REMOVAL MUST BE AN URGENT AND PRIME OBJECTIVE AND THAT UNDER EXISTING CONDITIONS THIS WOULD BE A HIGH PRIORITY OF OUR COVERT ACTION. HENCE WE WISH TO GIVE YOU WIDER AUTHORITY."

Sidney Gottlieb, the CIA's clubfooted master chemist, brought an airline carry-on bag containing vials of lethal toxins to the Congo and handed it to the station chief. It held a hypodermic syringe to inject the lethal drops into food, drink, or a tube of toothpaste. It was Devlin's job to deliver death to Lumumba. The two men held a nervous conversation in Devlin's apartment on or about the night of September 10. "I asked on whose orders these instructions were issued," Devlin said under oath in secret testimony declassified in 1998. The answer was "the President."

Devlin testified that he locked the toxins in his office safe and agonized over what to do. He remembered thinking: I'll be damned if I'm going to leave *that* lying around. In time, he took the poison vials out to the banks of the Congo River and buried them. He said he was ashamed of the order to kill Lumumba. He knew there were other means at the CIA's disposal.

The agency had already selected the Congo's next leader: Joseph Mobutu, "the only man in the Congo able to act with firmness," as Dulles told the president at the NSC meeting on September 21. The CIA delivered $250,000 to him in early October, followed by shipments of arms and ammunition in November. Mobutu captured Lumumba and, in Devlin's words, delivered him into the hands of a "sworn enemy." The CIA base in Elizabethville, deep in the heart of the Congo, reported that "a Belgian officer of Flemish origin executed Lumumba with a burst of submachine gun fire" two nights before the next president of the United States took office. With the unwavering support of the CIA, Mobutu finally gained full control of the Congo after a five-year power struggle. He was the agency's favorite ally in Africa and the clearinghouse for American covert action throughout the continent during the cold war. He ruled for three decades as one of the world's most brutal and corrupt dictators, stealing billions of dollars in revenues from the nation's enormous deposits of diamonds, minerals, and strategic metals, slaughtering multitudes to preserve his power.

"AN ABSOLUTELY UNTENABLE POSITION"

As the 1960 election drew nearer, it was clear to Vice President Nixon
that the CIA was far from ready to attack Cuba. At the end of September, Nixon nervously instructed the task force: "Don't do anything now;
wait until after the elections." The delay gave Fidel Castro a crucial edge.
His spies told him an American-backed invasion might be imminent, and
he built up his military and intelligence forces, cracking down hard on
the political dissidents whom the CIA hoped would serve as shock troops
for the coup. The internal resistance against Castro began to die that
summer, though the CIA never paid much heed to what was actually
happening on the island. Tracy Barnes privately commissioned a public-
opinion poll in Cuba—and it showed that people overwhelmingly supported Castro. Disliking the results, he discarded them.

The agency's effort to drop arms to rebels on the island was a fiasco.
On September 28, a pallet of machine guns, rifles, and Colt .45s for a
hundred fighters floated down to Cuba from a CIA plane flying out of
Guatemala. The drop missed its target by seven miles. Castro's forces
seized the arms, captured the Cuban CIA agent set to receive them, and
shot him. The pilot got lost on his way back and landed in southern
Mexico, where the local police seized the plane. In all, thirty such missions were flown; at most three succeeded.

By early October, the CIA realized that it knew next to nothing about
the anti-Castro forces inside Cuba. "We had no confidence that they
weren't penetrated" by Castro's spies, Jake Esterline said. He now was
certain that Castro could not be overthrown by subtle subversion.

"We had made a major effort at infiltration and resupply, and those
efforts had been unsuccessful," Bissell recalled. He decided that "what
was needed was a shock action"—a full-scale invasion.

The CIA had neither presidential approval nor the troops needed to
carry out that mission. The five hundred men undergoing training in
Guatemala were "a preposterously inadequate number," Bissell told Esterline. Both men realized that only a far larger force could succeed against
Castro, who had a sixty-thousand-man army with tanks and artillery,
along with an increasingly cruel and efficient internal-security service.

Bissell had the Mafia on one phone line, the White House on another.
The presidential election was looming. Sometime during the first week

of November 1960, the core concept of the Cuban operation cracked under the pressure. Esterline pronounced the plan unworkable, and Bissell knew he was right. But he told no one. In the months and weeks and days before the invasion, he retreated into deception.

"He was lying down and he was lying up," Jake Esterline said—down to the CIA's Cuba task force, up to the president and the new president-elect.

John Kennedy defeated Richard Nixon in November by fewer than 120,000 votes. Some Republicans thought the election was stolen in the political precincts of Chicago. Others pointed at vote buying in West Virginia. Richard Nixon blamed the CIA. He was convinced, wrongly, that "Georgetown liberals" like Dulles and Bissell had secretly aided Kennedy with inside information on Cuba before a crucial televised presidential debate.

President-elect Kennedy immediately announced the re-appointments of J. Edgar Hoover and Allen Dulles. That decision came from his father, and it was made for political and personal protection. Hoover knew some of the deeper secrets in the Kennedy family—including the president-elect's sexual dalliances during World War II with a suspected Nazi spy—and he had shared that knowledge with Dulles. Kennedy knew all this because his father, a former member of Eisenhower's board of foreign intelligence consultants, had told him on good authority.

On November 18, the president-elect met Dulles and Bissell at his father's retreat in Palm Beach, Florida. Three days before, Bissell had received a conclusive report from Esterline on the Cuban operation. "Our original concept is now seen to be unachievable in the face of the controls Castro has instituted," Esterline said. "There will not be the internal unrest earlier believed possible, nor will the defenses permit the type of strike first planned. Our second concept (1,500–3,000 man force to secure a beach with airstrip) is now also seen as unachievable, except as a joint Agency/DOD action."

In other words, to overthrow Castro, the United States would have to send in the marines.

"I sat there in my office at CIA," Esterline recounted, "and I said, 'Goddamn it, I hope Bissell has enough guts to tell John Kennedy what the facts are.' " But Bissell never breathed a word. The unachievable plan became a can-do mission.

The Palm Beach briefing placed the CIA leaders in "an absolutely untenable position," Bissell told an agency historian. Their notes for the meeting show that they had intended to discuss their past triumphs—particularly Guatemala—and a multitude of covert operations under way in Cuba, the Dominican Republic, Central and South America, and Asia. But they did not. Before the meeting, President Eisenhower told them to hew to "a narrow agenda"; they interpreted that as a ban on discussing anything that had transpired in the meetings of the National Security Council. As a result, crucial information about the CIA's covert operations was lost in transition from one president to another.

Eisenhower had never approved an invasion of Cuba. But Kennedy did not know that. What he knew was what Dulles and Bissell told him.

"AN EIGHT-YEAR DEFEAT"

For eight years, Allen Dulles had fended off all efforts by outsiders to change the CIA. He had a reputation to protect—the agency's and his own. Denying everything, admitting nothing, he had hidden the truth to conceal the failures of his covert operations.

From at least 1957 onward, he had shunned voices of reason and moderation, ignored the increasingly urgent recommendations of the president's intelligence consultants, brushed aside reports by his own inspector general, treated his underlings with contempt. "He was, by that time, a tired old man," whose professional conduct "could be, and usually was, trying in the extreme," said Dick Lehman, one of the best analysts the agency ever had. "His treatment of us reflected his sense of values. He was wrong, of course, but we had to live with it."

In his last days in office, President Eisenhower came to understand that he did not have a spy service worthy of the name. He came to that conclusion after reading through a thick stack of reports he had commissioned in the hope of changing the CIA.

The first, on December 15, 1960, was the work of the Joint Study Group, which he had created after the U-2 shootdown to survey the landscape of American intelligence. It was a terrifying picture of drift and disarray. It said Dulles never had addressed the problem of a surprise attack by the Soviets. He had never coordinated military intelligence and civilian analysis. He had never created the capability to provide warning in a crisis. He had spent eight years mounting covert operations instead of mastering American intelligence.

Then, on January 5, 1961, the President's Board of Consultants on Foreign Intelligence Activities issued its final recommendations. It called for "a total reassessment" of covert action: "We are unable to conclude that, on balance, all of the covert action programs undertaken by CIA up to this time have been worth the risk of the great expenditure of manpower, money and other resources involved." It warned that "CIA's concentration on political, psychological and related covert action activities have tended to distract substantially from the execution of its primary intelligence-gathering mission."

The board urged the president to consider the "complete separation" of the director of central intelligence from the CIA. It said Dulles was incapable of running the agency while carrying out his duties to coordinate American intelligence—the code making and code breaking of the National Security Agency; the dawning capabilities of spy satellites and space photoreconnaissance; the endless squabbles of the army, the navy, and the air force.

"I reminded the President that many times he had addressed himself to this general problem," his national-security aide, Gordon Gray, wrote after reviewing the report with Eisenhower. I know, Ike replied. I've tried. I cannot change Allen Dulles.

"A great deal has been accomplished," Dulles insisted to the president at the final gatherings of Eisenhower's National Security Council. Everything is well in hand, he said. I have fixed the clandestine service. American intelligence has never been more agile and adept. Coordination and cooperation are better than they ever have been. The proposals of the president's intelligence board were preposterous, he said, they were madness, they were illegal. I am responsible under the law for intelligence coordination, he reminded the president. I cannot delegate that responsibility. Without my leadership, he said, American intelligence would be "a body floating in thin air."

At the last, Dwight Eisenhower exploded in anger and frustration. "The structure of our intelligence organization is faulty," he told Dulles. It makes no sense, it has to be reorganized, and we should have done it long ago. Nothing had changed since Pearl Harbor. "I have suffered an eight-year defeat on this," said the president of the United States. He said he would "leave a legacy of ashes" to his successor.

PART THREE

Lost Causes

The CIA Under Kennedy and Johnson

1961 to 1968

17. "NOBODY KNEW WHAT TO DO"

The legacy was handed down on the morning of January 19, 1961, when the old general and the young senator met alone in the Oval Office. With a sense of foreboding, Eisenhower gave Kennedy a glance at the stratagems of national security: nuclear weapons and covert operations.

The two men emerged and met in the Cabinet Room with the old and new secretaries of state, defense, and the treasury. "Senator Kennedy asked the President's judgment as to the United States supporting the guerrilla operations in Cuba, even if this support involves the United States publicly," a note taker recorded that morning. "The President replied Yes as we cannot let the present government there go on. . . . The President also advised that the situation would be helped if we could handle the Dominican Republic at the same time." Eisenhower's idea that one Caribbean coup could counterbalance another was an equation no one in Washington had worked out.

As Kennedy arose the next morning for his swearing-in, the corrupt right-wing leader of the Dominican Republic, Generalissimo Rafael Trujillo, had been in power for thirty years. Support from the U.S. government and the American business community had helped keep him in office. He ruled by force, fraud, and fear; he took pleasure in hanging his enemies from meat hooks. "He had his torture chambers, he had his political assassinations," said Consul General Henry Dearborn, the ranking American diplomat in the Dominican Republic at the start of 1961. "But he kept law and order, cleaned the place up, made it sanitary, built public works and he didn't bother the United States. So that was fine with us." But Trujillo had become intolerable, Dearborn said. "About the time I got there his iniquities had gotten so bad that there was a lot of pressure from various political groups, civil rights groups and others, not only in the U.S., but throughout the hemisphere, that something just had to be done about this man."

Dearborn was left in charge of the American embassy in Santo Domingo after the United States severed diplomatic relations with the Dominican Republic in August 1960. All but a few of the American diplomats and spies left the island. But Richard Bissell had asked Dearborn to stay on and serve as the acting CIA station chief. The consul general agreed.

On January 19, 1961, Dearborn was advised that a shipment of small arms was on its way to a group of Dominican conspirators who aimed to kill Trujillo. The Special Group, Allen Dulles presiding, had made the decision one week before. Dearborn requested the agency's approval to arm the Dominicans with three carbine rifles left behind at the embassy by navy personnel. Bissell's covert-action deputy, Tracy Barnes, gave the green light. The CIA then dispatched three .38-caliber pistols to the Dominicans. Bissell authorized a second shipment of four machine guns and 240 rounds of ammunition. The machine guns remained at the American consulate in Santo Domingo after members of the new administration questioned what the world reaction might be if it were known that the United States was delivering murder weapons via diplomatic pouch.

Dearborn received a cable, personally approved by President Kennedy, which he read to say: "We don't care if the Dominicans assassinate Trujillo, that is all right. But we don't want anything to pin this on us." Nothing ever did. When Trujillo's killers shot him two weeks later, the smoking gun might or might not have been the agency's. There were no fingerprints. But the assassination was as close as the CIA had ever come to carrying out a murder at the command of the White House.

The attorney general of the United States, Robert F. Kennedy, jotted down some notes after he learned of the assassination. "The great problem now," he wrote, "is that we don't know what to do."

"I WAS ASHAMED OF MY COUNTRY"

As the CIA catapulted toward the invasion of Cuba, "the thing started to steamroller and get out of control," said Jake Esterline. Bissell was the driving force. He forged on, refusing to acknowledge that the CIA could not topple Castro, blinding himself to the fact that the secrecy of the operation had been blown long ago.

On March 11, Bissell went to the White House with four separate plots on paper. None satisfied President Kennedy. He gave the chief of the clandestine service three days to come up with something better. Bissell's brainstorm was his choice of a new landing zone—three broad beaches at the Bay of Pigs. The site satisfied a new political requirement from the administration: the Cuban invaders had to capture an airstrip upon landing, to establish a political beachhead for a new Cuban government.

Bissell assured the president that this operation would succeed. The worst that could happen was that the CIA's rebels would confront Castro's forces on the beaches and march on into the mountains. But the terrain at the Bay of Pigs was an impassible tangle of mangrove roots and mud. No one in Washington knew that. The crude survey maps in the CIA's possession suggesting that the swampland would serve as guerrilla country had been drawn in 1895.

The following week, the CIA's Mafia contacts took a swipe at killing Castro. They gave poison pills and thousands of dollars to one of the CIA's most prominent Cubans, Tony Varona. (Described by Esterline as "a scoundrel, a cheat, and a thief," Varona later met President Kennedy at the White House.) Varona managed to hand off the vial of poison to a restaurant worker in Havana, who was to slip it into Castro's ice cream cone. Cuban intelligence officers later found the vial in an icebox, frozen to the coils.

By spring, the president still had not approved a plan of attack. He did not understand how the invasion would work. On Wednesday, April 5, he met again with Dulles and Bissell, but could not make sense of their strategy. On Thursday, April 6, he asked them if their planned bombing of Castro's small air force would eliminate the invaders' element of surprise. No one had an answer.

On Saturday night, April 8, Richard Bissell answered the insistent ring of his home phone. Jake Esterline was calling from Quarters Eye, the CIA's Washington war room, saying he and Colonel Hawkins, his paramilitary planner, needed to see Bissell alone as soon as possible. Sunday morning, Bissell opened his front door to find Esterline and Hawkins in a state of barely controlled rage. They marched into his living room, sat down, and told him that the invasion of Cuba had to be called off.

It was too late to stop now, Bissell told them; the coup against Castro was set to begin in a week. Esterline and Hawkins threatened to resign. Bissell questioned their loyalty and patriotism. They wavered.

"If you don't want a disaster, we absolutely *must* take out *all* of Castro's air force," Esterline told Bissell, not for the first time. All three knew that Castro's thirty-six combat aircraft were capable of killing hundreds of the CIA's Cubans as they went ashore. Trust me, said Bissell. He promised to persuade President Kennedy to wipe out Castro's air force. "He talked us into continuing," Esterline recalled bitterly. "He said, 'I promise you that there will be no reductions of air raids.' "

But at the crucial hour, Bissell cut the American force sent to destroy Castro's aircraft in half, from sixteen to eight bombers. He did it to please the president, who wanted a quiet coup. Bissell deceived him into believing the CIA would deliver one.

On Saturday, April 15, eight American B-26 bombers struck three Cuban airfields as the CIA's brigade of 1,511 men headed for the Bay of Pigs. Five Cuban aircraft were destroyed and perhaps a dozen more damaged. Half of Castro's air force remained. The CIA's cover story was that the attacker was a sole Cuban air force defector who had landed in Florida. That day, Bissell sent Tracy Barnes to New York to peddle the tale to the American ambassador to the United Nations, Adlai Stevenson.

Bissell and Barnes played Stevenson for a fool, as if he were their agent. Like Secretary of State Colin Powell on the eve of the invasion of Iraq, Stevenson sold the CIA's story to the world. Unlike Powell, he discovered the next day that he had been had.

The knowledge that Stevenson was caught lying in public riveted Secretary of State Dean Rusk, who already had good reason to be enraged with the CIA. Only hours before, on the heels of another blown operation, Rusk had to send a formal letter of apology to Prime Minister Lee Kwan Yew of Singapore. The secret police in Singapore had burst into a CIA safe house, where a cabinet minister on the CIA's payroll was being interrogated. Lee Kwan Yew, a key American ally, said that the station chief offered him a $3.3 million bribe to hush up the matter.

At 6 p.m. on Sunday, April 16, Stevenson cabled Rusk from New York to warn of the "gravest risk of another U-2 disaster in such uncoordinated action." At 9:30 p.m. the president's national security adviser, McGeorge Bundy, called Dulles's deputy director, General Charles Pearre Cabell. Bundy said the CIA could not launch air strikes on Cuba unless "they could be conducted from a strip within the beachhead" at the Bay of Pigs. At 10:15 p.m., Cabell and Bissell rushed to the elegant seventh-floor offices of the secretary of state. Rusk told them the CIA's planes could go into battle to protect the beachhead, but not to attack Cuban airfields or harbors or radio stations. "He asked if I should like to speak to the President," Cabell wrote. "Mr. Bissell and I were impressed with the extremely delicate situation with Ambassador Stevenson and the United Nations and the risk to the entire political position of the United States"—a situation created by Bissell and Barnes's lies—and so "we saw no point in my speaking personally to the President." Trapped by his own cover stories, Bissell chose not to fight. In his memoirs, he attributed his silence to cowardice.

When Cabell returned to the CIA's war room to report what had happened, Jake Esterline seriously considered killing him with his own hands. The agency was going to leave its Cubans to die "like sitting ducks on that damn beach," Esterline said.

Cabell's cancellation order caught the CIA's pilots in Nicaragua in their cockpits, revving their engines. At 4:30 a.m. on Monday, April 17, Cabell called Rusk at home and pleaded for presidential authority for more air power to protect the CIA's ships, which were loaded to the gunwales with ammunition and military supplies. Rusk called President Kennedy at his Virginia retreat, Glen Ora, and put Cabell on the phone.

The president said he was unaware that there were going to be any air strikes on the morning of D-Day. Request denied.

Four hours later, a Sea Fury fighter-bomber swooped down on the Bay of Pigs. The American-trained pilot, Captain Enrique Carreras, was the ace of Fidel Castro's air force. He took aim at the *Rio Escondido,* a rust-bucket freighter out of New Orleans under contract to the CIA. Below him to the southeast, aboard the *Blagar,* a converted World War II landing craft, a CIA paramilitary officer named Grayston Lynch fired at the

Cuban fighter with a defective .50-caliber machine gun. Captain Carreras let loose a rocket that hit the forward deck of the *Rio Escondido* six feet below the railing, striking dozens of fifty-five-gallon drums filled with aviation gasoline. The fire ignited three thousand gallons of aircraft fuel and 145 tons of ammunition in the forward hold. The crew abandoned ship and started swimming for their lives. The freighter exploded in a fireball that sent a mushroom cloud rising half a mile high above the Bay of Pigs. From sixteen miles away, on a beach newly littered with the brigade's dead and wounded, the CIA commando Rip Robertson thought Castro had dropped an atomic bomb.

President Kennedy called on Admiral Arleigh Burke, the commander of the U.S. Navy, to save the CIA from disaster. "Nobody knew what to do nor did the CIA who were running the operation and who were wholly responsible for the operation know what to do or what was happening," the admiral said on April 18. "We have been kept pretty ignorant of this and have just been told partial truths."

For two miserable days and nights, Castro's Cubans and the CIA's Cubans killed one another. On the night of April 18, the commander of the rebel brigade, Pepe San Roman, radioed back to Lynch: "Do you people realize how desperate the situation is? Do you back us up or quit? . . . Please don't desert us. Am out of tank and bazooka ammo. Tanks will hit me at dawn. I will not be evacuated. Will fight to the end if we have to." Morning came and no help arrived. "We are out of ammo and fighting on the beach. Please send help. We cannot hold," San Roman shouted through his radio. His men were massacred standing knee-deep in the water.

"Situation for air support beachhead completely out of our hands," the agency's air operations chief told Bissell in a cable at noon. "Have now lost 5 Cuban pilots, 6 co-pilots, 2 American pilots, and one co-pilot." In all, four American pilots on contract to the CIA from the Alabama National Guard were killed in combat. For years the agency hid the cause of their deaths from their widows and families.

"Still have faith," said the air operation chief's cable. "Awaiting your guidance." Bissell had none to offer. At about two in the afternoon on April 19, San Roman cursed the CIA, shot his radio, and gave up the fight. In sixty hours, 1,189 members of the Cuban brigade had been captured and 114 killed.

"For the first time in my thirty-seven years," Grayston Lynch wrote, "I was ashamed of my country."

That same day, Robert Kennedy sent a prophetic note to his brother. "The time has come for a showdown, for in a year or two years the situation will be vastly worse," he wrote. "If we don't want Russia to set up missile bases in Cuba, we had better decide now what we are willing to do to stop it."

"TAKE THE BUCKET OF SLOP AND PUT ANOTHER COVER OVER IT"

President Kennedy told two of his aides that Allen Dulles had reassured him face-to-face in the Oval Office that the Bay of Pigs would be a sure-fire success: "Mr. President, I stood right here at Ike's desk and told him I was certain that our Guatemalan operation would succeed, and Mr. President, the prospects for this plan are even better than they were for that one." If so, it was an astonishing lie. Dulles in fact had told Eisenhower that the CIA's chances in Guatemala were one in five at best—and zero without air power.

At the hour of the invasion, Allen Dulles was making a speech in Puerto Rico. His public departure from Washington had been part of a deception plan, but now it looked like an admiral abandoning ship. Upon his return, Bobby Kennedy recounted, he looked like living death, his face buried in his trembling hands.

On April 22, the president convened the National Security Council, an instrument of government he had disdained. After ordering the distraught Dulles to start "stepping up coverage of Castro activities in the United States"—a task outside the CIA's charter—the president told General Maxwell Taylor, the new White House military adviser, to work with Dulles, Bobby Kennedy, and Admiral Arleigh Burke to perform an autopsy on the Bay of Pigs. The Taylor board of inquiry met that same afternoon, with Dulles clutching a copy of NSC 5412/2, the 1955 authorization for the covert operations of the CIA.

"I'm first to recognize that I don't think that the CIA should run paramilitary operations," Dulles told the board—a puff of smoke obscuring his decade of unblinking support for such operations. "I think, however, that rather than destroying everything and starting all over, we ought to take what's good in what we have, get rid of those things that are really beyond the competence of the CIA, then pull the thing together and make it more effective. We should look over the 5412 papers and revise them in such a manner that paramilitary operations are handled in some other way. It's not going to be easy to find a place to put them; it's very difficult to keep things secret."

The Taylor board's work soon made it clear to the president that he needed a new way of running covert operations. One of the last witnesses before the board was a dying man who spoke with a grave clarity on the deepest problems confronting the CIA. The testimony of General Walter Bedell Smith resounds with chilling authority today:

> QUESTION: How can we in a democracy use all our assets effectively without having to completely reorganize the Government?
>
> GENERAL SMITH: A democracy cannot wage war. When you go to war, you pass a law giving extraordinary powers to the President. The people of the country assume when the emergency is over, the rights and powers that were temporarily delegated to the Chief Executive will be returned to the states, counties and to the people.
>
> QUESTION: We often say that we are in a state of war at the present time.
>
> GENERAL SMITH: Yes, sir, that is correct.
>
> QUESTION: Are you suggesting that we should approximate the President's wartime powers?
>
> GENERAL SMITH: No. However, the American people do not feel that they are at war at the present time, and consequently they are not willing to make the sacrifices necessary to wage war. When you are at war, cold war if you like, you must have an amoral agency which can operate secretly. . . . I think that so much publicity has been given to CIA that the covert work might have to be put under another roof.
>
> QUESTION: Do you think we should take the covert operations from CIA?

GENERAL SMITH: It's time we take the bucket of slop and put another cover over it.

Three months later, Walter Bedell Smith died at age sixty-five.

The CIA's inspector general, Lyman Kirkpatrick, ran his own post-mortem on the Bay of Pigs. He concluded that Dulles and Bissell had failed to keep two presidents and two administrations accurately and realistically informed about the operation. If the CIA wanted to stay in business, Kirkpatrick said, it would have to drastically improve its organization and management. Dulles's deputy, General Cabell, warned him that if the report fell into unfriendly hands, it would destroy the agency. Dulles wholeheartedly agreed. He saw to it that the report was buried. Nineteen of the twenty printed copies were recalled and destroyed. The one that survived was locked away for almost forty years.

In September 1961, Allen Dulles retired as director of central intelligence. Workers were still putting the finishing touches on the grand new CIA headquarters he had fought for years to build in the Virginia woodlands above the west bank of the Potomac River, seven miles from the edge of the capital. He had commissioned an inscription from the Gospel of John to be engraved in its central lobby: "And ye shall know the truth, and the truth will make you free." A medallion in his image was hung in the same soaring space. *"Si monumentum requiris circumspice,"* it reads: If you seek his monument, look around you.

Richard Bissell stayed on another six months. He later confessed in secret testimony that the vaunted expertise of his clandestine service was a façade—it was "not the place where one would expect to look for professional competence." When he left, the president pinned the National Security Medal on his lapel. "Mr. Bissell's high purpose, unbounded energy, and unswerving devotion to duty are benchmarks of the intelligence service," he said. "He leaves an enduring legacy."

Part of that legacy was a broken confidence. For the next nineteen years, no president would place his full faith and trust in the Central Intelligence Agency.

"YOU ARE NOW LIVING ON THE BULL'S EYE"

In his wrath after the Bay of Pigs, John Kennedy first wanted to destroy the CIA. Then he took the agency's clandestine service out of its death spiral by handing the controls to his brother. It was one of the least wise decisions of his presidency. Robert F. Kennedy, thirty-five years old, famously ruthless, fascinated with secrecy, took command of the most sensitive covert operations of the United States. The two men unleashed covert action with an unprecedented intensity. Ike had undertaken 170 major CIA covert operations in eight years. The Kennedys launched 163 major covert operations in less than three.

The president had wanted to make RFK the new director of central intelligence, but his brother thought it best to choose a man who could afford the president political protection after the Bay of Pigs. After casting about for months, they settled on an Eisenhower elder statesman: John McCone.

Almost sixty years old, a deeply conservative California Republican, a devout Roman Catholic, and a fiery anticommunist, McCone would very likely have been secretary of defense had Nixon been elected in 1960. He had made a fortune building ships on the West Coast during World War II, then served as a deputy to Defense Secretary James Forrestal, hammering out the first budget of the new Department of Defense in 1948. As undersecretary of the air force during the Korean War, he had helped create the first truly global military power of the postwar world. As chairman of the Atomic Energy Commission under Eisenhower, he had overseen the nation's nuclear-weapons factories and held a seat on the National Security Council. McCone's new covert operations chief, Richard Helms, described him as "straight from central casting in Hollywood," with "white hair, ruddy cheeks, brisk gait, impeccable dark suits, rimless glasses, aloof manner, and unmistakable self-confidence."

The new director was "not a man that people were going to love," said Red White, his chief administrator, but he quickly became "very close with Bobby Kennedy." McCone first bonded with Bobby as a coreligionist and fellow anticommunist. The attorney general's big white clapboard house, Hickory Hill, was only a few hundred yards from the agency's new headquarters, and Kennedy often stopped by the CIA in the morning on his way to work downtown at the Justice Department, dropping in after McCone's daily 8:00 a.m. staff meeting.

McCone left a unique and meticulous daily record of his work, his thoughts, and his conversations, many first declassified in 2003 and 2004. His memoranda provide a moment-to-moment account of his years as director. Along with thousands of pages of conversations secretly recorded by President Kennedy inside the White House, many not accurately transcribed until 2003 and 2004, they detail the most dangerous days of the cold war.

Before his swearing-in, McCone tried to get the big picture of the agency's operations. He toured Europe with Allen Dulles and Richard Bissell, went on to a Far East station chiefs' meeting at a mountain retreat north of Manila, and immersed himself in paper.

But Dulles and Bissell left out some details. They never saw fit to tell McCone about the CIA's biggest, longest-lasting, and most illegal program in the United States: the opening of first-class mail coming in and out of the country. From 1952 onward, working at the main postal facility at the international airport in New York City, the CIA's security officers opened letters and Jim Angleton's counterintelligence staff sifted the information. Nor did Dulles and Bissell tell McCone about the CIA's assassination plots against Fidel Castro, temporarily suspended after the Bay of Pigs. Almost two years would pass before the director learned of the murder plans; he never found out about the mail openings until the rest of the nation did.

After the Bay of Pigs, President Kennedy was persuaded to rebuild the clearinghouses for covert action that he had torn down after his inauguration. The president's foreign intelligence board of advisers was reestablished. The Special Group (later renamed the 303 Committee) was reconstituted to oversee the clandestine service, and its chairman for the next four years would be the national security adviser: cool, clipped, correct McGeorge Bundy of Groton and Yale, the former dean of the arts and sciences at Harvard University. The members were McCone, the chairman of the Joint Chiefs, and senior deputies from Defense and State. But until very late in the Kennedy administration it was left to the CIA's covert operators to decide whether to consult with the Special Group. There were more than a few operations that McCone and the Special Group knew little or nothing about.

In November 1961, in the greatest secrecy, John and Bobby Kennedy created a new planning cell for covert action, the Special Group (Augmented). It was RFK's outfit, and it had one mission: eliminating Castro.

On the night of November 20, nine days before he took the oath of office as director, McCone answered his home telephone and heard the president summoning him to the White House. Arriving the following afternoon, he found the Kennedys in the company of a gangly fifty-three-year-old brigadier general named Ed Lansdale. His specialty was counterinsurgency, and his trademark was winning third-world hearts and minds with American ingenuity, greenback dollars, and snake oil. He had worked for the CIA and the Pentagon since before the Korean War, serving as Frank Wisner's man in Manila and Saigon, where he helped pro-American leaders take power.

Lansdale was introduced as the new chief of operations at the Special Group (Augmented). "The President explained that General Lansdale had been engaging in a study of possible action in Cuba, acting under the direction of the Attorney General, and he, the President, desired an immediate plan of action which could be submitted to him within two weeks," McCone recorded in his CIA files. "The Attorney General expressed grave concern over Cuba, the necessity for immediate dynamic action." McCone told them that the CIA and the rest of the Kennedy administration had been in a state of shock ever since the Bay of Pigs—"and, therefore, were doing very little."

McCone thought nothing short of a shooting war would knock out Castro. And he believed that the CIA was unfit to run a war, secret or not. He told President Kennedy that the agency could not continue to be seen as "a 'cloak and dagger' outfit . . . designed to overthrow governments, assassinate heads of state, involve itself in political affairs of foreign states." He reminded the president that the CIA had one fundamental responsibility under law—"to assemble *all* intelligence" gathered by the United States, and then analyze it, evaluate it, and report it to the White House. The Kennedys agreed, in a written order drafted by McCone and signed by the president, that he would be "the Government's principal intelligence officer." His job would be "the proper coordination, correlation, and evaluation of intelligence from all sources."

McCone also believed he had been hired to shape the foreign policy of the United States for the president. This was not, nor should it have been, the role of the nation's chief intelligence officer. But though his judgment often proved sounder than that of the Harvard men at the highest levels of the government, he quickly discovered that the Kennedys had a number of novel ideas about how he and the CIA were to serve American interests. On the day President Kennedy swore him in, he found out that he and RFK and the unctuous General Lansdale were in charge of Castro.

"You are now living on the bull's eye, and I welcome you to that spot," the president told McCone at his swearing-in.

"OUT OF THE QUESTION"

The president asked McCone from the outset to find a way to pierce the Berlin Wall. The wall had been erected—first barbed wire, then concrete—in August 1961. It could have been an enormous political and propaganda windfall for the West, hard evidence that the exorbitant lies of communism no longer served to keep millions of East German citizens from fleeing. It could have been a golden opportunity for the CIA.

The week that the wall went up, Kennedy sent Vice President Lyndon B. Johnson to Berlin, where he received a top secret briefing from the CIA's base chief, Bill Graver. LBJ gazed upon an impressively detailed chart showing all the CIA's agents in the East.

"I saw this briefing map," said Haviland Smith, then a rising star at the Berlin base. "If you *listened* to what Graver said, we had agents in the Karlsruhe compound"—the Soviet intelligence center—"agents in the Polish military mission, the Czech military mission—we had East Berlin absolutely penetrated up to the goddamn eyeballs. However, if you *knew* what we had, you knew that the penetration of the Polish military mission was the guy who sold newspapers on the corner. And you knew that this big penetration of the Soviet military compound was a *Dachermeister*—a master roofer, who fixed roofs."

"Berlin was a sham," he said. The agency was lying about its achievements to the next president of the United States.

David Murphy, then chief of the CIA's Eastern Europe division, met with President Kennedy at the White House the week after the wall went up. "The Kennedy administration pushed us very hard to persuade us to devise plans for covert paramilitary action and the fomenting of dissidence" in East Germany, he said, but "operations in East Germany were out of the question."

The reason finally emerged in a document declassified in June 2006, a devastating damage assessment drawn up by Dave Murphy himself.

On November 6, 1961, the West German chief of counterintelligence, Heinz Felfe, was arrested by his own security police. Felfe had been a hard-core Nazi who had joined the Gehlen organization in 1951, two years after the CIA took charge of it. He had risen rapidly through its ranks and kept rising after it became the official West German intelligence service, the BND, in 1955.

But Felfe had been working for the Soviets all along. He had penetrated the West German service and, through it, the CIA's station and bases. He was able to manipulate and deceive the CIA's officers in Germany until they had no idea whether the information they had gathered from behind the iron curtain was true or false.

Felfe could "initiate, direct, or halt any BND operations and later some of CIA's," Murphy noted glumly. He had revealed to the East German intelligence service the essential details of every important CIA mission against Moscow from June 1959 to November 1961. These included roughly seventy major covert operations, the identities of more than a hundred CIA officers, and some fifteen thousand secrets.

The agency was all but out of business in Germany and across Eastern Europe. It took a decade to repair the damage.

"THE PRESIDENT WANTS SOME ACTION, RIGHT NOW"

The Berlin Wall—and all else—paled before the Kennedys' desire to avenge the family honor lost at the Bay of Pigs. The overthrow of Castro was "the top priority in the United States Government," Bobby Kennedy told McCone on January 19, 1962. "No time, money, effort, or manpower is to be spared." But the new director warned him that the agency had little real intelligence on which to proceed. "Of the 27 or 28 agents CIA now has in Cuba, only 12 are in communication and these communications are infrequent," he told the attorney general. Seven of the CIA's Cubans had been captured four weeks before, after infiltrating the island.

On RFK's orders, Lansdale drew up a to-do list for the CIA: recruit and deploy the Catholic Church and the Cuban underworld against Castro, fracture the regime from within, sabotage the economy, subvert the secret police, destroy the crops with biological or chemical warfare, and change the regime before the next congressional elections in November 1962.

"Ed had this aura around him," said Sam Halpern, the new deputy chief of the Cuba desk, an OSS veteran who had known Lansdale for a decade. "Some people believed Ed was a kind of magician. But I'll tell you what he was. He was basically a con man. A Madison Avenue 'Man in the Grey Flannel Suit' con man. You take a look at his proposed plan for getting rid of Castro and the Castro regime. It's utter nonsense." The plan boiled down to an empty promise: to overthrow Castro without sending in the marines.

Halpern said to Richard Helms: "This is a political operation in the city of Washington D.C., and has nothing to do with the security of the United States." He warned that the CIA had no intelligence about Cuba. "We don't know what is going on," he told Helms. "We don't know who is doing what to whom. We haven't got any idea of their order of battle in terms of political organization and structure. Who hates whom? Who loves whom? We have nothing." It was the same problem the CIA would face when it confronted Iraq forty years later.

Helms agreed. The plan was a pipe dream.

The Kennedys did not want to hear that. They wanted swift, silent sabotage to overthrow Castro. "Let's get the hell on with it," the attorney general barked. "The President wants some action, right now." Helms saluted smartly and got the hell on with it. He created a new freestanding task force to report to Ed Lansdale and Robert Kennedy. He assembled a team from all over the world, creating the CIA's largest peacetime intelligence operation to date, with some six hundred CIA officers in and around Miami, almost five thousand CIA contractors, and the third largest navy in the Caribbean, including submarines, patrol boats, coast guard cutters, seaplanes, and Guantánamo Bay for a base. Some "nutty schemes" against Fidel were proposed by the Pentagon and the White House, Helms said. These included blowing up an American ship in Guantánamo Harbor and faking a terrorist attack against an American airliner to justify a new invasion.

The operation needed a code name, and Sam Halpern came up with Mongoose.

"THERE IS NOTHING ON PAPER, OF COURSE"

Helms chose William K. Harvey, the man who had built the Berlin Tunnel, to lead the Mongoose team. Harvey called the project "Task Force W," after William Walker, the American freebooter who led a private army into Central America and proclaimed himself the emperor of Nicaragua in the 1850s. It was a very odd choice—unless you knew Bill Harvey.

Harvey was introduced to the Kennedys as the CIA's James Bond. This seems to have mystified JFK, an avid reader of Ian Fleming's spy romances, for the only thing Bond and Harvey had in common was a taste for martinis. Obese, pop-eyed, always packing a pistol, Harvey drank doubles at lunch and returned to work muttering darkly, cursing the day he met RFK. Bobby Kennedy "wanted fast actions, he wanted fast answers," said McCone's executive assistant, Walt Elder. "Harvey did not have fast actions or fast answers."

But he did have a secret weapon.

The Kennedy White House twice had ordered the CIA to create an assassination squad. Under very close questioning by Senate investigators and a presidential commission in 1975, Richard Bissell said those orders had come from national security adviser McGeorge Bundy and Bundy's aide Walt Rostow, and that the president's men "would not have given such encouragement unless they were confident that it would meet with the president's approval."

Bissell had handed down the order to Bill Harvey, who did as he was told. He had returned to headquarters in September 1959 after a long tour as chief of the Berlin base to command Division D of the clandestine service. The division's officers broke into foreign embassies overseas to steal codebooks and ciphers for the eavesdroppers at the National Security Agency. They called themselves the Second-Story Men, and their skills ran from locksmithing to larceny and beyond. The division had contacts with criminals in foreign capitals who could be called on for cat burglaries, the kidnapping of embassy couriers, and assorted felonies in the name of American national security.

In February 1962, Harvey created an "executive action" program, code-named Rifle, and retained the services of a foreign agent, a resident of Luxembourg but a man without a country, who worked on contract for Division D. Harvey intended to use him to kill Fidel Castro.

In April 1962, the CIA's records show, Harvey took a second approach. He met the mobster John Rosselli in New York. He picked up a new batch of poison pills, designed to be dropped into Castro's tea or coffee, from Dr. Edward Gunn, the chief of the operations division of the CIA's Office of Medical Services. Then he drove to Miami and delivered them to Rosselli, along with a U-Haul truck filled with weapons.

On May 7, 1962, the attorney general was briefed in full on the Rifle project by the CIA's general counsel, Lawrence Houston, and the agency's security chief, Sheffield Edwards. RFK was "mad as hell"—not mad about the assassination plot itself, but about the Mafia's role in it. He did nothing to stop the CIA from seeking Castro's death.

Richard Helms, who had taken command of the clandestine service three months before, gave Harvey the go-ahead on Rifle. If the White House wanted a silver bullet, he believed it was the agency's job to try to find it. He thought it best not to tell McCone, correctly judging that the director would have the strongest religious, legal, and political objections.

I once put the question to Helms personally: Did President Kennedy want Castro dead? "There is nothing on paper, of course," he said evenly. "But there is certainly no question in my mind that he did."

Helms thought political assassination in peacetime was a moral aberration. But there were practical considerations as well. "If you become involved in the business of eliminating foreign leaders, and it is considered by governments more frequently than one likes to admit, there is always the question of who comes next," he observed. "If you kill someone else's leaders, why shouldn't they kill yours?"

"A TRUE UNCERTAINTY"

When John McCone took over as director of central intelligence, "CIA was suffering" and "morale was pretty well shattered," he recounted. "My first problem was to try to rebuild confidence."

But CIA headquarters was in an uproar six months into his reign. Mc-Cone started firing hundreds of clandestine service officers—aiming first to purge the "accident-prone," the "wife-beaters," and the "alcohol-addicted," noted his deputy director, General Marshall S. Carter. The dismissals, the aftershocks from the Bay of Pigs, and the almost daily beatings from the White House over Cuba were creating "a true uncertainty as to what the future of the Agency may be," McCone's executive director, Lyman Kirkpatrick, told him in a July 26, 1962, memorandum. He suggested that perhaps "something should be done immediately to restore morale in the Agency."

Helms determined that the only cure was a return to the basics of espionage. With some misgivings, he took his best men out of the paralyzed Soviet and Eastern Europe divisions and turned them on Castro's Cuba. He had a handful of officers under his command in Florida who had learned how to run agents and couriers in and out of communist-controlled zones such as East Berlin. The CIA set up a debriefing center in Opa-Locka to interview thousands of people who had left Cuba on commercial airliners and private boats. The center interrogated some 1,300 Cuban refugees; they provided the agency with political, military, and economic intelligence along with documents and the detritus of everyday life—clothes, coins, cigarettes—to help disguise agents infiltrating the island. The Miami station claimed to have forty-five men running information out of Cuba in the summer of 1962. Some arrived in Florida for a ten-day CIA crash course and returned by speedboat under cover of night. The small spy network they built inside Cuba was the sole achievement of the $50 million Mongoose operation.

Bobby Kennedy kept calling in vain for commandos to blow up Cuba's power plants, factories, and sugar mills in secret. "Can CIA actually hope to generate such strikes?" Lansdale asked Harvey. "Why is this now called a possibility?" Harvey replied that it would take two more years and another $100 million to create a force capable of overthrowing Castro.

The CIA was so busy carrying out covert action that it failed to see a threat to the national survival of the United States gathering in Cuba.

18. "WE HAD ALSO FOOLED OURSELVES"

On Monday, July 30, 1962, John F. Kennedy walked into the Oval Office and switched on the brand-new state-of-the-art taping system he had ordered installed over the weekend. The very first conversation he recorded was a plot to subvert the government of Brazil and oust its president, Joao Goulart.

Kennedy and his ambassador to Brazil, Lincoln Gordon, discussed spending $8 million to swing the next elections and to prepare the ground for a military coup against Goulart—"to push him out, if necessary," Ambassador Gordon told the president. The CIA station in Brazil would "make it clear, discreetly, that we are not necessarily hostile to any kind of military action whatsoever if it's clear that the reason for the military action is—"

"—against the Left," the president said. He would not let Brazil or any other nation in the Western Hemisphere become a second Cuba.

The money started flowing from the CIA into the political life of Brazil. One conduit was the American Institute for Free Labor Development, an arm of the AFL-CIO (British diplomats in the know called it the AFL-CIA). Another was the Institute for Social Research Studies, a newly formed organization of business and civic leaders in Brazil. The recipients were politicians and military officers who opposed President Goulart and who kept in close contact with the new American military attaché in Brazil—Vernon Walters, a future deputy director of central intelligence. The return on these investments would be paid in less than two years.

The White House tapes, transcribed in 2001, recorded a daily drum-beat of covert-action plans taking shape in the Oval Office.

On August 8, McCone met the president at the White House to dis-cuss the wisdom of dropping hundreds of Chinese Nationalist soldiers into Mao's China. The president had approved the paramilitary opera-tion. McCone was dubious. Mao had surface-to-air missiles, and the last U-2 flight that the CIA had sent over the Chinese mainland, McCone told the president, had been spotted and tracked by Chinese communist radars twelve minutes after takeoff from Taiwan. "That's humorous," said Kennedy's national-security aide, Michael Forrestal, the son of the late defense secretary. "We'll give the President another U-2 disaster." And what would the cover story be this time? the president joked. Everyone laughed. One month after this meeting, Mao's forces shot down a U-2 over China.

On August 9, Richard Helms went to the White House to discuss the chances for overthrowing Haiti, thirty miles from Cuba. Haiti's dictator, François "Papa Doc" Duvalier, had been stealing American economic aid and using American military support to shore up his corrupt regime. The president had authorized a coup. The CIA had given weapons to dissi-dents who hoped to topple the government by any means necessary. The question of whether Duvalier would be killed had been weighed. Mc-Cone had given the go-ahead.

But the CIA was bogged down. "I might say, Mr. President, that the plotting doesn't seem to be very successful," Helms said. He warned that Duvalier's "goon squads" were "a repressive force of no mean sub-stance," which "makes plotting a dangerous business." The CIA's best re-cruited agent, a former chief of the Haitian coast guard, lacked the will or the wherewithal to carry out the coup. Helms saw scant hope for suc-cess. "Another coup really doesn't do any good if you don't have any-body to work with," the president told Helms.

On August 10, John McCone, Robert Kennedy, and Defense Secretary Robert McNamara met in Secretary of State Dean Rusk's ornate confer-ence room on the seventh floor of the State Department. The subject was Cuba. McCone remembered "a suggestion being made to liquidate top people in the Castro regime," including Castro and his brother Raul, the Cuban defense minister, who had just returned from a weapons-buying trip to Moscow. He found the idea abhorrent. The director saw a greater danger ahead. He predicted that the Soviet Union was going to give Castro nuclear weapons—medium-range ballistic missiles capable of striking the United States. He had been worrying about that possibility for more than four months. He had no intelligence, nothing to go on save gut instinct.

McCone was the only one who saw the threat clearly. "If I were Khrushchev," he said, "I'd put offensive missiles in Cuba. Then I'd bang my shoe on the desk and say to the United States, 'How do you like looking down the end of a gun barrel for a change? Now, let's talk about Berlin and any other subject that I choose.' " No one seems to have believed him. "The experts unanimously and adamantly agreed that this was beyond the realm of possibility," notes an agency history of McCone's years. "He stood absolutely alone."

There was a growing skepticism about the agency's ability to predict the Soviets' behavior. Its analysts had been consistently wrong for a decade. "The CIA would come in and paint the most scary picture possible about what the Soviets would do to us—we were going to be second-rate; the Soviets were going to be Number One," said former president Gerald R. Ford, who in 1962 sat on the cloistered House subcommittee that provided the CIA's secret budget. "They had charts on the wall, they had figures, and their conclusion was that in ten years, the United States would be behind the Soviet Union in military capability, in economic growth," Ford said. "It was a scary presentation. The facts are they were 180 degrees wrong. These were the best people we had, the CIA's so-called experts."

"THE MOST DANGEROUS AREA IN THE WORLD"

On August 15, McCone returned to the White House to discuss how best to overthrow Cheddi Jagan, the prime minister of British Guiana, a wretched colony in the Caribbean mudflats of South America.

Jagan, an American-educated dentist married to a Marxist from Chicago named Janet Rosenberg, was descended from colonial plantation workers. He was first elected back in 1953. Shortly thereafter, Winston Churchill suspended the colonial constitution, ordered the government dissolved, and threw the Jagans in jail. They were freed after the British restored constitutional government. Jagan was twice re-elected, and he had visited the Oval Office in October 1961.

"I went to see President Kennedy to seek the help of the United States, and to seek his support for our independence from the British," Jagan remembered. "He was very charming and jovial. Now, the United States feared that I would give Guyana to the Russians. I said, 'If this is your fear, fear not.' We will not have a Soviet base."

John F. Kennedy publicly proclaimed—in a November 1961 interview with Khrushchev's son-in-law, the editor of *Izvestia*—that "the United States supports the idea that every people shall have the right to make a free choice as to the kind of government they want." Cheddi Jagan might be "a Marxist," he said, "but the United States doesn't object, because that choice was made by an honest election, which he won."

But Kennedy decided to use the CIA to depose him. Not long after Jagan left the White House, the cold war heated up in Georgetown, his capital. Previously unheard-of radio stations went on the air. Civil servants walked out. Riots took the lives of more than a hundred people. The labor unions revolted after taking advice and money from the American Institute for Free Labor Development, which in turn took cash and counsel from the CIA. Arthur Schlesinger, a special assistant and court historian for the Kennedy White House, asked the president: "Does CIA think that they can carry out a really *covert* operation—i.e., an operation which, whatever suspicions Jagan might have, will leave no visible trace which he can cite before the world, whether he wins or loses, as evidence of U.S. intervention?"

At the White House on August 15, 1962, the president, McCone, and national security adviser McGeorge Bundy decided it was time to bring matters to a head. The president launched a $2 million campaign that eventually drove Jagan from power. President Kennedy later explained to the British prime minister, Harold Macmillan: "Latin America was the most dangerous area in the world. The effect of having a Communist state in British Guiana . . . would be to create irresistible pressures in the United States to strike militarily against Cuba."

At the same August 15 meeting that sealed Jagan's fate, McCone handed President Kennedy the CIA's new doctrine on counterinsurgency. Along with it came a second document outlining covert operations under way in eleven nations—Vietnam, Laos, and Thailand; Iran and Pakistan; and Bolivia, Colombia, the Dominican Republic, Ecuador,

Guatemala, and Venezuela. That document was "highly classified because it tells all about the dirty tricks," McCone told the president. "A
marvelous collection or dictionary of your crimes," Bundy said, with a
laugh.

On August 21, Robert Kennedy asked McCone if the CIA could stage
a phony attack on the American military base at Guantánamo Bay as a
pretext for an American invasion of Cuba. McCone demurred. He told
John Kennedy in private the next day that an invasion could be a fatal
mistake. He warned the president for the first time that he thought the
Soviets might be installing medium-range ballistic missiles in Cuba. If so,
an American sneak attack might set off a nuclear war. He advocated raising a public alarm about the likelihood of a Soviet missile base. The president instantly rejected that idea, but he wondered aloud whether the
CIA's guerrillas or American troops would be needed to destroy the missile sites—if they existed. At that point, no one but McCone was convinced that they did.

Their conversation continued in the Oval Office, shortly after 6 p.m.
on August 22, when they were joined by Maxwell Taylor, the general
Kennedy trusted most. The president wanted to go over two other secret
operations before discussing Cuba. The first was the developing plan to
drop twenty Chinese Nationalist soldiers into mainland China during the
coming week. The second was a plan for the CIA to wiretap members of
the Washington press corps.

"How are we doing with that set-up on the Baldwin business?" the
president asked. Four weeks before, Hanson Baldwin, the national security reporter for *The New York Times,* had published an article on Soviet
efforts to protect intercontinental ballistic missile launch sites with concrete bunkers. Baldwin's highly detailed reporting accurately stated the
conclusions of the CIA's most recent national intelligence estimate.

The president told McCone to set up a domestic task force to stop the
flow of secrets from the government to the newspapers. The order violated the agency's charter, which specifically prohibits domestic spying.
Long before Nixon created his "plumbers" unit of CIA veterans to stop
news leaks, Kennedy used the agency to spy on Americans.

"CIA is completely in agreement with . . . setting up this task force,
which would be a continuing investigative group reporting to me," Mc-
Cone later told the president. The CIA kept watch on Baldwin, four
other reporters, and their sources from 1962 to 1965. By ordering the

director of central intelligence to conduct a program of domestic surveillance, Kennedy set a precedent that Presidents Johnson, Nixon, and
George W. Bush would follow.

At this same White House meeting, the conversation finally returned
to Castro. Thirty-eight Soviet ships had docked in Cuba in the past seven
weeks, McCone told the president. Their cargo "might contain missile
parts. We do not know." But either way the Soviets were working to
build up Cuba's military strength. "Now, that would be separate from the
question of whether they are building some missile bases, isn't it?" asked
the president. "Well, no," said McCone, "I think the two are related. I
think they're doing both."

McCone left Washington the next day for a long honeymoon. A recent widower who had just remarried, he planned to go to Paris and the
south of France. "I would be only too happy to have you call for me," he
wrote to the president, "and if you do, I would be somewhat relieved of
a guilty feeling that seems to possess me."

"PUT IT IN THE BOX AND NAIL IT SHUT"

A U-2 flight passed over Cuba on August 29. Its film was processed
overnight. On August 30, a CIA analyst bent over his light table and
shouted: I've got a SAM site! It was a surface-to-air missile, an SA-2, the
same Soviet weapon that had brought the U-2 down over Russia. That
same day, another U-2 was caught straying over Soviet airspace, violating a solemn American vow and prompting a formal protest from
Moscow.

The knowledge that Cuba had surface-to-air missiles created "an understandable reluctance or timidity" in the White House about authorizing new flights, McCone said later. JFK ordered General Carter, the
acting director of central intelligence during McCone's honeymoon, to
deep-six the report on the SAM. "Put it in the box and nail it shut," the
president said. He could not afford to let international tensions create a
domestic political uproar, not with elections two months away. Then, on
September 9, another U-2 was shot down over China. The spy plane and
its risks were now regarded, as a CIA report put it, with "universal re-

pugnance, or, at the very least, extreme uneasiness" at the State Department and the Pentagon. A furious McGeorge Bundy, spurred by Dean Rusk and acting in the president's name, canceled the next scheduled U-2 flight over Cuba and summoned James Q. Reber, the CIA veteran in charge of the Committee on Overhead Reconnaissance.

"Is there anyone involved in the planning of these missions who wants to start a war?" Bundy asked bluntly.

President Kennedy restricted U-2 flights from passing over Cuban airspace on September 11. Four days later, the first Soviet medium-range missiles docked at Mariel Harbor in Cuba. The photo gap—a blind spot at a decisive moment in history—went on for forty-five days.

McCone, keeping watch on CIA headquarters through incessant cables from the French Riviera, commanded the agency to warn the White House of the "danger of a surprise." It did not. The CIA estimated that there were 10,000 Soviet troops in Cuba. There were 43,000. The agency said Cuban troop strength stood at 100,000. The true number was 275,000. The CIA flatly rejected the possibility that the Soviets were building nuclear sites in Cuba.

"The establishment on Cuban soil of Soviet nuclear striking forces which could be used against the US would be incompatible with Soviet policy," the CIA's top experts concluded in a Special National Intelligence Estimate on September 19. In a classic example of mirror imaging, an uncertain CIA stated: "The Soviets themselves are probably still uncertain about their future military program for Cuba." The estimate stood as a high-water mark of misjudgment for forty years, until the CIA assayed the state of Iraq's arsenal.

McCone alone dissented. On September 20, in the last of his honeymoon cables to headquarters, he urged his agency to think again. The analysts sighed. Then they took another look at a message received at least eight days earlier from a road watcher, a Cuban agent at the lowest rung in the intelligence hierarchy. He had reported that a convoy of seventy-foot Soviet tractor-trailers was moving a mysterious canvas-covered cargo the size of thick telephone poles around the Cuban countryside near the town of San Cristobal. "I never knew his name," the CIA's Sam Halpern said. "This one agent, the only decent result out of Mongoose, this agent told us there's something funny going on. . . . And after ten days of arguing in front of the Committee on Overhead Reconnaissance, it was finally approved to have an overflight."

On October 4, McCone, back in command, raged against the U-2 ban imposed by the White House. There had been no spy flights over Cuba for nearly five weeks. At a Special Group (Augmented) meeting with Bobby Kennedy, "there arose a considerable discussion (with some heat)" as to who had stopped the flights. It was, of course, the president. Bobby Kennedy acknowledged the need for more intelligence on Cuba, but he said the president first and foremost wanted more sabotage: "He urged that 'massive activity' be mounted." He demanded that McCone and Lansdale send agents into Cuba to mine the harbors and kidnap Cuban soldiers for interrogation, an order that led to the final Mongoose mission in October, when some fifty spies and saboteurs were sent to Cuba by submarine at the height of the nuclear crisis.

While American intelligence flailed, ninety-nine Soviet nuclear warheads came into Cuba undetected on October 4. Each one was seventy times more powerful than the bomb that Harry Truman dropped on Hiroshima. With a single act of stealth, the Soviets had doubled the damage they could do to the United States. On October 5, McCone went to the White House to argue that the safety of the nation depended on more U-2 flights over Cuba. Bundy scoffed, saying he was convinced that there was no threat—and if one existed, the CIA could not find it.

"NEAR-TOTAL INTELLIGENCE SURPRISE"

The CIA's discovery of the missiles ten days thereafter has been portrayed as a triumph. Few of the men in power saw it that way at the time.

"The near-total intelligence surprise experienced by the United States with respect to the introduction and deployment of Soviet strategic missiles in Cuba resulted in large part from a malfunction of the analytic process by which intelligence indicators are assessed and reported," the president's foreign intelligence board reported a few months later. The president had been "ill served" by the CIA, which had "failed to get across to key Government officials the most accurate possible picture" of what the Soviets were doing. The board found that "clandestine agent coverage within Cuba was inadequate," and that "full use was not made of aerial photographic surveillance." It concluded: "The manner in which intelligence indicators were handled in the Cuba situation may well be the most serious flaw in our intelligence system, and one which, if uncorrected, could lead to the gravest consequences."

The flaws went uncorrected; the failure to see the true state of the Iraqi arsenal in 2002 played out in much the same way.

But at last, at McCone's insistence, the photo gap was closed. At first light on October 14, a U-2 aircraft, piloted by Air Force Major Richard D. Heyser of the Strategic Air Command, flew over western Cuba, taking 928 photographs in six minutes. Twenty-four hours later, the CIA's analysts gazed upon images of the biggest communist weapons they had ever seen. All day long on October 15, they compared the U-2 shots to photos taken of the Soviet missiles paraded through the streets of Moscow every May Day. They checked manuals of technical specifications supplied over the past year by Oleg Penkovsky, a colonel in the Soviet military intelligence service. He had spent four months, starting in the summer of 1960, trying to approach the CIA. But its officers had been too inexperienced, too wary, and too frightened to close the deal. He finally made contact with the British, who worked with him in concert with the CIA in London. At great risk, he had smuggled out some five thousand pages of documents, most of them providing insight into military technology and doctrine. He was a volunteer, and the first Soviet spy of consequence the CIA ever had. Exactly one week after the U-2 photos arrived in Washington, Penkovsky was arrested by Soviet intelligence.

By late afternoon on October 15, the CIA's analysts knew they were looking at SS-4 medium-range ballistic missiles capable of carrying a one-megaton warhead from western Cuba to Washington. President Kennedy was in New York, campaigning for candidates in the November election, now three weeks away. That night, McGeorge Bundy was at home, holding a farewell dinner for Chip Bohlen, the newly appointed American ambassador to France. At about 10 p.m. the telephone rang. It was Ray Cline, the CIA's deputy director of intelligence. "Those things we've been worrying about—it looks as though we've really got something," Cline said.

Richard Helms brought the U-2 photos to the attorney general's office at 9:15 a.m. on October 16. "Kennedy got up from his desk and stood for a moment staring out the window," Helms remembered. "He turned to face me. 'Shit,' he said loudly, raising both fists to his chest as if he were about to begin shadow boxing. 'Damn it all to hell and back.' These were my sentiments exactly."

Bobby Kennedy thought: "We had been deceived by Khrushchev, but we had also fooled ourselves."

19. "WE'D BE *DELIGHTED* TO TRADE THOSE MISSILES"

The CIA had fooled itself into thinking that the Soviets would never send nuclear weapons to Cuba. Now that it had seen the missiles, it still could not grasp the Soviet mindset. "I can't understand their viewpoint," President Kennedy lamented on October 16. "It's a goddamn mystery to me. I don't know enough about the Soviet Union."

General Marshall Carter was again the acting director; McCone had flown to Seattle for the funeral of his new stepson, killed in a car crash. Carter went to the Special Group (Augmented) meeting at 9:30 a.m. in the Situation Room, the underground command post at the White House, carrying new proposals for secret attacks on Cuba commissioned by Robert Kennedy. Carter, who privately compared Kennedy's performances at Mongoose meetings to the gnawing of an enraged rat terrier, listened silently as the attorney general approved eight new acts of sabotage, contingent on the president's go-ahead. Carter then met the CIA's chief photo interpreter, Art Lundahl, and the agency's top missile expert, Sidney Graybeal, upstairs at the White House. The three men brought blown-up U-2 images into the Cabinet Room, where the inner circle of the national-security establishment assembled shortly before noon.

The president flicked on his tape recorder. More than forty years went by before an accurate transcript of the Cuban missile crisis meetings was compiled.

"THAT'D BE *GODDAMN DANGEROUS*"

The president stared at the pictures. "How far advanced is this?" he asked. "Sir, we've never seen this kind of an installation before," Lundahl said. "Not even in the Soviet Union?" Kennedy said. "No, sir," Lundahl replied. "It's ready to be fired?" asked the president. "No, sir," said Graybeal. "How long have . . . we can't tell that, can we, how long before they fire?" Kennedy asked. No one knew. Where were the warheads? asked Defense Secretary McNamara. No one knew. Why had Khrushchev done this? wondered the president. No one knew. But Secretary Rusk had a good guess: "We don't really live under fear of his nuclear weapons to the extent that he has to live under ours," he suggested. "Also, we have nuclear weapons nearby, in Turkey and places like that."

The president was only dimly aware that those missiles were in place. He had all but forgotten that he had chosen to keep those weapons pointed at the Soviets.

JFK ordered three strike plans prepared: number one, to destroy the nuclear missile sites with air force or navy jets; number two, to mount a far bigger air strike; number three, to invade and conquer Cuba. "We're certainly going to do number one," he said. "We're going to take out these missiles." The meeting broke up at 1 p.m. after Bobby Kennedy argued for an all-out invasion.

At 2:30 p.m., RFK cracked the lash at the Mongoose team at his enormous office in the Justice Department, demanding new ideas, new missions. Passing on a question posed to him by the president ninety minutes earlier, he asked Helms to tell him how many Cubans would fight for the regime if the United States invaded. No one knew. At 6:30 p.m., the president's men reconvened in the Cabinet Room. Thinking of the Mongoose missions, President Kennedy asked if the MRBMs, the medium-range ballistic missiles, could be destroyed with bullets. Yes, General Carter told him, but these were mobile missiles; they could be moved to new hiding places. The problem of targeting mobile missiles has remained unsolved to this day.

The president now contemplated the question of a nuclear war over Cuba. He began to grasp how little he understood the Soviet leader. "We certainly have been wrong about what he's trying to do," the president said. "Not many of us thought that he was gonna put MRBMs on Cuba." Nobody save John McCone, Bundy muttered. Why had Khrushchev done it? the president asked. "What is the advantage of that? It's just as if we suddenly began to put a *major* number of MRBMs in Turkey," he said. "Now that'd be *goddamn dangerous,* I would think."

A moment of awkward silence fell. "Well, we *did* it, Mr. President," said Bundy.

The talk then turned to secret warfare. "We have a list of sabotage options, Mr. President," said Bundy. ". . . I take it you are in favor of sabotage." He was. Ten teams of five Mongoose agents were authorized to infiltrate Cuba by submarine. Their orders were to blow up Soviet ships with underwater mines in Cuban harbors, to attack three surface-to-air missile sites with machine guns and mortars, and perhaps to go after the nuclear missile launchers. The Kennedys were swinging wildly. The CIA was their blunt instrument.

The president walked out of the meeting, leaving two military options on the table: a sneak attack on Cuba and a full-bore invasion. His parting words were a request to see McCone the next morning before leaving for a campaign trip to Connecticut. General Carter, McNamara, Bundy, and a few others stayed behind.

Deputy Director of Central Intelligence Marshall Carter was sixty-one years old, short, squat, bald, and sharp-tongued. He had been chief of staff of NORAD, the North American Air Defense Command, under Eisenhower. He knew the nuclear strategies of the United States. Now, with the president out of the room, the CIA man voiced his deepest fear: "You go in there with a surprise attack," Carter said. "You put out all the missiles. This isn't the *end;* this is the *beginning.*" It would be the first day of World War III.

"THE COURSE WHICH I HAD RECOMMENDED"

The next day, Wednesday, October 17, John McCone and John Kennedy met at 9:30 a.m. "President seemed inclined to act promptly if at all, without warning," McCone noted in his daily memo for the record. The president then asked McCone to drive to Gettysburg, Pennsylvania, to brief Dwight D. Eisenhower. McCone arrived at noon carrying U-2 photos of the medium-range ballistic missiles. "Eisenhower seemed to lean toward (but did not specifically recommend) military action which would cut off Havana and therefore take over the heart of the government," McCone noted.

The director drove back to Washington and tried to pull together his thoughts. He was weary; he had been to the West Coast and back in less than forty-eight hours. The six single-spaced pages of notes he produced that afternoon were declassified in 2003. They reflect a search for a way to rid Cuba of the missiles without a nuclear war.

Given his background as a master shipbuilder, McCone understood the military, political, and economic power of ships at sea. The notes he drew up included the idea of imposing "an all-out blockade" on Cuba—"the interruption of all incoming shipping," backed up with the threat of an attack. In meetings with Bobby Kennedy, McNamara, Rusk, and Bundy that went on until nearly midnight, he elaborated on the blockade strategy. McCone's notes show that the idea received no evident support from the president's top advisers.

At 11 a.m. on Thursday, October 18, McCone and Art Lundahl went to the White House with new U-2 photos. These showed a new set of bigger missiles, each with a range of 2,200 miles, capable of hitting any major American city save Seattle. McCone said the missile bases were run by Soviet troops; McNamara pointed out that a surprise air strike on the bases would kill several hundred Soviets. Attacking them was an act of war against Moscow, not Havana. Then Undersecretary of State George Ball voiced what the CIA's Marshall Carter had said two nights before: "A course of action where we strike without warning is like Pearl Harbor."

The president said, "The question *really* is what action we take which *lessens* the chances of a nuclear exchange, which obviously is the final failure. . . . You have the blockade without any declaration of war. You've got a blockade with a declaration of war. We've got strikes one, two, and three. We've got invasion."

That day, McCone picked up two votes in favor of his argument for a blockade backed with threats of attack. One was Eisenhower's. The other was RFK's. They both had shifted to McCone's stance. They were still in the minority, but they turned the tide. The president told himself, sitting alone in the Oval Office at about midnight, speaking directly to the hidden microphones, that "opinions had obviously switched from the advantages of a first strike." The president called McCone at home on Sunday to say, as the director noted with satisfaction, that "he had made up his mind to pursue the course which I had recommended." The president announced that decision to the world in a televised address on Monday night, October 22.

"I WOULDA BEEN IMPEACHED"

The morning of Tuesday, October 23, began at the White House with a briefing by McCone. Intensely alert to the political damage the director could cause them as the only man in Washington who had accurately forewarned them of the threat, the Kennedys put McCone on spin patrol, briefing members of Congress and columnists. They also wanted him to stiffen the spine of Ambassador Adlai Stevenson, who needed to argue the American case at the United Nations.

From the White House, McCone called Ray Cline, his chief intelligence analyst, and told him to fly to New York with copies of the U-2 photographs. Stevenson's team was "in some difficulty putting together a convincing case to the Security Council," McCone explained. "See, they're in a little bad spot because at the time of the Bay of Pigs, why, Stevenson showed some fake pictures and they later turned out to be fake."

President Kennedy's twelve top national-security men then met to talk about how to manage the blockade, set to begin the next morning. It was technically an act of war. McCone reported corridor chatter at the United Nations, relayed by Ray Cline, suggesting that the Soviet vessels en route to Cuba might try to run past the American warships.

"*Now* what do we do tomorrow morning when these eight vessels continue to sail on?" asked President Kennedy. "We're all clear about how"—a beat of silence, a nervous chuckle—"we handle it?"

No one knew. Another brief silence fell.

"Shoot the rudders off 'em, don't you?" McCone replied.

The meeting broke up. Kennedy signed the quarantine proclamation. He and his brother were then alone for a few minutes in the Cabinet Room.

"Well, it looks like it's gonna be real *mean*. But on the other hand, there's really no choice," said the president. "If they get mean on this one—Jesus Christ! What are they gonna fuck up next?" His brother said: "There wasn't any choice. I mean, you woulda had a—you woulda been *impeached*." The president agreed: "I woulda been impeached."

At 10 a.m. on Wednesday, October 24, the blockade took effect, the American military went on its highest alert short of nuclear war, and McCone began his daily briefing at the White House. The director of central intelligence at last was serving as his charter commanded, bringing all of American intelligence to the president into a single voice. The Soviet army was not on full alert, but it was increasing its readiness, he reported, and the Soviet navy had submarines in the Atlantic trailing the fleet headed for Cuba. New photoreconnaissance showed storage buildings for nuclear warheads, but no sign of the warheads themselves. McCone took pains that day to point out to the president that the blockade would not stop the Soviets from readying the missile launching sites.

McNamara began to lay out his plans for intercepting the Soviet ships and submarines. Then McCone interrupted. "Mr. President, I have a note just handed me. . . . All six Soviet ships currently identified in Cuban waters . . . have either stopped or reversed course." Rusk said, "Whaddya mean, 'Cuban waters'?" The president asked, "The ships leaving Cuba or the ones coming in?" McCone got up, said, "I'll find out," and left the room. Rusk muttered: "Makes *some* difference."

McCone returned with the breaking news that the Soviet ships had been heading for Cuba, more than five hundred miles from the island, but had either stopped or reversed course. This is the moment when Rusk is supposed to have leaned over to Bundy and said: "We are eyeball to eyeball, and I think the other fellow just blinked."

The first part of McCone's strategy was working: the quarantine on Soviet shipping would hold. The second part would be much harder. As he kept reminding the president, the missiles were still there, the warheads were hidden somewhere on the island, and the danger was growing.

At the White House on October 26, Adlai Stevenson said it would take weeks, perhaps months of negotiations to get the missiles out of Cuba. McCone knew there was no time for that. At midday, he took the president aside (Bobby, if present, never spoke) for a private meeting, with only himself and the photo interpreter Art Lundahl, in the Oval Office. New photoreconnaissance showed that the Soviets had introduced short-range battlefield nuclear weapons. Newly camouflaged missile launchers were almost ready to fire. The missile sites each were manned by up to five hundred military personnel and guarded by three hundred more Soviets.

"I'm getting more concerned all the time," McCone told the president. "They could start at dark and have missiles pointing at us the next morning. For that reason, I'm growing increasingly concerned about following a political route."

"What other way?" asked the president. "The alternative course is we could do the air strike or an invasion. We are still gonna face the fact that, if we invade, by the time we get to these sites after a very bloody fight, we will have—they will be pointing at us. So it still comes down to a question of whether they're gonna fire the missiles."

"That's correct," McCone said. The president's mind now swerved from diplomacy to war. "I mean, there's no other action that, other than diplomatic, that we can take, which does not immediately get rid of these," Kennedy said. "The other way is, I would think, a combination of an air raid and probably invasion, which means that we would have to carry out both of those with the prospect that they might be fired."

McCone cautioned against an invasion. "Invading is going to be a much more *serious* undertaking than most people realize," he told the president. The Russians and the Cubans had "a *hell* of a lot of equipment. . . . Very lethal stuff they've got there. Rocket launchers, self-propelled gun carriers, half-tracks. . . . They'll give an invading force a pretty bad time. It would be no cinch by any manner or means."

That night, a long message from Moscow arrived at the White House. The cable took more than six hours to transmit and receive, and it was not complete until 9 p.m. It was a personal letter from Nikita Khrushchev decrying "the catastrophe of thermonuclear war" and proposing—so it seemed—a way out. If the Americans would promise not to invade Cuba, the Soviets would pull out the missiles.

On Saturday, October 27, McCone began the 10 a.m. White House meeting with the grim news that the missiles could be fired in as little as six hours. He had barely concluded his briefing when President Kennedy read a bulletin ripped from the Associated Press news ticker, datelined Moscow: "Premier Khrushchev told President Kennedy yesterday he would withdraw offensive weapons from Cuba if the United States withdrew its rockets from Turkey." The meeting went into an uproar.

No one bought the idea at first—except the president and McCone.

"Let's not kid ourselves," Kennedy said. "They've got a very good proposal."

McCone agreed: it was specific, serious, and impossible to ignore. The arguments over how to respond dragged on all day, punctuated by moments of terror. First a U-2 strayed into Soviet airspace off the coast of Alaska, prompting Soviet jets to scramble. Then, at about 6 p.m., McNamara suddenly announced that another U-2 had been shot down over Cuba, killing Air Force Major Rudolf Anderson.

The Joint Chiefs now strongly recommended that a full-scale attack on Cuba should begin in thirty-six hours. Around 6:30 p.m., President Kennedy left the room, and the talk immediately became less formal, more brutal.

"The military plan is basically invasion," McNamara said. "*When* we attack Cuba, we are going to *have* to attack with an *all-out* attack," he said. "This is *almost certain* to lead to an invasion." Or a nuclear war, Bundy muttered. "The Soviet Union *may*, and I think probably *will*, attack the Turkish missiles," McNamara continued. Then the United States would have to attack Soviet ships or bases in the Black Sea.

"And I would say that it is *damn dangerous*," said the secretary of defense. "Now, I'm not sure we can avoid anything like that if we attack Cuba. But I think we should make every effort to avoid it. And one way to avoid it is to defuse the Turkish missiles before we attack Cuba," McNamara said.

McCone exploded: "I don't see why you don't make the trade then!" And the ground shifted.

Other voices shouted out: Make the trade! Make the trade then! His anger rising, McCone went on: "We've talked about this, and we'd say we'd be *delighted* to trade those missiles in Turkey for the thing in Cuba." He pressed his point home. "I'd trade these Turkish things out *right now*. I wouldn't even talk to *anybody* about it. We sat for a *week* and there was—everybody was in favor of doing it"—until Khrushchev proposed it.

The president returned to the Cabinet Room at about 7:30 p.m., and suggested everyone take a dinner break. Then, in the Oval Office, he and his brother spoke with McNamara, Rusk, Bundy, and four other trusted aides. McCone was excluded. They discussed his idea, which was what the president wanted. Everyone in the room was sworn to secrecy. Bobby Kennedy left the White House and met with Soviet ambassador Anatoly

Dobrynin in his office at the Justice Department. He told Dobrynin that the United States accepted the quid pro quo on the missiles, provided it was never made public. The Kennedys could not be seen to be cutting a deal with Khrushchev. The attorney general deliberately falsified his memo of the meeting, deleting a drafted reference to the trade. The swap was kept a deep secret. John McCone said a quarter century later: "President Kennedy and Attorney General Bobby Kennedy insisted that they at no time discussed the missiles [in] Turkey with any representatives of the Soviets and that there was no such deal ever made."

For many years thereafter, the world believed that only President Kennedy's calm resolve and his brother's steely commitment to a peaceable resolution had saved the nation from a nuclear war. McCone's central role in the Cuban missile crisis was obscured for the rest of the twentieth century.

The Kennedys soon turned against McCone. The director let it be known throughout Washington that he had been the sole sentinel on the Cuban missiles; he testified to the president's foreign intelligence board that he had told the president about his hunch back on August 22. The gist of the board's report on the "photo gap" appeared in *The Washington Post* on March 4, 1963. That day, Bobby Kennedy told his brother that the CIA must have leaked the information to wound him.

"Yeah," said the president, "he's a real bastard, that John McCone."

"TO ELIMINATE FIDEL, BY EXECUTION IF NECESSARY"

At the height of the missile crisis, McCone had tried to put a leash on Mongoose and focus its considerable energies on gathering intelligence for the Pentagon. He thought he had succeeded. But the CIA's Bill Harvey concluded that the United States was about to invade Cuba and ordered his Mongoose saboteurs to attack.

When Bobby Kennedy, who had pushed the hardest for the Mongoose missions, found out about that dangerous failure of command, he went into a rage. After a screaming match, Harvey was banished from Washington. Helms sent him to Rome as chief of station—though not before the FBI took note of a drunken farewell meal Harvey had with

Johnny Rosselli, the Mafia hit man he had hired to kill Castro. In Rome, the hard-drinking Harvey became unhinged, driving his men as Bobby Kennedy had driven him.

Helms replaced him as the man in charge of Cuba with his Far East chief, Desmond FitzGerald, a Harvard man and a millionaire who lived in a red-brick Georgetown mansion with a butler in the pantry and a Jaguar in the garage. The president liked him; he fit the James Bond image. He had been hired out of his New York law firm by Frank Wisner at the start of the Korean War and instantly made executive officer of the Far East division of the clandestine service. He had helped run the disastrous Li Mi operation in Burma. Then he commanded the CIA's China Mission, which sent foreign agents to their deaths until 1955, when a headquarters review deemed the mission a waste of time, money, energy, and human life. FitzGerald then rose to deputy chief of the Far East, where he helped to plan and execute the Indonesian operation in 1957 and 1958. As Far East division chief, he presided over the rapid expansion of the CIA's operations in Vietnam, Laos, and Tibet.

Now the Kennedys ordered him to blow up Cuban mines, mills, power plants, and commercial ships, to destroy the enemy in hopes of creating a counterrevolution. The objective, as Bobby Kennedy told FitzGerald in April 1963, was to oust Castro in eighteen months—before the next presidential election. Twenty-five Cuban agents of the CIA died on those futile operations.

Then, in the summer and fall of 1963, FitzGerald led the final mission to kill Fidel Castro.

The CIA planned to use Rolando Cubela, its best-placed agent inside Cuba's government, as the hit man. A high-strung, loose-lipped, violent man who detested Castro, Cubela had held the rank of major in the Cuban army, served as its military attaché in Spain, and traveled widely. On August 1, 1963, in a conversation with a CIA officer in Helsinki, he volunteered "to eliminate Fidel, by execution if necessary." On September 5, he met with his CIA case officer, Nestor Sanchez, in Porto Alegre, Brazil, where he was representing the Cuban government at the international Collegiate Games. On September 7, the CIA duly noted that Castro had chosen a reception at the Brazilian embassy in Havana to deliver a long tirade to a reporter for the Associated Press. Castro said that "United States leaders would be in danger if they helped in any attempt to do away with Cuban leaders. . . . If they are aiding terrorist plots to eliminate Cuban leaders, they themselves will not be safe."

Sanchez and Cubela met again in Paris in early October, and the Cuban agent told the CIA officer that he wanted a high-powered rifle with a telescopic sight. On October 29, 1963, FitzGerald took a plane to Paris and met Cubela in a CIA safe house.

FitzGerald said that he was a personal emissary sent by Robert Kennedy, which was dangerously close to the truth, and that the CIA would deliver Cubela the weapons of his choosing. The United States, he said, wanted "a real coup" in Cuba.

20. "HEY, BOSS, WE DID A GOOD JOB, DIDN'T WE?"

Alone in the Oval Office on Monday, November 4, 1963, John F. Kennedy dictated a memo about a maelstrom he had set in motion half a world away—the assassination of an American ally, President Ngo Dinh Diem of South Vietnam.

"We must bear a good deal of responsibility for it," JFK said. He stopped for a moment to play with his children as they ran in and out of the room. Then he resumed. "The way he was killed"—and he paused again—"made it particularly abhorrent."

The CIA's Lucien Conein was Kennedy's spy among the mutinous generals who murdered Diem. "I was part and parcel of the whole conspiracy," Conein said in an extraordinary testament years later.

His nickname was Black Luigi, and he had the panache of a Corsican gangster. Conein had joined the OSS, trained with the British, and parachuted behind French lines. In 1945, he flew to Indochina to fight the Japanese; he was in Hanoi with Ho Chi Minh, and for a moment they were allies. He stayed on to become a charter member of the CIA.

In 1954, he was one of the first American intelligence officers in Vietnam. After Ho defeated the French at the battle of Dien Bien Phu, Vietnam was partitioned into North and South at an international conference in Geneva, where the United States was represented by Undersecretary of State Walter Bedell Smith.

For the next nine years, the United States backed President Diem as the man to fight communism in Vietnam. Conein served under the command of Ed Lansdale at the CIA's new Saigon Military Mission. Lansdale had "a very broad charter," said the CIA's Rufus Phillips. "It was literally, 'Ed, do what you can to save South Vietnam.' "

Conein went to North Vietnam on sabotage missions, destroying trains and buses, contaminating fuel and oil, organizing two hundred Vietnamese commandos trained by the CIA, and burying weapons in the cemeteries of Hanoi. He then returned to Saigon to help shore up President Diem, a mystic Catholic in a Buddhist country whom the CIA provided with millions of dollars, a phalanx of bodyguards, and a direct line to Allen Dulles. The agency created South Vietnam's political parties, trained its secret police, made its popular movies, and printed and peddled an astrological magazine predicting that the stars were in Diem's favor. It was building a nation from the ground up.

"THE IGNORANCE AND THE ARROGANCE"

In 1959, the peasant soldiers of North Vietnam began to carve the Ho Chi Minh Trail through the jungles of Laos; the footpaths were filled with guerrillas and spies heading for South Vietnam.

Laos, a preindustrial lotus land, became "a flashpoint where the U.S. saw its interests being challenged by the communist world," said John Gunther Dean, then a young State Department officer at the American embassy in Vientiane. The CIA set to work buying a new Lao government and building a guerrilla army to fight the communists and attack the trail. The North Vietnamese reacted by stepping up their attempts to infiltrate the country and train the local communists, the Pathet Lao.

The architect of the American political strategy in Laos was the CIA station chief, Henry Hecksher, a veteran of the Berlin base and the Guatemala coup. Hecksher began to build a network of American control by using junior diplomats as bagmen. "One day, Hecksher asked me whether I could take a suitcase to the Prime Minister," Dean remembered. "The suitcase contained money."

The cash made the leaders of Laos "realize that the real power at the Embassy was not the Ambassador but the CIA station chief," said Dean, later the American ambassador in Thailand, India, and Cambodia, among other nations. "The Ambassador was supposed to support the Lao

Government and basically not rock the boat. Henry Hecksher was committed to opposing the neutralist Prime Minister—and perhaps bring about his downfall. That is what happened."

The CIA forced out a freely elected coalition government and installed a new prime minister, Prince Souvanna Phouma. The prime minister's case officer was Campbell James, an heir to a railroad fortune who dressed, acted, and thought like a nineteenth-century British grenadier. Eight years out of Yale, he saw himself as a viceroy in Laos, and lived accordingly. James made friends and bought influence among the leaders of Laos at a private gambling club he created; its centerpiece was a roulette wheel borrowed from John Gunther Dean.

The real battle for Laos began after the CIA's Bill Lair, who ran a jungle warfare training school for Thai commandos, discovered a Lao mountain tribesman named Vang Pao, a general in the Royal Lao Army who led the hill tribe that called itself the Hmong. In December 1960, Lair told the Far East division chief Desmond FitzGerald about his new recruit. "Vang Pao had said: 'We can't live with the communists,' " Lair reported. " 'You give us the weapons, and we'll fight the communists.' " The next morning, at the CIA station, FitzGerald told Lair to write up a proposal. "It was an 18-page cable," Lair remembered. "The answer came back in a very short time. . . . That was the real go-ahead."

In early January 1961, in the final days of the Eisenhower administration, the CIA's pilots delivered their first weapons to the Hmong. Six months later, more than nine thousand hill tribesmen controlled by Vang Pao joined three hundred Thai commandos trained by Lair for combat operations against the communists. The CIA sent guns, money, radios, and airplanes to the Lao military in the capital and the tribal leaders in the mountains. Their most urgent mission was to cut the Ho Chi Minh Trail. Hanoi had now proclaimed a National Liberation Front in the south. That year, four thousand South Vietnamese officials died at the hands of the Vietcong.

A few months after President Kennedy took power, the fates of Laos and South Vietnam were seen as one. Kennedy did not want to send American combat troops to die in those jungles. Instead, he called on the CIA to double its tribal forces in Laos and "make every possible effort to launch guerrilla operations in North Vietnam" with its Asian recruits.

The Americans sent to Laos during the Kennedy years did not know the tribal name of the Hmong. They called them the Meo, an epithet somewhere between "barbarian" and "nigger." One of those young men was Dick Holm. Looking back, he rued "the ignorance and the arrogance of Americans arriving in Southeast Asia. . . . We had only minimal understanding of the history, culture, and politics of the people we wanted to aid. . . . Our strategic interests were superimposed onto a region where our president had decided to 'draw the line' against communism. And we would do it our way."

At CIA headquarters, "the activists were all for a war in Laos," said Robert Amory, Jr., the deputy director for intelligence. "They thought that was a great place to have a war."

"WE HARVESTED A LOT OF LIES"

The Americans sent to Vietnam had an equally profound ignorance of the country's history and culture. But the CIA's officers saw themselves as the point men in the global war on communism.

They had the run of Saigon. "They were under covers as varied as film and drama producers and industrial salesmen; they were trainers, weapons experts, merchants," said Ambassador Leonardo Neher, then a State Department officer in Saigon. "They had unbelievable funds. . . . They were having the time of their lives. They had everything they wanted."

What they lacked was intelligence about the enemy. That was the responsibility of William E. Colby, the station chief in Saigon from 1959 to 1961, soon to be chief of the Far East division of the clandestine service.

Colby, who had fought behind enemy lines as an OSS commando, did as he had done in World War II. He started an operation called Project Tiger to parachute some 250 South Vietnamese agents into North Vietnam. After two years, 217 of them were recorded as killed, missing, or suspected of being double agents. A final report listed the fate of fifty-two teams of agents, each team as large as seventeen commandos:

"Captured soon after landing."

"Hanoi Radio announced capture."

"Team destroyed."

"Team believed under North Vietnam control."

"Captured soon after landing."

"Doubled, played, terminated." That last phrase suggests that the United States discovered that a commando team was secretly working for North Vietnam and then hunted and killed its members. The reason for the failure of the missions eluded the CIA until after the cold war, when one of Colby's cohorts, Captain Do Van Tien, the deputy chief for Project Tiger, revealed that he had been a spy for Hanoi all along.

"We harvested a lot of lies," said Robert Barbour, the deputy chief of the American embassy's political section. "Some of them we knew were lies. Some of them we didn't."

In October 1961, President Kennedy sent General Maxwell Taylor to assess the situation. "South Vietnam is now undergoing an acute crisis of confidence," Taylor warned in a top secret report to the president. The United States had to "demonstrate by deeds—not merely words—the American commitment seriously to help save Vietnam." He wrote: "To be persuasive this commitment must include the sending to Vietnam of some U.S. military forces." That was a *very* deep secret.

To win the war, General Taylor continued, the United States needed more spies. In a secret annex to the report, the CIA's deputy station chief in Saigon, David Smith, said that a key battle would be fought within the government of South Vietnam. He said Americans had to infiltrate the Saigon government, influence it, "speed up the processes of decision and action" within it—and, if necessary, change it.

That job went to Lucien Conein.

"NOBODY LIKED DIEM"

Conein started working with President Diem's half-mad brother, Ngo Dinh Nhu, to establish the Strategic Hamlets program, which herded peasants from their villages into armed camps as a defense against communist subversion. Wearing the uniform of a U.S. Army lieutenant colonel, Conein burrowed deep into the decaying military and political culture of South Vietnam.

"I was able to go to every province, I was able to talk to unit commanders," he said. "Some of these people I had known for many years; some I had known even back in World War Two. Some of them were in powerful positions." His contacts soon became the best the agency had in Vietnam. But there was so much he did not know.

On May 7, 1963, the eve of the 2,527th birthday of the Buddha, Conein flew to Hue, where he found a large military entourage whose presence he did not understand. He was encouraged to leave on the next plane. "I wanted to stay," he remembered. "I wanted to see the celebration of the birthday of Buddha. I wanted to see the boats with the candles lit going down the perfumed river, but it was not to be." The next morning Diem's soldiers attacked and killed members of a Buddhist entourage in Hue.

"Diem had been out of touch with reality," Conein said. Diem's blue-uniformed scouts modeled on the Hitler Youth, his CIA-trained special forces, and his secret police aimed to create a Catholic regime in a Buddhist nation. By oppressing the monks, Diem had made them a powerful political force. Their protests against the government grew for the next five weeks. On June 11, a sixty-six-year-old monk named Quang Duc sat down and set himself ablaze in a Saigon intersection. The pictures of the immolation went around the world. All that was left of him was his heart. Now Diem began raiding the pagodas, killing monks and women and children to sustain his power.

"Nobody liked Diem," Bobby Kennedy said not long thereafter. "But how to get rid of him and get somebody who would continue the war, not split the country in two and, therefore, lose not only the war but the country—that was the great problem."

In late June and early July 1963, President Kennedy began to talk in private about getting rid of Diem. If it were to be done well, it had best be done in secret. The president began the change of regime by nominating a new American ambassador: the imperious Henry Cabot Lodge, a political rival he had twice defeated, once in the race for senator from Massachusetts and once as Richard Nixon's running mate. Lodge was happy to accept the job, once assured he would be provided with a viceroy's powers in Saigon.

On the Fourth of July, Lucien Conein received a message from General Tran Van Don, the acting chief of the joint staff of the army of South Vietnam, a man he had known for eighteen years. *Meet me at the Caravelle*

Hotel, the message said. That night, in the smoky, jam-packed basement nightclub at the hotel, General Don confided that the military was preparing to move against Diem.

"What will be the American reaction if we go all the way?" Don asked Conein.

On August 23, John F. Kennedy gave his answer.

He was alone on a rainy Saturday night in Hyannis Port, on crutches for his aching back, grieving for his stillborn son Patrick, buried two weeks before. Shortly after 9 p.m., the president took a call from his national-security aide Michael Forrestal, and without preamble approved an eyes-only cable for the newly arrived Ambassador Lodge, drafted by Roger Hilsman at the State Department. "We must face the possibility that Diem himself cannot be preserved," it told Lodge, and it urged him to "make detailed plans as to how we might bring about Diem's replacement." The secretary of state, the secretary of defense, and the director of central intelligence had not been consulted. All three were dubious about a coup against Diem.

"I should not have given my consent to it," the president told himself after the consequences became clear. Yet the order went forward.

Hilsman told Helms that the president had ordered Diem ousted. Helms handed the assignment to Bill Colby, the new chief of the CIA's Far East division. Colby passed it on to John Richardson, his choice to replace him as the station chief in Saigon: "In circumstance believe CIA must fully accept directives of policy makers and seek ways to accomplish objectives they seek," he instructed Richardson—though the order "appears to be throwing away bird in hand before we have adequately identified birds in bush, or songs they may sing."

On August 29, his sixth day in Saigon, Lodge cabled Washington: "We are launched on a course from which there is no turning back: the overthrow of the Diem government." At the White House, Helms listened as the president received that message, approved it, and ordered Lodge to make sure above all that the American role in the coup—Conein's role—would be concealed.

The ambassador resented the agency's exalted status in Saigon. He wrote in his private journal: "CIA has more money; bigger houses than diplomats; bigger salaries; more weapons; more modern equipment." He was jealous of the powers held by John Richardson, and he scoffed at the caution the station chief displayed about Conein's central role in the coup plotting. Lodge decided he wanted a new station chief.

So he burned Richardson—"exposed him, and gave his name publicly to the newspapers," as Bobby Kennedy said in a classified oral history eight months later—by feeding a coldly calculated leak to a journeyman reporter passing through Saigon. The story was a hot scoop. Identifying Richardson by name—an unprecedented breach of security—it said he had "frustrated a plan of action Mr. Lodge brought with him from Washington, because the Agency disagreed with it. . . . One high official here, a man who has devoted most of his life in the service of democracy, likened the CIA's growth to a malignancy, and added he was not sure even the White House could control it." *The New York Times* and *The Washington Post* picked up the story. Richardson, his career ruined, left Saigon four days later; after a decent interval, Ambassador Lodge moved into his house.

"We were fortunate when Richardson was recalled," said Conein's old friend, General Don. "Had he been there, he could have put our plan in great jeopardy."

"A COMPLETE LACK OF INTELLIGENCE"

Lucien Conein went to meet General Duong Van Minh, known as "Big Minh," at the Joint General Staff Headquarters in Saigon on October 5. He reported that the general raised the issue of assassination and the question of American support for a new junta. Dave Smith, the new acting station chief, recommended that "we do not set ourselves irrevocably against the assassination plot"—music to Ambassador Lodge's ears, anathema to McCone's.

McCone commanded Smith to stop "stimulating, or approving, or supporting assassination," and he rushed to the Oval Office. Careful to avoid using words that could link the White House to a murder, he later testified, he chose a sports analogy: Mr. President, if I were the manager of a baseball team, and I had only one pitcher, I'd keep him on the mound whether he was a good pitcher or not. On October 17, at a meeting of the

Special Group, and in a one-on-one with the president four days later, McCone said that ever since Lodge's arrival in August, American foreign policy in Vietnam had been based on "a complete lack of intelligence" on the politics of Saigon. The situation developing around Conein was "exceedingly dangerous," he said, and it threatened "absolute disaster for the United States."

The American ambassador reassured the White House. "I believe that our involvement to date through Conein is still within the realm of plausible denial," he reported. "We should not thwart a coup for two reasons. First, it seems at least an even bet that the next government would not bungle and stumble as much as the present one has. Secondly, it is extremely unwise in the long range for us to pour cold water on attempts at a coup. . . . We should remember that this is the only way in which the people in Vietnam can possibly get a change of government."

The White House cabled careful instructions for Conein. Find out the generals' plans, don't encourage them, keep a low profile. Too late: the line between espionage and covert action already had been crossed. Conein was far too famous to work undercover; "I had a very high profile in Vietnam," he said. Everyone who mattered knew exactly who he was and what he represented. They had faith that the CIA's point man spoke for America.

Conein met with General Don on the night of October 24 and learned that the coup was no more than ten days away. They met again on October 28. Don later wrote that Conein "offered us money and weapons, but I turned him down, saying that we still need only courage and conviction."

Conein carefully conveyed the message that the United States opposed assassination. The reaction of the generals, he testified, was: "You don't like it like that? Well, we'll do it our own way anyhow. . . . You don't like it, we won't talk about it anymore." He did not discourage them. If he had, he said, "I would then be cut off and blinded."

Conein reported back to Lodge that the coup was imminent. The ambassador sent the CIA's Rufus Phillips to see Diem. They sat in the palace and talked of war and politics. Then "Diem looked at me quizzically and said, 'Is there going to be a coup against me?' " Phillips remembered.

"I looked at him and just wanted to cry, and said, 'I am afraid so, Mr. President.' That was all we said about that."

"WHO GAVE THOSE ORDERS?"

The coup struck on November 1. It was noon in Saigon, midnight in Washington. Summoned at home by an emissary from General Don, Conein changed into his uniform and called Rufus Phillips to watch over his wife and infant children. Then he grabbed a .38-caliber revolver and a satchel with about $70,000 in CIA funds, hopped into his jeep, and rushed through the streets of Saigon to the Joint General Staff headquarters of the army of South Vietnam. The streets were filled with gunfire. The leaders of the coup had closed the airport, cut the city's telephone lines, stormed central police headquarters, seized the government radio station, and attacked the centers of political power.

Conein filed his first report shortly after 2 p.m. Saigon time. He stayed in contact with the CIA station over his jeep's secure communications link, describing shellings and bombings and troop movements and political maneuvers as they took place. The station relayed his reports to the White House and the State Department through encoded cables. It was as near to real-time intelligence as could be achieved in that day.

"Conein at JGS HQS/ from Gens Big Minh and Don and eyewitness observation," came the first flash cable. "Gens attempting contact Palace by telephone but unable to do so. Their proposition as follows: If the President will resign immediately, they will guarantee his safety and the safe departure of the President and Ngo Dinh Nhu. If the President refuses these terms, the Palace will be attacked within the hour."

Conein sent a second message a little more than an hour later: there would be "no discussion with the President. He will either say yes or no and that is the end of the conversation." General Don and his allies called President Diem shortly before 4 p.m. and asked him to surrender. They offered him sanctuary and a safe passage from the country. He refused. The president of South Vietnam then called the American ambassador. "What is the attitude of the United States?" Diem asked. Lodge said he had no idea. "It is 4:30 a.m. in Washington," he replied, "and the U.S. government cannot possibly have a view." Lodge then said, "I have a report that those in charge of the current activity offer you and your brother safe conduct out of the country. Have you heard this?"

"No," Diem lied. Then he paused, perhaps realizing that Lodge was in on the plot against him. "You have my telephone number," he said, and the conversation came to an end. Three hours later he and his brother fled to a safe house owned by a Chinese merchant who had financed Diem's private spy network in Saigon. The villa was equipped with a phone line hooked to the presidential palace, preserving the illusion that he remained at the seat of power. The battle went on all night; close to a hundred Vietnamese died as the rebels stormed the presidential palace.

At about 6 a.m., Diem telephoned General Big Minh. The president said he was ready to resign, and the general guaranteed his safety. Diem said he would be waiting at the Saint Francis Xavier church in the Chinese quarter of Saigon. The general sent an armored personnel carrier to fetch Diem and his brother, ordered his personal bodyguard to lead the convoy, and then raised two fingers on his right hand. It was a signal: kill them both.

General Don ordered his troops to clean up his headquarters, to bring in a large green-felt-covered table, and to prepare for a news conference. "Get the hell out," the general said to his friend Conein, "we're bringing in the press." Conein went home, only to be summoned by Lodge. "I went to the Embassy and I was informed that I had to find Diem," he said. "I was tired and fed up, and I said, 'Who gave those orders?' They let me know that those orders came from the President of the United States."

At about 10 a.m., Conein drove back to General Staff headquarters and confronted the first general he met. "Big Minh told me they committed suicide. I looked at him and said, where? He said they were in the Catholic Church in Cholon, and they committed suicide," Conein said in his classified testimony to the Senate committee investigating the assassination twelve years later.

"I think I lost my cool at that point," Conein said. He was thinking of mortal sin and his eternal soul.

"I told Big Minh, look, you're a Buddhist, I'm a Catholic. If they committed suicide at that church and the priest holds Mass tonight, that story won't hold water. I said, where are they? He said they are at the General Staff headquarters, behind the General Staff headquarters, did I want to see them? And I said no. He said, why not? And I said, well, if by chance one in a million of the people believe you that they committed suicide in church and I see that they have not committed suicide and I know differently, I am in trouble."

Conein returned to the American embassy to report that President

Diem was dead. He did not report the whole truth. "Informed by Viet counterparts that suicide committed en route from city," he cabled. At 2:50 a.m. Washington time came a reply signed in Dean Rusk's name: "News of Diem, Nhu suicide shocking here . . . important to establish publicly beyond question that deaths actually suicide if this true."

On Saturday, November 2, 1963, at 9:35 a.m., the president convened an off-the-record meeting at the White House with his brother, McCone, Rusk, McNamara, and General Taylor. Before long, Michael Forrestal ran in with a flash from Saigon. General Taylor recounted that the president leaped to his feet and "rushed from the room with a look of shock and dismay on his face which I had never seen before."

At 6:31 p.m., McGeorge Bundy cabled Lodge, with eyes-only copies to McCone, McNamara, and Rusk: "Deaths of Diem and Nhu, whatever their failings, has caused shock here and there is danger that standing and reputation of incoming government may be significantly damaged if conviction spreads of their assassination at direction of one or more senior members of incoming regime. . . . They should not be left under illusion that political assassination is easily accepted here."

Jim Rosenthal was the duty officer at the American embassy in Saigon on that Saturday. Ambassador Lodge sent him down to the front door to receive some important visitors. "I'll never forget the sight," he said. "This car pulled up to the Embassy, and the cameras were grinding away. Conein hops out of the front seat, opens the back door, and salutes, and these guys come out. As if he was delivering them to the Embassy, which he was. I just went up with them in the elevator, and Lodge greeted them. . . . Here were the guys who had just carried out a coup, killed the chief of state, and then they walk up to the Embassy, as if to say, 'Hey, boss, we did a good job, didn't we?' "

21. *"I* THOUGHT IT WAS A *CONSPIRACY"*

On Tuesday, November 19, 1963, Richard Helms carried a Belgian submachine gun concealed in an airline travel bag into the White House.

The weapon was a war trophy; the CIA had seized a three-ton arms cache that Fidel Castro had tried to smuggle into Venezuela. Helms had taken the gun to the Justice Department to show it off to Bobby Kennedy, who thought they should bring it to his brother. They went to the Oval Office, and they talked with the president about how to fight Fidel. The late autumn light was fading as the president arose from his rocking chair and stared out the window at the Rose Garden.

Helms slipped the weapon back into his bag and said: "I'm sure glad the Secret Service didn't catch us bringing this gun in here." The president, lost in thought, turned from the window and shook hands with Helms. "Yes," he said with a grin, "it gives me a feeling of confidence."

The following Friday, McCone and Helms were at headquarters, sharing a lunch of sandwiches in the director's suite. The tall wide windows on the seventh floor looked out over an unbroken field of treetops to the horizon. Then the terrible news broke.

The president had been shot. McCone clapped on his fedora and went to Bobby Kennedy's house, a minute away by car. Helms went down to his office and tried to draft a book message, a cable to be sent to every CIA station in the world. His thoughts at that moment were very close to Lyndon Johnson's.

"What raced through *my* mind," Johnson remembered, "was that, if they had shot our president . . . who would they shoot next? And what was going on in Washington? And when would the missiles be comin'? And *I* thought it was a *conspiracy*, and I raised that question. And nearly everybody that was *with* me raised it."

Over the next year, in the name of national security, the agency hid much of what it knew from the new president and the commission he created to investigate the killing. Its own internal investigation of the assassination collapsed in confusion and suspicion, casting shadows of doubt that still linger. This account is based on CIA records and the sworn testimony of CIA officers, all declassified between 1998 and 2004.

"THE EFFECT WAS ELECTRIC"

"Tragic death of President Kennedy requires all of us to look sharp for any unusual intelligence developments," Helms wrote in his worldwide message to CIA stations on November 22. At headquarters, Charlotte Bustos spotted one immediately. She managed the Mexico files of the clandestine service, and two minutes after the radio announced that the Dallas police had arrested Lee Harvey Oswald, she ran through the pastel corridors clutching Oswald's dossier, searching for her boss, John Whitten, the man in charge of the CIA's covert operations in Mexico and Central America. Whitten read quickly through the file.

"The effect was electric," he remembered.

The file said that at 10:45 a.m. on October 1, 1963, a man identifying himself as Lee Oswald had telephoned the Soviet embassy in Mexico City, asking what was happening with his standing request for a visa to travel to the Soviet Union. With the invaluable help of the Mexican secret police, the Mexico City station had wiretapped the Soviet and Cuban embassies in an operation code-named Envoy. The CIA had Oswald's call.

"Mexico had the biggest and most active telephone intercept operations in the whole world," Whitten said. "J. Edgar Hoover used to glow every time that he thought of the Mexico station"; more than a few American soldiers based in the southwestern United States had been caught trying to sell military secrets or defect to the Russians in Mexico City. The CIA also had photographic surveillance of the Soviet embassy and opened every piece of mail coming in and out of it.

But the eavesdropping operations were so big that they inundated the station, drowning it in useless information. It took eight days before the station listened to the October 1 tape, reported Oswald's visit, and asked CIA headquarters: Who is Lee Oswald? The CIA knew he was an American marine who had publicly defected to the Soviet Union in October 1959. It had in its files a collection of FBI and State Department reports detailing Oswald's attempts to renounce his American citizenship, his threats to tell the Soviets about secret American military installations in the Pacific, his marriage to a Russian woman, and his repatriation in June 1962.

During Oswald's stay in the Soviet Union, "CIA had no sources in a position to report on his activities or what the KGB might be doing with him," Whitten wrote in an internal report. But "it was suspected that Oswald and all other similar defectors were in the hands of the KGB. We were sure that all such defectors would be interrogated by the KGB, surrounded by KGB informants wherever they were resettled in the Soviet Union, and even possibly recruited by the KGB for a mission abroad later on."

Whitten realized that the man who had shot the president could be a communist agent. He picked up the telephone and asked Helms to order an immediate review of all the Envoy tapes and transcripts in Mexico City. The CIA chief of station, Win Scott, quickly called the president of Mexico, whose secret police worked all night with the CIA's eavesdroppers to listen for traces of Oswald's voice.

Word of the Oswald file spread as McCone returned to CIA headquarters. Six hours of hectic conferences ensued, the last one convening at 11:30 p.m. When McCone learned that the CIA had known beforehand of Oswald's trip to the Soviet embassy in Mexico City, he was enraged, ripping into his aides, furious at the way the agency was run.

The CIA's internal investigation took shape on Saturday morning, November 23. Helms met with the agency's barons, including James Angleton, chief of counterintelligence since 1954. Angleton fully expected to be handed the Oswald case. To his outrage, Helms put John Whitten in charge.

Whitten was a man who knew how to unravel a conspiracy. A skilled prisoner-of-war interrogator in World War II, he had joined the CIA in 1947. He was the first to employ the polygraph at the agency. In the early 1950s, he used the lie detector in hundreds of investigations of double agents, false defectors, and intelligence fabricators in Germany. He had uncovered some of the biggest hoaxes perpetrated on the agency, including the work of a con artist who sold the Vienna station a fake Soviet communications codebook. Another of the cases he cracked involved an agent Angleton had been running in Italy, a man whom Angleton launched against five different foreign intelligence services. The agent proved to be a fraud and a pathological liar; he had blithely disclosed to all five foreign services that he worked for the CIA, and he had been promptly doubled back to penetrate the agency by all five. This was not the only Angleton operation Whitten had exposed. In each case, Helms told Whitten to go into Angleton's dark and smoky office and confront him.

"I used to go in fingering my insurance policy, notifying my next of kin," Whitten said. The confrontations created "bitter feelings, the most bitter feelings" between the two men. From the moment Whitten was assigned the Oswald case, Angleton set out to sabotage him.

By midmorning on November 23, CIA headquarters knew that Oswald had visited both the Cuban and the Soviet embassies repeatedly in late September and October, trying to travel as quickly as possible to Cuba and stay there until his Soviet visa came through. "His having been to the Cuban and Soviet embassies in Mexico City obviously was a very important part of the initial impressions one had," Helms said. Shortly after noon, McCone rushed back downtown and broke the news of the Cuban connection to President Johnson, interrupting a long talk between LBJ and Dwight Eisenhower, who was warning him about the power that Robert Kennedy wielded over covert operations.

At 1:35 p.m., President Johnson called an old friend, a Wall Street power broker named Edwin Weisl, and confided: "This thing on the . . . this assassin . . . may have a lot more complications than you know about . . . it may lay deeper than you think." That afternoon, the U.S. ambassador in Mexico, Tom Mann, a Texan and a close LBJ confidant, relayed his own suspicion that Castro was behind the assassination.

On Sunday morning, November 24, McCone returned to the White House, where the funeral cortege that would take John Kennedy's casket to lie in state at the Capitol was assembling. McCone informed

Lyndon Johnson more fully about some of the CIA's operations to overthrow the government of Cuba. But Johnson still had no idea that the
United States had been trying to kill Castro for the better part of three
years. Very few people knew. One was Allen Dulles. Another was
Richard Helms. A third was Bobby Kennedy. A fourth was very likely Fidel Castro.

That same day, the CIA station in Mexico City determined without
question that Oswald had made his pleas for a visa to Soviet intelligence
officers on September 28. He had talked face-to-face with a man named
Valery Kostikov, who was thought to be a member of Department 13 of
the KGB—the department responsible for assassination.

The station sent headquarters a list of all the foreigners it suspected
had made contact with Soviet intelligence officers in Mexico City. One
of them was Rolando Cubela, the CIA's Cuban agent in the final plot to
kill Castro. Only two days before, at the hour of President Kennedy's
death, Cubela's CIA case officer, Nestor Sanchez, had given the Cuban a
pen rigged as a hypodermic syringe, filled with poison. The report from
the Mexico City station raised a harrowing question: was Cubela a double agent for Fidel?

The cortege to the Capitol was about to leave the White House when
Lee Harvey Oswald was murdered on live television in the Dallas police
station. The president ordered the CIA to give him everything it had on
Oswald, immediately. Whitten pulled together a summary and gave it to
Helms, who handed it over to the president a few hours later. The report
itself has been lost or destroyed. Its gist, Whitten said, was that the CIA
had no hard evidence that Oswald was an agent of Moscow or Havana—
but he might be.

"WE WERE TREADING VERY LIGHTLY"

John McCone delivered a formal intelligence briefing to the new president of the United States on Tuesday, November 26. "The President
noted with some considerable contempt the fact that certain people in
the Department of Justice had suggested to him on Saturday that an independent investigation of the President's assassination should be con-

ducted," McCone wrote in his daily memo for the record. "President Johnson rejected this idea."

Seventy-two hours later, against his instincts, Johnson reversed himself. On November 29, the day after Thanksgiving, he cajoled the reluctant chief justice of the Supreme Court, Earl Warren, to lead the investigation. He corralled the rest of the members of the Warren Commission in a furious five-hour round of telephone calls. Taking Bobby Kennedy's recommendation, the president rang an astonished and befuddled Allen Dulles at home. "You've considered the effect of my previous work and my previous job?" Dulles asked. LBJ hastily assured him he had, and hung up. Dulles immediately called James Angleton.

It was already dark outside, and the president was rushing to assemble the commission before the evening's newspaper deadlines. He ran down the list of the chosen. Discretion was the key, the president said: "We can't just have House and Senate and FBI and other people going around testifyin' that Khrushchev killed Kennedy, or Castro killed him." He impressed upon Representative Gerald R. Ford that he wanted men who knew how the CIA worked. His most important call came just before 9 p.m. Johnson's beloved mentor, the man who most closely watched the CIA in Congress, Senator Richard Russell, was on the line from Winder, Georgia. Though LBJ already had given his name to the wire services as a member of the Warren Commission, Russell tried to turn the president down.

"You're *goddamned sure gonna serve,* I'll tell you *that,*" the president yelled. "You're gonna lend your name to this thing because you're head of the CIA committee." Johnson repeated that there could be no loose talk about Khrushchev's killing Kennedy.

"Well, I don't think he did di-*rectly,*" Senator Russell said, but "I wouldn't be surprised if Castro had something to do with it."

The creation of the Warren Commission posed a crushing moral dilemma for Richard Helms. "Helms realized that disclosing the assassination plots would reflect very poorly on the Agency and reflect very poorly on him, and that it might indeed turn out that the Cubans had undertaken this assassination in retaliation for our operations to assassinate Castro. This would have a disastrous effect on him and the Agency," John Whitten testified.

Helms knew it all too well. "We were treading very lightly," he said in top secret testimony fifteen years later. "We were very concerned at the time as to what we might come up with. . . . Accusing a foreign government of having been responsible for this act is tearing the veil about as nastily as one can."

The question of disclosure of the plots against Castro also created an impossible burden for Bobby Kennedy. He kept his silence.

The president had ordered the FBI to investigate the killing of the president, commanded the CIA to cooperate fully, and told them to report their findings to the Warren Commission, which depended on them for the facts in the case. But their malfeasance was profound.

By early 1962, the CIA, the FBI, the Pentagon, the State Department, and the Immigration and Naturalization Service all had files on Oswald. In August 1963, in New Orleans, Oswald had a series of confrontations with members of the Cuban Student Directorate, a CIA-financed anti-Castro group, whose members reported to their case officer that they suspected Oswald was trying to infiltrate their ranks. By October 1963, the FBI knew him as a possibly deranged Marxist who supported the Cuban revolution, who was capable of violence, and who had been in recent contact with Soviet intelligence officers. On October 30, the bureau learned he was working at the Texas School Book Depository in Dallas.

In short, an angry defector who admired Castro, whom the CIA had reason to believe might be a recruited communist agent, who was urgently seeking to return to Moscow via Havana, was staking out the route of the president's motorcade in Dallas.

The CIA and the FBI never compared notes. The FBI never came close to tracking him down. This was a prelude to their performance in the weeks before September 11, 2001. It was "gross incompetency," J. Edgar Hoover declared in a December 10, 1963, memo that stayed secret until the turn of the century.

Cartha DeLoach, the assistant FBI director, urged Hoover not to discipline his agents for dereliction, for fear it would be seen as "a direct admission that we are responsible for negligence which might have resulted in the assassination of the President." Hoover nonetheless punished seventeen of his men. "We failed in carrying through some of the salient aspects of the Oswald investigation," Hoover wrote in October 1964. "It ought to be a lesson to us all, but I doubt if some even realize it now."

The members of the Warren Commission knew none of this. As John

Whitten soon learned, the CIA also concealed much of what it knew to be true from the commission.

Whitten had a terrible time sorting out the facts from an avalanche of falsehoods cascading in from the CIA's overseas stations. "Dozens of people were claiming that they had seen Oswald here, there, and everywhere in all kinds of conspiratorial circumstances, from the North Pole to the Congo," he remembered. Thousands of false leads propelled the CIA into a labyrinth. To sort out the facts of the case, Whitten had to depend on the FBI to share information with him. It took two weeks before he was allowed to read the FBI's preliminary investigative report on Oswald in December 1963. "For the first time," he testified years later, "I learned a myriad of vital facts about Oswald's background which apparently the FBI had known throughout the investigation and had not communicated to me."

The FBI routinely failed to share information with the CIA. But the president had ordered them to cooperate. The one man responsible for the CIA's liaison with the FBI was Jim Angleton, and "Angleton never told me of his talks with the FBI or of FBI information he gained in those meetings," Whitten said. Unable to influence the initial course of the investigation, Angleton had sandbagged Whitten, denounced his work, and doomed his efforts to uncover the facts of the case.

Helms and Angleton agreed to tell the Warren Commission and the CIA's own investigators nothing about the plots to kill Castro. That was "a morally reprehensible act," Whitten testified fifteen years later. "Helms withheld the information because it would have cost him his job." The knowledge would have been "an absolutely vital factor in analyzing the events surrounding the Kennedy assassination," Whitten said. Had he known, "our investigation of the Kennedy assassination would have looked much different than it did."

Angleton's clandestine conversations with Allen Dulles controlled the flow of information from the CIA. The decisions he and Helms made may have shaped the Warren Commission's conclusions. But Angleton testified that the commission could never have interpreted the significance of the Soviet and the Cuban connections the way that he and his small staff did.

"We would have seen it more sharply," he said. "We were more intensely engaged. . . . We had more experience in terms of Department

13 and the whole history of 30 years of Soviet sabotage and assassinations. We knew of cases and we knew of the modus operandi." He said there was no point in giving away secrets best kept in his hands.

His conduct was an obstruction of justice. He had only one defense. Angleton believed that Moscow had dispatched a double agent to cover up its role in the killing of John Kennedy.

"THE IMPLICATIONS . . . WOULD HAVE BEEN CATACLYSMIC"

His suspect was Yuri Nosenko, who had come to the United States as a KGB defector in February 1964, just as Angleton took over the CIA's investigation. Nosenko was a spoiled child of the Soviet elite: his father was the minister of shipbuilding, a member of the Central Committee of the Communist Party, buried in the Kremlin wall after he died. Yuri joined the KGB in 1953, at age twenty-five. In 1958, he worked in the KGB section that focused on American and British travelers in the Soviet Union. He transferred to the American department, spying on the U.S. embassy in 1961 and 1962, and then he became deputy chief of the tourist department.

His father's status protected him against his many stumbles, all created by his thirst for vodka, until he traveled to Geneva in June 1962 as the security officer for a Soviet delegation at an eighteen-nation conference on disarmament. He got very drunk on his first night, and he awoke to discover that a prostitute had robbed him of $900 worth of Swiss francs. The KGB's strictures on mishandling funds were severe.

Nosenko had identified—or, rather, misidentified—a member of the American diplomatic delegation named David Mark as a CIA officer, and Yuri went looking for him. Mark had arrived in Moscow five years before as the political and economic counselor at the American embassy. Though he was never a spy, he had done small favors for the CIA, and he was publicly declared persona non grata by the Soviets. It did not hurt his career; he later became an ambassador and the number-two man at the State Department's intelligence branch.

At the end of an afternoon meeting on the nuclear test ban treaty,

Mark remembered, Nosenko walked up to him and said, in Russian, "I'd like to talk to you. . . . But I don't want to talk here. I want to have lunch with you." It was an obvious pitch. Mark thought of a restaurant on the outskirts of town and made a date for the next day. "Of course, I told the CIA people about this right away, and they said, 'God, why did you pick that restaurant? That's where all the spies go.' " The American and the Russian broke bread, closely watched by two CIA officers.

Nosenko told Mark about the prostitute and the missing money. "I've got to make it up," Mark recalled him saying. "So I can give you some information that will be very interesting to the CIA, and all I want is my money." Mark warned him: "Now, look, you're going to commit treason." But the Russian was ready. So they arranged another meeting for the following day in Geneva. Two CIA officers rushed to the Swiss capital to lead the interrogation. One was Tennent Bagley, a Soviet division officer based in Bern, who spoke little Russian. The second was George Kisevalter, the CIA's premier Russian spy handler, who flew in from headquarters.

Nosenko arrived drunk for their first meeting. "Very drunk," he said many years later. The CIA taped him at great length, but the tape recorder malfunctioned. The record was patched together by Bagley, based on Kisevalter's memory. Much was lost in translation.

Bagley cabled headquarters on June 11, 1962, saying that Nosenko had "completely proven his bona fides," had "provided information of importance," and was completely cooperative. But over the next eighteen months, Angleton convinced Bagley that he had been duped; once Nosenko's staunchest supporter, Bagley became his angriest antagonist.

Nosenko had agreed to spy for the CIA in Moscow. He returned to Geneva with the Soviet disarmament delegation and met his CIA handlers at the end of January 1964. On February 3, the day the Warren Commission heard its first witness, he told the Americans that he wanted to defect immediately. Nosenko said he had handled the KGB's Oswald file, and nothing in it implicated the Soviet Union in the Kennedy assassination.

Angleton was certain that he was lying. This judgment had catastrophic consequences.

Nosenko produced a flood of secrets. But Angleton had already determined that he was part of a Soviet master plot. He believed that the KGB long ago had penetrated the CIA at a very high level. What else could explain the long litany of blown operations in Albania and Ukraine, Poland and Korea, Cuba and Vietnam? Perhaps all of the CIA's operations against the Soviets were known to Moscow. Perhaps they were controlled by Moscow. Perhaps Nosenko had been sent to protect the mole inside the CIA. The one and only defector Angleton ever embraced—Anatoly Golitsin, certified by CIA psychiatrists as clinically paranoid—confirmed and strengthened Angleton's deepest fears.

Angleton's highest duty as chief of counterintelligence was to protect the CIA and its agents against its enemies. But a great deal had gone wrong on his watch. In 1959, Major Pyotr Popov, the CIA's first spy of any note inside the Soviet Union, had been arrested and executed by the KGB. George Blake, the British spy for Moscow who blew the Berlin Tunnel before it was dug, had been exposed in the spring of 1961, forcing the CIA to consider that the tunnel had been used for Soviet disinformation. Six months later, Heinz Felfe, Angleton's West German counterpart, was exposed as a Soviet spy after inflicting deep damage on the CIA's operations in Germany and Eastern Europe. A year after that, the Soviets arrested Colonel Oleg Penkovsky, secret hero of the Cuban missile crisis. They executed him in the spring of 1962.

Then there was Kim Philby. In January 1963, Angleton's prime tutor in counterintelligence, his old confidant, his drinking partner, fled to Moscow. He was revealed at last as a Soviet spy who had served at the highest levels of British intelligence. Philby had been a suspect for twelve years. Back when he first fell under suspicion, Walter Bedell Smith had demanded reports from everyone having had contact with the man. Bill Harvey stated categorically that Philby was a Soviet agent. Jim Angleton stated categorically that he was not.

In the spring of 1964, after years of crushing failures, Angleton sought redemption. He believed that if the CIA could break Nosenko, the master plot might be revealed—and the Kennedy assassination solved.

Helms framed the problem in congressional testimony declassified in 1998:

> MR. HELMS: If the information that Nosenko had provided
> about Oswald was true, then it led to a certain conclusion
> about Oswald and his relationship to the Soviet authorities. If it
> was incorrect, if he was feeding this to the United States gov-
> ernment under instructions from the Soviet service, then it

would have led one to an entirely different conclusion. . . . If it were established beyond any doubt that he had been lying and, by implication, therefore, Oswald was an agent of the KGB, I would have thought that the implications of that—not for the CIA or for the FBI, but for the President of the United States and the Congress of the United States would have been cataclysmic.

QUESTION: Can you be more specific?

MR. HELMS: Yes, I can be specific. In other words, the Soviet government ordered President Kennedy assassinated.

Those were the stakes. In April 1964, with the approval of Attorney General Robert F. Kennedy, the CIA threw Nosenko into solitary confinement, first in a CIA safe house, and then at Camp Peary, the CIA's training site outside Williamsburg, Virginia. In the custody of the Soviet division, Nosenko received the treatment his fellow Russians received in the gulag. There were scanty meals of weak tea and gruel, a single bare light burning twenty-four hours a day, no human companionship. "I did not have enough to eat and was hungry all the time," Nosenko said in a statement declassified in 2001. "I had no contact with anyone to talk. I could not read. I could not smoke. I even could not have fresh air."

His testimony was remarkably similar to that of prisoners taken by the CIA after September 2001: "I was taken by guards, blindfolded and handcuffed in a car and delivered to an airport and put on a plane," he said. "I was taken to another location where I was put into a concrete room with bars on the door. In the room there was a single steel bed with a mattress." Nosenko was subjected to psychological intimidation and physical hardship for three more years. An audiotape of a hostile interrogation conducted by Tennent Bagley in the CIA's prison cell was preserved in the agency's files. Nosenko's low basso pleads in Russian: "From my soul . . . from my soul . . . I beg you to believe me." Bagley's high-pitched voice screams back in English, "That's bullshit! That's bullshit! That's bullshit!" For his work, Bagley was promoted to deputy chief of the Soviet division and awarded the Distinguished Intelligence Medal by Richard Helms.

In the late summer of 1964, the task of telling the Warren Commission about Yuri Nosenko fell to Helms. It was an excruciatingly delicate matter. Days before the commission concluded its work, Helms told the chief justice that the CIA could not accept Moscow's protestations of innocence in the assassination of the president. Earl Warren was not pleased by this last-minute development. The commission's final report never mentioned Nosenko's existence.

Helms himself came to fear the consequences of Nosenko's incarceration. "I recognized we couldn't keep him in durance vile, as we had, against the laws of the United States," he said. "Lord knows what would happen if we had a comparable situation today, because the laws haven't been changed, and I don't know what you do with people like Nosenko. We sought guidance from the Justice Department at the time. It was clear that we were holding him in violation of the law, but what were we to do with him? Were we going to release him and then a year later have it said, 'Well, you fellows should have had more sense than to do that. He was the whole key to who killed President Kennedy.' "

The CIA sent another team of interrogators to question Nosenko. They determined that he had been telling the truth. He was finally freed five years after his defection, paid $80,000, given a new identity, and placed on the CIA's payroll.

But Angleton and his circle never closed the case. Their search for the traitor within the CIA ripped the Soviet division apart. The mole hunt began by pursuing officers with Slavic surnames. It went up the chain of command to the Soviet division chief. It paralyzed the CIA's Russian operations for a decade, into the 1970s.

For twenty-five years after Nosenko's defection, the CIA struggled to write the last chapter of his story. In all, it conducted seven major studies of the case. Nosenko was convicted, exonerated, and re-indicted until a last judgment was levied by the CIA's Rich Heuer at the end of the cold war. Heuer had started out as a firm believer in the master plot. But then he weighed the value of what Nosenko had given the United States. The Russian spy had identified, or produced investigative leads on, some 200 foreigners and 238 Americans in whom the KGB had displayed interest. He had fingered some 300 Soviet intelligence agents and overseas contacts, and roughly 2,000 KGB officers. He had pinpointed fifty-two hidden microphones that the Soviets had placed in the American embassy in Moscow. He had expanded the CIA's knowledge of how the Soviets sought to blackmail foreign diplomats and journalists. To believe in the master plot, it was necessary to take four things on faith: First, that Moscow would trade all that information to protect one mole. Second, that all communist defectors were agents of deception. Third, that the immense Soviet intelligence apparatus existed solely to mislead the United States. And last, that an impenetrable communist conspiracy lay behind the Kennedy assassination.

For Richard Helms, the case remained an open book. Until the day that the Soviet and Cuban intelligence services turned over their files, he said, it would never be laid to rest. Either the killing of John Kennedy was the work of a deranged drifter with a cheap rifle and a seven-dollar scope, or the truth was more terrible. As Lyndon Johnson said toward the end of his presidency: "Kennedy was trying to get to Castro, but Castro got to him first."

22. "AN OMINOUS DRIFT"

The covert operations of the Kennedys haunted Lyndon Johnson all his life. He said over and over that Dallas was divine retribution for Diem. "We all got together and got a goddamn bunch of thugs and we went in and assassinated him," he lamented. In his first year in office, coup after coup wracked Saigon, a shadowy insurgency started killing Americans in Vietnam, and his fear that the CIA was an instrument of political murder festered and grew.

He now understood that Bobby Kennedy wielded great authority over covert operations. He saw him as a sworn rival for the presidency. At an Oval Office meeting with John McCone on December 13, 1963, Johnson asked bluntly if and when Kennedy would leave the government. McCone said that "the Attorney General intended to stay on as Attorney General, but it was not clear to what extent the President wished him to become involved [with] intelligence work, NSC problems, counterinsurgency matters." The answer soon became clear: Bobby's days as the whip hand of the clandestine service were over. He departed seven months later.

On December 28, McCone flew down to the LBJ Ranch in Texas for breakfast and a briefing after a trip to Saigon. "The President immediately brought up his desire to 'change the image of the CIA' from a cloak and dagger role," McCone recorded. The director could not have agreed more. The agency's only legal role was to gather, analyze, and report intelligence, McCone said, not to mount conspiracies to overthrow foreign states. Johnson said "he was tired of a situation that had been built up that every time my name or CIA's name was mentioned, it was associated with a dirty trick."

But Lyndon Johnson lay awake at night, trying to decide whether to go all-out in Vietnam or get out. Without American support, Saigon would fall. He did not want to plunge in with thousands of American troops. He could not be seen to pull out. The only path between war and diplomacy was covert action.

"NOBODY CAN RUN THE INTELLIGENCE BUSINESS"

In early 1964, McCone and his new Saigon station chief, Peer de Silva, had nothing but bad news for the president. McCone was "extremely worried about the situation." He thought that the intelligence data "on which we gauged the trend of the war were grossly in error." He warned the White House and the Congress that "the Viet Cong are receiving substantial support from North Vietnam and possibly elsewhere, and this support can be increased. Stopping this by sealing the borders, the extensive waterways, and the long coastline is difficult, if not impossible. The VC appeal to the people of South Vietnam on political grounds has been effective, gained recruits for their armed forces, and neutralized resistance."

Project Tiger, the Saigon station's two-year paramilitary program against North Vietnam, had ended in death and betrayal. Now the Pentagon proposed to begin again, in concert with the CIA. Its Operations Plan 34A was a yearlong series of covert raids intended to convince Hanoi to give up its insurgency in South Vietnam and Laos. The centerpiece was another set of airborne operations to drop intelligence and commando teams into North Vietnam, along with maritime assaults along the coast. The raiders would be South Vietnamese special-forces soldiers, supplemented by Nationalist Chinese and South Korean commandos, all of them trained by the CIA. McCone had no confidence that the attacks would change Ho Chi Minh's mind. "The President should be informed that this is not the greatest thing since peanut butter," he advised.

Under orders, the agency turned its network of Asian paramilitaries over to the Pentagon's Special Operations Group in Vietnam. Helms warned against "an ominous drift" that was pulling the CIA away from espionage and toward a role as a conventional military support staff. The agency's executive director, Lyman Kirkpatrick, foresaw "the fragmentation and destruction of CIA, with the clandestine service being gobbled up by the Joint Chiefs of Staff." These were prophetic fears.

In March 1964, the president sent McCone and McNamara back to Saigon. The director returned to tell the president that the war was not going well. "Mr. McNamara gave a very optimistic view that things were pretty good," McCone said in an oral history for the LBJ presidential library. "I had to take the position that as long as the Ho Chi Minh Trail was open and supplies and convoys of people could come in there without interruption, that we couldn't say things were so good."

That was the beginning of the end of John McCone's career as director of central intelligence. Lyndon Johnson closed the door to the Oval Office. Communication between the CIA and the president was limited to a twice-weekly written report on world events. The president read it at his leisure, if and when he wanted. On April 22, McCone told Bundy that he was "highly dissatisfied over the fact that President Johnson did not get direct intelligence briefings from me as was the custom with President Kennedy and had been the Eisenhower custom." A week later, McCone told LBJ that "I was not seeing very much of him, and this disturbed me." So Johnson and McCone played eight holes of golf together at the Burning Tree country club in May. But they did not have a substantial conversation until October. The president had been in office for eleven months before he asked McCone how big the CIA was, what it cost, and precisely how it could serve him. The director's advice was rarely heard and rarely heeded. Without the president's ear, he had no power, and without that power, the CIA began to drift into the dangerous middle passage of the 1960s.

McCone's split with McNamara over Vietnam revealed a deeper political fissure. Under law, the director of central intelligence was the chairman of the board of all American intelligence agencies. But the Pentagon had fought for two decades to make the director play second fiddle in the discordant band that people were now calling "the intelligence community." For six years, the president's board of intelligence advisers had suggested that the director should run the community and let a chief operating officer try to manage the CIA. Allen Dulles had adamantly re-

sisted the idea and refused to pay attention to anything but covert action. McCone kept saying he wanted to get out of the cloak-and-dagger
business. But in 1964, the CIA's clandestine service was consuming close
to two-thirds of the agency's budget and 90 percent of McCone's time.
He wanted to assert his statutory power over American intelligence. He
needed authority commensurate with his responsibility. He never received it. The Pentagon undermined him at every turn.

Three major branches of American intelligence had grown up over
the past decade. All three were under the director's titular leadership.
That power existed only on paper. The director was supposed to oversee
the National Security Agency, the increasingly gigantic global electronic-
eavesdropping arm of American intelligence. The NSA had been created
by Truman in 1952 at the urging of Walter Bedell Smith after the crushing surprises of the Korean War. But the secretary of defense was in
charge of its money and power. McNamara also controlled the new Defense Intelligence Agency, which he had created after the Bay of Pigs
with the intent of coordinating the jumble of information produced by
the army, the navy, the air force, and the marines. Then there was the
National Reconnaissance Office, born in 1962 to build spy satellites. In
the spring of 1964, air force generals tried to seize control of the billion-
dollar-a-year program from the CIA. The power grab fractured the frag-
ile reconnaissance office.

"I am just about ready to tell the Secretary of Defense and the President they can take NRO and shove it," McCone thundered. "I think the
thing I should do is call up the President and tell him to get a new Director of Central Intelligence. . . . The bureaucrats in the Pentagon are trying to screw things up so that nobody can run the intelligence business."

McCone tried to resign that summer, but Lyndon Johnson ordered
him to remain at his post until at least election day. The war in Vietnam
was now on in full, and the appearance of loyalty was utmost.

"SHOOTING AT FLYING FISH"

The war was authorized by the Gulf of Tonkin Resolution, rammed
through Congress after what the president and the Pentagon proclaimed

was an unprovoked attack by North Vietnam on American ships in international waters on August 4. The National Security Agency, which compiled and controlled the intelligence on the attack, insisted the evidence was ironclad. Robert McNamara swore to it. The navy's official history of the Vietnam War calls it conclusive.

It was not an honest mistake. The war in Vietnam began with political lies based on fake intelligence. Had the CIA been working as its charter intended, if McCone had fulfilled his duties under law as he saw them, the false reports might not have survived for more than a few hours. But the full truth did not come out until November 2005, in a highly detailed confession released by the National Security Agency.

In July 1964, the Pentagon and the CIA determined that the OPLAN 34A overland attacks begun six months before had been a series of pointless pinpricks, just as McCone had warned. The United States stepped up commando raids at sea, under the leadership of the CIA's Tucker Gougelmann, a battle-scarred marine who many years later became the last American to die in the war in Vietnam. To bolster his forces, Washington increased its surveillance on the North. The navy had started a program of eavesdropping on encoded enemy communications—the technical term is signals intelligence, or SIGINT—under an operation code-named Desoto. Those missions began inside a black box, the size of a cargo container, lashed to the deck of a destroyer off the coast of Vietnam. Inside each one were antennas and monitors operated by at least a dozen officers of the Naval Security Group. They listened in on North Vietnamese military chatter, and the data they collected was decrypted and translated by the National Security Agency.

The Joint Chiefs of Staff sent the USS *Maddox*, under the command of Captain John Herrick, on a Desoto mission with orders to "stimulate and record" North Vietnam's reactions to the commando raids. The *Maddox* had orders to stay eight nautical miles off the mainland and four knots off the coastal islands of North Vietnam in the Gulf of Tonkin. The United States did not recognize the international twelve-mile limit in Vietnam. On the last night of July and the first night of August 1964, the *Maddox* monitored an OPLAN 34A attack on Hon Me Island, off the central coast of North Vietnam in the Gulf of Tonkin. It tracked the North's counterattack, watching Soviet-made patrol boats armed with torpedoes and machines guns gathering off the island.

On the afternoon of August 2, the *Maddox* detected three of the boats

approaching. Captain Herrick sent a flash message to fellow commanders of the Seventh Fleet: he would fire on them if necessary. He requested help from the destroyer *Turner Joy* and the fighter jets of the
carrier *Ticonderoga*. Shortly after 3 p.m., the *Maddox* fired three times at
the North Vietnamese patrol boats. The shots were never reported or acknowledged by the Pentagon or the White House; they maintained that
the communists shot first. The *Maddox* was still firing when four navy
F-8E jets blasted the patrol boats, killing four sailors, heavily damaging
two of the ships, and winging the third. Their communist captains fled
and hid in coastal inlets, awaiting orders from Haiphong. The *Maddox*
had sustained one bullet hole from a machine gun.

On August 3, President Johnson proclaimed that American patrols
would continue in the Gulf of Tonkin, and the State Department announced that it had sent its first-ever diplomatic note to Hanoi, warning
of the "grave consequences" of "further unprovoked military action." At
that hour, another provocative OPLAN 34A maritime mission was dispatched to sabotage a radar station off the North Vietnamese coast, on
the island of Hon Matt.

Then, on the stormy night of August 4, the American captains of the
destroyers, the commanders of the Seventh Fleet, and their leaders in
the Pentagon all received an urgent alert from onshore SIGINT operators:
the three North Vietnamese patrol boats encountered off Hon Me Island
on August 2 were returning. In Washington, Robert McNamara called the
president. At 10 p.m. in the Gulf of Tonkin, 10 a.m. in Washington, the
American destroyers sent a flash message that they were under attack.

The radar and sonar operators aboard the *Maddox* and the *Turner Joy*
reported seeing ghostly blotches in the night. Their captains opened fire.
The NSA report declassified in 2005 described how "the two destroyers
gyrated wildly in the dark waters of the Gulf of Tonkin, the *Turner Joy*
firing over 300 rounds madly," both ships taking furious evasive maneuvers. "It was this high-speed gyrating by the American warships through
the waters that created all the additional sonar reports of more torpedoes." They had been firing at their own shadows.

The president immediately ordered an air strike against North Vietnamese naval bases to begin that night.

Within an hour, Captain Herrick reported: "ENTIRE ACTION LEAVES
MANY DOUBTS." Ninety minutes later, those doubts vanished in Washington. The NSA told the secretary of defense and the president of the

United States that it had intercepted a North Vietnamese naval communiqué reading: "SACRIFICED TWO SHIPS AND ALL THE REST ARE OKAY."

But after the American air strikes against North Vietnam had begun, the NSA reviewed the day's communications intercepts. There was nothing. Every SIGINT eavesdropper in South Vietnam and the Philippines looked again. Nothing. The NSA reexamined the intercept it had handed to the president, double-checking the translation and the time stamp on the original message.

Upon review, the message actually read: "WE SACRIFICED TWO COMRADES BUT ALL ARE BRAVE." The message had been composed either immediately before or at the moment when the *Maddox* and the *Turner Joy* opened fire on August 4. It was *not* about what had happened that night. It was about the first clash, two nights earlier, on August 2.

The NSA buried this salient fact. It told no one. Its analysts and linguists looked a third time, and a fourth time, at the time stamp. Everyone—everyone, even the doubters—decided to stay silent. The NSA's leadership put together five separate after-action reports and summaries between August 5 and August 7. Then it composed a formal chronology, the official version of the truth, the last word on what happened out in the Gulf of Tonkin, the history to be preserved for future generations of intelligence analysts and military commanders.

In the process, someone at the NSA destroyed the smoking gun—the intercept that McNamara had shown to the president. "McNamara had taken over raw SIGINT and shown the president what they thought was evidence of a second attack," said Ray Cline, then the CIA's deputy director of intelligence. "And it was just what Johnson was looking for." In a rational world, it would have been the CIA's task to take a hard look at the SIGINT from the Gulf of Tonkin and issue an independent interpretation of its meaning. It was no longer a rational world. "It was too late to make any difference," Cline said. "The planes had been launched."

As the NSA's November 2005 confession says: "The overwhelming body of reports, if used, would have told the story that no attack had happened. So a conscious effort ensued to demonstrate that the attack occurred . . . an active effort to make the SIGINT fit the claim of what happened during the evening of 4 August in the Gulf of Tonkin." The intelligence, the report concluded, "was deliberately skewed to support the notion that there had been an attack." American intelligence officers "rationalized the contradictory evidence away."

Lyndon Johnson had been ready to bomb North Vietnam for two months. On his orders, in June 1964, Bill Bundy, the assistant secretary of state for the Far East, brother of the national security adviser, and a veteran CIA analyst, had drawn up a war resolution to be sent to Congress when the moment was ripe.

The fake intelligence fit perfectly into the preconceived policy. On August 7, Congress authorized the war in Vietnam. The House voted 416–0. The Senate voted 88–2. It was a "Greek tragedy," Cline said, an act of political theater reprised four decades later when false intelligence on the Iraqi arsenal upheld another president's rationale for war.

It remained to Lyndon Johnson to sum up what really happened in the Gulf of Tonkin, which he did four years after the fact. "Hell," said the president, "those damn stupid sailors were just shooting at flying fish."

23. "MORE COURAGE THAN WISDOM"

"Vietnam was my nightmare for a good ten years," Richard Helms wrote. As he rose from chief of the clandestine service to become the director of central intelligence, the war was always with him. "Like an incubus, it involved efforts which were never to seem successful, and demands which could never be met but which were repeated, doubled, intensified, and redoubled.

"We tried every operational approach in the book, and committed our most experienced field operatives to the effort to get inside the government in Hanoi," Helms recounted. "Within the Agency, our failure to penetrate the North Vietnamese government was the single most frustrating aspect of those years. We could not determine what was going on at the highest levels of Ho's government, nor could we learn how policy was made or who was making it." At the root of this failure of intelligence was "our national ignorance of Vietnamese history, society, and language," he said.

We did not choose to know, so we did not know how much we did not know.

"The great sadness," Helms said in an oral history recorded for the LBJ Library, "was our ignorance—or innocence, if you like—which led us to mis-assess, not comprehend, and make a lot of wrong decisions."

Lyndon Johnson also had a recurring dream about Vietnam. If he ever wavered on the war, if he faltered, if he lost, "there would be Robert Kennedy out in front leading the fight against me, telling everyone that I had betrayed John Kennedy's commitment to South Vietnam. That I was a coward. An unmanly man. A man without a spine. Oh, I could see it coming, all right. Every night when I fell asleep I would see myself tied to the ground in the middle of a long, open space. In the distance I could hear the voices of thousands of people. They were all shouting and running toward me: 'Coward! Traitor! Weakling!' "

"McCONE'S WAR"

The strength of the Vietcong, the communist guerrillas in the south, continued to grow. A new ambassador, General Maxwell Taylor, late of the Special Group (Counterinsurgency), and Bill Colby, the CIA's Far East division chief, searched for a new strategy against the shadowy terrorists. "Counterinsurgency became an almost ridiculous battle cry," said Robert Amory, who had stepped down after nine years as the CIA's deputy director of intelligence to become the White House budget officer for classified programs. "It meant so many things to so many different people." But Bobby Kennedy knew its meaning, and he boiled it down to its essence. "What we needed," he said, "were people who could shoot guns."

On November 16, 1964, an explosive work by Peer de Silva, the CIA's station chief in Saigon, landed on John McCone's desk at headquarters. It was titled "Our Counterinsurgency Experiment and Its Implications." Helms and Colby had read it and approved it. It was a bold idea with one great risk: the potential "to turn 'McNamara's War' into 'McCone's War,' " as Deputy Director of Central Intelligence Marshall Carter bluntly warned his boss that day.

De Silva had been trying to extend the CIA's power in South Vietnam by creating paramilitary patrols in the provinces to hunt down the Vietcong. Working with the interior minister and the chief of the national police, de Silva bought an estate in the northeast corner of South Vietnam from a crooked labor-union kingpin and began offering a crash course in counterinsurgency for civilians. In the first week of November 1964, as Americans were electing President Johnson to a full term, de Silva had flown up to inspect his fledgling project. His officers had trained three teams of forty Vietnamese recruits who had reported killing 167 Vietcong while losing only 6 of their own. Now de Silva wanted to fly five thousand South Vietnamese citizens up to the estate from all over the country for a three-month education in military and political tactics taught by CIA officers and American military advisers. They would return home, in de Silva's words, as "counter-terror teams," and they would kill the Vietcong.

John McCone had a lot of faith in Peer de Silva, and he gave his approval. But he felt it was a losing battle. The day after de Silva's memo arrived, McCone walked into the White House and for the second time tendered his resignation to President Johnson. He offered a choice of qualified successors and begged to take his leave. Once again, not for the last time, the president ignored the director of central intelligence.

McCone stayed on while the crises confronting him piled up. He believed, as did the presidents he served, in the domino theory. He told the future president, Representative Gerald R. Ford, that "if South Vietnam fell to the communists, Laos and Cambodia would certainly go, followed by Thailand, Indonesia, Malaysia, and eventually the Philippines," which would have "a vast effect" on the Middle East, Africa, and Latin America. He did not think the CIA was equipped to fight insurgents and terrorists, and he feared that "the VC may be the wave of the future." He was quite certain that the CIA was incapable of combating the Vietcong.

De Silva later mourned the agency's "blindness" to the enemy and its strategy. In the villages, "the Vietcong use of terror was purposeful, precise, and frightful to behold," he wrote. The peasants "would feed them, recruit for them, conceal them, and provide them with all the intelligence the Vietcong needed." Then, at the end of 1964, the VC took the war to the capital. "The Vietcong use of terror within the city of Saigon was frequent, sometimes random, and sometimes carefully planned and executed," de Silva wrote. Secretary of Defense McNamara just missed being hit by a roadside bomb planted on the highway to the city from the airport. A car bomb destroyed the bachelor officers' quarters in Saigon on Christmas Eve 1964. Slowly the losses mounted as suicide bombers and sappers struck at will. At 2 a.m. on February 7, 1965, the Vietcong attacked an American base in Pleiku, the central highlands of Vietnam. Eight Americans died. When the firefight was over, the Americans searched the body of one of the Vietcong attackers and found a very precise map of the base in his pack.

We had more weapons, and bigger ones, but they had more spies, and better ones. It was a decisive difference.

Four days later, Lyndon Johnson lashed out. Dumb bombs, cluster bombs, and napalm bombs fell on Vietnam. The White House sent an urgent message to Saigon seeking the CIA's best estimate of the situation. George W. Allen, the most experienced Vietnam intelligence analyst at the Saigon station, said the enemy would not be deterred by bombs. It was growing stronger. Its will was unbroken. But Ambassador Maxwell Taylor went over the report line by line, methodically deleting each pessimistic paragraph before sending it on to the president. The CIA's men in Saigon took note that bad news was not welcome. The corruption of intelligence at the hands of political generals, civilian commanders, and the agency itself continued. There would not be a truly influential report from the CIA to the president on the subject of the war for three more years.

On March 8, the marines landed in Da Nang in full battle dress. Beautiful girls met them with garlands. In Hanoi, Ho Chi Minh prepared his own reception.

On March 30, Peer de Silva was in his second-floor office in the CIA station in Saigon, catercorner to the embassy, talking on the telephone with one of his officers and staring out the window at a man pushing an old gray Peugeot sedan up the street. De Silva looked down at the driver's seat and saw a detonator burning.

"My world turned to glue and slow motion as my mind told me this car was a bomb," de Silva remembered. "With the phone still in my hand and without conscious thought, I began falling away from the window and turned as I fell, but I was only halfway to the floor when the car exploded." Flying glass and shards of metal slashed de Silva's eyes and ears and throat. The blast killed at least twenty people in the street and de Silva's twenty-two-year-old secretary. Two CIA officers inside the station were permanently blinded. Sixty other CIA and embassy personnel were injured. George Allen suffered multiple contusions, cuts, and a concussion. De Silva lost the vision in his left eye. Doctors pumped him full of painkillers, swaddled his head in gauze, and told him he might go completely blind if he stayed on in Saigon.

The president wondered how to fight an enemy he could not see. "There must be somebody out there that's got enough brains to figure

out *some* way that we can find some special targets to hit on," Johnson
demanded as night fell in Saigon. He decided to pour thousands more
troops into battle and ratchet up the bombing campaign. He never once
consulted the director of central intelligence.

"A MILITARY EFFORT THAT WE CANNOT WIN"

On April 2, 1965, John McCone quit for the last time, effective as soon
as Lyndon Johnson selected a successor. He delivered a fateful prediction
for the president: "With the passage of each day and each week, we can
expect increasing pressure to stop the bombing," he said. "This will come
from various elements of the American public, from the press, the
United Nations and world opinion. Therefore time will run against us in
this operation and I think the North Vietnamese are counting on this."
One of his best analysts, Harold Ford, told him: "We are becoming pro-
gressively divorced from reality in Vietnam" and "proceeding with far
more courage than wisdom." McCone now understood that. He told Mc-
Namara that the nation was about to "drift into a combat situation
where victory would be dubious." His final warning to the President was
blunt as it could be: "We will find ourselves mired down in combat in the
jungle in a military effort that we cannot win, and from which we will
have extreme difficulty extracting ourselves."

Lyndon Johnson had stopped listening to John McCone long ago. The
director left office knowing he had had no impact whatsoever on the
thinking of the president of the United States. Like almost all who followed him, LBJ liked the agency's work only if it fit his thinking. When
it did not, it went into the wastebasket. "Let me tell you about these intelligence guys," he said. "When I was growing up in Texas, we had a
cow named Bessie. I'd go out early and milk her. I'd get her in the stan-
chion, seat myself, and squeeze out a pail of fresh milk. One day I'd
worked hard and gotten a full pail of milk, but I wasn't paying attention,
and old Bessie swung her shit-smeared tail through that bucket of milk.
Now, you know, that's what these intelligence guys do. You work hard
and get a good program or policy going, and they swing a shit-smeared
tail through it."

24. "THE BEGINNING OF A LONG SLIDE DOWNWARDS"

The president went looking for "a great man" to serve as the new director of central intelligence—"one that can light the fuse if it's just got to be done to save his country."

Deputy Director of Central Intelligence Marshall Carter warned against choosing an outsider. He said it would be "a grave error" to select a military yes-man and "a disaster" to choose a political crony; if the White House thought the CIA had no one from within who was worthy, "they had better close up the place and give it to the Indians." Richard Helms was the near-unanimous choice among the president's national-security team—McCone, McNamara, Rusk, and Bundy.

Johnson heeded none of them. On the afternoon of April 6, 1965, he placed a call to a fifty-nine-year-old retired admiral named Red Raborn, a native son of Decatur, Texas. Raborn had political credentials: he had won LBJ's affection by appearing in a paid television announcement during the 1964 campaign, calling the Republican candidate, Senator Barry Goldwater of Arizona, too dumb to be president. His claim to fame was managing the development of the Polaris nuclear missile for the navy's submarines, an effort that won him friends in Congress. He was a nice man with a nice job in the aerospace industry and a nice spread in Palm Springs overlooking the eleventh fairway of his favorite golf course.

Red Raborn stood at attention at the sound of his commander in chief's voice. "Now, I need you," Lyndon Johnson said, "and need you awful bad awful quick." They were quite a ways into their conversation before Raborn realized that LBJ wanted him to run the CIA. The president promised that Richard Helms, as the new deputy director, would do the heavy lifting. "You could take you a nap every day after lunch," he said. "We won't overwork you." Appealing to Raborn's patriotism, laying on the down-home charm, Johnson said: "I know what the old warhorse does when he hear the bell ring."

The admiral came aboard on April 28, 1965. The president put on a big show for his swearing-in at the White House, saying he had searched the nation far and wide and found only one man who could do the job. Tears of gratitude ran down Raborn's face. It was his last happy moment as director of central intelligence.

The Dominican Republic exploded that same day. The United States had tried and failed to make the nation the showplace of the Caribbean after the American-supported assassination of the dictator Rafael Trujillo in 1961. Now armed rebels were fighting in the streets of the capital. Johnson decided to send in four hundred U.S. Marines, along with the FBI and reinforcements for the CIA station. It was the first large-scale landing of American forces in Latin America since 1928, and the first armed adventure of its kind in the Caribbean since the Bay of Pigs.

At a full-dress White House meeting that night, Raborn reported—without evidence, and without qualification—that the rebels were controlled by Cuba. "In my opinion this is a real struggle mounted by Mr. Castro," Raborn said the next morning in a phone conversation with the president. "There is no question in my mind that this is the start of Castro's expansion."

The president asked: "How many Castro terrorists are there?"

Raborn replied: "Well, we have positively identified 8 of them. And I sent a list over to the White House about 6 o'clock—it should be in the Situation Room—who they are, what they are doing and what their training has been." The list of the eight "Castro terrorists" appeared in a CIA memorandum, which read: "There is no evidence that the Castro regime is directly involved in the current insurrection."

The president hung up the phone and decided to send a thousand more marines to the Dominican Republic.

Had there been any warning of the crisis from the CIA? the president asked his national security adviser that morning. "There was nothing," Bundy replied.

"Our CIA says this is a completely led . . . Castro operation," the president told his personal lawyer, Abe Fortas, as 2,500 army paratroopers landed in the Dominican Republic on April 30. "They *say* it is! Their people on the inside *tell* us! . . . There ain't no doubt about this being Castro now. . . . They are moving other places in the hemisphere. It may be part of a whole Communistic pattern tied in with Vietnam. . . . The worst domestic political disaster we could suffer would be for Castro to take over." The president prepared to send 6,500 more American soldiers to Santo Domingo.

But McNamara mistrusted what Raborn was telling the president. "You don't think CIA can document it?" Johnson asked the secretary of defense. "I don't think so, Mr. President," McNamara replied. "You don't know that Castro is trying to do anything. You would have a hard time proving to any group that Castro has done more than train these people, and we have trained a lot of people."

That gave the president pause. "Well, now, don't you think that's something that you and Raborn and I ought to talk about?" the president said. "CIA told me that there were two Castro leaders involved. And a little later, they told me eight, and a little later, they told me fifty-eight. . . ."

"I just don't believe the story," MacNamara said flatly.

The president nonetheless insisted in a speech to the American people that he would not allow "Communist conspirators" in the Dominican Republic to establish "another Communist government in the Western Hemisphere."

Raborn's reporting on the crisis did for LBJ what the U-2 had done for Eisenhower and the Bay of Pigs for Kennedy. It led directly to the first assertion by the American press that Lyndon Johnson had a "credibility gap." The phrase was first published on May 23, 1965. It stung, and it stuck.

The president took no further counsel from his new director of central intelligence.

Morale plunged at headquarters under Raborn's unsteady command. "It was tragic," said Ray Cline, the deputy director of intelligence, "the beginning of a long slide downwards." The bitter joke was that Dulles had run a happy ship, McCone a tight ship, and Raborn a sinking ship. "Poor old Raborn," said Red White, his third-in-command as executive director. "He came out there every morning at 6:30 and had breakfast thinking the President would call him someday." Johnson never did. It was painfully clear that Raborn was "not qualified to run the CIA," White said. The hapless admiral was "completely out in left field. If you talked about foreign countries, he wouldn't know if you were talking about a country in Africa or South America." The new director made a fool of himself while testifying in secret to Congress, Senator Richard Russell warned LBJ: "Raborn has got one failing that's going to get him in trouble. He won't ever admit he don't know. . . . If you ever decide to get rid of him, you just put that fellow Helms in there. He got more sense than any of them."

Richard Helms ran the CIA while Raborn fumbled and flailed. He had three major covert-action campaigns to fight that year. Each one had been started by President Eisenhower, then strengthened by President Kennedy, and now was central to LBJ's quest to win the war in Southeast Asia. In Laos, the CIA fought to cut the Ho Chi Minh Trail. In Thailand, it set out to fix the elections. In Indonesia, it provided secret support for leaders who massacred countless communists. All three nations were dominoes to the presidents who ordered the CIA to keep them in line, fearing that if one fell, Vietnam would fall.

On July 2, LBJ called Eisenhower for advice on escalating the war. The American death toll in Vietnam stood at 446. The ninth junta since the assassination of President Diem had just seized power, led by Nguyen Cao Ky, a pilot who had dropped paramilitary agents to their death on CIA missions, and by Nguyen Van Thieu, a general who later assumed the presidency. Ky was vicious, Thieu corrupt. Together they were the public face of democracy in South Vietnam. "You think that we can really beat the Vietcong out there?" the president asked. Victory depended entirely on good intelligence, Eisenhower replied, and "this is the hardest thing."

"A SACRED WAR"

Laos started out as an intelligence war. Under accords signed by the superpowers and their allies, all foreign fighters were supposed to leave the country. The newly arrived American ambassador, William Sullivan, had helped negotiate the accords himself. But Hanoi kept thousands of troops in the north, bolstering the communist forces, the Pathet Lao, and the CIA had its spies and shadow soldiers everywhere else in Laos. Station chiefs and their officers had orders to fight a war in secret, defying diplomatic niceties and the military facts on the ground.

In the summer of 1965, as Lyndon Johnson sent tens of thousands of American troops to Vietnam, the war in Laos was being run by about thirty CIA officers. Backed by military supplies flown in by agency pilots, they armed the Hmong tribesmen who served as guerrilla fighters, traveled to the edges of the Ho Chi Minh Trail, and oversaw Thai commandos trained by the CIA's Bill Lair.

Lair ran the war in Laos from a secret compound inside a base at Udorn, built by the CIA and the Pentagon, just across the Mekong River in Thailand. He was forty, and he had been working for the CIA in Southeast Asia for fourteen years. His forebears had lived in Texas since the Alamo, but he was married to a Thai woman, ate sticky rice with hot peppers, and drank Hmong firewater. When things went wrong in Laos, he locked the facts in his safe. When his fellow CIA officers died in battle, he kept their fates classified. The war was supposed to be "as invisible as possible," Lair said. "The idea then was to keep that secret because at the time we went in there, we didn't have no idea in the long range what the U.S. was going to do. . . . Once they got started on this tactic of keeping it secret, it's pretty hard to change it."

The CIA officer who fought hardest in Laos was Anthony Poshepny, known to all as Tony Poe. In 1965, he, too, was forty years old. Wounded in battle as a teenage marine at Iwo Jima, a veteran of the CIA's paramilitary missions in the Korean War, he was one of the five CIA officers who fled the island of Sumatra by submarine in 1958 as the coup in Indonesia collapsed. Poe lived at the CIA's base in the Long Tieng valley of central Laos, close to a hundred miles north of the capital. With a bottle of Scotch or Hmong rice whisky his constant companion, Tony Poe was the field commander of the secret war, walking point on the highland trails and valley paths with his Hmong and Thai troops. He had gone completely native and more than a little crazy.

"He did all these damn bizarre things," Lair said. "I knew if you shipped Tony home he wouldn't last five minutes in the hallways back there. He'd be out of the Agency. But, within the Agency you had a lot of those guys who admired him because they never were close to it, see, and he had done some good things. The big wheels at the Agency all knew exactly what was happening, too, and they didn't say a damn word."

Poe told his grunts to cut off the ears of the men they killed as proof of their victories in battle. He collected them in a green cellophane bag and, in the summer of 1965, he brought them to the CIA station in Vientiane and dumped them on the deputy chief's desk. Jim Lilley was the unfortunate recipient. If Tony Poe wanted to shock the new Ivy League big shot, he succeeded.

Lilley had signed up with the CIA fresh out of Yale in 1951. He joined the Far East division and spent the Korean War dropping agents into China and being swindled by Chinese Nationalists. He would go on to serve in Beijing, first as the station chief, then as the American ambassador.

In May 1965, Lilley landed in Laos as deputy chief of station, and when his boss burned out, he became the acting chief. He focused on political warfare in the capital. The CIA's cash flowed in "as part of our 'nation building' effort," he said, and "we pumped a relatively large amount of money to politicians who would listen to our advice." The results of the next election for the National Assembly in Laos would show fifty-four out of fifty-seven seats controlled by the CIA's chosen leaders. But Vientiane was a hard post.

"We saw some of our young guys killed in helicopter crashes," Lilley remembered. "We had coups d'etat, floods, and all kinds of things to deal with. We saw some of our people crack up who could no longer take it."

The normal problems of red-blooded Americans posted in a tropical war zone—sex, alcohol, madness—multiplied in Vientiane, most often at a nightclub called the White Rose. Lilley recalled the day that "one of our senior CIA officers briefed a visiting congressional delegation on the secret war up-country. That evening the delegation was taken to the White Rose for exposure to nightlife in Vientiane. Members of the delegation saw a large American man stark naked on the floor of the bar yelling, *I want it now!*' A hostess lifted up her skirt and sat on his face. It was the same officer who had briefed the delegation earlier in the day."

The CIA station fought to identify communist targets in Laos, to pinpoint the footpaths that wove together into the Ho Chi Minh Trail, and to hunt the enemy. "We tried to set up tribal teams," Lilley said. "They would report very high statistics of North Vietnamese killed, which I think were in part fabricated." They also spotted targets for American

bombing missions. Four times in 1965, the Americans destroyed innocent civilian targets in Laos, once bombing a friendly village that Ambassador Sullivan had blessed with a goodwill visit the day before. The
bombing run had been called in by Bill Lair, who was trying to rescue a
CIA pilot who had touched down in a hot landing zone and was captured by the Pathet Lao. The bombs fell twenty miles from their intended
target; the pilot, Ernie Brace, spent eight years as a prisoner of war in the
Hanoi Hilton.

In June 1965, one of Vang Pao's best officers was killed by ground fire
while standing in the open door of a helicopter trying to find a downed
American pilot forty miles inside North Vietnam. In August, an Air
America helicopter crashed into the Mekong River outside Vientiane,
killing Lewis Ojibway, the CIA's base chief in northwest Laos, and a Lao
army colonel who worked with him. The agency brass carved a star hon-
oring Ojibway into the marble entryway at CIA headquarters. In October, another chopper went down in the jungle near the Cambodian
border, killing Mike Deuel and Mike Maloney, two young sons of prominent CIA officers. Two more stars were hewn.

The CIA's war in Laos had started small, with "a great effervescence,
a sense that we had finally found people who would fight the communists and occasionally defeat them in guerrilla warfare," Lilley said. "It
was a sacred war. A good war."

Then the CIA outpost at Long Tieng started to sprawl: new roads,
warehouses, barracks, trucks, jeeps, bulldozers; a bigger airstrip, more
flights, more firepower, more air support. The Hmong stopped farming
when rice started falling out of the sky from CIA planes. "We increased
our personnel, doubling or tripling it," Lilley said. The newly arriving
CIA officers "really looked at Laos as a paramilitary problem. They really
had no grounding in the overall situation. . . . It became a little more like
Vietnam. And that's when the situation began to slip away from us."

That moment came in October 1965, when Bill Colby came to Laos
and flew up to Long Tieng on an inspection tour. The war in Vietnam
was now on full tilt; 184,000 troops were deployed by year's end. The
key to defeating the North still lay on the Ho Chi Minh Trail in Laos,
where the communists were moving men and materiel into battle faster
than the United States could destroy them. Colby was disheartened: the
enemy controlled strategic outposts throughout Laos, even on the outskirts of Vientiane.

He wanted a new station chief, a cold-blooded hard-charging commander. The man for the job was Ted Shackley.

"AN EXEMPLARY SUCCESS STORY"

When the call came, Shackley had been the CIA chief in Berlin for less than six months, following a long tour trying to overthrow Castro from Miami. His career had been focused on the Soviets, the Cubans, and the East Germans. He had never been anywhere near Asia. He flew to the Udorn base in Thailand, where American bulldozers were carving up the red-clay earth and camouflaged American jets were revving up for air strikes in Vietnam. Shackley remembered seeing the loaded bomb racks and thinking: "No one was talking theory here."

He wanted to take the war to the enemy, and he wanted instant results. He started building an empire in the jungle, with Jim Lilley as his deputy chief. They became close friends. Lilley's portrait of the man—"ambitious, tough-minded, and ruthless"—is telling. "What he was determined to do was to build up the station in Laos and play a critical role in the Vietnam War by hitting the Ho Chi Minh Trail," Lilley said. "He brought in the paramilitary assets that he had to bear on this key target. He didn't just sit around. He wanted to win wars."

Shackley brought in men he trusted from the Miami station and the Berlin base and told them to go out into the provinces, form village militias, and send them out to fight. The militias started out by spying on the Ho Chi Minh Trail and wound up in combat. He opened up new CIA bases all over Laos. The number of CIA officers working for him grew more than sevenfold, from 30 to 250. The Lao paramilitary forces under his command doubled to forty thousand men. He used them as forward air controllers to bring American air power raining down on Laos. By April 1966, twenty-nine CIA roadwatch teams in Southeast Laos were calling in enemy movements on the trail to the CIA base in Udorn, which dispatched American bombers to destroy them.

The U.S. Air Force started pounding the jungles of Laos into wasteland. B-52 bombers went to North Vietnam to destroy the villages and hamlets at the head of the Ho Chi Minh Trail. The army and the navy sent commandos to try to break the spine of the trail as it curved back into the South.

Shackley tallied the damage and the body counts. He concluded that his marriage of mountain tribesmen and American military technology had "revolutionized irregular warfare" and "put an essentially new weapon into the hands of American policy makers." Back in Washington, the president's men read Shackley's reports—so many thousands of Lao commandos recruited, so many communists killed per month, so many missions accomplished—and deemed his work "an exemplary success story." They approved tens of millions of dollars more for the CIA's war in Laos. Shackley thought he was winning the war. But the communists kept coming down the trail.

"AN ANCHOR LAND IN SOUTHEAST ASIA"

In Thailand, a more tricky political problem confronted the CIA: creating the illusion of democracy.

In 1953, Walter Bedell Smith and the Dulles brothers had sent an extraordinary American ambassador to Bangkok: Wild Bill Donovan. He was seventy years old, but he still had one fight left in him. "Ambassador Donovan recommended to President Eisenhower that they make a stand in Thailand, try to move from there back into some of these countries and to stop this onrush of communism" said Bill Thomas, the ambassador's chief information officer in Bangkok. "Money was no object."

Donovan set off a great surge in the CIA's covert operations throughout Southeast Asia after the Korean War. He was helped by the forty-thousand-strong Thai national police force, whose commander, underwritten by the CIA and Donovan's embassy, was an opium king. The agency and a rapidly expanding American military assistance group armed and trained the Thai military, whose commander controlled Bangkok's whorehouses, pork slaughterhouses, and liquor warehouses. Donovan publicly endorsed the Thai generals as defenders of democracy. The agency used its inroads with them to build its base near Udorn. Once a nerve center for covert operations throughout Southeast Asia, after 9/11 it served as a secret prison for the detention and interrogation of Islamic radicals.

Thailand remained under military dictatorship more than a decade after Donovan's departure. In 1965, under prodding from Washington, the generals proposed to hold elections someday. But they feared the left would rise at the ballot boxes. So the CIA set out to create and control the democratic process.

On September 28, 1965, Helms, covert-ops chief Desmond FitzGerald, and the Far East baron Bill Colby presented the White House with a proposal for "financing of a political party, electoral support for this party, and support for selected candidates for parliament from the party." Their plans were strongly endorsed by the wily and ambitious American ambassador in Thailand, Graham Martin, who considered the CIA his personal cashbox and constabulary. The problem was a delicate one, they reported. "Thailand today is still under martial law which does not permit political parties"; the Thai generals had "done little or nothing to develop and organize politically in preparation for the forthcoming elections." But under the firm hand of the ambassador and the CIA, they had agreed to join forces and form a new party. In return the CIA would provide millions to create the new political machine.

The goal was to continue "the leadership and control of the present ruling group" and "to ensure that the party created is successful in winning a comfortable and commanding majority in elections." The agency said it could begin "literally building a democratic electoral process from the ground up," so that the United States could depend on "a stable pro-Western regime in an anchor land in Southeast Asia." President Johnson personally approved the plan. The stability of Thailand was essential for an American victory in Vietnam.

"WE ONLY RODE THE WAVES ASHORE"

The CIA had warned the White House that a loss of American influence in Indonesia would make victory in Vietnam meaningless. The agency was working hard to find a new leader for the world's most populous Muslim nation.

Then, on the night of October 1, 1965, a political earthquake struck.

Seven years after the CIA tried to overthrow him, President Sukarno of Indonesia secretly launched what appeared to be a coup against his own government. After two decades in power, Sukarno, his health and his judgment failing, had sought to shore up his rule by allying himself with the Indonesian Communist Party, the PKI. The party had grown in strength, winning recruits with ceaseless reminders of the CIA's assaults on the nation's sovereignty. It was now the world's largest communist organization outside Russia and China, with 3.5 million nominal members.

Sukarno's lurch to the left proved a fatal mistake. At least five generals were assassinated that night, including the army chief of staff. The state-run radio announced that a revolutionary council had taken over to protect the president and the nation from the CIA.

The station in Jakarta had few friends within the army or the government. It had precisely one well-situated agent: Adam Malik, a forty-eight-year-old disillusioned ex-Marxist who had served as Sukarno's ambassador to Moscow and his minister of trade.

After a permanent falling-out with his president in 1964, Malik had met up with the CIA's Clyde McAvoy at a Jakarta safe house. McAvoy was the covert operator who a decade before had helped recruit the future prime minister of Japan, and he had come to Indonesia with orders to penetrate the PKI and the Sukarno government.

"I recruited and ran Adam Malik," McAvoy said in an interview in 2005. "He was the highest-ranking Indonesian we ever recruited." A mutual friend had introduced them, vouching for McAvoy; the go-between was a Japanese businessman in Jakarta and a former member of Japan's communist party. After Malik's recruitment, the CIA won approval for a stepped-up program of covert action to drive a political wedge between the left and the right in Indonesia.

Then, in a few terrifying weeks in October 1965, the Indonesian state split in two.

The CIA worked to consolidate a shadow government, a troika composed of Adam Malik, the ruling sultan of central Java, and an army major general named Suharto. Malik used his relationship with the CIA to set up a series of secret meetings with the new American ambassador in Indonesia, Marshall Green. The ambassador said he met Adam Malik "in a clandestine setting" and obtained "a very clear idea of what Suharto thought and what Malik thought and what they were proposing to do" to rid Indonesia of communism through the new political movement they led, the Kap-Gestapu.

"I ordered that all 14 of the walkie-talkies we had in the Embassy for emergency communications be handed over to Suharto," Ambassador Green said. "This provided additional internal security for him and his own top officers"—and a way for the CIA to monitor what they were doing. "I reported this to Washington and received a most gratifying telegram back from Bill Bundy," the assistant secretary of state for the Far East, and Green's good friend of thirty years from their days together at Groton.

In mid-October 1965, Malik sent an aide to the home of the American embassy's senior political officer, Bob Martens, who had served in Moscow while Malik was the Indonesian envoy. Martens gave the emissary an unclassified list of sixty-seven PKI leaders, a roster he had compiled out of communist press clippings. "It was certainly not a death list," Martens said. "It was a means for the non-communists that were basically fighting for their lives—remember, the outcome of a life-and-death struggle between the communists and non-communists was still in doubt—to know the organization of the other side." Two weeks later, Ambassador Green and the CIA station chief in Jakarta, Hugh Tovar, began receiving secondhand reports of killings and atrocities in eastern and central Java, where thousands of people were being slaughtered by civilian shock troops with the blessings of General Suharto.

McGeorge Bundy and his brother Bill resolved that Suharto and the Kap-Gestapu deserved American support. Ambassador Green warned them that the aid could not come through the Pentagon or the State Department. It could not be successfully concealed; the political risks were too great. The three old Grotonians—the ambassador, the national security adviser, and the assistant secretary of state for the Far East—agreed that the money had to be handled by the CIA.

They agreed to support the Indonesian army in the form of $500,000 of medical supplies to be shipped through the CIA, with the understanding that the army would sell the goods for cash, and provisionally approved a shipment of sophisticated communications equipment to Indonesian army leaders. Ambassador Green, after conferring with the CIA's Hugh Tovar, sent a cable to Bill Bundy recommending a substantial payment for Adam Malik:

This is to confirm my earlier concurrence that we provide Malik with fifty million rupiahs [roughly $10,000] for the activities of the Kap-Gestapu movement. This army-inspired but civilian-staffed action group is still carrying burden of current repressive efforts. . . . Our willingness to assist him in this manner will, I think, represent in Malik's mind our endorsement of his present role in the army's anti-PKI efforts, and will promote good cooperating relations between him and the army. The chances of detection or subsequent revelation of our support in this instance are as minimal as any black bag operation can be.

A great wave of violence began rising in Indonesia. General Suharto and the Kap-Gestapu massacred a multitude. Ambassador Green later told Vice President Hubert H. Humphrey, in a conversation at the vice president's office in the U.S. Capitol, that "300,000 to 400,000 people were slain" in "a blood bath." The vice president mentioned that he had known Adam Malik for many years, and the ambassador praised him as "one of the cleverest men he had ever met." Malik was installed as foreign minister, and he was invited to spend twenty minutes with the president of the United States in the Oval Office. They spent most of their time talking about Vietnam. At the end of their discussion, Lyndon Johnson said he was watching developments in Indonesia with the greatest interest, and he extended his best wishes to Malik and Suharto. With the backing of the United States, Malik later served as the president of the General Assembly of the United Nations.

Ambassador Green revised his guess of the death toll in Indonesia in a secret session of the Senate Foreign Relations Committee. "I think we would up that estimate to perhaps close to 500,000 people," he said in testimony declassified in March 2007. "Of course, nobody knows. We merely judge it by whole villages that have been depopulated."

The chairman, Senator J. William Fulbright of Arkansas, put the next question simply and directly.

"We were involved in the coup?" he asked.

"No, sir," said Ambassador Green.

"Were we involved in the previous attempt at a coup?" said the senator.

"No," said the ambassador. "I don't think so."

"CIA played no part in it?" asked Fulbright.

"You mean 1958?" said Green. The agency had run that coup, of course, from the bungled beginning to the bitter end. "I am afraid I cannot answer," the ambassador said. "I don't know for sure what happened."

A perilous moment, veering close to the edge of a disastrous operation and its deadly consequences—but the senator let it pass. "You don't know whether CIA was involved or not," Fulbright said. "And we were not involved in this coup."

"No sir," said the ambassador. "Definitely not."

More than one million political prisoners were jailed by the new regime. Some stayed in prison for decades. Some died there. Indonesia remained a military dictatorship for the rest of the cold war. The consequences of the repression resound to this day.

The United States has denied for forty years that it had anything to do with the slaughter carried out in the name of anticommunism in Indonesia. "We didn't create the waves," said Marshall Green. "We only rode the waves ashore."

"GENUINELY AND DEEPLY TROUBLED"

Twenty years earlier, Frank Wisner and Richard Helms had left Berlin together and flown to Washington, wondering if there would ever be a Central Intelligence Agency. Both had risen to lead the clandestine service. Now one was about to attain the pinnacle of power. The other had fallen into the abyss.

For months on end, Frank Wisner had been brooding in his lovely house in Georgetown, drinking from cut-glass tumblers filled with whisky, in a dark despair. Among the CIA's more closely held secrets was that one of its founding fathers had been in and out of the madhouse for years. Wisner had been removed as chief of station in London and forced to retire after his mental illness overtook him once again in 1962. He had been raving about Adolf Hitler, seeing things, hearing voices. He knew he would never be well. On October 29, 1965, Wisner had a date to go hunting at his estate on the Eastern Shore of Maryland with an old CIA friend, Joe Bryan. That afternoon, Wisner went up to his country house, took down a shotgun, and blew off his head. He was fifty-six years old. His funeral at the National Cathedral was magnificent. He was buried in Arlington National Cemetery, and his gravestone said: "Lieutenant, United States Navy."

The cold-war esprit de corps was starting to erode. Only a few weeks after Wisner was laid to rest, Ray Cline, the deputy director of intelligence, went to Clark Clifford, the chairman of the president's intelligence advisory board, and cut Red Raborn's throat.

Cline warned that the director was a danger to the nation. On January 25, 1966, Clifford told McGeorge Bundy, who was ready to quit after five exhausting years as national security adviser, that the intelligence board was "genuinely and deeply troubled about the leadership problem in CIA." A few days later a well-placed leak to the *Washington Star* let Raborn know he was on his way out. The admiral fought back. He sent a long list of his accomplishments to the president's aide Bill Moyers: the agency had weeded out stale and unproductive covert actions, installed a twenty-four-hour operations center to feed news and information to the president, doubled the strength of the counterterror teams in Vietnam, and tripled its overall effort in Saigon. He assured the White House that morale was great at headquarters and abroad. On the morning of February 22, 1966, President Johnson read Admiral Raborn's glowing self-assessment, picked up the phone, and called McGeorge Bundy.

Raborn was *"totally oblivious* to the fact that he is not highly regarded and he is not doing a good job," the president said. "He thinks that he's made a great improvement and he's a great success. And I'm afraid Helms lets him think that."

LBJ placed no one in charge of the covert-action review board, known as the 303 Committee, after Bundy resigned that week. Operations that needed White House attention hung in abeyance, including a plan to fix the elections in the Dominican Republic in favor of an exiled former president living in New York, and a fresh infusion of cash and weapons for the dictator of the Congo. Johnson left the chair empty through March and April 1966. At first he wanted Bill Moyers—later in life the most lucid leftist voice of public television—to take charge of the 303 Committee. Moyers attended one meeting on May 5, 1966, shuddered, and declined the honor. The president settled instead on his most loyal yea-sayer, Walt Whitman Rostow, as the new national security adviser and 303 chairman. The committee got back to work in May.

Despite the lull, it approved fifty-four major CIA covert operations that year, most of them in support of the war in Southeast Asia.

Finally, on the third Saturday of June 1966, the White House operator placed a call from the president to the home of Richard Helms.

Fifty-three, graying, trim from tennis, wound up like a Swiss watch, Helms drove his old black Cadillac to headquarters each morning at six-thirty, Saturdays included; this was a rare day off. What began for him as a wartime romance with secret intelligence had become an all-consuming passion. His marriage of twenty-seven years to Julia Shields, a sculptor six years older, was dying from inattention. Their son was off at college. His life was entirely devoted to the agency. When he answered the ringing phone, he heard his greatest wish fulfilled.

His swearing-in took place at the White House on June 30. The president brought in the Marine Band to perform. Helms now commanded close to twenty thousand people, more than a third of them spying overseas, and a budget of about a billion dollars. He was perceived as one of the most powerful men in Washington.

25. "WE KNEW THEN THAT WE COULD NOT WIN THE WAR"

A quarter of a million American soldiers were at war when Richard Helms took control at the CIA. One thousand covert operators in Southeast Asia and three thousand intelligence analysts at home were consumed by the growing disaster.

A battle was building at headquarters. The job of the analysts was to judge whether the war could be won. The job of the clandestine service was to help win it. Most analysts were pessimists; most operators were gung-ho. They worked in different worlds; armed guards stood between the directorates at headquarters. Helms felt he was "a circus rider standing astride two horses, each for the best of reasons going its own way."

One of the hundreds of new CIA recruits who arrived for work the summer that Helms took power was a twenty-three-year-old who had signed up on a lark, looking for a free trip to Washington during his senior year at Indiana University. Bob Gates, the future director of central intelligence and secretary of defense, rode an agency bus from downtown Washington into a driveway surrounded by a high chain-link fence topped with barbed wire. He entered a forbidding seven-story concrete slab topped with antennas.

"The inside of the building was deceptively bland," he remembered. "Long, undecorated hallways. Tiny cubicles to work in. Linoleum floors. Metal, government-issue furniture. It was like a giant insurance company. But, then again, it wasn't." The CIA made Gates a ninety-day wonder, an instant second lieutenant, and sent him off to Whiteman Air Force Base in Missouri to learn the science of nuclear targeting. From there the fledgling CIA analyst caught a chilling glimpse of the course of the war in Vietnam: the United States was running out of pilots, and white-haired colonels were being sent off to bomb the communists.

"We knew then," Gates remembered, "that we could not win the war."

"CIRCLE NOW SQUARED"

Helms and his Far East chief, Bill Colby, were career covert operators, and their reports to the president reflected the can-do spirit of the old clandestine service. Helms told LBJ, "This Agency is going flat out in its effort to contribute to the success of the total U.S. program in Vietnam." Colby sent the White House a glowing assessment of the CIA's Saigon station. While "the war is by no means over," he reported, "my Soviet or Chinese counterpart's report must exhibit great concern over the Viet Cong's mounting problems and the steady improvement in the ability of both the South Vietnamese and the Americans to fight a people's war." George Carver, whom Helms had chosen as his special assistant for Vietnamese affairs, was also a constant bearer of glad tidings for the White House.

Yet the CIA's best analysts had concluded in a book-length study, *The Vietnamese Communists' Will to Persist,* sent to the president and perhaps a dozen top aides, that nothing the United States was doing could defeat the enemy. When Secretary of Defense McNamara read that report on August 26, 1966, he immediately called Helms and asked to see the CIA's ranking expert on Vietnam. As it happened, Carver was on vacation that week. So his deputy, George Allen, was summoned to the inner sanctum of the Pentagon for his first and only one-on-one talk with the secretary of defense. He was scheduled for a half hour at 10:30 a.m. The conversation turned out to be the only true meeting of the minds of the CIA and the Pentagon during the presidency of Lyndon Johnson.

McNamara was fascinated to learn that Allen had spent seventeen years working on Vietnam. He did not know there was anyone who had devoted himself to the struggle for so long. Well, he said, you must have some ideas about what to do. "He wanted to know what I would do if I were sitting in his place," Allen remembered. "I decided to respond candidly."

"Stop the buildup of American forces," he said. "Halt the bombing of the North, and negotiate a cease-fire with Hanoi." McNamara called his secretary and told her to cancel the rest of his appointments until after lunch.

Why, the secretary of defense asked, would the United States choose to let the dominoes of Asia fall? Allen replied that the risk was no greater at the peace table than in the theater of war. If the United States stopped the bombing and started negotiating with China and the Soviet Union, as well as its Asian allies and enemies, there might be peace with honor.

After ninety minutes of this riveting heresy, McNamara made three fateful decisions. He asked the CIA to compile an order of battle, an estimate of the enemy forces arrayed against the United States. He told his aides to begin to compile a top secret history of the war since 1954—the Pentagon Papers. And he questioned what he was doing in Vietnam. On September 19, McNamara telephoned the president: "I myself am more and more convinced that we ought definitely to plan on termination of bombing in the North," he said. "I think also we ought to be planning, as I mentioned before, on a ceiling on our force levels. I don't think we ought to just look ahead to the future and say we're going to go higher and higher and higher and higher—six hundred thousand, seven hundred thousand, whatever it takes." The president's only response was an unintelligible grunt.

McNamara came to understand, too late, that the United States had dramatically underestimated the strength of the insurgents killing American soldiers in Vietnam, a fatal mistake that would be repeated many years later in Iraq. The order of battle study he commissioned set off a great struggle between the military commanders in Saigon and the CIA analysts at headquarters. Did the United States face a total of fewer than 300,000 communist fighters in Vietnam, as the military maintained, or more than 500,000, as most of the analysts believed?

The difference lay in the number of guerrillas, irregulars, militiamen—soldiers without uniforms. If the enemy stood half a million strong after two years of relentless bombings by American planes and intense attacks by American troops, it would be a sign that the war really could not be won. The lowball figure was an article of faith for General William Westmoreland, the American military commander in South Vietnam, and his aide, Robert Komer. Known as "Blowtorch Bob," Komer was a charter member of the CIA who ran Westmoreland's new and rapidly expanding counterinsurgency campaign, code-named Phoenix. He consistently sent eyes-only memos to LBJ saying victory was at hand. The real question, he asserted, was not whether we were winning, but how fast we wanted to win.

The argument went back and forth for months. Finally, Helms sent Carver out to Saigon to deal with Westmoreland and Komer. Their talks did not go well. The military was stonewalling. On September 11, 1967, the argument came to a head.

"You guys simply have to back off," Komer told Carver in an hour-long monologue over dinner. The truth would "create a public disaster and undo everything we've been trying to accomplish out here." Carver sent a cable to Helms saying the military would not be swayed. They had to prove that they were winning. They had underscored "their frustrating inability to convince the press (hence the public) of the great progress being made, and the paramount importance of saying nothing that would detract from the image of progress," Carver reported to the director. Quantifying the number of Vietcong irregulars in South Vietnam "would produce a politically unacceptable total of over 400,000." Since the military had "a pre-determined total, fixed on public-relations grounds, we can go no further (unless you instruct otherwise)."

Helms felt a crushing pressure to get on the team—and to trim the CIA's reporting to fit the president's policy. He caved in. He said the number "didn't mean a damn." The agency officially accepted the falsified figure of 299,000 enemy forces or fewer. "Circle now squared," Carver cabled back to the director.

The suppression and falsification of reporting on Vietnam had a long history. In the spring of 1963, John McCone had come under enormous pressure from the Pentagon to scuttle a pessimistic estimate that cited "very great weaknesses" in the government of South Vietnam—including poor morale among the troops, terrible intelligence, and communist penetration of the military. The CIA rewrote that estimate to read: "We believe that Communist progress has been blunted and that the situation is improving." The CIA did *not* believe that. A few weeks later came the riots in Hue, followed by the burning Buddhists, and the plotting to do away with Diem.

The pressure never stopped; the president's new national security adviser, Walt Rostow, constantly ordered the CIA to produce good news about the war for the White House. Whose side are you on, anyway? Rostow growled. But on the same day that Helms squared the circle, he also sent a brutally honest CIA study to the president. "The attached paper is sensitive, particularly if its *existence* were to leak," Helms's letter to the president began. "It has not been given, and will not be given, to any other official of the Government." The very title of the report—"Implications of an Unfavorable Outcome in Vietnam"—was explosive. "The compelling proposition," it said, was that "the U.S., acting within the constraints imposed by its traditions and public attitudes, cannot crush a revolutionary movement which is sufficiently large, dedicated, competent, and well-supported. . . . The structure of U.S. military power is ill-suited to cope with guerrilla warfare waged by a determined, resourceful, and politically astute opponent. This is not a novel discovery."

In Saigon, the CIA's best officers were making their own discovery. The more intelligence they gathered, the more they realized how little they knew.

But by now it hardly mattered what the CIA reported to Washington. Never had there been a war where more intelligence was placed in the hands of commanders: captured enemy documents, brutal interrogations of prisoners of war, electronic intercepts, overhead reconnaissance, field reports brought home to the Saigon station through the blood and mud of the front lines, careful analyses, statistical studies, quarterly syntheses of everything the CIA and American military commanders knew. Today an old torpedo factory not far from the Pentagon houses eight miles of microfilm, a small part of the archive of American intelligence from the war.

Never had so much intelligence meant so little. The conduct of the war had been set by a series of lies that the leaders of the United States told one another and the American people. The White House and the Pentagon kept trying to convince the people that the war was going well. In time, the facts on the ground would prevail.

26. "A POLITICAL H-BOMB"

On February 13, 1967, Richard Helms was in Albuquerque, at the end of a long day touring the American nuclear-weapons labs, when a highly agitated CIA communications officer met him at his hotel room with a message from the White House: Return to Washington immediately.

A little leftist monthly called *Ramparts* was about to publish a story saying that the National Student Association, a well-respected world-wide group of American collegians, had for years received a generous stipend from the agency. CIA headquarters had just warned the White House that there would be a firestorm "over CIA involvement with private voluntary organizations and foundations. The CIA will probably be accused of improperly interfering in domestic affairs, and of manipulating and endangering innocent young people. The Administration will probably come under attack."

When the story broke, President Johnson immediately announced that Nick Katzenbach, the number-two man at the State Department, would lead a top-down review of the relationships the CIA had forged with private voluntary organizations in the United States. Since Helms was the only one who knew precisely what had gone on, "LBJ left me the responsibility of pulling the Agency's scorched chestnuts out of the fire."

James Reston of *The New York Times* knowingly observed that the CIA's links to certain unnamed radio stations, publications, and labor unions were now also in jeopardy. In short order, two decades of secret work by the CIA was laid bare.

Radio Free Europe, Radio Liberty, and the Congress for Cultural Freedom were revealed as the agency's creations. All the influential little
magazines that had flourished under the banner of the anticommunist
liberal left, all the eminently respectable groups that had served as con-
duits for the CIA's money and people, such as the Ford Foundation and
the Asia Foundation—all were interwoven in a paper trail of dummy
corporations and front organizations linked to the CIA. When one was
blown, they all blew.

The radios were arguably the most influential political-warfare operations in the agency's history. The CIA had spent close to $400 million
subsidizing them, and it had reason to believe that millions of listeners
behind the iron curtain appreciated every word they broadcast. But their
legitimacy was undercut when they were revealed as the CIA's frequencies.

The agency had built a house of cards, and Helms knew it. The CIA's
support for the radios and the foundations were some of the biggest
covert-action programs the agency had run. But there was nothing truly
clandestine about them. Ten years before, Helms had talked to Wisner
about phasing out the secret subsidies and letting the State Department
handle the radios. They had agreed to try to convince President Eisenhower, but they never followed through. Since 1961, Secretary of State
Dean Rusk had been warning that the millions of dollars flowing from
the CIA to student groups and private foundations was "the subject of
common gossip, or knowledge, both here and abroad." For a year, *Ramparts* had been on the agency's radar; Helms had sent a memo to Bill
Moyers at the White House detailing the political and personal behavior
of its editors and reporters.

But the CIA was not the only party guilty of negligence when it came
to the control of covert action. For years, the White House, the Pentagon, and the State Department had failed to keep an eye on the agency.
More than three hundred major covert operations had been launched
since the inauguration of President Kennedy—and, except for Helms, no
one then in power knew about most of them. "We lack adequate detail
on how certain programs are to be carried out and we lack continuing
review of major ongoing programs," a State Department intelligence officer reported on February 15, 1967.

The mechanisms created to watch over the CIA and to invest its
clandestine service with presidential authority were not working. They

never had worked. There was a growing sense at the White House, the State Department, the Justice Department, and Congress that the agency had gone slightly out of control.

"WHAT THEY HAVE SPECIFICALLY IN MIND IS KILLING HIM"

On February 20, 1967, the president telephoned the acting attorney general of the United States, Ramsey Clark.

Five weeks before, LBJ and the syndicated columnist Drew Pearson had had an hour-long off-the-record conversation in the White House. Not for nothing was Pearson's column called *Washington Merry-Go-Round*. He had set the president's head spinning with a story about the Mafia's John Rosselli, the loyal friend of the CIA's Bill Harvey, who was the sworn enemy of Senator Robert F. Kennedy.

"This story going around about the CIA . . . sendin' in the folks to get Castro," LBJ said to Ramsey Clark. "It's *incredible."* He told the tale as he had heard it: "They have a man that was involved, that was brought in to the CIA, with a number of others, and instructed by the CIA and the Attorney General to assassinate Castro after the Bay of Pigs. . . . They had these pills." Every word of that was true. But the story went on. It took Johnson to a terrifying if unfounded conclusion: Castro had captured the plotters and "he tortured 'em. And they told him all about it. . . . So he said, 'Okay. We'll just take care of that.' So then he called Oswald and a group in, and told them to . . . get the *job* done." The job was the assassination of the president of the United States.

Johnson told Ramsey Clark to find out what the FBI knew about the connections among the CIA, and the Mafia, and Bobby Kennedy.

On March 3, Pearson's column reported that "President Johnson is sitting on a political H-bomb—an unconfirmed report that Senator Robert Kennedy may have approved an assassination plot which then backfired against his late brother." The item badly frightened Bobby Kennedy. He and Helms had lunch the next day, and the director brought the sole copy of the only CIA memo tying Kennedy to the Mafia plot against Castro.

Two days later, the FBI completed a report for the president with the pungent title "Central Intelligence Agency's Intentions to Send Hoodlums to Cuba to Assassinate Castro." It was clear and concise: the CIA had tried to kill Castro. The agency had hired members of the Mafia to do it. Robert Kennedy as attorney general knew about the CIA plot as it unfolded, and he knew the mob was involved.

President Johnson mulled the matter over for two weeks before he ordered Helms to undertake an official CIA investigation of the plots against Castro, Trujillo, and Diem. Helms had no choice. He told the CIA's inspector general, John Earman, to go to work. One by one, Earman called the handful of men who knew what had happened to his office; one by one, he pulled together the CIA's files, slowly assembling a detailed account.

Secretary of State Rusk ordered the chief of the State Department's intelligence bureau, Tom Hughes, to conduct his own independent review of the CIA's covert operations. On May 5, Hughes sat down with Rusk and Katzenbach in the secretary of state's chandeliered office. The three men weighed whether the president should sharply curtail the clandestine service. Hughes had come to believe that buying foreign politicians, supporting foreign coups, and running guns to foreign rebels could corrode American values. He proposed that the United States should cut covert action "to an irreducible minimum." They should go forward only when "the prospective results are essential to national security or national interests; are of such value as significantly to outweigh the risks; and cannot be effectively obtained in any other way." Rusk conveyed these thoughts to Richard Helms, who did not strongly disagree.

That same week, Helms read very carefully through the 133-page draft report of the CIA's inspector general. It said the killers of Diem and Trujillo had been "encouraged but not controlled by the U.S. government." But it dissected in grim detail the mechanics of the plots against Castro. "We cannot overemphasize the extent to which responsible Agency officers felt themselves subject to the Kennedy administration's severe pressures to do something about Castro," it said. "We find people speaking vaguely of 'doing something about Castro' when it is clear that what they have specifically in mind is killing him." Though the pressure had come from the highest levels of the government, the report was silent on the question of presidential authorization. The only man who could provide a definitive answer, Senator Robert F. Kennedy, was busy at that moment co-sponsoring a bill raising federal penalties for the desecration of the American flag.

The report implicated every living CIA officer who had served as chief of the clandestine service—Allen Dulles, Richard Bissell, Richard Helms, and Desmond FitzGerald—in conspiracies to commit murder. It placed a particularly heavy burden on FitzGerald. It said he had personally promised high-powered rifles with telescopic scopes to the Cuban agent Rolando Cubela, who had vowed to kill Castro, the week President Kennedy was assassinated. FitzGerald fervently denied it, but the chances that he was lying were high.

On May 10, Helms put his handwritten notes on the inspector general's report in his briefcase and went to see the president. No record of what they said is known to exist. On May 23, Helms testified before Senator Richard Russell's CIA subcommittee. Russell knew more than any outsider about the agency's affairs. He was closer to President Johnson than any man in Washington. He put a very pointed question to Helms in the context of political assassination. He asked about the CIA's "ability to keep former employees quiet."

Helms went back to headquarters that day and made sure that every piece of paper created by the inspector general's investigation was destroyed. He kept the sole copy of the report securely locked in his safe, where it sat untouched for the next six years.

Helms was well aware that the CIA officer who knew the most damning facts about the Castro conspiracy was the dangerously unstable Bill Harvey, who had been dismissed as station chief in Rome for chronic drunkenness but remained on the payroll, lurching around the corridors at headquarters. "Bill would show up at some meeting just crocked," said Red White, the CIA's executive director. "He'd drink those bathtub Martinis." White recalled meeting in Helms's office with Des FitzGerald and Jim Angleton in the last week of May 1967. The subject was what to do with Harvey. They eased him out of the agency with the greatest care and tried to make sure that he had a quiet retirement. The CIA's security director, Howard Osborn, took the washed-up officer out to lunch and recorded "his extreme bitterness toward the Agency and the Director," and his willingness to blackmail both if backed into a corner. Harvey would return to haunt the CIA before his death.

"A MAN OBSESSED"

It was a time of great professional peril for Helms. Throughout the spring of 1967, he faced another crisis at headquarters as grave as the ticking time bomb of the assassination plots. Some of his best officers had started an internal rebellion against the conspiracy theories of Jim Angleton.

For more than a decade, ever since Angleton had obtained, with Israel's help, a copy of Khrushchev's secret speech denouncing Stalin, he had enjoyed an exalted status at the CIA. He still controlled the Israeli account and liaison with the FBI along with his crucial role as chief of counterintelligence, the man who guarded the agency against penetration from communist spies. But his vision of a "master plot" run by Moscow had started to poison the agency. A secret CIA history of Richard Helms as director of central intelligence, declassified in February 2007, reveals in detail the precise tone and tenor of Angleton's work at headquarters:

> Angleton by the mid-1960s had come to hold a set of views that, if accurate, portended grave consequences for the United States. Angleton believed that the Soviet Union, guided by as skillful a group of leaders as ever served one government, was implacable in its hostility toward the West. International Communism remained monolithic, and reports of a rift between Moscow and Peking were only part of an elaborate "disinformation campaign." An "integrated and purposeful Socialist Bloc," Angleton wrote in 1966, sought to foster false stories of "splits, evolution, power struggles, economic disasters, [and] good and bad Communism" to present "a wilderness of mirrors" to the confused West. Once this program of strategic deception had succeeded in splintering Western solidarity, Moscow would find it an easy matter to pick off the Free World nations one by one. Only the Western intelligence services, in Angleton's view, could counter this challenge and stave off disaster. And because the Soviets had penetrated every one of these services, the fate of Western civilization rested, to a large extent, in the hands of the counterintelligence experts.

Angleton was unsound—"a man of loose and disjointed thinking whose theories, when applied to matters of public record, were patently unworthy of serious consideration," as an official CIA assessment later concluded. The consequences of believing in him were grave. In the spring of 1967, they included the continuing incarceration of Yuri Nosenko, the Soviet defector who was in his third year of illegal imprisonment under subhuman conditions in a CIA stockade; a cascade of false accusations against senior Soviet division officers wrongly suspected of spying for Moscow; and a refusal to accept the word of any and all Soviet defectors and recruited agents. "Loyal Agency employees had come under suspicion of treachery solely on the basis of coincidence and flimsy circumstantial evidence," says the secret CIA history of the Helms years. "Ongoing operations against Soviet targets had been shut down, new ones stifled, by the conviction that the Kremlin, tipped off by a mole within CIA, had doubled most Agency assets. Valuable information supplied by defectors and longtime sources was being ignored, for fear that it was somehow tainted."

A small but determined resistance to Angleton was growing within the clandestine service. "Rather than being disinformed by the enemy, we are deluding ourselves," a senior Soviet division officer named Leonard McCoy said in a memo that Helms first read in April 1967; he told Helms that the Angletonian mindset had created a complete "paralysis of our Soviet effort." In May, Howard Osborn, the director of the CIA's Office of Security, warned that the Nosenko case was a legal and moral abomination. Helms asked the deputy director of central intelligence, Admiral Rufus Taylor, to try to resolve the case. Taylor reported back that Nosenko was in no way a double agent, the CIA's Soviet division was being torn apart, and Helms had to set the prisoner free and make some major personnel changes to clear the air.

Angleton and his staff produced almost no intelligence reports for the rest of the agency; he considered himself the ultimate customer for his work and refused to circulate his conclusions in writing. He had sabotaged station chiefs throughout Europe, undermined allied intelligence services, and poisoned the well at headquarters—all without "one scrap of supportive evidence that there ever was or ever had been" a mole inside the Soviet division, as Rolfe Kingsley, the newly appointed chief of the division under Helms, protested without avail. Helms believed, in Admiral Taylor's words, that "Jim was a man obsessed. . . . Helms deplored that obsession but thought that Angleton was so valuable and so difficult to replace that his other attributes outweighed the disadvantages of that obsession."

Despite the blighted careers, the damaged lives, and the sheer chaos that Angleton created, Helms never broke faith with him. Why? First, as far as anyone knows, the CIA was never penetrated by a traitor or a Soviet spy during the twenty years that Angleton ran counterintelligence, and for this Helms was eternally grateful. Second, as the secret CIA history of the Helms years makes clear for the first time, Angleton was partly responsible for his greatest triumph as director of central intelligence: the CIA's accurate call of the Six-Day War.

On June 5, 1967, Israel launched an attack on Egypt, Syria, and Jordan. The CIA saw it coming. The Israelis had been telling the White House and the State Department that they were in great peril. Helms told the president that this was a calculated gambit, a white lie told in the hope of winning direct American military support. To Lyndon Johnson's great relief, Helms said that Israel would strike at the time and place of its choosing, and was likely to win swiftly—in a matter of days. The ultimate source of the confidently stated forecast was Angleton, who had gotten it from his friends at the highest levels of Israeli intelligence, and reported it directly and exclusively to Helms. His word was good. "The subsequent accuracy of this prediction established Helms's reputation in the Johnson White House," the CIA history recorded. "The experience almost certainly constituted the high point of Helms's service as Director. It also further solidified Angleton's standing in the DCI's estimation."

LBJ was duly impressed by the rare bull's-eye. Helms proudly recounted for the CIA's historians that Johnson, for the first time in his presidency, realized that "intelligence had a role in his life, and an important one at that. . . . This was the first time that he was really sort of jarred by the fact that 'those intelligence fellows had some insight that these other fellows don't have.' "

He offered Helms a seat at the president's Tuesday lunch—the best table in town, the highest council of the government, what Helms called the magic inner circle—alongside the secretary of state, the secretary of defense, and the chairman of the Joint Chiefs. Once a week, for the next eighteen months, the CIA had what it needed most of all: the attention of the president of the United States.

"AN ENORMOUS AMOUNT OF PLUMBING"

Helms wanted to keep the secrets of the CIA under control at home. To that end, he demanded no unpleasant surprises abroad. Under the prevailing political conditions, many of the agency's covert operations were potential H-bombs.

In June 1967, Helms told Desmond FitzGerald to evaluate every one of the CIA's overseas covert actions, ensure that the secrecy surrounding them was secure—and shut down every one that might blow. The agency could not withstand another public scandal or risk any more public scrutiny. The pressure on FitzGerald, on top of the onus placed upon him by the internal investigation of the Castro plots, proved too great. Five weeks later, a heart attack killed him as he played tennis with the British ambassador. Like Frank Wisner, he was fifty-six years old when he died.

After FitzGerald was buried, Helms selected a loyal old friend to lead the clandestine service: Thomas Hercules Karamessines, Tom K. to his friends, a charter member of the CIA and the former station chief in Athens, who lived in constant crippling pain from a twisted spine. Together, in the summer and fall of 1967, they continued the worldwide review of the CIA's covert operations. No nation on earth was neutral territory, and Helms aimed to give the agency a global reach.

In Saigon, the CIA had just started an excruciatingly sensitive operation, approved by President Johnson, code-named Buttercup. The agency was trying to put out peace feelers to North Vietnam by returning a politically astute Vietcong prisoner of war to Hanoi with a clandestine radio transmitter, seeking to open talks at the highest levels with the enemy. Nothing had come of it. The CIA had created and run the local Communist Party in several pro-American nations—among them Panama—hoping that the parties' leaders would be invited to Moscow and discover the secrets of Soviet doctrine firsthand. The lessons learned in the neverending battle to penetrate the Kremlin were slim. Helms was trying to mobilize the CIA's first worldwide cadre of deep-cover officers: spies who worked without the protection of a diplomatic passport, posing as international lawyers or traveling salesmen for *Fortune* 500 companies. The program, code-named Globe, had been under way for five years, but barely more than a dozen such officers were wandering the planet.

Good operations took years to develop. "You have to get the infra-structure, get the people who have to work with you," Helms once explained. "There is an enormous amount of plumbing to be put into the structure if it is to have any chance of success."

But patience, persistence, money, and cunning alone were not enough to fight communism. Real weapons needed to be placed in the hands of friendly rulers and their CIA-trained secret police and paramilitaries. President Eisenhower had created a one-size-fits-all plan called the Overseas Internal Security Program, run by the CIA in concert with the Pentagon and the State Department. The man who wrote the manifesto for the mission—"a democratic, unselfish, often unconditional approach to helping other countries to help themselves"—was the agency's own Al Haney, the con artist of the Seoul station and the field commander of Operation Success in Guatemala.

Haney proposed to police the world by arming America's third-world allies. "There have been charges that it is morally wrong for the U.S. to aid undemocratic regimes to strengthen their security systems, thereby serving to entrench them in power," he argued. But "the U.S. cannot afford the moral luxury of helping only those regimes in the free world that meet our ideals of self-government. Eliminate all the absolute monarchies, dictatorships and juntas from the free world and count those that are left and it should be readily apparent that the U.S. would be well on its way to isolation."

The program trained 771,217 foreign military and police officers in twenty-five nations. It found the most fertile ground in nations where covert action by the CIA had prepared the soil. It had helped create the secret police of Cambodia, Colombia, Ecuador, El Salvador, Guatemala, Iran, Iraq, Laos, Peru, the Philippines, South Korea, South Vietnam, and Thailand. In each of these nations, the interior ministries and the national police worked in close liaison with the CIA station. The agency also established an international police academy in Panama and a "bomb school" in Los Fresnos, Texas, which trained officers from Central and South America. Graduates included the future leaders of death squads in El Salvador and Honduras.

It was sometimes a short step from the classroom to the torture chamber. The CIA was on "dangerous ground," said Robert Amory, chief of the CIA's intelligence directorate under Eisenhower and Kennedy. "You can get into Gestapo-type tactics."

In the 1960s, the scope of the CIA's work expanded dramatically in Latin America. "Castro was the catalyst," said Tom Polgar, the Berlin base veteran who served as chief of the foreign intelligence staff of the Latin American division from 1965 to 1967. "The CIA and the propertied classes of Latin America had that one thing in common—that fear."

"My mission was to use the Latin American stations as a means to collect intelligence on the Soviet Union and Cuba," Polgar said. "To do that, you have to have a relatively stable government that will cooperate with the United States."

The CIA was backing the leaders of eleven Latin American nations—Argentina, Bolivia, Brazil, the Dominican Republic, Ecuador, Guatemala, Guyana, Honduras, Nicaragua, Peru, and Venezuela. Once a friendly government was in power, a CIA station chief had five paths to maintain American influence over foreign leaders. "You become their foreign intelligence service," Polgar said. "They don't know what's going on in the world. So you give them a weekly briefing—doctored to meet their sensibilities. Money, definitely—that's always welcome. Procurement—toys, games, weapons. Training. And you can always take a group of officers to Fort Bragg or to Washington—a wonderful holiday."

The agency held the position, duly stated in a formal estimate signed by Richard Helms, that Latin American military juntas were good for the United States. They were the only force capable of controlling political crises. Law and order were better than the messy struggle for democracy and freedom.

In LBJ's day, the counterinsurgency missions started by the Kennedys took root where Ike's internal-security programs had flourished and the CIA had installed military and political allies. In 1967, through the careful cultivation of dictators on two continents, the CIA scored one of its greatest cold-war victories: hunting down Che Guevara.

"REMEMBER, YOU ARE KILLING A MAN"

Che was a living emblem for the soldiers and the spies of the Cuban revolution. They served in outposts as far-flung as the Congo, where the power of the strongman Joseph Mobutu was threatened by a ragtag rebel force called the Simbas, whose warriors had kidnapped the CIA base chief in Stanleyville in 1964.

The Congo was a cockpit of the cold war, and Mobutu and the CIA worked in closest harmony. Gerry Gossens, the CIA's number-three man in the Congo, proposed that they create a new force to fight Soviet and Cuban influence in Africa. "Mobutu gave me a house, seven officers, and six Volkswagens, and I taught them how to conduct surveillance," Gossens said. "We set up a Congolese service reporting to the CIA. We directed them. We ran them. Eventually, with the President's blessing, we paid their operational expenses. I got the take, vetted it, edited it, and passed it on to Mobutu." Mobutu got whatever he wanted from the CIA—money and guns, planes and pilots, a personal physician, and the political security of close liaison with the American government—while the CIA built its bases and stations in the heart of Africa.

In a classic battle of the cold war, Che and his Cubans confronted the CIA and its Cubans on the western shores of Lake Tanganyika, in the heart of Africa. The agency's forces, equipped with recoilless rifles and warplanes, attacked several thousand Simbas and about a hundred of Che's Cuban soldiers. Under fire, Che sought new orders from Fidel. "Avoid annihilation," *el jefe maximo* advised.

Che made an inglorious retreat. On the run, he crossed the Atlantic, seeking to light the flames of revolution in Latin America. He wound up in the mountains of Bolivia, where the CIA tracked him down.

A right-wing general, Rene Barrientos, had seized power in that desperately poor nation, backed by more than $1 million from the CIA. The money served "to encourage," in the agency's words, "a stable government favorably inclined toward the United States," and "in support of the ruling Junta's plans to pacify the country." The general crushed his opponents with increasing force. Bill Broe, chief of the Latin American division of the clandestine service, wrote to Helms with satisfaction: "With the election of Rene Barrientos as President of Bolivia on July 3, 1966, this action was brought to a successful completion." The CIA sent its Barrientos file to the White House. National security adviser Walt Rostow handed it to the president and said: "This is to explain why General Barrientos may say thank you when you have lunch with him next Wednesday, the 20th."

In April 1967, Barrientos told the American ambassador, Douglas Henderson, that his officers were tracking Che in the mountains of

Bolivia. Ambassador Henderson was headed for Washington that week and he had brought the news to Desmond FitzGerald. "This can't be Che Guevara," FitzGerald had said. "We think that Che Guevara was killed in the Dominican Republic and is buried in an unmarked grave." Nevertheless, the CIA sent two Cuban veterans of the Bay of Pigs down to join the hunt with a squad of American-trained Bolivian Rangers.

One of the CIA's Cubans was Feliz Rodriguez, and he sent a series of stirring bulletins from the battlefront. His messages, declassified in 2004, are the only contemporary eyewitness accounts of a confrontation long shrouded by myth. From the village of Higueras, Rodriguez radioed John Tilton, the station chief in La Paz, who relayed the news to Bill Broe and Tom Polgar at headquarters. Their reports went to Helms, who handcarried them to the White House.

On October 8, 1967, Che was captured after a clash with the Bolivian Rangers. He had a wound in his leg but was otherwise in fair condition. His dreams of making a Vietnam in South America had evaporated in the thin air of the Bolivian highlands. His captors took him to a little schoolhouse. Rodriguez learned that the Bolivian high command in La Paz would decide Che's fate on the following day.

"I am managing to keep him alive," Rodriguez reported, "which is very hard."

At daybreak the following morning, Rodriguez tried to interrogate Che, who was sitting on the schoolhouse floor, his face in his hands, his wrists and ankles bound, the corpses of two Cuban *compañeros* beside him. They talked about the clash in the Congo and the course of the Cuban revolution. Che said that Castro had killed no more than 1,500 of his political enemies, apart from armed conflicts such as the Bay of Pigs. " 'The Cuban government, of course, executed all guerrilla leaders who invaded its territory,' " Che said, according to Rodriguez. "He stopped then with a quizzical look on his face and smiled as he recognized his own position on Bolivian soil." Rodriguez continued: "With his capture, the guerrilla movement had suffered an overwhelming setback. . . . He insisted that his ideals would win in the end. . . . He had not planned an exfiltration route from Bolivia in case of failure. He had definitely decided to fail or win."

The high command sent the order to kill Che at 11:50 a.m. "Guevara was executed with a burst of shots at 1:15 p.m.," Rodriguez radioed to Tilton. "Guevara's last words were: 'Tell my wife to remarry and tell Fidel Castro that the Revolution will rise again in the Americas.' To his executioner he said, 'Remember, you are killing a man.' "

Tom Polgar was the duty officer at headquarters when Tilton called in the news that Che was dead. "Can you send fingerprints?" Polgar asked.

"I can send fingers," Tilton replied. Che's executioners had cut off his hands.

"PARAMOUNT CONSIDERATIONS *MUST* BE POLITICAL SENSITIVITY"

There were few such triumphs to trumpet for Helms and his officers. They were outnumbered by a multitude of mistakes. "Once again CIA operations have created a major problem," the State Department's Egypt desk informed Luke Battle, the new assistant secretary of state for the Near East. Egypt's ruler, Gamal Abdel Nasser, was complaining—not for the first time, and not without cause—that the agency was trying to overthrow his government. "CIA appears to hope that these incidents can be swept under the rug," said the message to Battle. "This should not be allowed to happen."

Battle knew what the CIA's work in Egypt entailed. He had been the American ambassador when a happy-go-lucky case officer carelessly exposed the agency's relationship with a prominent Cairo newspaper editor named Mustapha Amin. Amin had been close to Nasser; the CIA paid him for information and for publishing pro-American news reports. The Cairo station chief had lied to the ambassador about the agency's relationship with Amin. "He had been on the U.S. payroll," Battle said. "Bruce Odell [the CIA case officer] had been meeting regularly with Mustapha Amin. I had been assured that no funds had been exchanged in Egypt, but a photograph of such a transaction was made when Mustapha Amin was arrested." The case made headlines around the world, prominently featuring Odell, who had worked under diplomatic cover. Amin was tried as a spy, brutally tortured, and imprisoned for nine years.

Helms tried to build confidence in the CIA. He had hoped that President Johnson would come out to Langley, Virginia, to address the troops at headquarters in September 1967, during ceremonies marking the agency's twentieth anniversary. But LBJ never once visited the CIA. He sent Vice President Humphrey for the ceremony, and Humphrey delivered a characteristically thumbs-up speech. "You will be criticized," he said. "The only people who aren't criticized are those who do nothing, and I would hate to see the Agency get in that state."

The CIA could not survive sustained criticism from within the government, much less from the public. It depended on secrecy to survive. When blown operations wound up in the newspapers, it eroded what faith remained in the agency.

On September 30, 1967, Helms laid out strict new guidelines for covert action and sent them to every station. For the first time in the history of the CIA, station chiefs and their superiors were instructed to err on the side of caution. "Review all projects which are politically sensitive," the order said. Inform headquarters of the identities of "foreign politicians, both governmental and opposition, as well as certain military leaders, on the U.S. covert payroll." No sum of money spent on covert action was too small to report. "Our paramount considerations *must* be the political sensitivity of the activity and its consistency with U.S. foreign policy."

The flow of cash to burned-out foreign agents, third-rate newspapers, also-ran political parties, and other unproductive operations began to dry up. The number of major political-warfare operations in Western Europe began to dwindle. The CIA would stay focused on the hot war in Southeast Asia and the cold war in the Middle East, Africa, and Latin America.

But there was a war going on at home as well. The president had just told Helms to undertake the most politically sensitive operation of all— the job of spying on Americans.

27. "TRACK DOWN THE FOREIGN COMMUNISTS"

President Johnson feared that the antiwar movement would drive him out of the White House. But in the end the war itself did it.

In October 1967, a handful of CIA analysts joined in the first big Washington march against the war. The president regarded the protesters as enemies of the state. He was convinced that the peace movement was controlled and financed by Moscow and Beijing. He wanted proof. He ordered Richard Helms to produce it.

Helms reminded the president that the CIA was barred from spying on Americans. He says Johnson told him: "I'm quite aware of that. What I want for you is to pursue this matter, and to do what is necessary to track down the foreign communists who are behind this intolerable interference in our domestic affairs." It is likely that LBJ expressed himself more plainly.

In a blatant violation of his powers under law, the director of central intelligence became a part-time secret police chief. The CIA undertook a domestic surveillance operation, code-named Chaos. It went on for almost seven years. Helms created a new Special Operations Group to run the spying on Americans, and he cannily hid it in the shadows of Angleton's counterintelligence staff. Eleven CIA officers grew long hair, learned the jargon of the New Left, and went off to infiltrate peace groups in the United States and Europe. The agency compiled a computer index of 300,000 names of American people and organizations, and extensive files on 7,200 citizens. It began working in secret with police departments all over America. Unable to draw a clear distinction between the far left and the mainstream opposition to the war, it spied on every major organization in the peace movement. At the president's command, transmitted through Helms and the secretary of defense, the National Security Agency turned its immense eavesdropping powers on American citizens.

Both the president and conservatives in Congress saw connections between the peace protests and the race riots rocking the United States. They wanted the CIA to prove that communists were behind them both. The agency tried its best.

In 1967, America's ghettoes had become war zones; seventy-five separate urban riots wracked the nation, resulting in 88 deaths, 1,397 injuries, 16,389 arrests, 2,157 convictions, and economic damage estimated at $664.5 million. Forty-three people had been killed in Detroit, twenty-six in Newark. Rage filled the streets of New York, Los Angeles, San Francisco, Boston, Cincinnati, Dayton, Cleveland, Youngstown, Toledo, Peoria, Des Moines, Wichita, Birmingham, and Tampa. On October 25, Senator John McClellan, an Arkansas Democrat and chairman of the Senate Permanent Subcommittee on Investigations, wrote to Helms seeking evidence that the Soviets were running the black-power movement in the United States. "The Subcommittee is very much interested in the operations of various militant organizations in this country," the senator wrote.

McClellan said that Moscow had created "an espionage or sabotage school in Ghana, Africa, for colored people" and that Americans had served as instructors. "Purportedly these teachers came from somewhere in California," the senator wrote. "It would be most helpful to the Subcommittee if the identity of any American teacher who returned to the United States were known as well as the identity of any student. . . . Your cooperation in this matter will indeed be appreciated."

The clandestine service cooperated. On October 31, 1967, Tom Karamessines sent a raw and unconfirmed rumor from a Miami Cuban to the White House. "A Negro training camp" had been established at a beach near Santiago de Cuba where "Negroes were being trained for subversive operations against the United States," the report said. "Their courses included English which was being taught by Soviet instructors." It continued: "Their subversive activities against the United States would include sabotage in connection with race riots directed at bringing a Negro revolution in the United States." It said that "150 Negroes are involved in the training program and some have already arrived in the United States."

Lyndon Johnson was enraged. "I'm *not* going to let the Communists take this government and *they're doing it right now,*" he told Helms, Rusk, and McNamara during a ninety-five-minute rant on a Saturday afternoon, November 4, 1967. "I've got my belly full of seeing these people put on a Communist plane and shipped all over this country. I want someone to carefully look at who leaves this country, where they go, why they are going." This last remark was aimed pointedly at Helms.

But the CIA never found a shred of evidence that linked the leaders of the American left or the black-power movement to foreign governments. Helms took this unhappy fact to the president on November 15, 1967. He reported that while the CIA suspected that some members of the American left might have ideological affinities with Moscow or Hanoi, no evidence showed "that they act under any direction other than their own." Lyndon Johnson ordered Helms to intensify the search. It produced nothing beyond a continuing violation of the CIA's charter.

For millions of Americans, the war came home every night on television. On January 31, 1968, 400,000 communist troops hit almost every major city and military garrison in South Vietnam. The attack came on the first night of Tet, the lunar new year, and the enemy laid siege to Saigon and the major American bases at Hue and Khe Sanh. On February 1, television and still cameras captured the Saigon police chief as he executed a Vietcong prisoner in cold blood with a pistol shot to the head. The assault went on and on. Though the American counterattack was overwhelming—100,000 tons of bombs fell around Khe Sanh alone—the shock of the surprise attack was a devastating psychological defeat for the United States. Helms concluded that the CIA could not have predicted the Tet offensive because it had next to no intelligence on the enemy's intent.

On February 11, 1968, Helms pulled all his Vietnam experts together at headquarters. All but one of them—George Carver, still an optimist, though not for long—agreed on the following points: General Westmoreland, the American commander in Saigon, had no coherent strategy. It was useless to send more American troops. If the government and the army of South Vietnam did not pull together and fight the enemy, the United States should get out. Helms sent George Allen back to Saigon to assess the damage and to meet with President Thieu and Vice President

Ky. Allen found the army of South Vietnam shattered and the two leaders at one another's throats. American soldiers were unable to defend the nation's cities; American spies were panicked and demoralized. Hanoi had won its greatest political victory since 1954, when it handed the French their final defeat at Dien Bien Phu.

Helms personally gave the president the deeply pessimistic conclusions. They destroyed all but the last of LBJ's enormous political will.

On February 19, as Hanoi mounted a second wave of Tet attacks, the president spoke privately with Dwight Eisenhower. The next day, at the Tuesday lunch at the White House, Helms listened as the president described the conversation.

"General Eisenhower said that Westmoreland carries more responsibility than any general in the history of this country," LBJ recounted. "I asked him how many allies he had under his command during World War II. He said, including U.S. and allied troops, he had about five million. I told him General Westmoreland had 500,000 men, so how could he say that Westmoreland had the greatest responsibility of any American general? He said it was a different kind of war and General Westmoreland doesn't know who the enemy is."

At last Lyndon Johnson understood that no strategy could survive the failure of intelligence in Vietnam. The United States could not defeat an enemy it could not understand. A few weeks later, he announced he would not seek re-election as the president of the United States.

PART
FOUR

"Get Rid of the Clowns"

The CIA Under Nixon and Ford

1968 to 1976

---

28. "WHAT THE HELL DO THOSE CLOWNS DO OUT THERE IN LANGLEY?"

In the spring of 1968, Richard Helms had good reason to fear that his next boss would be either Robert Kennedy or Richard Nixon. As attorney general, Kennedy had abused the powers of the agency. He had commandeered the CIA and treated Helms with cold disdain. As a candidate, or as a commander in chief, he would be threatened by the secrets in the agency's files. Helms was truly shocked when the senator was murdered on the campaign trail in June. But he was not truly saddened. For the rest of his life, Helms bore lasting scars from the lashings Kennedy had laid on him.

Richard Nixon was another problem altogether. Helms knew how deep his resentments ran. Nixon thought the agency was filled with eastern elitists, knee-jerk liberals, Georgetown gossips, Kennedy men. It was an open secret that Nixon held the CIA responsible for the greatest disaster in his life: his defeat in the 1960 election. He was convinced—wrongly—that secrets and lies leaked by Allen Dulles had helped John Kennedy score crucial points in the televised presidential debates. In his 1962 memoir, *Six Crises*, Nixon had written that if he had been elected president, he would have created a new organization outside the CIA for carrying out covert operations. It was an open threat to cut out the agency's heart.

On August 10, 1968, Nixon and Helms met for their first long talk. The president had invited the candidate down to the LBJ Ranch in Texas, fed him steak and corn on the cob, and drove him around the ranch in an open convertible. Then he turned to Helms for a tour of the world:

the confrontation between Czechoslovakia and the Soviet Union, Castro's continuing support for revolutionary movements, and finally the secret peace negotiations between the United States and North Vietnam.

Nixon turned directly to Helms with a pointed question.

"Do they still believe we have lost the war?" he asked.

"The North Vietnamese are convinced they won after Dien Bien Phu," Helms said. That was the last thing Nixon wanted to hear.

Three days after winning the election, Nixon placed a call to LBJ. "What do you think about Helms?" he asked. "Would you continue him?"

"Yes, I would," Johnson replied. "He's extremely competent. He's succinct. He tells you as it is, and he's loyal."

That was high praise. After a year and a half dining at the president's table, Helms had won LBJ's confidence and earned a reputation in Washington as a consummate professional. He believed that the CIA, after twenty years, had developed a cadre of analysts with unique expertise on the Soviet threat and a clandestine service capable of conducting espionage without getting caught. He saw himself as a loyal soldier in the service of his president.

Helms would soon find out the cost of that loyalty.

"INCURABLY COVERT"

"Richard Nixon never trusted anybody," Helms reflected twenty years later. "Here he had become President of the United States and therefore chief of the Executive branch, and yet he was constantly telling people that the Air Force in their bombings in Vietnam couldn't hit their ass with their hand, the State Department was just a bunch of pinstriped cocktail-drinking diplomats, that the Agency couldn't come up with a winning victory in Vietnam. . . . On and on and on. . . . 'They are dumb, they are stupid, they can't do this, and they can't do that.' "

At the White House in January 1969, a few days into the new administration, Helms sat in tense silence at lunch as Nixon picked at his cottage cheese and canned pineapple. The president ripped into the CIA while his national security adviser, Henry Kissinger, listened attentively.

"I haven't the slightest doubt," Helms recalled, "that Nixon's carping affected Kissinger."

The president-elect and the Harvard man had discovered they were kindred spirits. "Both were incurably covert, but Kissinger was charming about it," observed Thomas Hughes, the director of the State Department's intelligence bureau. "Both were inveterate manipulators, but Nixon was more transparent." They had reached an understanding: they alone would conceive, command, and control clandestine operations. Covert action and espionage could be tools fitted for their personal use. Nixon used them to build a political fortress at the White House, and Kissinger became, in the words of his aide Roger Morris, the acting chief of state for national security.

As a preemptive act of self-protection, Helms had created a committee of Wise Men called the Covert Operations Study Group to report to the president-elect on the value of the clandestine service—and to protect it from attack. The group was led by Franklin Lindsay, once Frank Wisner's right-hand man, housed at Harvard, and convened in secret; its foremost members were Richard Bissell and Lyman Kirkpatrick. It included half a dozen Harvard professors who had served the White House, the Pentagon, the State Department, and the CIA. Three of them were close enough to their colleague Henry Kissinger to know he would be the next president's national security adviser no matter who won the race, for Kissinger had simultaneously served both Nixon and Humphrey as a confidential consultant. Neither man ever considered anyone else for the job.

The Covert Operations Study Group's secret report was dated December 1, 1968. One of its recommendations particularly pleased Kissinger: it said the new president should give one senior White House official responsibility for watching over all covert operations. Kissinger would not merely watch them. He would run them.

The report urged the new president to "make it very clear to the Director of the CIA that he expects him to say 'No' when in the Director's judgment a proposed operation cannot be done." Nixon never heeded that advice.

"Covert operations can rarely achieve an important objective alone," the report continued. "At best, a covert operation can win time, forestall a coup, or otherwise create favorable conditions which will make it possible to use overt means to finally achieve an important objective." Nixon never understood this principle.

"An individual, a political party, or a government in office can be seriously injured or destroyed by exposure of covert assistance from CIA," the report said. "On balance, exposure of clandestine operations costs the United States in terms of world opinion. To some, exposure demonstrates the disregard of the United States for national rights and human rights; to others it demonstrates only our impotence and ineptness in getting caught. . . . The impression of many Americans, especially in the intellectual community and among the youth, that the United States is engaging in 'dirty tricks' tends to alienate them from their government," the report continued. "Disclosures in this atmosphere have created opportunities for the 'New Left' to affect a much wider spectrum of political opinion than otherwise would have been the case. The United States has been in the forefront of those nations concerned with expanding the rule of law in international affairs. Our credibility and our effectiveness in this role is necessarily damaged to the extent that it becomes known that we are secretly intervening in what may be (or appear to be) the internal affairs of others." Nixon and Kissinger willfully ignored all these ideas.

"It is our impression that CIA has become much too ingrown over the years," the report concluded. "Nearly all of the senior people have been in the organization on the order of 20 years. . . . There also is a strong tendency toward isolation and inwardness . . . a lack of innovativeness and perspective." This much Nixon believed. He set out to infiltrate that inner circle. He began by naming Marine Lieutenant General Robert Cushman, who had been his national security aide when he was vice president, as the deputy director of central intelligence under Helms. Cushman's mission was to spy on America's spies for the president.

Eager to curry favor with the president-elect, the CIA sent Nixon the same daily intelligence summaries that Lyndon Johnson had received. They piled up unread in a safe at Nixon's suite on the thirty-ninth floor at the Pierre Hotel in New York. The stack grew for a month, until Kissinger sent word in December that Nixon would never look at them. He made it clear that from now on anything the agency wanted to tell the president would have to be channeled through him. Neither Helms nor anyone else from the CIA would ever see Nixon alone.

From the start, Kissinger exerted an ever-tightening control over the

CIA's operations. In 1967 and 1968, the CIA's overseers at the 303 Committee had lively debates over the course of covert action. Those days were gone. Kissinger dominated every other member of the committee—Helms, Attorney General John Mitchell, and the number-two officers of the State Department and the Pentagon. It became a one-man show. During a thirty-two-month stretch, the committee technically approved nearly forty covert actions but never once actually convened. In all, more than three quarters of the covert-action programs of the Nixon administration never were considered formally by the committee. The black operations of the United States were approved by Henry Kissinger.

In 1969, as is well known, the president wiretapped private citizens to stop news leaks and to control the flow of information inside the government. His national security adviser went beyond that: Kissinger also used the CIA to spy on Americans, a fact that heretofore has escaped the attention of history.

After the antiwar movement called for a monthly national moratorium, a one-day suspension of American business as usual, Helms received an order from Kissinger to spy on its leaders. Recorded in the office diary of Robert L. Bannerman, a senior staff member in the CIA's Office of Security, the memo was titled "Dr. Kissinger—Information Request."

"Dr. Kissinger levied a request as to what information we have on the leaders of the groups that conducted the moratorium on Vietnam," the CIA memo reads. "After consideration this request was relayed to [*deleted*] who agreed to be the focal point for this report and work on this report was conducted over the weekend." This was not merely a continuation of Chaos, the CIA's ongoing search for sources of foreign support for the antiwar movement. It was a specific request from the president's national security adviser for CIA files on American citizens.

The record reflects no hesitation on the part of Richard Helms. Since 1962, three successive presidents had ordered the director of central intelligence to spy on Americans, regardless of the CIA's charter. Nixon believed that all presidential action is legal in the realm of national security. If the president does it, he said, it is not illegal. Among his successors, only George W. Bush fully embraced this interpretation of presidential power, rooted in the divine right of kings. But it was one thing for a president to issue such an order, and quite another for an unelected official to do so in the president's name.

"HIT THE SOVIETS, AND HIT THEM HARD"

Nixon and Kissinger operated at a level of clandestinity beyond the CIA's. When they dealt with the enemies of the United States—negotiating in secret with the Soviets, the Chinese, the North Vietnamese—the CIA knew little or nothing about it. There was a reason for that: the White House disbelieved much of what the CIA's experts said about the forces of communism, especially the agency's estimates of the military might of the Soviet Union.

"I don't mean to say that they are lying about the intelligence or distorting it, but I want you fellows to be very careful to separate facts from opinions," Nixon told Helms at a June 18, 1969, National Security Council meeting.

"The fact is that the intelligence projections for 1965, 1966, 1967, and 1968—and I've seen them all—have been up to fifty percent off in what the Russians were going to have—and on the low side," Nixon said. "We have got to start with fact, and all the facts, and reach the conclusions on the basis of hard fact. Is that understood now?"

Nixon was outraged when the agency argued that the Soviets had neither the intention nor the technology to launch a knockout nuclear first strike. That conclusion came in a flurry of formal estimates on Soviet strategic forces, all of which Nixon rejected. "Useless," he wrote in the margins of a memo from Helms on Moscow's nuclear capabilities. "A superficial mindless recitation of what we know from the daily press." The CIA's analyses flew in the face of Nixon's plans to build an antiballistic missile system—the prelude to the *Star Wars* fantasies of the future. "Whose side is the Agency on?" was the way Helms remembered the White House argument. "In other words, 'Let's all get together and trim the evidence.' "

In the end, that is exactly what Helms did, erasing a key passage of the CIA's most important estimate on Soviet nuclear forces in 1969. Once again, the agency was tailoring its work to fit the pattern of White House policy. His decision to go along with the White House "did not sit well with the Agency analysts," Helms recorded. "In their view, I had compromised one of the Agency's fundamental responsibilities—the mandate to evaluate all available data and express conclusions irrespective of U.S. policies." But Helms would not risk this battle: "I was convinced we would have lost the argument with the Nixon administration, and that in the process the Agency would have been permanently damaged." His analysts complained about the suppression of dissent and the failure to learn from past mistakes. But no plan to improve the analysis of Soviet capabilities and intentions came forth.

The CIA had been studying spy-satellite reconnaissance photos of the Soviet Union for eight years now, looking down from space and putting together a jigsaw puzzle of the Soviet military. The agency was working on the next generation of spy satellites, to be equipped with television cameras. Helms always had believed that gadgets were no replacement for spies. Nevertheless, he assured Nixon that they would give the United States the power to make sure that Moscow complied with agreements reached in SALT, the Strategic Arms Limitation Treaty talks then under way in Helsinki.

But the more raw data the CIA obtained on the Soviet military, the less clear the big picture became. Nixon rightly criticized the agency for having underestimated Soviet nuclear firepower in the 1960s; he pounded the agency on that account throughout his presidency. The result of that pressure is now evident: for thirteen years, from Nixon's era to the dying days of the cold war, every estimate of Soviet strategic nuclear forces *overstated* the rate at which Moscow was modernizing its weaponry.

Nixon nonetheless relied on the CIA to subvert the Soviet Union at every turn—not just in Moscow, but in every nation on earth.

"The President called Henry Kissinger and me into the Oval Office after the NSC meeting today for what turned out to be a 25-minute discussion of a variety of subjects, including SALT, Laos, Cambodia, Cuba, and black operations," Helms recorded in a March 25, 1970, memo. "With respect to black operations, the President enjoined me to hit the Soviets, and hit them hard, any place we can in the world. He said to 'just go ahead,' to keep Henry Kissinger informed, and to be as imaginative as we could. He was as emphatic on this as I have ever heard him on anything." Encouraged by this rare moment of presidential attention, Helms "took this moment to hit hard on the point that I felt strongly the United States should give up nothing which constituted a pressure on the Soviet Union or an irritation to them without exacting a specific price in return." He promised the president a new array of proposed covert actions against the Soviets.

Only one paragraph of the paper Helms sent to the White House the next week caught Nixon's eye.

Helms reviewed the work of Radio Free Europe and Radio Liberty—a twenty-year investment of more than $400 million—and the power of the radios to keep the fires of dissent alive behind the iron curtain. He detailed the work of Soviet dissidents such as the physicist Andrei Sakharov and the writer Alexander Solzhenitsyn, whose words had been played back to the Soviet Union by the CIA. Thirty million people in Eastern Europe heard Radio Free Europe, and Soviet citizens did their best to tune in Radio Liberty, though Moscow was spending $150 million a year jamming their signals. In addition, the Free Europe and Liberty organizations had distributed two and a half million books and periodicals in the Soviet Union and Eastern Europe since the late 1950s. The hope was that words, on the air and in print, could promote intellectual and cultural freedom.

All that was good—but it was also old hat to Nixon. What captured his imagination was the CIA's ability to swing elections.

"There have been numerous instances when, facing the threat of a Communist Party or popular front election victory in the Free World, we have met the threat and turned it successfully," Helms reminded the president. "Guyana in 1963 and Chile in 1964 are good examples of what can be accomplished under difficult circumstances. Similar situations may soon face us in various parts of the world, and we are prepared for action with carefully planned covert election programs." That was more like it. Money and politics were subjects close to Nixon's heart.

"THE ONLY WAY TO GO WAS THE OLD WAY"

The agency had secretly supported politicians in Western Europe throughout the cold war. The list included Chancellor Willy Brandt of Germany, Prime Minister Guy Mollet of France, and every Christian Democrat who ever won a national election in Italy.

The CIA had spent twenty years and at least $65 million buying influence in Rome and Milan and Naples. In 1965, McGeorge Bundy had called the covert-action program in Italy "the annual shame." Yet it went on. Foreign powers had been meddling in Italian politics for centuries; Washington was following "in the tradition of what the fascists, the communists, the Nazis, the British, and the French had done before," said Thomas Fina, the American consul general in Milan under Nixon and a veteran of American intelligence and diplomacy in Italy. The CIA had been "subsidizing political parties, withdrawing money from political parties, giving money to individual politicians, not giving it to other politicians, subsidizing the publication of books, the content of radio programs, subsidizing newspapers, subsidizing journalists," Fina noted. It had "financial resources, political resources, friends, the ability to blackmail."

Nixon and Kissinger revived that tradition. Their instrument was the CIA's Rome station and the extraordinary ambassador Graham Martin.

Kissinger called Martin "that cold-eyed fellow," and he meant it as a compliment. "He obviously admired somebody who could be as ruthless in the exercise of power as he could be," said Martin's chief political officer in Rome, Robert Barbour. Other American diplomats found Martin shadowy and strange, "slippery as a cold basket of eels." Martin had converted Marshall Plan funds to CIA cash at the American Embassy in Paris twenty years before. He had worked closely with the CIA as ambassador in Thailand from 1965 to 1968. No American diplomat was more deeply enamored of covert operations.

Nixon thought he was terrific. "I have great personal confidence in Graham Martin," he told Kissinger on February 14, 1969, and with that, the machine was in motion.

Martin's appointment as ambassador in Italy was the handiwork of a wealthy right-wing American named Pier Talenti, who lived in Rome, where he had raised hundreds of thousands of dollars for the 1968 Nixon campaign among his friends and political allies. That opened the door to the White House. Talenti went to see Colonel Alexander M. Haig, Jr., Kissinger's military aide, to deliver a warning that the socialists were on the verge of taking power in Italy and a proposal that a new American ambassador was needed to counter the left. He named Martin, and his message went right to the top. Martin had persuaded Nixon and Kissinger that "he was just the man, because he was tough as nails, to bring about a shift in Italian politics," said Wells Stabler, his deputy chief of mission in Rome.

"Martin decided that the only way to go was the old way," said

Stabler, who became a reluctant participant in the revival of American covert action in Italy. Beginning in 1970, after receiving formal approval from the Nixon White House, Martin oversaw the distribution of $25 million to both Christian Democrats and Italian neofascists, Stabler said. The money was divided "in the back room"—the CIA station inside the palatial American embassy—by "the Ambassador, myself, and the station chief," Stabler said. "Some was given to the parties, some to individuals. Sometimes the station chief or myself would recommend something, but it was the Ambassador who would give the approval." The station chief was Rocky Stone, the veteran of the Iran coup and the blown attempt to overthrow Syria, who had come to Rome after three years as chief of operations for the Soviet division.

Stone handed out about $6 million to the mainstream Christian Democrats. Millions more went to committees that pushed "ultra-conservative policies" in the party, Stabler said. And millions more went to a far-right underground.

The money, as Martin had promised, transformed the political face of Italy. The man he backed, Giulio Andreotti, won an election infused with the CIA's cash. But the covert financing of the far right fueled a failed neofascist coup in 1970. The money helped finance right-wing covert operations—including terrorist bombings, which Italian intelligence blamed on the extreme left. It also led to the worst political scandal in post-war Italy. Parliamentary investigations found that General Vito Miceli, the chief of the Italian military intelligence service, had taken at least $800,000 of the CIA's cash. Miceli was jailed for trying to take over the country by force. Andreotti, the most durable Italian politician in decades, spent the last years of his life fighting criminal charges, including murder.

The CIA's days of buying political influence in Italy finally ended when Graham Martin left Rome to become the next—and the last—American ambassador to South Vietnam.

"WE ARE CONSCIOUS OF WHAT IS AT STAKE"

Throughout 1969 and 1970, Nixon and Kissinger focused the CIA on the secret expansion of the war in Southeast Asia. They ordered the agency to make $725,000 in political payoffs to President Thieu of South Vietnam, manipulate the media in Saigon, fix an election in Thailand, and step up covert commando raids in North Vietnam, Cambodia, and Laos.

In a bleak dispatch on the eve of a world tour that took Nixon across Southeast Asia, Helms told the president about the CIA's long war in Laos. The agency "maintained a covert irregular force of a total of 39,000 men which has borne a major share of the active fighting" against the communists, he reminded Nixon. They were the CIA's Hmong fighters, led since 1960 by General Vang Pao. "These irregular forces are tired from eight years of constant warfare, and Vang Pao . . . has been forced to use 13- and 14-year-old children to replace his casualties. . . . The limits have largely been reached on what this agency can do in a paramilitary sense to stop the North Vietnamese advance." Nixon responded by ordering Helms to create a new Thai paramilitary battalion in Laos to shore up the Hmong. Kissinger asked where it would be best to bomb Laos with B-52s.

While their clandestine war in Southeast Asia intensified, Nixon and Kissinger made plans for a secret rapprochement with Chairman Mao Tse-tung. To clear the way to China, they strangled the agency's operations against the communist regime.

Over the past decade, in the name of combating Chinese communism, the CIA had spent tens of millions of dollars parachuting tons of weapons to hundreds of Tibetan guerrillas who fought for their spiritual leader, His Holiness Tenzen Gyatso, the fourteenth Dalai Lama. When Allen Dulles and Desmond FitzGerald briefed Eisenhower on the operation in February 1960, "the President wondered whether the net result of these operations would not be more brutal repressive reprisals by the Chinese Communists."

Ike approved the program nonetheless. The agency set up a training camp for the Tibetan fighters in the Rocky Mountains of Colorado. It had paid an annual subsidy of some $180,000 directly to the Dalai Lama, and it created Tibet Houses in New York and Geneva to serve as his unofficial embassies. The goal was to keep the dream of a free Tibet alive while harassing the Red Army in western China. The results to date had been dozens of dead resistance fighters, and one bloodstained satchel of invaluable Chinese military documents seized in a firefight.

In August 1969, the agency requested $2.5 million more to support Tibet's insurgents in the coming year, calling the 1,800-man paramilitary group "a force which could be employed in strength in the event of hostilities" against China. "Does this have any direct benefit to us?" Kissinger asked. He answered his own question. Though the CIA's subsidy to the Dalai Lama continued, the Tibetan resistance was abandoned.

Kissinger then scuttled the remains of the CIA's twenty-year mission to conduct clandestine operations against China.

The commando raids of the Korean War had dwindled down to desultory radio broadcasts from Taipei and Seoul, leaflets dropped on the mainland, fake news planted in Hong Kong and Tokyo, and what the agency described as "activities worldwide to denigrate and obstruct the People's Republic of China." The CIA kept working with Generalissimo Chiang Kai-shek in his doomed effort to free Taiwan, unaware that Nixon and Kissinger had plans to sit down with Chairman Mao and Prime Minister Chou En-lai in Beijing.

When Kissinger finally sat down with Chou, the prime minister asked about the latest Free Taiwan campaign: "The CIA had no hand in it?"

Kissinger assured Chou that "he vastly overestimates the competence of the CIA."

"They have become the topic of discussion throughout the world," Chou said. "Whenever something happens in the world they are always thought of."

"That is true," Kissinger replied, "and it flatters them, but they don't deserve it."

Chou was fascinated to learn that Kissinger personally approved the CIA's covert operations. He voiced his suspicions that the agency was still subverting the People's Republic.

Kissinger replied that most CIA officers "write long, incomprehensible reports and don't make revolution."

"You use the word revolution," Chou said. "We say subversion."

"Or subversion," Kissinger conceded. "I understand. We are conscious of what is at stake in our relationship, and we will not let one organization carry out petty operations that could hinder this course."

That was the end of that. The CIA was out of business in China for years to come.

"DEMOCRACY DOESN'T WORK"

The CIA fought on every front to shore up the war in Vietnam. One of its bigger efforts came to fruition three weeks after President Nixon took office. In February 1969, covert action created the appearance of democracy in Thailand.

A military junta had ruled Thailand for eleven years, and tens of thousands of American troops readied for battle against Hanoi at Thai military bases. The dictatorship did little to support the notion that Americans were fighting for democracy in Southeast Asia.

The CIA's election operation, code-named Lotus, was a straight-cash campaign first conceived by Ambassador Graham Martin in 1965, approved by President Johnson, and reaffirmed by President Nixon. The CIA station in Bangkok coaxed the junta toward holding a ballot; the generals kept putting them off. Finally the agency pumped millions of dollars into the politics of Thailand in 1968 and 1969; the cash financed the apparent transformation of the uniformed military into a ruling party ready to stand for elections. The CIA's bagman was Pote Sarasin— Thailand's ambassador to the United States from 1952 to 1957, the head of the Southeast Asia Treaty Organization from 1957 to 1964, and the leading civilian front man for the ruling junta.

The election came off and the ruling junta won handily. But the rulers grew impatient with the trappings of democracy. They soon ended the experiment, suspending the constitution and disbanding parliament. Pote Sarasin reassumed his position as the civilian face of martial law on the night of the bloodless coup, and he brought the generals to explain themselves to their friends at the American embassy in Bangkok that evening. They said they respected the principles of democracy and had tried to put them into action. But they said "it was clear that in Thailand today democracy doesn't work."

The CIA's covert action had been the thinnest veneer. "There should be no change in Thai relations with the U.S.," Kissinger told Nixon after the coup. "The leaders of the Revolutionary Council are in fact essentially the same ones with whom we have been dealing all along," he said. "We can anticipate that our programs in Thailand will continue without interruption."

"GET THE CIA JERKS WORKING"

In February 1970, the president urgently ordered the agency to get going in Cambodia. After a year of planning, his secret bombing campaign
against suspected Vietcong targets in that technically neutral nation was
set to begin on March 17. American B-52s would drop 108,823 tons of
bombs on six suspected communist camps that the CIA and the Pentagon had identified—incorrectly—as North Vietnam's hidden command
center.

Helms was trying to lay the foundations for a new CIA station in Cambodia when the nation's right-wing prime minister, Lon Nol, seized power.
The overthrow came on the day that the secret bombings began. The coup
shocked the CIA and the rest of the American government.

"What the hell do those clowns do out there in Langley?" Nixon
thundered.

"Get the CIA jerks working on Cambodia," he commanded. He told
Helms to ship thousands of AK-47 automatic rifles to Lon Nol, to print a
million propaganda leaflets, and to spread the word throughout the
world that the United States was ready to invade. Then he ordered the
CIA to deliver $10 million to the new Cambodian leader. "Get the money
to Lon Nol," he insisted.

Nixon had demanded an accurate tally of the arms and ammunition
flowing to the enemy through the Cambodian port of Sihanoukville. The
agency had been working on the question for five years without success.
Nixon suggested that the arms flow could be cut off if the CIA bribed the
right Cambodian generals. Helms demurred on practical grounds—the
generals were making millions off the arms trade and the agency did not
have the funds to buy or rent their loyalties. The argument did not im-
press the president. At a July 18, 1970, meeting with his foreign intelligence advisory board, Nixon savaged the agency's performance.

"CIA had described the flow of materials through Sihanoukville as
only a trickle," he said. In fact, the port was providing two thirds of the
communist arms in Cambodia. "If such mistakes could be made on a
fairly straightforward issue such as this one," he asked, "how should we
judge CIA's assessments or more important developments?"

"The U.S. is spending $6 billion per year on intelligence and deserves
to get a lot more than it is getting," Nixon said. The intelligence board's

minutes record his growing rage. The president said "he could not put up with people lying to him about intelligence. If intelligence is inadequate or if the intelligence depicts a bad situation, he wants to know about it and he will not stand being served warped evaluations."

"He understands that the intelligence community has been bitten badly a few times and thus tends to make its reports as bland as possible so that it won't be bitten again," the minutes say. "He believes that those responsible for the deliberate distortion of an intelligence report should be fired. He suggested that the time may be coming when he would have to read the riot act to the entire intelligence community."

At this delicate moment, Nixon ordered the CIA to fix the next election in Chile.

29. "USG WANTS A MILITARY SOLUTION"

By 1970, the CIA's influence was felt in every nation in the Western Hemisphere, from the Texas border to Tierra del Fuego. In Mexico, the president dealt exclusively with the station chief, not the ambassador, and he received a personal New Year's Day briefing at his home from the director of central intelligence. In Honduras, two successive station chiefs had privately pledged the support of the United States to the military junta, in defiance of the ambassadors they served.

Few Latin American nations paid more than lip service to the ideals of democracy and the rule of law. One of the few was Chile, where the CIA saw a red threat rising.

The leftist Salvador Allende was the front-runner in the presidential election, set for September 1970. The moderate Radomiro Tomic, backed by the Christian Democrats, traditional CIA favorites, looked like a very long shot. The right-winger Jorge Alessandri had a strong pro-American track record, but he was corrupt; the American ambassador, Edward Korry, found him insupportable. All bets were off.

The CIA had beaten Allende once before. President Kennedy first approved a political-warfare program to subvert him more than two years before the September 1964 Chilean elections. The agency put in the plumbing and pumped roughly $3 million into the political apparatus of Chile. It worked out to about a dollar a vote for the pro-American Christian Democrat Eduardo Frei. Lyndon Johnson, who approved the continuing operation, spent a lot less per voter when he won the American presidency in 1964. Frei's campaign received get-out-the-vote drives and political consultants along with suitcases full of cash. The CIA financed covert anti-Allende efforts by the Roman Catholic Church and trade unions. The agency pumped up the resistance to Allende in the Chilean military command and the national police. Secretary of State Rusk told President Johnson that Frei's victory was "a triumph for democracy," achieved "partly as a result of the good work of the CIA."

President Frei served for six years; the constitution limited him to one term. Now the question once again was how to stop Allende. For months, Helms had been warning the White House that if it wanted to keep Chile under control, it needed to approve a new covert action quickly. Winning foreign elections took time as well as money. The agency had one of its most durable and dependable men posted as station chief in Santiago— Henry Hecksher, who had spied on the Soviets from Berlin, helped overthrow Guatemala, and maneuvered Laos into the American camp. Now he strongly advised the White House to back Alessandri, the rightwinger.

Kissinger was preoccupied. He had a real war in Southeast Asia on his hands. He famously called Chile a dagger pointed at the heart of Antarctica. But in March 1970, he approved a $135,000 political-warfare program to crush Allende. On June 27, adding another $165,000, he observed: "I don't see why we have to let a country go Marxist just because its people are irresponsible." He backed the defeat of Allende, but the election of no one.

In the spring and summer of 1970, the CIA went to work. At home and abroad, it fed propaganda to prominent reporters who served as the agency's stenographers. "Particularly noteworthy in this connection was the *Time* cover story which owed a great deal to written materials and briefings provided by CIA," an in-house agency report noted. In Europe, senior representatives of the Vatican and Christian Democratic leaders in West Germany and Italy worked at the CIA's behest to stop Allende. In Chile, "posters were printed, news stories planted, editorial comment encouraged, rumors whispered, leaflets strewn, and pamphlets distributed," Helms recounted. The goal was to terrify the electorate—"to show that an Allende victory risked the destruction of Chilean democracy," Helms said. "It was a strenuous effort, but the discernable effect seemed minimal."

Ambassador Korry found the CIA's work appallingly unprofessional. "I had never seen such dreadful propaganda in a campaign anywhere in the world," he said many years later. "I said that the idiots in the CIA who had helped create the 'campaign of terror'—and I said this to the CIA—should have been sacked immediately for not understanding Chile and Chileans. This was the kind of thing I had seen in 1948 in Italy."

On September 4, 1970, Allende won the three-way election by a 1.5 percent margin, with less than 37 percent of the vote. Under Chilean law, the Congress had to ratify the result and affirm Allende's plurality fifty days after the election. It was a mere legal formality.

"YOU ALREADY HAVE YOUR VIETNAM"

The CIA had plenty of experience fixing an election before the ballot. It had never fixed one afterward. It had seven weeks to reverse the outcome.

Kissinger instructed Helms to weigh the chances for a coup. They were slim: Chile had been a democracy since 1932 and the military had not sought political power since. Helms sent station chief Henry Hecksher a cable ordering him to establish direct contacts with Chilean military officers who could take care of Allende. Hecksher had no such connections. But he did know Agustín Edwards, one of the most powerful men in Chile. Edwards owned most of the nation's copper mines; its biggest newspaper, *El Mercurio;* and its Pepsi-Cola bottling plant. A week after the election, Edwards flew north to see his good friend Donald Kendall, Pepsi's chief executive officer and one of President Nixon's most valued financial supporters.

On September 14, Edwards and Kendall had coffee with Kissinger. Then "Kendall went to Nixon and wanted some help to keep Allende out of office," Helms recalled. (Kendall later denied that role; Helms scoffed at the disavowal.) Helms met Edwards at midday at the Washington Hilton. They discussed the timing for a military coup against Allende. That afternoon, Kissinger approved $250,000 more for political warfare in Chile. In all, the CIA delivered a total of $1.95 million directly to Edwards, *El Mercurio*, and their campaign against Allende.

That same morning, Helms had told Tom Polgar, now the station chief in Buenos Aires, to get on the next plane for Washington—and to bring along the chief of the Argentine military junta, General Alejandro

Lanusse. The general was an unsentimental man who had spent four years in prison in the 1960s after a failed coup. The next afternoon, September 15, Polgar and Lanusse sat in the director's suite at CIA headquarters, waiting for Helms to return from a meeting with Nixon and Kissinger.

"Helms was very nervous when he returned," Polgar remembered, and with good reason: Nixon had ordered him to mount a military coup without telling the secretary of state, the secretary of defense, the American ambassador, or the station chief. Helms had scrawled the president's commands on a notepad:

> *One in 10 chance perhaps, but save Chile! . . .*
> *$10,000,000 available. . . .*
> *best men we have. . . .*
> *make the economy scream.*

Helms had forty-eight hours to give Kissinger a game plan and forty-nine days to stop Allende.

Tom Polgar had known Richard Helms for twenty-five years. They had started out together in the Berlin base in 1945. Polgar looked his old friend in the eye and saw a flicker of despair. Helms turned to General Lanusse and asked what it would take for his junta to help overthrow Allende.

The Argentine general stared at the chief of American intelligence.

"Mr. Helms," he said, "you already have your Vietnam. Don't make me have mine."

"WHAT WE NEED IS A GENERAL WITH BALLS"

On September 16, Helms called an early-morning meeting with his covert-action chief, Tom Karamessines, and seven other senior officers. "The President asked the Agency to prevent Allende from coming to power or to unseat him," he announced. Karamessines had overall command as well as the thankless job of keeping Kissinger posted.

The CIA divided the Allende operation into Track One and Track

Two. Track One was political warfare, economic pressure, propaganda, and diplomatic hardball. It aimed to buy enough votes in the Chilean Senate to block Allende's confirmation. If that failed, Ambassador Korry planned to persuade President Frei to create a constitutional coup. As a last resort, the United States would "condemn Chile and the Chileans to utmost deprivation and poverty," Korry told Kissinger, "forcing Allende to adopt the harsh features of a police state," and provoking a popular uprising.

Track Two was a military coup. Korry knew nothing about it. But Helms defied the president's order to exclude Henry Hecksher, and he told Tom Polgar to return to Argentina to bolster him. Hecksher and Polgar—Berlin base boys, the best of friends since World War II—were among the finest officers the CIA had. They both thought Track Two was a fool's errand.

Helms called in the station chief in Brazil, David Atlee Phillips, to lead the Chile task force. A CIA man since 1950, a veteran of Guatemala and the Dominican Republic, he was the best propaganda artist at the agency. He had no hope for Track One.

"Anyone who had lived in Chile, as I had, and knew Chileans, knew that you might get away with bribing one Chilean Senator, but two? Never. And three? Not a chance," he said. "They would blow the whistle. They were democrats and had been for a long time." As for Track Two, Phillips said, "the Chilean military was a very model of democratic rectitude." Their commander, General Rene Schneider, had proclaimed that the army would obey the constitution and refrain from politics.

For Track One, Phillips had twenty-three foreign reporters on his payroll to stir up international opinion. He and his colleagues had dictated the fierce anti-Allende story that ran on the cover of *Time*. For Track Two, he had a false-flag team of deep-cover CIA men with phony passports. One posed as a Colombian businessman, another as an Argentine smuggler, a third as a Bolivian military intelligence officer.

On September 27, the false-flaggers asked the U.S. Army attaché at the embassy, Colonel Paul Wimert, a longtime friend of the CIA, to help them find Chilean officers who would overthrow Allende. One of the very few generals who had tried to stir up a coup in the recent past, Roberto Viaux, was a candidate. But many of his fellow officers thought Viaux was a dangerous fool; some thought he was insane.

On October 6, one of the false-flaggers had a long talk with Viaux.

Within hours, Ambassador Korry learned for the first time that the CIA was plotting a coup behind his back. He had a screaming confrontation with Henry Hecksher. "You have twenty-four hours to either understand that I run you or you leave the country," the ambassador said.

"I am appalled," Korry cabled Kissinger. "Any attempt on our part actively to encourage a coup could lead us to a Bay of Pigs failure."

An apoplectic Kissinger ordered the ambassador to stop meddling. Then he summoned Helms once more to the White House. The result was a flash cable to the CIA station in Santiago: "CONTACT THE MILITARY AND LET THEM KNOW USG"—the U.S. government—"WANTS A MILITARY SOLUTION, AND THAT WE WILL SUPPORT THEM NOW AND LATER. . . . CREATE AT LEAST SOME SORT OF COUP CLIMATE. . . . SPONSOR A MILITARY MOVE."

On October 7, hours after that order left CIA headquarters, Helms took off on a two-week inspection tour of the stations in Saigon, Bangkok, Vientiane, and Tokyo.

That day, Henry Hecksher tried to knock down the idea of running a coup in concert with General Viaux. The station chief told headquarters that a Viaux regime "would be a tragedy for Chile and for the free world. . . . A Viaux coup would only produce a massive bloodbath." That went over poorly in Washington. On October 10, with two weeks left until the installation of Allende, Hecksher tried again to explain the facts to his superiors. "You have asked us to provoke chaos in Chile," Hecksher wrote. "Thru Viaux solution we provide you with formula for chaos which is unlikely to be bloodless. To dissimulate US involvement will clearly be impossible. Station team, as you know, has given serious consideration to all plans suggested by HQs counterparts. We conclude that none of them stand even a remote chance of achieving objective. Hence, Viaux gamble, despite high risk factors, may commend itself to you."

Headquarters hesitated.

On October 13, Hecksher cabled the news that Viaux was thinking about kidnapping the commander in chief of the Chilean army, the constitutionally minded General Schneider. Kissinger summoned Karamessines to the White House. On the morning of October 16, Karamessines cabled his orders to Hecksher:

IT IS FIRM AND CONTINUING POLICY THAT ALLENDE
BE OVERTHROWN BY A COUP. . . . IT WAS DETERMINED

THAT A VIAUX COUP ATTEMPT CARRIED OUT BY HIM
ALONE WITH THE FORCES NOW AT HIS DISPOSAL
WOULD FAIL. . . . ENCOURAGE HIM TO AMPLIFY HIS
PLANNING. . . . ENCOURAGE HIM TO JOIN FORCES WITH
OTHER COUP PLANNERS. . . . GREAT AND CONTINUING
INTEREST IN THE ACTIVITIES OF . . . VALENZUELA ET AL
AND WE WISH THEM OPTIMUM GOOD FORTUNE.

General Camilo Valenzuela, chief of the Santiago garrison, had been in touch with the CIA six days before. He had revealed that he was willing, perhaps able, but frightened. On the evening of October 16, one of Valenzuela's officers approached the CIA looking for money and guidance. *"Qué necesitamos es un general con cojones,"* the officer said. "What we need is a general with balls."

The next night, General Valenzuela sent two colonels to meet in secret with Colonel Wimert, the CIA's uniformed representative. Their plan—virtually identical to one first broached by Viaux—was to kidnap General Schneider, fly him to Argentina, dissolve Congress, and take power in the name of the armed forces. They received $50,000 cash, three submachine guns, and a satchel of tear gas, all approved at headquarters by Tom Karamessines.

On October 19, with five days to go, Hecksher pointed out that Track Two had been "so unprofessional and insecure that, in Chilean setting, it could stand a chance of succeeding." In other words, so many Chilean military officers knew that the CIA wanted Allende stopped that the odds of a coup were rising. "All interested military parties know our position," reads a CIA memo dated October 20. Richard Helms returned to the United States from his two-week tour of Asian stations the next day.

On October 22, fifty hours before Congress was to convene to confirm the election results, a gang of armed men ambushed General Schneider on his way to work. He was shot repeatedly and died in surgery shortly after Salvador Allende was affirmed by Congress as the constitutionally elected president of Chile by a vote of 153 to 35.

It took the CIA quite a few days to figure out who had killed General Schneider. At headquarters, Dave Phillips had assumed that the CIA's machine guns had done the job. To his great relief, it had been Viaux's men, not Valenzuela's, who pulled the trigger. The CIA plane once scheduled to smuggle a kidnapped General Schneider out of Santiago carried in his stead the Chilean officer who had received the agency's guns and money. "He came to Buenos Aires with a pistol in his pocket saying, 'I'm in big trouble, you got to help me,' " Tom Polgar remembered. The agency had started out buying votes in Chile, and it wound up smuggling automatic weapons to would-be assassins.

"THE CIA ISN'T WORTH A DAMN"

The White House was furious at the agency's failure to stop Allende. The president and his men believed that a liberal cabal at the CIA had sabotaged covert action in Chile. Alexander Haig, now a general and Kissinger's indispensable right hand, said the operation failed because the CIA's officers had let their political feelings "flavor their final assessments and their proposals for remedial action in the covert area." It was high time, Haig told his boss, to purge "the key left-wing dominated slots under Helms" and insist on "a major overhauling of the means, the attitude, and the conceptual basis on which CIA's covert programs should be carried out."

Nixon decreed that Helms could keep his job only if he cleaned house. The director immediately promised to dismiss four of his six deputies, retaining only Tom Karamessines for covert action and Carl Duckett for science and technology. In a memo to Kissinger, he warned obliquely that a continuing purge would threaten the morale and dedication of his men. The president responded by threatening over and over to cut hundreds of millions of dollars out of the agency's hide. "Nixon railed against the CIA and their lousy intelligence," recalled George P. Shultz, then his budget director. " 'I want you to cut the CIA's budget to one-third its present size,' " the president would say. " 'No, make it one-half its present size.' It was Nixon's way of venting his ire, but you didn't take it too seriously."

Nixon was not kidding. In December 1970, one of Kissinger's aides pleaded "that you privately urge the President not to make such a large, arbitrary, across-the-board cut. . . . A meat-ax approach could be disastrous." But the president held the knife at the CIA's throat for the next two years.

It proved simple for the Nixon White House to savage the CIA, but far harder to salvage it. That month, at the president's direction, Kissinger and Shultz deputized an ambitious ax-wielder at the budget office named James R. Schlesinger to lead a three-month review of the roles and responsibilities held by Richard Helms. Prematurely gray at forty-one, Schlesinger was a Harvard classmate of Kissinger's, every bit his equal in intellect, though lacking the essential quality of deceit. He had made his reputation at the Nixon White House by crashing into the underbrush of the government and chopping out dead wood.

Schlesinger reported that the cost of intelligence was soaring and the quality shrinking. Seven thousand CIA analysts swamped with data could not sort out the patterns of the present. Six thousand clandestine-service officers could not penetrate the high councils of the communist world. The director of central intelligence had no power to do anything except run covert action and produce intelligence reports that Nixon and Kissinger rarely read. The agency could not support Nixon's global ambitions—opening the door to China, standing up to the Soviets, ending the Vietnam War on American terms. "There is no evidence that the intelligence community, given its present structure, will come to grips with this class of problems," Schlesinger concluded.

He proposed the most radical reshaping of American espionage since 1947. A new czar to be known as the director of national intelligence would work at the White House and oversee the empire of intelligence. The CIA should be dismembered and a new agency invented to carry out covert action and espionage.

Haig, who had set the idea in motion, wrote a memo that it would be "the most controversial gutfight" undertaken in American government in memory. The problem was that Congress had created the CIA and it would have to play a part in its rebirth. This Nixon could not abide. It had to be done in secret. He ordered Kissinger to spend a month doing nothing else but making sure it happened. But Kissinger had no stomach for it. "I prefer to sit on it," he scribbled on Haig's memo. "I have no intention to bleed over it."

The long battle ended a year after Allende came to power. The president directly ordered Helms to hand over control of the CIA to his deputy director—Nixon's hired gun, General Cushman—and assume the role of figurehead emperor of American intelligence. Helms parried that deadly thrust with a deft riposte. He put Cushman in a freeze so deep that the general pleaded for a new billet as the commandant of the marines. The number-two job stayed open for six months.

With that, the idea died, except in the mind of Richard Nixon. "Intelligence is a sacred cow," he raged. "We've done nothing since we've been here about it. The CIA isn't worth a damn." He made a mental note to get rid of Richard Helms.

"THE NATURAL AND PROBABLE CONSEQUENCES"

The subversion of Salvador Allende went on. "Track Two never really ended," the CIA's Tom Karamessines said, and his notes from a December 10, 1970, White House meeting reflected what was to come: "Kissinger, in the role of the devil's advocate, pointed out that the proposed CIA program was aimed at supporting moderates. Since Allende is holding himself out as a moderate, he asked, why not support extremists?"

That is precisely what the agency did. It spent most of the $10 million authorized by Nixon sowing political and economic chaos in Chile. The seeds sprouted in 1971. The new chief of the Latin American division, Ted Shackley, back at CIA headquarters after chief-of-station stints in Laos and South Vietnam, told his superiors that his officers would "bring our influence to bear on key military commanders so that they might play a decisive role on the side of the coup forces." The new Santiago station chief, Ray Warren, built a web of military men and political saboteurs who sought to shift the Chilean military off its constitutional foundation. And President Allende made a fatal mistake. In reaction to the pressure placed upon him by the CIA, he built a shadow army called the Grupo de Amigos del Presidente, or the Friends of the President. Fidel Castro backed this force. The Chilean military could not conscience it.

Almost three years to the day after Allende's election, a young CIA officer in Santiago by the name of Jack Devine, who many years later became the acting chief of the clandestine service, flashed a bulletin that went straight to Kissinger, whom Richard Nixon had just nominated to be secretary of state. The cable said the United States would within minutes or hours receive a request for aid from "a key officer of the Chilean military group planning to overthrow President Allende."

The coup came on September 11, 1973. It was swift and terrible. Facing capture at the presidential palace, Allende killed himself with an automatic rifle, a gift from Fidel Castro. The military dictatorship of General Augusto Pinochet took power that afternoon, and the CIA quickly forged a liaison with the general's junta. Pinochet reigned with cruelty, murdering more than 3,200 people, jailing and torturing tens of thousands in the repression called the Caravan of Death.

"There is no doubt," the agency confessed in a statement to Congress after the cold war ended, "that some CIA contacts were actively engaged in committing and covering up serious human rights abuses." Chief among them was Colonel Manuel Contreras, the head of the Chilean intelligence service under Pinochet. He became a paid CIA agent and met with senior CIA officials in Virginia two years after the coup, at a time when the agency reported that he was personally responsible for thousands of cases of murder and torture in Chile. Contreras distinguished himself with a singular act of terror: the 1976 assassination of Orlando Letelier, who had been Allende's ambassador to the United States, and an American aide, Ronni Moffitt. They were killed by a car bomb fourteen blocks from the White House. Contreras then blackmailed the United States by threatening to tell the world about his relationship with the CIA, and blocked his extradition and trial for the murder. There was no question at the agency that Pinochet knew and approved of that terrorist killing on American soil.

The Pinochet regime held power for seventeen years. After it fell, Contreras was convicted by a Chilean court of the murder of Orlando Letelier and served a seven-year sentence. Pinochet died in December 2006 at age ninety-one, under indictment for murder and with $28 million in secret bank accounts abroad. At this writing, Henry Kissinger is being pursued in the courts of Chile, Argentina, Spain, and France by survivors of the Caravan of Death. When he was secretary of state, the White House counsel gave him fair warning that "one who sets in motion a coup attempt can be assessed with the responsibility for the natural and probable consequences of that action."

The CIA was incapable of "placing stop and go buttons on the machinery" of covert action, said Dave Phillips, the Chilean task force chief. "I thought that if there were a military coup, there might be two weeks of street fighting in Santiago, and perhaps months of fighting and thousands of deaths in the countryside," he testified in secret to a Senate committee five years after the initial failure of Track Two. "God knows I knew I was involved in something where one man might get killed."

His interrogator asked: What is the distinction that you draw between one death in an assassination and thousands in a coup?

"Sir," he replied, "what is the distinction I draw from the time I was a bombardier in World War Two and pushed a target button, and hundreds and perhaps thousands of people died?"

30. "WE ARE GOING TO CATCH A LOT OF HELL"

Under President Nixon, secret government surveillance reached a peak in the spring of 1971. The CIA, the NSA, and the FBI were spying on American citizens. Defense Secretary Melvin Laird and the Joint Chiefs of Staff were using electronic eavesdropping and espionage to keep tabs on Kissinger. Nixon, improving on the work of Kennedy and Johnson, had bugged the White House and Camp David with state-of-the-art voice-activated microphones. Nixon and Kissinger wiretapped their own close aides and Washington reporters, trying to stop leaks to the press.

But leaks were a spring that never failed. In June, *The New York Times* began publishing long excerpts from the Pentagon Papers, the secret Vietnam history commissioned by Defense Secretary Robert McNamara four years before. The source was Daniel Ellsberg, a former Pentagon whiz kid whom Kissinger had hired as a consultant to the National Security Council and invited into Nixon's California compound at San Clemente. Kissinger raged at the release, sending Nixon into a greater fury. The president turned to his domestic policy chief, John Ehrlichman, to stop the leaks. He assembled a team called the Plumbers, led by a very recently retired CIA officer who had played prominent roles in Guatemala and the Bay of Pigs.

Everette Howard Hunt, Jr., was "a unique character," said Ambassador Sam Hart, who met him when Hunt was chief of station in Uruguay in the late 1950s—"totally self-absorbed, totally amoral, and a danger to himself and anybody around him. As far as I could tell, Howard went from one disaster to another, rising higher and higher, everything floating just right behind him." Hunt had been a romantic young cold warrior when he signed up with the CIA in 1950. He had become a fantasist who funneled his talent into writing halfway decent spy novels. He had been retired from the CIA for less than a year when a casual acquaintance, Nixon's aide Chuck Colson, offered him an exciting new assignment running secret operations for the White House.

Hunt flew down to Miami to see his old Cuban American companion Bernard Barker, who was selling real estate, and they talked beside a monument to the dead of the Bay of Pigs. "He described the mission as national security," Barker said. "I asked Howard who he represented, and the answer he gave me was really something for the books. He said he was in a group at the White House level, under direct order of the President of the United States." Together they recruited four more Miami Cubans, including Eugenio Martinez, who had run some three hundred seagoing missions into Cuba for the CIA and remained on a $100-a-month retainer from headquarters.

On July 7, 1971, Ehrlichman telephoned Nixon's spy inside the CIA, the deputy director, General Cushman. The president's aide told him that Howard Hunt would be calling him directly and asking for assistance. "I wanted you to know that he was in fact doing some things for the President," Ehrlichman said. "You should consider he has pretty much carte blanche." Hunt's demands escalated—he wanted his old secretary back, he wanted an office with a secure telephone in New York, he wanted state-of-the-art tape recorders, he wanted a CIA camera to stake out a break-in at Ellsberg's psychiatrist's office in Beverly Hills, and he wanted the CIA to develop the film. Cushman belatedly informed Helms that the agency had given Hunt a set of disguises: a red wig, a voice-altering device, fake personal identification. Then the White House demanded that the agency produce a psychological profile of Daniel Ellsberg, a direct violation of the CIA's charter against spying on Americans. But Helms complied.

Helms pushed Cushman out of the agency in November 1971. Months went by before Nixon found the perfect candidate: Lieutenant General Vernon Walters.

General Walters had been conducting secret missions for presidents for the better part of twenty years. But Helms had never met him before he arrived as the new deputy director of central intelligence on May 2, 1972. "I had just come from running an operation which the CIA knew nothing about," General Walters recounted. "Helms, who had wanted someone else, said, 'I've heard about you; what do you know about intelligence?' I said, 'Well, I've been negotiating with the Chinese and the Vietnamese for three years, and I smuggled Henry Kissinger into Paris fifteen times without you or anybody else in the Agency knowing anything about it.' " Helms was duly impressed. But he soon had cause to wonder about his new deputy's loyalties.

"EVERY TREE IN THE FOREST WILL FALL"

Late on Saturday night, June 17, 1972, Howard Osborn, the chief of the CIA's Office of Security, called Helms at home. The director knew it could not be good news. This is how he remembered the conversation:

"Dick, are you still up?"

"Yes, Howard."

"I've just learned that the District police have picked up five men in a break-in at the Democratic Party National Headquarters at the Watergate. . . . Four Cubans and Jim McCord."

"McCord? Retired out of your shop?"

"Two years ago."

"What about the Cubans—Miami or Havana?"

"Miami . . . in this country for some time now."

"Do we know them?"

"As of now, I can't say."

"Get hold of the operations people, first thing. . . . Have them get on to Miami. Check every record here and in Miami. . . . Is that all of it?"

"No, not half," Osborn said heavily. "Howard Hunt also seems to be involved."

Hearing Hunt's name, Helms drew a deep breath. "What the hell were they doing?" he asked. He had a fair idea: McCord was an expert in electronic eavesdropping, Hunt was working for Nixon, and the charge was wiretapping, a federal crime.

Sitting on the edge of his bed, Helms tracked down the acting director of the FBI, L. Patrick Gray, at a hotel in Los Angeles. J. Edgar Hoover had died six weeks before, after forty-eight years in power. Helms told

Gray very carefully that the Watergate burglars had been hired by the White House and the CIA had *nothing to do with it.* Got that? Okay, good night then.

Helms convened the daily 9 a.m. meeting of senior CIA officers at headquarters on Monday, June 19. Bill Colby, now the CIA's executive director, the number-three man, remembered Helms saying: "We are going to catch a lot of hell, because these are formers"—that is, former CIA men—and "we knew they were working in the White House." The next morning, *The Washington Post* placed the responsibility for Watergate at the door of the Oval Office—although, to this day, no one really knows if Richard Nixon authorized the break-in.

On Friday, June 23, Nixon told his brutally efficient chief of staff, H. R. Haldeman, to call Helms and Walters into the White House and order them to wave off the FBI in the name of national security. They agreed to play ball at first—a very dangerous business. Walters called Gray and told him to stand down. But a line was crossed on Monday, June 26, when Nixon's counsel, John Dean, ordered Walters to come up with a large sum of untraceable hush money for the six jailed CIA veterans. On Tuesday, Dean repeated the demand. He later told the president that the price of silence would be $1 million over two years. Only Helms—or Walters, when Helms was outside the United States—could authorize a secret payment from the CIA's black budget. They were the only officials in the American government who could legally deliver a suitcase with a million dollars in secret cash to the White House, and Nixon knew it.

"We could get money anyplace in the world," Helms reflected. "We ran a whole arbitrage operation. We didn't need to launder money— ever." But if the CIA delivered the cash, "the end result would have been the end of the Agency," he said. "Not only would I have gone to jail if I had gone along with what the White House wanted us to do, but the agency's credibility would have been ruined forever."

Helms refused. Then, on June 28, he fled Washington for a three-week tour of intelligence outposts in Asia, Australia, and New Zealand, leaving Walters as the acting director. A week went by. Impatient FBI agents started to rebel against their orders to stand down. Gray told Walters he would need an order in writing from the CIA calling off the investigation on national-security grounds. Both men now understood the risks of a paper trail. They spoke on July 6, and shortly thereafter Gray called the president at his retreat in San Clemente. "People on your staff are trying to mortally wound you" by manipulating the CIA, he told Nixon. An awful silence followed—and then the president told Gray to go ahead with the investigation.

Shortly after Helms returned from his trip in late July, Jim McCord, awaiting trial and facing five years in prison, sent a message through his lawyer to the CIA. He said the president's men wanted him to testify that the Watergate break-in was an agency operation. Let the CIA take the rap, a White House aide told him, and a presidential pardon would follow. McCord responded in a letter: "If Helms goes and the Watergate operation is laid at CIA's feet, where it does not belong, every tree in the forest will fall. It will be a scorched desert. The whole matter is at the precipice right now. Pass the message that if they want it to blow, they are on exactly the right course."

"EVERYONE KNEW WE WERE IN FOR A BAD TIME"

On November 7, 1972, President Nixon was re-elected in one of the great landslides of American history. He vowed that day to run the CIA and the State Department with an iron hand in his second term, to destroy them and rebuild them in his image.

On November 9, Kissinger proposed replacing Helms with James Schlesinger, then the chairman of the Atomic Energy Commission. "Very good idea," Nixon responded.

On November 13, he told Kissinger that he intended "to ruin the Foreign Service. I mean ruin it—the old Foreign Service—and to build a new one. I'm going to do it." He settled on an inside man to do the job: the OSS veteran and champion Republican fund-raiser William J. Casey. In 1968, Casey had importuned President-elect Nixon to make him director of central intelligence, but Nixon handed him the chair at the Securities and Exchange Commission instead, a cunning decision that cheered corporate boardrooms across America. Now, in Nixon's second term, Casey would be named undersecretary of state for economic affairs. But his real assignment was to serve as Nixon's saboteur—"to tear up the Department," Nixon said.

On November 20, Nixon fired Richard Helms in a short, awkward

meeting at Camp David. He offered him the post of ambassador to the
Soviet Union. There was an uncomfortable pause as Helms considered
the ramifications. "Look, Mr. President, I don't think that would be a
very good idea, to send me to Moscow," Helms said. "Well, maybe not,"
Nixon replied. Helms proposed Iran instead, and Nixon urged him to
take it. They also reached an understanding that Helms would stay on
until March 1973, his sixtieth birthday, the formal retirement age at the
CIA. Nixon broke that pledge, a pointless act of cruelty. "The man was a
shit," Helms said, faintly shaking with rage as he told the story.

Helms believed to his dying day that Nixon fired him because he
wouldn't take a dive on Watergate. But the record shows that Nixon resolved long before the break-in to jettison Helms and gut the CIA. The
president actually believed that Helms was out to get *him.*

"Do you think there was, or could have been, a CIA conspiracy to remove you from office?" Nixon's friend and former aide Frank Gannon
asked him a decade later.

"Many people think so," Nixon responded. "The CIA had motive. It
was no secret that I was dissatisfied with the CIA, with its reports and
particularly with their appraisals of Soviet strength and our other problems around the world. . . . I wanted to get rid of some of the deadwood
and so forth. And they knew it. So they had a motive."

"Do you think they feared you?" Gannon asked.

"No question about it," Nixon replied. "And they had reason to."

On November 21, Nixon offered the CIA to James Schlesinger, who
accepted the president's offer with pleasure. Nixon was gratified "to put
his own man in—I mean one that really had R.N. tattooed on him—
which was Schlesinger," Helms said. Schlesinger's orders—like Casey's at
State—were to turn the place inside out. "Get rid of the clowns," the
president kept commanding. "What use are they? They've got 40,000
people over there reading newspapers."

On December 27, the president dictated a memo laying out the mission. Though Kissinger wanted dominion over American intelligence,
"Schlesinger must be the man in charge," Nixon said. If Congress ever
"got the impression that the President has turned all intelligence activities over to Kissinger all hell will break loose. If on the other hand I
name the new Director of CIA Schlesinger as my top assistant for intelligence activities, we can get it by the Congress. Henry simply doesn't
have the time. . . . I have been bugging him and Haig for over three

years to get intelligence reorganized with no success whatever." It was a strong echo of Eisenhower's final burst of anger at the end of his presidency, his fuming at his "eight-year defeat" in his battle to whip American intelligence into shape.

In his last days in office, Helms feared that Nixon and his loyalists would ransack the CIA's files. He did everything in his power to destroy two sets of secret documents that could have ruined the agency. One was the paper trail of the mind-control experiments with LSD and many other drugs that he and Allen Dulles had personally approved two decades before. Very few of those records survived.

The second was his own set of secret tapes. Helms had recorded hundreds of conversations in his executive office on the seventh floor during the six years and seven months that he had served as the director of central intelligence. By the date of his official departure on February 2, 1973, every one had been destroyed.

"When Helms left the building, all the troops jammed the headquarters entrance for his departure," said Sam Halpern, then the top aide at the clandestine service. "There wasn't a dry eye in the house. Everyone knew we were in for a bad time after that."

31. "TO CHANGE THE CONCEPT OF A SECRET SERVICE"

The collapse of the CIA as a secret intelligence service began on the day Helms left and James Schlesinger arrived at headquarters.

Schlesinger spent seventeen weeks as director of central intelligence. In that time, he purged more than five hundred analysts and more than one thousand people from the clandestine service. Officers serving overseas received unsigned coded cables informing them that they were fired. In response, he received anonymous death threats, and he added armed guards to his security detail.

He named Bill Colby as the new chief of the clandestine service, and then he sat him down to explain that it was time "to change the concept of a 'secret service.' " The dawn of technocracy had arrived, and the day of the old boys who had been at the game for twenty-five years was done. "He was hyper-suspicious of the role and influence of the clandestine operators," Colby recounted. "He felt the Agency had become complacent and bloated under their domination, that indeed there were far too many of these 'old boys' around the place doing little more than looking after each other, playing spy games, and reliving the halcyon past."

The old boys argued that every aspect of the CIA's work overseas was part of the struggle against the Soviets and the Red Chinese. Whether you were in Cairo or Kathmandu, you were always fighting Moscow and Beijing. But when Nixon and Kissinger clinked glasses with the leaders of the communist world, what was the point? Peace was at hand. The president's policy of détente was sapping the cold-war élan of the clandestine service.

Colby quickly undertook a survey of the CIA's capabilities. A decade before, half the CIA's budget had gone to covert operations. Under Nixon, that figure now was falling below 10 percent. The recruitment of new talent was flagging, and the war in Vietnam was the cause. The political climate was not conducive to the hiring of bright young college graduates; an increasing number of campuses barred CIA recruiters by popular demand. The end of the military draft meant a halt to the processions of junior officers rotating into the CIA's ranks.

The Soviet Union remained close to terra incognita for American spies. North Korea and North Vietnam were blanks. The CIA bought its best information from allied foreign intelligence services and from third-world leaders whom it owned outright. It was most effective on the peripheries of power, but those were the cheap seats, with obstructed views of the global stage.

The Soviet division was still paralyzed by the conspiracy theories of Jim Angleton, who remained in charge of American counterintelligence. "Angleton devastated us," said the CIA's Haviland Smith, who ran operations against the Soviet target in the 1960s and 1970s. "He took us out of the Soviet business." One of Bill Colby's many unhappy duties was to figure out what to do with the alcoholic spycatcher, who now had arrived at the conclusion that Colby himself was a mole for Moscow. Colby tried to persuade Schlesinger to fire Angleton. The new director demurred after he got the Briefing.

In his dark and smoky office, Angleton took the new boss on a fifty-year trip, back to the beginnings of Soviet communism, into the elaborate sting operations and political manipulations that the Russians ran against the West in the 1920s and 1930s, through the communist double-agent operations and disinformation campaigns of the 1940s and 1950s, winding up with the surmise that the CIA itself had been penetrated at or near the highest levels by Moscow in the 1960s. In short, the enemy had breached the CIA's defense and burrowed deep within.

Schlesinger bought the Briefing, entranced by Angleton's guided tour of hell.

"OUTSIDE THE LEGISLATIVE CHARTER OF THIS AGENCY"

Schlesinger said he saw the CIA as "the central intelligence agency—small 'c,' small 'i,' small 'a.' " It had become nothing more than "some component of the NSC staff" under Kissinger. He intended to hand it over to Deputy Director Vernon Walters while he dealt with the spy satellites of the National Reconnaissance Office, the electronic-eavesdropping colossus of the National Security Agency, and the military reports of the Defense Intelligence Agency. He intended to serve in the role he had imagined in his report to the president—as the director of national intelligence.

But his grand ambitions were shattered by the high crimes and misdemeanors of the White House. "The Watergate affair began to take over almost everything else," Schlesinger said, "and the desires that I had at the outset gradually were inundated by simply the necessity of protecting, arranging for the salvation of the Agency."

He had an unusual sense of how to save it.

Schlesinger thought that he had been told everything that the agency knew about Watergate. He was shocked when Howard Hunt testified that he and his Plumbers had ransacked Daniel Ellsberg's psychiatrist's office with the technical assistance of the CIA. A review by the agency of its own files turned up a copy of the film it had developed for Hunt after he cased the office. Further review disclosed the letters to the CIA from Jim McCord, which could be read as a threat to blackmail the president of the United States.

Bill Colby had jumped behind enemy lines with the OSS. He had spent six years supervising the killing of communists in Vietnam. He was not easily impressed by merely verbal violence. But he found Schlesinger's rage awesome. Fire everyone if you have to, the director ordered, tear the place apart, rip out the floorboards, uncover everything. Then Schlesinger drafted a memo to every employee of the CIA. The note was one of the most dangerous decisions a director of central intelligence had ever made. It was the legacy he chose to leave:

> I have ordered all senior operating officials of this Agency to re-
> port to me immediately on any activities now going on, or that

have gone on in the past, which might be construed to be outside the legislative charter of this Agency.

I hereby direct every person presently employed by CIA to
report to me on any such activities of which he has knowledge.
I invite all ex-employees to do the same. Anyone who has such
information should call . . . and say that he wishes to tell me
about "activities outside CIA's charter."

The CIA's exceedingly vague charter was clear on one point: the
agency could not be the American secret police. Yet over the course of
the cold war the CIA had been spying on citizens, tapping their telephones, opening first-class mail, and conspiring to commit murder on
orders from the White House.

Schlesinger's order was dated May 9, 1973, and effective immediately.
That same day, Watergate began to destroy Richard Nixon. He had been
forced to fire his palace guard, and only General Alexander Haig, the new
White House chief of staff, remained. Hours after the order was issued,
Haig called Colby to inform him that the attorney general was resigning,
the secretary of defense was taking his job, Schlesinger was leaving the
CIA for the Pentagon, and the president wanted Colby to be the next director of central intelligence. The government was in such disarray that
Colby was not sworn in until September. For four months, General Walters was the acting director and Colby the director-designate—an awkward state of affairs.

Colby was now fifty-three years old, with thirty years behind him in
the OSS and the CIA. He had been an avatar of covert action all his adult
life. Throughout the spring of 1973, he had been forced to serve as
Schlesinger's hit man, summoning his fellow officers and handing them
their walking papers. In the midst of all this, his eldest daughter, in her
midtwenties, had wasted away and died from anorexia. On May 21,
Colby sat down and began to read the initial compilation of the crimes
of the CIA, which eventually ran to 693 potential violations. The Senate's public hearings on the Watergate case had opened that week. The
news of Nixon and Kissinger's wiretapping of aides and reporters broke.
The appointment of a special prosecutor to investigate the crimes of Watergate was announced.

All his life, Colby had been a deeply devoted Roman Catholic, a man
who believed in the consequences of mortal sin. He now learned for the

first time that day of the plots against Fidel Castro and the central role of Robert F. Kennedy, the mind-control experiments and the secret prisons and the drug tests on unwitting human guinea pigs. The CIA's wiretapping and surveillance of citizens and reporters did not offend his conscience; clear orders from three presidents stood behind them. But he knew, given the tenor of the times, that if these secrets leaked the agency could be ruined. Colby locked them up and set about trying to run the CIA.

The White House was falling apart under the crushing weight of Watergate, and it sometimes seemed to Colby that the CIA was crumbling too. It was often a good thing that Nixon did not read the intelligence the agency provided him. When the holy days of Yom Kippur and Ramadan coincided in 1973, Egypt went to war against Israel and drove deep into Israeli-held territory. In striking contrast to its solid forecasts of the Six-Day War in 1967, the CIA had misread the gathering storm. "We did not cover ourselves with glory," Colby said. "We predicted the day before the war broke out that it was not going to break out."

The agency had assured the White House, a few hours before the war began: "Exercises are more realistic than usual. But there will be no war."

32. "A CLASSIC FASCIST IDEAL"

On March 7, 1973, President Nixon met in the Oval Office with Tom Pappas, a Greek American business magnate, political fixer, and friend of the CIA. Pappas had delivered $549,000 in cash to the 1968 Nixon campaign as a gift from the leaders of the Greek military junta. The money had been laundered through the KYP, the Greek intelligence service. It was one of the darker secrets of the Nixon White House.

Pappas now had hundreds of thousands of dollars more to offer the president—money to buy the silence of the CIA veterans jailed in the Watergate break-in. Nixon thanked him profusely: "I am aware of what you're doing to help out," he said. Most of it came from members and supporters of "the colonels"—the Greek junta that seized power in April 1967, led by George Papadopoulos, a recruited CIA agent since the days of Allen Dulles, and the KYP's liaison to the agency.

"These colonels had been plotting for years and years," said Robert Keeley, later the American ambassador to Greece. "They were fascists. They fitted the classic definition of fascism, as represented by Mussolini in the 1920s: a corporate state, uniting industry and unions, no parliament, trains running on time, heavy discipline and censorship . . . almost a classic fascist ideal."

Greek military and intelligence officers had worked in concert with seven successive station chiefs in Athens. They had a great friend in Thomas Hercules Karamessines, the Greek American chief of the clandestine service under Richard Helms, and they always had believed that "the Central Intelligence Agency was an effective and relatively direct route into the White House," said Norbert Anschutz, the ranking American diplomat in Athens during the 1967 coup.

Yet the colonels had taken the CIA by surprise. "The only time I saw Helms really angry was when the Greek colonels' coup took place in 1967," said the veteran analyst and current-intelligence chief Dick Lehman. "The Greek generals had been planning a coup against the elected government, a plan we knew all about and was not yet ripe. But a group of colonels had trumped their ace and acted without warning. Helms had been expecting to be warned of the generals' coup, and when a coup occurred, he naturally assumed it was this one, and he was furious." Lehman, who had read the overnight cables from Athens, "tried to cool Helms off by pointing out that this was a different coup, which we had no line on. This was a new thought."

Official American policy toward the colonels was cool and distant until the inauguration of Richard Nixon in January 1969. The junta used Tom Pappas, who had been working with the CIA in Athens for twenty years, as a courier to slip cash into the political coffers of Nixon and Vice President Spiro Agnew—the most powerful Greek American in the history of the United States. The payoff reaped benefits. Agnew came to Athens on an official visit. So did the secretaries of state, defense, and commerce. The United States sold tanks, aircraft, and artillery to the junta. The CIA's Athens station argued that the arms sales to the colonels "would bring them back to democracy," said Archer K. Blood, a political officer at the American embassy. That was "a lie," Blood said—but "if you said anything critical about the junta, the CIA would explode in anger."

By 1973, the United States was the only nation in the developed world on friendly terms with the junta, which jailed and tortured its political foes. "The CIA station chief was in bed with the guys who were beating up the Greeks," said Charles Stuart Kennedy, the American consul general in Athens. "I would raise issues of what would amount to human rights, and this would be discounted by the CIA." The agency "was too close to the wrong people," Kennedy said. "It seemed to have undue influence over the Ambassador," an old friend of Richard Nixon's named Henry Tasca.

In the spring of 1974, General Demetrios Ioannidis took over as the leader of the junta. He had been working with the CIA for twenty-two years. The agency was Ioannidis's sole contact with the government of

the United States; the ambassador and the American diplomatic establishment were out of the loop. Jim Potts, the CIA station chief, *was* the
American government, insofar as the junta was concerned. The agency
had "a major asset in Athens. They had a relationship with the guy who
ran the country, and they didn't want it disturbed," said the State Department's Thomas Boyatt, the Washington desk officer responsible for
Cyprus.

"CONNED BY A PISS-ANT GENERAL"

Cyprus, an island forty miles off the coast of Turkey and five hundred
miles from Athens, had been divided and conquered by Greek and Islamic armies since the days of the prophet Muhammad. The Greek
colonels had a deep hatred for the Cypriot leader, Archbishop Makarios,
and an abiding desire to overthrow him. The American deputy chief of
mission in Cyprus, William Crawford, had gotten wind of their scheming.

"I went up to Athens with what I considered proof positive that they
were going to pull the whole house of cards down," he remembered. "I
was told by our chief of station in Athens, Jim Potts, that that was just
absolutely impossible. He couldn't agree with me: these people were
friends with whom we'd worked for thirty years, and they would never
conduct anything so foolish."

By 1974, Tom Boyatt became convinced that the CIA's friends in
Athens wanted to do away with Makarios. He drafted a cable to Ambassador Tasca in Athens. Go talk to General Ioannidis, it said. Tell him—"in
words of one syllable that even he will understand"—that "the United
States strongly opposes any efforts by any element of the Greek government, overt or clandestine, to mess around in the Cyprus situation." Tell
him that "we particularly oppose any efforts to overthrow Makarios and
install a pro-Athens government. Because if that happens the Turks are
going to invade, and that's not good for any of us."

But Ambassador Tasca had never spoken to General Ioannidis in his
life. That role was reserved for the CIA station chief.

On Saturday, July 12, 1974, the State Department received a cable from
the CIA station in Athens. Rest assured, it said. The general and the junta

were not doing anything to overthrow Archbishop Makarios. "So, all right, we'd had it from the horse's mouth," Boyatt recounted. "I went home. And about 3:00 a.m. on Monday morning, I got a call from the Ops Center at the State Department, and the person said, 'You better get in here.' "

The junta had attacked. Boyatt rushed to the State Department, where a communications officer laid two pieces of paper in front of him. One was the CIA's intelligence brief for President Nixon and Secretary of State Kissinger: "We have been assured by General Ioannidis that Greece will not move its forces on Cyprus." The other was a cable from the American embassy in Cyprus: "The Presidential Palace is in flames. The Cypriot force has been decimated."

From Ankara came a flash that the Turkish forces had mobilized. Two NATO armies, the Greeks and the Turks, both trained and armed by the United States, were about to go to war with American weapons. The Turks hit the beach in northern Cyprus and cut the island in half with American tanks and artillery. There was a great slaughter of Greek Cypriots in the Turkish sector and a great slaughter of Turkish Cypriots in the Greek sector of the island. All through July, the CIA reported that the Greek army and the Greek people were solidly in support of General Ioannides. After the battle for Cyprus was joined, the Greek junta fell.

The CIA's failure to warn Washington about the war was an unusual case. There had been many such failures in the agency's annals, from the Korean War onward. In 1974 alone, a leftist military coup in Portugal and a nuclear test in India had come as complete surprises. But this was different: the CIA was in bed with the military men against whom it was supposed to warn.

"There we were," Boyatt said years later, "sitting there with the entire intelligence establishment of the United States in all of its majesty having been conned by a piss-ant Greek brigadier general."

"THE TERRIBLE PRICE"

On August 8, 1974, Richard Nixon resigned. The final blow was his admission that he had ordered the CIA to obstruct justice in the name of national security.

The next day, Secretary of State Kissinger read an extraordinary message from Tom Boyatt. It said the CIA had been lying about what it had been doing in Athens, deliberately misleading the American government—and those lies had helped start the war consuming Greece, Turkey, and Cyprus, a war in which thousands died.

The next week, gunfire broke out around the American embassy in Cyprus, and Ambassador Rodger P. Davies was killed by a bullet that tore his heart out. In Athens, hundreds of thousands of people marched on the American embassy; demonstrators tried to set the building on fire. The newly arrived ambassador there was Jack Kubisch, a veteran diplomat of broad experience, personally selected by Kissinger on the day that Nixon resigned.

He requested a new station chief, and the CIA sent Richard Welch, who had learned his Greek at Harvard and had served as chief in Peru and Guatemala. Welch took up residence in the mansion where every one of his predecessors had lived. The address was widely known. "It was a very serious problem," Ambassador Kubisch said. "I had made arrangements for him to go into a different residence and to live in a different part of town, to try and help conceal who he was and to give him some cover." Given the anti-American fervor in Athens, that seemed prudent. But "neither Welch nor his wife seemed to be at all concerned about this," he said. "They just didn't think that in Athens there was any real severe threat to them."

Welch and his wife went to a Christmas party at the ambassador's residence, just a few blocks from the CIA's mansion in the hills. When they returned home, a small car with four people in it was waiting in the driveway. Three of them forced the station chief out of his car. "They fired three slugs from a .45 into his chest and killed him," Ambassador Kubisch said. "They got into their car and sped off." It was the first time in the history of the CIA that a station chief had been assassinated. But it was part of a pattern of the past.

Ambassador Kubisch said that he had seen in Athens, for the first time in his life, "the terrible price the U.S. Government must pay when it associates itself so intimately . . . with a repressive regime." Part of the cost was the consequence of letting the CIA shape the foreign policy of the United States.

33. "THE CIA WOULD BE DESTROYED"

"Let me start by mentioning a problem we have concerning the use of classified material," President Gerald R. Ford said as he opened one of his first National Security Council meetings in the White House Cabinet Room on October 7, 1974.

The survivors of Watergate—Secretary of State Kissinger, Secretary of Defense Schlesinger, Deputy Director of Central Intelligence Walters, and the ambitious and influential White House staffer Donald Rumsfeld—were enraged by the latest leak. The United States was preparing to ship billions of dollars' worth of weapons to Israel and Egypt. The newspapers had printed the Israeli shopping list and the American response.

"This is intolerable," Ford said. "I have discussed several options for how to deal with it with Don Rumsfeld." The president wanted a plan within forty-eight hours on how to stop the press from printing what it knew. "We don't have the tools we need," Schlesinger warned him. "We need an Official Secrets Act," he said, but "the present climate is bad for this sort of thing."

The power of secrecy had been undone by the lies of presidents, told in the name of national security of the United States. The U-2 was a weather plane. America would not invade Cuba. Our ships were attacked in the Gulf of Tonkin. The Vietnam War was a just cause. The fall of Richard Nixon showed that these noble lies would no longer serve in a democracy.

Bill Colby leaped at the chance to renew the CIA's standing with the

White House, for he knew that the assault on secrecy threatened the agency's survival. He had cultivated Ford from the moment he became vice president, delivering a copy of the president's daily brief by messenger, and keeping him posted on the CIA's secret $400 million project to raise a sunken Soviet submarine from the bottom of the Pacific Ocean (the salvage operation failed when the sub broke in two). He wanted Ford to know "everything the President knew," he said. "We didn't want another situation like when Truman was unaware of the Manhattan Project."

But President Ford never telephoned him or sought his private counsel. Ford restored the National Security Council as it was under Eisenhower, and Colby attended, but he was never admitted to the Oval Office alone. Colby tried to become a player on the great issues of the day, but he remained an outsider. With Kissinger and Haig as gatekeepers and guardians, Colby never penetrated the inner circle at the Ford White House. And whatever chance he might have had to repair the CIA's reputation died in December 1974.

A *New York Times* reporter, Seymour Hersh, had uncovered the secret of the agency's spying on Americans. He had gotten the gist of the story from months of reporting, and on Friday, December 20, 1974, he received a long-sought interview with Colby at headquarters. Colby, who secretly taped the conversation, tried to convince Hersh that the illegal surveillance was of no great importance, a small affair, best left unspoken. "I think family skeletons are best left where they are—in the closet," he said to Hersh. But, he conceded, it had happened. Hersh wrote all night and into Saturday morning.

The story ran December 22, 1974, on page one of the Sunday paper. The banner headline read: HUGE C.I.A. OPERATION REPORTED IN U.S. AGAINST ANTI-WAR FORCES.

Colby tried to protect the agency by laying the issue of illegal domestic surveillance at the doorstep of Jim Angleton, who had been opening first-class mail in partnership with the FBI for twenty years. He called Angleton up to the seventh floor and fired him. Out in the cold, Angleton spent the rest of his life spinning myths about his work. He summed it up when he was asked to explain why the CIA had not fulfilled an order from the White House to destroy the agency's stockpile of poisons. "It is inconceivable," he said, "that a secret arm of the government has to comply with all the overt orders of the government."

"DEAD CATS WILL COME OUT"

On Christmas Eve, Colby sent a long note to Kissinger summarizing the secrets compiled at Schlesinger's command. In the wake of Watergate, their release could wreck the agency. Kissinger boiled them down in a five-page, single-spaced memo to President Ford on Christmas Day. It took Congress a year of investigation, all of 1975, to dig out some of the facts in this memo.

Kissinger informed the president that the CIA had indeed spied on the left, wiretapped newspaper reporters and placed them under surveillance, conducted illegal searches, and opened uncounted sacks of mail. But there was much more, and far worse. Kissinger did not dare put in writing what he had learned from what he called "the horrors book." Some of the CIA's actions "clearly were illegal," he warned Ford. Others "raise profound moral questions." Though he had served a decade on the small CIA subcommittee in the House of Representatives, President Ford had never heard a whisper of these secrets—domestic spying, mind control, assassination attempts. The conspiracies to commit murder had started in the White House under Eisenhower, the most revered Republican president of the twentieth century.

Then on Friday, January 3, 1975, Ford received another bulletin, this one from the acting attorney general of the United States, Laurence Silberman.

Silberman learned that day about the thick file that held the secrets of the CIA's wrongdoing. It lay in Colby's office safe, and Silberman surmised that it held evidence of federal crimes. The nation's highest law enforcement officer mousetrapped the director of central intelligence. He would have to hand over the files, or he might face a charge of obstruction of justice. It was no longer a question of whether Colby wanted to spill the secrets. It was a question of going to prison to protect them.

Silberman—later in life a federal appeals court judge and the leader of a devastating investigation of the CIA in 2005—came perilously close to becoming the director of central intelligence himself at this dangerous moment. "Ford asked me to come into the White House to run intelligence, but I declined," Silberman said in an oral history. "I was seriously considered at that point to be CIA director. I did not wish to do that for a whole host of reasons." He knew that the agency was about to face a howling storm.

In his January 3 memo to the president, Silberman raised two issues. One: "Plans to assassinate certain foreign leaders—which, to say the least, present unique questions." Two: "Mr. Helms may have committed perjury during the confirmation hearings on his appointment as Ambassador to Iran." Helms had been asked, under oath, about the overthrow of President Allende of Chile. Did the CIA have anything to do with that? No, sir, Helms had answered. Sworn to secrecy but sworn to tell the truth, Helms eventually had to stand before a federal judge and face a charge of lying—a misdeameanor count of failing to tell Congress the whole truth.

On the evening of January 3, Ford told Kissinger, Vice President Nelson Rockefeller, and Donald Rumsfeld that "the CIA would be destroyed" if the secrets leaked. At noon on Saturday, January 4, Helms came to the Oval Office. "Frankly, we are in a mess," Ford told him. The president said that Rockefeller would run a commission to investigate the domestic activities of the CIA, but only the domestic activities. Ford hoped it could hew to that narrow charter. "It would be tragic if it went beyond it," he told Helms. "It would be a shame if the public uproar forced us to go beyond and to damage the integrity of the CIA. I automatically assume what you did was right, unless it's proven otherwise."

Helms saw what lay ahead.

"A lot of dead cats will come out," he warned the president. "I don't know everything which went on in the Agency. Maybe no one does. But I know enough to say that if the dead cats come out, I will participate."

Helms tossed one over the White House fence that day, telling Kissinger that Bobby Kennedy had personally managed the assassination plots against Castro. Kissinger passed the news to the president. The horror deepened. Ford had first come to national prominence through his service on the Warren Commission. Now he understood that there were aspects to the Kennedy assassination he had never known, and the missing pieces of the puzzle haunted him. Near the end of his life, he called the agency's withholding of evidence from the Warren Commission "unconscionable." The CIA "made a mistake in not giving us all of the data they had available," Ford said. "Their judgment was not good in not giving us the full story."

The White House now faced eight separate congressional investigations and hearings on the CIA. Rumsfeld explained how the White House was going to head them all off at the pass with the Rockefeller

Commission, whose members would be "Republican and right." One was already listed in his files: "Ronald Reagan, political commentator, former President of the Screen Actors' Guild, and former Governor of California."

"What should the final report be?" the president asked. All present agreed in principle that damage control was of the utmost importance. "Colby must be brought under control," Kissinger said. If he did not stay silent, "this stuff will be all over town soon."

On January 16, 1975, President Ford hosted a luncheon at the White House for senior editors and the publisher of *The New York Times*. The president said that it was decidedly not in the national interest to discuss the CIA's past. He said the reputation of every president since Harry Truman could be ruined if the deepest secrets spilled. Like what? an editor asked. Like assassinations! Ford said. Hard to say which was stranger— what the president had said, or that the editors managed to keep the statement off the record.

The new Congress, elected three months after Nixon's resignation, was the most liberal in memory. "The question is how to plan to meet the investigation of the CIA," President Ford told Rumsfeld on February 21; Rumsfeld pledged to mount "a damage-limiting operation for the President." He took charge of determining how many—if any—of the CIA's secrets Ford and Rockefeller would share with Capitol Hill.

On March 28, Schlesinger told the president that it was imperative to cut back on "the prominence of CIA operations" around the world. "Within the CIA there is bitter dissension," said Schlesinger, who had helped to sow it. The clandestine service was "full of tired-out old agents," men who might spill secrets. Colby was being "too damned co-operative with the Congress." The danger of disclosure was growing by the day.

34. "SAIGON SIGNING OFF"

On April 2, 1975, Bill Colby warned the White House that the United States was about to lose a war.

"Let me get a grasp on the situation," Kissinger said. "Is there anywhere the South Vietnamese have a chance of establishing a line and of stopping the North Vietnamese?"

"North of Saigon here," Colby said, pointing to a line on a map.

"That's hopeless!" Schlesinger shouted.

Was South Vietnam going to collapse? Kissinger asked. It seemed inevitable to Colby.

"I think Martin"—Ambassador Graham Martin—"should begin preparing a plan of evacuation," Kissinger said. "I think we owe—it's our duty—to get the people who believed in us out. . . . We have to take out these people who participated in the Phoenix program." This was the paramilitary campaign of arrest, interrogation, and torture that Colby had helped run as a civilian, with the rank of ambassador, from 1968 to 1971. At a minimum, Phoenix had killed more than twenty thousand Vietcong suspects.

"The real question now," said Colby, "is do we try for a redoubt around Saigon?" Or negotiate a face-saving, possibly life-saving, settlement so as to evacuate the capital without bloodshed?

No negotiations, Kissinger said—"not as long as I am in this chair." Keep the weapons flowing to Saigon and let the North and the South work it out. "We can save nothing," he said.

"Nothing but lives," Colby replied. But Kissinger was adamant. He would not negotiate a peaceful end to the war.

On April 9, Colby went back to the White House to try to focus President Ford on the fact that communist armies were closing in on the capitals of South Vietnam, Laos, and Cambodia. Twenty years of struggle by the military and intelligence forces of the United States were going down the drain.

"The Communists have begun a new round of fighting, with Saigon as the ultimate target," Colby told the president and the National Security Council on April 9. The United States needed to start evacuating everyone it could—Americans and Vietnamese—as soon as possible, he said. There would surely be vengeance when Saigon fell. Thousands of Americans and tens of thousands of political, military, and intelligence allies among the South Vietnamese were at risk if they remained.

"The North Vietnamese now have 18 infantry divisions in South Vietnam," Colby said. "We believe Hanoi will take whatever action is necessary to force the war to an early conclusion—probably by early summer." He was off by two months. The city of Saigon, where six thousand American military officers, spies, diplomats, and government aid workers still labored, would fall within three weeks. Colby told the president that "we should ask Congress to commit money to carry out the pledge to let the Vietnamese, perhaps one to two million, leave." This would have been the biggest emergency evacuation in the history of the United States.

Colby's warning did not register anywhere in Washington, not at the White House, not with Congress, not in the Pentagon, and not in the mind of the American ambassador in Saigon. One man understood all too well: the Saigon station chief, Tom Polgar.

"IT HAS BEEN A LONG FIGHT AND WE HAVE LOST"

At 4 a.m. on April 29, 1975, Polgar awoke to the sound of rockets and artillery. The airport was under fire. Seven Air America helicopters—the CIA's shuttle service in South Vietnam—were destroyed. Polgar had

hundreds of people to look after. The Americans who worked for him
were one problem. The Vietnamese who worked for the CIA, and their
families, were another. They were desperate to leave, but getting fixed-
wing aircraft in and out of the airport would be impossible now.

Polgar dressed quickly in a blue shirt and tan slacks, instinctively put
his passport in his pocket, and sped to the American embassy. The streets
of Saigon, a city of four million people, were empty, under twenty-four-
hour curfew. He called Ambassador Martin. Suffering from emphysema
and bronchitis, Martin was reduced to anguished whispers. Polgar then
contacted Kissinger and the American commander in chief in the Pacific,
Admiral Noel Gayler, the former director of the National Security
Agency. He received new orders from Washington: push the evacuation
of nonessential personnel to the utmost. Kissinger offered no instructions beyond that as to who would stay and who would go and how they
would leave.

The South Vietnamese army was collapsing into chaos. The national
police dissolved. The once-silent streets were anarchy.

President Ford ordered a reduction of the embassy from 600 people to
150. Fifty among those to remain were CIA officers. Polgar did not quite
envision the North Vietnamese allowing a robust CIA station to go on
working after Saigon fell.

Inside the embassy, Polgar saw people in states of rage smashing and
trampling photographs of Nixon and Kissinger. The embassy had become,
in Polgar's words, "a thirty-three-ring circus, without a ringmaster."

At 11:38 a.m. Ford ordered the American mission in Saigon to shut
down. Now all Americans had to be out of the city by nightfall. The embassy was surrounded by thousands of panicked Vietnamese, a wall of
desperate people. There was only one way in and out, a secret passage-
way from the parking lot to the garden of the French embassy. Ambassador Martin used it to round up his wife and their servants. Polgar
called home. His maid told him he had visitors: a deputy prime minister,
a three-star general, the chief of the nation's communications intelligence agency, the chief of protocol, senior military officers and their
families, and many more Vietnamese who had worked with the CIA.

Three hours after President Ford issued the evacuation order, the first
American helicopters arrived from eighty miles offshore. The marine pilots performed with skill and daring, shuttling out about a thousand

Americans and close to six thousand Vietnamese. A famous photograph shows one of the last helicopters leaving Saigon, perched on a rooftop, as a trail of people climb a ladder to safety. That photo, for many years, was mislabeled as a shot of the embassy. But in fact it was a CIA safe house, and those were Polgar's friends clambering aboard.

Polgar burned all the CIA's files, cables, and codebooks that evening. Not long after midnight, he composed his farewell: "THIS WILL BE FINAL MESSAGE FROM SAIGON STATION. . . . IT HAS BEEN A LONG FIGHT AND WE HAVE LOST. . . . THOSE WHO FAIL TO LEARN FROM HISTORY ARE FORCED TO REPEAT IT. LET US HOPE THAT WE WILL NOT HAVE ANOTHER VIETNAM EXPERIENCE AND THAT WE HAVE LEARNED OUR LESSON. SAIGON SIGNING OFF."

Then he blew up the machine that sent the message.

Thirty years later, Polgar remembered the final moments of the American war in Vietnam: "As we stepped up the narrow metal stairs to the helicopter pad on the roof, we knew we were leaving behind thousands of people in the Embassy's logistics compound. We all knew how we felt, leaders of a defeated cause."

"FIFTEEN YEARS OF HARD WORK THAT TURNED TO NOTHING"

The CIA's long war in Laos came to an end two weeks later in a valley surrounded by tall shafts of limestone. The communists surrounded the agency's central outpost in Long Tieng. The ridge above the valley was covered with North Vietnamese soldiers. Tens of thousands of the Hmong—the CIA's fighters and their families—were gathering at the primitive airstrip, hoping for a flight. The agency had no plans to save them after fifteen years of paramilitary missions.

One CIA officer remained at Long Tieng: Jerry Daniels, a onetime Montana smoke jumper known to his Hmong friends as "Sky." He was thirty-three years old and he had been up-country for close to ten years. He was the case officer for General Vang Pao, the military and political leader of the Hmong and the agency's greatest asset in Laos since 1960.

Daniels was one of seven CIA officers—Bill Lair and Ted Shackley included—who had been awarded the Order of the Million Elephants and the White Parasol by the king of Laos in gratitude for their work.

Daniels pleaded with Dan Arnold, the station chief in Laos, to send planes to Long Tieng. It was "imperative that the evacuation proceed without delay," Arnold said in an oral history. But there weren't any planes. "Of course the authorization for an airlift had to go to Washington, and this was done with the highest precedence," Arnold said. "This went from CIA to the White House. . . . Washington was repeatedly requested to urgently arrange for additional airlift capability because we had drawn down so heavily. The problem was occasioned by delays at the highest political level."

On May 12, 1975, the CIA scoured up the last two C-46 aircraft in Thailand. The planes, roughly the size of a DC-3, belonged to Continental Air Services, a private contractor for the agency. Over the years, hundreds of planes of that size had landed on the Long Tieng airstrip carrying cargo. But they always left empty, barely clearing the high ridgeline. No one had ever flown a loaded C-46 *out* of Long Tieng. The planes were built to carry thirty-five passengers. With twice that number aboard, and thousands clamoring to get on each flight, they slowly began the evacuation.

In Bangkok, on the morning of May 13, Air Force Brigadier General Heinie Aderholt, chief of the U.S. Military Assistance Command in Thailand, got a call from a stranger. General Aderholt, who had worked alongside the CIA on air operations for twenty years, ran the only functioning American military operation remaining in Southeast Asia. "The guy did not identify himself by name," the general remembered. "He said the U.S. was abandoning the Hmong at Long Tieng. He used that word, '*abandoning.*' " The stranger asked Aderholt to send a four-engine C-130—a midsized cargo transport plane—to save the Hmong. Aderholt somehow found an American pilot who was minutes from clearing the departure lounge at the Bangkok airport and offered him $5,000 in cash to fly the C-130 to Long Tieng. Then he called the chairman of the Joint Chiefs of Staff, General George Brown, for authority to carry out the mission. That afternoon, the C-130 arrived. Hundreds of Hmong loaded themselves within a few minutes; the plane departed and returned the next morning.

The CIA's Jerry Daniels was running the evacuation, serving as bodyguard to General Vang Pao, working as flight controller at the airstrip, and holding a lifeline for fifty thousand panicked people. Daniels and Vang Pao could not be seen to abandon the troops and their families. When the C-130 returned on the morning of May 14, thousands of Hmong ran for its rear cargo door. It was a scene of fury and despair. Vang Pao stole away to a helicopter landing zone a few miles away; a CIA crew spirited him away.

Daniels procured a plane for himself. The flight log reads: "All was in turmoil. . . . We took off at 10:47 and this ended the secret CIA base at Long Tieng, Laos." A CIA contract pilot on the scene, Captain Jack Knotts, recorded an audiotape memorializing the final minutes of the long war in Laos. Daniels, carrying a briefcase and a case of Olympia beer, rolled up to the landing zone in his white-and-blue Ford Bronco. He stepped out of the car and then stopped dead. "He won't get in the chopper," Knotts said. "He doesn't want to leave yet! He gets his brief-case out of the back, and then he starts talking on the radio. He messes around and messes around and finally—and this is a very bad thing be-cause he's been there for so long—he salutes. He comes to attention, just like he is saluting the jeep. But he is really saluting ten or fifteen years of hard work that turned to nothing."

Richard Helms called Laos "the war we won." It was hard to see how. Ford and Kissinger forced a political arrangement that certified communist control of the country. "And then we left," said the CIA's Dick Holm, who had started his thirty-five-year career at the CIA in Laos. Those among the Hmong who survived wound up in refugee camps or in exile. "Their way of life has been destroyed," Holm wrote. "They can never return to Laos." The United States, he said, "failed to assume the moral responsibility that we owed to those who worked so closely with us during those tumultuous years."

Jerry Daniels died of gas poisoning at his apartment in Bangkok seven years after the evacuation of Long Tieng. He was forty years old. No one knows if he took his own life.

35. "INEFFECTIVE AND SCARED"

The CIA was being sacked like a conquered city. Congressional committees were combing through its files, the Senate focusing on covert action, the House homing in on failures of espionage and analysis. In the streets of Washington, handmade posters of Bill Colby had appeared, inscribed with skulls and crossbones and the ace of spades. The agency's senior officers feared personal and professional ruin. The White House feared political destruction. In the Oval Office on October 13, 1975, the president and his men met to weigh the damage.

"Any document which officially shows American involvement in an assassination is a foreign policy disaster," Colby told the president. "They also want to go into sensitive covert operations"—like Laos. Would the White House go to the courts to stop Congress? "We are better off with a political confrontation than a legal one," said Don Rumsfeld. To prepare for that fight, the president shook up his cabinet at the end of October 1975.

The move was instantly called the Halloween Massacre. Jim Schlesinger was dismissed and Don Rumsfeld became secretary of defense. Dick Cheney took his place as White House chief of staff. And, in an uncharacteristically Machiavellian move, Ford neutralized a potentially troublesome challenger for the 1976 presidential nomination by firing Bill Colby and making George Herbert Walker Bush the next director of central intelligence. It was on its face a strange choice.

Bush was not a general, an admiral, or a spy. He knew almost nothing about intelligence. He was a politician pure and simple. The son of

Prescott Bush, a patrician U.S. senator from Connecticut who had been a
good friend to Allen Dulles, he had moved to Texas to seek his fortune in
the oil business. He served two terms in Congress. He ran for the Senate
twice and lost. He had been United Nations ambassador for twenty-two
months and Nixon's relentlessly cheery Republican National Committee
chairman during Watergate. In August 1974, Ford had come very close to
making Bush vice president. His failure to win the job was the worst blow
of his political life. His consolation prize was a choice of prestigious am-
bassadorships, and he had chosen China. From Beijing, Bush had seen
the struggles of the CIA through a thick prism, relying on the radio reports of the Voice of America and clippings from week-old newspapers.

But his political instincts told him what the job had to offer. "Bury
Bush at the CIA?" he asked himself. "It's a graveyard for politics," he
wrote. He told Ford: "I see this as the total end of any political future."
The prospect depressed him. But his sense of propriety impelled him to
say yes.

Within weeks after becoming director at the end of January 1976,
Bush discovered that he loved the agency—the secrecy, the camaraderie,
the gadgetry, the international intrigue. The CIA was Skull and Bones
with a billion-dollar budget. "This is the most interesting job I've ever
had," he wrote to a friend in March. In less than eleven months at the
helm, he bucked up morale at headquarters, defended the CIA against
all critics, and deftly used the agency to build a political base for his soaring ambitions.

Beyond that, he accomplished little. From the start, Bush ran headlong into Secretary of Defense Rumsfeld, who had control over 80 percent of the intelligence budget. That money belongs to me, Rumsfeld
said; spy satellites and electronic surveillance and military intelligence
were all battlefield support for American soldiers. Though the American
military was in full retreat, Rumsfeld stiff-armed Bush. He was strongly
disinclined to let the director of central intelligence have a say in shap-
ing the secret spending. Rumsfeld was "paranoid" about the CIA and,
convinced that the agency was out to "spy on him," cut off long-
standing channels of communication and cooperation between the Pentagon and the CIA, the veteran analyst George Carver said in a CIA oral
history interview.

The recruitment of new officers in the wake of Watergate and Vietnam
was extraordinarily difficult. The agency was top-heavy with middle-

aged bureaucrats playing for time; Bush eased out twelve of the sixteen most senior officers at headquarters to try to make some headroom. He wanted to name his own chief of the clandestine service, so he called in Colby's chief, Bill Nelson, and said it was time for him to leave. Nelson saluted and left, but not before dropping a memo on Bush's desk that told him that the clandestine service had two thousand too many officers. Bush, in the tradition of Allen Dulles, buried the study.

"THE CIA WAS CUT OFF"

"This is a turbulent and troublesome period for the Agency," Bush wrote to President Ford on June 1, 1976. "The intensive investigations by both Houses of the Congress for more than a year now have resulted in extensive public disclosures of past and current covert action operations." The investigations led the Senate to create an intelligence oversight committee while Bush was director; the House set one up a year later. If only the president could find a way to shield the CIA from Congress, Bush wrote, then "covert action operations will continue to make the positive contribution to our foreign policy that they have made over the past twenty-eight years."

But the agency, under a newly vigilant Congress, had very few new covert-action operations under way. In a written response to questions from the author, Bush contended that the congressional investigations did long-lasting damage to the agency. They "set back our liaison relationships around the world"—the CIA's links with foreign intelligence services, the source of so much of the information it gathered—and "they caused many people abroad to pull away from cooperating with the CIA." Worst of all, he said, "they devastated the morale of perhaps the finest group of public servants this country has."

Continuing failures in the field also sapped the CIA's spirit in 1976. Among the biggest was in Angola. Two months after the fall of Saigon, President Ford approved a big new operation to secure Angola against communism. The country had been Portugal's biggest prize in Africa, but Lisbon's leaders had been among the worst of the European colonialists, and they sacked Angola as they withdrew. The country was coming apart as rival forces went to war.

The CIA shipped $32 million in cash and $16 million worth of weapons to Angola through the agency's great ally, President Mobutu of the Congo. The weapons went to an unruly gang of anticommunist guerrillas, commanded by Mobutu's brother-in-law and aligned with the white South African government. The program was aided by President Kenneth Kaunda of Zambia, a genial leader who had long received under-the-table support from the United States and the CIA. It was coordinated at Kissinger's State Department by a talented young diplomat—Frank G. Wisner, Jr., the son and namesake of the late chief of covert operations.

"We had been forced out of Vietnam," Wisner said. "There was a real concern on the part of the Administration that the United States would now be tested" by the forces of communism across the world. "Were we going to see a new seemingly communist-led offensive move in, take over oil-rich Angola and begin to carry the Cold War into southern Africa, or were we going to try to stop it?"

"We weren't going to be able to walk down to Congress, in the aftermath of Vietnam, and say, 'Look, let's send American military trainers and equipment over there to Mobutu,' so Kissinger and the President made the decision to go to the Agency," Wisner said. But the CIA-backed troops in Angola faltered, and their enemies, strongly supported by Moscow and Havana, took control of the capital. Kissinger ordered up another $28 million in secret support. There was no money left in the CIA's contingency budget. Early on in Bush's short year at the CIA, Congress publicly banned covert support for the Angolan guerrillas and killed the operation while it was in progress. Nothing of the kind had ever happened before. "The CIA was cut off, and we were driven back," Wisner said.

"I FEEL LIKE I HAVE BEEN HAD"

On the bicentennial day of July 4, 1976, Bush prepared to meet the governor of Georgia at a hotel in Hershey, Pennsylvania. He had been extraordinarily responsive when Jimmy Carter requested intelligence briefings from the CIA even before winning the Democratic presidential nomination. No candidate had ever made such a request so early in the game. Bush and his national intelligence deputy, Dick Lehman—who had grown so frustrated watching Allen Dulles hefting reports instead of reading them—found Carter extremely interested. Their discussion ranged from spy satellites to the future of white minority rule in Africa. They agreed that the briefings could continue later in July at Carter's home in the hamlet of Plains, Georgia.

The director had a hard time getting there. The CIA's Gulfstream jet could not handle the sod airstrip in Plains. The agency sought logistical help from the Pentagon and learned that Bush would have to take a helicopter to Peterson Field. The CIA aircrew checked their maps. Where the hell was Peterson Field? Another phone call to Plains and they understood: "Peterson's field" was some farmer's forty acres on the edge of town.

The six-hour session touched on Lebanon, Iraq, Syria, Egypt, Libya, Rhodesia, and Angola. China took thirty minutes. The Soviet Union took ten times as long. The CIA's men talked all afternoon and into the evening. Carter, who had been a nuclear engineer in the navy, grasped the arcane details of the American strategic arsenal. He was particularly interested in the evidence spy satellites obtained about Soviet weapons, and he understood that the intelligence they gleaned would play a vital role in arms control. He learned that the Soviets would never show their hand with an accurate statement of the size of their nuclear forces; the American side had to come to the negotiating table and tell the Soviets how many missiles *they* had and how many *we* had. This gave Carter pause: the notion that the Soviets lied seemed to be a new idea to him.

Bush assured him that the photographs provided by the first generation of spy satellites had provided Presidents Nixon and Ford with the information they needed to pursue SALT, the Strategic Arms Limitation Treaty, with the Soviets, and to keep a close eye on whether the Soviets would abide by their agreements. A new generation of satellites was coming on line that summer. Code-named Keyhole, they provided real-time television images instead of slow-to-develop photos. The CIA's science and technology division had been working on Keyhole for years, and it was a great breakthrough.

Carter's running mate, Senator Walter Mondale of Minnesota, asked about covert action and the agency's liaisons with foreign intelligence services. Mondale had been a member of the Church Committee, the Senate panel that investigated the CIA. Its final report had come out two months before. The committee is remembered today chiefly for its chairman's statement that the agency had been "a rogue elephant"—a pronouncement that badly missed the point by absolving the presidents who had driven the elephant. Bush, infuriated by the very existence of the Church Committee, refused to answer Mondale's questions.

Eight CIA officers joined Bush in Plains two weeks later, sitting in a circle in Carter's family room as his daughter and her cat wandered in and out. To their surprise, Carter seemed to have a highly nuanced understanding of the world. When Carter and Ford went head-to-head in the first televised presidential debates since Kennedy and Nixon, the governor cleaned the president's clock on foreign policy. He also took a hard swipe at the agency, saying: "Our system of government—in spite of Vietnam, Cambodia, CIA, Watergate—is still the best system of government on Earth."

On November 19, 1976, there was one final, awkward meeting between Bush and President-elect Carter in Plains. "Bush wanted to be kept on" at the CIA, Carter remembered. "If I had agreed to that, he never would have become President. His career would have gone off on a whole different track!"

Bush's memo of the meeting shows that he revealed a handful of ongoing operations to the president-elect, including the CIA's financial support for heads of state such as King Hussein of Jordan and President Mobutu of the Congo and strongmen such as Manuel Noriega, the future dictator of Panama. Bush observed that Carter seemed strangely turned off. His impression was correct. The president-elect found the CIA's subsidies for foreign leaders reprehensible.

By the end of 1976, Bush was in bad odor with some of his former fans at the agency. He had made a baldly political decision to let a team of neoconservative ideologues—"howling right-wingers," Dick Lehman called them—rewrite the CIA's estimates of Soviet military forces.

William J. Casey, the most vociferous member of the President's Foreign Intelligence Advisory Board, had been talking with some of his friends and associates in the intelligence community. They were convinced that the CIA was dangerously underestimating Soviet nuclear strength. Casey and his fellow members of the advisory board pressed

President Ford to let an outside group write their own Soviet estimate. The team, whose members were deeply disenchanted with détente and handpicked by the Republican right, included General Daniel O. Graham, America's leading advocate of missile defense, and Paul Wolfowitz, a disillusioned arms-control negotiator and a future deputy secretary of defense. In May 1976, Bush approved "Team B" with a cheery scribble: "Let her fly!! O.K. G.B."

The debate was highly technical, but it boiled down to a single question: what is Moscow up to? Team B portrayed a Soviet Union in the midst of a tremendous military buildup—when in fact it was cutting military spending. They dramatically overstated the accuracy of Soviet intercontinental ballistic missiles. They doubled the number of Backfire bombers the Soviet Union was building. They repeatedly warned of dangers that never materialized, threats that did not exist, technologies that were never created—and, most terrifying of all, the specter of a secret Soviet strategy to fight and win a nuclear war. Then, in December 1976, they selectively shared their findings with sympathetic reporters and opinion columnists. "The B Team was out of control," Lehman said, "and they were leaking all over the place."

The uproar Team B created went on for years, fueled a huge increase in Pentagon weapons spending, and led directly to the rise of Ronald Reagan to the top of the list of front-runners for the 1980 Republican nomination. After the cold war was over, the agency put Team B's findings to the test. Every one of them was wrong. It was the bomber gap and the missile gap all over again.

"I feel like I have been had," Bush told Ford, Kissinger, and Rumsfeld at the last National Security Council meeting of the outgoing administration.

Intelligence analysis had become corrupted—another tool wielded for political advantage—and it would never recover its integrity. The CIA's estimates had been blatantly politicized since 1969, when President Nixon forced the agency to change its views on the Soviets' abilities to launch a nuclear first strike. "I look upon that as almost a turning point from which everything went down," Abbot Smith, who ran the agency's Office of National Estimates under Nixon, said in a CIA oral history interview. "The Nixon administration was really the first one in which intelligence was just another form of politics. And that was bound to be disastrous, and I think it was disastrous." John Huizenga, who succeeded

Smith in 1971, put it even more bluntly to the CIA's historians, and his thoughts rang true in decades to come, into the twenty-first century:

> In retrospect, you see, I really do not believe that an intelligence organization in this government is able to deliver an honest analytical product without facing the risk of political contention. By and large, I think the tendency to treat intelligence politically increased over this whole period. And it's mainly over issues like Southeast Asia and the growth of Soviet strategic forces that were extremely divisive politically. I think it's probably naïve in retrospect to have believed what most of us believed at one time ... that you could deliver an honest analytical product and have it taken at face value. . . . I think that intelligence has had relatively little impact on the policies that we've made over the years. Relatively none. In certain particular circumstances, perhaps insights and facts that were provided had an effect on what we did. But only in a very narrow range of circumstances. By and large, the intelligence effort did not alter the premises with which political leadership came to office. They brought their baggage and they more or less carried it along. Ideally, what had been supposed was that ... serious intelligence analysis could ... assist the policy side to reexamine premises, render policymaking more sophisticated, closer to the reality of the world. Those were the large ambitions which I think were never realized.

These thoughts did not trouble the director of central intelligence and the future president of the United States.

"THE GREATNESS THAT IS CIA"

In his farewell to the employees at CIA headquarters, Bush delivered a fond thank-you note, as was his wont. "I hope I can find some ways in the years ahead to make the American people understand more fully the greatness that is CIA," he wrote. He was the last director of central intelligence who received something approaching full support from his troops at headquarters. In their eyes, it was to his great credit that he had tried to save the clandestine service. But to his shame, in the end, he had let the CIA be cowed by politics.

"I find no degradation in the quality of intelligence analysis," Kissinger said at their last meeting before the inauguration of Jimmy Carter. "The opposite is true, however, in the covert action area. We are unable to do it anymore."

"Henry, you are right," said George Herbert Walker Bush, one of the greatest boosters the CIA had ever had. "We are both ineffective and scared."

PART
FIVE

―――――

Victory Without Joy

The CIA Under Carter, Reagan, and George H. W. Bush

1977 to 1993

―――――

36. "HE SOUGHT TO OVERTHROW THEIR SYSTEM"

Running for president, Jimmy Carter had condemned the CIA as a national disgrace. Once in power, he wound up signing almost as many covert-action orders as Nixon and Ford. The difference was that he did it in the name of human rights. The problem was harnessing the agency's atrophied powers to that new mission.

His search for a new director of central intelligence went poorly. Thomas L. Hughes, the former chief of the State Department's Bureau of Intelligence and Research, declined the honor. The nomination went instead to the Kennedy speechwriter Ted Sorensen. "Somewhat to my surprise, Carter called me and asked me if I would come on down to Plains," Sorensen recounted. "I had a brother who had worked for CIA undercover for years. I went down there and I had a brief conversation with Carter and the very next day he presented me with the job." But he had been a conscientious objector in World War II, and his nomination died, the first time such a thing had happened in the history of the CIA. "Carter failed to give me any support while I was dangling there," Sorensen remembered bitterly.

On the third try, the new president selected a near stranger: Admiral Stansfield Turner, commander of the southern flank of NATO, based in Naples, Italy. Turner would be the third admiral in the history of the agency who found the CIA a hard vessel to handle. He was the first to admit his unfamiliarity with the agency. But he was quick to assert his authority.

"THAT WAS NOT THE RIGHT WAY TO PLAY THE GAME"

"Lots of people think President Carter called me in and said, 'Clean the place up and straighten it out.' He never did that," Turner said. "From the very beginning he was intensely interested in having good intelligence. He wanted to understand the mechanisms from our satellites to our spies to our methods of analyzing what was happening. He was extremely supportive of the intelligence operations. At the same time I knew full well just from his character that we were to operate within the laws of the United States of America. I knew also that there were ethical limits as to what President Carter would want us to do and whenever I came close to questioning whether we were close to those limits I went to him and I got his decisions on it. Almost always those decisions were to go ahead.

"The Carter administration had no bias against covert action," Turner said. "The CIA had a problem with covert action itself because it was in this state of shock from the criticisms it had gone through."

Early on, the clandestine service presented Turner with a life-and-death dilemma. "They came to me and said: 'We have an agent almost inside this terrorist organization, but they've asked him to do one more thing to prove his bona fides. He's to go out and murder one of the members of the government. Do we permit him to do that?' And I said: 'No, we pull him out.' You know, it's a trade-off. Maybe he could have saved some lives. But I was not going to have the United States party to a murder in order to take that chance. This was a real life right now and this was the reputation of our country. And I thought that was not the right way to play the game."

Turner quickly grasped the basics of the tug-of-war between spies and gadgets. He pulled for machines over men, spending much of his time and energy trying to improve the global coverage of American reconnaissance satellites. He tried to organize the "intelligence community" into a confederation, creating a coordinating staff and a unified budget. Those who served the cause were appalled at the disarray. "I was in charge of human intelligence collection," remembered John Holdridge, who had been Bush's deputy chief of mission in Beijing before joining the intelligence community staff. "I would look at these pie-in-the-sky operations which were presented to me and wonder who in the dickens

dreamed these up. They seemed to be so dreadfully impractical and unworkable."

Nor did the analysts receive high marks. President Carter pronounced
himself puzzled at the fact that the CIA's daily brief recapitulated what
he read in the newspapers. He and Turner wondered why the agency's
estimates seemed shallow and irrelevant. The agency was off to a rocky
start with the new president.

"CARTER HAD CHANGED THE LONG-STANDING RULES"

Carter's new national-security team had five ranking members with four
different agendas. The president and vice president dreamed of a new
American foreign policy founded on the principles of human rights. Secretary of State Cyrus Vance thought arms control was paramount. Secretary of Defense Harold Brown tried to produce a new generation of
military and intelligence technology for a few billion dollars less than the
Pentagon planned. National security adviser Zbigniew Brzezinski was
the hawk among these owls and doves. Centuries of Warsaw's woes at
the hands of Moscow shaped his thinking. He wanted to help the United
States win hearts and minds in Eastern Europe. He harnessed this ambition to the president's foreign policy and tried to hit the Soviets where
they were weakest.

President Ford and the Soviet leader, Leonid Brezhnev, had signed an
agreement in Helsinki in 1975 endorsing "the free movement of people
and ideas." Ford and Kissinger saw it as window dressing. But others
were dead serious: a generation of dissidents in Russia and Eastern Europe fed up with the evil banality of the Soviet state.

Brzezinski ordered—and Carter approved—an array of CIA covert actions aimed at Moscow, Warsaw, and Prague. They commanded the
agency to publish books and to subsidize the printing and distribution of
magazines and journals in Poland and Czechoslovakia, to help distribute
the written work of dissidents in the Soviet Union, to back the political
work of Ukrainians and other Soviet ethnic minorities, to place fax machines and tape cassettes in the hands of free-minded people behind the

iron curtain. They wanted to subvert the control of information that was the foundation of repression in the communist world.

The political warfare that Jimmy Carter waged opened a new front in the cold war, said the CIA's Bob Gates, then serving as a Soviet analyst on Brzezinski's National Security Council staff: "Through his human rights policies, he became the first president since Truman to challenge directly the legitimacy of the Soviet government in the eyes of its own people. And the Soviets immediately recognized this for the fundamental challenge it was: they believed he sought to overthrow their system."

Carter's aims were more modest: he wanted to alter the Soviet system, not abolish it. But the clandestine service of the CIA did not want to take on the task. The White House faced resistance to the stepped-up covert-action orders from the chiefs of the Soviet/East Europe division. They had a reason: they had a prized agent to protect in Warsaw, and they did not want the White House's ideals about human rights to threaten him. A Polish colonel named Ryszard Kuklinski was giving the United States a long hard look at the Soviet military. He was the highest-ranking source that the agency had behind the iron curtain. "Colonel Kuklinski was himself never in a strict sense a CIA agent," Brzezinski said. "He volunteered. He operated on his own." He had secretly offered his services to the United States during a visit to Hamburg. Keeping in touch with him was difficult; six months at a stretch went by in silence. But when Kuklinski traveled through Scandinavia and Western Europe, he always left word. During 1977 and 1978, until he began to fall under suspicion and surveillance in Warsaw, he delivered information that revealed how the Soviets would put all the armies of Eastern Europe under the Kremlin's control if war came. He told the agency how Moscow would run that war in Western Europe; its plans provided for the use of forty tactical nuclear weapons against the city of Hamburg alone.

Freed from the paranoia of the Angleton era, the Soviet division was beginning to recruit real spies behind the iron curtain. "We had moved away from all the grand and glorious traditions of the OSS and become an espionage service, dedicated to gathering foreign intelligence," said the CIA's Haviland Smith. "By God, we could go over to East Berlin and not get caught. We could recruit Eastern Europeans. We were going after and recruiting Soviets. The only thing missing is—we don't have anything on Soviet intentions. And I don't know how you get that. And that's *the charter of the clandestine service.* If we had been able to recruit a member of the Politburo, we would have had everything."

The Politburo of the late 1970s was a corrupt and decrepit gerontocracy. Its empire was dangerously overextended, dying from within. The politically ambitious Soviet intelligence chief, Yuri Andropov, had created a false image of the Soviet Union as a superpower for his doddering superiors in the Kremlin. But the Soviets' Potemkin village fooled the CIA as well. "We were appreciating as early as '78 that the Soviet economy was in serious trouble," Admiral Turner said. "We didn't make the leap that we should have made, I should have made, that the economic trouble would lead to political trouble. We thought they would tighten their belt under a Stalin-like regime and continue marching on."

Jimmy Carter's instinctive decision to assert the principles of human rights as an international standard was seen as an act of piety by many members of the clandestine service. His modest mobilization of the CIA to probe that weak chink in the armor of the iron curtain was a cautious challenge to the Kremlin. Nevertheless, he hastened the beginning of the end of the Soviet Union. "Carter had, in fact, changed the long-standing rules of the Cold War," Bob Gates concluded.

"FROM A BLACK-WHITE CONFLICT INTO A RED-WHITE CONFLICT"

President Carter also tried to use the CIA to undermine apartheid in South Africa. His stance changed the course of thirty years of cold-war foreign policy.

On February 8, 1977, in the White House Situation Room, the president's national-security team agreed that it was time for the United States to try to change the racist South African regime. "The possibilities are there to change this from a black-white conflict into a red-white conflict," Brzezinski said. "If this is the beginning of a long and bitter historical process, it is in our interest to accelerate this process." It was not about race but about getting on the right side of history.

The acting director of central intelligence, Enno Knoche, said: "We are seeking changes in their fundamental attitudes. This will require very close observation." In other words, the United States was going to have to start spying on South Africa. On March 3, 1977, at a full-dress National Security Council meeting, Carter commanded the CIA to explore how to bring economic and political pressure to bear on South Africa and its racist ally, Rhodesia.

The problem was that "nobody wanted to pay attention to Africa," said Carter's deputy director of central intelligence, Frank Carlucci. "We were very much focused on the Soviet Union. One of the main purposes of having people in stations in Africa was to try and recruit the Soviets who were stationed there. That was the number-one priority."

The Soviets supported the strongest enemy of apartheid, the African National Congress. The ANC's leader, Nelson Mandela, had been arrested and imprisoned in 1962, thanks in part to the CIA. The agency had worked in the closest harmony with the South African BOSS, the Bureau of State Security. The CIA's officers had stood "side-by-side with the security police in South Africa," said Gerry Gossens, a station chief in four African nations under Presidents Nixon, Ford, and Carter. "The word was that they had fingered Mandela himself."

In 1977, Gossens went to work on the hard-core white supremacist Ian Smith, who ruled in Rhodesia, as well as the pro-American Kenneth Kaunda, the president of Zambia. As station chief in the capital, Lusaka, Gossens met regularly with President Kaunda and his security service. He began to develop a picture of the black and white armed forces arrayed against one another throughout southern Africa: "We needed to know how many Soviets and Czechs and East Germans and North Koreans were providing arms and training. Could they overwhelm the Rhodesians? We needed human penetrations into the frontline governments."

Then, in 1978, Gossens became the new station chief in Pretoria. His orders from Washington were to spy on the white government of South Africa. Now the CIA was part of an ambitious American effort to push the Soviets out of southern Africa while winning support from black African governments.

"For the first time in history," he said, "I was instructed to begin unilateral operations against BOSS. I got in new people who were undeclared to the government. I got new targets in the South African military, their nuclear program, and their policy vis-à-vis Rhodesia. The Embassy was full-bore on the question: what is the South African government up to?" For two years, the CIA started gathering intelligence on the apartheid regimes. Then the secret police in Rhodesia arrested three CIA officers who had bungled their way into a trap. South African intelligence betrayed a fourth. Frank G. Wisner, Jr., came out to Zambia as the new American ambassador, where he remembered: "My greatest single crisis, my most difficult moment, came as the result of a spy scandal with a CIA officer."

Panicked by the blown missions, agency headquarters started shutting down operations and pulling out its spies. The CIA's efforts to fulfill the human-rights policies of the president came up short.

"THEY'RE A UNIQUE CULTURE"

The morals of the Carter administration were not good for morale at CIA headquarters. Admiral Turner tried to hew to Carter's pledge about never lying to the American people. This was a dilemma for the chief of a secret intelligence service, whose operators depended on deceit to succeed. What little confidence Turner had in the clandestine service was constantly chiseled away by acts of subversion.

In 1978, the American ambassador in Yugoslavia, Lawrence Eagleburger, who later served as secretary of state in the first Bush administration, came across a directive from the clandestine service at headquarters to every station chief in the world. Behind Turner's back, someone very senior had sent instructions to keep major operations secret from ambassadors everywhere abroad. The message was in direct violation of standing presidential orders going back seventeen years.

"I asked my station chief if it were true," Eagleburger said. "He said, yes, it was true. I said, 'Fine, I want you to send a message back to Admiral Turner.'" It was succinct: "You are out of business in Yugoslavia until such time as that order is rescinded. I mean by that, you're not to come into the office, and you're not to conduct any business in Belgrade or in Yugoslavia: you are simply to close up shop."

Turner was a Christian Scientist who drank hot water with lemon instead of coffee or tea. The old boys preferred whisky in their water. They

scorned Turner in word and deed. Turner wrote years later that his enemies within the clandestine service tried to discredit him with disinformation campaigns—"one of their basic skills." Chief among these was a
story that has persisted for a quarter century: that Turner was single-
handedly responsible for the gutting of the clandestine service in the
1970s. The first deep cuts had been ordered by Nixon. One thousand
covert operators had been let go by James Schlesinger. George Bush, under Ford, had chosen to ignore a recommendation from his own covert-
action chief that 2,000 more should depart. Turner wound up cutting
precisely 825, starting with the bottom 5 percent on the performance
charts. He had the president's support. "We were aware that some of
the unqualified and incompetent personnel whom he discharged were
deeply resentful, but I fully approved," Jimmy Carter said in a letter to
the author.

The old boys fought hard against Turner when he selected John
McMahon to lead the clandestine service. McMahon was not one of
them. He had started out carrying Allen Dulles's suitcases and now ran
the agency's directorate of science and technology, the branch that produced the hardware and software of espionage. He told Turner: "No, I'm
the wrong guy for it. They're a unique culture. They work best with their
own and you have to understand how they think. My last exposure to
them was back in the early fifties over in Germany. And times have
changed."

In January 1978, after resisting for half a year, McMahon became the
third chief of the clandestine service in eighteen months. Three weeks
after he took over, he was called to appear at the first meeting of the new
House intelligence oversight committee. The clandestine service rebelled. "Talk about apoplexy—they went bonkers," McMahon said. "But
what I knew was that the congressmen didn't understand CIA or clandestine operations. And I was going to go down there and educate
them." He gathered up a shopping bag of spy gear and gadgets—
miniature cameras and audio bugs and the like—and went up to the Hill.
"I said: 'Let me tell you what it's like to operate in Moscow.' " McMahon
had never been to Moscow in his life. "I said, 'Now, here is some of the
equipment we use.' And I started passing it out. And they looked at
all these gadgets . . . and they were just mesmerized." The spellbound
committee gave the spies a far bigger budget than the president had
requested. The rebuilding of the clandestine service, ravaged and demor-

alized by cuts going back to the Nixon years, began then and there, in the fall of 1978.

But the mood remained grim at the citadel of American intelligence. "In spite of its current (and worsening) morale problems CIA will still come up with some imaginative ideas, I suspect," Brzezinski's liaison to the agency advised him on February 5, 1979. "We must not deceive ourselves, however: the capabilities that used to exist in CIA are very *thin* right now and there are very few officers disposed to take risks of the kind that used to be routinely taken to get things done."

That same week, the world started falling in on the CIA.

"A SPECTATOR SPORT"

On February 11, 1979, the army of the shah collapsed and a fanatic ayatollah took control in Tehran. Three days later, a few hundred miles to the west, came a killing that would come to bear the same heavy weight for the United States.

The American ambassador in Afghanistan, Adolph "Spike" Dubs, was snatched off the streets of Kabul, kidnapped by Afghan rebels fighting the pro-Soviet puppet regime, and killed when Afghan police—accompanied by Soviet advisers—attacked the hotel where he was held. It was a clear sign that Afghanistan was spinning out of control. The Islamic rebels, supported by Pakistan, were gearing up for a revolution against their godless government. The geriatric leaders of the Soviet Union looked south in fear. More than forty million Muslims lived in the Soviet republics of central Asia. The Soviets saw the flames of Islamic fundamentalism burning toward their borders. At an extended Politburo meeting that began on March 17, the Soviet intelligence chief, Yuri Andropov, declared that "we cannot lose Afghanistan."

Over the next nine months, the CIA failed to warn the president of the United States of an invasion that changed the face of the world. The agency had a fair grasp of Soviet capabilities. It understood nothing of Soviet intentions.

"The Soviets would be most reluctant to introduce large numbers of ground forces into Afghanistan," the CIA's *National Intelligence Daily*, its top secret report to the White House, the Pentagon, and the State Department, confidently stated on March 23, 1979. That week, thirty thousand Soviet combat troops began to deploy near the Afghan border in trucks, tanks, and armored personnel carriers.

In July and August, the Afghan rebels' attacks grew, Afghan army garrisons began to mutiny, and Moscow flew a battalion of airborne combat units into the Bagram air base outside Kabul. Prompted by Brzezinski, President Carter signed a covert-action order for the CIA to provide the Afghan rebels with medical aid, money, and propaganda. The Soviets sent thirteen generals to Kabul, led by the commander of Soviet ground forces. Still, the CIA assured the president on August 24 that "the deteriorating situation does not presage an escalation of Soviet military involvement in the form of a direct combat role."

On September 14, Admiral Turner told the president that "Soviet leaders may be on the threshold of a decision to commit their own forces to prevent the collapse of the regime" in Afghanistan—but only bit by bit, with small groups of military advisers, and some few thousands of troops. Unsure of that assessment, the CIA gathered all its expertise and every element of American military intelligence, electronic-eavesdropping transcripts, and spy-satellite reconnaissance together for a full-dress review of the evidence. On September 28, the experts unanimously concluded that Moscow would not invade Afghanistan.

The Soviet troops kept coming. On December 8, a second airborne battalion landed at Bagram. The *National Intelligence Daily* assessed their presence as a move to beef up defenses against rebel attacks at the air base. The next week, the CIA station chief in Kabul reported secondhand sightings of Soviet special-forces commandos on the streets of the city.

On Monday morning, December 17, Admiral Turner went to a White House meeting of the president's most senior aides, the Special Coordination Committee. Among those present were Vice President Walter Mondale, Zbigniew Brzezinski, Secretary of Defense Harold Brown, and the deputy secretary of state, Warren Christopher. Turner told them that there were now 5,300 Soviet soldiers at the Bagram air base and two new Soviet command posts just north of the Afghan border. Then he said: "CIA does not see this as a crash buildup." It was "perhaps related to Soviet perceptions of a deterioration of the Afghan military forces and the need to beef them up at some point." The word *invasion* did not cross his lips.

The CIA's best Soviet analysts—among them Doug MacEachin, later the deputy director for intelligence—worked around the clock to marshal their knowledge for the president. On December 19, they issued their final formal judgment. "The pace of Soviet deployments does not suggest . . . urgent contingency," they said. "Anti-insurgent operations on a countrywide scale would require mobilization of much larger numbers of regular ground forces." In short, the Soviets did not intend to attack.

Three days later, Vice Admiral Bobby Ray Inman, the director of the National Security Agency, the American electronic-eavesdropping empire, got a flash message from the field: the invasion of Afghanistan was imminent. In fact, it was under way. More than a hundred thousand Soviet troops were seizing the country. Carter immediately signed a covert-action order for the CIA to begin arming the Afghan resistance, and the agency began to build a worldwide arms pipeline to Afghanistan. But the Soviet occupation was an accomplished fact.

The CIA not only missed the invasion, it refused to admit that it had missed it. Why would anyone in his right mind invade Afghanistan, graveyard of conquerors for two thousand years? A lack of intelligence was not the cause of the failure. A lack of imagination was.

So the Soviet invasion became "a spectator sport" for the United States, the agency's star analyst Doug MacEachin wrote more than twenty years later. "The U.S. could make a lot of noise from the stands, but could not have much impact on the playing field. That would have to wait until the next round of the Great Game."

37. "WE WERE JUST PLAIN ASLEEP"

Ever since the CIA secured his throne in 1953, the shah of Iran had been the centerpiece of American foreign policy in the Middle East. "I just wish there were a few more leaders around the world with his foresight," President Nixon reflected in April 1971. "And his ability to run, basically, let's face it, a virtual dictatorship in a benign way."

Nixon may not have intended to send a message by sending Richard Helms out as the American ambassador to Iran in 1973. But he did. "We were amazed that the White House would send a man who, after all, had such associations with the CIA, which was deemed by every Iranian responsible for the fall of Mossadeq," said Henry Precht, the American embassy's chief political officer. "It seemed to us to abandon any pretense of a sort of a neutral America and to confirm that the shah was our puppet."

On December 31, 1977, in a toast to the shah at a glittering state dinner, President Carter called the monarchy "an island of stability in a sea of turmoil," a view that had been confirmed and repeated by the CIA's spies and analysts for fifteen years beforehand. It was, in fact, the very phrase the shah used to describe himself.

But when Howard Hart, one of the bravest officers the clandestine service ever produced, came to Tehran a few weeks later and started doing what he did best—skulking around the streets and reporting on the real world—he reached the opposite conclusion. His work was so pessimistic that his superiors suppressed it. It directly contradicted everything the CIA had said about the shah since the 1960s.

The agency had reported nothing to suggest that the shah was in trouble. It lacked the ability to question twenty-five years of its own reporting. In August 1978, the agency told the White House that Iran was nowhere near a revolution. Weeks later, there were riots in the streets. As they spread, the CIA's top analysts sent Admiral Turner a draft National Intelligence Estimate for his signature. It said the shah might survive for another ten years. Or he might not. Turner read it, deemed it useless, and shelved it.

On January 16, 1979, the shah fled Tehran. A few days later, Howard Hart's view from the streets grew decidedly darker.

He was waylaid by an armed gang—followers of a seventy-seven-year-old religious zealot, Ayatollah Ruhollah Musavi Khomeini, who was preparing to return to Tehran from exile. Hart was an investment banker's son who had spent three years as a young child interned in a Japanese prison camp in the Philippines during World War II. He was now a prisoner once more. His captors roughed him up, held a kangaroo court, proclaimed him a CIA spy, and prepared to execute him on the spot. Proclaiming his innocence, pleading for his life, preparing to die, Hart asked to see the nearest mullah. A young cleric arrived to find the blond, blue-eyed, hard-muscled spy in the clutches of rough justice.

"I said, 'This is wrong—nowhere in the Holy Koran is this sanctioned,' " Hart remembered. The mullah pondered the question and agreed. Hart went free.

"WE DID NOT UNDERSTAND WHO KHOMEINI WAS"

A few days later, on February 1, 1979, the popular revolution that pushed the shah from the Peacock Throne opened the way for Khomeini's return to Tehran. Thousands of Americans, including most of the embassy's staff, were evacuated as the chaos in the streets grew. A secular prime minister still held power alongside a Revolutionary Council, and the CIA tried to work with him, influence him, and mobilize him against Saddam Hussein. "Some very, very sensitive classified conversations occurred at the level of Prime Minister," said Bruce Laingen, the chargé d'affaires at the American embassy. "We went to the degree of actually sitting down with them and giving them highly classified intelligence on Iraq."

Laingen had been the youngest officer at the American embassy in Tehran in 1953. He was the most senior officer in 1979. In the intervening years a succession of station chiefs and ambassadors had become far too cozy with the shah, far too fond of his caviar and his champagne. "We paid for it," Laingen said. "We are there to find out how people are thinking and why they are thinking that way and behaving that way. And if we get too comfortable in believing something that fits our purposes—well, we are in hellish trouble."

The idea that religion would prove to be a compelling political force in the late twentieth century was incomprehensible. Few at the CIA believed that an ancient cleric could seize power and proclaim Iran an Islamic republic. "We did not understand who Khomeini was and the support his movement had," Turner said—or what his seventh-century view of the world might mean for the United States.

"We were just plain asleep," he said.

On March 18, 1979, Howard Hart, now the acting chief of station, had a 2 a.m. meeting with a high-ranking officer of SAVAK, the shah's brutal secret police, who had served the station loyally as an agent and informer. After passing the officer money and false documents to help him flee Tehran, Hart ran into a cordon of Khomeini's Revolutionary Guards. They beat him brutally, shouting "CIA! CIA!" Flat on his back, Hart drew his pistol and killed them both with two shots. Many years later, he remembered the glittering zeal he saw in their eyes. It was the face of holy war. "We haven't a clue as a nation," he reflected, "as to what the hell this is."

"IT WAS BEYOND INSULT"

Iranians from all walks of life, well-educated elites and wild-eyed radicals alike, thought the CIA was an omnipotent force with immense power over their lives. They could not have believed the truth: in the summer of 1979, the CIA station was a four-man operation, and all four were newly arrived in Iran. Howard Hart had returned to headquarters in July, leaving behind a new station chief, Tom Ahern, who had spent the past thirteen years in Japan; an experienced case officer, Malcolm Kalp; a communications technician, Phil Ward; and a thirty-two-year-old marine veteran, William J. Daugherty, who had joined the CIA nine months before. Daugherty had flown seventy-six combat missions during the Vietnam War. Tehran was his first CIA tour.

"I knew little about Iran," he recalled. "I knew even less about Iranians. My entire exposure to Iran, beyond the evening television news and a three-week area studies course at the State Department, consisted of what I had picked up during five weeks on the desk reading operational files."

Five months before, a rabble of Iranian Marxists had overrun the American embassy. The ayatollah's followers led a counterattack, threw the communists out, and set the Americans free. No one thought it could happen again. "Don't worry about another embassy attack," the CIA's Iran branch chief at headquarters had assured the Tehran station. "The only thing that could trigger an attack would be if the Shah was let into the United States—and no one in this town is stupid enough to do that."

On October 21, 1979, Daugherty stared at a new cable from headquarters. "I could not believe what I was reading," he recalled.

Under intense political pressure from friends of the shah—notably, Henry Kissinger—President Carter, against his better judgment, had decided that day to admit the exiled monarch to the United States for medical treatment. The president had agonized about this decision, fearing that Americans would be taken hostage in reprisal. "I shouted, *'Blank* the Shah! He's just as well off playing tennis in Acapulco as he is in California,' " Carter recalled. " 'What are we going to do if they take twenty of our Marines and kill one of them every morning at sunrise? Are we going to go to war with Iran?' "

No one at the White House thought to ask the agency for its opinion.

Two weeks later, a group of Iranian students, all followers of the ayatollah, seized the American embassy. They held fifty-three hostages for the rest of the Carter administration, 444 days and nights. Daugherty spent the last weeks of 1979 in solitary confinement. He recalled six interrogations between November 29 and December 14, starting at nightfall and going on until dawn, led by Hossein Sheik-ol-eslam, a future deputy foreign minister of Iran. After midnight on December 2, Hossein handed him a cable. "I thought my life was over," he wrote in a memoir for the CIA's in-house journal. "The cable gave my true name and stated clearly that I was to be assigned to the station in Teheran. It also mentioned the special program under which I had come into the Agency 10 months previously. When I looked up at Hossein and his stooges, they were grinning like a trio of Cheshire cats."

His interrogators "said they knew that I was the head of the CIA's entire Middle East spy network, that I had been planning Khomeini's assassination, and that I had been stirring up the Kurds to revolt against the Teheran government. They accused me of trying to destroy their country," Daugherty remembered. "These Iranians found it inconceivable that the CIA would ever send to such a critical place as Iran someone who was so ignorant of the local culture and language. It was so inconceivable to them that weeks later, when they at last came to realize the truth, they were personally offended. It had been difficult enough for them to accept that the CIA would post an inexperienced officer in their country. But it was beyond insult for that officer not to speak the language or know the customs, culture, and history of their country."

After each night's interrogation ended, Daugherty slept fitfully on a foam-rubber pad in the station chief's office. As hundreds of thousands of Iranians chanted in the streets outside the walled American compound, he dreamed of flying a warplane over the wide boulevards and incinerating the crowds with napalm.

The CIA could do nothing to free him and his fellow hostages at the American embassy. But in January 1980, the agency executed a classic espionage operation to extract six State Department employees who had managed to find refuge across town at the Canadian embassy.

The operation was the brainchild of the CIA's Tony Mendez, whose specialties were forgery and disguise. Mendez and his crew were the people who perfected the *Mission Impossible* masks that allowed white officers to disguise themselves as Africans, Arabs, and Asians. He was a rare exemplar of intuitive genius at the CIA.

As a cover for the mission in Iran, Mendez created Studio Six, a bogus Hollywood film production company; rented office space in Los Angeles; and took out full-page ads in *Variety* and *The Hollywood Reporter* announcing the upcoming filming of *Argo*, a science-fiction fantasy with location shots in Iran. The script for the movie—and for the operation—included documents and masks for the six Americans. Armed with a portfolio of forged passports and phony publicity, he cleared his entry to

Iran with the proper authorities, flew in on a commercial flight from Bonn, checked into the Tehran Sheraton, obtained Swissair reservations to Zurich for the coming Monday, and took a taxi to the Canadian embassy to meet his six fellow Americans. Mendez brought the *Argo* operation off with barely a hitch. One of the Americans he freed punched him in the arm as they boarded the Swissair flight and said, "You arranged for everything, didn't you?" He was pointing at the name painted on the nose of the airplane—"Argau," a canton in Switzerland.

"We took it as a sign that everything would be all right," Mendez remembered. "We waited until the plane took off and had cleared Iranian airspace before we could give the thumbs up and order Bloody Marys."

"AN ACT OF VENGEANCE"

No such magic freed the remaining prisoners. The Pentagon's special-operations forces were in charge of Desert One, the April 1980 mission to save the hostages at the American embassy. "The effort relied very heavily on the CIA," said Anthony Quainton, the government's chief counterterrorism coordinator from 1978 to 1981. The agency provided intelligence on the probable location of the hostages inside the embassy compound. Its pilots flew a small plane undetected into the Iran desert to test the landing site for the mission. Howard Hart helped create the immensely complicated plan to extract the hostages and fly them to freedom. But the mission ended in catastrophe; eight commandos died in the Iranian wasteland after crashing a helicopter into a transport plane.

Life became much worse for the hostages. Bill Daugherty was taken from the embassy and thrown into prison. He spent most of the next nine months in solitary, in a cell barely big enough to hold his six-foot-three-frame. He ended up weighing 133 pounds. He and the rest of the hostages finally were freed by the consent of their captors at the hour that President Carter left the White House for the last time. Their release had nothing to do with covert action or American intelligence. It was a political statement devised to humiliate the United States.

The next day, Jimmy Carter, private citizen, came to meet the freed Americans at a military base in Germany. "I still have the photo stashed away somewhere," Daugherty recorded. "The former President looks awkward, and I look like an unsmiling cadaver."

The taking of the hostages was an "act of vengeance" for the CIA's 1953 coup in Iran, wrote Ken Pollack, a veteran CIA analyst of the Middle East. But the legacy of that long-ago operation went far beyond the Americans' ordeal. The zeal of the Iranian revolution would haunt the next four presidents of the United States and kill hundreds of Americans in the Middle East. A blaze of glory for the covert operators of the CIA's greatest generation became a tragic conflagration for their heirs.

38. "A FREELANCE BUCCANEER"

On October 4, 1980, the director of central intelligence and three of his top aides drove out to Wexford, a millionaire's estate in the Virginia horse country once owned by John and Jackie Kennedy. They came to brief the Republican candidate for president, Ronald Reagan. He had agreed to give the CIA an hour of his time.

Admiral Turner had fifteen minutes to cover Saddam Hussein's recent invasion of Iran. Fifteen minutes more went to the nine-month-old Soviet occupation of Afghanistan and the CIA's arms shipments to support the Afghan resistance. Bob Ames, the agency's expert on the Middle East, did fifteen minutes on the kingdom of Saudi Arabia and the theocracy of Ayatollah Khomeini. Members of Reagan's entourage, flush with the prospect of certain victory in the upcoming election, rushed in and out of the room like characters in a screwball comedy. The hour was over in a flash.

Reagan knew little more about the CIA than what he had learned at the movies. But he pledged to unleash it, and he was good to his word. The man he chose for the job was his brilliant and devious campaign manager, William J. Casey.

Casey, in thrall to his memories of his days as an OSS intelligence chief in London, hung a signed portrait of Wild Bill Donovan on his office wall at headquarters, and for the next six years Donovan gazed down upon him. In a global and totalitarian war, Wild Bill had said, intelligence must be global and totalitarian. This was Bill Casey's credo. He aimed to revive that fighting spirit at the CIA. "His view of how you fight

a war against a totalitarian power had clearly been shaped in World War
Two," said Bob Gates, who served six years at his side. "Where there
were no holds barred. Where everything went."

Casey made a bid to become secretary of state, but the idea appalled
Reagan's intimates. It was a question of appearances. Casey was no
statesman: he looked like an unmade bed, mumbled unintelligibly, and
ate like a stumblebum. The first-lady-in-waiting could not bear the
thought of Casey at a formal state dinner, spilling food down his cum-
merbund. Sensing the opposition, Casey was bitter, but he won a hand-
shake deal with Reagan: he would accept the CIA, but he had to have
cabinet rank, the first director to do so, and he had to have the ability to
see the president in private. He would use those powers not merely to
execute American foreign policy but to make it, as if he were the secretary of state after all. All Casey needed was a few minutes with the president, a wink and a nod, and he was off.

Casey was a charming scoundrel, an old-time Wall Street operator
whose fortune came from selling tax-shelter strategies. His talent lay in
bending rules to the breaking point. "By God, we've got to get rid of the
lawyers!" he once muttered to William Webster, Reagan's FBI director. "I
don't think he meant to say 'scrap the Constitution,' " said Webster, who
was a lawyer to the soles of his wingtips. "But he tended to feel the constraints of the law. He wanted a way out of them."

Reagan trusted him. Others did not. "I was absolutely surprised when
President Reagan selected Casey," Gerald R. Ford said. "He was not qualified to be the head of the CIA." Ford's own director of central intelligence agreed wholeheartedly. "Casey was an inappropriate choice," said
George H. W. Bush.

But Casey believed that he was responsible for Reagan's election and
that they had a historic role to play together. Like Reagan, Casey had big
visions. Like Nixon, he believed that if it's secret, it's legal. Like Bush, he
thought the CIA embodied the best American values. And, like the Soviets, he reserved the right to lie and cheat.

The Reagan years started out with a burst of new covert operations
approved by the small National Security Planning Group, which met in
the Situation Room, down in the basement of the White House. The
group was the laboratory for covert action in the Reagan years. At the
start, its core members were the president; Vice President Bush; Secretary of State Alexander M. Haig, Jr.; Secretary of Defense Caspar W.

Weinberger; the national security adviser and the chairman of the Joint Chiefs; the United Nations ambassador, Jeane Kirkpatrick; and her close friend Bill Casey. Casey dominated the first meeting, and in the first two months of the new administration, the group gave him the go-ahead for sweeping covert operations aimed at Central America, Nicaragua, Cuba, northern Africa, and South Africa.

On March 30, 1981, a lunatic shot the president on a sidewalk in Washington. Reagan came very close to dying that day, a fact the American people never knew.

When Al Haig—hoarse, sweating, trembling—grabbed the press-room podium at the White House with white-knuckled hands and proclaimed himself in charge, he did not inspire confidence. The president's recovery was slow and painful. So was Haig's meltdown. Throughout 1981, "there was an underlying problem," said Vice Admiral John Poindexter, then a National Security Council staffer. "Who was going to be in charge of foreign policy?" That question was never answered, for Reagan's national-security team was in a never-ending state of war with itself, riven by fierce personal and political rivalries. The State Department and the Pentagon fought like opposing armies. Six different men served as national security adviser over the course of eight tumultuous years. Reagan never tried to stop the backstabbing.

Casey gained the upper hand. When George P. Shultz took over from Haig as secretary of state, he was astonished to find Casey freelancing plans such as an invasion of Suriname, on the northeastern shoulder of South America, with 175 Korean commandos backed by the CIA. "It was a hare-brained idea," said Shultz, who killed it. "Crazy. I was shaken to find such a wild plan put forward." He quickly came to understand that "the CIA and Bill Casey were as independent as a hog on ice and could be as confident as they were wrong."

"A BLINDERED FRATERNITY"

Bill Casey was as smart, as capable, and as inspirational a leader as any man who ever ran the CIA. He was also "a freelance buccaneer," said Admiral Bobby Ray Inman, who was the director of the National Security

Agency when President Reagan ordered him to serve as Casey's number-two in 1981.

"Casey told me very directly that he did not want to be the traditional Director of Central Intelligence," Inman said. "He did want to be the President's intelligence officer, and he was going to run the clandestine service of the CIA."

Casey believed that the clandestine service had become "a blindered fraternity living on the legends and achievements of their forebears of the 1950s and 1960s," said his first chief of staff, Bob Gates. It needed fresh blood. He did not give a damn for the CIA's organizational chart; he would reach down into the bowels of the agency, or outside it, to find people who would do his bidding.

So he shoved John McMahon out as chief of the clandestine service. "He viewed me as a slow mover when it came to covert action—that I didn't have that fire in the belly," McMahon said. "He knew I was a cautionary influence on what he or the agency might want to do."

Casey replaced the thirty-year CIA veteran with an old friend named Max Hugel, who had raised money and gotten out votes for Reagan. Hugel was a foul-mouthed business mogul who had started out in Japan after the war as a used-car salesman. He knew nothing about the CIA, which was instantly evident. A tiny man with a toupee, he once showed up for work at the agency wearing a lavender jumpsuit open to the navel, gold chains nestled in his graying chest hair. To a man, the CIA's covert operators, serving and retired, rebelled against him. They dug up dirt on him, fed it to *The Washington Post*, and forced him out in less than two months. He was replaced by John Stein, who had helped Mobutu rise to power and had created the Cambodia station during the war in Vietnam. Stein, the fifth new chief of covert action in five years, soon also proved too cautious for Casey's taste. He would be cast off for a truly bold covert operator, Clair George. Having tossed McMahon out of the clandestine service, Casey ordered him to reshape the directorate of intelligence and shake up its analysts. McMahon made a start on the first major reorganization of the directorate in thirty years.

But it was nothing compared to what Bob Gates did when he took over from McMahon at the start of 1982. At age thirty-eight, Gates had won the promotion with an attention-grabbing memo to Casey. "CIA is slowly turning into the Department of Agriculture," he wrote. The agency had "an advanced case of bureaucratic arteriosclerosis." The halls were filled with plodding mediocrities counting the days until retire-ment—and they were the principal cause of "the decline in the quality of our intelligence collection and analysis over the last fifteen years."

Gates told the CIA's analysts they were "close-minded, smug, arro-gant" people; their work was "irrelevant, uninteresting, too late to be of value, too narrow, too unimaginative, and too often just flat out wrong"; their ranks were filled with amateurs "pretending to be experts." They had missed almost every important development in the Soviet Union and its advances into the third world over the past decade. It was time to shape up or ship out.

Shape up meant get in line. When Casey disagreed with his analysts, as he often did, he rewrote their conclusions to reflect his views. When he told the president, "This is what the CIA thinks," he meant, "This is what *I* think." He chased independent-minded, let-the-chips-fall-where-they-may analysts out of the CIA, and among the last to leave was Dick Lehman, the current-intelligence chief who had endured Allen Dulles when the old man judged his work by hefting its weight rather than reading it. "Working for Casey was a trial for everybody, partly because of his growing erraticism and partly because of his own right-wing ten-dencies," Lehman said. "He was amenable to argument, but it took a hell of a lot of argument."

Like a newspaper bent by its publisher's prejudices, the analytical pow-ers of the CIA became one man's opinion. "The CIA's intelligence was in many cases simply Bill Casey's ideology," Secretary of State Shultz said.

"I'LL TAKE CARE OF CENTRAL AMERICA"

After publicly denouncing everything Jimmy Carter represented, Reagan and Casey embraced seven major covert-action programs that he had started. Arms shipments to Afghanistan and political-warfare programs to support dissidents in the Soviet Union, Poland, and Czechoslovakia would prove to be among the most important CIA operations of the cold war. But Casey was more interested in a real war in America's backyard.

"Sometime in the dark of night," said Clair George, Casey had reassured Ronald Reagan: "I'll take care of Central America. Just leave it to me."

In 1980, President Carter had approved three small covert-action programs in Central America. They took aim at the Sandinistas, the leftists who had taken power in Nicaragua, wresting it from what remained of the brutal forty-three-year-old right-wing dictatorship of the Somoza family. The Sandinistas' mixture of nationalism, liberation theology, and Marxism was tilting ever closer to Cuba's. Carter's covert actions committed the CIA to support pro-American political parties, church groups, farmer's co-ops, and unions against the spread of the Sandinistas' socialism.

Casey turned the small-bore operations into a huge scattershot paramilitary program. In March 1981, President Reagan authorized the CIA to provide guns and money "to counter foreign-sponsored subversion and terrorism" in Central America. The White House and the agency told Congress that the goal was to defend El Salvador, run by right-wing politicians and their death squads, by cutting off Nicaraguan arms shipments to leftists. This was a calculated ruse. The real plan was to train and arm Nicaraguans in Honduras—the *contras*—and to use them to recapture their country from the Sandinistas.

Casey convinced the president that the CIA's little army could take Nicaragua by storm. If they failed, he warned Reagan, an army of Latino leftists could roll northward from Central America to Texas. The CIA's analysts tried to contradict him. The *contras* are not going to win, they said; they do not have popular support. Casey ensured that the naysayers' reporting never reached the White House. To counteract them, he built a Central American Task Force with its own "war room," where covert-action officers cooked the books, inflated the threats, exaggerated the prospects for success, and pumped up reports from the field. Gates says he "raised hell with Casey" about the war room for years, to no avail.

Casey gave his plans a kick-start by selecting Duane Clarridge as the Latin American division chief of the clandestine service. Just shy of fifty, hard-drinking and cigar-puffing despite an early heart attack, Clarridge never had worked in Latin America, spoke no Spanish, and knew next to nothing about the region. "Casey said, 'Take off a month or two and basically figure out what to do about Central America,' " Clarridge said. "That was the sum total of his approach. And it didn't take rocket science to understand what needed to be done." Clarridge said he came up with a two-point plan: "Make war in Nicaragua and start killing Cubans. This was exactly what Casey wanted to hear and he said, 'Okay, go ahead and do it.' "

Reagan's ambassador to Nicaragua, Anthony Quainton, arrived to take up his post on the day of the opening shot. "The secret war began on March 15, 1982, when the CIA, using Nicaraguan agents, blew up the bridges that connected Nicaragua with Honduras," he said. "I stepped off the plane with my wife in a blaze of klieg lights and microphones and was asked what I thought about the developments that morning, the blowing up of the bridges, and how that would affect bilateral relations between the United States and Nicaragua.

"I had not been told that this event was to take place on this day," Ambassador Quainton said. "The CIA had a planning process of their own."

The secret war did not stay secret for long. On December 21, 1982, Congress passed a law restricting the CIA to its stated mission of cutting off the flow of communist arms in Central America. The agency was prohibited from using its funds to oust the Sandinistas. President Reagan stuck with the cover story, maintaining the fiction that the United States was not seeking to topple the Nicaraguan regime, giving his assurances to a joint session of Congress. That was the first time the well-loved president lied to Congress to protect the CIA's covert operations, but not the last.

"FUCK THE CONGRESS"

Congress gave Casey hundreds of millions of dollars in new funds for the clandestine service during his first two years in power. Spending on American intelligence, buried inside the Pentagon's accounts, shot past $30 billion as the agency's own budget rose above $3 billion. The money supercharged the CIA's ambitions and the scope of covert action.

Casey used part of his windfall to hire close to two thousand new officers for the clandestine service, reversing the cuts made under Presidents Nixon, Ford, and Carter. The new hires knew far less about the world than their predecessors. They were far less likely to have served in the military or lived overseas. They were "proof positive that the CIA was no longer attracting America's brightest," Clarridge said—"yuppie spies who cared more about their retirement plan and health insurance benefits than about protecting democracy."

Congress strongly supported a bigger, better, stronger, smarter CIA. But it did not support a war in Central America. Neither did the American people. Reagan never took the trouble to explain why that war was a good idea. Nor would most Americans approve of some of the CIA's allies—leaders of the dictatorial Nicaraguan national guard, shock troops from the Argentine military junta, murderous colonels from the Honduran army, and death-squad leaders from Guatemala.

The powers of Congress to oversee the CIA had slowly evolved into a workable system by 1981. Now two select intelligence committees, one in the Senate, one in the House, were supposed to receive and review presidential covert-action plans. These checkreins never slowed Casey. "Casey was guilty of contempt of Congress from the day he was sworn in," said Bob Gates. Called to testify, he would mumble and obfuscate and occasionally lie through his teeth. "I hope that will hold the bastards!" he said on emerging from one hearing. The deceit spread downward from the director's office. Many of Casey's senior officers learned the fine art of testifying in ways that were "specifically evasive," in the words of his Central America Task Force chief, Allen Fiers. Others resisted. Admiral Inman resigned as Casey's deputy director after fifteen months because "I caught him lying to me in a number of cases."

Casey's lies were designed to slip a tightening legal leash. If Congress would not finance the CIA's operations in Central America, he would work around the law, looking for private financiers or a foreign potentate to give him the money.

Despite Casey's open disdain, the congressional intelligence committees gave him great power under "global findings," authorizations signed by President Reagan that covered covert-action campaigns against real and perceived threats anywhere in the world. Many of the CIA's operations were conceived by Casey as grand designs to boost an American ally or bleed an American enemy. But they boiled down to running guns to warlords. One of the first got under way ten days after Casey took office. It lasted for ten years.

A January 1981 global finding ordered the CIA to do something about the Libyan dictator Muhammar Qaddafi, who was serving as a one-stop weapons depot for radical movements all over Europe and Africa. Seek-

The Directors of Central Intelligence
1946–2005

The spirit of Wild Bill Donovan, the American spymaster of World War II, drove many future CIA officers who served under him, among them William Casey, director of central intelligence from 1981 to 1987. *Above:* Casey speaks at an OSS reunion, Donovan's image above him. *Bottom left:* President Truman pins a medal on the first director, Rear Admiral Sidney Souers. *Bottom right:* General Hoyt Vandenberg, the second director, testifies before Congress.

General Walter Bedell Smith, director from 1950 to 1953, was the first real leader of the CIA. *Top left:* With Ike on V-E Day; *top right:* with Truman in the White House. *Below:* In an October 1950 photo taken at CIA headquarters, Bedell Smith, left, takes command from the ineffectual Rear Admiral Roscoe Hillenkoetter, in light suit. *Far right:* A worried Frank Wisner, who ran the CIA's covert operations from 1948 until his mental breakdown in 1958, stares into space.

Top left: Allen Dulles at his headquarters office in 1954. *Top right:* JFK replaced Dulles with John McCone after the Bay of Pigs. McCone became close to Attorney General Robert Kennedy (*bottom left*), who played a central role in covert operations. President Johnson rejected McCone and hired the hapless Admiral Red Raborn (*bottom right*), at the LBJ Ranch in April 1965.

Richard Helms, director from 1966 to 1973, sought and won respect from President Johnson. *Above:* The week before his appointment as deputy director in 1965, Helms gets to know the president. *Below:* In 1968, a confident Helms briefs LBJ and Secretary of State Dean Rusk at the Tuesday lunch—the best table in Washington.

Top left: President Nixon presses the flesh at CIA headquarters in March 1969. Nixon distrusted the agency and scorned its work. *Below:* Saigon is falling as director Bill Colby, far left, briefs President Ford in April 1975. Flanking Ford are Secretary of State Henry Kissinger and, far right, Secretary of Defense James Schlesinger. *Top right:* George H. W. Bush and President Gerald R. Ford discussing evacuating Americans from Beirut with L. Dean Brown, special envoy to Lebanon, June 17, 1976.

Above: In November 1979, Director Stansfield Turner brings up the rear as President Carter calls his top military and diplomatic advisers to Camp David to assess the plight of the American hostages in Iran. *Below:* In June 1985, President Reagan and his national security team in the White House Situation Room during the hijacking of a TWA flight bound for Beirut, a hostage drama that ended with a secret deal; Bill Casey is at far right.

The end of the cold war created a revolving door at the top of the CIA—five directors in six years. The constant changes coincided with an exodus of expertise among covert operators and analysts. *Above, left to right:* William Webster; Robert Gates, the last career CIA officer to lead the agency; and Jim Woolsey.

Bottom left: John Deutch. *Bottom right:* George Tenet, with a wheelchair-bound President Clinton, tried desperately to rebuild the CIA for seven years.

Left: George Tenet at the White House with President Bush and Vice President Cheney as the war on Iraq begins in March 2003. Tenet confidently stood by the CIA in saying that Saddam Hussein's arsenal bristled with weapons of mass destruction. *Below, center:* His successor, Porter Goss, with Bush at CIA headquarters in March 2005, proved to be the last director of central intelligence.

Right: As its sixtieth year approached, the CIA ceased to be first among equals in American intelligence. In March 2006, General Mike Hayden was sworn in as CIA director at headquarters. The new boss, Director of National Intelligence John Negroponte, applauded as Wild Bill Donovan's statue stood watch.

ing a base for operations against Libya, the CIA set out to control the government of its next-door neighbor, Chad, one of Africa's poorest and most isolated nations. The agent for this mission was Hissan Habré, Chad's defense minister, who had broken with his government and holed up with about two thousand fighters in western Sudan. "American aid started to flow, the result of a Casey decision," said Ambassador Don Norland, the senior American diplomat accredited to Chad at the start of the Reagan era. "The CIA was deeply involved in the whole operation. Habré was getting assistance directly and indirectly."

The official foreign policy of the United States was to promote a peaceful resolution of the factional fighting in Chad. Habré had committed countless atrocities against his own people; he could only rule by brute force. The CIA, knowing little about Habré and his history, helped him take over Chad in 1982. It supported him because he was Qaddafi's enemy.

CIA supply planes flew the weapons into North Africa in shipments coordinated by the National Security Council. This was the first major covert operation in which a young lieutenant colonel on the NSC staff named Oliver North caught Bill Casey's eye. David Blakemore, a military aide in the Chad operation, took an urgent call from North on a Friday night in late 1981. "He asked what the delay was in getting the equipment out to Chad. He wanted to see it move immediately."

"I said, 'Well, Colonel North, that is fine. We have notified the Congress and we have to wait so many days and then we will get it moving. We understand the urgency.'

"North's reply was: 'Fuck the Congress. Send the stuff now.' Which we did."

Thousands died as Habré and his forces fought for control of Chad. As the fighting intensified, the agency armed him with Stinger missiles, the world's best shoulder-carried anti-aircraft weapon. Ambassador Norland said it cost the United States "perhaps a half-billion dollars to put him in power and keep him there for eight years." American support for Chad—Casey's policy—was "a misguided decision," he said. But few Americans had ever heard of the country, much less cared about its fate. Fewer still knew that throughout the 1980s, the CIA's ally Habré received direct support from Saddam Hussein.

On the eve of the 1991 Gulf War against Iraq, the CIA realized that a dozen or so of the Stingers that it had sent to Chad were missing and unaccounted for—and possibly in Saddam's hands. When Secretary of State James A. Baker III heard that, he was thunderstruck. Baker had been the White House chief of staff when the covert action began, but he had lost track of the operation. He wondered aloud: "What the hell did we give Stinger missiles to Chad for?"

"SOMEDAY THE UNITED STATES WILL NOT BE HERE"

The CIA's biggest gunrunning mission was its global pipeline to the mujahideen, the holy warriors of Afghanistan, who were fighting the 110,000-man Soviet army of occupation. It began under Jimmy Carter in January 1980. Because it was Carter's idea, Casey did not embrace it wholeheartedly—not at first. But soon he saw the opportunity at hand.

"I was the first chief of station ever sent abroad with this wonderful order: 'Go kill Soviet soldiers,'" said Howard Hart, who arrived as the chief in Pakistan in 1981. "Imagine! I loved it." It was a noble goal. But the mission was not to liberate Afghanistan. No one believed that the Afghans could actually win.

From the start, the Saudis matched the CIA's support for the rebels, dollar for dollar. The Chinese kicked in millions of dollars' worth of weapons, as did the Egyptians and the British. The CIA coordinated the shipments. Hart handed them over to Pakistani intelligence. The Pakistanis skimmed off a large share before delivering them to the exiled political leaders of the Afghan resistance in Peshawar, east of the Khyber Pass, and the rebel leaders cached their own share before the weapons ever got to Afghanistan.

"We didn't try to tell the Afghan rebels how to fight the war," John McMahon said. "But when we saw some of the Soviet successes against the mujahideen, I became convinced that all the arms that we had provided were not ending up in Afghan shooters' hands." So he went to Pakistan and convened a meeting of the seven leaders of the Afghan rebel groups, who ranged from Parisian exiles wearing soft loafers to rough-hewn mountain men. "I told them I was concerned that they were siphoning off the arms and either caching them for a later day or, I said, 'God forbid, you're selling them.' And they laughed. And they

said, 'You're absolutely right! We're caching some arms. Because someday the United States will not be here, and we'll be left on our own to
carry on our struggle.' "

The Pakistani intelligence chiefs who doled out the CIA's guns and
money favored the Afghan factions who proved themselves most capable in battle. Those factions also happened to be the most committed Is-
lamists. No one dreamed that the holy warriors could ever turn their
jihad against the United States.

"In covert action," McMahon said, "you always have to think of the
endgame before you start it. And we don't always do that."

"A BRILLIANT PLAN"

In May 1981, the Soviets weighed the rhetoric and the realities of the
Reagan administration and began to fear a surprise attack by the United
States. They went on a global nuclear alert that lasted for two years. The
superpowers came too close for comfort to an accidental war without the
CIA's ever realizing it, Bob Gates concluded a decade later. "We did not
then grasp the growing desperation of the men in the Kremlin. . . . how
pedestrian, isolated, and self-absorbed they were; how paranoid, fearful
they were," said Gates, the agency's foremost Soviet analyst and the
strongest defender of its performance in his field.

If the Soviets had eavesdropped on a private conversation between
President François Mitterrand of France and President Reagan that summer, they might have had good reason to fear.

In July 1981, Mitterrand pulled Reagan aside at an economic summit
in Ottawa. Translators who doubled as spies passed the word: French intelligence was running a KGB defector, Colonel Vladimir Vetrov, and
Mitterrand thought the United States should have a look at his work. His
file, code-named the Farewell dossier, was handed on to Vice President
Bush and Bill Casey. It took six months for the National Security Council staff and the CIA to absorb its meaning. By that time, Vetrov had gone
mad and murdered a fellow KGB officer. He was arrested, interrogated,
and executed.

The Farewell dossier held four thousand documents detailing a decade's

worth of work by a unit inside the KGB's directorate for science and technology. The group was called Line X. It worked with every major intelligence service in Eastern Europe. It stole American know-how—especially
software, a field where the United States then held a ten-year lead on the
Soviets. The KGB's efforts at technology theft extended from the dullest
international trade fairs to the dramatic docking of the *Apollo* and the *Soyuz*
spacecraft in 1975.

The dossier contained clues that the Soviets had cloned American
software for airborne radar systems. It suggested the ambitions of Soviet
military designers to pursue a new generation of military aircraft and the
ever-elusive goal of a defense against ballistic missiles. It identified scores
of Soviet intelligence officers assigned to steal American technology in
the United States and Western Europe.

America struck back. "It was a brilliant plan," said Richard V. Allen,
Reagan's first national security adviser, whose staffers devised it. "We
started in motion feeding the Soviets bad technology, bad computer
technology, bad oil drilling technology. We fed them a whole lot, let
them steal stuff that they were happy to get." Posing as traitorous employees of the American military-industrial complex, FBI officers sent a
procession of technological Trojan horses to Soviet spies. The time bombs
included computer chips for weapons systems, a blueprint for a space
shuttle, engineering designs for chemical plants, and state-of-the-art tur-
bines.

The Soviets were trying to build a natural-gas pipeline from Siberia
into Eastern Europe. They needed computers to control its pressure
gauges and valves. They sought the software on the open market in the
United States. Washington rejected the request but subtly pointed to a
certain Canadian company that might have what Moscow wanted. The
Soviets sent a Line X officer to steal the software. The CIA and the Cana-
dians conspired to let them have it. For a few months, the software ran
swimmingly. Then it slowly sent the pressure in the pipeline soaring. The
explosion in the wilds of Siberia cost Moscow millions it could ill afford
to spare.

The silent attack on Soviet military and state engineering programs
went on for a year. Casey capped it by sending John McMahon to Western Europe to hand friendly foreign intelligence services the identities of
some two hundred Soviet officers and agents identified in the Farewell
dossier.

The operation used almost every weapon at the CIA's command—psychological warfare, sabotage, economic warfare, strategic deception, counterintelligence, cyberwarfare—all in collaboration with the National Security Council, the Pentagon, and the FBI. It destroyed a vigorous Soviet espionage team, damaged the Soviet economy, and destabilized the Soviet state. It was a smashing success. Had the tables been turned, it could have been seen as an act of terror.

39. "IN A DANGEROUS WAY"

For more than a decade, terrorists had been hijacking airplanes, taking hostages, and killing American ambassadors. Neither the CIA nor any other branch of the American government had a clear idea of what to do about it.

On the last Saturday of January 1981, Anthony Quainton, then still serving as the government's counterterrorism coordinator, received an urgent phone call from Secretary of State Haig: on Monday at one o'clock, Quainton would brief the White House on his work. "I gave that briefing to the President, who was joined by the Vice President, the head of CIA, the head of the FBI, and a number of National Security Council members," Ambassador Quainton said. "After a couple of jelly beans, the President dozed off. That in itself was quite unnerving."

That same week, Haig announced that international terrorism would replace human rights as the number-one issue for the United States. Soon thereafter, Haig proclaimed that the Soviets were secretly directing the dirty work of the world's worst terrorists. He asked the CIA to prove this bold assertion. Casey privately agreed with Haig, but he had no facts to prove the case. The CIA's analysts could not provide them, despite bitter tongue-lashings from the boss. Under pressure, the CIA produced a fraud—Casey's conclusions placed precariously atop an analysis that could not support them. The attempt to place the blame on the Kremlin was a failure to understand the true nature of terror in the Middle East.

The CIA once had possessed an exceptionally well-placed source: Ali Hassan Salameh, chief of intelligence for the Palestine Liberation Organization and henchman in the murder of eleven Israeli athletes at the 1972 Munich Olympics. The information he offered was an olive branch being extended to the United States by the PLO's chairman, Yasser Arafat. His case officer was Bob Ames, who worked the streets of Beirut before rising to deputy chief of the Near East division at the clandestine service. Starting at the end of 1973, Salameh and Ames negotiated an understanding that the PLO would not attack Americans. For four years, they shared intelligence on their mutual enemies in the Arab world. During that time, the CIA's reporting on terrorism in the Middle East was better than it ever had been, or ever would be again. It showed an understanding that terrorism transcended state sponsorship, that it was rooted in the rage of the dispossessed. An April 1976 CIA study concluded that "the wave of the future" was "the development of a complex support base for transnational terrorist activity that is largely independent of—and quite resistant to control by—the state-centered international system."

This line of thought disappeared from the CIA's reporting after 1978, when Israeli intelligence assassinated Salameh in revenge for Munich. It did not reappear for a generation. When President Reagan took office, the CIA had next to no good sources on terrorism in the Middle East.

"TOO LITTLE INTELLIGENCE FOR A LONG TIME"

On Friday, July 16, 1982, the day he was sworn in as secretary of state, George Shultz confronted an international crisis in Lebanon. The second telephone call he placed from his new office that day was to Bob Ames, who had become the leading CIA analyst of the Arab world.

Ames was the most influential CIA officer of his generation—a "uniquely talented" man, Bob Gates said. Tall, handsome, fond of hand-tooled cowboy boots, he dealt personally with Arafat, King Hussein of Jordan, and the leaders of Lebanon. Among his recruited agents was a political strongman in Beirut named Bashir Gemayel, a Christian of the Maronite sect and the CIA's most highly placed source in Lebanon.

The agency's Maronite network was a controlling force in Beirut. The CIA's reliance on it blinded the agency to how deeply the majority of

Lebanese despised the power of the Maronite minority. That anger was a principal cause of the civil war that shattered the nation and opened the path for the Israeli invasion of June 1982.

By August, the country was flying apart—Muslim against Christian, Muslim against Muslim. Gemayel, with the strong backing of the United States and Israel, was selected as president by Lebanon's parliament. The CIA once again had a national leader on its payroll. Gemayel personally assured the agency that Americans would be safe in Lebanon, once the PLO's armed forces were evacuated and Israel ended its brutal shelling of Beirut.

On September 1, President Reagan announced a grand strategy to transform the Middle East. It had been put together in secret by a small team that included Bob Ames. Its success depended on a harmonic convergence in which Israel, Lebanon, Syria, Jordan, and the PLO cooperated at the command of the United States. It lasted all of two weeks.

On September 14, President Gemayel was assassinated when a bomb destroyed his headquarters. In revenge, the CIA's Maronite allies, abetted by Israel's troops, slaughtered some seven hundred Palestinian refugees stranded in the slums of Beirut. Women and children were buried under rough stones. In the wake of the killings and the outrage they engendered, President Reagan sent a contingent of U.S. Marines to serve as peacekeepers. There was no peace to keep.

As the marines landed, "the Agency people were busy trying to recreate some of their disrupted networks," said Robert S. Dillon, the American ambassador in Lebanon. "They remained involved—probably in a dangerous way—with the Maronites."

As the CIA fought to rebuild in Beirut, it did not see a new force rising from the rubble. An assassin named Imad Mughniyah, a chieftain of the violent terrorist group called Hezbollah, the Party of God, was gathering money and explosives, training his thugs for a series of bombings and kidnappings that would paralyze the United States for years to come. He reported to Tehran, where the Ayatollah Khomeini was creating an Office of Liberation Movements to further his messianic vision of conquering Iraq, seizing the holy shrine of Karbala, and marching onward across the River Jordan to Jerusalem.

Mughniyah's name has been forgotten now, but he was the Osama bin Laden of the 1980s, the scowling face of terror. As of this writing, he remains at large.

On Sunday, April 17, 1983, Bob Ames flew into Beirut, dropped by the American embassy on his way from the airport, and then sat down to supper with three fellow officers at the home of Jim Lewis, the deputy chief of station, who had survived a year at the Hanoi Hilton after being captured up-country in Laos fifteen years before.

Ames had been away from Beirut for five years. "He was exhilarated to be back," said the CIA's Susan Morgan, who was at the table Sunday night. He had returned to try to resurrect what the agency had lost with Gemayel's assassination.

On Monday morning, Ames called Morgan and invited her to supper that night at the Mayflower Hotel. Then Morgan went off to a luncheon in Sidon, south of Beirut. As the plates were being cleared, her hostess told her that there had been a radio report about an explosion at the American embassy. Morgan drove back to Beirut in a daze, barely seeing the ruined villages around her, destroyed during the Israeli army's assault. She had to walk past a police cordon on the Corniche to get to the embassy. It had been destroyed. Ames and his fellow officers had been killed instantly by the shock wave and buried in stone and steel and ash. It was two-thirty in the morning when they found him in the rubble. Morgan retrieved his passport, his wallet, and his wedding ring.

Sixty-three people were dead, among them seventeen Americans, including the Beirut station chief, Ken Haas, a veteran of the Tehran station; his deputy, Jim Lewis; and a CIA secretary, Phyllis Filatchy, who had toughed it out through years in the provinces of South Vietnam. In all, seven CIA officers and support staff were killed, the deadliest day in the history of the agency. The blast was the work of Imad Mughniyah, supported by Iran.

The obliteration of the Beirut station and the death of Robert Ames destroyed the agency's capability for gathering information in Lebanon and in much of the Middle East, "leaving us with too little intelligence for a long time thereafter," said Sam Lewis, the American ambassador to Israel at the time. "It made us very dependent on Israeli intelligence." The CIA would see the Islamic threat in the Middle East through an Israeli prism for the rest of the cold war.

Now Beirut was a battleground for the United States. But the CIA's reports, bereft of sources, had no impact whatsoever. American marines were siding with the Christians, American jets were dropping bombs on Muslims, and American ships were lobbing one-ton shells into the hills of Lebanon without knowing what they were hitting. The White House had gone to war in the Middle East with no idea of what it was getting into.

On October 23, 1983, Mughniyah's terrorists drove a truck bomb into the American barracks at Beirut International Airport and killed 241 marines. The blast was estimated at the kiloton level, the metric used for tactical nuclear weapons.

"OPERATING VIRTUALLY IN THE DARK"

Thirty-six hours after the barracks bombing, with the dead and wounded still being counted in Beirut, the White House, the Pentagon, and the CIA diverted America's attention to a nasty little Marxist insurgency in Grenada, a tiny island in the Caribbean crawling with a Cuban brigade of military construction workers. The island's leader, Maurice Bishop, had been killed in a power struggle, and that death provided "an excuse to go deal with that problem," said Duane Clarridge, chief of the Latin America division and one of three principal planners of the Grenada invasion.

"Our intelligence about Grenada was lousy," Clarridge said. "We were operating virtually in the dark." That contributed to the confusion of an operation in which nineteen Americans died and at least twenty-one patients at a mental hospital were killed by an American bombing raid.

The CIA staged its part of the invasion out of a hotel in Barbados. Clarridge's deputy handed the agency's proposal for a new Grenadian government to his State Department counterpart, Tony Gillespie. "The CIA had a plan to form a government," Gillespie recalled. "This was a top secret list, with all kinds of code words on it." He ran it past the most experienced American diplomats in the region. "They looked at it and then just threw up their hands. They said: 'These are some of the worst people in the Caribbean. You don't want them anywhere near this island.' " The list included "the worst crumb-bums . . . narcotics traffickers and crooks." These miscreants were the CIA's paid sources. As Allen Dulles had judged the value of his analysts' work by its weight, his successors assayed the value of secret information by virtue of what it cost. That was the rule in Beirut, in Barbados, and around the world.

The good vibrations resounding from the liberation of Grenada had faded by the time the last of the American marines left Beirut on February 26, 1984, their failed deployment doomed by a near-total lack of accurate intelligence. The mission had left 260 American soldiers and spies dead and America's enemies in control.

Casey had looked long and hard to find a new station chief with the courage to restore the CIA's eyes in Lebanon. The only candidate was an experienced but aging officer, Bill Buckley, who had served before in Beirut and whose cover had been blown. Casey decided it was worth the risk to send him back.

Eighteen days after the last marine left Lebanon, Buckley was kidnapped on his way to work. He was in enemy hands.

40. "HE WAS RUNNING A GREAT RISK"

The agency had some experience with hostages. One of its officers had just been freed from forty days of harsh captivity.

Timothy Wells, a thirty-four-year-old combat-wounded Vietnam veteran, had been sent to Addis Ababa, the capital of Ethiopia, in 1983. The nation was controlled by the Marxist dictator Haile Mengistu, whose palace guard, provided by Moscow, was led by East German intelligence officers. Wells was on his second tour of duty with the CIA. His orders were to create a political uprising. "There was a presidential finding signed by Ronald Reagan," Wells said. "It was a mandate. I was there to help overthrow the goddamn government."

Ten years before, Wells had been a marine guard at the American embassy in Khartoum when Palestinian gunmen took the American ambassador and the departing chargé d'affaires hostage at a reception. President Nixon made a no-concessions statement off the top of his head. The PLO chairman Yasser Arafat answered with a go-ahead to kill the Americans. The harrowing experience made Wells change his life. He returned to the United States, went back to college, and joined the CIA. He underwent eighteen months of training for the clandestine service and arrived in Ethiopia after a two-year tour in Uganda. He was posted under State Department cover as a commercial officer. The United States had little commerce with Ethiopia at the time. Mengistu had made the White House's most-wanted list.

Under President Carter, the CIA had a minuscule covert-action project of financial support for an exile group called the Ethiopian People's

Democratic Alliance. Under President Reagan, the program became a no-holds-barred multimillion-dollar affair. Wells inherited a network of Ethiopian intellectuals, professors, and businesspeople that he suspected had been penetrated by Mengistu's security forces. His mission was to keep them supplied with money and propaganda written by an exiled former Ethiopian minister of defense who worked with the agency. Posters, pamphlets, and bumper stickers arrived in diplomatic pouches at the embassy, where CIA personnel outnumbered State Department officials two to one.

Wells knew that he was being tailed. Yet he persisted. "I'm surprised it took them as long as they did to get me," he said.

On December 20, 1983, Mengistu's thugs burst in on a meeting Wells was holding in an upper-middle-class neighborhood and arrested three leaders of the opposition—a seventy-eight-year-old aide to the late emperor Haile Selassie; a fifty-year-old businessman; and his niece, a biologist. Wells hid for two days and two nights in a closet where the propaganda was kept. Then Mengistu's palace guard found him. They hogtied Wells, brought the three dissidents back to the house, and began to torture them. Wells heard their screams and confessed that he was a CIA officer. His captors blindfolded him, tossed him in a car, and drove him away. On Christmas Eve, they took him to a safe house south of the city, in a place called Nazaret. He spent the next five weeks being interrogated and beaten. His skull was fractured and his shoulders dislocated.

"To save his own ass, this American rolls up the rest of the organization, gives it away," said Joseph P. O'Neill, the deputy chief of mission at the American embassy. Scores of Ethiopians were jailed, tortured, or killed as a consequence.

At the end of the five weeks of torture, the Ethiopians sent word through the Israeli embassy in Nairobi that they had imprisoned a CIA officer. Within a day, President Reagan dispatched his ambassador-at-large, General Vernon Walters, who was in Africa at the time, to free Wells.

On February 3, 1984, the former deputy director of central intelligence, sixty-seven years old and riddled with gout, came lumbering off a plane in Addis Ababa, flopped into a car, and rode up to the embassy, gasping in the thin air at 8,300 feet. "What are you going to say to Mengistu?" O'Neill asked. Walters replied: "The President of the United States wishes to have back Mr. Timothy Wells." He had no intention of negotiating.

Walters went up to the presidential palace in Asmara, where Mengistu gave him a three-hour lecture on Ethiopian history. Wells was set free the next day. His hair had turned gray. He had told his captors the identities of the four other members of the CIA station. "COUNTERREVOLUTIONARY ELEMENTS CAUGHT RED-HANDED," said the morning headline in the *Ethiopian Herald*, the English-language newspaper in the capital. It ran alongside a front-page picture of eighteen terrified Ethiopians standing in front of a table littered with weapons, pamphlets, and cassettes. Most if not all of the people in the picture later died in confinement.

Wells flew back to Washington in a Lear jet. A team of CIA officers met the plane. It was not a welcoming party. They suspected him of treason. They took him to a safe house in the Virginia suburbs and interrogated him for six weeks. "If I had wanted to stay a captive I would have stayed in Ethiopia," Wells told them.

"I had wanted to join the agency because they took care of their own," he said. "They did not take care of me in any way, shape, or form. They thought I was a traitor for talking. I was asked to resign. That was devastating to me." The pain remained more than twenty years later.

"The Reagan Administration took a covert operation that had been begun on a very small scale under Carter and made it into an activity to be carried on inside of Ethiopia," said David Korn, the American chargé d'affaires in Addis Ababa when Wells was taken hostage. "This was something I didn't believe could go undiscovered and tried to get stopped. I was sure that given the surveillance the Ethiopian government exercised over us that this would be discovered. It was."

"WHAT THE HELL KIND OF INTELLIGENCE AGENCY ARE YOU RUNNING?"

On March 7, 1984, Jeremy Levin, the CNN bureau chief in Beirut, was kidnapped. On March 16, Bill Buckley, the CIA's station chief, disappeared. On May 8, the Reverend Benjamin Weir, a Presbyterian missionary, vanished from the streets of the city. In all, fourteen American hostages were taken in Beirut during the Reagan years.

But Buckley always was uppermost in Bill Casey's mind, and with good reason, for the director was personally responsible for his plight.

Casey played a tape of Buckley being tortured to President Reagan. By all accounts, it had a profound effect.

The CIA came up with at least a dozen plans to free Buckley, but it never had enough intelligence to execute them. In frustration, the clandestine service set out to try to kidnap Imad Mughniyah. "The President had approved Director of Central Intelligence Casey's recommendation to kidnap Mughniyah," said the government's counterterrorism coordinator, Robert Oakley. The CIA thought he was in Paris. Alerted by the agency, French intelligence officers raided the hotel room where the CIA said they would find him. They found a fifty-year-old Spanish tourist where a twenty-five-year-old Lebanese terrorist was supposed to be.

One of the many sources that the CIA station in Paris had cultivated in the name of counterterrorism was an Iranian swindler named Manucher Ghorbanifar, a wheeler-dealer who had been an agent of SAVAK, the shah's secret police. Fat, balding, goateed, clad in fancy suits, carrying at least three fake passports, Ghorbanifar had fled Iran after the fall of the old regime. He had been selling dubious information to the CIA and Israeli intelligence ever since. Ghorbanifar had a pattern of predicting events after they happened; his information was carefully crafted to create cash payoffs. One day after Buckley was kidnapped, Ghorbanifar met with CIA officers in Paris, and said he had information that could free him. The agency subsequently subjected him to three lie-detector tests. The last time, he flunked every question but his own name and nationality. On July 25, 1984, the CIA officially certified Ghorbanifar as a consummate liar—"an intelligence fabricator and a nuisance"—and issued a rare worldwide burn notice in his name, an order stating that the truth was not in him and his word was never to be trusted. Nonetheless, on November 19, 1984, Ghorbanifar lured the veteran CIA officer Ted Shackley to a three-day meeting at a four-star hotel in Hamburg.

After a ruthlessly ambitious rise to second-in-command at the clandestine service, Shackley had been forced into retirement by Admiral Turner five years before, to the great relief of some of his CIA colleagues. His name had become synonymous with professional dishonesty at the agency. He now worked as a private intelligence broker—a seller of secrets, like Ghorbanifar. He had represented himself in meetings with various Iranian exiles as an emissary of the president of the United States.

Shackley listened with interest as Ghorbanifar discussed ways to free the American hostages. Perhaps it could be a secret ransom, a straight-cash deal. Or perhaps it could be profitable. The United States could ship missiles to Iran, using a trading firm called Star Line, which Ghorbanifar ran in tandem with the Israeli intelligence service. The sale of weapons would create goodwill in Tehran, millions for the private traders involved, and a large cash ransom to free Bill Buckley and his fellow American hostages. Shackley reported the conversation to the ubiquitous Vernon Walters, who passed it on to the counterterrorism czar Robert Oakley.

On December 3, 1984, Peter Kilburn, a librarian at the American University in Beirut, was kidnapped. In Washington, the families of the American hostages begged the White House to do something. Their pleas wounded the president, who asked Casey constantly what the CIA was doing to set them free. "Reagan was preoccupied with the fate of the hostages and could not understand why CIA could not locate and rescue them," said Bob Gates. "He put more and more pressure on Casey to find them. Reagan's brand of pressure was hard to resist. No loud words or harsh indictments—none of the style of Johnson or Nixon. Just a quizzical look, a suggestion of pain, and then the request—'We just have to get those people out'—repeated nearly daily, week after week, month after month. Implicit was the accusation: *What the hell kind of intelligence agency are you running if you can't find and rescue these Americans?*"

"IT WAS OF OUR OWN MAKING"

In December 1984, as Washington prepared for Reagan's second inauguration, Ghorbanifar's offer to facilitate a profitable arms-for-hostages deal still stood. Casey kept it alive. That same month, he formally proposed that the CIA should finance its war in Central America with money from abroad. He had been kicking the idea around at the White House for half a year.

Congress outlawed American funding for the war shortly before election day 1984. Two snafus at the clandestine service had compelled the cutoff. First there was the comic-book fiasco. Since Casey had exhausted the CIA's small reservoir of paramilitary expertise in Central America, "the Agency had to reach outside itself and bring in people who could conduct that war for them," said Deputy Director of Central Intelligence John McMahon. "That was mainly done through retirees from the Special Forces who had learned their trade in Vietnam." One of these veterans had an old comic book that had been used to train Vietnamese peasants how to take over a village by murdering the mayor, the chief of police, and the militia. The CIA translated it into Spanish and distributed it to the *contras*. It quickly became public, and when it did, some high-ranking officers at the agency thought that "somebody's pulling a covert action against us," McMahon said. "This has to be absurd. And it turned out it was of our own making." Casey issued reprimands to five senior CIA officers over the comic book. Three refused to sign them. Their insubordination went unpunished.

Then there were the mines. Aiming to destroy what was left of Nicaragua's economy, Casey had authorized the mining of the Nicaraguan port of Corinto—an act of war. This was a Duane Clarridge brainstorm, born of desperation after the funds for the *contras* started running dry. "I was sitting at home one night—frankly, having a glass of gin—and I said, you know, the mines has got to be the solution!" Clarridge said. The agency made them on the cheap, out of sewer pipe. Casey had notified Congress about the mining with an inaudible mumble. When Senator Barry Goldwater, the Republican chairman of the intelligence committee, raised a ruckus about it, CIA officers defamed him as a muddleheaded drunk.

Congress, wary of Casey's ways, had specifically prohibited the agency from soliciting funds from third countries to evade the ban on aid to the *contras*. Casey nevertheless arranged for Saudi Arabia to kick in $32 million, Taiwan another $2 million, the money flowing through a Swiss account controlled by the agency. But it was a stopgap.

In January 1985, at the start of the second Reagan administration, the director faced two urgent commands from the president. Free the hostages. Save the *contras*. The missions commingled in his mind.

Casey saw life as an enterprise. He believed in the end that politics, policy, diplomacy, and intelligence were all business deals. He saw how the hostage crisis and the cash crunch confronting the *contras* could be resolved through a grand bargain with Iran. The director would have preferred to run the Iranian operation by himself, but he faced the universal opposition of his clandestine service to working with the notorious Manucher Ghorbanifar, and the CIA had no other channel into Iran.

Casey would have loved to save the *contras* single-handedly, too, but the CIA was prohibited from providing them with direct assistance. His solution was to run both operations outside the government.

He conceived what he believed to be the ultimate covert action. It lasted less than two years from conception to destruction, and it came dangerously close to ruining President Reagan, Vice President Bush, and the agency itself.

"He was running a great risk," Bob Gates reflected, "jeopardizing the President, himself, and CIA."

41. "A CON MAN'S CON MAN"

On June 14, 1985, Hezbollah, the Party of God, hijacked TWA Flight 847 out of Athens en route to Rome and New York. They took the plane to Beirut, hauled a U.S. Navy diver out of his seat, shot him in the head, and dumped his body on the tarmac, not far from where the American marines had died in their barracks twenty months before.

The hijackers demanded the release of 17 jailed terrorists held in Kuwait—one of whom was Mughniyah's brother-in-law—and 766 Lebanese prisoners held by Israel. President Reagan privately pressured Israel, and 300 of the prisoners were set free. At the request of the White House, Ali Akbar Hashemi Rafsanjani, the speaker of Iran's parliament, helped negotiate an end to the hijacking.

The ordeal taught Casey a lesson: Reagan was willing to make deals with terrorists.

That same week, the Iranian wheeler-dealer Manucher Ghorbanifar got a message through to the director via an indicted Iranian American arms trafficker who was a relative of Rafsanjani's. It was a bracing bulletin: Hezbollah held the hostages. Iran held sway over Hezbollah. An arms deal with Iran could free the Americans.

Casey carefully explained this proposition to the president. On July 18, 1985, Reagan wrote in his diary: "It could be a breakthrough on getting our seven kidnap victims back." On August 3, the president gave Casey formal approval to cut a deal.

With that go-ahead, the Israelis and Ghorbanifar sent two shipments containing a total of 504 American TOW missiles to Tehran. The Iranians paid about $10,000 per missile, the middleman pocketed a modest profit, and Iran's Revolutionary Guards took the weapons. On September 15, hours after the second shipment arrived, the Reverend Benjamin Weir was set free after sixteen months of captivity.

Two pillars of Reagan's foreign policy—no deals with terrorists, no arms for Iran—tumbled down in secret.

Three weeks later, Ghorbanifar sent word that all six remaining hostages could be freed in exchange for several thousand American HAWK anti-aircraft missiles. The price kept going up: three hundred, four hundred, five hundred missiles for a life. On November 14, Casey and McMahon met with national security adviser Robert McFarlane and his deputy, Admiral John Poindexter. All four thought that Israel would deliver the American weapons to a faction within the Iranian military that wanted to overthrow Ayatollah Khomeini. But that was a lie, a smoke screen devised by Ghorbanifar and his Israeli backers, who stood to gain millions for the operation—the more arms delivered, the more profit to be pocketed.

To watch over the middlemen, Casey chose Richard Secord, a retired American general turned private arms dealer, as the CIA's representative. Secord had been a loyal soldier in the global underground effort to arm and finance the *contras* behind the back of Congress. His job was to ensure that a share of the profits wound up in the right hands.

"THIS REALLY ISN'T WORTH IT"

Shortly after 3 a.m. on Friday, November 22, 1985, Duane Clarridge, now chief of the European division of the clandestine service, was awakened by a frantic phone call from Lieutenant Colonel Oliver North. They met on the sixth floor of CIA headquarters about an hour later.

The HAWK flight to Iran was becoming a debacle. The Israelis had packaged eight hundred technologically outmoded missiles on an El Al 747. The idea was for the Israelis to fly the weapons to Lisbon and transfer them to a Nigerian cargo plane leased by Secord, which would take them to Tehran. But no one had secured landing rights in Lisbon for the Israeli plane, which was at that moment somewhere over the Mediterranean.

North said the plane was filled with oil-drilling equipment bound for Iran, and could Clarridge please move heaven and earth to clear its landing in Portugal? This gave Clarridge, who was neither a fool nor a stickler for rules and regulations, a moment's pause. It didn't matter whether drill bits or baby bottles or bazookas were aboard the flight, he observed. Sending *anything* to the Iranians was against the law and the foreign policy of the United States. But North assured him that the president had lifted the embargo and approved a secret deal to free the hostages.

Clarridge worked the problem all weekend. One flight was scrubbed, then another. Finally he secured a CIA 707 in Frankfurt. The smaller plane managed to fly from Tel Aviv to Tehran and deliver a fraction of the cargo—eighteen HAWK missiles—to the Iranians on Monday, October 25. The government of Iran was unhappy with the quantity and the quality of the out-of-date weapons, not to mention their Hebrew lettering.

No one was less happy than Deputy Director of Central Intelligence John McMahon, who arrived at work at 7 a.m. on Monday to discover that the CIA had broken the law. Only weeks before, McMahon had beaten back an attempt by the National Security Council staff to violate a presidential ban on political assassinations. "We received a draft secret executive order telling us to go knock off terrorists in pre-emptive strikes," McMahon recalled. "I told our folks to send it back and tell them: 'When the President revokes the executive order which precludes CIA from assassinations, then we'll take this on.' That hit the guys on the NSC staff. They went ballistic."

The flight of the CIA 707 was a covert action that required a finding, a signed presidential order. McMahon knew that Reagan had approved an arms-for-hostages deal in principle. But in practice the CIA's participation required the president's signature. McMahon ordered the CIA's in-house general counsel to draw up a *retroactive* finding—backdated, like a bad check—authorizing "the provision of assistance by the Central Intelligence Agency to private parties in their attempt to obtain the release of Americans held hostage in the Middle East." It continued: "As part of these efforts certain foreign materiel and munitions may be provided to the Government of Iran which is taking steps to facilitate the release of the American hostages."

There it was in black and white. The CIA sent the finding to the White House. On December 5, 1985, the president of the United States signed it. Under its terms, and under a second finding drawn up a few weeks later, Casey was the man ultimately responsible for the arms-for-hostages deal.

Casey summoned Ghorbanifar to Washington to anoint him as the CIA's Iranian agent in the operation. Clair George pleaded with him to stop: "Bill, the guy really is no good," he said. "This really isn't worth it." So did the CIA's Charles Allen, the chief of the agency's Hostage Location Task Force. On January 13, 1986, he met with Ghorbanifar and then went to see Casey.

"I described him as a con man to the Director," Allen said. Casey replied, "Well, maybe this is a con man's con man." Casey insisted that the CIA would keep using Ghorbanifar as its arms merchant and interlocutor with the government of Iran. Charlie Allen knew there was only one conceivable reason to use him. The Iranian shyster told the CIA officer that the arms deal could spin off money for "Ollie's boys in Central America."

On January 22, 1986, North secretly tape-recorded a conversation with Ghorbanifar. "I think this is, Ollie, the best chance," the go-between said with a laugh. "We never will find such a good time again, never get such good money, we do everything free of charge, we do hostages free of charge, we do all terrorists free of charge, Central America free of charge."

After a long haggle, the first HAWK transaction had concluded with $850,000 left over in a Swiss bank account controlled by Richard Secord. Colonel North took the money and gave it to the *contras*. Iran was now a source of covert funds for the war in Central America.

Now the Iranians sent word that they wanted battlefield intelligence for the war against Iraq. The CIA already had provided intelligence for Iraq to use against Iran. This was too much for McMahon. In a January 25, 1986, cable to Casey, who was meeting his Pakistani colleagues in Islamabad, McMahon warned that the CIA was "aiding and abetting the wrong people. Providing defensive missiles was one thing but when we provide intelligence on the order of battle, we are giving the Iranians the wherewithal for offensive action."

Casey rejected his advice. McMahon retired not long thereafter as the number-two man at the CIA, closing out a thirty-four-year career on a bitter note. Bob Gates took his place.

The deal went ahead.

"A NEAT IDEA"

Oliver North's role in the underground effort to keep the war against the Sandinistas going had been an open secret in Washington since midsummer 1985. That winter, reporters were working on detailed accounts of what North was doing in Central America. But not a soul outside a very small circle at the CIA and the White House knew what he was doing in Iran.

North had worked out the money end of the arms-for-hostages swap. The Pentagon would transfer thousands of TOW missiles to the CIA. The cost to the agency was a cut-rate $3,469 per missile, a crucial fact known to very few people. Secord, on behalf of the CIA, would pay $10,000 apiece, generating $6,531 in gross profits, pocketing his fair share, and then transferring the net to the *contras* in Central America. Ghorbanifar would cover the $10,000 cost and then some by marking up the missiles again when he sold them to the Iranians. Depending on how many weapons the United States could sell to Tehran, the *contras* stood to gain millions.

In late January, Defense Secretary Weinberger ordered his chief aide, the future secretary of state, Colin Powell, to transfer one thousand TOW missiles from a Pentagon warehouse to the custody of the CIA. The missiles went through Richard Secord and Manucher Ghorbanifar into Iran in February. The Iranian broker marked up his prices munificently before the weapons reached Tehran. When the cash flowed back, the CIA reimbursed the Pentagon with a technique familiar to money launderers everywhere. Its checks were broken up into sums of $999,999.99 or less. CIA financial transfers of $1 million or more required a routine legal notification to Congress. Secord received $10 million for the one thousand missiles from Ghorbanifar. Most of the profit was earmarked for the *contras*.

In an April 4, 1986, memo, Lieutenant Colonel North laid out the big picture for Vice Admiral John Poindexter, the new national security adviser to the president. Once everyone's costs were covered, he reported, "$12 million will be used to purchase critically needed supplies for the Nicaraguan Democratic Resistance Forces." As North famously observed, "it was a neat idea."

Only one element was missing from this elaborate calculus: the hostages. Four hostages were being held in July 1986. Six months later

there were twelve. The willingness of the Americans to provide weapons
to the Iranians only increased the appetite for hostages.

"North's rationale, which was supported by those in the CIA who
were helping him, was that the kidnappers in Lebanon were a different
group from those who were getting the payoffs," said the American ambassador in Lebanon, John H. Kelly. " *'Our Shi'ites are reliable. It is a different group of Shi'ites that are doing the kidnapping.'* It was total hogwash!"

Casey and a handful of his loyal analysts concocted the notion that
the weapons deals would signal support to political moderates in the
government of Iran. This was a grievous example of the way in which
"the CIA was corrupted" during the Reagan administration, in the words
of Philip C. Wilcox, Jr., the State Department's principal intelligence officer and its highest-ranking liaison to the CIA in the late 1980s. There
weren't any moderates left in the government of Iran. They had all been
killed or jailed by the people receiving the weapons.

"I HOPE IT WILL NOT LEAK"

The proceeds of the arms sales and the millions Casey had finagled from
the Saudis put the CIA back in business in Central America.

The agency set up an air base and a network of safe houses for
weapons shipments outside San Salvador. The base was run by two veteran anti-Castro Cubans on the CIA's payroll. One was Felix Rodriguez,
the man who had helped capture Che Guevara. The other was Luis
Posada Carriles, who had just escaped from a Venezuelan jail, where he
was being held for his central role in the terrorist bombing of a Cuban
passenger jet that killed seventy-three people.

By the summer of 1986 they were dropping ninety tons of guns and
ammunition to the *contras* in southern Nicaragua. In June Congress did
an about-face and authorized $100 million in support for the war in
Central America, effective October 1. On that date, the CIA would have
its hunting license back. For a moment, it looked like the war was going
their way.

But the CIA's elaborately concealed arms network was coming apart.
The station chief in Costa Rica, Joe Fernandez, was serving as an air traf-

fic controller for the weapons shipments, and he had a rough airstrip cleared for clandestine flights. But the new president of Costa Rica, Oscar Arias, who was working for a negotiated peace in Central America, had warned Fernandez to his face not to use the airstrip to arm the *contras*. On June 9, 1986, a CIA plane loaded with weapons took off from the secret air base outside San Salvador in bad weather, made an unscheduled landing at the airstrip, and sank axle-deep into the mud. Shaking with fear and anger, Fernandez got on the phone, called San Salvador, and ordered his CIA colleague to "get that plane the hell out of Costa Rica!" It took two days.

That same month, Felix Rodriguez began to realize that someone in the supply line—he suspected General Secord—was profiting from their patriotism. On August 12, he tried to blow the whistle in a meeting with another old friend—Vice President Bush's national security adviser, the CIA veteran Don Gregg. It was, Gregg concluded, "a very murky business."

On October 5, 1986, a teenage Nicaraguan soldier fired a missile that brought down an American C-123 cargo plane ferrying weapons from San Salvador to the *contras*. The sole survivor, an American cargo handler, told reporters that he worked under contract for the agency. Felix Rodriguez made a panicked call to the office of the vice president of the United States. When the plane went down, North was in Frankfurt trying to cut a new arms-for-hostages deal with Iran.

On November 3, weeks after the tale of the secret deals was first revealed in anonymous leaflets scattered on the streets of Tehran, it was published by a little weekly in Lebanon. It would be months before the full story came out: Iran's Revolutionary Guards had received two thousand antitank missiles, eighteen sophisticated anti-aircraft missiles, two planeloads of spare parts, and some useful battlefield intelligence through the good offices of the CIA. The arms shipments "added significantly to Iranian military capabilities," said Robert Oakley, the counterterrorism coordinator. "The intelligence we passed to them was also of significant help." But the Iranians had been cheated. They were complaining, with good reason, that they had been overcharged 600 percent for the last shipment of HAWK parts. Ghorbanifar himself had been caught short; his creditors were pursuing him for millions, and he threatened to expose the operation to save his skin.

Casey's covert operation was coming undone. "The person who

managed this whole affair was Casey," said the State Department's in-house counsel, Abraham Sofaer. "I don't have any doubt about it. I knew Casey from before. I admired and liked him, and when I blew the whis-tle on the whole thing, it was Casey who, I felt, regarded what I had done as treason."

On November 4, 1986, election day, Rafsanjani, the speaker of Iran's parliament, revealed that American officials had been to Iran bearing gifts. The next day, Vice President Bush recorded in his taped diary: "On the news at this time is the question of the hostages. I'm one of the few people that know fully the details. . . . This is one operation that had been held very, very tight, and I hope it will not leak."

On November 10, Casey went to an extraordinarily tense meeting of the members of the National Security Council. He steered Reagan toward making a public statement that the United States was working on a long-term strategic plan to foil the Soviets and the terrorists in Iran—not trading weapons for hostages. The president parroted the line. "We did not—repeat—did not trade weapons or anything else for hostages," Reagan told the nation on November 13. Once again, as in the U-2 shootdown, as at the Bay of Pigs, as in the war in Central America, the president lied to protect the covert operations of the CIA.

This time very few people believed him.

It took five more years to free the last American hostages. Two never came back. Peter Kilburn was murdered. After enduring months of tor-ture and interrogation, the CIA's Bill Buckley died in chains.

"NO ONE IN THE U.S. GOVERNMENT KNEW"

The congressional intelligence committees wanted a word with Bill Casey, but he chose to follow tradition and leave the country at a mo-ment of crisis for the CIA.

On Sunday, November 16, Casey flew south to review the troops in Central America, leaving his deputy Bob Gates to clean up the mess. The hearings were reset for the coming Friday. The five intervening days were among the worst in the agency's history.

On Monday, Gates and his subordinates started trying to piece together a chronology of what had happened. The director put Clair George and his clandestine service in charge of preparing his testimony to Congress. The intent was not to tell the truth.

On Tuesday, staff members of the intelligence committee summoned George to a closed hearing in a sealed and electronically secured vault in the dome of the Capitol. He knew that a year earlier the CIA, without legal authorization, had traded arms for hostages. Under close questioning, he did exactly as the president had done five days before: he lied.

Overnight, Gates sent another of Casey's assistants down to Central America to deliver a draft copy of Casey's proposed testimony and to bring the director back to headquarters. On Wednesday, Casey started writing a new version on a legal pad as he flew back to Washington. But he soon found that he could not read his own handwriting. He started dictating flowery prose into a tape recorder. It was a jumble. He tossed the work aside.

On Thursday, Casey carried the original draft in his briefcase to the White House for a meeting with North and Poindexter. As they put their heads together, Casey scrawled a note on his draft saying that "No one in the U.S. Government knew" about the November 1985 HAWK flight of the CIA. It was an extraordinarily bold lie. He returned to headquarters and met in the director's seventh-floor conference room with most of the agency's leadership and many of the officers directly involved in the Iran arms shipments.

"The meeting was an unmitigated disaster," remembered Casey's executive staff director, Jim McCullough. Dave Gries, another of Casey's closest aides, said that "no one present was able—or perhaps willing—to fit together all elements of the Iran-contra puzzle."

"The atmosphere at the meeting was surreal," Gries recalled. "Many of the participants seemingly were more interested in protecting themselves than in assisting Casey, who was visibly exhausted and at times incoherent. It was clear to McCullough and me that the next morning we would be accompanying a badly confused Director to Congress."

On Friday, Casey delivered closed-door testimony to the congressional intelligence committees. It was a farrago of evasion and befuddlement, accompanied by one riveting fact. A senator asked if the CIA had been shipping secret support to both Iran and Iraq as the two nations slaughtered each other. Yeah, Casey said, we've been aiding Iraq for three years.

Over the weekend, North's memo to Poindexter about skimming

millions from the Iran arms sales and funneling the money to the *contras* turned up. Both men had been shredding and destroying documents furiously for weeks, but North somehow missed that one.

On Monday, November 24, Vice President Bush dictated a note for his diary: "A real bombshell. . . . North had taken the money and put it in a Swiss bank account . . . to be used for the contras. . . . It's going to be a major flap." It was the biggest political uproar in Washington since Richard Nixon left town.

Four days later, Casey convened a conference of American intelligence chieftains from CIA, State, and the Pentagon. "Feel very good about our community having worked together for six years more effectively than most of our government without any significant failures," his talking points read. "No scandal and a good many solid successes."

"THE SILENCE SEEMED TO LAST FOREVER"

Ever since Watergate, it was not the crime but the cover-up that destroyed the powers of Washington. Casey was in no shape to cover up. He staggered and stumbled through a week of incoherent testimony on Capitol Hill, lurching in his chair, unable to string sentences together. He could barely hold up his head. His aides were aghast. But they kept pushing him.

"Bill Casey had a lot to answer for," said Jim McCullough, his staff man and a thirty-four-year CIA veteran. "It is doubtful that the operation would have ever gotten off the ground—much less be sustained for well over a year—without his acquiescence and support."

Casey attended a memorial dinner for the slain CIA officer Bob Ames in Philadelphia on the evening of Thursday, December 11. He returned to headquarters at 6:00 a.m. on Friday for an interview with a *Time* magazine reporter named Bruce van Voorst. The agency had often turned to *Time* for a public-relations boost in moments of crisis. Van Voorst was a dependable man. He had served for seven years at the CIA.

The agency set the ground rules: thirty minutes for Iran-*contra*, thirty minutes for a review of the CIA's many accomplishments under Casey's command. McCullough had heard Casey give the good-news spiel many times before. He was confident the director could recite his lines even in a state of exhaustion. The first half hour proved an ordeal, but when it was over, the softball question came right down the plate: "Mr. Casey, could you talk a little about some of the Agency's accomplishments under your leadership?"

"We all breathed a sigh of relief and relaxed," McCullough recalled. "But Casey stared at van Voorst as if he could not believe or did not understand the question. He said nothing. The silence seemed to last forever."

Monday morning, December 15, Casey had a seizure in his seventh-floor office. He was wheeled out on a stretcher before anyone really grasped what had happened. At Georgetown University Hospital, his doctors determined that he had an undiagnosed central nervous system lymphoma—a malignant spider's web spreading in his brain, a rare disease, difficult to detect. It often led to inexplicably bizarre behavior in the twelve to eighteen months before it was discovered.

Casey would never return to the CIA. Bob Gates went to see him at the hospital on January 29, 1987, on orders from the White House, carrying a resignation letter for the director to sign. Casey could not hold the pen. He lay back on the bed, tears in his eyes. Gates went back to the White House the next day and the president of the United States offered him the job—"a job no one else seemed to want," Gates reflected. "No wonder."

Gates served as acting director of central intelligence for five excruciating months, until May 26, 1987, but his nomination was doomed. He would have to wait for the wheel to turn again. "It quickly became clear that he was too close to whatever Casey was or was not doing," said the next director of central intelligence, William Webster. "Bob's approach had been that he did not want to know. In these circumstances, that was not acceptable."

Webster had been running the FBI for nine long years. He was a square-jawed, squeaky-clean, apolitical Carter appointee, one of the few emblems of moral rectitude left standing in the Reagan administration after the Iran-*contra* imbroglio. He once had been a federal judge and preferred to be addressed by the honorific. The attraction of appointing a man named "Judge" to run the CIA was obvious at the White House. Like Admiral Turner, he was an upright Christian Scientist and a man of moral conviction. He was not a Reagan man; he had no political or personal connection with the president. "He never asked me for anything," Webster said. "We never talked business. It was not a buddy-buddy relationship. Then, at the end of February 1987, I got a call." Reagan was all business now. On March 3, the president announced Webster's nomination as director of central intelligence and praised him as "a man who is committed to the rule of law."

The same was never said about Bill Casey. After he died on May 6, at age seventy-four, his own bishop denounced him from the pulpit at his funeral, as Presidents Reagan and Nixon listened in silence.

Casey had nearly doubled the size of the CIA over six years; the clandestine service now had some six thousand officers. He had built a $300 million glass palace to house his new hires at headquarters; he had mobilized secret armies around the world. Yet he left the agency far weaker than he found it, shattered by his legacy of lies.

Bob Gates learned a simple lesson serving under Casey. "The clandestine service is the heart and soul of the agency," he said. "It is also the part that can land you in jail."

42. "TO THINK THE UNTHINKABLE"

The president of the United States confessed to the American people that he had lied to them about trading arms for hostages. The White House tried to spin the political whirlwind toward Casey and the CIA. Neither the man nor the institution could put up a defense. Congress summoned Casey's officers and agents to testify. They left the impression that the United States had hired a gang of con men and thieves to run its foreign affairs.

The arrival of Judge Webster heralded a hostile takeover at the CIA. Congress and an independent counsel set out to determine what exactly Casey had been up to. Operations were suspended, plans shelved, careers shattered. Fear shot through agency headquarters as three dozen FBI agents carrying subpoenas stalked through the corridors, opened double-locked safes, and thumbed through top secret files, gathering evidence for obstruction of justice and perjury charges. The leaders of the clandestine service underwent interrogations and envisioned indictments. Casey's vision of a CIA free from the restraints of law had brought them to grief.

"It took me months to get a clear understanding of what had happened, and who had done what to whom," Webster said. "Casey left behind a *lot* of problems." Chief among them, Webster thought, was a tradition of defiant insubordination. "People out in the field had felt they needed to act on their own," he said. "They weren't supposed to act without approval from the boss. But chiefs of station felt: I *am* the boss."

The officers of the clandestine service were sure that Webster—

instantly dubbed "Mild Bill"—had no grasp of who they were, what they did, or the mystique that held them together. "No one else can understand it," said Colin Thompson, who had served in Laos, Cambodia, and Vietnam. "It's a mist you dip into and hide behind. You believe you have become an elite person in the world of American government, and the agency encourages that belief from the moment you come in. They make you a believer."

To outsiders they looked like members of a Virginia men's club, a white-shirt southern culture. But they saw themselves as a camouflaged combat battalion, a blood brotherhood. The friction with Webster was white-hot from the start. "We probably could have overcome Webster's ego, his lack of experience with foreign affairs, his small-town America world perspective, and even his yuppier-than-thou arrogance," the CIA's Duane Clarridge complained. "What we couldn't overcome was that he was a lawyer.

"All of his training as a lawyer and a judge was that you didn't do illegal things. He could never accept that this is *exactly* what the CIA does when it operates abroad. We break the laws of their countries. It's how we collect information. It's why we're in business. Webster had an insurmountable problem with the raison d'être of the organization he was brought in to run."

Within weeks of Webster's arrival, the word went out from Clarridge and his colleagues to the White House: the man was a lightweight, a dilettante, a half-bright social butterfly. He recognized the rebellion he faced and tried to beat it back with advice from Richard Helms, who had emerged from his brush with the criminal courts as a respected gray eminence. "A point Dick Helms made with me: because we have to lie and do those things overseas, it is very important that we do not lie to each other and subvert each other," Webster remembered. "The message I wanted to send was that you can do so much more when people trust you. I don't know how much difference it made. People listened very carefully. But the question at the agency was: does he mean it? There was always a question in their minds."

Webster vowed that the agency would keep no secrets from Congress. But the congressional intelligence committees had been burned too often. They decided that the lesson of Iran-*contra* was that the agency needed to be managed from Capitol Hill. Congress could impose its will because, under the Constitution, it ultimately controlled the checkbook of the government. Webster raised the white flag, and with his surrender, the CIA was no longer an instrument of purely presidential power. It was poised, precariously, between the commander in chief and the Congress.

The clandestine service fought hard against giving Congress a role in running the CIA. It feared that among the 535 elected representatives, there might be 5 who understood the first thing about the agency. So the staffs of the congressional oversight committees were quickly seeded with career CIA officers who could look after their own.

The committees had a knife out for Clair George, still the chief of the clandestine service. He had been Casey's special liaison to Congress and a master of the art of deception. Casey had loved his charm and his cunning, but these two qualities were not in demand at Webster's CIA. "Clair had a glibness about him that endeared one to him," Webster said. "But he thought the way to handle a question from Congress was to dance around it."

At the end of November 1987, Webster called him on the carpet and said: "The fact is that Congress doesn't believe you. I'm going to have to have your job." George considered this for a moment. "He said: 'I really think I *should* retire—and maybe I'll take some people with me who ought to retire too.' " Three weeks later, Duane Clarridge was having a stiff noontime cup of Christmas cheer with George when Webster summoned him upstairs and told him it was time to go. Clarridge briefly considered fighting back, first by blackmailing Webster, and then by using his connections in the White House. He had just received a nice note from his good friend the vice president of the United States. "You have my friendship," George Bush wrote, "my respect and high esteem. That won't ever change." But Clarridge decided that a covenant of loyalty had been broken. He quit.

A cadre of covert operators with two thousand years' experience among them walked out the door with him.

"AMERICAN INTELLIGENCE WAS GENEROUS"

What haunted Clair George the most in his retirement was not the blown operations or the prospect of indictment, but the shadow of a mole inside the CIA.

On his watch, during 1985 and 1986, the Soviet/Eastern Europe division of the clandestine service had lost every one of its spies. Its dozen Soviet agents-in-place had been arrested and executed, one by one. The small CIA stations in Moscow and East Berlin ceased to function, the officers' covers blown, their operations destroyed. In 1986 and 1987, the division was collapsing like a dynamited building caught on slow-motion film. The CIA had no idea why. At first it thought a rookie officer named Ed Howard was the traitor within. He had joined the clandestine service in 1981 and was selected to serve on his first tour abroad as a deep-cover officer in Moscow. He had gone through two years of training. A few personal details about Howard had escaped the CIA's notice until the last possible minute: he was a drunk, a liar, and a thief. The agency let him go, and he had defected to Moscow in April 1985.

As part of his training, Howard had read the files on some of the best spies the CIA had in Moscow, among them Adolf Tolkachev, a military scientist who had for four years delivered documents on cutting-edge Soviet weapons research. Tolkachev was regarded as the CIA's greatest Soviet source in twenty years.

When the Politburo met in the Kremlin on September 28, 1986, the KGB chairman, Viktor Chebrikov, proudly informed Mikhail Gorbachev that Tolkachev had been executed for treason the day before. "American intelligence was generous with him," Gorbachev remarked. "They found two million rubles on him." That was more than half a million dollars. The KGB now knew the going rate for world-class spies.

The agency believed that Howard might well have betrayed Tolkachev. But he could not possibly have been responsible for more than three of the dozen deaths that had wiped out the CIA's roster of Soviet spies. Something or someone else was to blame. The President's Foreign Intelligence Advisory Board looked into the case and reported "a fundamental inability of anyone in the Soviet division to think the unthinkable"—that a traitor might be hiding inside the clandestine service. Casey had read the report and reprimanded Clair George. "I am appalled," he had written, at the "astonishing complacency" in the face of "this catastrophe." But in private, Casey shrugged it off. He placed three people—one of them part-time—on the investigation of the deaths of the CIA's most prized foreign agents.

It was a measure of the trust placed in Webster by the senior officers of the clandestine service that they never told him the whole truth about the case. He never knew that it constituted the worst penetration in the agency's history. He knew there was a low-level investigation—"an exercise, nothing more. If they found something, fine," he said. "If they didn't find a sinister reason, maybe they'd find another reason, or no reason at all," he said. "That's all I ever heard about it."

The investigation collapsed and the counterintelligence nightmare confronting the CIA grew under Webster.

In June 1987, Major Florentino Aspillaga Lombard, the chief of Cuban intelligence in Czechoslovakia, drove across the border to Vienna, walked into the American embassy, and defected to Jim Olson, the CIA chief of station. He revealed that every Cuban agent recruited by the agency over the past twenty years was a double—pretending to be loyal to the United States while working in secret for Havana. It was a genuine shock, and hard to believe. But CIA analysts glumly concluded after a long and painful review that the major was telling the truth. That same summer, a trickle of fresh intelligence about the deaths of the CIA's agents began coming in from a new set of Soviet and Soviet-bloc military and intelligence officers. It grew to a stream, and then a flowing river, and seven years passed before the terrible realization that it was disinformation delivered to mystify and mislead the CIA.

"THEY ACTUALLY DID SOMETHING RIGHT"

Webster turned to Bob Gates shortly after his swearing-in and asked, Well, Bob, what's going on in Moscow? What's Gorbachev up to? He never was satisfied with the answers. "I had my glass half-full guys and my glass half-empty guys," Webster sighed. "On the one hand this, on the other hand that."

The CIA did not know that Gorbachev had told the Warsaw Pact meeting in May 1987 that the Soviets would never invade Eastern Europe to shore up their empire. The CIA did not know that Gorbachev had told the leader of Afghanistan in July 1987 that the Soviets were going to start pulling their occupying troops out soon. And the agency was flabbergasted in December 1987, when throngs of adoring American citizens hailed Gorbachev as a hero on the streets of Washington. The man in the street seemed to understand that the leader of the communist world wanted to end the cold war. The CIA did not grasp the concept. Bob Gates spent the next year asking his underlings why Gorbachev consistently surprised them.

Over the course of more than thirty years, the United States had spent close to a quarter of a *trillion* dollars on spy satellites and electronic-eavesdropping equipment built to monitor the Soviet military. These programs were on paper the responsibility of the director of central intelligence but in reality run by the Pentagon. They provided the data for the endless Strategic Arms Limitation Treaty negotiations with the Soviets, and it could be argued that those talks helped keep the cold war cold. But Washington and Moscow never gave up a single weapons system that they had wanted to build. Their arsenals remained capable of blowing up the world a hundred times over. And in the end the United States abrogated the very idea of arms control.

But in August 1988 a payoff came in a moment of perfect irony. Frank Carlucci, now Reagan's secretary of defense, went to Moscow for meetings with his counterpart, Soviet defense minister Dmitri Yazov, and he lectured generals and admirals at the Voroshilov military academy. "How is it you know so much about us?" one of them asked Carlucci. "We have to do it from satellites," he replied. "It would make it a lot easier for us if you'd just do what we do and publish your military budget." The room exploded in laughter, and afterward Carlucci asked his Russian escort officer what was so funny. "You don't understand," the Russian said. "You attacked the heart of their system"—secrecy. The face-to-face contacts between American and Soviet military chiefs made the Russians realize two things. First, the Americans did not want to kill them. Second, they might be every bit as strong as the Americans in nuclear missiles, but it made no difference whatsoever. They were far weaker in every other regard. They knew then that their closed system, built on secrecy and lies, could never defeat an open society.

They saw that the game was up. The agency did not.

The CIA still managed to achieve three stirring successes that year. The first came after Colonel Chang Hsien-yi, the deputy director of Taiwan's nuclear energy research institute, defected to the United States. For twenty years, he had worked in secret for the United States, ever since the CIA recruited him as a military cadet. His institute, ostensibly established for civilian research, had been built with the aid of American plutonium,

South African uranium, and international expertise. Taiwan's leaders had created a cell within it to build a nuclear bomb. That weapon had only one conceivable target: the Chinese mainland. China's communist leaders had vowed to attack if Taiwan deployed a nuclear weapon. The United States demanded a halt to the program. Taiwan lied about it and continued apace. Among the few Americans who knew about Colonel Chang's long service was the CIA's Jim Lilley, who had served as station chief in China and Taiwan and was soon to become the U.S. ambassador to China. "You pick a comer, put the right case officer on him, and recruit him carefully on an ideological basis—although money was involved—and keep in touch," Lilley said. Colonel Chang sent out an alert to his case officer, defected, and delivered proof positive of the nuclear weapons program's progress. A CIA spy of twenty years' standing had helped stop the spread of weapons of mass destruction. "This was a case where they actually did something right," Lilley said. "They got the guy out. They got the documentation. And they confronted the Taiwanese." Armed with the evidence, the State Department leaned hard on the government of Taiwan, which finally announced that it had the ability to build nuclear weapons but no intent to do so. This was arms control at its best.

Then came a brilliant plot against the Abu Nidal Organization, a gang that had been killing, hijacking, and terrorizing Westerners across Europe and the Middle East for a dozen years. It involved three foreign governments and a former president of the United States. It grew out of the new counterterrorism center at the CIA, and it began after Jimmy Carter delivered a package of intelligence on Abu Nidal to the president of Syria, Hafiz al-Assad, in a March 1987 meeting. Assad expelled the terrorist. Over the next two years, with the help of the PLO and the Jordanian and Israeli intelligence services, the agency waged psychological warfare against Abu Nidal. A strong and steady flow of disinformation convinced him that his top lieutenants were traitors. He killed seven of them and dozens of their underlings over the next year, crippling his organization. The campaign peaked when two of Abu Nidal's men defected and mounted an attack on his headquarters in Lebanon, killing eighty of his men. The organization was shattered, a stirring victory for the CIA's counterterrorism center and the Near East division under Tom Twetten, who would be promoted to chief of the clandestine service.

The third great success—so it seemed to everyone at the time—was the triumph of the Afghan rebels.

Every other force among the CIA's freedom fighters was falling apart. The *contras* signed a cease-fire days after the agency's secret support was cut off for the last time. Ballots replaced bullets in Nicaragua. A lost patrol of anti-Qaddafi warriors was wandering around in the Sudan. The CIA had to demobilize this half-baked insurgency and extract its troops from North Africa, taking them first to the Congo, then to California. Diplomacy supplanted covert action in southern Africa, and the flow of arms from Washington and Moscow ran dry. Casey's program to back a Cambodian rebel army fighting Hanoi's forces—a grudge match against the winners of the Vietnam War—was badly mismanaged, with money and guns winding up in the hands of corrupt Thai generals. And it placed the CIA's allies in alignment with the butchers of Cambodia, the Khmer Rouge. Colin Powell, serving as Reagan's deputy national security adviser after the Iran-*contra* housecleaning, cautioned that the White House should think twice about the operation. In time, it was shut down.

Only the mujahideen, the Afghan holy warriors, were drawing blood and scenting victory. The CIA's Afghan operation was now a $700-million-a-year program. It represented about 80 percent of the overseas budget of the clandestine service. Armed with Stinger anti-aircraft missiles, the Afghan rebels were killing Soviet soldiers, downing Soviet helicopter gunships, and inflicting deep wounds on the Soviet self-image. The CIA had done what it set out to do: to give the Soviets their Vietnam. "One by one we killed them," said Howard Hart, who had run the mission to arm the Afghans from 1981 to 1984. "And they went home. And that was a terrorist campaign."

"WE WALKED AWAY"

The Soviets announced that they would pull out for good as soon as the Reagan administration left office. The CIA's briefing books never answered the question of what would happen when a militant Islamic army defeated the godless invaders of Afghanistan. Tom Twetten, the number-two man in the clandestine service in the summer of 1988, had the task of figuring out what would become of the Afghan rebels. He said it quickly became clear to him that "we don't have any plan." The CIA simply decided: "There'll be 'Afghan democracy.' And it won't be pretty."

The Soviet war was over. But the CIA's Afghan jihad was not. Robert Oakley, the American ambassador to Pakistan from 1988 to 1991, argued that the United States and Pakistan should "drastically reduce our assistance to the real radicals" in Afghanistan, and work to make the mujahideen more moderate. "But the CIA couldn't or wouldn't get its Pakistani partners in line," he said. "So we continued to support some of the radicals." Chief among them was the Afghan rebel leader Gulbuddin Hekmatyar, who had received hundreds of millions of dollars in arms from the CIA and hoarded much of them. He was about to turn those weapons against the people of Afghanistan in a drive for total power.

"I had another problem with the Agency," Ambassador Oakley said. "The same people who were fighting the Soviets were also profiting from the narcotics trade." Afghanistan was, and remains, the world's single greatest source of heroin, with endless acres of opium poppies harvested twice a year. "I suspect that the Pakistani intelligence services may have been involved and that CIA was not going to rock their relationships over this issue," Oakley said.

"I kept asking the Station to obtain information on this traffic from its sources inside Afghanistan," he said. "They denied that they had any sources capable of doing so. They could not deny that they had sources, since we were getting information on weapons and other matters.

"I even raised the matter with Bill Webster," Oakley said. "Never got a satisfactory answer. Nothing ever happened."

Webster invited the leaders of the Afghan rebels to lunch in Washington. "This was not an easy crowd," he remembered. Hekmatyar was among the honored guests. When I met Hekmatyar in Afghanistan a few years later, he vowed to create a new Islamic society, and if it took a million more deaths, he said, so be it. At this writing, the CIA is still hunting for him in Afghanistan, where he and his forces are killing American soldiers and their allies.

The last Soviet soldier left Afghanistan on February 15, 1989. The CIA's weapons kept flowing. "None of us really foresaw the major consequence," Ambassador Oakley said. Within a year, white-robed Saudis began to appear in the provincial capitals and ruined villages of Afghanistan. They proclaimed themselves emirs. They bought the loyalties of village leaders and they began to build little empires. They were emissaries of a new force abroad in the world that came to be called al Qaeda.

"We walked away from it," Webster said. "We should not have walked away."

43. "WHAT ARE WE GOING TO DO WHEN THE WALL COMES DOWN?"

The agency celebrated when George H. W. Bush was sworn in as president on January 20, 1989. He was one of them. He loved them. He understood them. He was, in truth, the first and only commander in chief who knew how the CIA worked.

Bush became his own director of central intelligence. He respected Judge Webster, but he knew the troops did not, and he shut him out of his inner circle. Bush wanted daily briefings from professionals, and if they did not satisfy him, he wanted raw reports. If something was cooking in Peru or Poland, he wanted to hear from the station chief, pronto. His faith in the agency bordered on religious belief.

It was sorely tested in Panama. On the campaign trail in 1988, Bush denied that he had ever met General Manuel Noriega, that nation's notorious dictator. But there were pictures that proved it. Noriega had been on the CIA payroll for many years. Bill Casey had welcomed the general at headquarters annually and had flown down to Panama at least once to see him. "Casey saw him as a protégé," said Arthur H. Davis, Jr., the American ambassador to Panama under Reagan and Bush.

In February 1988, the general was indicted in Florida as a cocaine kingpin, but he remained in power, sneering at the United States. By then it was public knowledge that Noriega was a murderer as well as a long-standing friend of the CIA. The impasse was excruciating. "The CIA, who had dealt with him for so long, didn't want to end the relationship," said the National Security Council staffer Robert Pastorino, who had met for many hours with Noriega as a senior Pentagon civilian during the 1980s.

After the indictment, the Reagan White House twice ordered the agency to find a way to dislodge Noriega, and shortly after his inauguration, President Bush again instructed the CIA to overthrow the dictator. Each time the agency balked. General Vernon Walters, then the American ambassador to the United Nations, was particularly wary. "As a former deputy director of the CIA—just like some people in the Pentagon who had been at Southcom, the U.S. Forces Southern Command—he was not eager to see Noriega brought to the U.S. and put on trial for anything," said Stephen Dachi, who knew both General Walters and General Noriega personally and served as the number-two man at the American embassy in Panama during 1989. Noriega's old friends in the agency and the military did not want him testifying about them under oath in an American courtroom.

On President Bush's orders, the agency spent $10 million backing the opposition in a May 1989 election. Noriega outmaneuvered the CIA's fourth operation against him. President Bush approved a fifth covert action against Noriega, including paramilitary support for a coup. Forget about it, the covert operators said: only a full-scale military invasion could dislodge Noriega. Some of the agency's most experienced Latin America hands—including the station chief in Panama, Don Winters—were loath to go up against the general.

Furious, Bush let it be known that he was learning more about events in Panama from CNN than CIA. That was the end of William Webster's standing as director of central intelligence. From then on, the president made plans to topple Noriega in concert with Defense Secretary Dick Cheney, whose skepticism about the agency deepened with every passing day.

The CIA's failure to unseat its old ally in secret forced the United States to mount its biggest military operation since the fall of Saigon. During Christmas week of 1989, smart bombs blasted Panama City slums into rubble while Special Forces soldiers fought their way through the capital. Twenty-three Americans and hundreds of innocent Panamanian civilians died in the two weeks it took to arrest Noriega and to bring him in chains to Miami.

The CIA's Don Winters testified for the defense at Noriega's trial, where the United States admitted paying the dictator at least $320,000 through the agency and the American military. Winters described Noriega as the CIA's trusted liaison between the United States and Fidel Castro, a loyal ally in the war against communism in Central America, and a linchpin for American foreign policy—he had even sheltered the exiled shah of Iran. Noriega was convicted on eight counts of drug trafficking and racketeering. Thanks in great part to posttrial testimony by Winters, Noriega's sentence as a prisoner of war was reduced by a decade and his parole date was reset to September 2007.

"I CAN NEVER TRUST CIA AGAIN"

In 1990, another dictator challenged the United States: Saddam Hussein.

During the eight-year Iran-Iraq war, President Reagan had dispatched Don Rumsfeld as his personal envoy to Baghdad to shake Saddam's hand and offer him American support. The agency had given Saddam military intelligence, including battlefield data from spy satellites, and the United States granted him high-technology export licenses, which Iraq used to try to build weapons of mass destruction.

Skewed intelligence from Bill Casey and the CIA was a decisive factor in these decisions. "Saddam Hussein was known to be a brutal dictator, but many thought he was the lesser of two evils," said Philip Wilcox, the State Department liaison to the agency. "There were intelligence estimates about the threat from Iran that, in retrospect, exaggerated Iran's ability to prevail in that war. . . ."

"We did indeed tilt toward Iraq," he said. "We provided Iraq with intelligence, took Baghdad off the list of state sponsors of terrorism, and viewed positively comments from Saddam Hussein suggesting that he supported an Arab-Israeli peace process. Many began to view Iraq optimistically as a potential factor for stability, and Saddam Hussein as a man with whom we could work."

The return on the investment in Iraq was exceedingly slight. No intelligence flowed back. The agency never penetrated the Iraqi police state. It had next to no firsthand knowledge about the regime. Its network of Iraqi agents consisted of a handful of diplomats and trade officials at overseas embassies. These men had little insight on the secret councils of Baghdad. At one point, the CIA was reduced to recruiting an Iraqi hotel clerk in Germany.

The CIA still maintained a network of more than forty Iranian agents, including midlevel military officers who knew something about the Iraqi army. The CIA's station in Frankfurt communicated with them through the ancient technique of invisible ink. But in the fall of 1989 a CIA clerk mailed letters to all of the agents, all at the same time, all from the same mailbox, all in the same handwriting, all to the same address. When one of the agents was unmasked, the whole network was exposed. It was a failure of Tradecraft 101. Every one of the CIA's Iranian spies was imprisoned, and many were executed for treason.

"The arrested agents were tortured to death," said Phil Giraldi, then the deputy chief of base in Istanbul. "Nobody in CIA was punished," he said, "and the chief of the field element responsible was, in fact, promoted." The collapse of the agent network closed the CIA's window both on Iraq and on Iran.

In the spring of 1990, when Saddam began mobilizing his military again, the CIA missed it. The agency sent a special national intelligence estimate to the White House saying that Iraq's armed forces were exhausted, that they would need years to recover from the war with Iran, and that Saddam was unlikely to embark on any military adventures in the near future. Then, on July 24, 1990, Judge Webster brought spy satellite images to President Bush showing two Republican Guard divisions—tens of thousands of Iraqi troops—massing at the border of Kuwait. The headline on the CIA's *National Intelligence Daily* the next day read: "Is Iraq Bluffing?"

Only one prominent CIA analyst, Charles Allen, the national intelligence officer for warning, judged the chances for war at better than even. "I did sound the warning bell," Allen said. "Surprisingly, there were very few listeners."

On July 31, the CIA called an invasion unlikely; Saddam might make a limited grab for some oil fields or a handful of islands, but no more. Not until the next day—twenty hours before the invasion—did Deputy Director of Central Intelligence Richard J. Kerr warn the White House that an Iraqi attack was imminent.

President Bush did not believe his CIA. He speed-dialed the president of Egypt, the king of Saudi Arabia, and the emir of Kuwait, and they all told him Saddam would never invade. King Hussein of Jordan told the president, "On the Iraqi side, they send their best regards and highest esteem to you, sir." Bush went to sleep reassured. Hours later, the first wave of 140,000 Iraqi soldiers poured over the border to seize Kuwait.

The president's most trusted intelligence adviser, Bob Gates, was having a family picnic outside Washington. A friend of his wife's joined him. What are you doing here? she asked. What are you talking about? Gates replied. The invasion, she said. What invasion? Gates asked. In short, "there wasn't much intelligence on what was going on inside Iraq," noted Secretary of State James Baker.

For the next two months, the CIA "behaved in an unfortunately quite typical pattern," said Chas W. Freeman, Jr., the American ambassador to Saudi Arabia. It swung to the opposite extreme. On August 5, it reported that Saddam would attack Saudi Arabia. He never did. It assured the president that Iraq did not have chemical warheads for its short-range and medium-range missiles. Then it asserted with increasing confidence that Iraq *did* have chemical warheads—and Saddam was likely to use them. There was no hard evidence behind the warnings. Saddam never came close to using chemical weapons during the Gulf War. But there was great fear when Iraqi Scud missiles started falling on Riyadh and Tel Aviv.

In the weeks before the seven-week air war on Iraq began on January 17, 1991, the Pentagon invited the CIA to pick bombing targets. The agency selected, among many other sites, an underground military bunker in Baghdad. On February 13, the air force blew it up, but the bunker was being used as a civilian air raid shelter. Hundreds of women and children died. The agency was not called upon to pick targets after that.

Then a brutal argument broke out between the CIA and the American commander of Operation Desert Storm, General Norman Schwarzkopf. The fight was over the battle-damage assessment—the daily reports on the military and political impact of the bombing. It was imperative for the Pentagon to assure the White House that American bombers had destroyed enough Iraqi missile launchers to protect Israel and Saudi Arabia, and enough Iraqi tanks and armor to protect American ground forces. The general assured the president and the public that the job was well done. The CIA's analysts told the president that he was exaggerating the damage done to Iraqi forces—and they were right. But the agency broke its sword when it challenged Schwarzkopf. The agency was banned from

conducting battle-damage assessments. The Pentagon took away the job
of interpreting spy-satellite photos. Congress forced the agency to assume a subservient role in its relations with the American military. After
the war it was compelled to create a new office of military affairs to serve
solely as second-echelon support for the Pentagon. The CIA spent the
next decade answering thousands of questions from military men: How
wide is that road? How strong is that bridge? What's over that hill? For
forty-five years, the CIA had answered to civilian leaders, not uniformed
officers. It had lost its independence from the military chain of command.

The war ended with Saddam still in power but the CIA weakened.
The agency, taking the word of Iraqi exiles, reported the potential for a
rebellion against the dictator. President Bush called on the Iraqi people
to rise up and overthrow him. The Shiites of the south and the Kurds in
the north took Bush at his word. The agency used every means at its
disposal—chiefly propaganda and psychological warfare—to promote an
uprising. Over the next seven weeks, Saddam crushed the Kurds and
Shiites mercilessly, murdering thousands and sending thousands more
fleeing into exile. The CIA began working with the leaders of those exiles in London and Amman and Washington, building networks for the
next coup, and the next.

After the war, a United Nations Special Commission went into Iraq
looking for chemical, biological, and nuclear weapons. Its investigators
included CIA officers carrying the United Nations flag. Richard Clarke,
an unusually intense National Security Council staffer, remembered
their raid on the Iraqi agricultural ministry, where they discovered the
core of Saddam's nuclear weapons directorate. "We went there, broke
down doors, blew off locks, got into the sanctum sanctorum," Clarke recalled fifteen years later for a *Frontline* television documentary. "The
Iraqis immediately reacted, surrounded the facility and prevented the
U.N. inspectors from getting out. We thought that might happen, too, so
we had given them satellite telephones. They translated the nuclear reports on-site into English from the Arabic and read them to us over the
satellite telephones." They determined that Iraq was probably nine to
eighteen months away from having its first nuclear weapon detonation.

"CIA had totally missed it," Clarke said. "We had bombed everything
we could bomb in Iraq, but missed an enormous nuclear-weapons development facility. Didn't know it was there, never dropped one bomb on

it. Dick Cheney looked at that report and said, 'Here's what the Iraqis themselves are saying: that there's this huge facility that was never hit during the war; that they were very close to making a nuclear bomb, and CIA didn't know it.' "

Clarke concluded: "I'm sure he said to himself, 'I can never trust CIA again to tell me when a country is about to make a nuclear bomb.' There's no doubt that the Dick Cheney who comes back into office nine years later has that as one of the things burnt into his memory: *'Iraq wants a nuclear weapon. Iraq was that close to getting a nuclear weapon. And CIA hadn't a clue.'* "

"AND NOW THE MISSION IS OVER"

The CIA "had no idea in January 1989 that a tidal wave of history was about to break upon us," said Bob Gates, who had left headquarters that month—for good, he thought—to become President Bush's deputy national security adviser.

The agency had pronounced the dictatorship of the Soviet Union untouched and untouchable at the hour it was starting to vanish. On December 1, 1988, the month before Bush came to office, the CIA issued a formal report confidently stating that "the basic elements of Soviet defense policy and practice thus far have not been changed by Gorbachev's reform campaign." Six days later, Mikhail Gorbachev stood at the podium of the United Nations and offered a unilateral cut of 500,000 troops in the Soviet military. It was unthinkable, Doug MacEachin, then the CIA's chief of Soviet analysis, told Congress the next week: even if the CIA had concluded that such earthshaking changes were about to sweep the Soviet Union, "we never would have been able to publish it, quite frankly," he said. "Had we done so, people would have been calling for my head."

While the Soviet state withered away, the CIA was "constantly reporting that the Soviet economy was growing," said Mark Palmer, one of the Bush administration's most experienced Kremlinologists. "They used to simply take what the Soviets officially announced, discount it a percent, and put it out. And it was just wrong, and anybody who had spent time in the Soviet Union, in the villages and towns, could look around and see that this was just crazy." This was the work of the CIA's best thinkers—like Bob Gates, for years the chief Soviet analyst—and Palmer found that fact infuriating. "He'd never actually been to the Soviet Union! He'd never once been there, and he was the top so-called expert in the CIA!"

The agency had somehow missed the fact that its main enemy was dying. "They talked about the Soviet Union as if they weren't reading the newspapers, much less developed clandestine intelligence," said Admiral William J. Crowe, Jr., chairman of the Joint Chiefs of Staff under Bush. When the first deep cracks in the Soviet republics started to develop in the spring of 1989, the CIA did indeed get its information from reading the local papers. They were three weeks old when they arrived.

No one at the agency asked the question that Vernon Walters, Bush's newly appointed ambassador to Germany, put to his officers in May 1989: "What are we going to do when the Wall comes down?"

The Berlin Wall had stood for nearly thirty years, the greatest symbol of the cold war. When it began to crack one night in November 1989, the chief of the Soviet division of the clandestine service, Milt Bearden, sat speechless at headquarters, staring at CNN. The upstart network had become a huge problem for the agency. In a crisis, it provided what passed for real-time intelligence. How could the CIA top that? Now the White House was on the line: What's happening in Moscow? What are our spies telling us? It was hard to confess that there were no Soviet spies worth a damn—they all had been rounded up and killed, and no one at the CIA knew why.

The agency wanted to drive eastward like conquering heroes and capture the intelligence services of Czechoslovakia, Poland, and East Germany, but the White House advised caution. The best the CIA could do at first was to train the security staffs of new leaders such as the Czech playwright Vaclav Havel, and to bid the highest dollar for the purloined files of the Stasi, which started floating out a window in East Berlin one fine day, tossed into the streets by a ransacking crowd overthrowing the secret police.

The intelligence services of Soviet communism were enormous and precise instruments of repression. They had served above all to spy on their own citizens, to terrify them, to try to control them. Bigger and more ruthless than the CIA, they had beaten their enemies in many battles overseas, but they lost the war, undone by the brutality and the banality of the Soviet state.

The loss of the Soviets tore out the CIA's heart. How could the agency live without its enemy? "It was easy, once upon a time, for the CIA to be unique and mystical," Milt Bearden said. "It was not an institution. It was a mission. And the mission was a crusade. Then you took the Soviet Union away from us and there wasn't anything else. We don't have a history. We don't have a hero. Even our medals are secret. And now the mission is over. *Fini.*"

Hundreds of veterans of the clandestine service declared victory and pulled out. One among many was Phil Giraldi, who had started out as a field officer in Rome and ended up sixteen years later as chief of base in Barcelona. His partner in the Rome station had been a Ph.D. in Italian politics. In Barcelona, she was an English major who spoke no Spanish.

"The ultimate tragedy is spiritual," he said. "Most of the younger officers I knew have resigned. These were the best and the brightest. Eighty or ninety percent of the people I knew, halfway through their careers, have packed it in. There was very little motivation left. The enthusiasm was gone. When I joined the agency, back in '76, there was a tribalism. The esprit de corps that the agency had was created by this tribalism, and it served a good purpose." And now it was gone, and most of the clandestine service was gone with it.

As early as 1990, "this was rapidly evolving into a very bad situation," said Arnold Donahue, an agency veteran in charge of national-security budgets under Bush. Whenever the White House wanted "ten or fifteen more clandestine people on the ground to find out what was happening" in Somalia or the Balkans—wherever the crisis of the moment arose—it asked the CIA: "Is there a cadre of people ready to go?" And the answer was always: "Absolutely not."

"ADJUST OR DIE"

On May 8, 1991, President Bush called Bob Gates up to the front cabin aboard *Air Force One* and asked him to take the job of director of central intelligence. Gates was both thrilled and slightly terrified. His confirmation hearings became a bloodbath; the ordeal went on for six months. He was battered for Bill Casey's sins and belittled by his own people. Gates had wanted to address the future of the CIA, but the hearings became a battle about its past. They gave voice to an angry crowd of analysts whom Gates and Casey had whipsawed for years. Their anger was professional and personal. They attacked a culture of deceit and self-deception at the CIA. Harold Ford, who had served with distinction over the course of forty years, said that Gates—and the CIA itself—had been "dead wrong" on the facts of life inside the Soviet Union. Those two words called into question the rationale for the Central Intelligence Agency.

Badly shaken, Gates felt like a prizefighter barely able to answer the bell for the next round. But he managed to convince the senators that they would be his partner in "a not-to-be-missed opportunity to reassess the role, mission, priorities and structure of American intelligence." He owed the votes he won in no small part to the staff director and stage manager of the Senate intelligence committee, the future director of central intelligence George J. Tenet. Thirty-seven years old, fantastically ambitious, ferociously gregarious, the son of Greek immigrants who ran a hamburger joint on the edge of Queens called the 20th Century Diner, Tenet was the quintessential staff man: hardworking, loyal to his bosses, eager to please. He marshaled the evidence for the senators who only wanted proof that Gates would cede them power to gain a measure of his own.

While Gates agonized in Washington, the CIA experienced some dizzying moments overseas. In August 1991, as a coup against Gorbachev fizzled and the Soviet Union began to fall, the CIA was reporting live from Moscow, from the best seat in the house—Soviet intelligence headquarters in Dzerzhinsky Square. One of the stars of the Soviet division, Michael Sulick, drove into Lithuania as it proclaimed its independence, becoming the first CIA officer to set foot in a former Soviet republic. He openly introduced himself to the fledgling nation's new leaders and offered to help them create an intelligence service. He found himself invited to work in the offices of the new vice president, Karol Motieka. "Sitting alone in the vice president's office was surrealistic for a CIA officer who had spent his entire career combating the Soviet Union," Sulick wrote in the agency's journal. "If I had been alone just months before in the office of the vice president of a Soviet republic, I would have thought I had struck an intelligence mother lode. As I sat behind Motieka's desk, documents strewn about, my only purpose was to phone Warsaw."

The bits and pieces of intelligence so painstakingly smuggled out by spies had never come close to providing a big picture of the Soviet Union. Over the whole course of the cold war, the CIA had controlled precisely three agents who were able to provide secrets of lasting value on the Soviet military threat, and all of them had been arrested and executed. Spy satellites had counted tanks and missiles precisely but the numbers now seemed immaterial. Bugs and taps had picked up billions of words, and now they had lost their meaning.

"New world out there. Adjust or die," Gates wrote on a notepad before two days of meetings with the leaders of the clandestine service on November 7 and 8, 1991, immediately after he was sworn in as director of central intelligence. The next week, Bush sent a signed order to the members of his cabinet, labeled National Security Review 29. Gates had drafted it over the past five months. It called on every arm of the government to define what it wanted from American intelligence for the next fifteen years. "This effort," Gates announced to an audience of hundreds of CIA employees, was "a monumental and historic undertaking."

The national security review carried Bush's signature. But it was a plea from Gates to the rest of the government: *just tell us what you want.* He knew the agency had to be seen to change in order to survive. Richard Kerr, the deputy director of central intelligence for four years under Bush, wondered aloud whether there was going to be a CIA in days to come. The agency was "in as much of a revolution as the former Soviet Union," he said. "We have lost the simplicity of purpose or cohesion that essentially has driven not only intelligence but has driven this country for forty-plus years." The consensus on where American interests lay and how the CIA might serve them was gone.

Gates put out a press release calling the national-security review "the most far-reaching directive to assess future intelligence needs and priorities since 1947." But what were those needs? During the cold war, no president and no director of central intelligence ever had to ask. Should the CIA now focus on the wretched of the earth or the rise of global markets? What was more threatening, terrorism or technology? Over the winter, Gates compiled his to-do list for the new world, completed it in February, and presented it to Congress on April 2, 1992. The final draft included 176 threats, from climate change to cybercrime. At the top were nuclear, chemical, and biological weapons. Then came narcotics and terrorism—the two were twinned as "drugs and thugs"; terrorism was still a second-tier issue—and after that, world trade and technological surprise. But they did not add up to the immensity of the Soviet Union.

President Bush decided to reduce the size and refocus the scope of the agency. Gates agreed. It was a reasonable response to the end of the cold war. So the power of the CIA was diminished by design. Everyone thought the CIA would be smarter if it were smaller. The intelligence budget began going down in 1991, and it fell for the next six years. The cuts were taking a toll in 1992, at the moment when the CIA was instructed to dramatically increase its support for day-to-day military operations. More than twenty CIA outposts were shuttered, some large stations in major capitals downsized by more than 60 percent, and the number of clandestine service officers working overseas plummeted. The analysts were hit harder. Doug MacEachin, now their chief, said he found it hard to do serious analysis with "a bunch of 19-year-olds on two-year rotations." That was something of an exaggeration, but not much.

"Tensions rising as budget pinches," Gates wrote in a private work diary not long after his swearing-in. The cuts kept coming, and in years to come, Bush and many others blamed them on knee-jerk liberals. The record shows they were equally his work. They were in the spirit of the times, captured in a television commercial Bill Colby taped for an advocacy group called the Coalition for Democratic Values as the 1992 election season started.

"I'm William Colby, and I was head of the CIA," he said. "The job of intelligence is to warn us of dangers to our military. Now the cold war is over, and the military threat is far less. Now it is time to cut our military spending by fifty percent and invest that money in our schools, health care and our economy." This was the famous peace dividend.

But this peace proved as fleeting as it had been after World War II, and this time there were no victory parades, and the cold war's veterans had cause to mourn the vanquished enemy.

"If you're going to be involved with espionage you've got to be motivated," Richard Helms once said to me, his eyes narrowed and his voice low and urgent. "It's not fun and games. It's dirty and dangerous. There's always a chance you're going to get burned. In World War Two, in the

OSS, we knew what our motivation was: *to beat the goddamn Nazis.* In the cold war, we knew what our motivation was: *to beat the goddamn Russians.* Suddenly the cold war is over, and what is the motivation? What would compel someone to spend their lives doing this kind of thing?"

Gates spent a year trying to answer those questions—days on end testifying on Capitol Hill, shoring up political support, making public speeches, leading task forces and roundtables, promising more intelligence for the military, less political pressure on analysts, an all-out attack on the top ten threats, a new CIA, a better CIA. He never had time to realize any of these visions. He had been in office for ten months when he had to set his work aside to fly to Little Rock and brief the man who would be the next president of the United States.

PART
SIX

The Reckoning

The CIA Under Clinton and George W. Bush

1993 to 2007

---

44. "WE HAD NO FACTS"

No commander in chief since Calvin Coolidge had come to the White House thinking less about the wider world than Bill Clinton. When he spun the globe, it always came back to rest on the United States.

Born in 1946, no older than the CIA, Clinton was shaped by the national resistance to Vietnam and the military draft, perfected as a politician by the local and state affairs of Arkansas, and elected on a promise to revive the American economy. No aspect of foreign policy made the top five items on his agenda. He had no deep thoughts about American strategic interests after the cold war. He saw his time in office as "a moment of immense democratic and entrepreneurial opportunity," in the words of his national security adviser, Tony Lake. The administration was eight months old before Lake pronounced the new foreign policy of the United States: increasing the number of the world's free markets. This was more of a business plan than a policy. Clinton equated free trade and freedom, as if selling American goods would spread American values abroad.

Clinton's national-security team was second-string. He selected the high-minded but scatterbrained congressman Les Aspin for secretary of defense; Aspin lasted less than a year. He chose the high-collared attorney Warren Christopher for secretary of state; Christopher was formal and distant, handling great global issues as if they were case law. And, at the last minute, Clinton picked a high-strung veteran of Richard Nixon's National Security Council staff for director of central intelligence.

R. James Woolsey, Jr., was a fifty-one-year-old lawyer and an experi-

enced arms-control negotiator who had served as undersecretary of the
navy under President Carter. His bulging temples and biting wit gave the
impression of a highly intelligent hammerhead shark. A month after
Clinton's election, Woolsey gave a well-noticed speech saying the United
States had fought a dragon for forty-five years, and finally had slain it,
only to find itself in a jungle filled with poisonous snakes. No one had
articulated a more vivid vision for American intelligence after the cold
war. He got the call a few days later, flew to Little Rock, and met Clinton after midnight on December 22. The laid-back president-elect chat-
ted about his youth in Arkansas and asked about Woolsey's boyhood
next door in Oklahoma, taking him on a short trip down a 1950s memory lane. At dawn Woolsey learned he would be the next director of central intelligence.

Fifteen minutes before the formal announcement that morning, Dee
Dee Myers, Clinton's press secretary, glanced at her notes and said: "Admiral, I didn't know you served in the Bush administration as well."

"Dee Dee, I'm not an admiral," Woolsey said. "I never got above captain in the army."

"Whoops," she said. "We'd better change the press release."

He fled as fast as he could. With the airport fogged in, Woolsey shanghaied a CIA officer to drive him to Dallas so he could fly to California for
Christmas. It would be his last act of free will for a long time. He was
about to become a prisoner of war at the CIA.

He met precisely twice with the president of the United States in the
course of the next two years—an all-time low in the agency's annals. "I
didn't have a bad relationship with the president," he said years later. "I
just didn't have one at all."

The CIA's top officers served a director who they knew had no clout
and a president who they thought had no clue. "We had a fabulous relationship with the White House under Bush—Christmas parties at
Camp David, that sort of thing," said Tom Twetten, chief of the clandestine service from the start of 1991 through the end of 1993. "And we
went from that to nothing. After about six months under Clinton, it
dawns on us that nobody's seen the president or the National Security
Council." The CIA was powerless without direction from the president.
It was a ship in irons, adrift.

Though Clinton came to office in a state of willful ignorance about the
CIA, he quickly turned to the clandestine service to solve his problems

overseas, and ordered up dozens of covert-action proposals during his first two years in office. When they failed to produce quick fixes, he was forced to turn to his military commanders, who almost to a man scorned him as a draft dodger. The results were dreadful.

"THERE WAS NO INTELLIGENCE NETWORK"

"No harsher test was there than Somalia," said Frank G. Wisner, Jr., the son of the founder of the CIA's clandestine service.

Somalia was a casualty of the cold war. The wholesale provision of weapons to its competing factions by the United States and the Soviet Union left enormous arsenals for warring clans. The day before Thanksgiving 1992, President Bush had authorized an American military intervention for humanitarian purposes. Half a million people had died from starvation in Somalia; ten thousand a day were dying as the Bush administration came to a close. Now the clans were stealing food aid and killing one another. The mission of feeding dying people quickly mutated into a military operation against the strongest Somali warlord, General Mohamed Farah Aideed. On inauguration day 1993, after serving for a moment as the acting secretary of state, Wisner moved to the Pentagon as the undersecretary of defense for policy. He looked to Somalia and he found a blank. The Bush administration had closed down the American embassy and the CIA station two years earlier.

"We had no facts," Wisner said. "There was no intelligence network. There was no way of knowing the dynamics." This was Wisner's problem to solve, with the help of the CIA. He set up a Somalia Task Force, which deployed American special-forces commandos, and turned to the agency to serve as its eyes and ears on the ground. That job fell to Garrett Jones, the newly appointed station chief in Somalia. Once a Miami police detective, Jones was dropped into the middle of nowhere, with seven officers beneath him and the task of overthrowing an army of warriors before him. His headquarters was a ransacked room of the ambassador's abandoned residence in Mogadishu. Within days, his best Somali agent shot himself in the head, another was killed by a rocket fired from an American helicopter, his deputy chief of station was shot in the neck by a sniper and nearly died, and Jones found himself leading the manhunt for Aideed and his lieutenants down a series of blind alleys. That path led to the death of 18 American soldiers in a clash that killed 1,200 Somalis.

A postmortem on Somalia came from Admiral William Crowe, who had retired as chairman of the Joint Chiefs of Staff to become the leader of the President's Foreign Intelligence Advisory Board, the council of elders created by Eisenhower. The board investigated and concluded that "the intelligence failure in Somalia was right in the National Security Council," Admiral Crowe said. "They expected intelligence to make their decisions for them, not just give them information about what was going on there. They couldn't understand why intelligence didn't advise them correctly on what to do.

"It made for considerable confusion right at the top as to what was going out to Somalia," Crowe said. "The President himself wasn't very interested in the intelligence, which was most unfortunate."

The result was an ever-deepening distrust between the White House and the CIA.

"RETALIATING QUITE EFFECTIVELY AGAINST IRAQI CLEANING WOMEN"

At the start of 1993, terrorism was not an issue at the forefront of most minds at the agency. The United States had undertaken no meaningful action against the sources of terror since it had been caught selling missiles to Iran. The American hostages taken during the Reagan years had all come home from Beirut by 1991, though Bill Buckley came home in a box. In 1992, there was serious talk about shutting down the CIA's counterterrorism center. Things had been quiet. People thought perhaps the problem had solved itself.

Not long after dawn on January 25, 1993, the fifth day of the Clinton administration, Nicholas Starr, a sixty-year-old career CIA officer, was first in line at the stoplight outside the main entrance to the agency's headquarters. The light takes forever to turn green, and cars back up to the horizon on Route 123, waiting to enter the tranquil woods of the

CIA's headquarters. At 7:50 a.m., a young Pakistani stepped out of his car and began firing an AK-47 assault rifle. First he shot Frank Darling, twenty-eight, who worked as a covert-operations communicator, hitting him in the right shoulder, as Darling's wife screamed in horror. The gunman wheeled, shot, and killed Dr. Lansing Bennett, sixty-six, a CIA physician. He turned and hit Nick Starr in the left arm and shoulder, then shot Calvin Morgan, sixty-one, a CIA engineer, and Stephen Williams, forty-eight, later identified in court records as a CIA employee. The killer turned again and blew Darling's head off. And then he drove away. It was all over in half a minute. Grievously wounded, Nick Starr somehow reached the guardhouse at the CIA's gates and raised the alarm.

President Clinton never came to the CIA to pay his respects to the dead and wounded. He sent his wife instead. It is hard to exaggerate how much fury this created at headquarters. When Fred Woodruff, the acting station chief in Tbilisi, Georgia, was shot and killed in an apparently random murder that summer while on a sightseeing trip, Woolsey made a point of flying halfway around the world to receive his mortal remains.

On February 26, 1993, one month after the shooting at the agency's gates, a bomb went off in the subterranean parking garage of the World Trade Center. Six people were killed and more than one thousand injured. The FBI thought at first it was Balkan separatists, but within a week, it became clear that the bombers were the acolytes of a blind Egyptian sheik who lived in Brooklyn—Omar Abdel Rahman. His name rang a very loud bell at CIA headquarters. The blind sheik had recruited many hundreds of Arab fighters for the war against the Soviets in Afghanistan under the banner of Al Gama'a al Islamiyya, the Islamic Group. Tried and acquitted in the 1981 assassination of President Anwar el-Sadat, he had nonetheless remained under house arrest in Egypt until 1986. As soon as he got out of prison in Egypt, he started trying to get into the United States. He succeeded in 1990. But how? The sheik was a known seditionist—and, as it developed, the spiritual leader of a conspiracy to kill Americans by the thousands.

His visa had been issued in the capital of Sudan—"by a member of the Central Intelligence Agency in Khartoum," said Joe O'Neill, the chargé d'affaires at the American embassy. "The Agency knew that he was traveling in the area looking for a visa, and never told us." It must have been a mistake, O'Neill thought: "That name should have shown up like a shot." In fact, CIA officers had reviewed seven applications by Abdel Rahman to enter the United States—and said yes six times. "I can't tell you what a terrible thing it is that that had happened," O'Neill said. "It was atrocious."

On April 14, 1993, George H. W. Bush arrived in Kuwait to commemorate the victory in the Gulf War. His wife, two of his sons, and former secretary of state Jim Baker were among his entourage. On that trip, the Kuwaiti secret police arrested seventeen men and charged them with a plot to kill Bush with a car bomb—close to two hundred pounds of plastic explosives hidden in a Toyota Land Cruiser. Under torture, some of the suspects confessed that Iraq's intelligence service was behind the assassination attempt. On April 29, the CIA's technicians reported that the construction of the bomb bore an Iraqi signature. A few days later, the FBI started interrogating the suspects. Two said they had been sent by Iraq. The only part of the puzzle that did not seem to fit was the suspects themselves. Most of them were whisky smugglers, hashish peddlers, and shell-shocked veterans. But the CIA eventually concluded that Saddam Hussein had tried to kill President Bush.

Over the next month, President Clinton weighed a response. At about 1:30 a.m. on June 26, on the Muslim Sabbath, twenty-three Tomahawk missiles landed in and around Iraqi intelligence headquarters, a complex of seven large buildings inside a walled compound in downtown Baghdad. At least one of the missiles struck an apartment building and killed several innocent civilians, including a prominent Iraqi artist and her husband. General Colin Powell, chairman of the Joint Chiefs of Staff, said the bombing was intended to be "proportionate to the attack on President Bush."

The director of central intelligence was enraged by the president's sense of proportion. "Saddam tries to assassinate former President Bush," Woolsey said years later, "and President Clinton fires a couple of dozen cruise missiles into an empty building in the middle of the night in Baghdad, thereby retaliating quite effectively against Iraqi cleaning women and night watchmen, but not especially effectively against Saddam Hussein." Not long thereafter, he noted, "our helicopters were shot down in Mogadishu and—as in Beirut ten years earlier—we left."

With the images of dead Army Rangers being dragged through the streets of Mogadishu still fresh in American minds, Clinton set out to restore the power of the elected president of Haiti, the leftist priest Jean-

Bertrand Aristide. He genuinely viewed Aristide as the legitimate ruler of the Haitian people and he wanted to see justice done. This required undoing the military junta that had ousted Aristide. Many of its leaders had been on the CIA's payroll for years, serving as trusted informants for the clandestine service. This fact was an unpleasant surprise for the White House. So was the revelation that the agency had created a Haitian intelligence service whose military leaders did little but distribute Colombian cocaine, destroy their political enemies, and preserve their power in the capital, Port-au-Prince. The agency was now placed in the awkward position of overthrowing its own agents.

This put Clinton and the CIA in direct conflict. So did the CIA's accurate assessment that Aristide was not a pillar of strength or virtue. Woolsey painted the conflict as ideological. The president and his aides "desperately wanted us at the CIA to say that Aristide was effectively going to be the Thomas Jefferson of Haiti," he recalled. "We somewhat grumpily declined to do that and pointed out both his short side as well as some of the positive things about him. We were not popular because of that." Woolsey was only partly right. The White House found the CIA's analysis of Aristide's weaknesses inconvenient. But it also found the agency's old allies in Haiti appalling.

Furious when the CIA crossed swords with him on Haiti, paralyzed by his inability to formulate a foreign policy, shell-shocked by the shootdown in Somalia, the president wanted to withdraw from third-world adventures for a while. But as soon as American soldiers and spies started pulling out of the Horn of Africa, where they had gone on a humanitarian mission and wound up killing and being killed, they were called upon to go save lives in Rwanda, where two tribes were at each other's throats.

At the end of January 1994, the White House studiously ignored a CIA study saying half a million people might die in Rwanda. Soon the conflict exploded into one of the great man-made disasters of the twentieth century. "Nobody was really focused on how serious the situation was until things were out of control," said Mort Halperin, then a member of Clinton's National Security Council staff. "There weren't any visuals and there wasn't a lot of information." Reluctant to become involved in nations whose sufferings were not televised, the Clinton administration refused to call the one-sided massacres genocide. The president's response to Rwanda was a decision to narrowly define America's national interest in the fate of faraway failed states whose collapse would not directly affect the United States—places such as Somalia, Sudan, and Afghanistan.

"BLOW IT UP"

Woolsey lost almost every fight he picked, and there were plenty. When it became clear that Woolsey could not restore the CIA's money and power, most of the remaining stars among the cold-war generation began flicking out the lights and going home. The veterans had been the first to vanish. Then the up-and-coming officers in their thirties and early forties bailed out to start new careers. Recruiting new talent, people in their twenties, was harder and harder every year.

The intellectual and operational powers of the CIA were fading away. Headquarters was run by professional clerks who meted out dwindling funds without any understanding of what worked and what did not work in the field. They had no system of distinguishing programs that succeeded from those that did not. Without a scorecard of successes and failures, they had little understanding of how to field their players. As the number of experienced CIA operators and analysts dwindled, the authority of the director of central intelligence was sapped by his own bloated middle management, an ever-growing cadre of special assistants, staff aides, and task forces that overflowed from headquarters into rented offices in the shopping malls and industrial parks of Virginia.

Woolsey found himself presiding over a secret bureaucracy increasingly disconnected from the rest of American government. Like a big-city hospital whose poor practices made its patients sick, the CIA was making mistakes as part of its everyday operations. American intelligence had started to resemble "Frankenstein's creature," wrote James Monnier Simon, Jr., the CIA's chief administrative officer at the turn of the century—"an amalgamation of ill-fitting pieces put together at differing times by different, and sometimes indifferent, workmen," suffering from "a defective nervous system that cripples its coordination and balance."

The problems were too complicated for a quick fix. Like the space shuttle, the agency was a complex system that could explode if a simple component failed. The only person with the power to start to make the pieces fit was the president of the United States. But Clinton did not find the time to understand what the CIA was, how it worked, or where it fit in with the rest of the American government. The president delegated all of that to George Tenet, whom he brought to the White House as the National Security Council's staff director for intelligence.

Fourteen months into the Clinton administration, Tenet was musing over a double espresso and a cigar at a sidewalk café two blocks from the White House. What did he think should be done to change the CIA? "Blow it up," Tenet said. He meant, of course, a creative destruction, a rebuilding from the ground up. But it was a vivid choice of words.

45. "WHY IN THE WORLD DIDN'T WE KNOW?"

Fred Hitz, the CIA's inspector general, said his job was to walk through the battlefield while the smoke cleared and shoot the wounded. His internal investigations were painstaking and pitiless. He was old-school agency, recruited in his senior year at Princeton after being tapped by the dean of students. As fate would have it, his biggest case concerned his classmate from the CIA's career-training cadre of 1967, an alcoholic burnout from the old Soviet division by the name of Aldrich Hazen Ames.

On Presidents' Day, February 21, 1994, a team of FBI agents hauled Ames out of his Jaguar as he left his suburban home for headquarters, slapped on the handcuffs, and took him away forever. I went to see him in the Alexandria county jail after his arrest. He was a gray man of fifty-three who had been spying for the Soviets for nearly nine years. He would soon be sent to a lifetime of solitary confinement, and he was eager to talk.

Ames was a malcontent and a malingerer who got a job with the agency because his father had once worked there. He spoke passable Russian and wrote readable reports when sober, but his personnel records were a chronicle of drunkenness and ineptitude. He had failed upward for seventeen years. In 1985, he had reached a pinnacle: chief of counterintelligence for the Soviet Union and Eastern Europe. He was known to be an alcoholic malcontent. Yet the agency gave him access to the files of nearly every important spy working for the United States behind the iron curtain.

He had become contemptuous of the CIA. He thought it absurd to say that the Soviet threat to the United States was immense and growing. He decided that he knew better. "I know what the Soviet Union is really all about, and I know what's best for foreign policy and national security," he remembered thinking. "And I'm going to act on that."

Ames obtained permission from his superiors to meet with an officer from the Soviet embassy in Washington, pretending that he could recruit the Russian. In April 1985, in exchange for $50,000, he had handed the Soviet intelligence officer the names of three Soviet citizens who were working with the CIA. Then, a few months later, he named every name he knew. Moscow set $2 million aside for him.

One by one, America's spies inside the Soviet Union were arrested, tried, imprisoned, and executed. As they died, Ames said, "bells and whistles" went off inside the clandestine service. "It was as if neon lights and searchlights lit up all over the Kremlin, shone all the way across the Atlantic Ocean, saying, 'There is a penetration.' " Yet the CIA's leaders refused to believe that one of their own had betrayed them. Using double agents and deception, the KGB skillfully manipulated the CIA's perceptions of the case. It had to be a bug. It could not be a mole.

Ames also gave Moscow the identities of hundreds of his fellow CIA officers and a thorough rundown on their work. "Their names were given to the Soviet intelligence service, as were the details of a number of operations that the United States was engaged in," Hitz said. "This began in 1985, but continued until one or two years before his arrest, and Ames was an avid gatherer of information to supply to his Soviet case officer. So in strict intelligence terms it was a horror."

The agency knew that something had destroyed its Soviet operations. But it took seven years to begin to face the facts. The CIA was unable to investigate itself, and Ames knew it. "You would wind up with people throwing up their hands and saying, 'We can't do it,' " he said with a smirk. "You've got two or three or four thousand people running around doing espionage. You can't monitor it. You can't control it. You can't check it. And that's probably the biggest problem with an espionage service. It has to be small. The minute you get big, you get like the KGB, or you get like us."

"A VIOLATION OF COMMANDMENT NUMBER ONE"

It took Hitz more than a year after the arrest to assess the damage Ames had wrought. In the end, he found that the CIA itself had been part of an elaborate deception.

Among the most highly classified papers that the agency produced during and after the cold war were "blue border" reports, with a blue stripe on the side signifying their importance, assessing the strength of Moscow's missiles, tanks, jets, bombers, strategy, and tactics. They were signed by the director of central intelligence and sent to the president, the secretary of defense, and the secretary of state. "That is what the intelligence community exists to do," Hitz said.

For eight years, from 1986 to 1994, the senior CIA officers responsible for these reports had known that some of their sources were controlled by Russian intelligence. The agency knowingly gave the White House information manipulated by Moscow—and deliberately concealed the fact. To reveal that it had been delivering misinformation and disinformation would have been too embarrassing. Ninety-five of these tainted reports warped American perceptions of the major military and political developments in Moscow. Eleven of the reports went directly to Presidents Reagan, Bush, and Clinton. They distorted and diminished America's ability to understand what was going on in Moscow.

"This was an incredible discovery," Hitz said. The most senior CIA official responsible for these reports insisted—as Ames had done—that he knew best. He knew what was real and what was not. The fact that the reporting had come from agents of deception meant nothing. "He made that decision himself," Hitz said. "Well, that was shocking."

"What came out of this whole episode was a feeling that the agency couldn't be trusted," Hitz said. "In short, it was a violation of Commandment Number One. And that's why it had such a destructive impact." By lying to the White House, the CIA had broken "the sacred trust," Hitz said, "and without that, no espionage agency can do its job."

"THE PLACE JUST NEEDS A TOTAL OVERHAUL"

Woolsey acknowledged that the Ames case revealed an institutional carelessness that bordered on criminal negligence. "One could almost conclude not only that no one was watching, but that no one cared," he said. But he announced that no one would be dismissed or demoted for the "systemic failure" of the CIA in the Ames case. Instead, he sent letters of reprimand to six former senior officers and five still on duty, including the chief of the clandestine service, Ted Price. He defined the failures as sins of omission and blamed them on a flawed culture within the CIA, a tradition of arrogance and denial.

Woolsey presented his decision to the House intelligence committee on the afternoon of September 28, 1994. He made a bad impression. "You have to wonder whether the CIA has become no different from any other bureaucracy," the committee's chairman, Dan Glickman, a Kansas Democrat, said upon emerging from the meeting. "You have to wonder if it has lost the vibrancy of its unique mission."

The Ames case created an attack on the CIA that was unprecedented in its intensity. It came from the right and it came from the left and it came from the dwindling center of American politics. Anger mixed with ridicule—a deadly brew—flowed from the White House and Congress. There was a strong sense that the Ames case was not an isolated aberration but evidence of a structural dry rot. Lieutenant General Bill Odom, who had run the National Security Agency under President Reagan, said the solution was radical surgery.

"I would disembowel the CIA," he said. "It's contaminated. And if you take halfhearted measures it will remain contaminated."

Striving to defend the agency from without and within, Woolsey promised the American people that they had a right to ask where the CIA was headed. But he had lost his ability to chart that course. So on September 30, 1994, Congress created a commission on the future of the CIA and gave it the power to blaze a new path for the agency in the twenty-first century. The Ames case had created a once-in-a-generation chance for change.

"The place just needs a total overhaul," said Senator Arlen Specter of Pennsylvania, a Republican who had served six years on the Senate intelligence committee.

What was needed was a push from the president of the United States, which never came. It took three months to select the seventeen members of the commission, four months to draft an agenda, and five months before the panel held its first formal meeting. The commission was dominated by members of Congress, notably Representative Porter J. Goss of Florida, a conservative Florida Republican. Goss had spent an undistinguished stint with the clandestine service in the 1960s, but he was the only member of Congress who could claim hands-on experience at the agency. The commission's most distinguished outsider was Paul Wolfowitz, who came to the table thinking that the CIA's ability to gather intelligence through espionage had collapsed, and who would be among the most influential members of the next president's inner circle.

The commission was led by Les Aspin, who had lost his job as secretary of defense nine months before, fired for his inability to make decisions. Clinton had named him chairman of the President's Foreign Intelligence Advisory Board. Depressed and disorganized, Aspin asked big questions without clear answers: "What does it all mean now? What are the targets now? What are you trying to do?" When he died suddenly of a stroke at fifty-six a few months later, the commission's staff was despondent and its work went adrift. The commissioners headed in a dozen different directions, unable to decide on a destination.

The staff director, Britt Snider, proclaimed: "Our goal is to sell intelligence." But many of the witnesses were warning that salesmanship was not the issue. It was the product.

The commission finally convened and took testimony. Bob Gates, who had drawn up the long list of 176 threats and targets three years before, now said the agency was overwhelmed by the multiplicity of tasks. Case officers and station chiefs said the clandestine service was drowning under too many requests to do too many small-bore things too far afield. Why was the White House asking the CIA to report on the growth of the evangelical movement in Latin America? Was that really important to the national security of the United States? The agency was only capable of a few major missions. Tell us what you want us to do, the CIA's officers begged.

But nothing focused the commission. Not the March 1995 attack by a religious cult that poured sarin gas into the Tokyo subways, killing 12 people and injuring 3,769, an event that signified the transformation of terrorism from nation-states to the self-anointed. Not the April 1995 bombing of the federal headquarters in Oklahoma City, which killed 169 people, the deadliest attack on American territory since Pearl Harbor. Not the discovery of a plot by Islamic militants to blow up a dozen American airliners over the Pacific and crash a hijacked jet into CIA headquarters. Not the warning from a CIA officer that someday the United States would face "aerial terrorism"—an airplane dive-bombing a target. Not the fact that a total of three people in the American intelligence community had the linguistic ability to understand excited Muslims talking to each other. Not the realization that the ability of the CIA to analyze information was being drowned by the explosion of e-mail, personal computers, cellular telephones, and publicly available encryption for private communications. Not the growing realization that the CIA was in a state of collapse.

The report, seventeen months in the making, had no weight and no impact. "Counterterrorism received little attention," said Loch Johnson, a member of the commission's staff. "The limits of covert action were never defined; the weaknesses in accountability went largely unaddressed." No one who read it bought the anodyne arguments that a little fine-tuning would fix the machine.

As the commission completed its report, a total of twenty-five people were enrolled at the CIA's career training center for young new recruits. The agency's ability to attract talent was at an all-time low. So was its reputation. The Ames case had made the CIA's future a casualty of its history.

The clandestine service was "terribly concerned about what they feel are inadequate numbers of people on the front line," Fred Hitz said at the time. "Getting the right people and getting them in the right place is already a different problem to solve. We've got good people but not enough of them, and not enough of them in the places where we need them. If the president of the United States and the Congress of the United States don't help, then the one thing that will bring us around will bring us around too late. Some horrible event happening somewhere in the world, maybe in our own nation, that makes us all wake up as Pearl Harbor made us wake up and say—why in the world didn't we know?"

46. "WE'RE IN TROUBLE"

At the end of 1994, Jim Woolsey recorded a farewell address to his troops at the CIA, sent a letter of resignation to the White House by courier, and left town in a hurry. Bill Clinton searched the government for someone willing and able to take the job.

"The president asked me whether I was interested in being the director of central intelligence," said his deputy secretary of defense, John Deutch. "I made it very clear to him that I was not. I saw my friend Jim Woolsey having tremendous difficulties as director. I didn't think that there was any reason for me to think I could do better."

Fine, Clinton replied, find someone who can. Six weeks went by before Deutch managed to press-gang a retired air force general named Mike Carns for the job. Six more weeks passed before the nomination wobbled, plummeted, and crashed.

"The president pressed on me the view that I really had to do it," Deutch said. Thus began a short and bitter lesson in the political science of American intelligence. Deutch had good reason to dread the assignment. He had been in and around national-security circles for three decades, and he knew that no director of central intelligence ever had succeeded in fulfilling his charter—serving simultaneously as the chairman of American intelligence and the chief executive of the CIA. He requested and received cabinet rank, as Bill Casey had, to ensure himself some access to the president. He had hopes that he might become the secretary of defense if Clinton was re-elected in 1996. But he knew that the CIA was in a state of turmoil that could not be repaired in a year or two.

"Plagued by poor leadership, the Agency is adrift," a veteran CIA analyst, John Gentry, wrote during the days that Deutch first came to office. "It has a palpable malaise. The unhappiness level of employees well into management ranks is very high. Senior officers are floundering as well." The agency was led by "a corps of senior officers so devoid of real leadership skills that it is largely incapable of independent creative action." With Clinton apparently content to get his intelligence from CNN, Gentry wrote, the CIA had "no one left to pander to."

As deputy secretary of defense, Deutch had been through a yearlong review of American intelligence with Woolsey, trying for a truce in the endless wars over money and power between the Pentagon and the CIA. They would pick an issue—say, the proliferation of nuclear weapons—and at the end of the day they would conclude that much more had to be done. Counterintelligence? After Ames, definitely more. Support to military operations? Hugely important. Human intelligence? More spies. Better analysis? Absolutely crucial. At the end of the review it was clear that there were an infinite number of needs and a finite amount of money and personnel available to meet them. American intelligence could not be reformed from within, and surely it was not being reformed from without.

Deutch and Woolsey both had the well-known I'm-the-smartest-guy-in-the-room syndrome. The difference was that Deutch often *was* the smartest. He had been the dean of science and the provost at the Massachusetts Institute of Technology; his field was physical chemistry, the science of the transformation of matter at the molecular, atomic, and subatomic levels. He could explain how a lump of coal becomes a diamond. He set out to transform the CIA under that type of pressure. At his confirmation hearings, he had vowed to change the culture of the CIA's clandestine service, "down to the bare bones," but he had no clear idea how. Like his predecessors, he went to learn at the feet of Richard Helms.

Helms, now eighty-two, carried himself with the bearing of a British peer. Shortly after his skull session with the new director, I had lunch with him at a restaurant two blocks from the White House. Helms sipped a noontime beer, sitting beneath slowly revolving ceiling fans, and con-

fided that Deutch was instinctively drawing away from the clandestine
service—"seeing it as nothing but trouble. Nor is he the first to be dis-
tancing himself. He's got to do a job convincing them he's on the team."

In May 1995, a few days after Deutch showed up for work at CIA
headquarters, the leaders of the clandestine service, always conscious of
the need to recruit a new boss, presented him with a glossy brochure titled "A New Direction. A New Future." It was the list of their top ten targets: loose nukes, terrorism, Islamic fundamentalism, support for military
operations, macroeconomics, Iran, Iraq, North Korea, Russia, China. The
new director and his spies all knew that the White House wanted to use
the CIA as a private Internet, a database on everything from tropical rain
forests to compact-disc counterfeiters, and that its attention needed a far
sharper focus. "The trouble is there's too much to do," Deutch said. "You
get requests: What's going to happen in Indonesia? What's going to happen in Sudan? What's going to happen in the Middle East?" The call for
global coverage was impossible to fulfill. Let us concentrate on a few hard
targets, the spies said. Deutch could not settle the argument.

Instead, he worked for five months trying to get a handle on the clandestine service. He flew off to CIA stations around the world, listening,
questioning, and weighing what he had to work with. He said he found
"tremendously poor morale." He was shocked by the inability of his spies
to solve their own problems. He found them in a state approaching
panic.

He compared them to the American military after Vietnam. Back
then, as Deutch put it in September 1995, a lot of smart lieutenants and
colonels had looked at one another and said: " 'We're in trouble. We've
got to change. We've got to figure out a way to do this differently. We're
either leaving or we're going to change the system.' And the people who
stayed did change the system." Deutch wanted the clandestine service to
solve its own problems. But he found his people incapable of change.
"Compared to uniformed officers," he said of his spies, "they certainly
are not as competent, or as understanding of what their relative role is
or what their responsibilities are." The clandestine service "was not confident of carrying out its day-to-day activity."

This crisis of confidence took many forms. Some were made manifest
in misguided operations that backfired. Others were continuing failures
of collection and analysis. Some were breathtaking lapses in judgment.

In Bosnia, on July 13, 1995, as the world's press reported mass killings of Muslims by Serbs, a spy satellite sent back pictures of prisoners being guarded by gunmen in fields outside the town of Srebrenica. No one at the CIA looked at that picture for three weeks. No one had thought that the Serbs would conquer the town. No one anticipated a slaughter. No one paid heed to human-rights groups, the United Nations, or the press. The CIA had no officers and no agents in the field to corroborate what they were reporting. It had no information about any atrocities. It had been ordered to devote itself to supporting military operations in the region, and it had neither time nor talent to spare to check out reports from terrified refugees.

Two weeks after the first press accounts of a slaughter, the CIA sent a U-2 over Srebrenica; the plane recorded images of freshly dug mass graves in the fields where the prisoners had stood. Those photos arrived at the CIA on a regular military courier flight three days later. And three days after that, a CIA photo analyst matched up the location of the first satellite image of the prisoners in the field with the second U-2 image of burial sites. The analysis landed at the White House on August 4, 1995.

Thus did the CIA report, three weeks after the fact, the biggest mass murder of civilians in Europe since Hitler's death camps fifty years before. Eight thousand people were dead, and the agency had missed it.

On the other end of Europe, the CIA's Paris station had run an elaborate operation trying to steal the French negotiating position on trade talks. Locked into the idea that free trade was the guiding force of American foreign policy, the White House had aggravated the CIA's woes by demanding more and more economic intelligence. The Paris station was pursuing secrets of minimal importance to the national security of the United States—such as how many American movies would be shown on French screens. The French interior ministry ran a counterespionage operation that included the seduction of a CIA officer working under nonofficial cover as a businesswoman. There was pillow talk, and secrets were spilled. The government publicly expelled the Paris station chief— Dick Holm, a genuine hero at the clandestine service, who had run field operations in Laos and barely survived a fiery plane crash in the Congo thirty years before, and who was on his last tour before retirement. Four hapless and humiliated CIA officers were kicked out of France with him.

Another blown operation, another public embarrassment for the clandestine service, and "another public example of a situation where its ability to carry out its function as its own standards required came into question," Deutch said. He asked his officers time and again: "What are the professional standards of carrying out your very difficult mission? And are you doing it well all over the world?" His answer to that last question was a resounding no.

"IT WAS CLEARLY MALICE"

The problems at the Paris station were a passing annoyance compared to what went on in the Latin American division of the clandestine service. The division was a world apart at the CIA, dominated by veterans of the war against Fidel Castro, men who had their own set of rules and disciplines. Since 1987, station chiefs in Costa Rica, El Salvador, Peru, Venezuela, and Jamaica had been accused of lying to superiors, sexually harassing coworkers, stealing money, threatening underlings at gunpoint, running a counternarcotics operation in which a ton of cocaine wound up on the streets of Florida, and keeping sloppy accounts involving $1 million in government funds. It was the only division in the clandestine service in which station chiefs were removed from their posts for misconduct on a regular basis. The division's isolation flowed in part from the internal politics of the countries it covered. Throughout the cold war, the CIA had worked with military regimes against left-wing insurgencies in Latin America. The old bonds were hard to break.

In Guatemala, 200,000 civilians had died during forty years of struggle following the agency's 1954 coup against an elected president. Between 90 and 96 percent of those deaths came at the hands of the Guatemalan military. In 1994, the CIA's officers in Guatemala still went to great lengths to conceal the nature of their close relations to the military and to suppress reports that Guatemalan officers on its payroll were murderers, torturers, and thieves. This concealment violated a balancing test that Woolsey had started in 1994. The test, called "agent validation," was supposed to weigh the quality of an agent's information against the perfidiousness of his conduct.

"You don't want to be in a position of dealing with military officials or officials in that government who are known by everyone to have blood on their hands unless there is a legitimate intelligence goal to be served," said Inspector General Fred Hitz. "Unless that person knows that there's a cache in southern Guatemala where biological weapons are being put together and they're going to be sold on the open market and he's your only source for it. If a person is notorious for butchering people, breaking the law, then the fact that the CIA is in contact with that individual has to be balanced against the information that individual is likely to provide. If the information is the keys to the holy mystery, we'll take the chance. But let's do it with our eyes open and not because of inertia or momentum."

This problem boiled over when a Guatemalan colonel on the CIA's payroll was implicated in the cover-up of the murders of an American innkeeper and a Guatemalan guerrilla married to an American lawyer. The outcry over the innkeeper's murder had led the Bush administration to cut off millions of dollars in military aid to Guatemala, though the agency continued its financial support for Guatemalan military intelligence. "The CIA station in Guatemala was about twice the size it needed to be," said Thomas Stroock, the American ambassador to Guatemala from 1989 to 1992, but it could not seem to bring itself to report accurately on the case. The station chief, Fred Brugger, failed to tell Ambassador Stroock that the colonel, a prime suspect, was a CIA agent. "Not only did they not tell me," Ambassador Stroock said, "they did not tell my boss, the secretary of state, or the Congress. That was stupid."

Folly turned to malevolence in 1994, when Dan Donahue became the station chief. While the new American ambassador, Marilyn McAfee, was preaching human rights and justice, the CIA stayed loyal to the murderous Guatemalan intelligence service.

The embassy split in two. "The chief of station came into my office and showed me a piece of intelligence, which came from a Guatemalan source, suggesting that I was having an affair with my secretary, whose name was Carol Murphy," Ambassador McAfee remembered. The Guatemalan military had bugged the ambassador's bedroom and recorded her cooing endearments to Murphy. They spread the word that the ambassador was a lesbian. The CIA station transmitted this piece of intelligence—later known as "the Murphy memo"—to Washington, where it was widely distributed. "The CIA sent this report to the Hill," ambassador McAfee said. "It was clearly malice. The CIA had defamed an ambassador by back channels."

The ambassador was a conservative person from a conservative family, she was married, and she was not sleeping with her secretary.

"Murphy" was the name of her two-year-old black standard poodle. The bug in her bedroom had recorded her petting her dog.

The CIA station had shown a stronger affinity for its friends in the Guatemalan military than for the American ambassador. "There was a division between intelligence and policy," Ambassador McAfee said. "That's what scares me."

It scared Deutch too. On September 29, 1995, toward the end of his fifth month in office, Deutch went to the Bubble—the once-futuristic six-hundred-seat amphitheater near the entrance to CIA headquarters—to deliver some bad news to the clandestine service. An internal-review board at the CIA had weighed the evidence in Guatemala and told Deutch that he should dismiss Terry Ward, the Latin American division chief of the clandestine service from 1990 to 1993, then serving as the chief of station in Switzerland. It said he should dismiss the former Guatemala station chief Fred Brugger too, and discipline his successor Dan Donahue severely, making sure he never served as a station chief again.

Deutch said there were "tremendous deficiencies in the way the agency carried out its business" in Guatemala. The problem was lying—or, as he put it, "a lack of candor"—between the chief of station and the American ambassador, the station and the Latin American division, the division and headquarters, and finally between the agency and Congress.

It was rare—very rare—for anyone to be fired from the clandestine service. But Deutch said he was going to do exactly as the review board recommended. The announcement did not go over well at the Bubble. The hundreds of officers gathered there were ferociously angry. Deutch's decision signified to them a suffocating political correctness. The director told them that they had to keep going out into the world and taking risks in the name of national security. A low growl rose from the back of the Bubble, a bitter laugh signifying: Yeah. Sure. That was the moment when the director and the clandestine service washed their hands of one another. It sealed his fate at the CIA.

"WE WANT TO GET THIS RIGHT"

The break was unbridgeable. Deutch decided to hand the portfolio of problems at the clandestine service to his number-two man—George Tenet, the deputy director of central intelligence. Now forty-two years old, Tenet, always the tireless and loyal aide, had spent five years as staff director of the Senate intelligence committee and two years as the National Security Council's point man for intelligence. He had vital insights in managing the CIA's tortured relationships with the Congress and the White House. And he soon came to see the clandestine service differently than Deutch did—not as a problem to be solved but a cause to be championed. Tenet would do his utmost to lead them.

"Let me explain life to you," Tenet said he told the clandestine service chiefs. "Here are the ten or fifteen things, that we cannot tolerate to fail against, to advance the national-security interests of the United States. This is what we want you to devote your money, your people, your language training, and your skills to. We want to get this right."

Terrorism soon rose to the top of Tenet's list. In the fall of 1995, a barrage of threatening reports started coming from the CIA station in the Sudan to the agency headquarters and the White House counterterrorism czar, Richard Clarke. They were based on the word of a single recruited CIA agent. They warned of an imminent attack against the station, the American embassy, and a prominent member of the Clinton administration.

"Dick Clarke came to me and said, 'They're going to blow you up,' " remembered Tony Lake, the president's national security adviser. *Who* is going to blow me up? Lake asked. Maybe the Iranians, Clarke replied, maybe the Sudanese. "So I went to live in a safe house and drove to work in a bulletproof car," Lake said. "They could never show it was real. I suspect not."

The Sudan was an international clearinghouse for stateless terrorists in those days. Among them was Osama bin Laden. The agency first knew him in the late 1980s as a rich Saudi who supported the same Afghan rebels that the agency armed in their fight against their Soviet oppressors. He was known as a financier of people who had grand visions of attacking the enemies of Islam. The CIA never pulled together its shards and fragments of intelligence on bin Laden and his network into a coherent report for the White House. No formal estimate of the terrorist threat he represented was published until after the entire world knew his name.

Bin Laden had returned to Saudi Arabia to rail against the presence of American troops after the 1991 Gulf War. The Saudi government expelled him, and he settled in the Sudan. The CIA's station chief in the Sudan, Cofer Black, was an old-school operator of considerable courage and cunning who had helped hunt down the burned-out terrorist known as Carlos the Jackal. Black tracked bin Laden's movements and motives in the Sudan as best he could. In January 1996, the CIA created a counterterrorism unit of a dozen people devoted entirely to the Saudi—the bin Laden station. There was a sense that he might start taking aim at American targets abroad.

But in February 1996, the CIA, heeding the warnings of its recruited agent, shut down its operations in the Sudan, blinding itself to fresh intelligence on its new target. The station and the American embassy were shuttered and their personnel moved to Kenya. The decision came over the strongest objections of the American ambassador, Timothy Carney, a man of military discipline along with diplomatic sensibilities. He argued that for the United States to withdraw from the Sudan was a dangerous mistake. He questioned the CIA's warnings about an imminent attack, and he was proved right. The agent who had raised the alarm was later found to be a fabricator, and the CIA formally withdrew roughly one hundred reports based on his information.

Shortly thereafter, bin Laden moved to Afghanistan. The chief of the bin Laden station, Mike Scheuer, saw this as a tremendous opportunity. The CIA had reestablished contacts with a network of Afghan exiles in the tribal northwest territories of Pakistan. The "tribals," as the CIA called them, were helping in the hunt for Mir Amal Kansi, the gunman who had killed two agency officers outside headquarters.

The hope was that they could help kidnap or kill bin Laden someday. But that day would have to wait. The CIA had another man in its crosshairs at that moment.

The chief of the Near East division of the clandestine service, Stephen Richter, had been working for two years on a plan to support a military coup against Saddam Hussein. The order had come from President Clinton, the third such command from the White House to the CIA in five years. In Jordan, a team of CIA officers met with Mohammed Abdullah Shawani, a former commander of Iraqi special forces. In London, the agency conspired with an Iraqi exile named Ayad Alawi, who headed a network of rebellious Iraqi military officers and Ba'ath Party leaders. The CIA backed him with money and guns. In northern Iraq, the CIA gathered the tribal leaders of the stateless Iraqi Kurds, renewing an old and troubled romance.

Despite the CIA's best efforts, none of these disparate and fractious forces came together. The agency invested many millions trying to recruit key members of Saddam's military and political circles, hoping they would rise up. But the plot was penetrated and subverted by Saddam and his spies. On June 26, 1996, Saddam began arresting at least two hundred officers in and around Baghdad. He executed at least eighty of them, including General Shawani's sons.

"The Saddam case was an interesting case," Mark Lowenthal, who had been staff director of the House intelligence committee and a senior CIA analyst, said after the coup collapsed. "All right, so we get rid of Saddam Hussein, good thing. But who do we get after him? Who's our guy in Iraq? Anybody that we put in power in Iraq is likely to have the staying power of a flea. So this was a case where you had policy makers saying *do something*. This *do something* urge really expressed their frustration." They failed to see that the CIA "had no way to deal with Saddam Hussein," he said. "The problem with the operation was that there were no reliable Iraqis to deal with. And the reliable Iraqis you're looking at have no access to do what you want to them to do. So the operation was a bust. It wasn't feasible. But it's very hard for an operator to say, 'Mr. President, we can't do that.' So you end up with an operation that probably shouldn't have been started in the first place."

"FAILURE IS INEVITABLE"

Deutch infuriated Clinton by telling Congress that the CIA might never solve the problem of Saddam Hussein. His seventeen-month tenure as director of central intelligence ended in bitterness. In December 1996, after Clinton was re-elected, he dismissed Deutch from the government and turned to his national security adviser, Tony Lake, to take the job so few coveted.

"It would have been a great challenge," Lake mused. "What I had in mind was pushing the analytical side to make intelligence—both its sources and its products—fit in with the world of the mid-1990s. What we got was too often an overnight parsing of the news."

But Lake would not be confirmed. The Republican chairman of the Senate intelligence committee, Richard Shelby of Alabama, decided to make him a whipping boy for everything that conservatives found wrong with the Clinton administration's conduct of foreign policy. The appearance of bipartisanship that the intelligence committees had maintained for the better part of twenty years evaporated. There was also an undercurrent of opposition to Lake from inside the clandestine service. The message was: don't send us any more outsiders.

"To the CIA, everyone is an outsider," Lake observed.

It was not even close to a fair hearing. On March 17, 1997, Lake withdrew in anger, telling the president that he was not going to spend three more months as "a dancing bear in a political circus." So the poisoned chalice was handed to George Tenet—the only choice remaining. Tenet was already running the agency as the acting chief. He would become the fifth director of central intelligence in six years.

"It is impossible to overstate the turbulence and disruption that that much change at the top caused," the CIA's Fred Hitz said. "Its impact on morale is hard to overstate, in terms of its destructiveness. You have the feeling—who's in charge here? Can't anybody up there play this game? Don't they understand what we're about? Don't they realize what our mission is?"

Tenet knew what the mission was: save the CIA. But the agency approached the end of the American Century burdened by a personnel system invented in the 1880s, an information conveyor belt resembling assembly lines of the 1920s, and a bureaucracy dating to the 1950s. It moved people and money around in ways that summoned up memories of Stalin's Five-Year Plans. Its ability to collect and analyze secrets was falling apart as the information age exploded and the Internet made encryption—the transformation of language into code—a universal tool. The clandestine service had become a place where "great successes are rare and failure is routine," a report by the House intelligence committee noted.

Those failures once again were front-page news. The CIA's capacity for spying had once again been wounded by a traitor from within. Harold J. Nicholson, who had been station chief in Romania, had taken up a two-year posting as a head instructor at the Farm, the CIA's training school outside Williamsburg, Virginia. He had been spying for Moscow since 1994, selling the Russians files on dozens of CIA officers stationed abroad and the identities of every new officer graduated from the Farm in 1994, 1995, and 1996. The CIA told the federal judge who sentenced Nicholson to twenty-three years in prison that it would never be able to calculate the damage he had done to its operations worldwide. The careers of three years' worth of CIA trainees were blighted; once burned, they could never serve overseas.

On June 18, 1997, three weeks before Tenet's swearing-in, a new report by the House intelligence committee erased the remnants of the prideful notion that the CIA served as America's first line of defense. The committee, led by Porter J. Goss, said the agency was filled with inexperienced officers unable to speak the languages or understand the political landscapes of the countries they covered. It said the CIA had a small and dwindling capability to gather intelligence through espionage. It concluded that the CIA lacked the necessary "depth, breadth, and expertise to monitor political, military, and economic developments worldwide."

Later that summer, a career intelligence officer named Russ Travers published a haunting essay in the CIA's in-house journal. He said America's abilities to gather and analyze intelligence were falling apart. For years, he wrote, the leaders of American intelligence had been insisting that they were putting the agency on the right track. This was a myth. "We fine-tune our structures and marginally change our programs . . . getting the deck chairs on the *Titanic* nice and neat." But "we are going to begin making more and bigger mistakes more often," he warned. "We have gotten away from basics—the collection and unbiased analysis of facts."

He offered a prophecy for the future leaders of the CIA. "The year is 2001," he wrote. "By the turn of the century, analysis had become dangerously fragmented. The Community could still collect 'facts,' but analysis had long ago been overwhelmed by the volume of available information and were no longer able to distinguish between significant facts and background noise. The quality of analysis had become increasingly suspect. . . . The data were there, but we had failed to recognize fully their significance.

"From the vantage point of 2001," he wrote, "intelligence failure is inevitable."

47. "THE THREAT COULD NOT BE MORE REAL"

George Tenet was sworn in as the eighteenth director of central intelligence on July 11, 1997. He boasted to me back then, knowing his words would appear in *The New York Times*, that the CIA was far smarter and more skilled than any outsider could know. This was public relations. "We were nearly bankrupt," he confessed seven years later. He had inherited a CIA "whose expertise was ebbing" and a clandestine service "in disarray."

The agency was preparing to mark its fiftieth anniversary that September, and it had put together a list of the fifty greatest CIA officers as part of the celebration. Most were either old and gray or dead and gone. The greatest among the living was Richard Helms. He was not in a celebratory mood. "The only remaining superpower doesn't have enough interest in what's going on in the world to organize and run an espionage service," Helms said to me that month. "We've drifted away from that as a country." His successor, James Schlesinger, felt much the same. "The trust that was reposed in the CIA has faded," he said. "The agency is now so battered that its utility for espionage is subject to question."

Tenet started rebuilding. He called old stars out of retirement, including Jack Downing, who had served as station chief in Moscow and Beijing and agreed to run the clandestine service for a year or two. Tenet also sought a multibillion-dollar cash infusion for the agency. He promised that the CIA could be restored to health in five years' time, by 2002, if the money started flowing immediately. Porter Goss, who held the agency's purse strings in the House, arranged for secret "emergency assistance" of several hundred million dollars, followed by a onetime $1.8 billion shot in the arm. It was the biggest intelligence spending increase in fifteen years, and Goss promised to find more.

"Intelligence isn't just something for the cold war," Goss said back then. "When you think back to Pearl Harbor, you can understand why. Unpleasant surprises are out there."

"CATASTROPHIC SYSTEMIC INTELLIGENCE FAILURE"

Tenet lived in a state of foreboding, awaiting the next snafu. "I will not allow the CIA to become a second-rate organization," he proclaimed at a headquarters pep rally. A few days later, on May 11, 1998, the agency was caught by surprise again when India exploded a nuclear bomb. The test remade the balance of power in the world.

The new Hindu nationalist government had vowed openly to make nuclear weapons part of its arsenal. India's atomic weapons commissioner had said he was ready to test if political leaders gave the go-ahead. Pakistan had fired off new missiles, all but daring New Delhi to respond. So a nuclear blast by the world's largest democracy should not have come as a shock—but it did. The reporting from the CIA's station in New Delhi was lazy. The analysis at headquarters was fuzzy. The warning bell never rang. The test revealed a failure of espionage, a failure to read photographs, a failure to comprehend reports, a failure to think, and a failure to see. It was "a very disturbing event," said Charles Allen, the CIA's longtime chief of warning, whom Tenet recalled from retirement to serve as his assistant director of central intelligence for collection. It was a clear sign of a systemic breakdown at the CIA.

People started having premonitions of a catastrophe. "The likelihood of a cataclysmic warning failure is growing," Tenet's successor at the National Security Council, Mary McCarthy, wrote in an unclassified report shortly after the Indian test. "Disaster looms!"

Tenet had a reason to be looking the other way at the time of the nuclear test. His troops were rehearsing an operation to capture Osama bin Laden. In February 1998, bin Laden had proclaimed that he was on a mission from God to kill Americans. In Afghanistan, he was gathering the shock troops and camp followers of the holy war against the Soviets for a new jihad against the United States. In Pakistan, the CIA's station chief, Gary Schroen, was perfecting a plan to use the agency's old Afghan allies to snatch bin Laden as he traveled to his mud-walled compound in the southern city of Kandahar. On May 20, 1998, they began a final, four-day, full-scale dress rehearsal. But on May 29, Tenet decided to cancel the operation. Success depended on coordination with Pakistan—which had now exploded its own nuclear test in response to India. The Pakistanis were pounding the war drums. The Afghans were unreliable. Failure was not an option—it was a probability. The chances for capturing bin Laden were slim to start, and the world was now too unstable to risk it.

June passed without the promised attack from bin Laden, then July. On August 7, 1998, President Clinton was awakened by a 5:35 a.m. call reporting the bombings of the American embassies in Nairobi, Kenya, and Dar es Salaam, Tanzania. The explosions took place four minutes apart. The damage in Nairobi was horrific; I saw it with my own eyes. Twelve Americans, including a young CIA officer, died in that blast, which killed hundreds and wounded thousands of Kenyans in the streets and office buildings outside the embassy walls.

The next day, George Tenet went to the White House with the news that bin Laden was heading to an encampment outside Khost, Afghanistan, near the border with Pakistan. Tenet and Clinton's national-security aides agreed to hit the camp with cruise missiles. They wanted a second target to even the score, and they chose al Shifa, an industrial plant outside Khartoum, the capital of Sudan. An Egyptian agent of the CIA had delivered a soil sample from outside the plant suggesting the presence of a chemical used to make VX nerve gas.

The evidence was a very slender reed. "We will need much better intelligence on this facility" before bombing it, warned Mary McCarthy at the National Security Council. None ever appeared.

Navy ships in the Arabian Sea fired a barrage of million-dollar cruise missiles at both targets on August 20. They killed perhaps twenty Pakistanis passing through Khost—bin Laden was long gone—and a night watchman in Sudan. Clinton's inner circle claimed that the evidence for attacking Sudan was airtight. First they said al Shifa was a weapons factory working for bin Laden. In fact, it was a pharmaceutical plant, and the link to bin Laden vanished. Then they said it was part of an Iraqi scheme to distribute nerve weapons. But the Iraqis had not weaponized VX, as tests by United Nations inspectors confirmed. The soil sample might have been a VX precursor, and it might as well have been weed killer.

The case was a dozen dots connected by inference and surmise. Nothing ever corroborated the decision to strike al Shifa. "It was a mistake," said Donald Petterson, the American ambassador to Sudan from 1992 to 1995. "The administration failed to produce conclusive evidence that chemical weapons were being made at the pharmaceutical factory. The administration had grounds for suspicion, but to commit an act of war, which the missile attack was, the evidence should have been iron-clad." His successor, Ambassador Tim Carney, said with deliberate restraint: "The decision to target al Shifa continues a tradition of operating on inadequate intelligence about Sudan." The Clinton administration's counterterrorist attack went off half-cocked.

Three weeks later, Tenet met with the rest of the leaders of the American intelligence community. They agreed that they had to make "substantial and sweeping changes" in the way the nation collected, analyzed, and produced information. If they did not, they said, the result would be "a catastrophic systemic intelligence failure." The date was September 11, 1998.

"WE WILL CONTINUE TO BE SURPRISED"

If the CIA did not reinvent itself, and soon, "in ten years we won't be relevant," Tenet told me in October, his first on-the-record interview as director of central intelligence. "Unless you develop the expertise, we won't achieve what we want to achieve."

Since 1991, the agency had lost more than three thousand of its best people—about 20 percent of its senior spies, analysts, scientists, and technology experts. Roughly 7 percent of the clandestine service was headed out the door annually. That added up to a loss of about a thousand experienced spies, and it left not many more than a thousand in place. Tenet knew he could not guard against the future with so weak a force out on the front lines.

"There will always be days where we have to race to catch up to events we did not foresee, not because somebody is asleep at the switch, but because what's going on is so complicated," he said. "There is an expectation that we have built a no-fault intelligence system, that intelligence is expected not only to tell you about the trends and to tell you about events and give you insight, but in each and every case has a responsibility to tell you when the date, time, and place of an event is." The CIA itself had created that hope and expectation long ago. It was an illusion. "We will continue to be surprised," Tenet said.

He began to organize a nationwide talent hunt, painfully aware that his battle to rebuild the CIA would take many years, many billions of dollars, and many thousands of new officers. It was a desperate struggle against time. It takes five to seven years to turn a novice into a case officer capable of working in the rougher capitals of the world. American-born citizens who were both fluent in foreign cultures and willing and able to work for the CIA were hard to come by. A spy must know how "to use deception, to use manipulation, to use, frankly, dishonesty in the pursuit of his job," said Jeffrey Smith, the CIA's general counsel in the mid-1990s. "The management of the agency must always worry about finding that extraordinarily rare individual who has the talent to deal in this deceptive and manipulative world and keep his or her own moral ballast." Finding, hiring, and keeping such exceptional minds had been a job that never was done.

Over the years, the CIA had become less and less willing to hire "people that are a little different, people who are eccentric, people who don't look good in a suit and tie, people who don't play well in the sandbox with others," Bob Gates said. "The kinds of tests that we make people pass, psychological, and everything else, make it very hard for somebody who may be brilliant or have extraordinary talents and unique capabilities to get into the agency." As a consequence of its cultural myopia, the CIA misread the world. Very few of its officers could read or speak Chinese, Korean, Arabic, Hindi, Urdu, or Farsi—the languages of three billion people, half the planet's population. Far too few had ever haggled in an Arab bazaar or walked through an African village. The agency was unable to dispatch "an Asian-American into North Korea without him being identified as some kid who just walked out of Kansas, or African-Americans to work around the world, or Arab-Americans," Gates said.

In 1992, when Gates was director of central intelligence, he wanted

to hire an American citizen raised in Azerbaijan. "He spoke Azeri flu-
ently, but he didn't write English very well," he recalled. "And so he was
rejected because he didn't pass our English test. And when I was told
this, I just went crazy. I said: 'I've got thousands of people here who can
write English, but I don't have anybody here who can speak Azeri. What
have you done?' "

The agency started combing the cities and the suburbs of America
looking for the children of immigrants and refugees, young men and
women who grew up in first-generation Asian and Arab households,
reaching out with ads in ethnic newspapers throughout the United
States. The harvest was thin. Tenet knew the agency would live or die in
years to come by virtue of its ability to project an image of international
intrigue and intellectual adventure to smart young people. But new
blood was only part of the cure. The recruitment drive never resolved a
fundamental question at the agency—could the CIA recruit the kind of
person it would need five or ten years down the road? It did not know
where the road would lead. It only knew it could not survive in the state
into which it had fallen.

"WE'RE GOING TO BOMB THIS"

The enemy was growing stronger as the agency grew weaker. The failed
attack on bin Laden supercharged his status and attracted thousands of
new recruits to his cause. The urgency of the CIA's campaign against al
Qaeda escalated in concert with his popularity.

Tenet revived the plans to use Afghan proxies to capture him. In September and October 1998, the Afghans claimed they had mounted four
failed ambushes against bin Laden—which the CIA strongly doubted.
But they convinced the agency's field officers that they could track him
as he traveled from camp to camp inside Afghanistan. They reported on
December 18 that bin Laden was heading back to Kandahar, and that he
would spend the night of December 20 at a house inside the governor's
compound there. Station chief Gary Schroen sent word from Pakistan:
strike tonight—there may never be a better chance. The cruise missiles
were spinning in their chambers and locked on the target. But the intel-

ligence was one man's word and hundreds of people were sleeping in the compound that night. Tenet's desire to do away with bin Laden was overcome by his doubts. The word from on high was no go. Courage gave way to caution and gung-ho became go slow.

From the fall of 1998 onward, "the United States had the capability to remove Osama bin Laden from Afghanistan or to kill him," but it quailed when it came time to pull the trigger, said John MacGaffin, the number-two officer in the clandestine service earlier in the Clinton years. "The CIA knew bin Laden's location almost every day—sometimes within fifty miles, sometimes within fifty feet." At least fifteen American special-forces soldiers were killed or injured in training missions for the antici-pated assault. Commanders in the Pentagon and civilian leaders in the White House continually backed down from the political gamble of a military mission against bin Laden.

They left the job to the CIA. And the agency could not execute it.

The Afghans reported in the first weeks of 1999 that bin Laden was headed for a hunting camp south of Kandahar favored by wealthy falcon-ers. A spy satellite looked down on the camp on February 8 and fixed its location. A government aircraft from the United Arab Emirates—an American ally—was parked there. The lives of the emirs could not be sac-rificed to kill bin Laden and the cruise missiles stayed in their launchers.

The Afghans kept tracking bin Laden's travels in and out of Kandahar throughout April 1999. They locked onto him for thirty-six straight hours in May. Gary Schroen's agents delivered detailed reports on his whereabouts. The intelligence would never be better, said Tenet's deputy director of central intelligence, General John Gordon.

Three times the chance came to strike with cruise missiles. Three times Tenet said no. His confidence in the CIA's ability to pick its targets had been badly shaken days before.

A NATO bombing campaign against Serbia had been launched with the intent of forcing President Slobodan Milosevic to withdraw his troops from Kosovo. The CIA had been invited to pick targets for Amer-ican warplanes. The task was assigned to the agency's counterprolifera-tion division, the group that analyzed intelligence on the spread of weapons of mass destruction. The analysts identified their best target as the Yugoslav Federal Directorate of Supply and Procurement, at 2 Umet-nosti Boulevard in Belgrade. They used tourist maps to help them fix the location. The targeting flowed up through the CIA's machinery to the

Pentagon, and the coordinates were loaded onto a B-2 stealth bomber's circuitry.

The target was destroyed. But the CIA had misread its maps. The building was not Milosevic's military depot. It was the Chinese embassy.

"The bombing of the Chinese embassy in Belgrade was an acutely unpleasant experience for me," said Vice Admiral Thomas R. Wilson, who became director of the Defense Intelligence Agency in July 1999. "I was the one who showed the picture of the Chinese embassy to the President of the United States—among 900 other pictures I showed him—and said, 'We're going to bomb this, because it's the Yugoslav department of military procurement.' " He had gotten that picture from the CIA.

This mistake cut deeper than anyone could know. It would be a long time before the White House and the Pentagon would trust the agency to put anything—or anyone—in the crosshairs of an American missile.

"YOU AMERICANS ARE CRAZY"

The military and intelligence services of the United States were still set up to work against armies and nations—hard to kill, but easy to find on the map of the world. The new enemy was a man—easy to kill, but hard to find. He was a wraith moving around Afghanistan at night in a Land Cruiser.

President Clinton signed secret orders that he thought gave the CIA the power to kill bin Laden. In the throes of his impeachment, he daydreamed aloud about American ninjas rappelling out of helicopters to grab the Saudi. He made Tenet the commander of a war against one man.

Tenet fought his own doubts about the CIA's intelligence and its covert-action capabilities. But he had to devise a new plan of attack before bin Laden struck again. With his new counterterrorism chief, Cofer Black, he laid out a new strategy at the end of the summer of 1999. The agency would work with old friends and old foes around the world to kill bin Laden and his allies. Black deepened his ties to foreign military, intelligence, and security services in places such as Uzbekistan and Tajikistan, on the Afghan border. The hope was that they would help CIA officers put their boots on the ground inside Afghanistan.

The goal was to link up with the Afghan warrior Ahmed Shah Massoud at the redoubt he had held for nearly twenty years, since the early days of the Soviet occupation, deep in a mountain valley northeast of Kabul. Massoud, a noble and courageous fighter who wanted to be the king of Afghanistan, proposed a grand alliance to his old contacts from the agency. He offered to attack bin Laden's strongholds—and, with the help of the CIA and American arms, to overthrow the Taliban, the rabble of peasants, mullahs, and jihad veterans that ruled in Kabul. He could help the agency establish a base that would let it get bin Laden on its own. Cofer Black was all for it. His deputies were ready to go.

But the chances of failure were too high for Tenet. Once again, he said no—getting in and out was too risky. Reporters and foreign aid workers took those risks all the time in Afghanistan. The CIA at headquarters would not.

Massoud laughed when he heard that. "You Americans are crazy," he said. "You guys never change."

As the millennium approached, Jordan's intelligence service, created and long supported by the CIA, arrested sixteen men whom it believed were prepared to blow up hotels and tourist sites during Christmas. The agency thought that this plot prefigured a global attack by al Qaeda timed for the new year. Tenet went into overdrive, contacting twenty foreign intelligence chiefs in Europe, the Middle East, and Asia, telling them to arrest anyone associated with bin Laden. He sent an urgent message to all CIA officers overseas. "The threat could not be more real," it said. "Do whatever is necessary." The millennium passed without a catastrophic attack.

The president was briefed on the CIA's covert-action plans against bin Laden in February and March 2000, and he said the United States surely could do better. Tenet and Jim Pavitt, the new chief of the clandestine service, said they would need millions in new funds to do the job. The White House counterterrorism czar, Richard Clarke, thought that the CIA's will, not its wallet, was too thin; he said the agency had been given "a lot of money to do it and a long time to do it, and I didn't want to put more good money after bad."

The political season brought the return of the tradition inaugurated by President Truman: the intelligence briefing for the opposition. The acting deputy director of central intelligence, John McLaughlin, and the deputy chief of the counterterrorist center, Ben Bonk, went down to Crawford,

Texas, and led a four-hour seminar for Governor George W. Bush over Labor Day in September. It was Bonk's unhappy duty to tell the Republican candidate that Americans would die at the hands of foreign terrorists at some time in the coming four years.

The first deaths came five weeks later. On October 12, in the harbor of Aden, the capital of Yemen, two men in a speedboat stood and bowed as they approached an American warship, the USS *Cole*. The explosion killed seventeen, wounded forty, and ripped a $250 million hole in one of the American navy's most sophisticated vessels.

Al Qaeda was the obvious suspect.

The CIA set up a satellite office in Crawford to keep Bush posted on that attack and other world events during the long struggle over the 2000 election. In December, after the Supreme Court declared Bush the victor, Tenet personally briefed the president-elect on bin Laden. Bush remembered specifically asking Tenet if the CIA could kill the guy; Tenet replied that killing him would not end the threat he represented. Bush then met alone with Clinton for two hours to talk about national security.

Clinton remembers telling him: "Your biggest threat is bin Laden." Bush swore that he never heard those words.

48. "THE DARK SIDE"

"American intelligence is in trouble," James Monnier Simon, Jr., the assistant director of central intelligence for administration, warned shortly after Bush took office in January 2001. The CIA "has had its centrality compromised," he said. It lacked the power to collect and analyze the intelligence needed to protect the nation.

"The United States in 2001 is faced with a growing, almost dizzying disparity between its diminished capabilities and the burgeoning requirements of national security," Simon said. "The disconnect between what we are planning for and the likelihood of what the United States will face has never been so stark." The time would come when the president and Congress would have to explain "why a foreseeable disaster went unforeseen."

American intelligence was almost as divided and diffused as it had been in 1941. Eighteen consecutive directors of central intelligence had failed in their duty to unify it. Now the agency was about to fail as an institution of American government.

The CIA stood at seventeen thousand people, about the size of an army division, but the great majority of them were desk jockeys. Roughly one thousand people worked abroad in the clandestine service. Most officers lived comfortably in suburban cul-de-sacs and townhouses in the orbit of the Washington beltway. They were unused to drinking dirty water and sleeping on mud floors. They were unsuited for lives of sacrifice.

Two hundred officers had joined the CIA's clandestine service as char-

ter members in September 1947. Perhaps two hundred were capable and
courageous enough to tough it out in hardship posts in January 2001.
The full complement of CIA personnel focused on al Qaeda amounted to
perhaps twice that number. Most of them were staring at computers at
headquarters, cut off from the realities of the outside world by their antiquated information technologies. To expect them to protect the United
States from attack was at best a misplaced faith.

"A HOLLOW SHELL OF WORDS WITHOUT DEEDS"

Tenet was in the good graces at the White House, having formally renamed the CIA's headquarters the Bush Center for Intelligence after the
president's father, and the new commander in chief liked Tenet's tough-
guy attitude. But the agency received the barest support from President
Bush during his first nine months in office. He gave the Pentagon an immediate 7 percent budget increase. The CIA and the rest of the intelligence community received a boost of three-hundredths of one percent.
The difference was set in meetings at Donald Rumsfeld's Pentagon,
where not a single representative of the intelligence community was
present. Rumsfeld and Vice President Dick Cheney, partners in the politics of national security since the days of Nixon and Ford, held enormous
power in the new administration. They shared an abiding distrust in the
capabilities of the CIA.

Bush and Tenet met at the White House almost every morning at
eight. But nothing Tenet said about bin Laden fully captured the president's attention. Morning after morning at the eight o'clock briefing,
Tenet told the president, Cheney, and national security adviser Condoleezza Rice about portents of al Qaeda's plot to strike America. But
Bush was interested in other things—missile defense, Mexico, the Middle East. He was struck by no sense of emergency.

During the Reagan administration, when the president was hard of
hearing and the director of central intelligence mumbled unintelligibly,
aides used to joke that there was no telling what went on between them.
Bush and Tenet had no such infirmities. The problem lay in a lack of
clarity at the CIA and a lack of focus at the White House. *It's not enough*

to ring the bell, Richard Helms used to say. *You've got to make sure the other guy hears it.*

The noise—the volume and frequency of fragmentary and uncorroborated information about a coming terrorist attack—was deafening. Tenet could not convey a coherent signal to the president. As the klaxon sounded louder and louder in the spring and summer of 2001, every nerve and sinew of the agency strained to see and hear the threat clearly. Warnings were pouring in from Saudi Arabia and the Gulf states, Jordan and Israel, all over Europe. The CIA's frayed circuits were dangerously overloaded. Tips kept coming in. They're going to hit Boston. They're going to hit London. They're going to hit New York. "When these attacks occur, as they likely will," Clarke e-mailed Rice on May 29, "we will wonder what more we could have done to stop them."

The agency feared an onslaught overseas during the July 4 holiday, when American embassies across the world traditionally let down their defenses and open their doors to celebrate the American Revolution. In the weeks before the holiday, Tenet had called upon the chiefs of foreign intelligence services in Amman, Cairo, Islamabad, Rome, and Ankara to try to destroy known and suspected cells of al Qaeda and its affiliates throughout the world. The CIA would supply the intelligence, and the foreign services would make the arrests. A handful of suspected terrorists were jailed in the Gulf States and in Italy. Maybe the arrests had disrupted plans of attack against two or three American embassies, Tenet told the White House. Maybe not. Impossible to tell.

Tenet now had to make a life-and-death decisions unlike any that had ever confronted a director of central intelligence. A year before, after a seven-year struggle between the CIA and the Pentagon, a small pilotless aircraft equipped with video cameras and spy sensors called the Predator had been declared ready to be deployed over Afghanistan. The first flight had come on September 7, 2000. Now the agency and the air force had figured out how to put antitank missiles on the Predator. In theory, for an investment of a few million dollars a CIA officer at headquarters would soon be able to hunt and kill bin Laden with a video screen and a joystick. But what was the chain of command? Tenet wondered. Who gives the go-ahead? Who pulls the trigger? Tenet thought he had no license to kill. The idea of the CIA launching a remote-control assassination on its own authority appalled him. The agency had made too many mistakes picking targets in the past.

On August 1, 2001, the Deputies Committee—the second-echelon national-security team—decided that it would be legal for the CIA to kill bin Laden with the Predator, an act of national self-defense. But the agency came back with more questions. Who would pay for it? Who would arm the aircraft? Who would be the air traffic controller? Who would play the roles of pilot and missile man? The hand-wringing drove counterterrorism czar Clarke crazy. "Either al Qaeda is a threat worth acting against or it is not," he fumed. "CIA leadership has to decide which it is and cease these bi-polar mood swings."

The agency never had answered a question put to it by President Bush: could an attack come in the United States? Now was the time: on August 6, the president's daily brief began with the headline "Bin Ladin Determined to Strike in US." The warning beneath the headline was a very weak piece of reporting. The freshest intelligence in it dated from 1999. It was a work of history, not a news bulletin. The president continued his vacation, chopping brush in Crawford, unwinding for five weeks.

The long White House holiday ended on Tuesday, September 4, when Bush's first-string national security team, the Principals Committee, sat down together for the first meeting it ever held on the threat of bin Laden and al Qaeda. Clarke sent an agonized note that morning to Condoleezza Rice, begging the national security adviser to envision hundreds of Americans lying dead from the next attack. He said the agency had become "a hollow shell of words without deeds," relying on foreign governments to stop bin Laden, leaving the United States "waiting for the big attack." He implored her to move the CIA to action that day.

"WE'RE AT WAR"

Intelligence fails because it is human, no stronger than the power of one mind to understand another. Garrett Jones, the CIA station chief during the disastrous American expedition in Somalia, put it plainly: "There are going to be screw-ups, mistakes, confusion, and missteps," he said. "One hopes they won't be fatal."

September 11 was the catastrophic failure Tenet had predicted three years before. It was a systemic failure of American government—the White House, the National Security Council, the FBI, the Federal Aviation Administration, the Immigration and Naturalization Service, the congressional intelligence committees. It was a failure of policy and diplomacy. It was a failure of the reporters who covered the government to understand and convey its disarray to their readers. But above all it was a failure to know the enemy. It was the Pearl Harbor that the CIA had been created to prevent.

Tenet and his counterterror chief, Cofer Black, were at Camp David on Saturday, September 15, laying out a plan to send CIA officers into Afghanistan to work with local warlords against al Qaeda. The director returned to headquarters late Sunday and issued a proclamation to his troops: "We're at war."

The agency, as Cheney said that morning, went over to "the dark side." On Monday, September 17, President Bush issued a fourteen-page top secret directive to Tenet and the CIA, ordering the agency to hunt, capture, imprison, and interrogate suspects around the world. It set no limits on what the agency could do. It was the foundation for a system of secret prisons where CIA officers and contractors used techniques that included torture. One CIA contractor was convicted of beating an Afghan prisoner to death. This was not the role of a civilian intelligence service in a democratic society. But it is clearly what the White House wanted the CIA to do.

The CIA had run secret interrogation centers before—beginning in 1950, in Germany, Japan, and Panama. It had participated in the torture of captured enemy combatants before—beginning in 1967, under the Phoenix program in Vietnam. It had kidnapped suspected terrorists and assassins before—most famously in 1997, in the case of Mir Amal Kansi, the killer of two CIA officers. But Bush gave the agency a new and extraordinary authority: to turn kidnapped suspects over to foreign security services for interrogation and torture, and to rely on the confessions they extracted. As I wrote in *The New York Times* on October 7, 2001: "American intelligence may have to rely on its liaisons with the world's toughest foreign services, men who can look and think and act like terrorists. If someone is going to interrogate a man in a basement in Cairo or Quetta, it will be an Egyptian or a Pakistani officer. American intelligence will take the information without asking a lot of lawyerly questions."

Under Bush's order, the CIA began to function as a global military police, throwing hundreds of suspects into secret jails in Afghanistan, Thailand, Poland, and inside the American military prison in Guantánamo,
Cuba. It handed hundreds more prisoners off to the intelligence services
in Egypt, Pakistan, Jordan, and Syria for interrogations. The gloves were
off. "Our war on terror begins with al Qaeda, but it does not end there,"
Bush told the nation in an address to a joint session of Congress on September 20. "It will not end until every terrorist group of global reach has
been found, stopped, and defeated."

"I COULD *NOT* NOT DO THIS"

There was a war at home as well, and the CIA was part of it. After 9/11,
James Monnier Simon, Jr., the assistant director of central intelligence,
was placed in charge of homeland security for the intelligence community. He went to a meeting at the White House with Attorney General
John Ashcroft. The subject was the creation of national identity cards for
Americans. "What would it have? Well, a thumbprint," Simon said.
"Blood type would be useful, as would a retinal scan. We would want
your picture taken a special way so that we could pick your face out of
a crowd even if you were wearing a disguise. We would want your voice
print, because the technology is coming up that will pick your voice out
of every other voice in all the cell phones on earth, and your voice is
unique. In fact, we would like to have a bit of your DNA in there, so if
something ever happens to you we can identify the body. By the way,
we would want the chip to tell us where this card is, so that if we needed
to find you we could. Then it dawned on us that if we did that, you could
set the card down. So we would put the chip in your bloodstream."

Where would this drive for security end? Simon wondered. The
names of Stalin's and Hitler's intelligence services sprang to his mind. "It
could in fact end up being the KGB, NKVD, Gestapo," he said. "We, the
people, need to watch and be involved." Precisely how the American
people were supposed to watch was a problematic question. What a representative of the director of central intelligence was doing at the White
House discussing the implantation of microchips in American citizens

was another. The national identity card never materialized. But Congress did give the CIA new legal powers to spy on people in the United States. The agency was now permitted to read secret grand jury testimony, without a judge's prior approval, and obtain private records of institutions and corporations. The agency used the authority to request and receive banking and credit data on American citizens and companies from financial corporations. The CIA had never had the formal power to spy inside the borders of the United States before. It did now.

Tenet talked to General Michael Hayden, the director of the National Security Agency, shortly after the attacks. "Is there anything more you can do?" he asked. "Not within my current authorities," Hayden answered. Tenet then "invited me to come down and talk to the administration about what more could be done." Hayden came up with a plan to eavesdrop on the communications of suspected terrorists within the United States without judicial warrants. It was arguably illegal but arguably justified on a theory of "hot pursuit"—chasing suspects beyond the borders of the map and outside the limits of the law. President Bush ordered him to execute the plan on October 4, 2001. It had to be done, Hayden said: "I could *not* not do this." The NSA once again began to spy within the United States.

Cofer Black ordered his counterterror corps to bring him bin Laden's head in a box. The Counterterrorist Center, born fifteen years before as a small freestanding unit of the clandestine service, still working in the basement at headquarters, was now the heart of the CIA. Retired officers returned to duty and new recruits joined the agency's tiny cadre of paramilitary commandos. They flew into Afghanistan to make war. The agency's men handed out millions of dollars to marshal the loyalties of Afghan tribal leaders. They served nobly for a few months as advance troops for the American occupation of Afghanistan.

By the third week of November 2001, the American military knocked out the political leadership of the Taliban, leaving behind the rank and file, but paving the way for a new government in Kabul. It left tens of thousands of Taliban loyalists unscathed. They trimmed their beards and melted into the villages; they would return when the Americans began to tire of their war in Afghanistan. They would live to fight again.

It took eleven weeks to organize the hunt for Osama bin Laden. When that hunt began in earnest, I was in eastern Afghanistan, in and around Jalalabad, where I had traveled on five trips over the years. An old acquaintance named Haji Abdul Qadir had just reclaimed his post as the provincial governor, two days after the fall of the Taliban. Haji Qadir was an exemplar of Afghan democracy. A well-educated and highly cultured Pathan tribal leader in his early sixties, a wealthy dealer in opium and weapons and other basic staples of the Afghan economy, he had been a CIA-supported commander in the fight against the Soviet occupation, the governor of his province from 1992 to 1996, and a close associate of the Taliban in their time. He personally welcomed Osama bin Laden to Afghanistan and helped him establish a compound outside Jalalabad. Now he welcomed the American occupation. Haji Qadir was a good host. We walked in the gardens of the governor's palace, through swayback palms and feathery tamarisks. He was expecting a visit from his American friends any day now, and he was looking forward to the renewal of old ties and the ritual exchange of cash for information.

Haji Qadir had gathered the village elders of his province at the governor's palace. On November 24, they reported that bin Laden and the Arab fighters of al Qaeda were holed up in an isolated mountain hideout thirty-five miles south-by-southwest of the city, near the village of Tora Bora.

On November 28, at about five in the morning, as the first call to prayer sounded, a small plane landed at the rocket-pocked runway of the Jalalabad airport with a delegation of CIA and Special Forces officers aboard. They were carrying bales of $100 bills. They met with Haji Zaman, the newly appointed Jalalabad commander of the self-proclaimed government. He told the Americans he was "90 percent sure" that bin Laden was in Tora Bora. The dusty road south from Jalalabad to Tora Bora ended in a rough mountain trail impassable to all but men and mules. The trailhead connected with a network of smugglers' routes leading to mountain passes into Pakistan. Those routes had been a supply line for the Afghan rebels, and Tora Bora had been a place of great renown in the fight against the Soviets. A cave complex dug deep into the mountainside had been built, with the CIA's assistance, to meet NATO military standards. An American commander with orders to destroy Tora Bora would have been well advised to use a tactical nuclear weapon. A CIA officer with orders to capture bin Laden would have needed to requisition the Tenth Mountain Division.

On December 5, as American B-52 bombers pounded away at that stony redoubt, I watched the attack from a few miles' distance. I wanted to see bin Laden's head on a pike myself. He was within the agency's reach, but beyond its grasp. He could only be taken by siege, and the CIA could not mount one. Those who went after al Qaeda in Afghanistan were the best the agency had, but they were too few. They had come armed with lots of cash, but too little intelligence. The futility of hunting bin Laden with dumb bombs was soon made manifest. Moving from camp to camp in the Afghan borderlands, bin Laden was protected by a phalanx of hundreds of battle-hardened Afghan fighters and thousands of Pathan tribesmen who would sooner die than betray him. He had the CIA outnumbered and outmaneuvered in Afghanistan, and he escaped.

Tenet was red-eyed, furious, gnawing on cigar stubs, near the limits of his endurance. His counterterror troops were pushed beyond their capacity. Alongside American special-operations soldiers, they were hunting, capturing, and killing bin Laden's lieutenants and foot soldiers in Afghanistan, Pakistan, Saudi Arabia, Yemen, and Indonesia. But they started hitting the wrong targets again. Armed Predator attacks killed at least twenty-four innocent Afghans in January and February 2002; the CIA handed out $1,000 in reparations to each of their families. Fanning out across Europe, Africa, and Asia, working with every friendly foreign intelligence service on earth, CIA officers snatched and grabbed more than three thousand people in more than one hundred countries in the year after 9/11, Tenet said. "Not everyone arrested was a terrorist," he cautioned. "Some have been released. But this worldwide rousting of al Qaeda definitely disrupted its operations." That was inarguable. But the fact remained that as few as fourteen men among the three thousand seized were high-ranking authority figures within al Qaeda and its affiliates. Along with them, the agency jailed hundreds of nobodies. They became ghost prisoners in the war on terror.

The focus and intensity of the mission to kill or capture bin Laden began to ebb in March 2002, after the failed assault on Tora Bora. The CIA had been commanded by the White House to turn its attention to Iraq. The agency responded with a fiasco far more fatal to its fortunes than the 9/11 attacks.

49. "A GRAVE MISTAKE"

"There is no doubt that Saddam Hussein now has weapons of mass destruction," Vice President Dick Cheney said on August 26, 2002. "There is no doubt he is amassing them to use against our friends, against our allies, and against us." Secretary of Defense Don Rumsfeld said the same: "We know they have weapons of mass destruction," he said. "There isn't any debate about it."

Tenet provided his own grim warnings in a secret hearing before the Senate intelligence committee on September 17: "Iraq provided al Qaeda with various kinds of training—combat, bomb-making, and chemical, biological, radiological and nuclear." He based that statement on the confessions of a single source—Ibn al-Shakh al-Libi, a fringe player who had been beaten, stuffed in a two-foot-square box for seventeen hours, and threatened with prolonged torture. The prisoner had recanted after the threat of torture receded. Tenet did not correct the record.

On October 7, on the eve of congressional debate over whether to go to war with Iraq, President Bush said that Iraq "possesses and produces chemical and biological weapons." He went on to warn that "Iraq could decide on any given day to provide a biological or chemical weapon to a terrorist group or individual terrorist." This created a dilemma for Tenet. Days before, his deputy, John McLaughlin, had contradicted the president in testimony to the Senate intelligence committee. On orders from the White House, Tenet issued a statement saying, "There is no inconsistency between our view of Saddam's growing threat and the view as expressed by the President in his speech."

It was the last thing he should have said, and he knew it. "It was the wrong thing to do," Tenet testified almost four years later. Throughout his years of public service, Tenet had been a fundamentally decent man. But under the enormous pressures he faced after 9/11, his one flaw, his all-consuming desire to please his superiors, became a fault line. Tenet's character cracked, and the CIA did too. Under his leadership, the agency produced the worst body of work in its long history: a special national intelligence estimate titled "Iraq's Continuing Programs for Weapons of Mass Destruction."

A national estimate is the best judgment of the American intelligence community, produced and directed by the CIA, and distributed with the authority and imprimatur of the director of central intelligence. It is his word.

The estimate was commissioned by members of the Senate intelligence committee, which thought it might be wise to review the evidence before going to war. At their request, the CIA's analysts spent three weeks gathering and reviewing everything the agency knew from spy satellites; from foreign intelligence services; and from recruited Iraqi agents, defectors, and volunteers. The CIA reported in October 2002 that the threat was incalculable. "Baghdad has chemical and biological weapons," the top secret estimate said. Saddam had bolstered his missile technology, bulked up his deadly stockpiles, and restarted his nuclear weapons program. "If Baghdad acquires sufficient fissile material from abroad," said the estimate, "it could make a nuclear weapon within several months." And most terrifying of all, the CIA warned that Iraq could conduct chemical and biological attacks inside the United States.

The CIA confirmed everything the White House was saying. But the agency was saying far more than it knew. "We did not have many Iraqi sources," Jim Pavitt, the chief of the clandestine service, admitted two years later. "We had less than a handful." The agency produced a ton of analysis from an ounce of intelligence. That might have worked if the ounce been solid gold and not pure dross.

The CIA as an institution was betting that American soldiers or spies would find the evidence after the invasion of Iraq. It was a hell of a gamble. It would have appalled Richard Helms, who died at age eighty-nine on October 22, 2002, after the estimate was completed. In tribute to his legacy, the CIA reprinted parts of a speech he had made years before. The full text was buried in the agency's archives, but its power had not dimmed. "It is sometimes difficult for us to understand the intensity of our public critics," Helms had said. "Criticism of our efficiency is one thing, criticism of our responsibility quite another. I believe that we are, as an important arm of government, a legitimate object of public concern. . . . I find it most painful, however, when public debate lessens our usefulness to the nation by casting doubt on our integrity and objectivity. If we are not believed, we have no purpose."

"WE HAD NO ANSWERS"

To understand how the CIA was able to say that Iraq's weapons of mass destruction existed, go back to 1991 and the end of the first Gulf war. After the war came seven years of intensive international scrutiny, led by United Nations inspectors looking for evidence that Saddam had a hidden arsenal. They combed the country and captured what they could.

In the mid-1990s, Saddam feared international economic sanctions more than another attack from the United States. He destroyed his weapons of mass destruction in compliance with the commands of the United Nations. But he kept his weapons-production facilities, he lied about it, and the United States and the United Nations knew he was lying. That legacy of lying caused the inspectors and the CIA to distrust everything Iraq did.

In 1995, General Hussein Kamal, Saddam's son-in-law, defected along with a few of his aides. Kamal confirmed that Saddam had destroyed the weapons. The CIA disregarded what he said, judging it as deception. The fact that Kamal went back to Iraq and was assassinated by his father-in-law did not alter the agency's belief.

His aides told the CIA about Iraq's National Monitoring Directorate, which aimed to conceal Saddam's military intentions and capabilities from the world. The CIA wanted to pierce that system of concealment, and a stroke of good fortune made it possible. Rolf Ekeus, the chairman of the United Nations inspection team, was Swedish. So was Ericsson, the telecommunications giant that made the walkie-talkies used by the National Monitoring Directorate. The CIA, the NSA, Ekeus, and Ericsson devised a way to tap the Iraqis' telecommunications. In March 1998, a

CIA officer in the guise of a United Nations weapons inspector went to Baghdad and installed the eavesdropping system. Intercepted conversations were beamed to a computer in Bahrain, which searched for key words such as *missile* and *chemical*. A sterling operation, with one exception: the CIA learned nothing about the existence of any weapons of mass destruction in Iraq.

That spring, the weapons inspectors found what they thought were remnants of VX nerve gas in Iraqi missile warheads. Their report was leaked to *The Washington Post*. Baghdad called it an American lie. Charles Duelfer, who had led some of the inspection teams in the 1990s and returned to Iraq as Tenet's lead weapons hunter in 2004, concluded, "Ultimately, I think, the Iraqis were right. They did not weaponize VX."

The confrontation over the VX report was a turning point. Iraq no longer trusted the inspectors, who had never trusted Iraq. In December 1998, the United Nations pulled its inspectors out and the United States once again started bombing Baghdad. The information the CIA had gleaned from its Ericsson taps was used to target American missiles on the people and institutions it penetrated—including the home of the man who ran the National Monitoring Directorate.

Iraq declared to the United Nations that it had rid itself of weapons of mass destruction. The declarations were essentially accurate; the substantial violations were minor. But Saddam had been deliberately ambiguous about his arsenal, fearing he would stand naked before his enemies if they believed he did not have the capability to produce the weapons. He *wanted* the United States, his foes in Israel and Iran, his internal enemies, and above all his own troops to believe that he still had the weapons. Illusion was his best deterrent and his last defense against attack.

This was the state of affairs that confronted the CIA after 9/11. Its last reliable reports from inside Iraq were very old news. "We were bereft of any human intelligence—zero, nada, in terms of agents on the ground," said David Kay, who also had led the United Nations team and preceded Duelfer as the CIA's chief weapons hunter in Iraq. The White House wanted answers. "We had no answers," Kay said.

Then, in 2002, "suddenly, what looked like a golden source of human intelligence stepped forward: defectors," he said. "These defectors coming out of Saddam's regime told us about his weapons programs and weapons progress. Not all of them came out to the United States; many came out to the intelligence services of France, Germany, Britain, and other countries. The information seemed to be unbelievably good." One of the most riveting stories was the one about mobile biological weapons laboratories. The source was an Iraqi in the hands of the German intelligence service, code-named Curveball.

"The Iraqi defectors understood two things: one, we shared a mutual interest in regime replacement; and, two, the U.S. was very concerned about weapons of mass destruction in Iraq," Kay said. "So they told us about weapons in order to get us to move against Saddam. It was basic Newtonian physics: give me a big enough lever and a fulcrum, and I can move the world."

Only one thing was worse than having no sources, and that was to be seduced by sources telling lies.

The clandestine service had produced little information on Iraq. The analysts accepted whatever supported the case for war. They swallowed secondhand and thirdhand hearsay that conformed to the president's plans. Absence of evidence was not evidence of absence for the agency. Saddam once had the weapons. The defectors said he still had them. Therefore he had them. The CIA as an institution desperately sought the White House's attention and approval. It did so by telling the president what he wanted to hear.

"FACTS AND CONCLUSIONS BASED ON SOLID INTELLIGENCE"

President Bush presented the CIA's case and more in his State of the Union speech on January 28, 2003: Saddam Hussein had biological weapons sufficient to kill millions, chemical weapons to kill countless thousands, mobile biological weapons labs designed to produce germ-warfare agents. "Saddam Hussein recently sought significant quantities of uranium from Africa," he said. "Our intelligence sources tell us that he has attempted to purchase high-strength aluminum tubes suitable for nuclear weapons production."

All of this was terrifying. None of it was true.

On the eve of the war, on February 5, 2003, Secretary of State Colin

Powell, whose international stature was unmatched in the Bush administration, went to the United Nations. With George Tenet at his shoulder, ever the loyal aide, his presence a silent affirmation—and the American ambassador to the United Nations, the future director of national intelligence, John Negroponte, at his side—the secretary of state began: "Every statement I make today is backed up by sources, solid sources. These are not assertions. What we are giving you are facts and conclusions based on solid intelligence."

Powell said: "There can be no doubt that Saddam Hussein has biological weapons and he has the ability to dispense these lethal poisons and diseases in ways that can cause massive death and destruction." He again warned of Iraq's mobile biological-weapons laboratories, how they could park in a shed, make their poison, and move on undetected. He said Saddam had enough lethal chemical weaponry to fill sixteen thousand battlefield rockets. And perhaps worst of all, there was the threat of the "much more sinister nexus between Iraq and the al Qaeda terrorist network."

This was not a selective use of intelligence. It was not "cherry-picking." It was not fixing the facts to fit the war plans. It was what the intelligence said, the best intelligence the agency had to offer. Powell had spent days and nights with Tenet, checking and rechecking the CIA's reporting. Tenet looked him in the eye and told him it was rock solid.

On March 20, 2003, the war began ahead of schedule with a bad tip from the CIA. Tenet ran to the White House with a flash report that Saddam Hussein was hiding at a compound south of Baghdad called Doura Farms. The president ordered the Pentagon to destroy the compound. The bunker-busting bombs and the cruise missiles rained down. Vice President Cheney said, "I think we did get Saddam Hussein. He was seen being dug out of the rubble and wasn't able to breathe." It was a false report: Saddam was nowhere to be found. The first targeting failure of the war was not the last. On April 7, 2003, the CIA reported that Saddam and his sons were meeting at a house next to the Saa Restaurant in the Mansur district of Baghdad. The air force dropped four one-ton bombs on the house. Saddam was not there either. Eighteen innocent civilians were killed.

The agency had predicted that thousands of Iraqi soldiers and their commanders would surrender all along the route of the attack once it was launched over the border from Kuwait. But the American invading force had to fight its way through every town of any size on the road to Baghdad. The CIA envisioned the wholesale capitulation of Iraqi military units, and its intelligence was specific: the Iraqi division based at An Nasiriya would lay down its arms. The first American troops into the city were ambushed; eighteen marines were killed, some by friendly fire, in the first major combat of the war. American forces were told they would be welcomed by cheering Iraqis waving American flags—the clandestine service would provide the flags—and showered with candy and flowers on the streets of Baghdad. In time, they were met with bullets and bombs.

The CIA compiled a list of 946 suspect sites where Saddam's arsenals of mass destruction might be found. American soldiers were wounded and killed hunting for the weapons that never were. The agency missed the threat posed by the assault rifles and rocket-propelled grenades stockpiled by the Fedayeen, the irregular forces led by Saddam's son Uday Hussein. The failure led to the first major series of combat deaths of American soldiers. "The Fedayeen and other paramilitary forces proved more of a threat than anyone had expected," wrote the authors of *On Point,* the U.S. Army's official history of the invasion of Iraq. "The intelligence and operations communities had never anticipated how ferocious, tenacious, and fanatical they would be."

The CIA organized a paramilitary squad of Iraqis called the Scorpions to conduct sabotage before and during the war. During the occupation, the Scorpions distinguished themselves by beating an Iraqi general to death. Major General Abed Hamed Mowhoush, who was suspected of directing insurgent attacks but had turned himself in voluntarily to American forces, was clubbed senseless with sledgehammer handles by the Scorpions in the presence of a CIA officer who led them, a retired Special Forces officer who had signed on with the agency for the war. Mowhoush died of his injuries two days later, on November 26, 2003. Earlier that month, an Iraqi prisoner named Manadal al-Jamadi was tortured to death at the Abu Ghraib prison while in the custody of a CIA officer. The brutal interrogations were part of what the White House had called upon the agency to do when the gloves came off.

As the CIA concluded three years after the invasion, the American occupation of Iraq became "the cause celebre for jihadists, breeding a deep resentment of U.S. involvement in the Muslim world and cultivating supporters for the global jihadist movement." The assessment came far too late to be much use to American forces. "Every Army of liberation has a half-life beyond which it turns into an Army of occupation," wrote Lieutenant General David H. Petraeus, who commanded the 101st Airborne Division in the first year of the war, oversaw the effort to train the Iraqi army on a second tour, and returned as the commander of American forces in 2007.

"Intelligence is the key to success," he said. Without it, military operations fall into "a catastrophic downward spiral."

"JUST GUESSING"

The agency went pouring into Baghdad when the war was over. "As Iraq transitions from tyranny to self-determination, Baghdad is home to the largest CIA station since the Vietnam war," proclaimed Jim Pavitt, the chief of the clandestine service. "I am extremely proud of our performance in Iraq, and of our role in liberating its people from decades of repression." The officers at the Baghdad station worked with Special Forces soldiers, trying to create a new political climate in Iraq, selecting local leaders, paying off politicians, trying to rebuild society at the grass roots. They tried to work with their British counterparts to create a new Iraqi intelligence service. But very little came of all that. When the Iraqi insurgency began to rise up against the American occupation, those projects started to fall apart and the leadership at the CIA's Baghdad station began breaking down.

As the occupation spun out of control, the CIA's officers found themselves pinned down at the American embassy compound in the capital, unable to escape the protection of the high walls and razor wire. They became prisoners of the Green Zone, powerless to comprehend the Iraqi insurgency, spending far too many hours drinking at the Babylon bar, run by the Baghdad station. Many would not accept a rotation of more than one to three months, barely enough time to get their bearings in Baghdad.

The station, whose ranks approached five hundred officers, ran through three chiefs in the course of a year. The CIA simply could not find a replacement for the first station chief in 2003. "They had grave,

grave difficulty finding a competent individual to go out," said Larry Crandall, a veteran Foreign Service officer who had worked closely with the CIA during the Afghan jihad and served as the number-two manager of the $18 billion American reconstruction program in Iraq. The agency had no one from the clandestine service willing or able to serve. It finally selected an analyst with next to no experience in running operations. He lasted for a matter of months. It was an extraordinary failure of leadership in a time of war.

The CIA sent the best of the American inspectors who had hunted down Saddam's arsenal in the 1990s back to Iraq. David Kay led a team of 1,400 specialists, the Iraq Survey Group, working directly for the director of central intelligence. Tenet continued to stand by the CIA's reporting, rejecting the growing criticism as "misinformed, misleading, and just plain wrong." But the survey group scoured Iraq and found nothing. When Kay returned to report that, Tenet put him in purgatory. Kay nonetheless went before the Senate Armed Services Committee on January 28, 2004, and spoke the truth.

"We were almost all wrong," he said.

When it became certain that the agency had only imagined Iraq's doomsday arsenal, a moral exhaustion began to settle over the CIA. A dark bitter anger overtook the fiery spirit that had gripped it after 9/11. It was evident that it no longer mattered much to the White House or the Pentagon or the State Department what the agency had to say.

President Bush disdained the CIA's increasingly dire reports on the course of the occupation. The agency was "just guessing," he said.

This was a death knell. *If we are not believed, we have no purpose.*

"THE EVIDENCE WAS COMPLETELY FRAIL"

"We're at war," said Judge Laurence Silberman, whom President Bush appointed on February 6, 2004, to lead an investigation into the ways in which the CIA had conjured Saddam's weaponry. "If the American Army had made a mistake anywhere near as bad as our intelligence community, we would expect generals to be cashiered."

He continued: "It would have been eminently justifiable to have told the President and the Congress that it was likely that Saddam had weapons of mass destruction based on his past use, insufficient indications of destruction, and his deceptive behavior." But the CIA had made "a grave, grave mistake in concluding that there was a ninety percent degree of certainty that he had weapons of mass destruction. And it was a grave mistake not based on hindsight," he said. "The evidence was completely frail, some quite faulty, and their tradecraft wasn't good. Moreover, there was such an abysmal lack of internal communication within the intelligence community that often the left hand didn't know what the right hand was doing."

The CIA had reached its conclusions on Iraqi chemical weapons solely on the basis of misinterpreted pictures of Iraqi tanker trucks. The CIA had based its conclusions on Iraqi biological weapons on one source— Curveball. The CIA had based its conclusions on Iraqi nuclear weapons almost entirely on Saddam's importation of aluminum tubes intended for conventional rocketry. "It's almost shockingly wrong to conclude that those aluminum tubes were appropriate or designed for centrifuges for nuclear weapons," Judge Silberman said.

"What was such a disaster," he said, "was for Colin Powell to have gone to the United Nations and set forth that absolutely unmistakable certain case which was based on really bad, bad stuff."

Judge Silberman and his presidential commission received unprecedented permission to read every article on Iraq's weapons of mass destruction from the president's daily brief. They found that the CIA's reports for the president's eyes were no different from the rest of its work, including the infamous estimate—except in one regard. They were "even more misleading," the commission found. They were, "if anything, more alarmist and less nuanced." The president's daily briefs, "with their attention-grabbing headlines and drumbeat of repetition, left an impression of many corroborating reports where in fact there were very few sources. . . . In ways both subtle and not so subtle, the daily reports seemed to be 'selling' intelligence—in order to keep its customers, or at least the First Customer, interested."

"WE DIDN'T GET THE JOB DONE"

George Tenet saw that his time was over. He had done his best to revive and renew the agency. Yet he would always be remembered for one thing: reassuring the president that the CIA had "slam dunk" evidence on Iraq's weapons of mass destruction. "Those were the two dumbest words I ever said," Tenet reflected. No matter how long he lived, no matter what good deeds he might do in years to come, they would feature in the first paragraph of his obituary.

Tenet, to his credit, asked Richard Kerr, the former deputy director of central intelligence, to investigate what had gone wrong with the Iraq estimate. The study was classified upon completion in July 2004 and stayed that way for nearly two years thereafter. When it was unsealed, it was clear why the agency had kept it under wraps. It was an epitaph. It said the CIA had all but ceased to be when the cold war came to a close; the fall of the Soviet Union had an impact on the agency "analogous to the effect of the meteor strikes on the dinosaurs."

In the case of Iraq, and in many other cases as well, analysts were routinely forced to "rely on reporting whose sourcing was misleading and even unreliable." In the infamous case of Curveball, CIA officers had fair warning that the man was a liar. This warning went unheeded. That was not dereliction of duty, but it came close.

The clandestine service routinely "used different descriptions for the same source," so that the readers of its reports believed they had three corroborating sources of information when they had one. This was not fraud, but it came close.

The CIA had been working on the questions of the Iraqi arsenal for more than a decade, and yet Tenet had gone to George Bush and Colin Powell on the eve of war brandishing falsehoods cloaked as hard truths. That was not a crime, but it came close.

Tragically, this was Tenet's legacy. He finally conceded that the CIA was wrong—not for "political reasons or a craven desire to lead the country to war" but because of its incompetence. "We didn't get the job done," he said.

The meaning of that failure was left for the CIA's chief weapons inspector, David Kay, to explain in full. "We think intelligence is important to win wars," he said. "Wars are not won by intelligence. They're won by the blood, treasure, courage of the young men and women that we put in the field. . . . What intelligence really does when it is working well is to help avoid wars." That, in the end, was the ultimate intelligence failure.

50. "THE BURIAL CEREMONY"

On July 8, 2004, seven years after he took office, George Tenet resigned. In his farewell at CIA headquarters, he summoned up the words of Teddy Roosevelt: *It is not the critic who counts, nor the man who points out how the strong man stumbles, or where the doer of deeds could have done them better. The credit belongs to the man who is actually in the arena, whose face is marred by dust and sweat and blood.* Richard Nixon had quoted the same speech the day before he left the White House in disgrace.

Tenet retreated to write a painful personal memoir of his time at the CIA. It was a prideful, bitter book. He justly boasted of the CIA's success—with invaluable help from British intelligence—at dismantling secret weapons programs in Pakistan and Libya. He maintained that he had transformed the agency from a shambles into a dynamo. But the machine had broken down under intolerable pressure. Tenet could not strike at al Qaeda before 9/11: "In the absence of hard intelligence," he wrote, "covert action is a fool's game." And ever since the attacks, he had been swamped by tidal waves of threats that never materialized. Every day he conveyed the newest fears to the White House, and "you could drive yourself crazy believing all or even half" of what he reported. He nearly had. Gripped by uncertainty, he and the CIA had convinced themselves that Iraq's arsenal existed. "We were prisoners of our own history," he wrote, for the only hard facts they had were four years old. He confessed error, but it was a condemned man's plea for absolution. Tenet came to believe that the White House wanted to blame the decision to go to war on him. It was too great a weight to bear.

And now the critic took his turn as the man in the arena.

Porter Goss had never been a great success at the CIA. Recruited in his junior year at Yale in 1959, he joined the clandestine service and served under Allen Dulles, John McCone, and Richard Helms. He had worked in the Latin American division for a decade, focused on Cuba, Haiti, the Dominican Republic, and Mexico. The highlight of his time in the Miami station was running Cuban agents on and off the island in small boats under the cover of the night in the fall of 1962.

Nine years later, Goss was serving at the London station when a bacterial infection seized his heart and lungs and nearly killed him. He retired, recovered, bought a small newspaper in Florida, and parlayed the paper into a seat in Congress in 1988. He had a net worth of $14 million, a gentleman's farm in Virginia, an estate on Long Island Sound, and a viceroy's dominion over the CIA as chairman of the House intelligence committee.

He was modest about his accomplishments at the agency. "I couldn't get a job with CIA today," he said in 2003. "I am not qualified." He was right about that. But he had decided that he and he alone should be the next director of central intelligence. He had taken aim at Tenet with a vicious fusillade. His weapons were the words of the intelligence committee's annual report on the agency.

"IT WILL TAKE US ANOTHER FIVE YEARS"

Published on June 21, 2004, three weeks before Tenet stepped down, the Goss report warned that the clandestine service was becoming "a stilted bureaucracy incapable of even the slightest bit of success." Though 138,000 Americans had applied to work at the CIA in the previous year, few made the grade as spies. Tenet had just testified that "it will take us another five years of work to have the kind of clandestine service our country needs."

Goss seized on that sad truth: "We are now in the eighth year of rebuild, and still we are more than five years away from being healthy. This is tragic."

Goss then turned his fire on the CIA's intelligence directorate for producing spot news of scant value instead of the long-range strategic intelligence that had been the initial reason for creating the agency. Goss was

right about that, too—and everyone in the intelligence world knew it.
"We haven't done strategic intelligence for so long that most of our analysts don't know how to do it anymore," said Carl W. Ford, Jr., the assistant secretary of state for intelligence and research from May 2001 to
October 2003, and a former CIA officer.

"As long as we rate intelligence more for its volume than its quality,
we will continue to turn out the $40 billion pile of crap we have become
famous for," Ford said. He was incensed that the agency, while transfixed
by the chimerical arsenal of Saddam Hussein, had learned nothing about
the nuclear weapons programs of the rest of the president's axis of evil.
"We probably knew a hundred times more about Iraq's nuclear program
than Iran's and a thousand times more than Korea's," Ford said. North
Korea was a blank, as it had always been. The CIA had tried to rebuild a
network of agents in Iran but failed. Now Iran was a blank, too; the
agency actually knew less about those nuclear programs than it had
known five or ten years before.

The CIA was in ruins, Ford said: "It's broken. It's so broken that nobody wants to believe it." The Goss report made that clear. "There is a
dysfunctional denial of any need for corrective action," it said. "CIA continues down a road leading over a proverbial cliff."

Goss was sure he had the answers. He knew that the CIA had been
fooling itself and others about the quality of its work. He knew that most
of the clandestine service had spent four decades of the cold war waiting
and hoping for Soviets to volunteer their services as spies. He knew that
its overseas officers in the war on terror spent days and nights waiting
and hoping for their counterparts in Pakistan and Jordan and Indonesia
and the Philippines to sell them information. He knew that the solution
was to overhaul the agency.

The 9/11 Commission created by Congress was about to issue its final
report. The commission did a splendid job reconstructing the events leading up to the attacks. It did not chart a clear path forward. Nor had Congress done much to fix the agency since 9/11, other than giving it billions
of dollars and plenty of free advice. The commission correctly described
congressional oversight of intelligence as "dysfunctional"—the same epithet Goss hurled at the agency. For years, there had been next to no engagement on the life-and-death issues that confronted the CIA by the
House and Senate intelligence committees. The House committee under
Goss had produced its last substantive report on the conduct of the CIA in

1998. A quarter of a century of congressional oversight of the agency had produced little of lasting value. The intelligence committees and their staffs had applied an occasional public whipping and a patchwork of quick fixes for ever-present problems.

It was known that the 9/11 Commission would recommend the creation of a new national intelligence director. The idea had been kicked around since Allen Dulles's heyday. It offered no real solution to the crisis at the CIA. Rearranging the boxes on the flowchart of the government would not make it easier to run the CIA.

"It is an organization that thrives through deception," said John Hamre, a former deputy secretary of defense and the president of the Center for Strategic and International Studies in Washington. "How do you manage an organization like that?"

It was one of many questions the CIA and Congress never had answered. How do you run a secret intelligence service in an open democracy? How do you serve the truth by lying? How do you spread democracy by deceit?

"IN THE END, THEY WON'T STAY"

The myth about the CIA dated back to the Bay of Pigs: that all its successes were secret, that only its failures were trumpeted. The truth was that the CIA could not succeed without recruiting and sustaining skilled and daring officers and foreign agents. The agency failed daily at that mission, and to pretend otherwise was a delusion.

To succeed, the CIA needed to find men and women with the discipline and self-sacrifice of the nation's best military officers, the cultural awareness and historical knowledge of the nation's best diplomats, and the sense of curiosity and adventure possessed by the nation's best foreign correspondents. It would help if those recruits were able to pass for Palestinians, Pakistanis, or Pathans. Americans like that were hard to find.

"Can CIA meet the ongoing threat? The answer at this moment is no—absolutely not," said Howard Hart, who had put his life on the line to run agents in Iran, smuggled guns to the Afghan rebels, and led the agency's paramilitary officers. Hart said he took offense when Goss called the CIA "a bunch of dysfunctional jerks" and "a pack of idiots." But he conceded that "CIA's clandestine service can be criticized for not having done as well as it should have. That is a fair statement. Because we have people who just don't pull their weight. And the reason that most of them are there is that we have no way to replace them."

President Bush pledged to increase the agency's ranks by 50 percent. But quality, not quantity, was the crisis at hand. "What we don't need is more money and people, at least not for now," Carl Ford said. "Fifty percent more operators and fifty percent more analysts equals fifty percent more hot air." The personnel problem was the same one Walter Bedell Smith had faced as director of central intelligence while the Korean War was raging: "We can't get qualified people. They just simply don't exist."

The CIA could not find enough talented Americans to serve as spies on a government salary. Hundreds had resigned at headquarters and in the field during 2004, infuriated and humiliated at the collapse of credibility and authority at the agency. Recruiting, hiring, training, and retaining young officers still remained the most difficult task at the agency.

Goss vowed to find them. He went to his Senate confirmation hearings with a swagger on September 14, 2004, saying he could fix the CIA once and for all. "I don't want to give aid and comfort to the enemy by telling you how bad I think the problem is," he said before the cameras, but the problem would be solved. Upon his confirmation by a 77-to-17 vote from the full Senate, Goss went straight to CIA headquarters in a state of exhilaration.

"I never in my wildest dreams expected I'd be back here," he told the men and women he had roundly condemned three months before. "But here I am." He proclaimed that his powers would be "enhanced by executive orders" from the president: he would be Bush's intelligence briefer, the head of the CIA, director of central intelligence, national intelligence director, and chief of a new national counterterrorism center. He would not wear two hats, like his predecessors. He would wear five.

On his first day of work, Goss began a purge more swift and sweeping than any in the history of the Central Intelligence Agency. He forced almost every one of the CIA's most senior officers out the door. He created a bitterness that had not been seen at headquarters in nearly thirty years. The resentment over the expulsion of Stephen Kappes as chief of the clandestine service was ferocious. Kappes, an ex-marine and former station chief in Moscow, represented the very best of the CIA. In partnership

with the British intelligence service, he had only recently played a leading role in a triumph of intelligence and diplomacy by persuading Libya
to abandon its long-running program to develop weapons of mass destruction. When he questioned Goss's judgment, he was shown the door.

The new director surrounded himself with a team of political hacks he
had imported from Capitol Hill. They believed they were on a mission
from the White House—or some higher power—to rid the CIA of left-
wing subversives. It was the perception at headquarters that Goss and
his staff, the "Gosslings," prized loyalty to the president and his policies
above all, that they did not want the agency athwart of the White House,
and that those who challenged them would pay the price. The scourging
of the CIA was rightly a question of competence. It wrongly became a
question of ideology.

The director issued orders against dissent from the president's policies.
His message was clear: get with the program or get out. The latter choice
looked more and more attractive for the talented tenth of the CIA's personnel. A huge homeland security industry was growing at the outer
edge of the beltway, selling its services to a government outsourcing expertise. The best of the agency's people sold out. The CIA had been top-
heavy with aging cold warriors fifteen years before. Now it was
bottom-heavy with beginners. By 2005, half of the CIA's workforce—
operators and analysts alike—had five years' experience or less.

The president's offhand proclamation that the agency was "just guessing" about Iraq ignited a smoldering anger that burned throughout the
ranks of those professionals who remained. The CIA's officers in Baghdad
and in Washington tried to warn that the path the president was pursuing in Iraq was disastrous. They said the United States could not run a
country it did not understand. Their words carried no weight at the
White House. They were heresy in an administration whose policies were
based on faith.

Four former chiefs of the clandestine service tried to contact Goss to
advise him to go slow, lest he destroy what remained of the CIA. He
would not take their calls. One of them went public: "Goss and his min-
ions can do a great deal of damage in short order," Tom Twetten wrote in
an opinion piece published in the *Los Angeles Times* on November 23,
2004. "If the professional employees in the agency don't believe the
agency's leadership is on their side, they won't take risks for it and, in the
end, they won't stay." The next day, John McLaughlin, who had held

the agency together as acting director after Tenet's resignation, delivered another riposte. The CIA was not "a 'dysfunctional' and 'rogue' agency," he wrote in *The Washington Post.* "The CIA was not institutionally plotting against the president." Haviland Smith, who had retired as chief of the counterterrorism staff, weighed in. "Porter Goss and his troops from the Hill are wreaking havoc," he wrote. "Purging the CIA at this unfortunate moment, when we need to be dealing with real issues of terrorism, is cutting off our nose to spite our face." In all the years that the agency had been battered in the press, never had the director been attacked in print, on the record, by the most senior veterans of American intelligence.

The façade was falling. The CIA was tearing itself apart.

"Here is one of the most peculiar types of operation any government can have," President Eisenhower had said fifty years before. "It probably takes a strange kind of genius to run it." Nineteen men had served as director of central intelligence. Not one met the high standard Eisenhower had set. The agency's founders had been defeated by their ignorance in Korea and Vietnam and undone by their arrogance in Washington. Their successors were set adrift when the Soviet Union died and caught unaware when terror struck at the heart of American power. Their attempts to make sense of the world had generated heat but little light. As it was in the beginning, the warriors of the Pentagon and the diplomats of State held them in disdain. For more than half a century, presidents had been frustrated or furious when they turned to the directors for insight and for knowledge.

The job, having proved impossible to fill, now would be abolished.

In December 2004, with the upheaval at the agency in full force, Congress passed and the president signed a new law establishing the director of national intelligence, as the 9/11 Commission had urged. Hastily drafted, hurriedly debated, the law did nothing to ease the chronic and congenital problems that had plagued the agency since birth. It was continuity masquerading as change.

Goss thought the president would choose him. The call never came. On Feburary 17, 2005, Bush announced that he was nominating the American ambassador to Iraq, John D. Negroponte. A diplomat of rigorously conservative stripe, suave, subtle, a skilled infighter, he had never worked a day in the world of intelligence, and he would not long serve in it.

As in 1947, the new czar was given responsibility without commensurate authority. The Pentagon still controlled the great bulk of the na-

tional security budget, now approaching $500 billion a year, of which
the CIA's share was roughly 1 percent. The new order served only as a
formal recognition that the old order had failed.

"FAILURE CANNOT BE EXPLAINED"

The CIA was gravely wounded. In accordance with the laws of the jungle and the ways of Washington, stronger beasts fed upon it. The president gave great power over espionage, covert action, eavesdropping, and
reconnaissance to the Pentagon's undersecretary for intelligence, and el-
evated that job to the number-three position at the Department of Defense. "That sent seismic shudders through the intelligence community,"
said Joan Dempsey, who was a deputy director of central intelligence
and executive director of the foreign intelligence advisory board under
Bush. "That's much more of a Kremlin approach."

The Pentagon moved stealthily and steadily into the fields of overseas
covert operations, usurping the traditional roles, responsibilities, authorities, and missions of the clandestine service. It recruited the most promising young paramilitary officers and retained the most experienced
ones. The militarization of intelligence accelerated as the nation's civilian intelligence service eroded.

Negroponte's new chief analyst, Thomas Fingar, had run the State Department's small but first-rate office of intelligence and research. He surveyed the state of the agency's directorate of intelligence and quickly
determined that "nobody had any idea of who was doing what where."
He moved to pull the functioning remains of the CIA's analytic machinery under his aegis. The best and the brightest thinkers left at the agency
signed on with him.

The agency as constituted was vanishing. The building was still there,
and there would always be an institution in it. But on March 30, 2005,
a wrecking ball struck what remained of the spirit of the CIA. It came in
the form of the six-hundred-page report of Judge Silberman's presidential commission. The judge was as rigorous a thinker as could be found
in the capital. His intellectual badge was as strong as his intensely conservative credentials. He had twice come close to being named director

of central intelligence. In fifteen years as a federal appeals court judge in Washington, he had consistently supported the means and ends of national security, even when they encroached on the ideals of liberty. His staff, unlike the 9/11 Commission's, was deeply experienced in intelligence operations and analysis.

Their judgment was brutal and final. The realm of the director of central intelligence was "a closed world" with "an almost perfect record" of resisting change. The director had presided over a "fragmented, loosely managed, and poorly coordinated" patchwork of intelligence collection and analysis. The agency was "often unable to gather intelligence on the very things we care the most about" and its analysts "do not always tell decision-makers just how limited their knowledge really is." The CIA was "increasingly irrelevant to the new challenges presented by weapons of mass destruction." Its overriding flaw was "poor human intelligence"—an inability to conduct espionage.

"We recognize that espionage is always chancy at best; fifty years of pounding away at the Soviet Union resulted in only a handful of truly important human sources," the commission said. "Still, we have no choice but to do better." The CIA "needs fundamental change if it is to successfully confront the threats of the 21st century." That was "a goal that would be difficult to meet even in the best of all possible worlds. And we do not live in the best of worlds."

On April 21, 2005, the office of director of central intelligence disappeared into history. Goss called Negroponte's swearing-in "the burial ceremony" for the agency of old. On that day, the new boss received an odd blessing: "I hope the spirit of Wild Bill Donovan guides and inspires his efforts," said Senator John Warner of Virginia, chairman of the Armed Services Committee.

A bronze statue of Donovan stands guard at the entrance to CIA headquarters, where every living former director of central intelligence gathered at Goss's invitation on August 21, 2005, to receive medallions commemorating their service and to mark the end of their long line. George H. W. Bush was there, at the center that bore his name. So were Jim Schlesinger and Stan Turner, so bitterly resented as outsiders; Bill Webster and Bob Gates, failed reformers and restorers; Jim Woolsey, John Deutch, and George Tenet, who had fought to right a ship that had lost its bearings. Some of these men cheerfully despised one another; others shared deep bonds of trust. It was a pleasant enough wake, with a touch of pomp. There was a luncheon and a lecture on the vanished office from the CIA's chief historian, David S. Robarge. Goss sat in the front row, writhing inside. He had spent weeks agonizing over an inspector general's report he himself had demanded while still chairman of the House intelligence committee. It was a scathing look at the flaws that contributed to the 9/11 attacks, a knife in the agency's heart, a surgical examination of its inability to wage anything resembling a war against the nation's enemies. In the tradition of Allen Dulles, Goss had decided to bury it. The agency would never account for its failure to protect the United States. But in truth the reckoning had come to pass.

The CIA's historian recalled President Eisenhower's words when he came to lay the cornerstone for the agency's headquarters on November 3, 1959:

> America's fundamental aspiration is the preservation of peace. To this end we seek to develop policies and arrangements to make the peace both permanent and just. This can be done only on the basis of comprehensive and appropriate information.
>
> In war nothing is more important to a commander than the facts concerning the strength, dispositions, and intentions of his opponent, and the proper interpretation of those facts. In peacetime the necessary facts . . . and their correct interpretation are essential to the development of policy to further our long-term national security and best interests. . . . No task could be more important. Upon the quality of your work depends in large measure the success of our effort to further the nation's position in the international scene. . . . This agency demands of its members the highest order of dedication, ability, trustworthiness, and selflessness—to say nothing of the finest type of courage, whenever needed. Success cannot be advertised: failure cannot be explained. In the work of intelligence, heroes are undecorated and unsung.

"On this spot will rise a beautiful and useful structure," the president had concluded. "May it long endure, to serve the cause of America and of peace."

As Americans died in battle for want of the facts, the directors of central intelligence arose, shook hands, walked out into the heat of the summer afternoon, and went on with their lives. As the old soldier feared long ago, they had left a legacy of ashes.

"ADMIT NOTHING, DENY EVERYTHING"

On May 5, 2006, President Bush fired Porter Goss after nineteen months of ceaseless backstabbing at the CIA. The fall of the last director of central intelligence was swift and inglorious, and the bequest he left was bitter.

The next day, Goss got on a plane and delivered the commencement address at Tiffin University, ninety miles west of Cleveland, Ohio. "If this were a graduating class of CIA case officers, my advice would be short and to the point," he said. "Admit nothing, deny everything, and make counter-accusations." With those words, he disappeared from view, leaving behind the weakest cadre of spies and analysts in the history of the CIA.

One week after Goss resigned, a team of FBI agents raided CIA headquarters. They seized control of the office of Dusty Foggo, who had just stepped down as executive director, the third-highest job at the agency. This was the man whom Goss had inexplicably put in charge of running the CIA from day to day. In his previous post, Foggo had been quartermaster for the clandestine service. Based in Frankfurt, he kept CIA officers from Amman to Afghanistan supplied with everything from bottled water to body armor. Among his tasks was ensuring that his own accountants and cargo-kickers complied with the CIA's rules and regulations. "Having been the 'Ethic's Guy,'" he wrote to a fellow officer, "I wish you the best with this annual exercise." Foggo evidently had trouble with the word *ethics*.

The indictment in *United States of America v. Kyle Dustin Foggo* was painfully specific in its particulars. Unsealed on February 13, 2007, it charged Foggo with fraud, conspiracy, and money laundering. It said Foggo had fixed million-dollar contracts for a close friend who had wined and dined him in high style, treated him to extravagant trips to Scotland and Hawaii, and promised him a lucrative job—old-fashioned palm greasing. There had never been a case remotely like it in the history of the CIA. At this writing, Foggo has entered a plea of not guilty. He faces twenty years in prison if convicted.

On the same day that Foggo was indicted, a federal judge in North Carolina sentenced a CIA contract worker named David Passaro to eight years and four months in prison for beating a man to death in Afghanistan. Passaro served with a CIA paramilitary team based in Asadabad, the capital of Kunar Province, a few miles west of the border with Pakistan. The agency had hired Passaro despite his history of criminal violence; he had been fired from the police force in Hartford, Connecticut, after he was arrested for beating a man in a brawl.

The man who died at his hands was Abdul Wali, a well-known local farmer who had fought the Soviets in the 1980s. Wali had heard that he was wanted for questioning after a series of rocket attacks near the American base. He came to the Americans of his own free will, and he said he was innocent. Passaro doubted his word and threw him in a cell. He beat Wali so badly that the prisoner pleaded to be shot to end his pain; he died of his injuries two days later. Passaro was indicted and convicted under a provision of the Patriot Act allowing American citizens to be tried for crimes committed on territory claimed by the United States overseas. The judge noted that the absence of an autopsy had shielded him from a charge of murder.

The court received a letter from the former governor of Kunar, who said that Wali's death had done grievous damage to the American cause in Afghanistan and served as powerful propaganda for the resurgent forces of al Qaeda and the Taliban. "The distrust of the Americans increased, the security and reconstruction efforts of Afghanistan were dealt a blow, and the only people to gain from Dave Passaro's actions were al Qaeda and their partners," the governor wrote.

Three days after Passaro was sentenced, a judge in Italy ordered the indictment of the CIA's Rome station chief, the Milan base chief, and two dozen more officers in the abduction of a radical cleric who spent years under brutal interrogation in Egypt. A court in Germany charged thirteen CIA officers for the wrongful kidnapping and imprisonment of a Lebanese-born German citizen. The government of Canada formally apologized and paid a $10 million settlement to one of its citizens, Maher Arar, who had been seized by the CIA while changing planes in New York after a family vacation, transported to Syria, and subjected to the cruelest interrogation for ten months.

By then, the CIA's prison system had been condemned. It could not long survive when it was no longer secret. Americans were asked to take it on faith that the kidnapping, imprisonment, and torture of innocent people had been part of a program essential to preventing another attack on the United States. It may be so, but the evidence is scant. It is unlikely that we will ever know.

Porter Goss was succeeded at the CIA by General Michael Hayden, the deputy director of national intelligence, the former chief of the National Security Agency, the executor of President Bush's orders to train electronic eavesdropping on American targets, the first man to hold the diminished title of director of the Central Intelligence Agency, and the first active-duty military officer to run the CIA since Walter Bedell Smith left in 1953. General Hayden declared at his Senate confirmation that "amateur hour" was over at the CIA. But it was not.

By the CIA's own standards, roughly half its work force were still trainees. Few were ready and able to produce results. But there was nothing to be done about it; the CIA had no choice but to promote them beyond their levels of ability. As youngsters in their twenties replaced people in their forties and fifties, the result was an abridgment of intelligence. The clandestine service began to abandon the techniques of the past—political warfare, propaganda, and covert action—because it lacked the skills to conduct them. The agency remained a place where few people spoke Arabic or Persian, Korean or Chinese. It still denied employment to patriotic Arab Americans on security grounds if they had relatives living in the Middle East—as most did. The information revolution had left officers and analysts no more capable of comprehending the terrorist threat than they had understood the Soviet Union. And as the agency's reporting was overtaken by catastrophe in Iraq, the fifth Baghdad station chief in less than four years packed his bags for the closed world of the Green Zone.

The CIA was at a nadir. It no longer had the president's ear, and American leaders were looking elsewhere for intelligence—to the Pentagon and private industry.

"THE DISASTROUS RISE OF MISPLACED POWER"

Bob Gates took over the Pentagon on December 18, 2006—the only entry-level analyst ever to run the CIA and the only director ever to become secretary of defense. Two weeks later, John Negroponte, the new national intelligence czar, resigned after nineteen months to become the number-two man at the State Department. He was replaced by a retired admiral, Mike McConnell, who had run the National Security Agency during its first great collapse at the dawn of the digital age and who had spent the past decade making money as a military contractor at Booz Allen Hamilton.

When Gates settled in at the Pentagon, he looked around at the American intelligence establishment and he saw stars: a general was running the CIA, a general was the undersecretary of defense for intelligence, a general was in charge of State Department's counterterrorism programs, a lieutenant general was the Pentagon's deputy undersecretary for intelligence, and a major general was running spies at the CIA. Every one of these jobs had been held by civilians, going back many years. Gates saw a world in which the Pentagon had crushed the CIA, just as it had vowed to do sixty years before. He wanted to close the military prison at Guantánamo Bay, bring the suspected terrorists from Cuba to the United States, and either convict them or recruit them. He wanted to contain the Defense Department's dominance over intelligence. He longed to reverse the decline in the CIA's central role in American government. But there was very little he could do.

The decline was part of a slow rot undermining the pillars of American national security. After four years of war in Iraq, the military was exhausted, bled by leaders who had invested far more in futuristic weapons than in uniformed soldiers. After five years of defending a foreign policy based on born-again faith, the State Department was adrift, unable to give voice to the values of democracy. And after six years of willful ignorance imposed by know-nothing politicians, congressional oversight of the agency had collapsed. The 9/11 Commission had said that of all the tasks facing American intelligence, strengthening congressional oversight might be the most difficult, and the most important. In 2005 and 2006, Congress responded by failing to pass the annual authorization bill for the CIA, the basic law governing the agency, its policies, and its spending. The roadblock was a single Republican senator who obstructed the bill because it ordered the White House to file a classified report on the CIA's secret prisons.

The failure of authority made the congressional intelligence committees irrelevant. Not since the 1960s had there been so little congressional control over the agency. Now a far different force gained great influence over intelligence: corporate America.

At the end of Dwight Eisenhower's years as president, a few days after he lamented the legacy of intelligence failures he would pass on to his successors, he gave his farewell address to the nation and famously warned: "We must guard against the acquisition of unwarranted influence, whether sought or unsought, by the military-industrial complex. The potential for the disastrous rise of misplaced power exists and will persist." Little more than half a century later, the surge of secret spending on national security after 9/11 had created a booming intelligence-industrial complex.

Corporate clones of the CIA started sprouting all over the suburbs of Washington and beyond. Patriotism for profit became a $50-billion-a-year business, by some estimates—a sum about the size of the American intelligence budget itself. This phenomenon traced back fifteen years. After the cold war, the agency began contracting out thousands of jobs to fill the perceived void created by the budget cuts that began in 1992. A CIA officer could file his retirement papers, turn in his blue identification badge, go to work for a much better salary at a military contractor such as Lockheed Martin or Booz Allen Hamilton, then return to the CIA the next day, wearing a green badge. After September 2001, the outsourcing went out of control. Green-badge bosses started openly recruiting in the CIA's cafeteria.

Great chunks of the clandestine service became wholly dependent on contractors who looked like they were in the CIA's chain of command, but who worked for their corporate masters. In effect, the agency had two workforces—and the private one was paid far better. By 2006 something on the order of half the officers at the Baghdad station and the new National Counterterrorism Center were contract employees, and Lockheed Martin, the nation's biggest military contractor, was posting help-wanted ads for "counterterrorism analysts" to interrogate suspected terrorists at the Guantánamo prison.

Fortunes could be made in the intelligence industry. The money was a powerful attractor, and the result was an ever-accelerating brain drain—the last thing the CIA could afford—and the creation of companies like Total Intelligence Solutions. Founded in February 2007, Total Intel was run by Cofer Black—the chief of the CIA's counterterrorist center on 9/11. His partners were Robert Richer, who had been the number-two man at the clandestine service, and Enrique Prado, Black's chief of counterterror operations. All three had decamped from the Bush administration's war on terror in 2005 to join Blackwater USA, the politically wired private security company that served, among many other things, as the Praetorian Guard for Americans in Baghdad. They learned the tricks of the government-contracting trade at Blackwater, and within little more than a year Black and company were running Total Intel. These were among the best of the CIA's officers. But the spectacle of jumping ship in the middle of a war to make a killing was unremarkable in twenty-first-century Washington. Legions of CIA veterans quit their posts to sell their services to the agency by writing analyses, creating cover for overseas officers, setting up communications networks, and running clandestine operations. Following their example, new CIA hires adopted their own five-year plan: get in, get out, and get paid. A top secret security clearance and a green badge were golden tickets for a new breed of Beltway bandits. The outsourcing of intelligence was a clear sign that the CIA could not perform many of its basic missions unaided after 9/11.

Above all, it could not help the army impose democracy at gunpoint in Iraq. Action without knowledge was a dangerous business, as Americans found to their sorrow.

"TO ORGANIZE AND RUN AN ESPIONAGE SERVICE"

In the cold war, the CIA was condemned by the American left for what it did. In the war on terror, the CIA was attacked by the American right for what it could not do. The charge was incompetence, leveled by such men as Dick Cheney and Don Rumsfeld. Say what one may about their leadership, they knew from long experience what the reader now knows: the CIA was unable to fulfill its role as America's intelligence service.

The fictional CIA, the one that lives in novels and movies, is omnipotent. The myth of a golden age was of the CIA's own making, the product of the publicity and the political propaganda Allen Dulles manufactured in the 1950s. It held that the agency could change the world, and it helps explain why the CIA is so impervious to change. The legend was perpetuated in the 1980s by Bill Casey, who tried to revive the devil-may-care

spirits of Dulles and Wild Bill Donovan. Now the agency has revived the
fable that it is America's best defense. With orders to train and retain
thousands of new officers, it needs to project an image of success to survive.

In truth, there haven't been many halcyon days. But there have been
a few. When Richard Helms was in charge, the agency spoke the truth
to Lyndon Johnson and Robert McNamara about the war in Vietnam,
and they listened. There was another such fleeting moment when Bob
Gates ran the CIA; he kept calm and carried on as the Soviet Union
crumbled. But fifteen years have passed since then, and the glory is
gone. The CIA found itself unable to see the way forward in a battle
where information and ideas were the most powerful weapons.

For sixty years tens of thousands of clandestine service officers have
gathered only the barest threads of truly important intelligence—and
that is the CIA's deepest secret. Their mission is extraordinarily hard. But
we Americans still do not understand the people and the political forces
we seek to contain and control. The CIA has yet to become what its creators hoped it would be.

"The only remaining superpower doesn't have enough interest in
what's going on in the world to organize and run an espionage service,"
Richard Helms said a decade ago. Perhaps a decade from now the agency
will rise from the ashes, infused with many billions of dollars, inspired
by new leadership, invigorated by a new generation. Analysts may see
the world clearly. American spies may become capable of espionage
against America's enemies. The CIA someday may serve as its founders
intended. We must depend on it. For the war in which we are now engaged may last as long as the cold war, and we will win or lose by virtue
of our intelligence.

ACKNOWLEDGMENTS

I am fortunate to have spent part of the past twenty years talking with CIA directors and officers whose professional lives spanned the course of six decades. I am particularly grateful to Richard Helms, William Colby, Stansfield Turner, William Webster, Bob Gates, John Deutch, George Tenet, John McMahon, Tom Twetten, Milt Bearden, Tom Polgar, Peter Sichel, Frank Lindsay, Sam Halpern, Don Gregg, Jim Lilley, Steve Tanner, Gerry Gossens, Clyde McAvoy, Walter Pforzheimer, Haviland Smith, Fred Hitz, and Mark Lowenthal. A tip of the hat goes to the men and women of the CIA's history staff, who do their part for the cause of openness in the face of fierce resistance from the clandestine service, and to present and former members of the agency's public affairs staff.

I am deeply in debt to the work of Charles Stuart Kennedy, a retired Foreign Service officer and the founder and director of the Foreign Affairs Oral History Program. The library he has created is a unique and invaluable resource. The State Department's historians, who produce *The Foreign Relations of the United States*, the official record of American diplomacy, published since 1861, have done more in the past decade to unseal secret documents than any other arm of government. They, along with the staffs of the presidential libraries, deserve the thanks of a grateful nation.

A reporter is lucky to have one great editor in a lifetime. I have had more than my share, and over the years they have given me time to think and freedom to write. Gene Roberts gave me my start at the *Philadelphia Inquirer*. Bill Keller, Jill Abramson, Andy Rosenthal, and Jon Landman help make *The New York Times* a daily miracle. They are keepers of a public trust.

Three tireless researchers helped create this book. Matt Malinowski transcribed interview tapes, Zoe Chace dug into the diplomatic history and the National Security Council files, and Cora Currier did groundbreaking research at the National Archives. I am grateful to my high school chum Lavinia Currier for introducing me to her fiercely intelligent daughter. Zoe is the daughter of the late James Chace and the sister of Beka Chace, two friends whose spirits sustain me.

I want to salute the journalists who have covered the CIA, the struggles in Iraq and Afghanistan, and the agonies of American national security since 9/11. Among them are John Burns, Dexter Filkins, Matt Purdy, Doug Jehl, Scott Shane, Carlotta Gall, John Kifner, and Steve Crowley of *The New York Times;* Dana Priest, Walter Pincus, and Pam Constable of *The Washington Post;* Vernon Loeb, Bob Drogin, and Megan Stack of the *Los Angeles Times;* and Andy Maykuth of *The Philadelphia Inquirer.* We remember our brothers and sisters who gave their lives to get the news, among them Elizabeth Neuffer, Mark Fineman, Michael Kelly, Harry Burton, Azizullah Haidari, Maria Grazia Cutuli, and Julio Fuentes.

My gratitude goes to Phyllis Grann, who had the good grace to edit and publish this book, and to Kathy Robbins, the world's most brilliant literary agent.

Legacy of Ashes took shape at Yaddo, the retreat for artists and writers in Saratoga Springs, New York. For two months, the good people of Yaddo housed and fed me while thousands of words a day went pouring into my ThinkPad. I was honored to be the first recipient of the Nora Sayre Endowed Residency for Nonfiction, created in her memory to support her literary legacy. A thousand thanks to the poet Jean Valentine for introducing me to Yaddo; to Elaina Richardson, president of the Corporation of Yaddo; and to the trustees, supporters, and employees of this magnificent refuge.

The book grew longer and stronger at the house of my in-laws, Susanna and Boker Doyle, who supported me with their great good nature.

My will to write began when I first saw my mother, Professor Dora B. Weiner, working on a book in the basement of our home in the quiet before dawn. Forty-five years later, she is still writing and teaching and inspiring her students and her sons. All of us wish my father were here to hold this book in his hands.

Legacy of Ashes ends as it began, with a dedication to the love of my life, Kate Doyle; to our daughters, Emma and Ruby; and to the rest of our lives together.

NOTES

PRIMARY SOURCES

—Central Intelligence Agency records obtained from the CIA Records Search Technology at the National Archives and Records Administration (CIA/CREST)

—CIA records released or reprinted by the CIA's Center for the Study of Intelligence (CIA/CSI)

—CIA records obtained from the Declassified Documents Records System (CIA/DDRS)

—National Archives and Records Administration (NARA)

—*The Foreign Relations of the United States* (FRUS). CIA records in the FRUS volume "Emergency of the Intelligence Establishment, 1945–1950," are hereinafter "FRUS Intelligence."

—Foreign Affairs Oral History (FAOH)

—Franklin D. Roosevelt Presidential Library, Hyde Park, NY (FDRL)

—Harry S. Truman Presidential Library, Independence, MO (HSTL)

—Dwight D. Eisenhower Presidential Library, Abilene, KS (DDEL)

—John F. Kennedy Presidential Library, Boston, MA (JFKL)

—Lyndon B. Johnson Presidential Library, Austin, TX (LBJL)

—Richard M. Nixon Presidential Library. Yorba Linda, CA (RMNL)

—Gerald R. Ford Presidential Library, Grand Rapids, MI (GRFL)

—Jimmy Carter Library, Atlanta, GA (JCL)

—George H.W. Bush Library, College Station, TX (GHWBL)

—Hoover Institution Archives, Stanford University, Stanford, CA

—The records of the Senate Select Committee to Study Governmental Operations with Respect to Intelligence Activities (hereinafter "Church Committee")

CIA clandestine service histories were obtained through declassification and
through unofficial sources. The CIA has reneged on pledges made by three consecutive directors of central intelligence—Gates, Woolsey, and Deutch—to de-
classify records on nine major covert actions: France and Italy in the 1940s and
1950s; North Korea in the 1950s; Iran in 1953; Indonesia in 1958; Tibet in the
1950s and 1960s; and the Congo, the Dominican Republic, and Laos in the
1960s. The Guatemala documents were finally released in 2003, most of the Bay
of Pigs documents are out, and the Iran history was leaked. The rest remain under official seal. While I was gathering and obtaining declassification authorizations for some of the CIA records used in this book at the National Archives, the
agency was engaging in a secret effort to reclassify many of those same records,
dating back to the 1940s, flouting the law and breaking its word. Nevertheless,
the work of historians, archivists, and journalists has created a foundation of
documents on which a book can be built.

PART ONE
Chapter One

3   *"When I took over"*: Truman to David M. Noyes, December 1, 1963, David
    M. Noyes papers, HSTL.
3   *"In a global and totalitarian war"*: Donovan to Joint Psychological Warfare
    Committee, October 24, 1942, NARA.
4   *"capabilities, intentions and activities of foreign nations"* . . . *"subversive opera-*
    tions abroad": Donovan to Roosevelt, "Substantive Authority Necessary in
    Establishment of a Central Intelligence Service," November 18, 1944,
    reprinted in Thomas F. Troy, CIA/CSI, republished as *Donovan and the CIA*
    (Frederick, MD: University Publications of America, 1981), pp. 445–447.
4   *"lay the keel"*: Donovan to Roosevelt, OSS folder, President's Secretary's file,
    FDRL. Roosevelt once said, not without malice, that Donovan could have
    been president had he not been an Irishman, a Catholic, and a Republican.
4   *"His imagination was unlimited"*: Bruce cited in Dulles speech, "William J.
    Donovan and the National Security," undated but probably 1959,
    CIA/CSI.
5   *"an extremely dangerous thing in a democracy"*: Bissell cited in Troy, *Donovan*
    and the CIA, p. 243. This was a widely held view. Yet the army had done
    worse during the war. The chief of army intelligence, Major General
    George Strong, had cast a gimlet eye at Donovan's new and independent
    OSS and decided to set up his own intelligence shop. He instructed the
    chief of the War Department's Military Intelligence Service, Brigadier
    General Hayes Kroner, to create this organization in October 1942. Kro-
    ner, in turn, plucked a renegade U.S. Army captain named John

"Frenchy" Grombach out of Donovan's organization and handed him some extraordinary marching orders: to focus on spying and subversion against the United States by its wartime allies, the British and the Soviets. Grombach called his intelligence outfit The Pond. It was uncontrolled by higher authority and undermined by the utter unreliability of its reporting. By Grombach's own account, 80 percent of his work wound up in the trash. The Pond succeeded mainly at keeping itself secret. "Its existence was not known," General Kroner said; only a handful of men, including "the President himself, who had to know by virtue of his approving certain operations, knew it existed." Grombach's ambitious orders were, however, a milestone: "He would not only institute a secret intelligence service, looking to the current war effort, but he would lay the foundation for a perpetual, a far-seeing, a far-distant, continuing secret intelligence service," Kroner said. "That was the birth of high-level intelligence, secret intelligence operations in our government." National Security Act of 1947, Hearing Before the Committee on Expenditures in the Executive Departments, June 27, 1947. See Mark Stout, "The Pond: Running Agents for State, War, and the CIA," *Studies in Intelligence,* Vol. 48, No. 3, CIA/CSI, available online at https://www.cia.gov/csi/studies/vol48no3/article07.html.

6   *a short row of wooden filing cabinets at the State Department*: In October 1941, Captain Dean Rusk, the future secretary of state, was ordered to organize a new army intelligence section covering a great swath of the world, from Afghanistan through India to Australia. "The need for information," Rusk said, "cannot be exaggerated. We were running into this factor of ignorance." He asked to see what files the United States had on hand: "I was shown one file drawer by an old lady named Mrs. North. In that file drawer was one copy of 'Murphy's Tourist Handbook' to India and Ceylon which had been stamped Confidential because it was the only copy in town, and they wanted to keep track of it; one 1925 military attaché report from London on the British Army in India, and then a considerable number of clippings from The New York Times that this old lady, Mrs. North, had been clipping since World War One, and that was it." In World War II, when American pilots crossed the Himalayas from India to China and back, they were flying blind, Rusk remembered: "I didn't even have maps that would show us the scale of one to one million in the terrain in which we were operating." When Rusk tried to organize a Burmese-language unit for the army, "we looked around the United States for a native Burman. . . . We finally found one and we looked him up and he was in an insane asylum. Well, we fished him out of the insane asylum and made a Burmese language instructor out of him." Rusk testimony, President's Commission on CIA Activities

(Rockefeller Commission), April 21, 1975, pp. 2191–2193, Top Secret, declassified 1995, GRFL.

6 *half the night*: Troy, *Donovan and the CIA*, p. 265.

6 *"What do you think it means . . . ?"*: Casey cited in Joseph E. Persico, *Casey: The Lives and Secrets of William J. Casey: From the OSS to the CIA* (New York: Viking), p. 81.

6 *"serious harm to the citizens"*: Park report, Rose A. Conway files, OSS/Donovan folder, HSTL.

7 *"The defects and the dangers"*: Donovan to Truman, "Statement of Principles," FRUS Intelligence, pp. 17–21.

Chapter Two

9 *"What you have to remember"*: Helms interview with author.

10 *"most inadvisable"*: Stimson to Donovan, May 1, 1945, CIA Historical Intelligence Collection, CIA/CSI.

10 *"the continuing operations of OSS must be performed in order to preserve them"*: McCloy to Magruder, September 26, 1945, FRUS Intelligence, pp. 235–236. The records detailing the survival of Central Intelligence after Truman's abolition of the OSS are in FRUS Intelligence, pp. 74–315; see especially Magruder's essay on clandestine intelligence operations and the Lovett report.

10 *"the holy cause of central intelligence"*: Magruder cited in Michael Warner, "Salvage and Liquidation: The Creation of the Central Intelligence Group," *Studies in Intelligence*, Vol. 39, No. 5, 1996, CIA/CSI.

10 *"it was very clear our primary target was going to be what the Russians were up to"*: Polgar interview with author.

11 *"we were seeing the total takeover by the Russians of the East German system"*: Sichel interview with author.

11 *a successful liaison*: Wisner to Chief/SI, March 27, 1945, CIA/DDRS.

12 *"Clandestine intelligence operations"*: Magruder to Lovett, "Intelligence Matters," undated but likely late October 1945, FRUS Intelligence, pp. 77–81.

12 *"The intelligence collection effort more or less came to a standstill"*: William W. Quinn, *Buffalo Bill Remembers: Truth and Courage* (Fowlerville, MI: Wilderness Adventure Books, 1991), p. 240.

12 *"transparently jerry-built"*: Richard Helms with William Hood, *A Look over My Shoulder: A Life in the Central Intelligence Agency* (New York: Random House, 2003), p. 72.

Colonel Quinn had been the chief intelligence officer for the Seventh Army in North Africa, France, and Germany, working in direct liaison with OSS. He faced fierce opposition to the new intelligence service in Washington. He brought a package of inside information on the Soviet

Baltic Fleet to an admiral at the Office of Naval Intelligence. "Your organization is infiltrated with communists," replied the admiral. "I couldn't possibly accept anything that you might want to give me." There were several such rejections. So Quinn decided he needed a clean bill of health from the only man in Washington who could grant it: J. Edgar Hoover of the FBI. He went to Hoover, stated his case, and watched as Hoover smiled and fairly licked his lips as he considered the problem. "You know, this is quite a relief," Hoover said. "Colonel, I fought that Bill Donovan tooth-and-nail, particularly regarding operations in South and Central America." The FBI had been ordered out of every nation south of the Rio Grande after the war; Hoover's G-men burned their intelligence files rather than turn them over to Central Intelligence, the beginning of a never-ending battle. Now, for the moment, Quinn's coming to the FBI hat in hand took some of the heat out of Hoover's hatred. "I admired Donovan, but I was certainly not fond of him," Hoover continued. "So here we are at the end of that road. What do you want me to do?"

"Mr. Hoover," Quinn replied, "the simple answer to your question is to find out if I have any commies in my organization."

"Well, we can do that," said Hoover. "We can run a national check."

"While you're doing it subversively, would you please check them criminally as well?"

"All right."

"Before we decide on how to do it, for posterity, and for ultimate co-operation, I would like to ask that you send me a representative to be your liaison with my organization."

At this, Hoover almost fell out of his seat. "I knew what was going on in his mind," Quinn recalled. "He was probably thinking, my God, this guy is asking for a direct penetration in his agency." Quinn had just invited the FBI to spy on his spies. He needed the anticommunist inoculation from Hoover for the outfit to survive at the beginning of the great red scare that gripped Washington for nearly a decade. His decision temporarily increased the standing and reputation of Central Intelligence at home.

Colonel Quinn was placed in charge of the Office of Special Operations, in charge of espionage and covert action overseas, by Director of Central Intelligence Vandenberg in July 1946. He found his new assignment "contrary to any principles of organization, command and control that I had ever experienced." In search of cash, he went to Capitol Hill and sought $15 million for espionage from a few members of Congress. "I just knew that these people didn't know what we did," he said. So Quinn asked for a secret executive session, and he told the members a stirring tale about a cleaning woman in Berlin who had been recruited as a spy, photographing Soviet documents at night. The congressmen were rapt. Quinn got his money, under the table, and it helped to keep American intelligence alive.

He also tried to re-enlist OSS veterans like Bill Casey, who would take over as director of central intelligence thirty-five years later. But in 1946, Casey wanted to make money on Wall Street more than he wanted to continue serving his country. He and his OSS friends feared that intelligence would remain a cross-eyed stepchild of the military services, run by generals and admirals in thrall to transient tactics rather than skilled civilians focused on the big strategic picture. The future of American intelligence was threatened, Casey wrote to Donovan, by "today's moral and political climate, which I attribute to a considerable degree to our late Commander in Chief," President Roosevelt. Casey's list of recommendations to Quinn included Hans Tofte, who later tried to run covert operations against China during the Korean War, and Mike Burke, who tried to run operations across the iron curtain in the early 1950s. Quinn, *Buffalo Bill Remembers*, pp. 234–267. J. Russell Forgan letter to Quinn, May 8, 1946; Casey letter to Forgan, January 25, 1966; Casey letter to Donovan, August 20, 1946; all three letters in J. Russell Forgan papers, Hoover Institution, Stanford University.

13 *"I don't suppose there had ever been or could ever be sadder or more tormented period of my life"*: Sherman Kent, *Reminiscences of a Varied Life*, n.d., privately printed, pp. 225–231. Kent wrote in 1946: "From the very beginning, there was administrative trouble of a high order, much of it avoidable; personnel actions—new appointments, replacements, and overdue promotions—moved with the ponderous slowness of the glacier or not at all. Life outside the government [became] more and more attractive to irreplaceable professionals. They began to leave in the order of their importance to the organization; and as replacements did not appear, morale declined." "Prospects for the National Intelligence Service," *Yale Review*, Vol. 36, No. 1, Autumn 1946, p. 116. William Colby, the future director of central intelligence, wrote that the separation of the scholars of the research and analysis division from the spies of the clandestine service created two cultures within the intelligence profession, separate, unequal, and contemptuous of each other. That critique remained true throughout the CIA's first sixty years.

13 *Smith warned the president*: The warning, declassified by the White House in 2004, was titled "Intelligence and Security Activities of the Government" and dated September 20, 1945, the day the president ordered the OSS abolished.

13 *"royally bitched up"*: Harold D. Smith papers, "Diaries—Conferences with the President," 1945, FDRL.

13 *"a disgraceful way"*: Leahy cited in Smith memo, "White House Conference on Intelligence Activities," January 9, 1946, FRUS Intelligence, pp.
170–171.

13 *"At lunch today in the White House"*: Diary of William D. Leahy, January
24, 1946, Library of Congress; Warner, "Salvage and Liquidation,"
CIA/CSI.

14 *Truman said he only needed a daily intelligence digest*: Russell Jack Smith,
later the CIA's deputy director for intelligence, remembered that when
the Central Intelligence Group was first established in January 1946,
"Truman began asking daily, 'Where's my newspaper?' It seemed almost
that the only CIG activity President Truman deemed important was the
daily summary." His predecessor, Sherman Kent, wrote in 1949 that the
CIA should strive to resemble "great metropolitan newspapers," with
"small forces of decorous and highly intelligent salesmen" to "push the
product"—the product being, as it turned out, the president's newspaper.
The newspaper became known as the President's Daily Brief. Delivered
by courier to the president for nearly six decades, it was the CIA's one
constant source of power. But the last thing a spy engaged in the business of espionage wants (or needs) is the daily demands of newspaper
deadlines. Spying does not produce a steady flow of news to meet a daily
deadline. It is a slow search to find ground truths, to know the mind of
the enemy by silently stealing secrets of state. There was, and remains, "a
conflict between the real demands of espionage and the reportorial needs
of current intelligence," wrote William R. Johnson, a twenty-eight-year
veteran of the CIA's clandestine service. Was the job of American intelligence to beg or borrow or purvey information and sell it, repackaged, to
the president? Or was it to steal state secrets abroad? This conflict was not
resolved in favor of espionage. Johnson concluded, and he spoke for
much of the clandestine service after three decades of toil, that the business of current intelligence lay outside the CIA. And for good measure,
he wrote: "As for the political action people, the media planters and the
grey radio broadcasters, and the corrupters of venal politicians, let them
make their accommodation wherever it suits. Their work is not clandestine. . . . Let the Security Council find a place for them somewhere
removed from the conduct of espionage." William R. Johnson, "Clandestinity and Current Intelligence," *Studies in Intelligence*, Fall 1976,
CIA/CSI, reprinted in H. Bradford Westerfield (ed.), *Inside CIA's Private
World: Declassified Articles from the Agency's Internal Journal 1955–1992* (New
Haven, CT: Yale University Press, 1995), pp. 118–184.

14 *"There is an urgent need"*: Souers, "Development of Intelligence on USSR,"
April 29, 1946, FRUS Intelligence, pp. 345–347.

15 *"We had accustomed ourselves"*: Kennan interview for the CNN Cold War

series, 1996, National Security Archive transcript, available online at
http://www.gwu.edu/~nsarchiv/coldwar/interviews/-espisode-1/kennan1
.html.
15 *"the best possible tutor"*: Walter Bedell Smith, *My Three Years in Moscow*
     (Philadelphia: Lippincott, 1950), p. 86.
16 *On a cold, starry night in April 1946*: Ibid., pp. 46–54.
17 *"an apprentice juggler"*: Helms, *A Look over My Shoulder*, p. 67.
17 *"throwing money at a problem"*: Ibid., pp. 92–95. Berlin base chief Dana
     Durand confessed that the intelligence he and his men had produced was
     shot through with "rumors, high level gossip, political chitchat." Durand
     to Helms, "Report on Berlin Operations Base," April 8, 1948, declassified
     1999, CIA. In one of many such intelligence swindles, Karl-Heinz
     Kramer, "the Stockholm Abwehr," sold the Americans highly detailed re-
     ports on the Russian airframe industry, which he claimed came from his
     extensive network of agents inside the Soviet Union. In reality, his source
     was a set of aircraft manuals bought from a Stockholm bookstore. James
     V. Milano and Patrick Brogan, *Soldiers, Spies, and the Rat Line: America's Un-
     declared War against the Soviets* (Washington, DC: Brassey's, 1995), pp.
     149–150. In another scam, Central Intelligence bought a chunk of "ra-
     dioactive uranium" advertised as having been swiped from a shipment in
     East Germany bound for Moscow. The hot potato was a hunk of lead
     wrapped in aluminum foil. This kind of fiasco led General Leslie Groves,
     the man who ran the Manhattan Project, the secret program that created
     the atomic bomb, to set up his own intelligence unit, dedicated to deter-
     mining every possible source of uranium in the world and tracking the
     development of atomic weapons in the Soviet Union. General Groves,
     judging Helms's men "unable to function satisfactorily" and thus inca-
     pable of keeping an eye on Stalin's plans to build a Soviet atomic bomb,
     kept the existence of this unit and its mission secret from Vandenberg
     and his men at Central Intelligence. That contributed to the failure of the
     CIA to accurately predict when America's monopoly on weapons of mass
     destruction might end. "Minutes of the Sixth Meeting of the National In-
     telligence Authority," August 21, 1946, FRUS Intelligence, pp. 395–400;
     Groves memo to the Atomic Energy Commission, November 21, 1946,
     FRUS Intelligence, pp. 458–460.
18 *an "operating agency"*: Elsey memorandum for the record, July 17, 1946,
     CIA/CSI.
18 *"intelligence agents all over the world"*: "Minutes of the Fourth Meeting of
     the National Intelligence Authority," July 17, 1946, FRUS Intelligence,
     pp. 526–533. For the context of the war scare of 1946, see Eduard Mark,
     "The War Scare of 1946 and Its Consequences," *Diplomatic History*, Vol. 21,
     No. 3, Summer 1997.

18 *"conspiracy, intrigue, nastiness"*: Hostler interview with author. Hostler spent the closing months of the war on an interim assignment in Italy, working at a 1,200-room royal palace outside Naples, helping James J. Angleton of the OSS in "strengthening his control over the various Italian intelligence and security networks." For the background of the Romanian fiasco, see Charles W. Hostler, *Soldier to Ambassador: From the D-Day Normandy Landing to the Persian Gulf War, A Memoir Odyssey* (San Diego: San Diego State University Press, 1993), pp. 51–85; and Elizabeth W. Hazard, *Cold War Crucible* (Boulder, CO: Eastern European Monographs, 1996). Hazard is the daughter of Frank Wisner.

Chapter Three

20 *"extraordinarily important events"*: Wisner quoted in C. David Heymann, *The Georgetown Ladies' Social Club* (New York: Atria, 2003), pp. 36–37.

21 *the ideas of this obscure diplomat*: Kennan would in time disavow his intellectual constructs for the Truman Doctrine and the CIA. The Truman Doctrine, Kennan wrote two decades later, built "the framework of a universal policy" out of a unique problem: "All another country had to do, in order to qualify for American aid, was to demonstrate the existence of a Communist threat. Since almost no country was without a Communist minority, this assumption carried very far." But the doctrine was read by almost all Americans in 1947 as a ringing proclamation for the forces of freedom. The American intelligence officer James McCargar was working in Budapest on the day of Truman's speech. For months on end, spirits at the American Legation there had been "going down and down, because we saw that the Russians were getting away with what they wanted to do, which was to take over Hungary entirely." The story was the same across the Balkans and perhaps—who knew?—all of Europe: "There was no question whatsoever that this was going to be a contest, a real confrontation" between the United States and the Soviet Union. "We became more and more depressed"—until the day the Truman Doctrine was proclaimed. "We all went out into the streets that morning with our heads held high," McCargar said. "We were going to back up democratic forces as much as we could anywhere around the world." George F. Kennan, *Memoirs 1925–50* (New York: Pantheon, 1983), p. 322; McCargar oral history, FAOH; McCargar interview with author; Vandenberg memo, "Subject: Special Consultant to the Director of Central Intelligence," June 27, 1946, CIA/CSI.

The origins of the Truman Doctrine trace back to the war scare of 1946. Late in the afternoon on Friday, July 12, 1946, as the first covert operation and the first war plans against the Soviets began to take shape,

Harry Truman had a bourbon or two in the White House with his counsel, Clark Clifford. He asked him to pull together something on the mystery of the Soviets, something his Central Intelligence news service seemed unable to do to his satisfaction. Clifford, already a little addled by his proximity to power, decided to take on the job himself. No one as close to Truman was less qualified. "I had no real background" in foreign policy or national security, Clifford said. "I had to learn as I went; it was catch as catch can." Truman was not the first president to set up his own amateur intelligence shop at the White House. He would not be the last. Clifford's work, written with Truman's aide George Elsey, was delivered in early September 1946. It borrowed and built on Kennan's words, and then took a long leap into the unknown. Clifford oral history, HSTL. "The Joint Intelligence Committee," CIA/CSI, 2000.

The United States had to assume that the Soviets could attack anywhere at any time, and so the president had to be ready to wage "atomic and biological warfare" against the Soviet Union, for "the language of military power is the only language" the Soviets understood, it said. The only true alternative would be a worldwide effort by the United States to "support and assist all democratic countries which are in any way menaced or endangered by the U.S.S.R." To do that, the nation had to build a new and unified set of foreign policies, military plans, economic aid programs, and intelligence operations to blunt the Soviets. The United States had to lead the rest of Western civilization "in an attempt to build up a world of our own."

Director of Central Intelligence Vandenberg caught wind of Clifford's endeavor. Not to be outdone, a week after Truman commissioned Clifford's report Vandenberg told Ludwell Lee Montague, his chief reports officer, to deliver a blockbuster on the military and foreign policies of the Soviet Union, and to have it on his desk by Tuesday. Montague, without any competent staff, did it all by himself. Sleeping very little over the next hundred hours, he delivered on deadline the first analysis of the Soviets ever published by Central Intelligence. Montague concluded that while Moscow anticipated a clash with the capitalist world and would strive to solidify control of all the lands behind the iron curtain, it would not provoke the next war and could not afford a direct conflict with the United States in the foreseeable future. It was as good a guess as any. This report was the first Soviet estimate, the first of hundreds, one of the most difficult and least satisfying jobs the CIA undertook. Like those that followed, it was based on few hard facts, proof of the wisdom put forth by Sherman Kent that "estimating is what you do when you do not know." The report sank like a stone. It painted shades of gray when what was wanted at the White House was black-and-white. And it suffered one fundamental weakness: the army, the navy, and the State Department still would not share their thinking, much less their secrets, with the upstarts at Central Intelligence. Sherman Kent, "Estimates and Influence," *Foreign Service Journal,* April 1969. See also Ludwell L. Montague, *General Walter Bedell Smith as Director of Central Intelligence* (University Park, PA: Penn State University Press, 1992), pp. 120–123 [hereinafter CIA/LLM]. This is a CIA history, declassified in part. Ludwell Lee Montague, "Production of a 'World Situation Estimate,' " CIA, FRUS Intelligence, pp. 804–806.

This was a crippling blow. Over the next four years, Montague later wrote, Central Intelligence consistently failed to deliver what Truman wanted: knowledge from all known sources. The one insurmountable obstacle was the military. They wanted to do their own thinking and predicting and threat analysis, as they still do. Montague's work was the last big think piece on the Soviet Union that Central Intelligence would submit to the president for nearly two years. The bitter lesson would deepen with time: the CIA would wield power in Washington only when it had gathered its own unique secrets.

Clifford, by contrast, had the clout that Central Intelligence lacked. He had the finest office in the West Wing of the White House and he met with the president a half-dozen times a day. He had the president's ear. He demanded and received the secrets of the State, War, and Navy Departments in the president's name. The report he and Elsey delivered in September lifted liberally from the work of the Joint Chiefs' own intelligence staff. Yet it, too, had a fatal flaw: no one in the U.S. government had any way of accurately reading Moscow's military capabilities and intentions. The best information on the Soviets available to the U.S. government back then, Richard Helms reflected fifty years later, was sitting in the stacks of the Library of Congress. But Clifford, working off the cuff, had done precisely what Central Intelligence was supposed to do. He gathered the government's thoughts. Clifford-Elsey memo, draft copy, September 1946, CIA/DDRS. See also James Chace, *Acheson* (New York: Simon and Schuster, 1998), p. 157; and Clark M. Clifford with Richard Holbrooke, *Counsel to the President* (New York: Anchor, 1992) pp. 109–129.

22 *"Mr. President"*: Chace, *Acheson,* pp. 162–165; Dean Acheson, *Present at the Creation: My Years in the State Department* (New York: W. W. Norton, 1969), p. 219.

23 *"The oceans have shrunk"*: Statement of Lieutenant General Hoyt S. Vandenberg on S. 758, National Security Act of 1947, NARA. "It takes time," Vandenberg said, "to start something that we are 400 years behind the times on today."

23 *"and probably never should have been"*: CIA/LLM, p. 4. Souers, Vandenberg,
    and Hillenkoetter were among a dozen of the nineteen directors of cen-
    tral intelligence who were unprepared or unsuited for office. "This as-
    signment was definitely unsought," Hillenkoetter wrote to Wild Bill
    Donovan on May 21, 1947. "As you are the past master in this art, I am
    presuming to ask you if you will give me some advice as well as your
    ideas on the subject." Hilly would need all the help he could get. Letter
    to Donovan, Forgan papers, Hoover Institution, Stanford University.

24 *Room 1501 of the Longworth Office Building*: Dulles's testimony is recorded
    in Hearing Before the Committee on Expenditures in the Executive De-
    partments, June 27, 1947. In 1982, Representative Jack Brooks, chair of
    the House Committee on Government Operations, and Representative
    Edward Boland, chair of the House Permanent Select Committee on In-
    telligence, had their staffs unearth the transcript and printed it with an
    introduction on its unusual history. Representative Clare E. Hoffman of
    Michigan, the Republican chair of the House Committee on Expenditures
    in the Executive Departments, led the session in 1947. The witnesses tes-
    tified under code names (Mr. A, Mr. B, Mr. C). Hoffman had kept the
    only transcript of the hearing; in October 1947, he loaned it to the leg-
    islative counsel of the CIA, Walter Pforzheimer, who made a copy, stored
    it in a safe, and returned the original. Hoffman destroyed the original in
    1950. The sole surviving copy was unearthed from CIA archives thirty-
    two years later.

    The other major witnesses at the hearing were Director of Central In-
    telligence Vandenberg and John "Frenchy" Grombach, leader of The
    Pond, the spy service created by army intelligence back in 1942. "We are
    not playing with marbles," Grombach told the committee. "We are play-
    ing with our national security, and our lives" by letting Central Intelli-
    gence run clandestine operations. Let the army spy for the United States,
    he argued, and let Central Intelligence write reports. Any other way
    would be "wrong and dangerous."

    Vandenberg struck back. The real danger, he testified, was The Pond—
    "a gravy train," a "commercial concern," filled with mercenary amateurs
    who babbled secrets in barrooms. The clandestine collection of secret in-
    telligence was a difficult business that had to be conducted by tightly con-
    trolled professionals.

    Vandenberg went on to explain how to build a proper intelligence
    network. "The clandestine field, sir, is a very complicated one," he testi-
    fied. "The way it works is that you have an expert in the clandestine field,
    or as near an expert as the United States has, and who we can hire for
    the money that we can pay. . . . He then builds a chain of people that he
    knows. Then, we have to have another man picked, in whom we have

full confidence, who builds a chain alongside, who is just watching . . . to make sure that this man is not giving you information and receiving pay from a foreign government. . . . The man who originally set up the net ostensibly has no connection with any person or any department of the Government." He cautioned: "The chances of the U.S. Government in peacetime getting into tremendous difficulties behooves us to keep it right under our thumb; and you cannot keep it under your thumb if you are contracting for it [by hiring] some chap who comes into the office and tells you he would be very glad if you would give him $500,000 a year. . . . It might very well be that that man is paid by another government and is feeding you the information that that government would like for you to have."

That was an accurate outline of the challenges the CIA faced at its creation—more so than what followed from Allen Dulles: "I do not believe in a big agency," he said. "You ought to keep it small. If this thing gets to be a great big octopus, it should not function well. Abroad, you will need a certain number of people, but it ought not to be a great number. It ought to be scores rather than hundreds." He inherited nearly ten thousand people when he took over in 1953 and built from there past fifteen thousand, toward twenty thousand, and most of them were charged with running covert operations abroad. Covert operations were a task Dulles never got around to mentioning.

24 *"the greatest cemetery for dead cats"*: Walter Millis (ed.) with E. S. Duffield, *The Forrestal Diaries* (New York: Viking, 1951), p. 299.

25 *"I had the gravest forebodings"*: Acheson, *Present at the Creation*, p. 214.

25 *hundreds of major covert actions—eighty-one of them during Truman's second term*: a number published in "Coordination and Policy Approval of Covert Actions," a coordinated NSC/CIA document dated February 23, 1967, and declassified after a long struggle in 2002.

25 *The CIA's counsel, Lawrence Houston*: Houston told Hillenkoetter that the act gave the CIA no legal authority for anything resembling covert action. Nor was there any implied intent of Congress to be read between the lines of the law. If the NSC gave orders for that kind of mission, and if the CIA went back to Congress and specifically requested and received the authority and the money for a covert operation, that might be another matter. Thirty years passed before his advice was heeded. Houston to Hillenkoetter, "CIA Authority to Perform Propaganda and Commando Type Functions," September 25, 1947, FRUS Intelligence, pp. 622–623.

25–26 *"guerrilla warfare".* . . . *"fight fire with fire"*: Kennan to Forrestal, September 26, 1947, Record Group 165, ABC files, 352:1, NARA.

26 *In a bitter memo*: Penrose to Forrestal, January 2, 1948, FRUS Intelligence, pp. 830–834.

26   *"covert psychological operation"*: NSC 4/A, December 14, 1947.

What was psychological warfare? The first CIA officers wondered. A war of words? If words were weapons, should they be true or false? Was the CIA supposed to sell democracy on the open market or smuggle it into the Soviet Union? Was this about beaming radio broadcasts or dropping leaflets behind the iron curtain? Or was it a command to mount clandestine operations designed to break enemy morale? The dark arts of strategic deception had fallen into disuse since D-Day. No one had developed a new doctrine of conducting warfare without weapons. From his command post in Europe, General Eisenhower urged fellow officers "to keep alive the arts of psychological warfare." Eisenhower memo, June 19, 1947, RG 310, Army Operations, P & O 091.412, NARA; Memo from Director of Central Intelligence, "Psychological Warfare," October 22, 1947, FRUS Intelligence, pp. 626–627.

But Brigadier General Robert A. McClure, the future father of American special-operations forces, found that American "ignorance . . . about psychological warfare . . . is astounding." McClure to Propaganda Branch, MID War Department, Record Group 319, Box 263, NARA; Colonel Alfred H. Paddock, Jr., "Psychological and Unconventional Warfare, 1941–1952," U.S. Army War College, Carlisle Barracks, PA, November 1979.

Hillenkoetter searched for a chief of a new "Special Procedures Branch" who could cut through the murk. Kennan and Forrestal wanted Allen Dulles for the job. They got Thomas G. Cassady, an old OSS man, a broker and banker from Chicago. Cassady was a disaster. He tried to set up a radio station for transmissions behind the iron curtain, and a printing press for propaganda in Germany, but nobody could come up with the right words to win the hearts and minds of the oppressed. His big idea was Project Ultimate: sending high-level balloons into the Soviet Union with leaflets bearing messages of brotherly love. Why not an airlift of Mickey Mouse watches? asked a skeptic at the State Department.

26   *"the most ancient seat of Western Culture"*: "Consequences of Communist Accession to Power in Italy by Legal Means," CIA, Office of Research and Estimates, March 5, 1948.

27   *"We were going beyond our charter"*: Wyatt interview with author. See also his interview for the CNN Cold War series, 1998 National Security Archive transcript available online at http://www.gwu.edu/~nsarchiv/coldwar/interview/episode-3/wyatt1.html.

The Italian operation became one of the most expensive, longest-running, and richly rewarding political-action operations in the agency's first twenty-five years. In November 1947, at the start of the operation, James J. Angleton returned from his post as station chief in Rome to organize a Soviet division inside Galloway's struggling Office of Special Operations. Angleton had built a substantial stable of agents in Italy, in part by offering some very tough customers immunity from war crimes prosecutions, and he had been thinking about the coming elections and laying plans for many months. Angleton's executive officer in Rome, Ray Rocca, an Italian American from San Francisco, was left in charge of the first phases of the operation. In retrospect, William Colby felt there was no magic to the operation; it was a straight-cash proposition. It would remain straight cash for a quarter century. The miracle of 1948 was that the center held and that the CIA could claim credit for the victory. In the run-up to that election, the center-right Christian Democrats, allied with the Vatican and led by Alcide De Gasperi, were neck and neck with the Communist Party, whose leaders looked to Moscow and claimed a rank-and-file membership of two million loyalists. "They were the big parties," said the CIA's Mark Wyatt. "The neo-fascists were out of the picture. The monarchists were dead." Three minor parties remained: Republicans, Liberals, and Social Democrats. The CIA decided in March to split its own vote, as it were, by supporting minor-party candidates as well as the Christian Democrats. Overviews of the operation are in Ray S. Cline, *Secrets, Spies, and Scholars: Blueprint of the Essential CIA* (Washington, DC: Acropolis, 1976), pp. 99–103, and Peter Grose, *Operation Rollback: America's Secret War Behind the Iron Curtain* (Boston: Houghton Mifflin, 2000), pp. 114–117. Cline was deputy director of intelligence at the CIA from 1962 to 1966; Grose unearthed telling congressional testimony describing the uses of the Treasury Department's Exchange Stabilization Fund.

There are no records of what the Italian operation cost, though estimates run from $10 million to $30 million. The black bags of money were filled, in part, with bonds of friendship and trust. Treasury Secretary Snyder had a close friend in A. P. Giannini, the Italian American financier who ran Transamerica Corporation, a holding company that controlled the Bank of America and some two hundred smaller banks. Giannini, in turn, was put in touch with Wyatt, a fellow San Franciscan. "I had many contacts with prominent Italian-Americans in this country: bankers, industrialists, that were full of ideas, and some of them were very aberrant ideas," such as a coup d'état if the covert plan failed, Wyatt said. Giannini was among his contacts, as were "powerful political leaders in this country, not just Tammany Hall and Cook County, Illinois, but outstanding ones that knew how to win elections." Muscle as well as money was involved. An apocryphal story about the 1948 Italian operation holds that three CIA contract agents went to Palermo to do something about the situation on the docks, where they turned to members of the local Mafia to address the problem. They succeeded in getting American arms shipments past communist longshoremen, but headquarters was not happy with their methodology. Assessing precisely how crucial the CIA was to the American cause in the 1948 elections is like unscrambling an egg. The flood of American weapons and armor to Italy, the American ships that delivered tons of food, and waves of international news amplified by the shock of the fall of Czechoslovakia all contributed to the victory and to the cementing of the long relationship between the CIA and the increasingly corrupt Italian political elite. Joe Greene, who divided his time between the State Department and the Office of Policy Coordination, recalled that the Italians "announced they wanted to give the U.S. a token of their appreciation for all the Americans had done from the end of the war, when they changed sides, up to the early '50s. They offered enormous bronze equestrian statues that are on the northwest end of the Memorial Bridge in Washington. De Gasperi came over for that and Truman attended the dedication ceremony. It was a great show." The horses are still there. Greene oral history, FAOH.

28 *The CIA station chief in Prague, Charles Katek*: The exfiltration of Katek's Czech agents was described in interviews by Tom Polgar and Steve Tanner, both CIA officers in Germany in 1948. But the CIA performed less nobly when called upon to save the life of Michael Shipkov, a Bulgarian who served as chief translator for the American Legation in that newly Stalinist state. The legation asked the army for help in getting Shipkov out of the country, said Raymond Courtney, the American vice consul: "They came back with a really childish, impossible scheme: have him set out on the road by night and make his way, not by road but cross country over the mountains with five or six feet of snow, down to the Greek border and try to make a clandestine meeting in a graveyard there. I put Shipkov out on the road about 3 o'clock in the morning and sent the poor guy on his way. Well, he made the first safe house all right and the second safe house, but then the couriers didn't turn up and he didn't want to compromise his hosts any further so he tried to set out on his own without any guidance or assistance. The militia picked him up. We learned later that the reason the couriers had not shown was that they had both gone down with flu and had laid over 24 hours in a haystack. Shipkov's capture was announced over the State radio with a great blare of publicity. Shipkov was given a very, very bad time. After 15 years of that he was released from prison." Courtney oral history, FAOH.

28 *the Marshall Plan*: the CIA's use of Marshall Plan funds is described in "A Short History of the PSB," December 21, 1951, NSC Staff Papers, White House Office Files, DDEL. The diversion of Marshall Plan funds for covert action was detailed in an October 17, 1949, memo for Frank Wisner, chief of the Office of Policy Coordination: "CIA Responsibility and Ac-

countability for ECA Counterpart Funds Expended by OPC," classified Secret, reprinted in Michael Warner (ed.), *CIA Cold War Records: The CIA Under Harry Truman* (Washington, DC: CIA History Staff, 1994). This was a rare accounting: under "general and specific agreements" made in secret among a handful of men in the know, "the 5% counterpart funds of ECA are made available to CIA" for covert operations, according to the CIA document. The ECA, or Economic Cooperation Administration, administered the Marshall Plan.

There was always plenty of cash. "Of course, we had money," said Melbourne L. Spector, a Marshall Plan administrator in Paris. "We had counterpart funds just coming out of our ears." Spector oral history, FAOH.

28 *"Tell them to stick their hand in our pocket"*: Griffin oral history, HSTL.

29 *"the inauguration of organized political warfare"*: Kennan unsigned memo, May 4, 1948, FRUS Intelligence, pp. 668–672.

29 *NSC Directive 10/2 called for covert operations*: the fighting words in full were as follows:

> The National Security Council, taking cognizance of the vicious covert activities of the USSR, its satellite countries and Communist groups to discredit and defeat the aims and activities of the United States and other Western powers, has determined that, in the interests of world peace and US national security, the overt foreign activities of the US Government must be supplemented by covert operations . . . so planned and executed that any US Government responsibility for them is not evident to unauthorized persons and that if uncovered the US Government can plausibly disclaim any responsibility for them. Specifically, such operations shall include any covert activities related to: propaganda, economic warfare; preventive direct action, including sabotage, anti-sabotage, demolition and evacuation measures; subversion against hostile states, including assistance to underground resistance movements, guerrillas and refugee liberation groups, and support of indigenous anti-communist elements in threatened countries of the free world.

Kennan was indisputably the directive's chief intellectual author. A generation later he rued it all, saying that the push for political warfare was his greatest mistake, that covert operations clashed with American traditions, that "excessive secrecy, duplicity and clandestine skullduggery are simply not our dish." Few in power said so at the time. The conventional wisdom among the cognoscenti was clear. If America was to stop the Soviets, it was going to need an army of secret soldiers. Kennan managed to write more than a thousand pages of memoirs without any mention of his role as the progenitor of covert action. His justly acclaimed work was thus a small masterpiece of duplicity as well as a magnificent diplomatic history. See also Kennan's "Mortality and Foreign Policy," *Foreign Affairs*, Winter 1985–1986; and his statement that the political warfare initiative was "the greatest mistake I ever made" in his testimony to the Church Committee, October 28, 1975, quoted in the committee's final report, Vol. 4, p. 31.

Director of Central Intelligence Hillenkoetter was aghast at the very idea of the new clandestine service. He made plain his belief that the United States should never engage in covert action in peacetime. Nor was he the only one to wonder about the costs of secret subversion. Sherman Kent, the greatest of the CIA's cold-war analysts, had committed the following thought to paper: To send "clandestine operatives into a foreign country against which the United States is not at war and instruct these agents to carry out 'black' operations," he wrote, "not only runs counter to the principles upon which our country was founded but also those for which we recently fought a war." Robin Winks, *Cloak and Gown: Scholars in the Secret War, 1939–1961* (New Haven, CT: Yale University Press, 1987), p. 451.

29 *"rumor-spreading, bribery, the organization of non-communist fronts"*: Edward P. Lilly, "The Development of American Psychological Operations, 1945–1951," National Security Council, Top Secret, DDEL, c. 1953.

30 *The CIA's Berlin base*: Sichel and Polgar interviews with author; "Subject: Targets of German Mission, January 10, 1947," CIA/CREST. For a reliable overview of the CIA's Berlin Operations Base, see David E. Murphy, Sergei A. Kondrashev, and George Bailey, *Battleground Berlin: CIA vs. KGB in the Cold War* (New Haven, CT: Yale University Press, 1997). Murphy later served as base chief.

31 *"a zeal and intensity"*: Helms's eulogy at a memorial service for Wisner at CIA headquarters, January 29, 1971. Helms summoned up some lines from Robert Frost's "Once by the Pacific" when he remembered the cold warrior in Wisner:

> *It looked as if a night of dark intent*
> *Was coming, and not only a night, an age.*
> *Someone had better be prepared for rage.* . . .

Wisner was described as "a singular choice to create a covert organization from scratch" in "Office of Policy Coordination, 1948–1952," unsigned, undated, declassified with redactions in March 1997, CIA/CREST. The author was Gerald Miller, Wisner's Western Europe operations chief.

Chapter Four

32 *battle plans for the next five years*: Wisner's ambitions are detailed in his
   memo "Subject: OPC Projects," October 29, 1948, FRUS Intelligence,
   pp. 730–731; author's interviews with Wisner's contemporaries, including Richard Helms, Franklin Lindsay, Sam Halpern, Al Ulmer, and
   Walter Pforzheimer; and "Office of Policy Coordination, 1948–1952,"
   CIA/CREST.

33 *LeMay told Wisner's right-hand man Franklin Lindsay*: Lindsay interview
   with author. Lindsay fought as an OSS guerrilla alongside Tito's partisans
   in Yugoslavia. After the war, alongside Allen Dulles, he served on the
   staff of the congressional committee that authorized the Marshall Plan.
   In September 1947, he had led a group of members of Congress on that
   committee, including Richard Nixon, to the occupied city of Trieste,
   where they witnessed a tense confrontation between a Yugoslav tank
   column and American forces on the eve of Trieste's transition to a free
   territory. Yugoslavia was still in the Soviet orbit; Tito would not break
   with Stalin for another nine months. It was a hair-trigger moment. The
   Allied commander in Trieste, General Terence Airey, warned the American and British governments: "If this matter is not handled very carefully
   a third World War might start here." Upon returning to Washington,
   Lindsay and his predecessor as the chief of the wartime military mission
   to Tito's forces, Charles Thayer, proposed a guerrilla warfare corps to battle the Soviets—"fighting fire with fire"—an idea that caught Kennan's
   eye just as Lindsay caught Wisner's.

34 *"the most secret thing"*: James McCargar oral history, FAOH. McCargar had
   worked in secret for The Pond in Hungary, serving both the State Department and the army's covert intelligence network from April 1946 to December 1947.

35 *"We were in charge"*: Ulmer interview with author.

35 *First in Athens*: The CIA's Thomas Hercules Karamessines, a Greek American from Staten Island, started out in Athens in 1947 and befriended up-
   and-coming officers. After the Greek military took over the country
   twenty years later, they had a friend in Karamessines, who had risen to
   become the chief of covert action.

35 *"Individuals, groups, and intelligence services quickly came to see"*: "Office of
   Policy Coordination, 1948–1952," CIA/CREST.

35 *Wisner flew to Paris . . . to talk . . . with Averell Harriman*: Franklin Lindsay
   was working for Harriman in the Paris headquarters of the Marshall Plan
   in the fall of 1948, witnessed the conversation, and then immediately
   went to work as an operations chief for Wisner. "Harriman knew all
   about OPC," Lindsay said. Wisner fully briefed Harriman on November

16, 1948. After that, money was never an object: "I had a budget of as many millions as I could spend, and I couldn't spend it all," McCargar recounted. For Harriman's knowledge of Wisner's plans, see Wisner's memorandum for the file, FRUS Intelligence, pp. 732–733. Wisner's visit to Dick Bissell came shortly thereafter. Richard M. Bissell, Jr., with Jonathan E. Lewis and Frances T. Pudlo, *Reflections of a Cold Warrior: From Yalta to the Bay of Pigs* (New Haven, CT: Yale University Press, 1996), pp. 68–69.

The connections among the diplomats, the money men, and the spies were cozy. The ECA chief in Paris was David K. E. Bruce, late of the OSS. Harriman's chief deputy was Milton Katz, head of the secret intelligence division of the OSS in London under William Casey, the future director of central intelligence.

The Marshall Plan, in addition to money and cover, chipped in with personnel on covert propaganda and anticommunist actions aimed at labor unions in France and Italy. Some Marshall Plan officials ran covert operations for Wisner for three years after he sealed the deal with Averell Harriman. Wisner also briefed John McCloy, then the senior American civilian in Germany (and the War Department chieftain who helped preserve American intelligence in the face of Truman's death sentence back in September 1945). Wisner recorded that he "explained to Mr. McCloy the general significance and origin of OPC" and detailed "certain aspects of our present and prospective operations in Germany." He noted that McCloy "seemed to be impressed by my statement that the original architects of the whole deal included Messrs. Lovett, Harriman, Forrestal, Kennan, Marshall, et al." FRUS Intelligence, pp. 735–736.

36 *the well-greased palms of Corsican gangsters*: Gerald Miller's OPC history records that Wisner "initially concentrated its efforts within the circumference of the trade union movement." The earliest of these efforts, Operations Pikestaff and Largo, are documented in declassified CIA records, complete with Kennan's authorizing signature, dated October 1948. "In the early days of the Marshall Plan," said Victor Reuther, the Congress of Industrial Organizations' representative in Europe in those days, "when there were some political strikes called by communist trade union forces and perhaps communist political elements to try to defeat the Marshall Plan and to try to block foreign aid from being unloaded, it became a matter of breaking these strikes. And the U.S. government, through Central Intelligence, called upon Irving Brown and Jay Lovestone to try to organize a countermove. And of course, if you want to break a strike, you go to boys who have big bare knuckles and who know how to wield cudgels. And they turned to what can best be described as the Corsican Mafia." A CIA officer who later handled that account, Paul Sakwa, said he cut off the pay-

ments to the chief of the Corsican mob, Pierre Ferri-Pisani, in 1953, when the Marshall Plan's run was over. "There was nothing for Ferri-Pisani to do at the time," Sakwa said, "and probably he was involved in smuggling heroin going through Marseille, and he did not need our money." Reuther and Sakwa interviews, "Inside the CIA: On Company Business," a 1980 documentary directed by Allan Francovich, transcript courtesy of John Bernhart. The present author interviewed Mr. Sakwa in 1995. The relationship of Wisner, Lovestone, and Brown is detailed in the Free Trade Union Committee's files and Lovestone's own records at the AFL-CIO International Affairs Department Collections, George Meany Memorial Archives, Silver Spring, MD, and in the Lovestone Collection at the Hoover Institution, Stanford University. See also Anthony Carew, "The Origins of CIA Financing of AFL Programs," *Labor History,* Vol. 39, No. 1, 1999.

Lovestone served the CIA for a quarter of a century, earning a reputation as a brilliant manipulator. His first case officer was Wisner's aide, Carmel Offie, who oversaw labor and émigré affairs as well as the National Committee for Free Europe, and created the first big security scare inside the CIA. Offie was a flamboyant homosexual in an age when deviance was deemed politically dangerous. The CIA's security officers found a police report showing that Offie had been arrested for soliciting sex in a men's room a block from the White House. They handed it to J. Edgar Hoover. He hounded Offie, who was quietly dismissed from the CIA and went on the American Federation of Labor's payroll. FBI agents tapped Lovestone's phone and recorded him railing to Wild Bill Donovan that the CIA was filled with "Park Avenue socialites and incompetents and degenerates. . . . That whole organization is thoroughly mismanaged, thoroughly inefficient, thoroughly irresponsible." This was the purest catnip for Hoover.

36 *"a vast project targeted on the intellectuals"*: Braden in Granada Television documentary, "World in Action: The Rise and Fall of the CIA," June 1975. Among the budding authors who wrote books while working with the CIA in Paris was Peter Mathiessen, one of the greatest writers of his generation and a noted liberal.

37 *The report, which remained classified for fifty years*: "The Central Intelligence Agency and National Organization for Intelligence: A Report to the National Security Council," also known as the Dulles-Jackson-Correa report, January 1, 1949, CIA/CREST.

37 *"the heat of confusion"*: Roosevelt to Acheson, February 1, 1949, HSTL.

37 *"The greatest weakness of CIA"*: Ohly to Forrestal, February 23, 1949, HSTL.

38 *After fifty haunted nights*: Forrestal's suicide followed months of "a severe and progressive fatigue," Townsend Hoopes and Douglas Brinkley, *Driven Patriot: The Life and Times of James Forrestal* (New York: Vintage, 1993), pp.

448–475. Dr. Menninger said he suffered from "an extreme impulsive drive to self-destruction." Menninger letter to Captain George Raines, Chief of Neuropsychiatry, U.S. Naval Hospital, Bethesda, MD, in "Report of Board of Investigation in the Case of James V. Forrestal," National Naval Medical Center, 1949. President Truman replaced Forrestal with Louis Johnson, a wealthy campaign contributor who had been clamoring for the job for months. Johnson was a man with few redeeming virtues, so given to seething rages and staggeringly illogical table-pounding rants that Dean Acheson, who served alongside him as secretary of state, was convinced that he was either brain-damaged or mentally ill. General Omar Bradley, the chairman of the Joint Chiefs, concluded that "Truman had replaced one mental case with another." As this drama played out at the Pentagon, Truman himself wondered whether he had put a madman in charge of American national security. Dean Acheson, *Present at the Creation: My Years in the State Department* (New York: W. W. Norton, 1969), p. 374; Omar N. Bradley and Clay Blair, *A General's Life: An Autobiography* (New York: Simon and Schuster, 1983), p. 503.

Chapter Five

39 *"run the railroads"*: Richard Helms with William Hood, *A Look over My Shoulder: A Life in the Central Intelligence Agency* (New York: Random House, 2003), p. 82.

39 *Many among them were desperate refugees*: In 1948, John W. McDonald, an American officer, was serving as the district attorney of Frankfurt under the American occupation when he encountered the CIA at work. He told the story as follows:

> The police had captured a ring of eighteen people. The number-one person was a Pole named Polansky, a displaced person. He had done a brilliant job of making these plates for fifty-dollar U.S. greenbacks. We caught him and a hundred thousand dollars in counterfeit currency, and the presses and the plates and the ink—everything you could possibly ask for. He also had a U.S. Army uniform. He had an ID card and an Army .45-pistol and a PX card. The whole bit. So I thought this was great. We were about to go to trial with the whole group of them when I was visited one day by a Major, who came into the office.

The conversation went like this:

> "I'm Overt."
> "Major Overt, it's a pleasure to meet you."

"No, you don't understand. Overt as opposed to Covert."

"Who are you?"

"I'm a member of the CIA."

"What can I do for you?"

"You have this Pole in prison, named Polansky. He's one of us."

"What do you mean, one of us?"

"He's on our payroll. He's part of the CIA."

"Since when does the CIA employ counterfeiters of U.S. dollars?"

"No, no, no. He did that on his own time."

"So it doesn't count, is that right?"

"Well, yes, it doesn't count. He is our best maker of documents, passports and all kinds of things like that that we use for going Eastward."

"Well, that's fine, but he has still committed a crime and I couldn't care less about who he is working for."

McDonald continued: "I showed him the door. The next day a Colonel came to see me about the same case and we had exactly the same discussion. I was unimpressed. Two days after that a Major General came to see me. Now that is a lot of brass in those days. It was very serious, I could see that. But he was smarter than the other two, he said, 'As you know by now, this man worked for us. We are the ones who gave him the uniform, and the .45 and all the ID cards and so forth. I would very much appreciate it if you would drop those charges, so that we will not be publicly embarrassed.' I went on and a week or so later went to trial and of course got the maximum of ten years, which was the maximum under German law for counterfeiting. But I've never forgotten Major Overt. My first encounter with the CIA was not a very auspicious one." McDonald oral history, FAOH.

39 *"encouraging resistance movements into the Soviet World"*: Wisner cited in Kevin C. Ruffner, "Cold War Allies: The Origins of CIA's Relationship with Ukrainian Nationalists," Central Intelligence Agency, 1998.

39 *"a reserve for a possible war emergency"*: "U.S. Policy on Support for Covert Action Involving Emigrés Directed at the Soviet Union," December 12, 1969, FRUS, 1969–1970, Vol. XII, document 106.

39 *a CIA history*: Ruffner, "Cold War Allies."

40 *"We will just have to tell the House"* and *"The less we say about this bill, the better"*: Both in Hearings Before the House Committee on Armed Services, as declassified, 81st Congress, 1st session, 1949.

41 *Mikola Lebed*: Norman J. W. Goda, "Nazi Collaborators in the United States," in *U.S. Intelligence and the Nazis*, National Archives, pp. 249–255. Army intelligence officers had already started a touch-and-go relation-

ship with the Ukrainians, using them to try to gather information on the Soviet military and Soviet spies in postwar Germany. Their first hireling in Munich had been Myron Matvieyko, a German intelligence agent during the war, a murderer and counterfeiter afterward. Suspicions soon grew that he was a mole for Moscow; his subsequent defection to the Soviet Union confirmed that fear.

41 *"rendering valuable assistance"* and *"of inestimable value"*: The Dulles and Wyman letters are in the National Archives, Record Group 263, Mikola Lebed name file, made public in 2004. After Lebed was admitted to the United States, the agency maintained an operational relationship with his Ukrainians that proved to be one of its most resilient alliances with anticommunist émigré groups. His Supreme Council for the Liberation of the Ukraine eventually turned to less lethal forms of resistance activity. The CIA set up a publishing house for Lebed in New York in the 1950s. He lived to see the Soviet Union fall and Ukraine free to chart its own difficult destiny.

41 *"however slim the possibility of success or unsavory the agent"*: Ruffner, "Cold War Allies."

42 *General Reinhard Gehlen*: Allen Dulles had the last word on Gehlen: "There are few archbishops in espionage. He's on our side and that's all that matters. Besides, one needn't ask him to one's club." The American rationale for recruiting Nazi spies was clear to men like army captain John R. Boker, Jr., as early as the summer of 1945. "Now was the ideal time to gain intelligence of the Soviet Union if we were ever going to get it," said Boker, a skilled interrogator with deep German roots who started nosing around for Nazis days after their surrender. Boker found his man in Reinhard Gehlen. The American captain regarded the German general as "a goldmine that we had found." Both men agreed that a new war with the Soviets was coming soon and that their nations should make common cause against the communist threat. Brigadier General Edwin L. Sibert, the army intelligence chief in Europe and soon to be the CIA's first assistant director for covert operations, bought this pitch. He decided to hire Gehlen and his spy ring. He did not clear his decision with his superiors—Generals Dwight D. Eisenhower and Omar Bradley—on the sound assumption that they would have rejected it. On Sibert's say-so, General Gehlen and six of his fellow German spies flew to Washington on the personal plane of the future director of central intelligence General Walter Bedell Smith. The Germans were vetted and debriefed for ten months at a secret military installation within Fort Hunt, outside Washington, before they were returned to their fatherland to work against the Russians. This was the birth of a long partnership between America's intelligence officers and Hitler's washed-up spies. John R. Boker, Jr., "Report of Initial Contacts with General Gehlen's

Organization," May 1, 1952. This debriefing and a host of CIA documents on the Gehlen organization are collected in *Forging an Intelligence Partnership: CIA and the Origins of the BND,* edited by Kevin C. Ruffner of the CIA's History Staff, printed by CIA's Directorate of Operations, European Division, and declassified in 2002. The documents include Gehlen's statements enclosed in James Critchfield [Chief of Station, Karlsruhe] to Chief, FBM, CIA HQ, February 10, 1949; "Report of Interview with General Edwin L. Sibert on the Gehlen Organization," March 26, 1970; "SS Personnel with Known Nazi Records," Acting Chief, Karlsruhe Operations Base, to Chief, FBM, August 19, 1948.

42   *"a rich blind man"*: Chief, Munich Operations Base, to Acting Chief of Station, Karlsruhe, July 7, 1948.

42   *"no question the Russians know"*: Helms to ADSO, Col. Donald Galloway, March 19, 1948.

42   *"We did not want to touch it"*: Sichel interview with author.

43   *"given how hard it was for us"*: Tanner interview with author.

Tanner, who retired from the CIA in 1970, added the following contribution, written in the third person, to the previously untold story of the agency's support for the Ukrainian insurgents:

> Tanner found only one group meeting his criteria, namely the Supreme Council for the Liberation of the Ukraine (UHVR). Surprisingly, no Russian émigré group qualified. UHVR not only had overland courier contact with the Ukrainian Insurgent Army in the Carpathian Mountains, but also received some reports from Ukraine via couriers, Catholic clerics, plus occasional travelers and escapees.
>
> The key interests of the UHVR and CIA seemed to dovetail: both desperately wanted radio contact with insurgent headquarters, "behind enemy lines." Policy bigwigs in Washington approved this formula, which had worked well in wartime France, Italy and Yugoslavia.
>
> Over nine months, two couriers were trained under Tanner's supervision in radio operation, enciphered codes, parachuting and target practice for self-defense. They parachuted onto a mountain meadow near Lvov the night of September 5, 1949. This first air drop and the next one in 1951 produced radio contact, but no earthshaking information. The final two missions were definitely compromised via Angleton's briefings to Philby and the unlucky courier groups were arrested on the spot by Soviet NKVD "welcoming committees."
>
> To Ukrainian nationalists in the USSR, the first air drop

was a huge morale boost and must have led to exaggerated expectations. By mid-1953, however, the Soviets had effectively overwhelmed armed insurgent resistance.

Four errors and stellar stupidities in the postwar era stuck in Tanner's mind. First, at the end of World War Two, the Allies forcibly repatriated Soviet citizens. When they found out they were about to be handed back to the Russians, many committed suicide. And those handed back never reached Soviet soil, but were shot or hung in Eastern Europe by Security Service death squads.

Second, the cover of CIA's Munich base personnel was blown skyhigh by an error in the 1949 U.S. Army phone book: names listed with no unit designation all belonged to CIA people. The Army might as well have placed an asterisk next to their names.

Thirdly, after World War Two parachute experts and trainers left OSS as the need for their services was over. There were two results: a Serbo-American OSS veteran who had parachuted into wartime Yugoslavia taught the two Ukrainian couriers to somersault backwards when they hit the ground, despite the four-foot carbines strapped to their sides. Also, for the September 1949 drop Washington advised using the wrong freight chute and the crate holding 1400 pounds of equipment burst into small pieces upon impact.

Fourthly, and worst of all, James Angleton briefed Kim Philby, the Soviet mole in British intelligence, about the RED-SOX program [the overall effort to infiltrate former Soviet and ethnic foreign nationals behind the iron curtain].

46 *"What had we done wrong?"*: John Limond Hart's convincing critique of Angleton is in his posthumous memoir, *The CIA's Russians* (Annapolis, MD: Naval Institute Press, 2002), especially pp. 136–137. Hart was called out of retirement in 1976 to assay the damage Angleton had done to the CIA as its counterintelligence chief. On the Albanian operation: McCargar oral history, FAOH; Michael Burke, *Outrageous Good Fortune* (Boston: Little, Brown, 1984), pp. 140–169. Wisner picked Mike Burke to train the Albanians. Burke, later the president of the New York Yankees, was an OSS veteran and he liked the covert life. He signed on as a $15,000-a-year contract agent and was off to Munich, where he met the Albanian politicos at a safe house in a working-class district of the city. "As the youngest person in the room, representing a young and rich country, I commanded their attention," Burke wrote. He believed that he and the

exiles understood one another. The Albanians saw things differently: "The Americans who prepared our men for these missions knew nothing of Albania, the Albanian people or their mentality," said Xhemal Laci, an Albanian monarchist who recruited men for the cause in Germany. The operation was so completely compromised from the start that it was anyone's guess where the deepest roots of the disaster lay. McCargar, who was a good friend of Angleton's, concluded: "The Albanian community in Italy was so thoroughly penetrated, not only by the Italians but by the Communists, that to me that was where the Russians were getting their information, as were the Albanian Communist authorities."

47 *"The ends don't always justify the means"*: Coffin interview with author.

47 *"assistance to the émigrés for the eventuality of war"*: This retrospective look is in "U.S. Policy on Support for Covert Action Involving Emigrés Directed at the Soviet Union."

48 *the CIA confidently declared*: CIA Intelligence Memorandum No. 225, "Estimate of Status of Atomic Warfare in the USSR," September 20, 1949, reprinted in Michael Warner (ed.), *CIA Cold War Records: The CIA Under Harry Truman* (Washington, DC: CIA History Staff, 1994). The full text: "The earliest possible date by which the USSR might be expected to produce an atomic bomb is mid-1950 and the most probable date is mid-1953." The assistant director of the CIA's Office of Scientific Intelligence, Willard Machle, reported to Director of Central Intelligence Hillenkoetter that the agency's work on Soviet atomic weapons had been an "almost total failure" at every level. The spies had "failed completely" to gather scientific and technical data on the Soviet bomb, and the CIA's analysts had resorted to "geological reasoning" based on guesstimates of the Soviets' ability to mine uranium.

In Machle's memo to Hillenkoetter, "Inability of OSI to Accomplish Its Mission," dated September 29, 1949, he lamented that it had "proved difficult to find persons with acceptable qualifications who could be prevailed upon to accept employment in the Agency." Machle memo, in George S. Jackson and Martin P. Claussen, *Organizational History of the Central Intelligence Agency, 1950–1953*, Vol. 6, pp. 19–34, DCI Historical Series HS-2, CIA Historical Staff, 1957, Record Group 263, NARA.

The in-house CIA historian Roberta Knapp noted that as of September 1949, "the official coordinated statement on Soviet completion of an atomic weapon was to be found in an estimate that predicted three different dates for it—1958, 1955, and 'between 1950 and 1953'—all wrong." This, she concludes, "constituted clear evidence of disarray." As a consequence, the CIA's Office of Reports and Estimates (ORE) was "doomed," according to another CIA historian, Donald P. Steury in "How the CIA Missed Stalin's Bomb," *Studies in Intelligence*, Vol. 49, No. 1, 2005,

CIA/CSI. This internal history notes that many ORE analysts were nuclear physicists and engineers from the Manhattan Project who had the optimistic notion that they could track the progress of the Soviet nuclear program by reading published scientific papers, supplemented by evidence from clandestine sources. By 1948 there was no useful evidence in open-source literature emerging from the Soviet Union. But since 1947, a German source at the former I. G. Farben complex (makers, among other things, of Nazi death-camp gases) had reported that the Soviets were importing thirty tons of distilled metallic calcium a month from the plant. The quantity of the pure calcium, which was used to refine uranium ore, was roughly eighty times the annual U.S. output. The source's reporting was independently corroborated. It should have raised an alarm. It did not.

Chapter Six

49   *"One is God, and the other is Stalin"*: "Nomination of Lt. Gen. Walter Bedell Smith to Be Director of Central Intelligence Agency," Executive Session, August 24, 1950, CIA, Walter Bedell Smith papers, DDEL.

49   *"I expect the worst"* and *"It's interesting to see all you fellows here"*: David S. Robarge, "Directors of Central Intelligence, 1946–2005," *Studies in Intelligence*, Vol. 49, No. 3, 2005, CIA/CSI.

50   *"It was the place where all the money was spent"*: Bedell Smith quoted in "Office of Policy Coordination, 1948–1952," CIA/CREST.

50   *"the heart and soul of CIA"*: Bedell Smith quoted in George S. Jackson and Martin P. Claussen, *Organizational History of the Central Intelligence Agency, 1950–1953*, Vol. 9, Part 2, p. 38. This 1957 history was declassified in 2005. DCI Historical Series HS-2, CIA Historical Staff, Record Group 263, NARA.

50   *"an impossible task"*: Sherman Kent, "The First Year of the Office of National Estimates: The Directorship of William L. Langer," CIA/CSI, 1970.

50   *"estimating is what you do when you do not know"*: Sherman Kent, "Estimates and Influence," *Foreign Service Journal*, April 1969.

50–51   *Four hundred CIA analysts*: Jackson and Claussen, *Organizational History of the Central Intelligence Agency, 1950–1953*, Vol. 8, p. 2.

51   *The CIA found itself manipulated*: James Lilley, former CIA station chief in Beijing, interview with author. The problem persisted well into the late 1960s, when Lilley found that "the same sort of fabricated Chinese intelligence networks that we had resisted and thrown out 15 years ago" were back in business, picking up tidbits from provincial newspapers in China and selling them to American spies in Hong Kong.

51   *"the most significant intelligence loss in U.S. history"*: David A. Hatch with Robert

Louis Benson, "The Korean War: The SIGINT Background," National Security Agency, available online at http://www.nsa.gov/publications/publi000 22.cfm. Weisband's role in the history of American intelligence has been misrepresented for decades. The magisterial *KGB: The Inside Story* by Christopher Andrew, one of the world's preeminent intelligence historians, and Oleg Gordievsky, the defector from Soviet intelligence, devotes three sentences to Weisband and incorrectly gives the date of his recruitment by Soviet intelligence as 1946. According to the official National Security Agency and CIA histories of the case, Weisband was recruited by the Soviets in 1934. An aircraft industry worker in California told the FBI in 1950 that Weisband had been his KGB handler during the war. Weisband was born in Egypt to Russian parents in 1908, came to the United States in the late 1920s, and became an American citizen in 1938. He joined the Army Signals Security Agency in 1942 and was assigned to North Africa and Italy before returning to Arlington Hall. Weisband was suspended from his work at the security agency and then failed to appear at a federal grand jury hearing on Communist Party activity. Convicted of contempt, he was sentenced to a year in prison—and there the matter ended, for to accuse him openly of espionage would have deepened the problems of American intelligence. Weisband died suddenly in 1967, apparently of natural causes, at age fifty-nine.

52 *"no convincing indications"*: The only thing the CIA at headquarters knew for sure was that General MacArthur believed that the Chinese were not coming. CIA reporting and analysis on Korea from June to December 1950 reflected that fallacy. The reporting is detailed in P. K. Rose, "Two Strategic Intelligence Mistakes in Korea, 1950," *Studies in Intelligence*, Fall/Winter, No. 11, 2001; CIA Historical Staff, "Study of CIA Reporting on Chinese Communist Intervention in the Korean War, September–December 1950," prepared in October 1955 and declassified in June 2001; and Woodrow J. Kuhns, "Assessing the Soviet Threat: The Early Cold War Years," CIA Directorate of Intelligence, Center for the Study of Intelligence, 1997.

53 *an impossible tangle*: Before Bill Jackson resigned as Bedell Smith's deputy director in 1951, he gave the general a report on Wisner's operations. "Subject: Survey of Office of Policy Coordination by Deputy Director of Central Intelligence," May 24, 1951, CIA/CREST. It said: "The job . . . exceeds the capacity of any one man." The Office of Policy Coordination was trying to build "a world-wide machine, comparable in many ways to a military force" without adequate levels of competent control, personnel, training, logistics, or communications. "There is a great discrepancy between the most highly qualified Division Chiefs and the least qualified," he reported. "The burdens of operational commitments have overtaken the capacity to recruit highly qualified personnel."

53 *It was $587 million*: "CIA/Location of Budgeted Funds/Fiscal Year 1953," a
    document from the files of Representative George Mahon, one of four
    members of Congress with knowledge of the CIA's budget. When Profes-
    sor David Barrett of Villanova University found this document in 2004, it
    changed history. For almost thirty years, every book about the CIA has
    faithfully reprinted the 1976 finding of Senate investigators that Wisner's
    budget was $82 million in 1952. That figure is clearly erroneous. The
    OPC's budget in 1952 was in fact roughly four times bigger than previ-
    ously reported.

53 *"a distinct danger"*: Director's meeting, November 14, 1951, CIA/CREST.
    The minutes of the daily meetings of the director of central intelligence,
    his deputies, and his staff, contained in newly declassified records ob-
    tained through CREST, give the flavor of the struggles of the CIA. The
    minutes of this meeting state: "The Director wants them [Dulles and Wis-
    ner] to take a very close look at OPC. Paramilitary operations should be
    sorted out from the rest of the budget as should all operations that do not
    contribute to intelligence. He believes we have arrived at a point where
    the size of our OPC operations have become a distinct danger to CIA as
    an intelligence agency."

    Bedell Smith saw that United States "had no strategy for conducting
    this kind of war," meaning Wisner's kind of war. "Preliminary Staff
    Meeting, National Psychological Strategy Board," May 8, 1951,
    CIA/CREST. He told Dulles and Wisner, "You do not have in government
    a basic approved strategy for this kind of war. . . . While we have the
    equipment and the power, we are not doing the job we should."

    Bedell Smith tried more than once to remove Wisner from control of
    paramilitary operations. Director's meeting, April 16, 1952, CIA/CREST.
    He argued in vain that they far exceeded what had been contemplated in
    NSC 10/2, the political-warfare manifesto of 1948. But State and Defense
    all wanted an expansion of covert action—one of "great magnitude." Be-
    dell Smith to NSC, "Scope and Pace of Covert Operations," May 8, 1951,
    CIA/CREST. Bedell Smith's warning not "to withhold" or "to whitewash
    unfortunate incidents or serious errors" came at the August 21, 1951,
    daily staff meeting, CIA/CREST. He had days before implored Wisner and
    other senior intelligence officers "to give serious attention to the prob-
    lems of fabrication and duplication in intelligence sources." Minutes of
    meeting, August 9, 1951, CIA/CREST.

    The newly available CREST records show that Bedell Smith had inher-
    ited "a sort of Holy Roman Empire in which the feudal barons pursued
    their respective interests subject to no effective direction and control by
    their titular emperor," in the words of Ludwell Lee Montague, his per-
    sonal representative on the National Security Council staff, who recorded

that the general "came to suspect that Dulles and Wisner . . . would eventually lead him into some ill-conceived and disastrous misadventure." CIA/LLM, pp. 91–96, 264.

54 *The classified CIA histories*: The classified Central Intelligence Agency histories are "CIA in Korea, 1946–1965," "The Secret War in Korea, June 1950–June 1952," and "Infiltration and Resupply of Agents in North Korea, 1952–1953." They were first cited by Michael Haas, a retired air force colonel, in his monograph, *In the Devil's Shadow: U.N. Special Operations during the Korean War* (Annapolis, MD: Naval Institute Press, 2000).

54 *"They were suicide missions"*: Sichel interview with author.

55 *"a great reputation and a terrible record"*: Gregg interview with author. In the case of Korea, the record has been obscured or falsified. For instance, John Ranelagh, *The Agency* (New York: Simon and Schuster, 1986), long considered a standard reference on the CIA, contains three paragraphs on covert paramilitary activities during the Korean War. It claims that OPC operations chief Hans Tofte successfully placed agents all over Korea, China, and Manchuria: "These 'closed' areas were successfully penetrated with Korean and Chinese CIA agents," and Tofte's "multifaceted and complex" operations used "trained guerrillas to operate in North Korea" and placed "agents across Korea who could act as guides and provide hideouts for lost airmen" (pp. 217–218). This is false, as the CIA's operational histories of Korea show. Tofte was a fabricator. He faked film footage of CIA guerrillas operating in North Korea; the fraud was quickly unmasked when someone back in Washington wondered why commando missions were being launched in broad daylight. More to the point, the actual missions, as opposed to the staged one, were by and large disasters. The CIA's own internal histories flatly contradict the pretty picture of Korean War operations represented in *The Agency*.

56 *"controlled by the other side"*: Thomas oral history, FAOH.

56 *"a hard look at the miraculous achievements"*: John Limond Hart's posthumous memoir, *The CIA's Russians* (Annapolis, MD: Naval Institute Press, 2004), spells out his extraordinary experiences in succeeding Al Haney as station chief in Seoul.

57 *"The CIA, being a new"*: Hart quoted in Christopher Andrew, *For the President's Eyes Only: Secret Intelligence and the American Presidency from Washington to Bush* (New York: Harper Perennial, 1996), pp. 193–194.

Hart's reports of Haney's fraud were buried, as were Haney's mistakes. Haney himself later noted, "There was considerable talk during and after Korea by many responsible senior officers that CIA should profit from its experience and be better prepared for the next Korea." But, he concluded, "I seriously doubt if CIA has profited at all from Korea or that the experiences there have even been catalogued let alone studied for lessons for the future." Haney to Helms, "Subject: Staff Study re Improvement of CIA/CS Manpower Potential Thereby Increasing Operational Capability," November 26, 1954, declassified April 2003, CIA/CREST. Haney survived his incredible performance in the Korean War because at the end of his tour in November 1952, he had helped arrange for the transportation of a grievously wounded marine lieutenant in Korea from the battlefield to the hospital ship *Constellation* to the United States, where seven weeks later the brain-damaged soldier was photographed receiving a rare kiss from his father, Allen W. Dulles. The photo was taken the day before the elder Dulles's confirmation hearings to become director of central intelligence. Dulles paid his debt of gratitude by making Haney the Florida-based commander of Operation Success in 1954.

57–58 *"Blown operations indicate a lack of success"*: Becker to Wisner, undated but December 1952 or January 1953, CIA/CREST. Before resigning as deputy director of intelligence, Loftus Becker told his colleagues that he was "distressed to learn how uninformed our people in the field were" and expressed his doubts about the CIA's ability to gather intelligence anywhere in Asia. Deputy director's meeting, December 29, 1952, CIA/CREST. Then he confronted Frank Wisner directly.

58 *"CIA was being duped"*: Kellis made his accusations of false testimony by senior CIA officials in a letter to President Dwight D. Eisenhower, May 24, 1954, DDEL.

58 *"We are all aware that our operations in the Far East are far from what we would like"*: Wisner, "[*Deleted*] Report on CIA Installations in the Far East," March 14, 1952, CIA/CREST.

58 *The officers on the agency's China operations desk*: The history of American intelligence operations in and around China in the years between the end of World War II and the beginning of Mao's dictatorship has never been completely recounted. A score of OSS veterans had hung on in China under military cover after Truman's abolition order, taking the name External Security Detachment 44. Lieutenant Colonel Robert J. Delaney first ran ESD-44; he later became chief of the CIA's tiny Tokyo station in 1947, and then the number-two man at OPC's Western Enterprises operation on Taiwan. In 1945, when the war was over, Delaney wrote of the tasks ahead in a dispatch sent from Shanghai. He noted that American intelligence officers faced a vast terrain as unfamiliar as the mountains of the moon, great swaths of land running from the South China Sea west to Afghanistan, from Saigon north to Siberia. They had to know the capabilities and intentions of the Soviet, communist Chinese, and Nationalist Chinese military and intelligence services, and they had to puzzle out the particulars of all the politics and pressure groups in the Far East. These tasks would take the better part of fifty years. They were complicated by

CIA's conventional wisdom: Mao's Chinese, Ho Chi Minh's Vietnamese, and Kim Il-sung's Koreans all were creatures of the Kremlin, an immutable monolith, of one mind, made in Moscow. The OSS and early CIA men of the Far East sent bales of intelligence back to Washington. Much of it went unread, "locked up in archives in the company of silence and rats." Maochun Yu, *OSS in China: Prelude to Cold War* (New Haven: Yale University Press, 1997), pp. 258–259.

The CIA's first officers in China were commanded by Amos D. Moscrip, who worked out of a French outpost in Shanghai, where he played the socialite, drank hard, and slept with a White Russian girlfriend. Some State Department diplomats thought they could do business with Mao, who after all had worked with the OSS against the Japanese. But the communists clearly suspected that Americans in China, diplomats or not, would try to subvert them. By October 1948, the State Department wanted all American diplomatic outposts in China evacuated, because anyone who could remotely be connected by the communists to espionage on behalf of the United States faced prison or perhaps worse. In Mukden, a city of two million in Manchuria, those evacuation orders arrived as the American consul general, Angus Ward, and his twenty-one-member staff were placed under a yearlong house arrest after refusing to surrender the consulate to Mao's troops. "He was accused of espionage, which, frankly, he was guilty of!" remembered John F. Melby, then a State Department political officer reporting out of Chungking. "He'd been working with what was known as ESD-number something or other, which was a CIA outpost. He was up to his eyeballs, working with the crew that he had up there with him in Manchuria." Melby oral histories, HSTL, FAOH.

The chief of "the crew" was Jack Singlaub, one of the more audacious cold warriors of the 1970s and 1980s. In 1948, Singlaub had been conspiring with the Chinese Nationalists, attempting to insert a network of White Russians into the Soviet Union, and seeking ways to plant spies in Soviet-occupied North Korea. Singlaub did in fact manage to run some Korean agents through Manchuria into North Korea in 1948. He dispatched dozens of men who had been prisoners of war held by the Japanese with orders to try to join the communist military in the North and report back on their intentions and capabilities. A handful seemed at first to have succeeded. But when he tried to find safe houses for those spies in Seoul, he was thwarted by MacArthur's resistance. Singlaub sent an extraordinary request through CIA channels to the White House—it was addressed "Eyes Only Moscrip, For the President"—pleading for Truman to arm the Chinese Nationalists with American war stockpiles on Okinawa. The president was unmoved. With the fall of Mukden imminent, Singlaub cabled

the nearest American naval commander: "IMPERATIVE I NOT BE CAP-
TURED." He flew out under artillery attack, passing a reconnaissance
plane with a red star insignia, knowing this battle of the cold war was lost.
John K. Singlaub, *Hazardous Duty: An American Soldier in the Twentieth Century* (New York: Summit, 1992), pp. 132–149.

In Shanghai, the station chief, Fred Schultheis, had been building a
fair-size network of agents and informers in the city, in part because he
spoke impeccable Chinese, which he honed by reading anything he could
get his hands on, from newspapers to comic books. He was, among
Americans, an old China hand, having been stationed in country with
the army throughout the war. With Mao on the march, winning city after city in late 1948, Schultheis couldn't wait to get out. He went to Hong
Kong as chief of station in 1949, and soon became convinced that Hong
Kong, too, was about to come under communist attack. He began sending out terrifying reports based on speculation and surmise, warning that
the city was the next domino to fall. One State Department officer and
OSS veteran stationed with him in Hong Kong, Joseph A. Yager, remembered that fear vividly: "We had various intelligence that seemed to indicate that an attack was coming. It turned out to be wrong." But
"Schultheis was convinced that it was coming. He was very alarmist. He
said, 'This time, it won't be Stanley. It will be Belsen.' Stanley was Stanley Peninsula, where the Japanese had interned the foreigners. That was
pretty bad. They had nearly starved them to death. Of course, Belsen was
one of the death camps of the Germans." Yager oral history, FAOH.

At headquarters in 1950, Singlaub, installed as the CIA's China desk
officer after Mao's triumph, oversaw stations abandoned and operations
routed. He worked feverishly to maintain the dwindling network of CIA
officers and stay-behind agents in China, and to re-establish broken espionage networks in Manchuria and North Korea.

In Tihwa, the capital of Xinjiang, in China's desolate wild west, Douglas Mackiernan was the CIA man at the two-man American consulate.
He had been posted there during the war as an army air force officer and
knew the terrain, rich with uranium, oil, and gold. He lived about as far
from Western civilization as any American on earth. Finally forced to
abandon the consulate in the face of communist forces, Mackiernan was
stranded. He would have to find his own way out. At the end of a seven-
month, 1,200-mile trek out of China, he was shot, pointlessly, by a Tibetan border guard, the first CIA officer to die in the line of duty.

In Shanghai, Hugh Redmond, who had been Singlaub's underling in
Mukden, tried to operate under a thin cover as the local representative
of a British import-export firm. "He was a likeable guy, but not terribly
effective," Singlaub observed. "It was the height of folly to believe that an

amiable young amateur like Hugh Redmond, no matter how dedicated, could function well against a ruthless totalitarian foe." Chinese security forces arrested Redmond as a spy. He killed himself after almost two decades in prison. Robert F. Drexler, a longtime China intelligence hand at the State Department, received Redmond's mortal remains. "His ashes, I can still see them," Drexler remembered, "an enormous package, about two feet long and one foot square, with a muslin covering and the large letters of his name on the side. And this was set on my desk. Perfectly horrible. The Chinese told us he committed suicide, after being held for 20 years, with a razor blade in a Red Cross package. The Red Cross told us they never put razor blades in their packages." On Mackiernan and Redmond: Drexler oral history, FAOH; Ted Gup, *The Book of Honor: The Secret Lives and Deaths of CIA Operatives* (New York: Anchor, 2002).

58 *"We haven't even a policy on Chiang Kai-shek"*: Bedell Smith, preliminary staff meeting, National Psychological Strategy Board, May 8, 1951, CIA/CREST.

59 *"they tested me on my loyalty"*: Kreisberg oral history, FAOH.

59 *"Luckily for me"*: Coe interview with author. Mike Coe was sent to White Dog Island, off the China coast, where the futility of the mission was considerably eased by the camaraderie. His companions on the island included Phil Montgomery, born Philippe-Louis de Montgomery, an heir to the Noilly Prat vermouth fortune, who kept the bar well stocked; and the legendary R. Campbell James, Jr., who drained it as best he could. "Zup" James, Yale '50, with the mannerisms and clipped mustache of a British grenadier, was the last Western Enterprises officer to leave Taiwan in 1955. He went on to Laos, where he recruited the nation's leaders over cocktails and roulette.

60 *the CIA decided that there had to be a "Third Force" in China*: Lilley and Coe interviews with author. Lilley FAOH.

60 *arms and ammunition for 200,000 guerrillas*: "OPC History," Vol. 2, p. 553, CIA.

60 *Dick Fecteau and Jack Downey*: The CIA recently declassified its first formal admission of the deaths of its agents in the Third Force fiasco and the bungling that led to the capture of Fecteau and Downey: Nick Dujmovic, "Two CIA Prisoners in China, 1952–1973," *Studies in Intelligence*, Vol. 50, No. 4, 2006:

> The first Third Force team to be airdropped did not deploy until April 1952. This four-man team parachuted into southern China and was never heard from again. The second Third Force team comprised five ethnic Chinese dropped into the Jilin region of Manchuria in mid-July 1952. Downey was

well known to the Chinese operatives on this team because
he had trained them. The team quickly established radio contact with Downey's CIA unit outside of China and was resup-
plied by air in August and October. A sixth team member,
intended as a courier between the team and the controlling
CIA unit, was dropped in September.

In early November, the team reported contact with a local
dissident leader and said it had obtained needed operational
documents such as official credentials. They requested air exfiltration of the courier, a method he had trained for but that
the CIA had never attempted operationally. . . . Pilots Norman Schwartz and Robert Snoddy had trained in the aerial
pickup technique during the fall of 1952 and were willing to
undertake the mission. . . . Late on 29 November, Downey
and Fecteau boarded Schwartz and Snoddy's olive-drab C-47
on an airfield on the Korean peninsula and took off for the
rendezvous point in Chinese Communist Manchuria, some
400 miles away . . . heading for a trap.

The agent team, unbeknownst to the men on the flight,
had been captured by Communist Chinese security forces
and had been turned. The request for exfiltration was a ruse,
and the promised documentation and purported contact with
a local dissident leader were merely bait. The team members
almost certainly had told Chinese authorities everything they
knew about the operation and about the CIA men and facilities associated with it. From the way the ambush was conducted, it was clear that the Chinese Communists knew
exactly what to expect. . . . As the C-47 came in low for the
pickup, flying nearly at its stall speed of around sixty knots,
white sheets that had been camouflaging two antiaircraft
guns on the snowy terrain flew off and gunfire erupted at the
very moment the pickup was to have been made. The guns,
straddling the flight path, began a murderous crossfire. . . .
Fecteau later remembered standing outside the aircraft with
Downey, both stunned but conscious, telling each other that
they were "in a hell of a mess." The Chinese security forces
descended on them, "whooping and hollering," and they
gave themselves up to the inevitable.

[T]here is the question of whether the field ignored warnings that the deployed team had been turned by the communists. . . . A former senior operations officer who, as a young
man, had served in Downey and Fecteau's unit in 1952 . . .

asserts that, in the summer before the November flight, an analysis of two messages sent by the team made it "90 percent" certain, in his view, that the team had been doubled. Bringing his concerns to the attention of the unit chief, the officer was rebuffed for lack of further evidence. When he persisted, he was transferred to another CIA unit. After Downey and Fecteau's flight failed to return, the unit chief called the officer back and told him not to talk about the matter, and he followed instructions—much to his later regret. . . .

No record of an inquiry into the decision to send Downey and Fecteau on the flight appears to exist. It is clear that no one was ever disciplined for it. . . . Many years later, Downey told a debriefer that he felt no bitterness toward the man who sent him on the mission: "I felt for him. It turned out to be such a goddamned disaster from his point of view."

61 *the Li Mi operation*: The operation would have terrible consequences. The first of these came after the CIA neglected to inform the American ambassador in Burma, David M. Key, about Li Mi. When he found out, he was furious. He cabled Washington, protesting that the operation was becoming an open secret in the Burmese capital and in Bangkok as well, and that the trampling of Burma's sovereignty was doing deep damage to American interests. The assistant secretary of state for the Far East, Dean Rusk, instructed his ambassador to shut up: he was to categorically deny any American involvement in the operation and blame it all on freelance gunrunners. Li Mi and his forces later turned their guns on the Burmese government, whose leaders, suspecting American connivance, severed relations with the United States and began a half century of isolation from the West that produced one of the world's more repressive regimes. Aspects of the Li Mi operation are in Major D. H. Berger, USMC, "The Use of Covert Paramilitary Activity as a Policy Tool: An Analysis of Operations Conducted by the United States Central Intelligence Agency, 1949–1951," available online at http://www.global security.org/intell/library/reports/1995/BDH.htm. Further details were supplied by Al Ulmer, who succeeded Desmond FitzGerald as Far East division chief; Sam Halpern, FitzGerald's executive officer; and James Lilley.

The CIA's Thai allies were deeply into Li Mi's heroin trade. Things almost got out of hand in Bangkok in 1952. The CIA's Lyman Kirkpatrick, then the assistant director for special operations and thought to be in line to succeed Wisner, flew out to Asia in late September 1952, along with his counterpart, Wisner's assistant director, Colonel Pat Johnston. At least one

American mixed up with the drug dealing was dead, and the matter appears to have been referred to the attorney general of the United States. None of it was sorted out to anyone's satisfaction. Colonel Johnston resigned his post immediately thereafter. Kirkpatrick contracted polio during the trip and nearly died. He returned to the CIA a year later, was passed over for promotion, and spent the rest of his life in a wheelchair, serving as the CIA's brooding inspector general, a study in frustrated ambition.

61 *"I have found, through painful experience"*: Smith to Ridgway, April 17, 1952, CIA, DDEL.

61 *A postscript to the CIA's Korean calamities*: On the effort to supplant Syngman Rhee: "Rhee was becoming senile, and the CIA sought ways to replace him. . . ," The Ambassador in Korea (John Muccio) to the Assistant Secretary of State for Far Eastern Affairs (John Allison), Secret, February 15, 1952, FRUS, Vol. XV, pp. 50–51. An NSC memo to Secretary of State Dulles, dated February 18, 1955, said that President Eisenhower had approved an operation "to select and encourage covertly the development of new South Korean leadership" and to bring it to power if needed. Peer de Silva's recounting of the CIA's near-shooting of President Rhee is in his memoir, *Sub Rosa: The CIA and the Uses of Intelligence* (New York: Times Books, 1978), p. 152.

62 *"Our intelligence is so bad that it approaches malfeasance in office"*: Melby, FAOH.

62 *"people who are ready and willing to stand up and take the consequences"*: Dulles in transcript of "Proceedings at the Opening Session of the National Committee for a Free Europe," misdated but May 1952, declassified May 28, 2003, DDEL.

Chapter Seven

63 *"If we are going to move in and take the offensive"*: Dulles transcript, "Proceedings of the National Committee for a Free Europe," misdated but May 1952, declassified May 28, 2003, DDEL.

63 *"a major covert offensive against the Soviet Union," aimed at "the heartland of the communist control system"*: The orders were to "contribute to the retraction and reduction of Soviet power," and to "develop underground resistance and facilitate covert and guerrilla operations in strategic areas." They came from Admiral L. C. Stevens, a senior war planner from the Joint Chiefs of Staff who had been Smith's naval attaché in Moscow. Admiral L. C. Stevens memo to Wisner, "Subject: OPC Strategic Planning," July 13, 1951, CIA/CREST. The goal was to "place the maximum strain on the Soviet structure of power." NSC staff memo, "Scope and Pace of Covert Operations," June 27, 1951, CIA/CREST.

64 *"Like Guantánamo"*: Polgar interview with author. Bedell Smith's orders to Truscott are dated March 9, 1951, CIA/CREST.

65 *a program code-named Project Artichoke*: Untitled memo for deputy director of central intelligence, May 15, 1952; memo for director of central intelligence, "Subject: Successful Application of Narco-Hypnotic Interrogation (Artichoke)," July 14, 1952, CIA/CREST. This second report noted that Dulles had met with military intelligence service chiefs in April 1951 to seek their help with Project Artichoke; only the navy liaison had come through. The result of the navy's assistance was the Panama brig. A follow-up memo, sent to Bedell Smith, reported that two Russians had been interrogated for two weeks in June 1952 by a joint Navy-CIA team under Project Artichoke, and a combination of drugs and hypnosis had proved useful. All of this was an outgrowth of the national emergency created by the Korean War and the suspicion that American prisoners were being brainwashed in North Korea. Senate investigations got to the margins of this program thirty years ago, but the paper trail had largely been destroyed. Project Artichoke, the investigators reported in four terse paragraphs, included "overseas interrogations" involving both "a combination of sodium pentothal and hypnosis" and "special interrogation techniques" including "truth serums." The nature of the "overseas interrogations" was not explored by Congress.

66 *"special interrogation" techniques continued for several years thereafter*: Senate investigators confirmed that plans for overseas interrogations were a topic of monthly meetings at the CIA from 1951 to at least 1956, and probably for several years thereafter: "The CIA maintains that the project ended in 1956, but evidence suggests that Office of Security and Office of Medical Services use of 'special interrogation' techniques continued for several years thereafter." Report of the Senate Select Committee on Intelligence, "Testing and Use of Chemical and Biological Agents by the Intelligence Community," Appendix I, August 3, 1977.

66 *a group called the Young Germans*: Tom Polgar and McMahon interviews with author.

67 *the CIA's Free Jurists*: Polgar and Peter Sichel interviews with author, see also David E. Murphy, Sergei A. Kondrashev, and George Bailey, *Battleground Berlin: CIA vs. KGB in the Cold War* (New Haven, CT: Yale University Press, 1997), pp. 113–126.

67 *"Poland represents"*: Smith and Wisner at deputies' meeting, August 5, 1952 CIA/CREST. For Shackley's encounter with WIN, see Ted Shackley with Richard A. Finney, *Spymaster: My Life in the CIA* (Dulles, VA: Potomac, 2005), pp. xvi–20.

68 *"CIA had clearly thought"*: Loomis oral history, FAOH.

68 *Frank Lindsay . . . told Dulles and Wisner*: Lindsay's prophetic report was called "A Program for the Development of New Cold War Instruments,"

March 3, 1953, declassified in part July 8, 2003, DDEL. Lindsay interview with author. Dulles did his best to suppress the report. The leaders of the CIA never took time to assess the consequences of covert action's failures, or accept criticism that could cost them their jobs if it ever leaked out. Nor did they heed one of their best spies, Peter Sichel, Helms's chief of espionage operations for Eastern Europe in the early 1950s, who warned that the only way to fight the enemy was to know the enemy. Sichel said he argued that "the minute you get involved in ideology you are no longer going to have dependable intelligence. You are exposing intelligence agents to danger. You can't be a political agent without exposing yourself to the system that you are trying to undermine. If you're trying to undermine a political system that's autocratic, you're going to get hurt."

68 *"Our insight into the Soviet Union was zero"*: McMahon interview with author.

69 *"We can't get qualified people"*: Smith quoted in *CIA Support Functions: Organization and Accomplishments of the DDA-DDS Group, 1953–1956*, Vol. 2, Chap. 3, p. 128, Director of Central Intelligence Historical Series, declassified March 6, 2001, CIA/CREST.

69 *"improperly trained or inferior personnel"*: Minutes of meeting, October 27, 1952, CIA/CREST.

69 *"A word about the future"*: Richard Helms with William Hood, *A Look over My Shoulder: A Life in the Central Intelligence Agency* (New York: Random House, 2003), pp. 102–104.

Part Two
Chapter Eight

73 *"We have no reliable inside intelligence"*: The report, "Intelligence on the Soviet Bloc," is cited in Gerald Haines and Robert Leggett (eds.), *CIA's Analyses of the Soviet Union, 1947–1991: A Documentary History,* CIA History Staff, 2001, CIA/CSI.

73 *Eisenhower fumed*: Emmet J. Hughes, *The Ordeal of Power: A Political Memoir of the Eisenhower Years* (New York: Atheneum, 1963), p. 101. The president was equally unhappy to learn that the agency had no riposte for the Soviet peace offensive that followed soon after Stalin's funeral—a crude, cynical, occasionally effective propaganda campaign to convince the world that the Kremlin had copyrighted the concepts of Justice and Freedom.

73 *"Stalin never did anything to provoke a war with the United States"*: Jerrold Schecter and Vyacheslav Luchkov (trans. and ed.), *Khrushchev Remembers: The Glasnost Tapes* (Boston: Little, Brown, 1990), pp. 100–101.

75 *"any prior warning"*: NSC minutes, June 5, 1953, declassified February 12, 2003, DDEL.

75 *"as though the hour of decision were at hand"*: NSC minutes, September 24, 1953, declassified September 29, 1999, DDEL.

75 *"the Russians could launch an atomic attack"* ... *"We could lick the whole world"*: NSC minutes, October 7, 1953, declassified February 28, 2003, DDEL.

76 *The uprising was crushed*: The June 1953 East Berlin uprising is conclusively documented by the CIA's David Murphy in *Battleground Berlin: CIA vs. KGB in the Cold War* (New Haven, CT: Yale University Press, 1997), pp. 163–182. The endlessly repeated story—see, among many, John Ranelagh, *The Agency* (New York: Simon and Schuster, 1986), p. 258— that the CIA's Berlin base wanted to distribute weapons to the East German protestors is false. The figure of 370,000 protestors comes from James David Marchio, "Rhetoric and Reality: The Eisenhower Administration and Unrest in Eastern Europe, 1953–1959" (Ph.D. diss., American University, 1990), cited in Gregory Mitrovich, *Undermining the Kremlin: America's Strategy to Subvert the Soviet Bloc, 1947–1956* (Ithaca, NY: Cornell University Press, 2000), pp. 132–133.

76 *"train and equip underground organizations"*: NSC 158, "United States Objectives and Actions to Exploit the Unrest in the Satellite States," DDEL. Eisenhower signed the order on June 26, 1953.

76 *170 new major covert actions*: In "Coordination and Policy Approval of Covert Actions," February 23, 1967, NSC/CIA.

77 *Dulles polished the public image*: A partial list of news organizations that cooperated with the CIA under Allen Dulles includes CBS, NBC, ABC, the Associated Press, United Press International, Reuters, Scripps-Howard Newspapers, Hearst Newspapers, Copley News Service, and the Miami Herald. For a comprehensive list of war-propaganda veterans running American newsrooms in 1953, see Edward Barrett, *Truth Is Our Weapon* (New York: Funk and Wagnalls, 1953), pp. 31–33. This is a story that remains to be told, although Carl Bernstein had a very good cut at it in "The CIA and the Media," *Rolling Stone*, October 20, 1977. Bernstein got it precisely right in this passage: "Many journalists who covered World War II were close to people in the Office of Strategic Services, the wartime predecessor of the CIA; more important, they were all on the same side. When the war ended and many OSS officials went into the CIA, it was only natural that these relationships would continue. Meanwhile, the first postwar generation of journalists entered the profession; they shared the same political and professional values as their mentors. 'You had a gang of people who worked together during World War II and never got over it,' said one Agency official. 'They were

genuinely motivated and highly susceptible to intrigue and being on the inside.' "

77 *The minutes of the daily meetings of Dulles and his deputies*: The records were obtained from the CREST system at the National Archives in 2005 and 2006. They reflect a grinding fear that the CIA's weaknesses would be exposed to public view.

At the meetings of August 28 and September 23, 1953, CIA inspector general Lyman Kirkpatrick warned that military officers were leaving CIA in droves, and "with an unfriendly attitude." The agency's personnel policies were "causing disgruntlement and leaving the door wide open for these individuals to approach members of Congress."

On June 13, 1955, Kirkpatrick asked Dulles whether a CIA officer "recently convicted of manslaughter . . . as a result of a fight with an RAF officer should be terminated or allowed to resign." On October 5, 1955, Deputy Director of Intelligence Robert Amory noted that "the Army is presently preparing a history of Korea, which if published as presently written will put CIA in a bad light."

The station chief in Switzerland who killed himself was James Kronthal, an OSS veteran who had succeeded Allen Dulles in Bern and had served there since 1946. He was a homosexual suspected of succumbing to Soviet blackmail. The case was not proven. He committed suicide in Washington during Dulles's first days as director in March 1953.

The 17 percent annual turnover rate—one in six CIA personnel left in 1953—was a finding of the "Final Report on Reasons for Low Morale Among Junior Officers," November 9, 1953, CIA/CREST. The survey of 115 CIA officers recorded deep unhappiness at corruption, waste, and misdirected missions.

79 *"a major personnel crisis"*: House Permanent Select Committee on Intelligence, IC21, "Intelligence Community Management," p. 21.

79 *a man he regarded as a pompous blowhard*: CIA historians have surmised that Bedell Smith expected Ike to name him chairman of the Joint Chiefs of Staff, did not want to serve as undersecretary of state, did not like John Foster Dulles, and was uneasy about Allen Dulles's appointment as director of central intelligence. John L. Helgerson, "Getting to Know the President: CIA Briefings of Presidential Candidates, 1952–1992," CIA/CSI.

79 *"a couple of drinks would loosen his tongue"*: Transcript of Nixon interview with Frank Gannon, April 8, 1983, Walter J. Brown Media Archives, University of Georgia, available online at http://www.libs.uga.edu/media/collections/nixon.

Chapter Nine

This chapter is based in part on two classified CIA clandestine service histories: "Zindabad Shah!" obtained by the author, dated 2003, with redactions, and "Overthrow of Premier Mossadeq of Iran," written in March 1954 by Donald Wilber, the propaganda chief for Operation Ajax, and published on the Web site of *The New York Times* in 2000. "Overthrow" is the official authorized American intelligence version of the coup, a digest of what the CIA officers on the scene recorded and reported to their headquarters at the time. But it is not close to the full truth. The officers on the scene, like Kim Roosevelt, all but ceased relaying the news back home in the final days of the coup, because the news was almost all bad. The CIA history ignores the rationales behind the operation and strenuously downplays the central British role in the overthrow of Mossadeq. It explains President Eisenhower's reflection that "reports from observers on the spot in Tehran during the critical days sounded more like a dime novel than historical fact." Wilber, the author of "Overthrow," was also the rewrite man on the script for the coup itself. Every facet of the plot was polished in May 1953 at the British intelligence station in Nicosia, Cyprus, by Wilber, an OSS veteran who had served in Iran during the war and returned to the Tehran station, and his British counterpart Norman Darbyshire. What emerged was a play in which the Iranians were puppets.

81   *"When is our goddamn operation going to get underway?"*: Kermit Roosevelt, *Countercoup: The Struggle for Control of Iran* (New York: McGraw-Hill, 1979), pp. 78–81, 107–108. The book is much more novel than fact, but the cited quotation has the ring of authenticity. Kim Roosevelt, born to wealth, schooled in muscular Christianity at Groton, cut his teeth on secret intelligence at the OSS station in Cairo. Donovan's spies claimed a network of five hundred Arab agents by the war's end, across the Middle East, in every nation except Saudi Arabia. After the war, Roosevelt returned to the Middle East, ostensibly working for the *Saturday Evening Post* and gathering material for his 1947 book, *Arabs, Oil and History*. When the call came to join Frank Wisner's clandestine service, Kim heard it clearly. The legacy of big-stick diplomacy he inherited from his grandfather, the man who seized the Panama Canal and the Philippines, compelled him to become Wisner's grand vizier of the nations of Islam in 1950. As chief of the Near East division, Kim spent eight years trying to cajole the leaders of Egypt, Iraq, Syria, Lebanon, Jordan, and Saudi Arabia into pledges of American allegiance, using guns and money and promises of American support as inducements, and mounting the occasional coup when those means failed. He put young King Hussein of Jordan on the CIA's payroll, and he dispatched a corps of General Reinhard Gehlen's former storm troopers to train the secret service of the new Egyptian leader, Gamal Abdel Nasser.

The agency had a little experience in running Middle Eastern operations before Ajax. In the early 1950s. Miles Copeland, an Arabic-speaking smoothie from Alabama and the CIA's first station chief in Damascus, worked closely with the American military attaché in Syria, Stephen J. Meade, on a plan to back an "army supported dictatorship," to quote a December 1948 cable by Meade to the Pentagon. Their man was Colonel Husni Za'im, described by Copeland as an officer known for "his will of iron and brain to match." Copeland encouraged the colonel to overthrow his president, who had blocked an Arabian-American Oil Company pipeline across Syria, and he promised that President Truman would grant him political recognition. Za'im toppled the government on March 30, 1949, pledged complete cooperation with the pipeline project, and, as Meade reported, threw "over 400 Commies" into prison. The iron-brained colonel lasted less than five months before he was overthrown and executed. Back to the drawing board, Copeland cheerfully conceded.

The CIA's 1953 coup in Iran could never have started without the British, and it likely would not have succeeded. British intelligence had a deep understanding of the underlying political intrigues of Iran, gleaned from their agents in the government, the bazaar, and the underworld. The British government had an immense economic motive. And their plot to do away with Mossadeq had a powerful political impetus. It was driven forward by Sir Winston Churchill himself.

83 *"unseat Mossadeq"*: The longtime deputy director of intelligence Robert Amory recorded in his official diary for November 26, 1952, a discussion with the director concerning an "effort to unseat Mossadeq" and a subsequent lunch at which the main topic was Iran and the participants included Wisner, Ambassador Loy Henderson, and, though his name is deleted from the declassified record, doubtlessly Monty Woodhouse.

83 *"CIA makes policy by default"*: Deputies' meeting, August 10, 1953, CIA/CREST.

84 *"consequences of Soviet take over"*: Dulles briefing notes for NSC meeting, March 4, 1953, CIA/CREST.

84 *a $100 million loan*: NSC meeting minutes, March 4, 1953, DDEL.

84 *They could not maintain that Mossadeq was a communist*: Soviet intelligence reports in 1953 more concisely judged Mossadeq as "a bourgeois nationalist," and no ally in Moscow's eyes. Vladislav M. Zubok, "Soviet Intelligence and the Cold War: The 'Small' Committee of Information, 1952–53," *Diplomatic History*, Vol. 19, Summer 1995, pp. 466–468.

85 *"rescued by the Americans"*: Stutesman oral history, FOAH.

87 *"to liquidate the Mossadeq government"*: "Radio Report on Coup Plotting,"

July 7, 1953, National Security Archive, CIA/Freedom of Information Act (FOIA) release.

87 *Brigadier General Robert A. McClure*: General McClure's central role in the coup has gone unrecognized; the CIA's official in-house history of the plot all but erases him. The agency deliberately downplayed his work, for the general was no great friend of the CIA. See Alfred H. Paddock, Jr., *U.S. Army Special Warfare: Its Origins* (Washington, DC: National Defense University Press, 1982). I am grateful to Paddock for sharing the insights he derived from reading McClure's personal papers. McClure's "very fine relationships with the Shah" were mentioned in a note from Eisenhower to Army Secretary Robert Ten Broeck Stevens, April 2, 1954, Presidential Papers of Dwight David Eisenhower, document 814.

90 *"The failure of the military coup"*: CIA Office of Current Intelligence, "Comment on the Attempted Coup in Iran," August 17, 1953, declassified November 16, 2006.

90 *" 'After you, Your Majesty' "*: The dialogue is reproduced in the classified CIA history of the coup titled "Zindabad Shah!" (Victory to the Shah!)

90 *"an almost spontaneous revolution"*: Rountree oral history, FAOH.

91 *One was the Ayatollah*: It has been alleged that Ayatollah Kashani was in the pay of the CIA. Mark J. Gasiorowski, "The 1953 Coup D'Etat in Iran," *International Journal of Middle East Studies*, Vol. 19, 1987, pp. 268–269. But Reuel Marc Gerecht, who joined the CIA in 1985 as a member of the Iran desk of the clandestine service, wrote that Kashani was "beholden to no foreigner." Gerecht read the CIA's history of Operation Ajax, and he said the lesson in it was this: "One has to be generous to give American operatives in Iran much credit for restoring the Shah. Virtually every detail of their plan went awry. The principal American operatives at our embassy didn't speak Persian. When Teheran started to boil and it was impossible to make contact with the usual English- and French-speaking Iranian sources, the CIA station went blind. The coup succeeded only because Iranians who were neither on the American or British payrolls nor under foreign control seized the initiative to topple Prime Minister Mossadeq." Reuel Marc Gerecht, "Blundering Through History with the C.I.A.," *The New York Times*, April 23, 2000.

91 *"his old friend Bedell Smith"*: Roosevelt's recounting of this scene appears in chapter 9 of "Overthrow," the official CIA history.

92 *"Romantic gossip about the 'coup' in Iran"*: Ray S. Cline, *Secrets, Spies, and Scholars: Blueprint of the Essential CIA* (Washington, DC: Acropolis, 1976), p. 132. Note the quotation marks Cline placed around *coup*.

92 *"CIA's greatest single triumph"*: Killgore oral history, FAOH.

Chapter Ten

This chapter is based on the richest documentation of a CIA covert operation now available. In May 2003, the State Department published a supplemental volume of *The Foreign Relations of the United States* covering the role of the United States in the overthrow of the Guatemalan government in 1954 (available online at http://www.state.gov/r/pa/ho/frus/ike/guat/), along with a chronological, collated collection of 5,120 redacted CIA documents on the covert operation made public that same day (available online at http://www.foia.cia.gov/guatemala.asp). The publication of these documents was the result of a twenty-year struggle, and it represented a high-water mark in CIA historiography.

Unless otherwise noted, the quotations in this chapter are taken verbatim from these primary documents and from the CIA's own internal history of the coup, written by Nicolas Cullather, published in redacted form as *Secret History: The CIA's Classified Account of Its Operations in Guatemala, 1952–1954* (Stanford, CA: Stanford University Press, 1999).

The role of William Pawley at the crucial hour of the coup was revealed by the historian Max Holland in "Private Sources of U.S. Foreign Policy: William Pawley and the 1954 Coup d'État in Guatemala," *Journal of Cold War Studies*, Vol. 7, No. 4, 2005, pp. 46–73. Holland uncovered Pawley's unpublished memoirs at the George C. Marshall Library in Lexington, Virginia.

The memoirs of the key players include Dwight Eisenhower, *The White House Years: Mandate for Change, 1953–1956* (Garden City, NY: Doubleday, 1963); Richard Bissell, Jr., with Jonathan E. Lewis and Frances T. Pudlo, *Reflections of a Cold Warrior: From Yalta to the Bay of Pigs* (New Haven, CT: Yale University Press, 1996); and David Atlee Phillips, *The Night Watch: 25 Years of Peculiar Service* (New York: Atheneum, 1977). Phillips gives the players cover names, but the declassified documents make that cover transparent.

The Guatemalan operation began under General Walter Bedell Smith. On January 24, 1952, Allen Dulles told a State Department official overseeing Latin America that the "CIA was giving consideration to the possibility to rendering assistance to a group headed by Colonel Carlos Castillo Armas plotting the overthrow of the Government of Guatemala." Castillo Armas sought the help from Latin America's most powerful dictators—Nicaragua's Somoza, the Dominican Republic's Trujillo, Cuba's Batista—as his proposal gradually filtered up to the CIA's chiefs. In the spring and summer of 1952, Bedell Smith and Undersecretary of State David Bruce repeatedly discussed plans for a CIA-backed coup. The operation was code-named Fortune and the job was handed to J. C. King, the chief of the CIA's newly formed Western Hemisphere Division.

King devised a plan to ship weapons and $225,000 to Castillo Armas and his allies. In October 1952, he packed up 380 pistols, 250 rifles, 64 machine guns, and 4,500 hand grenades, all labeled as farm machinery, and he was set to ship them south from New Orleans. But the Nicaraguan dictator Somoza and his son Tacho had talked freely about the plot. Word filtered back to Washington that its cover was blown, and David Bruce called the whole thing off. But behind the State Department's back, with Bedell Smith's approval, King requisitioned an aging navy transport to carry the weapons to Nicaragua and Honduras. On its first trip, the ship was spied by several hundred curious Nicaraguans as it sought to land on a supposedly deserted island; on its second voyage, its engines conked out and the navy had to send a destroyer to rescue the crew and cargo.

A trickle of CIA aid reached Castillo Armas nonetheless, and in March 1953 he and most of his followers, about two hundred strong, tried to seize a remote Guatemalan army garrison. They were crushed, and while Castillo Armas escaped to Honduras, his movement was badly wounded. Operation Fortune had failed.

When it was revived as Operation Success, Bedell Smith played his role as undersecretary of state to the fullest. The American ambassadors in Guatemala, Honduras, and Nicaragua reported to the CIA through Bedell Smith. All shared the sense that "Communism is directed by the Kremlin all over the world, and anybody who thinks differently doesn't know what he is talking about," as Ambassador Peurifoy said. But the Kremlin thought little about Latin America in the days before Fidel Castro came to power. It had all but ceded the terrain to the United States, the dominant force in the hemisphere since the nineteenth century. Had the CIA infiltrated Guatemala's small but influential communist party, it would have known that the Guatemalans were not in touch with the Soviets.

The agency nevertheless saw Guatemala's President Arbenz as a Red puppet marching to music from Moscow. He had instituted the most ambitious and successful program of land reform in all of Latin America, taking fallow fields from corporations such as United Fruit and deeding them to hundreds of thousands of peasants. United Fruit felt threatened, and the CIA knew it; the company had tremendous political power in Washington and made its anger known at the highest levels of the government. But the CIA was not fighting for bananas. It saw Guatemala as a Soviet beachhead in the West and a direct threat to the United States. It also saw United Fruit and its lobbyists as an irritating impediment; it tried to shove them out of the picture as the operation gained steam.

94 *the classic CIA résumé of the 1950s—Groton, Yale, Harvard Law*: Perhaps too much has been made of the influence brought to bear at the CIA by the school of muscular Christianity practiced at Groton. But Operation Ajax in Iran was led by Kermit Roosevelt, class of 1936, with help from his cousin Archie Roosevelt, class of 1934. The planning and execution of Operation Success was led by Tracy Barnes, class of 1932, and Richard Bissell, class of 1931. Bissell, Barnes, and John Bross, the senior prefect

of the class of 1932, led the charge at the Bay of Pigs. And the toxins that the CIA aimed to use to kill Fidel Castro were prepared in an agency lab run by Cornelius Roosevelt, class of 1934.

94 *"Barnes proved unable"*: Richard Helms with William Hood, *A Look over My Shoulder: A Life in the Central Intelligence Agency* (New York: Random House, 2003), pp. 175–177.

96 *"Dulles's apprentice"*: Bissell, *Reflections of a Cold Warrior*, pp. 84–91.

99 *"What we wanted to do was to have a terror campaign"*: E. Howard Hunt interview for the CNN Cold War series, 1998, National Security Archive transcript available online at http://www.gwu.edu/~nsarchiv/coldwar/interviews/episode-18/hunt1.html.

101 *"we were all at our wit's end"*: Bissell, *Reflections of a Cold Warrior*, pp. 84–91.

104 *"we really didn't think it was much of a success"*: Esterline oral history in James G. Blight and Peter Kornbluh (eds.), *Politics of Illusion: The Bay of Pigs Invasion Reexamined* (Boulder, CO: Lynne Rienner, 1998), p. 40.

Chapter Eleven

105 *"Secrecy now beclouds"*: *Congressional Record* 2811–14 (1954).

105 *"CIA success stories"*: Deputies' meeting, February 29, 1956, CIA/CREST.

105 *"risky or even unwise"*: Dulles, "Notes for Briefing of Appropriations Committee: Clandestine Services," March 11, 1954, CIA/CREST. Such candor before Congress was exceedingly rare. John Warner, one of Allen Dulles's in-house lawyers at the CIA, recalled a far more typical encounter between Dulles and the House Appropriations Committee chairman, Clarence Cannon of Missouri. Cannon was close to eighty years old at the time: "Cannon greets Dulles; 'Oh, it's good to see you again, Mr. Secretary.' He thinks it's Foster Dulles. . . . They swap stories for two hours. And at the end—'Well, Mr. Secretary, have you got enough money in your budget for this year, the coming year?'—'Well, I think we are all right, Mr. Chairman. Thank you very much.' That was the budget hearing."

105 *"the CIA had unwittingly hired"*: Roy Cohn, *McCarthy* (New York: New American Library, 1968), p. 49.

106 *"CIA was neither sacrosanct"*: Transcript of telephone conversation between Allen and Foster Dulles, cited in David M. Barrett, *The CIA and Congress: The Untold Story from Truman to Kennedy* (Lawrence: University of Kansas Press, 2005), p. 184.

106 *a down-and-dirty covert operation*: The declassified CIA history outlining the CIA's work against McCarthy is Mark Stout, "The Pond: Running Agents for State, War, and the CIA," *Studies in Intelligence*, Vol. 48, No. 3, 2004, CIA/CSI. The congressional testimony came from William J. Morgan, a Yale-trained psychologist and OSS veteran who had been the CIA's

deputy chief of training, in a March 4, 1954, hearing before the Mc-Carthy committee titled "Alleged Threats Against the Chairman." The transcript was unsealed in January 2003. Morgan, who was detailed to Walter Bedell Smith's Operations Coordinating Board, testified that his superior, a CIA officer named Horace Craig, suggested that "the best thing to do was penetrate the McCarthy organization." Failing that, Craig speculated, more severe measures might be taken:

> Senator Charles E. Potter (R., Ill.): He stated in essence that this man should be liquidated, referring to Senator McCarthy?
> Dr. Morgan: It may be necessary.
> Senator Potter: And that there are madmen—
> Dr. Morgan: For a price willing to do the thing.

No other known evidence corroborates the charge that the CIA was thinking about killing McCarthy. The senator drank himself to death in good time.

107 *A congressional task force led by Eisenhower's trusted colleague General Mark Clark*: Clark's secret report, declassified in 2005, called the CIA "virtually a law unto itself," its conduct "unique and in many ways strange to our democratic form of government." See Michael Warner and J. Kenneth McDonald, "US Intelligence Community Reform Studies Since 1947," 2005, CIA/CSI.

107 *an extraordinary six-page letter*: Kellis to Eisenhower, May 24, 1954, DDEL.

108 *Doolittle went to see the president*: President's meeting with Doolittle Committee, October 19, 1954, DDEL. The notes from this meeting, hastily taken, convey the awkwardness of a bearer of bad news.

108 *The Doolittle report*: Special Study Group, "Report on the Covert Activities of the Central Intelligence Agency," September 30, 1954, declassified August 20, 2001, CIA/CREST.

109 *"sensitive and/or delicate operations"*: Director's meeting, October 24, 1954, CIA/CREST. The problem of uncontrolled secret operations persisted in the Dulles years. The director had determined that he could decide whether his superiors needed to know what he was up to. Some of his underlings felt the same way about him and his top aides. A senior CIA officer, John Whitten, gave secret Senate testimony in 1978 stating that "there were a number of operations in the clandestine services that neither the DDO nor the ADDO knew" in the 1950s and early 1960s. The DDO was the deputy director for operations—the chief of the clandestine service—and the ADDO his top assistant. Deposition of John Whitten, *Assassination Transcripts of the Church Committee*, May 16, 1978, pp. 127–128. Whitten testified under the alias "John Scelso"; his true identity was declassified by the CIA in October 2002.

109 *not even Wisner*: At a deputies' meeting on November 8, 1954, Wisner asked Dulles if he would be allowed to read the Doolittle report. Dulles refused the request. He allowed Wisner to see a brief version of the report's recommendations, but not the devastating critique itself.

110 *Dulles was desperate*: John Maury and Edward Ellis Smith interviews, R. Harris Smith papers, Hoover Institute, Stanford University.

110 *"Let's not have another Pearl Harbor"*: NSC minutes, March 3, 1955, DDEL.

111 *A secret CIA history of the Berlin tunnel*: "Clandestine Services History: The Berlin Tunnel Operation, 1952–1956," CIA, August 25, 1967, declassified February 15, 2007.

112 *glimmer of warning that Moscow intended to go to war*: The CIA officers who had started out at the Berlin base under Richard Helms still saw the city and the techniques they had learned there as the best windows into Moscow. Helms and his men thought that the big CIA stations in Germany and Austria and Greece should carefully and patiently establish resident agents inside Eastern Europe. These networks of trusted foreigners would recruit other like-minded spies, coming closer and closer to the seats of power, each creating sources of information that, when analyzed and sifted, would become intelligence for the president. That was the way to know your enemy, they believed, and by the mid-1950s they were starting to think that they might be starting to see a picture emerging out of the darkness.

   The CIA found its first real Russian spy as the Berlin Tunnel project got under way. The Vienna station was in contact with Major Pyotr Popov, an actual Soviet military intelligence man, the first Russian spy of lasting value that the CIA ever had. He knew a thing or two about tanks and tactical missiles and Russian military doctrine, and over the course of five years he betrayed the identities of some 650 of his fellow officers. Frank Wisner, inevitably, had wanted to turn Popov into the leader of an underground network of resistance fighters. The espionage side of the house fought hard and this time wore Wisner down; the bitterness over this fight lingered for years. Popov was not a perfect spy; he drank like a fish, forgot things, and ran terrible risks. But for five years, he was unique. The CIA would claim with conviction that Popov saved the United States half a billion dollars in military research and development. He cost the CIA about $4,000 a year. The British mole George Blake, betrayer of the Berlin tunnel, exposed Popov too. The major died before a KGB firing squad in 1959.

112 *"Those of us who knew"*: Polgar interview with author.

113 *"We obtain little significant information"*: Technological Capabilities Panel, "Report to the President," February 14, 1955, DDEL.

113 *"one of these machines is going to be caught"*: James R. Killian, *Sputnik, Scien-*

tists and Eisenhower: A Memoir of the First Assistant to the President for Science and Technology (Cambridge, MA: MIT Press, 1967), pp. 70–71.

113 *"the last refuge of organizational privacy"*: Bissell, "Subject: Congressional Watchdog Committee on CIA," February 9, 1959, declassified January 29, 2003, CIA/CREST.

113 *Bissell saw the U-2*: Bissell's thoughts about the U-2 are in his memoir, *Reflections of a Cold Warrior: From Yalta to the Bay of Pigs* (New Haven, CT: Yale University Press, 1996), pp. 92–140. Reber's observation that "we didn't raise the right questions" is on p. 105. Helms knew the U-2 was no silver bullet. He once told a meeting of clandestine service officers in the days when Bissell's star was at its zenith that "a good reporter does not need a magical black box to get useful information. . . . As long as there has been an airplane, pictures have been taken from it. CIA needs to use every collection device it can. . . . But in the final analysis, the only way you can get at what a man thinks is to talk to him."

115 *A five-volume CIA history*: Wayne G. Jackson, *Allen Welsh Dulles as Director of Central Intelligence*, declassified 1994, Vol. 3, 1973, pp. 71ff., CIA.

115 *"There are some things he doesn't tell the President"*: Eleanor Dulles's remark is recorded in Ambassador William B. Macomber, Jr., oral history, FAOH. Macomber was assistant secretary of state for congressional relations under Eisenhower.

Chapter Twelve

The relationship between the CIA and the leaders of Japan in the 1950s was detailed in the author's interviews with Al Ulmer, CIA's Far East division chief from 1955 to 1958; Clyde McAvoy, Kishi's CIA case officer in the mid-1950s; Horace Feldman, a former CIA station chief in Tokyo; Roger Hilsman and U. Alexis Johnson, senior State Department officials under Presidents Kennedy and Johnson; Jim Lilley and Don Gregg, formerly CIA station chiefs and U.S. ambassadors in Beijing and Seoul, respectively; and Douglas MacArthur II, the U.S. ambassador in Tokyo under Eisenhower.

The relationship was first limned in the author's *New York Times* article, "CIA Supported Japanese Right in '50s and '60s," October 9, 1994. That article had its origins in a struggle then ongoing between the CIA and the State Department over the release of a volume of *The Foreign Relations of the United States* covering Japan in the 1960s. Twelve years later, in July 2006, the State Department belatedly acknowledged that "the U.S. Government approved four covert programs to try to influence the direction of Japanese political life." The statement described three of the four programs. It said that the Eisenhower administration authorized the CIA before the May 1958 elections for the Japanese House of Representatives to provide "a few key pro-American and conservative politicians" with money. It said the Eisenhower administration also authorized the CIA "to institute a covert program to try to split off the moderate wing of the leftist opposition in the hope that a more pro-American and 'responsible' opposition party would emerge." In addition, "a broader covert program, divided almost equally between propaganda and social action," sought to encourage the Japanese people to embrace the ruling party and reject the influence of the left. The deep relationship with the rising politician and future prime minister Kishi was not acknowledged. FRUS, 1964–1968, Vol. XXIX, Part 2.

After Japan fell, the American occupation led by General MacArthur purged and imprisoned right-wing militarists such as Kishi and his allies. But things changed after George Kennan was sent to Japan in 1948 by Secretary of State Marshall to try to persuade MacArthur to change his views. An example of MacArthur's policies could be seen on the docks of Osaka, where dismantled machinery from Japanese industries was being greased, crated, and shipped at great expense to China as part of a war reparations program. Americans were paying to take Japan apart and support China at the moment it was being overrun by the communists. Kennan argued that the United States should move as fast as possible from the reformation of Japan toward its economic recovery. This about-face required an end to MacArthur's purges. It meant that accused war criminals such as Kishi and Kodama would be released. It led to their recruitment by the CIA and the eventual restoration of powerful leaders, business cartels, internal security forces, and political parties.

"The U.S. should do what it can to encourage effective conservative leadership in Japan," said the Operations Coordinating Board, in a report to the White House dated October 28, 1954, and declassified fifty years later. If the conservatives were united, they could work together to control Japan's political life, the board said, and "to take legal measures against Communists, and to combat the neutralist, anti-American tendencies of many of the individuals in Japan's educated groups." This is precisely what the CIA did from 1954 onward.

117 *The CIA provided $2.8 million in financing*: Japanese conservatives needed money. The American military needed tungsten. "Somebody had the idea: Let's kill two birds with one stone," said John Howley, a New York lawyer and OSS veteran who helped arrange the transaction. The Kodama-CIA operation smuggled tons of tungsten out from Japanese military caches into the United States and sold it to the Pentagon for $10 million. The smugglers included Kay Sugahara, a Japanese American recruited by the OSS from an internment camp in California during World War II. His files, researched by Howard Schonberger, a University of Maine professor writing a book nearly completed at his death in 1991, described the operation in detail. The proceeds were pumped into the campaigns of conservatives during Japan's first post-occupation elections

in 1953. Howley said: "We had learned in O.S.S., to accomplish a purpose, you had to put the right money in the right hands."

117 *"He is a professional liar"*: "Background on J.I.S. and Japanese Military Personalities," September 10, 1953, National Archives, Record Group 263, CIA Name File, box 7, folder: Kodama, Yoshio.

118 *"Strange, isn't it?"*: Dan Kurzman, *Kishi and Japan: The Search for the Sun* (New York: Obolensky, 1960), p. 256.

118 *"It was clear that he wanted at least the tacit backing of the United States government"*: Hutchinson oral history, FAOH.

120 *"He and I pulled off a great coup that day"*: McAvoy interview with author.

120 *"if Japan went Communist"*: MacArthur interview with author.

121 *Kaya became a recruited agent*: The records of Kaya's relationship with the CIA are in the National Archives, Record Group 263, CIA Name File, box 6, folder: Kaya, Okinori.

121 *"we ran it in a different way"*: Feldman interview with author.

Chapter Thirteen

122 *"He would heft them and decide"*: Lehman oral history interview, "Mr. Current Intelligence," *Studies in Intelligence,* Summer 2000, CIA/CSI.

123 *NSC 5412/2*: "Directive on Covert Operations," December 28, 1955, DDEL.

124 *The division was dysfunctional*: "Inspector General's Survey of the Soviet Russia Division, June 1956," declassified March 23, 2004, CIA/CREST.

125 *"'indict the whole Soviet system'"*: Ray Cline oral history, March 21, 1983, LBJL.

125 *His interference created a split signal at Radio Free Europe*: The radios' director, OSS veteran Bob Lang, complained about "the intrusion in each and every element of our affairs" by Wisner and his lieutenants. The CIA's Cord Meyer, the division chief in charge of Radio Free Europe, said he felt "pressure to distort the purpose of the radios."

125 *Vice President Nixon argued*: NSC minutes, July 12, 1956, DDEL; NSC 5608/1, "U.S. Policy Toward the Soviet Satellites in East Europe," July 18, 1956, DDEL. Under the auspices of the Free Europe program, the CIA already had floated 300,000 balloons containing 300 million leaflets, posters, and pamphlets from West Germany into Hungary, Czechoslovakia, and Poland. The balloons carried an implicit message: the Americans could cross the iron curtain with more than tin medals and radio waves.

126 *"CIA represented great power"*: Ray Cline, *Secrets, Spies, and Scholars, Blueprint of the Essential CIA* (Washington, DC: Acropolis, 1976), pp. 164–170.

127 *"dead wrong"*: NSC minutes, October 4, 1956, DDEL.

128 *Dulles assured Eisenhower*: Memorandum of conference among Eisenhower, Allen Dulles, and acting secretary of state Herbert Hoover, Jr.,

July 27, 1956, DDEL; Eisenhower diary, October 26, 1956, Presidential
Papers of Dwight David Eisenhower, document 1921; Dillon oral history,
FAOH; deputies' meeting notes from October, November, and December
1956, CIA/CREST.

129 *"wishful blindness"*: The state of Wisner's operations in Hungary is described in two clandestine service histories: *The Hungarian Revolution and
Planning for the Future: 23 October–4 November 1956*, Vol. 1, January 1958,
CIA; and *Hungary, Volume I [deleted]* and *Volume II: External Operations,
1946–1965*, May 1972, CIA History Staff, all declassified with deletions in
2005.

130 *"Freedom or Death!"*: Transcripts of Radio Free Europe programs, October
28, 1956, in Csasa Bekes, Malcolm Byrne, and Janos M. Rainer (eds.),
The 1956 Hungarian Revolution: A History in Documents (Budapest: Central
European University Press, 2002), pp. 286–289.

130 *"terrible mistakes and crimes of these past ten years"*: "Radio Message from
Imre Nagy, October 28, 1956," in Bekes, Byrne, and Rainer, *The 1956
Hungarian Revolution*, pp. 284–285.

Few knew that Wisner had more than one frequency to fight with. In
Frankfurt, the Solidarists, the neofascist Russians who had worked for
the CIA since 1949, began broadcasts into Hungary saying an army of exile warriors was heading for the border. They sent their message in the
name of Andras Zako, who had served as a general in the fascist wartime
Hungarian government and ran an Iron Cross outfit called the League of
Hungarian Veterans. "Zako was the very model of an intelligence entre-
preneur," Richard Helms noted. He had sold millions of dollars' worth of
fabricated intelligence to every major American military and intelligence
service from 1946 to 1952. The general had earned the rare distinction of
a "burn notice," a worldwide CIA order barring him from doing business
with the agency.

Reflecting on the CIA's decision to amplify and beam back the low-
wattage broadcasts of Hungarian partisans—using its own frequencies to
broadcast their pleas for violent struggle against the Soviets—John
Richardson, Jr., the president of Radio Free Europe, said: "The freedom
fighters would be telling the folks whatever they wanted to tell them and
whatever they'd believe. Then RFE would pick that up and rebroadcast
it. That was, I think, the single most serious mistake that was made."
Richardson oral history. FAOH.

130 *"What had occurred there was a miracle"*: NSC minutes, November 1, 1956,
DDEL.

131 *"the promise that help would come"*: William Griffith, Radio Free Europe,
"Policy Review of Voice for Free Hungary Programming" (December 5,
1956), in Bekes, Byrne, and Rainer, *The 1956 Hungarian Revolution*, pp.

464–484. This document constitutes an official acknowledgment of a fact long denied by the CIA: that RFE implied or stated to its Hungarian listeners that help was on the way. RFE's Hungarian desk was purged after Griffith's detailed but self-absolving report. Two years later, its voice had changed. It inaugurated a hugely popular and truly subversive program that captured the popular imagination: a rock 'n' roll show called *Teenager Party*. See also Arch Puddington, *Broadcasting Freedom: The Cold War Triumph of Radio Free Europe and Radio Liberty* (Lexington: University Press of Kentucky, 2000), pp. 95–104; and George R. Urban, *Radio Free Liberty and the Pursuit of Democracy: My War Within the Cold War* (New Haven, CT: Yale University Press, 1997), pp. 211–247.

131 *"headquarters was caught up in the fever of the times"*: Peer de Silva, *Sub Rosa: The CIA and the Uses of Intelligence* (New York: Times Books, 1978), p. 128.

132 *a fresh but false report from Allen Dulles that the Soviets were ready to send 250,000 troops to Egypt*: Eisenhower diary, November 7, 1956, DDEL.

132 *"near a nervous breakdown"*: William Colby, *Honorable Men: My Life in the CIA* (New York: Simon and Schuster, 1978), pp. 134–135.

132 *"revved up"*: John H. Richardson, *My Father the Spy: A Family History of the CIA, the Cold War and the Sixties* (New York: HarperCollins, 2005), p. 126.

132 *"We are well-equipped"*: Director's meeting, December 14, 1956, CIA/CREST.

133 *Bruce's personal journals*: Bruce's journals are at the University of Virginia. They show that as the American ambassador in Paris, Bruce had heard through the grapevine in June 1950—on a day he lunched with Allen Dulles—about "the horrible possibility" that he might be asked to become director of central intelligence. Walter Bedell Smith took the job instead.

133 *His top secret report*: Though the report from the president's board of intelligence consultants has become known as the "Bruce-Lovett report," its style clearly shows that David Bruce wrote it. The investigation team was Bruce; former secretary of defense Robert Lovett; and a former deputy chief of naval operations, retired admiral Richard L. Conolly. Until recently, the only evidence of the existence of the report was a set of notes taken by the historian Arthur Schlesinger from a document now said to have disappeared from the John F. Kennedy Memorial Library. The declassified version of the document—long excerpts from a collection of Eisenhower-era intelligence reports compiled for the Kennedy White House after the Bay of Pigs—appears here for the first time in book form, with abbreviations spelled out for clarity, typographical errors corrected, and the CIA's deletions noted.

The conception, planning and, even on occasion the approval itself [*deleted*] of covert operations, enormously significant to our military and foreign policies, is becoming more and more exclusively the business of the CIA—underwritten heavily by unvouchered CIA funds. (This is only the inevitable result of the structure, system and personalities concerned with the initiation and conduct of such operations.) The CIA, busy, monied and privileged, likes its "King-making" responsibility (the intrigue is fascinating—considerable self-satisfaction, sometimes with applause, derives from successes—no charge is made for "failures"—and the whole business is very much simpler than collecting covert intelligence on the USSR through the usual CIA methods!).

Although these extremely sensitive, costly operations are justifiable only insofar as they are in support of U.S. military and foreign policies, the responsible long-range planning and sustained guidance for these, which should be forthcoming from both the Defense and State Departments, appear too often to be lacking. There are always, of course, on record the twin, well-worn purposes of "frustrating the Soviets" and keeping others "pro-western" oriented. Under these almost any psychological warfare and paramilitary action can be and is being justified [*deleted*].

Initiative, and continuing impetus for psychological warfare and paramilitary operations, for the most part, reside in CIA. And, once having been conceived, the final approval given to any project (at informal meetings of the Operations Coordinating Board inner group) can, at best, be described as pro forma.

Upon approval, projects in most instances pass to the management of the CIA and remain there to conclusion. Since these operations are so inextricably interwoven with (and, on occasion, dictate the course of) our other foreign policy operations, it would appear they should have not only the prior approval of the National Security Council (rather than OCB) itself, but also the continuous surveillance of that body.

As a matter of fact, in most instances, approval of any new project would appear to comprise simply the endorsement of a Director of Central Intelligence proposal, usually without demurrer, from individuals preoccupied with other important matters of their own. Of course there is a preliminary (CIA proprietary) staffing of each project and an eventual (after the fact) reporting of its results to the NSC—but even after this report is rendered orally by the Director of Central Intelligence on an "off the record"—and on a naturally understandable, biased basis.

Psychological warfare and paramilitary operations themselves, at any one time, whether through personal arrangement between the Secretary of State and the DCI (deciding between them on any one occasion to use what they regard as the best "assets" available) or undertaken at the personal discretion of the DCI, frequently and in direct and continuing dealings between CIA representatives and the heads of foreign states [*deleted*]. Oftentimes such dealings are in reality only the continuation of relationships established at a time when the foreign personalities involved may have been "the opposition." (It is somewhat difficult to understand why anyone less than the Senior U.S. Representative [i.e., the Ambassador] in any country should deal directly with its Head in any matter which involves the official relationships of the two countries.) One obvious, inevitable result of this is to divide U.S. foreign policy resources and to incline the foreigner—often the former "opposition" now come into power (and who *knows* with whom he is dealing)—to play one U.S. agency against the other or to use whichever suits his current purpose [*deleted*].

A corollary to this is the exclusion of responsible American officials from knowledge they should have to properly discharge their obligation. (It has been reported by people in its intelligence area that there is great concern throughout the State Department over the impacts of CIA psychological warfare and paramilitary activities on our foreign relations. The State Department people feel that perhaps the greatest contribution this board could make would be to bring to the attention of the President the significant, almost unilateral influences that CIA psychological warfare and paramilitary activities have on the actual formation of our foreign policies and our relationships with our "friends.")

CIA support and its maneuvering of local news media, labor groups, political figures and parties and other activities which can have, at any one time, the most significant impacts on the responsibilities of the local Ambassador are sometimes completely unknown to or only hazily recognized by him. . . . Too often differences of opinion regarding the U.S. attitude toward local figures or organizations develop, especially as between the CIA and the State Department. . . . (At times, the Secretary of State–DCI brother relationship may arbitrarily set "the U.S. position.")

. . . CIA is in propaganda programs [*five lines deleted, probably dealing with the agency's financing of dozens of magazines, journals, publishing houses, and the Congress of Cultural Freedom*] which are difficult to identify as part of the responsibilities assigned to it by Congress and the National Security Council. . . .

The military expects that it will be responsible for the conduct of unconventional warfare (and there is difference of opinion here as to the extent of that responsibility); it is not quite sure who will be responsible for other psychological warfare and paramilitary operations in time of war—or how (or when) the responsibilities for them will be distributed.

Psychological warfare and paramilitary operations (often growing out of the increased mingling in the internal affairs of other nations of bright, highly graded young men who must be doing something all the time to justify their reason for being) today are being conducted on a world-wide basis by a horde of CIA representatives [*deleted*] many of whom, by the very nature of the personnel situation [*deleted*] are politically immature. (Out of their "dealings" with shifty, changing characters their applications of "themes" suggested from headquarters or developed by them in the field—sometimes at the suggestion of local opportunists—strange things are apt to, and do, develop.)

Fortunately in some instances, unfortunately in others, the results of many of these operations are comparatively short-lived [*seven lines deleted*]. If exposed these operations couldn't possibly be "plausibly denied"—indeed it would seem to be utterly naïve for anyone to think that the American hand in these operations is not only well known to both local country and Communist Party officials, but to many others (including the press)—and in derogation of the specific caveat contained in NSC [orders that the American role in covert operations remain unseen].

Should not someone, somewhere in an authoritative position in our government, on a continuing basis, be counting the immediate costs of disappointments (Jordan, Syria, Egypt, et al.), calculating the impacts on our international position, and keeping in mind the long-range wisdom of activities which have entailed the virtual abandonment of the international "golden rule," and which, if successful to the degree claimed for them, are responsible, in a great measure, for stir-

ring up the turmoil and raising the doubts about us that exist
in many countries of the world today? What of the effects on
our present alliances? Where will we be tomorrow?

We are sure that the supporters of the 1948 decision to
launch this government on a positive psychological warfare
and paramilitary program could not possibly have foreseen
the ramifications of the operations which have resulted from
it. No one, other than those in the CIA immediately concerned with their day to day operation, have any detailed
knowledge of what is going on. With the world situation in
the state it is today now would appear to be the time to engage in a reappraisal and realistic adjustment of that program
with perhaps some accompanying "unentanglement" of our
involvement, and a more rational application of our activities
than is now apparent.

135 *"a strange kind of genius"*: Ann Whitman memo, October 19, 1954, DDEL.

Chapter Fourteen

136 *"If you go and live with these Arabs"*: NSC minutes, June 18, 1959, DDEL.
136 *"a target legally authorized by statute for CIA political action"*: Archie Roo-
     sevelt, *For Lust of Knowing: Memoirs of an Intelligence Officer* (Boston: Little,
     Brown, 1988), pp. 444–448.
136 *few CIA officers spoke the language*: "Inspector General's Survey of the CIA
     Training Program," June 1960, declassified May 1, 2002, CIA/CREST;
     Matthew Baird, CIA Director of Training, "Subject: Foreign Language De-
     velopment Program," November 8, 1956, declassified August 1, 2001,
     CIA/CREST.
137 *"the 'holy war' aspect"* and *"a secret task force"*: Goodpaster memorandum
     of conference with the president, September 7, 1957, DDEL. Eisen-
     hower's hopes for military action to protect Islam against militant athe-
     ism and his meetings with Rountree to orchestrate secret American
     military aid to Saudi Arabia, Jordan, Iraq, and Lebanon were recorded by
     his staff secretary, General Andrew J. Goodpaster, in memos dated Au-
     gust 23 and August 28, 1957, DDEL.
137 *"These four mongrels"*: Symmes oral history, FAOH.
137 *Frank Wisner's proposal*: Frank G. Wisner, memorandum for the record,
     "Subject: Resume of OCB Luncheon Meeting," June 12, 1957, CIA/
     CREST. The memo says that "Wisner pushed need for across-the-board
     assistance to Jordan," in addition to CIA support. "The Agency is strongly
     in favor of getting Saudi Arabia and Iraq to put up as much as they can."

137   *"Let's put it this way"*: Symmes oral history, FAOH.

138   *"a likeable rogue"*: Miles Copeland, *The Game Player* (London: Aurum, 1989), pp. 74–93.

138   *"ripe for a military coup d'etat"*: Dulles in NSC minutes, March 3, 1955. The best account of the CIA's work in the region is Douglas Little, "Mission Impossible: The CIA and the Cult of Covert Action in the Middle East," *Diplomatic History*, Vol. 28, No. 5, November 2004. Little's essay is a tour de force based on primary documents. Copeland's memoirs are strong on atmosphere but untrustworthy on telling details unless independently confirmed by scholarship like Little's.

138   *A document discovered in 2003*: The British document describing the joint CIA-SIS plot against Syria was discovered by Matthew Jones and detailed in his monograph "The 'Preferred Plan': The Anglo-American Working Group Report on Covert Action in Syria, 1957," *Intelligence and National Security*, September 2004.

139   *"The officers with whom Stone was dealing"*: Curtis F. Jones oral history, FAOH. "We were trying to overcome more than the Rocky Stone episode," Jones said. "For example, we had financed arms purchases by Armenians who buried them in Syria"—until Syrian intelligence dug up the arms caches and broke up the underground battalion.

139   *"particularly clumsy CIA plot"*: Charles Yost, *History and Memory: A Statesman's Perceptions of the Twentieth Century* (New York: Norton, 1980), pp. 236–237.

140   *"some soul-searching"* and *"pulling the strings"*: Deputies' meeting, May 14, 1958, CIA/CREST.

140   *"caught completely by surprise"*: Gordon oral history, FAOH.

140–41 *"the most dangerous place in the world"*: NSC minutes, May 13, 1958, DDEL.

141   *"We have no evidence that Qasim is a communist"*: CIA briefing to NSC, January 15, 1959, CIA/CREST.

141   *"The only effective and organized force in Iraq"*: Deputies' meeting, May 14, 1959, CIA/CREST.

141   *another failed assassination plot*: In 1960, Critchfield proposed the poisoned handkerchief. Helms endorsed it. So did Bissell. Dulles approved. All believed they were carrying out the wishes of the president of the United States.

141   *"We came to power on a CIA train"*: Sa'adi quoted in Said Aburish, *A Brutal Friendship: The West and the Arab Elite* (New York: St. Martin's, 2001). Aburish was a committed Ba'athist who broke with Saddam and chronicled the brutality of his regime. He gave an instructive interview to *Frontline*, published on the Web site of the PBS documentary series (http://www.pbs.org/wgbh/pages/frontline/shows/saddam/interviews/aburish.html). "The U.S. involvement in the coup against Kassem in Iraq

in 1963 was substantial," he said. "There is evidence that CIA agents were in touch with army officers who were involved in the coup. There is evidence that an electronic command center was set up in Kuwait to guide the forces who were fighting Kassem. There is evidence that they supplied the conspirators with lists of people who had to be eliminated immediately in order to ensure success. The relationship between the Americans and the Ba'ath Party at that moment in time was very close indeed. And that continued for some time after the coup. And there was an exchange of information between the two sides. For example it is one of the first times that the United States was able to get certain models of MiG fighters and certain tanks made in the Soviet Union. That was the bribe. That was what the Ba'ath had to offer the United States in return for their help in eliminating Kassem." James Critchfield, who orchestrated the operation as the Near East chief of the clandestine service, said to the Associated Press shortly before he died in April 2003: "You have to understand the context of the time and the scope of the threat we were facing. That's what I say to people who say, 'You guys in the CIA created Saddam Hussein.' "

Chapter Fifteen

142 *"measures by this Government that would cause the fall of the new regime in Indonesia"*: NSC minutes, September 9, 1953, DDEL.

143 *"a tremendous hold on the people; is completely noncommunist"*: "Meeting with the Vice President, Friday, 8 January, 1954," CIA/DDRS.

143 *"There was planning of such a possibility"*: Bissell testimony, President's Commission on CIA Activities (Rockefeller Commission), April 21, 1975, Top Secret, declassified 1995, GRFL.

143 *"all feasible covert means"*: NSC 5518, declassified 2003, DDEL.

144 *"a number of political figures"*: Bissell oral history, DDEL.

144 *"God, we had fun"*: Ulmer interview with author.

144 *fire-breathing cables*: CIA report summaries, "NSC Briefing: Indonesia," February 27 and 28, March 5 and March 14, and April 3 and 10, 1957; CIA deputies' meeting, March 4, 1957; CIA estimate, "The Situation in Indonesia," March 5, 1957.

145 *"Sumatrans prepared to fight"*: "NSC Briefing: Indonesia," April 17, 1957; CIA chronology, "Indonesian Operation," March 15, 1958, declassified January 9, 2002. All CIA/CREST.

145 *"attempt to find out State Department policy on Indonesia"*: Director's meeting, July 19, 1957, CIA/CREST.

145 *"subversion by ballot"*: F. M. Dearborn to White House, "Some Notes on Far East Trip," November 1957, declassified August 10, 2003, DDEL.

Dearborn personally reported on his trip in a face-to-face meeting with Eisenhower on November 16, according to the president's diary. CIA, "Special Report on Indonesia," September 13, 1957, declassified September 9, 2003, DDEL. "Indonesian Operation," March 5, 1958, CIA/CREST.

145 *Al Ulmer believed*: Ulmer and Sichel interviews with author. In the summer of 1957, Ulmer sent out a call to clandestine service officers to monitor Sukarno during his annual jaunt on a chartered Pan Am jet to Asia's most exclusive bordellos. The fruits of his mission were limited to a sample of Sukarno's stool for medical analysis, obtained by the chief of the Hong Kong station, Peter Sichel, with the help of a patriotic Pan Am crew in the CIA's pay. In the absence of knowledge, all evidence was germane.

146 *"beyond the point of no return"*: NSC minutes, August 1, 1957, DDEL.

146 *"utmost gravity"*: Deputies' meeting, August 2, 1957, CIA/CREST.

147 *"the dismemberment of Indonesia"*: Cumming Committee, "Special Report on Indonesia," September 13, 1957, declassified July 9, 2003, DDEL.

At this time, Ambassador Allison accepted a summons to come over to the presidential palace for an informal chat. Sukarno wanted Eisenhower to come to Indonesia, to see the country for himself, to be the very first head of state to visit the lovely new guest house he was building on Bali. When the cold rejection from Washington arrived two weeks later, Allison handed it over with a shudder: "I literally saw Sukarno's jaw drop as he read President Eisenhower's letter. He couldn't believe it." Allison's views and quotations cited in this chapter are in John M. Allison, *Ambassador from the Prairie, or Allison Wonderland* (Boston: Houghton Mifflin, 1973), pp. 307–339.

147 *Eisenhower ordered the agency*: The language of the order is printed in the CIA's chronology, "Indonesian Operation," March 15, 1958, CIA/CREST.

147 *Wisner flew to the CIA station in Singapore*: CIA records show two trips to the region in the fall of 1957 and the spring of 1958. Wisner sought to make sure that the State Department knew as little as possible about his covert-action plans. The minutes of the director's meeting on December 26, 1957, say that he had meetings scheduled with State Department officials set for December 30 "concerning the Indonesian situation. Mr. Wisner expressed the hope that these discussions could be fairly well limited to policy matters rather than permitted to slice over into operational matters."

148 *The CIA's Jakarta station*: "Indonesian Operation," March 15, 1958, CIA/CREST. The paramilitary operation is detailed in Kenneth Conboy and James Morrison, *Feet to the Fire: CIA Covert Operations in Indonesia, 1957–1958* (Annapolis, MD: Naval Institute Press, 1999), pp. 50–98. The background of the political-warfare programs is in Audrey R. Kahin and George M. T. Kahin, *Subversion as Foreign Policy: The Secret Eisenhower and Dulles Debacle in Indonesia* (Seattle: University of Washington Press, 1995).

148 *"sons of Eisenhower"*: Office of U.S. Army attaché, Jakarta, to State, May 25, 1958, cited in Kahin and Kahin, *Subversion as Foreign Policy*, p. 178.

The CIA asked the Pentagon to help find more English-speaking Indonesian Army officers who wanted to seize power with the CIA's assistance. Memo to Allen W. Dulles from Major General Robert A. Schow, the army's intelligence chief, February 5, 1958.

The responses should have given the Americans some pause. General Nasution, the professional military officer who led the Indonesian Army and stayed loyal to the government, assured the U.S. Army attaché in Jakarta, Major George Benson, that he already was purging every suspected communist from any position of influence. Lieutenant Colonel D. I. Pandjaitan, an Indonesian military attaché based in Bonn—and a Christian, his American counterparts noted—proclaimed: "If the U.S. knows of any Communists, let them tell us, and we will have them removed. . . . We will do anything except shoot Sukarno or attack the Communists without proof of illegal actions on their part. In our country now we cannot arrest Communists just because they are Communists; we will remove them"—and here the colonel stabbed at the air as if holding a knife—"if they step out of line." Memorandum of conversation with Indonesian army officers, date unclear but probably early 1958, declassified April 4, 2003, CIA/CREST.

149 *Foster said he was "in favor of doing something"*: JFD telephone call transcripts, DDEL.

149 *"the United States faced very difficult problems"*: NSC minutes, February 27, 1958, DDEL.

151 *"It was a very strange war"*: NSC minutes, April 25, 1958, DDEL.

151 *"any operations partaking of a military character in Indonesia"*: NSC minutes, April 14, 1958, DDEL. John Foster Dulles, memorandum of conversation with the president, April 15, 1958, DDEL.

151 *"I enjoyed killing Communists"*: Pope interview with author.

151 *"almost too effective"*: NSC minutes, May 1, 1958, DDEL.

151 *"stirred great anger"*: NSC minutes, May 4, 1958, DDEL.

152 *"it could not be conducted as a completely covert operation"*: "Indonesian Operation," March 15, 1958, CIA/CREST. Incredibly, Allen Dulles pleaded poverty as the reason for the failed mission. The CIA needed at least $50 million more in its covert action budget, he told Eisenhower: "We were quite thin in our resources to meet situations such as that in Indonesia."

152 *"They convicted me of murder"*: Pope interview with author. Sukarno waited two years before putting Pope on trial. The CIA pilot was held at a summer resort on the slopes of Mount Merapi, where his guards took him hunting and gave him every chance to escape. He calculated this as a plot, a way for the government to turn a strapping blond, blue-eyed

American prisoner over to the Communist Party of Indonesia. After four years and two months of captivity, he was set free in July 1962 at the personal request of the attorney general of the United States, Robert F. Kennedy. He went back to flying for the CIA in Vietnam for the rest of the 1960s. In February 2005, at age seventy-six, Al Pope was awarded the Legion of Honor by the government of France for his role in the resupply of besieged French forces at Dien Bien Phu in 1954.

153 *"glaring mix-up"*: Director's meeting, May 19, 1958, CIA/CREST.

153 *favorable to the United States*: "NSC Briefing: Indonesia," May 21, 1958, declassified January 15, 2004, CIA/CREST.

153 *"The operation was, of course, a complete failure"*: Bissell oral history, DDEL.

153 *"Dissident B-26 aircraft shot down"*: "NSC Briefing: Indonesia," May 21, 1958, CIA/CREST.

153 *He came back from the Far East in June 1958 at the edge of his sanity, and at summer's end he went mad*: But Wisner had been demonstrably unsound since late 1956, and so had the clandestine service. Paul Nitze, a good friend who had worked closely with Wisner as Kennan's successor at the State Department, observed that "the upshot of the strains of that Hungarian episode and the Suez episode were more than Frank could bear and he had a nervous breakdown after that. I think that the difficulties [at the clandestine service] began after Frank had a nervous breakdown. . . . They began after Frank was no longer competent to run it." Nitze oral history, HSTL. Wisner suffered through "a very hard time" during his treatment, Dulles wrote to his old deputy director, Bill Jackson, in December 1958. "I hope it will not now be many weeks before he is out of the sanitarium." Allen Dulles papers, declassified February 13, 2001, CIA. At the time, electroshock was "used for a variety of disorders, frequently in high doses and for long periods. . . . Many of these efforts proved ineffective, and some even harmful." See "Report of the National Institute of Mental Health Consensus Development Conference on Electroconvulsive Therapy," *Journal of the American Medical Association*, Vol. 254, 1985, pp. 2103–2108.

154 *"at a loss"*: Director's meeting, June 23, 1958, CIA/CREST.

154 *"We had constructed"*: Smith cited in Douglas Garthoff, "Analyzing Soviet Politics and Foreign Policy," in Gerald K. Haines and Robert E. Leggett (eds.), *Watching the Bear: Essays on CIA's Analysis of the Soviet Union* CIA/CSI, 2003.

154 *a report from his intelligence board*: "Subject: Third Report of the President by the President's Board of Consultants on Foreign Intelligence Activities" and memorandum of conference with the president [by the board], December 16, 1958, CIA/DDEL. At this meeting with the president, former defense secretary Robert Lovett "reinforced the views of the Board

that the present organization is weak by citing the example of Indonesia," read the top secret minutes of the meeting. "Mr. Lovett pointed out by way of general summary that we have two basic ways of obtaining reliable information, through gadgets and through individual secret agents. It is in this latter field, the secret agents, that he feels we will obtain our best information. . . . We are not good in this field and we should get better."

154 *"our problems were getting greater every year"*: Dulles, minutes of senior staff meeting, January 12, 1959, CIA/CREST.

Chapter Sixteen

155 *Richard Bissell became the chief*: Bissell's ambitions for the CIA were great; the obstacles against them were greater. He told his senior officers that his mandate was to merge the "Hot War plans and Cold War capabilities" of the United States—to make the CIA more sword than shield in the battle against the Soviets. He created a new division, Development Projects, that allowed him to run covert action programs out of his hip pocket. He saw the CIA as an instrument of American power no less potent—and much more useful—than the nuclear arsenal or the 101st Airborne Division. "Mr. Bissell's Remarks, War Planners Conference," March 16, 1959, declassified January 7, 2002, CIA/CREST.

Bissell knew the agency was dangerously short on the talent needed to achieve his goals. His own "sheer brilliance," said one of his top assistants, Jim Flannery, "could not overcome the fact that the clandestine service is basically people." Flannery quoted in Peter Wyden, *Bay of Pigs: The Untold Story* (New York: Simon and Schuster, 1979), p. 320.

Bissell immediately ordered his division chiefs to "identify substandard employees and dispose of them." He wanted an "unrelenting and constant" culling of the herd. "Look beyond the case of inefficiency or wrongdoing," he instructed his underlings. "Identify and terminate those employees who are not carrying, can not, or will not carry their fair share of the work." Richard Bissell, "Subject: Program for Greater Efficiency in CIA," February 2, 1959, declassified February 12, 2002, CIA/CREST.

A detailed internal survey of the CIA's clandestine service in November 1959 showed the source of Bissell's concerns: the recruitment of talented young officers had dwindled while the ranks of the mediocre and middle-aged swelled. "A very considerable percentage" of the CIA's officers soon would be at least fifty years old; they were the World War II generation, and in three short years they would start retiring en masse after twenty years of military and intelligence service. "There is a strong feeling of frustration widespread among the best Clandestine Service officers which has its origin in the Agency's apparent inability to solve the manpower problem," the internal CIA study showed. That problem remains unsolved today. "Subject: A Manpower Control Problem for the Clandestine Services Career Program," November 4, 1959, declassified August 1, 2001, CIA/CREST.

155 *A secret CIA history*: Unless otherwise noted, quotations and citations on the CIA and Cuba in this chapter are taken from the CIA's clandestine history of the planning on the Bay of Pigs operation: Jack Pfeiffer, *Evolution of CIA's Anti-Castro Policies, 1951–January 1961*, Vol. 3 of *Official History of the Bay of Pigs Operation*, CIA, NARA (hereinafter cited as Pfeiffer).

Pfeiffer was named the CIA's chief historian in 1976; he retired in 1984 and spent a decade thereafter unsuccessfully suing the CIA to release this work. His three-hundred-page history turned up in the National Archives in June 2005, unearthed by Professor David Barrett of Villanova University.

155 *Jim Noel*: Noel quoted in Pfeiffer. Ambassador William Attwood, who served as President Kennedy's personal back channel to Castro in the summer of 1963, remembered: "I was in Cuba, in '59, and I met CIA people there whose main sources were members of the Havana country club. . . . They didn't get out among the people." Attwood oral history, FAOH.

155 *Al Cox*: Cox quoted in Pfeiffer.

155 *Robert Reynolds*: Reynolds made the remark to the author and several other reporters attending a conference on the Bay of Pigs in Havana in 2001.

155 *"a new spiritual leader"*: Quoted in Pfeiffer.

156 *"Though our intelligence experts backed and filled"*: Dwight D. Eisenhower, *Waging Peace: The White House Years: 1956–1961* (Garden City, NY: Doubleday, 1965), p. 524.

155 *"the elimination of Fidel Castro"*: Authorship of the memo may be credited to J. C. King, then finishing his ninth year as chief of the Western Hemisphere division. The editing by Dulles is in Pfeiffer.

156 *"anybody with eyes could see"*: Unless otherwise noted, quotations from Jake Esterline in this book are from videotaped interviews with Peter Kornbluh of the National Security Archive or from Esterline's remarks at transcripts of conferences on the Bay of Pigs conducted at the Musgrove Plantation in Georgia in 1996. The Musgrove conference is in James G. Blight and Peter Kornbluh (eds.), *Politics of Illusion: The Bay of Pigs Invasion Reexamined* (Boulder, CO: Lynne Rienner, 1998).

157 *"The Dripping Cuban"*: Helms and the dripping Cuban are in Pfeiffer. "Helms completely divorced himself from this thing. I mean absolutely!"

Dick Drain, chief of operations for the Cuba task force, recounted. "The third time that he said, 'You know I have nothing to do with this project,' I said, 'Well, Mr. Helms, I don't want to be fatuous about this, but I wish to Christ that you did because we could use your expertise.' He said, 'Hahaha . . . yes . . . well, thank you very much,' and that was the end of that. He avoided the thing like the plague."

158 *It had four*: Raymond L. Garthoff, "Estimating Soviet Military Intentions and Capabilities," in Gerald K. Haines and Robert E. Leggett (eds.), *Watching the Bear: Essays on CIA's Analysis of the Soviet Union*, CIA/CSI, 2003.

159 *"provocative pin-pricking"*: Goodpaster memo, October 30, 1959, DDEL.

160 *"the lie we told about the U-2"*: Ike made the remark to journalist David Kraslow; it is cited in several sources, including David Wise, *The Politics of Lying: Government Deception, Secrecy, and Power* (New York: Random House, 1973).

161 *"Bissell probably believed"*: Michael Warner, "The CIA's Internal Probe of the Bay of Pigs Affair," *Studies in Intelligence*, Winter 1998–1999, CIA/CSI.

162 *should be eliminated*: The evidence that Eisenhower wanted Lumumba dead is overwhelming. "The President did want a man whom he regarded (as did lots of others, myself included) as a thorough scoundrel and a very dangerous man, got rid of," Bissell said later in an oral-history interview for the Eisenhower presidential library. "I have not the slightest doubt that he wanted Lumumba got rid of and he wanted it badly and promptly, as a matter of urgency and of very great importance. Allen's cable reflected that sense of urgency and priority." NSC secretary Robert Johnson's testimony on Eisenhower's order to kill Lumumba at the NSC meeting on August 18, 1960, and Devlin's quoted testimony on his orders coming from "the President" were given to investigators for the Church Committee. Devlin testified on August 25, 1975; Johnson testified on June 18 and September 13, 1975. On the murder of Lumumba, see "Conclusions of the Enquiry Committee," a thousand-page parliamentary report published by the government of Belgium in December 2001. See also NSC minutes, September 12 and 19, 1960, DDEL. Steve Weissman, former staff director, House of Representatives subcommittee on Africa, granted the author an illuminating interview on the structure of the covert operation in the Congo; see also Weissman's "Opening the Secret Files on Lumumba's Murder," *Washington Post*, July 21, 2002. After the killing, Nikita Khrushchev had a conversation with the American ambassador in Moscow, who reported in an eyes-only cable to Washington: "With respect to Congo K said what had happened there and particularly murder of Lumumba had helped communism. Lumumba was not Communist and he doubted if he would have become one." FRUS, 1961–1963, Vol. X, document 51. Moscow nonetheless established the

Patrice Lumumba Friendship University for students from Africa, Asia, and Latin America, and the KGB used it as a rich recruiting ground. But Soviet intelligence would never return to the Congo under Mobutu, who personally staged a mock execution of the last Soviet intelligence officer he expelled from the capital.

163 *The CIA delivered $250,000*: Personal testimony on the payoffs to the CIA's allies in the Congo comes from Owen Roberts, later a U.S. ambassador under President Ronald Reagan. Roberts was the ranking expert on the Congo at the State Department's intelligence and research bureau in Washington in 1960. He had served for two years in the Congolese capital and was the first American foreign service officer who knew all the new leaders personally. He was working on a book-length study of the country financed by the CIA in 1960, and he served as the escort officer when Prime Minister Lumumba, President Joseph Kasavubu, and eighteen of their ministers visited Washington and the United Nations, where the general assembly convened in September 1960. "The CIA made some payoffs, I know," to the Congolese delegation at the United Nations, Ambassador Roberts said. Roberts oral history, FAOH.

164 *"We had made a major effort"*: Bissell interview in Piero Gleijeses, "Ships in the Night: The CIA, the White House, and the Bay of Pigs," *Journal of Latin American Studies*, Vol. 27, 1995, pp. 1–42.

166 *"a tired old man"*: Lehman oral history, "Mr. Current Intelligence," *Studies in Intelligence*, Summer 2000, CIA/CSI.

167 *"worth the risk"*: "Report from the Chairman of the President's Board of Intelligence Consultants" and "Sixth Report of the President's Board of Consultants," January 5, 1961, DDEL; "Report of the Joint Study Group," December 15, 1960, DDEL; Lyman Kirkpatrick, memorandum for director of central intelligence, "Subject: Summary of Survey Report of FI Staff, DDP," undated, CIA/CREST; NSC minutes, January 5 and 12, 1961, DDEL.

167 *"I reminded the President"*: Gordon Gray, memorandum of meeting with President Eisenhower, January 18, 1961, DDEL.

167 *"an eight-year defeat"* and *"a legacy of ashes"*: Memorandum of discussion at the 473rd meeting of the NSC, January 5, 1961, DDEL; memorandum from Director of Central Intelligence Dulles, January 9, 1961 (Dulles claiming that he had "corrected deficiencies" in the clandestine service and that everything there was "now satisfactory"); memorandum of discussion at the 474th meeting of the NSC, January 12, 1961, DDEL (Dulles saying that American intelligence was "better than it ever had been," that creating a director of national intelligence would be "illegal," and that such a director would be "a body floating in thin air"). The declassified NSC minutes, published in 2002, are not verbatim notes, but

they preserve the president's anger and frustration. All are collected in FRUS, 1961–1963, Vol. XXV, released in March 7, 2002.

PART THREE
Chapter Seventeen

171 *"Senator Kennedy asked the President's judgment"*: "Transfer: January 19, 1961, Meeting of the President and Senator Kennedy," declassified January 9, 1997, DDEL.

171 *"He had his torture chambers"*: Dearborn oral history, FAOH. This is a remarkably candid interview.

172 *"The great problem now"*: RFK notes cited in Church Committee report.

173 *The worst that could happen*: Unless otherwise indicated, the reconstruction of the Bay of Pigs invasion in this chapter is drawn directly from *The Foreign Relations of the United States, 1961–1963*, Vol. 10, *Cuba, 1961–1962*, declassified in 1997, and its microfiche supplements, published in 1998, Vol. 11; *Cuban Missile Crisis and Aftermath, 1962–1963*, declassified in 1996, and its 1998 supplements; and Jack Pfeiffer, *Evolution of CIA's Anti-Castro Policies, 1951–January 1961*, Vol. 3 of *Official History of the Bay of Pigs Operation*, CIA, NARA. Quotes from Jake Esterline are from the Musgrove conference transcript, in James G. Blight and Peter Kornbluh (eds.), *Politics of Illusion: The Bay of Pigs Invasion Reexamined* (Boulder, CO: Lynne Rienner, 1998).

174 *another blown operation*: The station chief who tried to buy off the government was Art Jacobs, Frank Wisner's law school friend and gatekeeper in the early days of the CIA, a diminutive man known in those days as Ozzard of Wiz. "We had a bandit down in Singapore, a cabinet minister who was on the CIA payroll," remembered Ambassador Sam Hart, then a political officer at the American embassy in Malaysia. "One night they had him wired to a polygraph in a safehouse. . . . The Singapore M-5 burst in on the safehouse and there's this cabinet minister wired to the polygraph." Hart oral history, FAOH. The subsequent letter from Rusk read: "Dear Mr. Prime Minister: I am deeply distressed . . . regret very much . . . unfortunate incident . . . improper activities . . . very serious . . . reviewing activities of these officials for possible disciplinary actions."

175 *could not launch air strikes*: Cabell and Bissell, memorandum for General Maxwell D. Taylor, "Subject: Cuban Operation," May 9, 1961, JFKL, DDRS.

175 *The president said he was unaware that there were going to be any air strikes on the morning of D-Day*: FRUS, Vol. XI, April 25, 1961 (Taylor Board).

177 *"The time has come for a showdown"*: Robert F. Kennedy to the president,

April 19, 1961, JFKL, cited in Aleksandr Fursenko and Timothy Naftali, *One Hell of a Gamble* (New York: Norton, 1997), p. 97.

177　*"Mr. President, I stood right here"*: The aides were Theodore Sorensen and Arthur Schlesinger, and their accounts are, respectively, *Kennedy* (New York: Harper and Row, 1965), and *Robert Kennedy and His Times* (Boston: Houghton Mifflin, 1978).

177　*an instrument of government he had disdained*: President Kennedy had torn out the wiring in the White House for governing the use of secret power. Eisenhower had exerted the presidential power through a rigorous staff system, like the army's. Kennedy had tossed it around like a pigskin at a touch football game. Days after taking office, he had abolished the president's panel of intelligence consultants and the Operations Coordinating Board. They were assuredly imperfect institutions, but they were better than nothing, which was what John Kennedy had built in their place. The post–Bay of Pigs meeting of the NSC was the first serious roundtable discussion of covert action in the Kennedy administration.

177　*"I'm first to recognize"*: Dulles quoted in "Paramilitary Study Group Meeting" (Taylor Board), May 11, 1961, declassified March 2000 and available online at http://www.gwu.edu/nsarchiv/NSAEBB/NSAEBB29/06-01.htm.

179　*"take the bucket of slop"*: Smith quoted in "Paramilitary Study Group Meeting" (Taylor Board), May 10, 1961, NARA.

179　*"He leaves an enduring legacy"*: Bissell, *Reflections of a Cold Warrior: From Yalta to the Bay of Pigs* (New Haven, CT: Yale University Press, 1996), p. 204. Bissell came to believe he had left the CIA with "a legacy that has still not been put to rest historically and perhaps never will be." In secret testimony declassified in 1996, Bissell gave this assessment of the CIA's clandestine service: "In part because of my own failings and shortcomings, by the late '60s the Agency already had, I thought, a rather lamentable record. . . . Reviewing the whole range of different kinds of covert operations—they involved propaganda operations, paramilitary operations, political action operations, and the whole range—the Clandestine Service is not the place where one would expect to look for professional competence." Bissell said that basic skills in military affairs, political analysis, and economic analysis had not been developed at the CIA. The agency had become nothing more than a secret bureaucracy—and a "very sloppy" one at that. Bissell testimony, President's Commission on CIA Activities (Rockefeller Commission), April 21, 1975, GRFL.

180　*"and unmistakable self-confidence"*: Richard Helms with William Hood, *A Look over My Shoulder: A Life in the Central Intelligence Agency* (New York: Random House, 2003), p. 195.

180　*"not a man that people were going to love"*: James Hanrahan, "An Interview with Former CIA Executive Director Lawrence K. 'Red' White," *Studies in Intelligence*, Vol. 43, No. 1, Winter 1999–2000, CIA/CSI.

181 *McCone tried to get the big picture*: On his worldwide tour to meet the troops, at the Far East station chiefs' retreat at the mountain resort of Baguio in the Philippines in October 1961, McCone chose a new deputy director to serve as the CIA's chief intelligence analyst: Ray Cline, then chief of station in Taipei.

181 *There were more than a few operations that McCone and the Special Group knew little or nothing about*: Division chiefs such as J. C. King, who had served a decade under Dulles, thought nothing of running operations as they saw fit. McCone also never knew that his appointment had set off an internal rebellion at the agency. "I, for one, underestimated the strength of the opposition in the second and third levels of CIA," McGeorge Bundy told the president. "Some very good men are disquieted." Robert Amory, the deputy director of intelligence, called McCone's appointment "a cheap political move." Other foes within the CIA feared McCone would sacrifice the agency to the young lions at the White House. Still others at the clandestine service were unhappy at an outsider's coming to power.

182 *"The President explained"*: McCone memo, November 22, 1961, FRUS, Vol. X.

182 *"a 'cloak and dagger' outfit"*: McCone memorandum for the file, January 13, 1964: "I have felt, and expressed myself to the late President Kennedy, to President Johnson, and to Secretary Rusk and others, that the DCI and CIA image must be changed. Its basic and primary responsibilities by law are to assemble all intelligence, analyze, evaluate, estimate and report such intelligence for the benefit of policy makers. This function has been submerged and CIA has been consistently referred to as a 'cloak and dagger' outfit whose activities involve (almost exclusively) operations designed to overthrow governments, assassinate Heads of State, involve itself in political affairs of foreign states. . . . I wish to attempt to change this image." FRUS, 1964–1968, Vol. XXXIII, document 184. McCone was "a man who believed he had two hats: one hat was running the Agency, and the other hat was as one of the President's policymakers." Richard Helms oral history, September 16, 1981, LBJL. McCone said he consistently argued that the CIA "had through the years been subordinated to operational activities"—and "this had to be changed." McCone memo, "Discussion with Attorney General Robert Kennedy," December 27, 1961, CIA/CREST. He drafted and received a written understanding that he would be "the Government's principal intelligence officer." JFK to McCone, January 16, 1962, CIA/CREST.

183 *"You are now living on the bull's eye"*: David S. Robarge, "Directors of Central Intelligence, 1946–2005," *Studies in Intelligence*, Vol. 49, No. 3, 2005, CIA/CSI.

183 *"Berlin was a sham"*: Smith interview with author.

183 *"operations in East Germany were out of the question"*: Murphy, CNN Interactive chat transcript, 1998, available online at http://www.cnn.com/SPECIALS/cold.war/guides/debate/chats/murphy/.

184 *The agency was all but out of business*: Murphy to Helms, "Subject: Heinz Felfe Damage Assessment," February 7, 1963, declassified June 2006, CIA.

184 *"the top priority"*: Helms to McCone, January 19, 1962, FRUS, Vol. X.

184 *"Of the 27 or 28 agents"*: McCone memo, "Discussion with Attorney General Robert Kennedy, 2:45 P.M., 27 December 1961," FRUS, Vol. X.

185 *the Catholic Church and the Cuban underworld*: Lansdale to McCone, December 7, 1961, FRUS, Vol. X.

185 *"Ed had this aura around him"*: Esterline, Musgrove transcript, *Politics of Illusion*, p. 113.

185 *"Let's get the hell on with it"*: Helms, *A Look over My Shoulder*, p. 205.

186 *"he wanted fast answers"*: Elder statement to Church Committee investigators, August 13, 1975, declassified May 4, 1994.

186 *"it would meet with the president's approval"*: The question of whether president Kennedy authorized the CIA to kill Castro can be answered, at least to my satisfaction. In 1975, Bissell testified to the presidential commission led by Vice President Nelson Rockefeller on the question of presidential authorization of assassinations by the CIA.

Rockefeller questioned Bissell:

> Q: Any assassination or assassination attempt would have to have the highest approval?
> A: That's correct.
> Q: From the President?
> A: That is correct.

187 *"mad as hell"*: Houston to the historian Thomas Powers: "Kennedy was mad," Houston said. "He was mad as hell. . . . He was not angry about the assassination plot, but about our involvement with the Mafia." Powers, "Inside the Department of Dirty Tricks," *Atlantic Monthly*, August 1979.

187 *"no question in my mind that he did"*: Helms interview with author. This seems to me to settle the question of JFK's authorization, taken together with Bissell's testimony and the overwhelming weight of circumstantial evidence. The counterargument is that John Kennedy would never have done such a thing, and that argument has worn very thin.

187 *"why shouldn't they kill yours?"*: The full context of Helms's observation is worth reproducing, now that the CIA is back in the business of targeted killings. "Let's leave aside the notion of theology and the morality of all good men for just a moment," he said in 1978. "Leaving that aside, one comes smack up against the fact that if you hire someone to kill some-

body else, you are immediately subject to blackmail, and that includes individuals as well as governments. In short, these things inevitably come
out. That is the most compelling reason for not getting involved. But then
there is an ancillary consideration. If you become involved in the business of eliminating foreign leaders, and it is considered by governments
more frequently than one likes to admit, there is always the question of
who comes next. . . . If you kill someone else's leaders, why shouldn't
they kill yours?" The question was very much on Helms's mind after November 22, 1963. Helms interview with David Frost, 1978, full transcript
reprinted in *Studies in Intelligence*, September 1993, CIA/CSI.

187 *"CIA was suffering" and "morale was pretty well shattered"*: McCone oral history, August 19, 1970, LBJL. McCone recounted his first meeting with
President Kennedy, when he was offered the job as director of central intelligence: "[JFK said]: 'Now, there are only four people besides Allen
Dulles that know that we are having this discussion: Bob McNamara and
his deputy Roswell Gilpatric, and Dean Rusk, and [Chairman of the Senate Atomic Energy Committee] Senator Clinton Anderson.' And he said,
'I don't want anybody else to know about it, because if these liberal
s.o.b.'s that work in the basement of this building hear that I am talking
to you about this, they'd destroy you before I can get you confirmed.' "
McCone oral history, April 21, 1988, Institute of International Studies,
University of California at Berkeley.

188 *"accident-prone" . . . "alcohol-addicted" . . . "something should be done immediately to restore morale in the Agency"*: Lyman B. Kirkpatrick, Jr., "Report of
the Task Force on Personnel Management in CIA," July 26, 1962,
CIA/CREST; Kirkpatrick's handwritten notes from an August 6, 1962,
Executive Committee meeting on the report, CIA/CREST.

188 *1,300 Cuban refugees*: Harvey to Lansdale, May 24, 1962, CIA/DDRS

188 *"forty-five men"*: Lansdale to Special Group (Augmented), July 5, 1962,
FRUS, Vol. X.

188 *"Can CIA actually hope to generate such strikes?"*: Lansdale to Harvey, August
6, 1962, FRUS, Vol. X.

Chapter Eighteen

189 *John F. Kennedy walked into the Oval Office and switched on the brand-new
state-of-the-art taping system*: Direct quotations in this chapter are drawn
from the recently transcribed Kennedy White House tapes, unless otherwise cited. The tapes, McCone's newly declassified memos, and more
than one thousand pages of internal CIA records create a rich mosaic of
the daily life of the agency in the summer and fall of 1962. The White
House tapes from July 30 through October 28, 1962, are compiled in

Timothy Naftali, Philip Zelikow, and Ernest May (eds.), *The Presidential Recordings: John F. Kennedy,* 3 vols. (New York: Norton, 2001), produced by the Miller Center of Public Affairs. The cited McCone memos are from three sources: FRUS, CREST, and DDRS. The internal CIA records were obtained by the author from CREST.

189 *The return on these investments:* Two years after this Oval Office conversation, Goulart was overthrown, and Brazil was on the road to a police state. Bobby Kennedy had gone to Brazil to see the situation for himself: "I didn't like Goulart," he said. The 1964 coup backed by the CIA led to the first in a series of military dictatorships that ruled Brazil for the better part of twenty years.

190 *McCone had given the go-ahead:* The director drew a distinction in his own mind between a coup in which there might be a bloodbath and a targeted assassination attempt against a head of state. One was moral, the other was not; a coup in which a president was killed might be deplorable, but not reprehensible.

190 *On August 10 . . . The subject was Cuba:* Almost every record of this meeting has been destroyed, but fragments were painstakingly reassembled by State Department historians from the files of the director of central intelligence: "McCone maintained at the meeting that the Soviet Union had in Cuba an asset of such importance that 'the Soviets will not let Cuba fail.' To prevent such a failure McCone expected that the Soviet Union would supplement economic, technical, and conventional military aid with medium-range ballistic missiles, which they would justify by reference to U.S. missile bases in Italy and Turkey. . . . [T]he issue of the assassination of Cuban political leaders came up during the discussion. According to an August 14 memorandum from Harvey to Richard Helms, the issue was raised during the meeting by McNamara. . . . On April 14, 1967, McCone sent a memorandum from his retirement to Helms, who had become Director of Central Intelligence, in which he wrote of the discussion at the August 10 meeting: 'I recall a suggestion being made to liquidate top people in the Castro regime, including Castro. I took immediate exception to this suggestion, stating that the subject was completely out of bounds as far as the USG and CIA were concerned and the idea should not be discussed nor should it appear in any papers, as the USG could not consider such actions on moral or ethical grounds.' " FRUS, Vol. X, editorial note, document 371. McCone first raised the question of nuclear weapons in Cuba at a March 12, 1962, Special Group meeting: "Could we now develop a policy for action if missile bases are placed on Cuban soil?" FRUS, Vol. X, document 316. But on August 8, 1962, only two days before delivering his first warning that Soviet missiles would be sent to Cuba, McCone had told a gathering of twenty-six Republican sen-

ators that he was "positive that there were no missiles or missile bases in Cuba." "Luncheon Meeting Attended by the DCI of Senate Republican Policy Committee," August 8, 1962, declassified May 12, 2005, CIA/ CREST.

191 *"If I were Khrushchev"*: Walter Elder, "John McCone, the Sixth Director of Central Intelligence," draft copy, CIA History Staff, 1987, partially declassified and released in 1998.

191 *"the Soviets were going to be Number One"*: Ford quoted in John L. Helgerson, "CIA Briefings of Presidential Candidates," May 1996, CIA/CSI.

191 *"They had charts on the wall"*: Ford cited by the author, *The New York Times,* July 20, 1997.

192 *"I went to see President Kennedy"*: Jagan interview with author.

192 *"the United States supports the idea"*: "Interview Between President Kennedy and the Editor of *Izvestia,"* November 25, 1961, FRUS, Vol. V.

192 *"a really* covert *operation"*: Schlesinger memo, July 19, 1962, FRUS, Vol. XII.

192 *time to bring matters to a head*: Memo to Bundy, August 8, 1962.

192 *The president launched a $2 million campaign*: The author laid out some of its consequences in "A Kennedy-C.I.A. Plot Returns to Haunt Clinton," *The New York Times,* October 30, 1994. The article touched on the struggle over the declassification of the government records about the covert operation. In 2005, the State Department published the following "editorial note" in FRUS, 1964–1968, Vol. XXXII: "During the Johnson administration, the U.S. Government continued the Kennedy administration's policy of working with the British Government to offer encouragement and support to the pro-West leaders and political organizations of British Guiana as that limited self-governing colony moved toward total independence. The Special Group/303 Committee approved approximately $2.08 million for covert action programs between 1962 and 1968 in that country. U.S. policy included covert opposition to Cheddi Jagan, the then pro-Marxist leader of British Guiana's East Indian population. A portion of the funds authorized by the Special Group/303 Committee for covert action programs was used between November 1962 and June 1963 to improve the election prospects of the opposition political parties to the government of Jagan's People's Progressive Party. The U.S. Government successfully urged the British to impose a system of proportional representation in British Guiana (which favored the anti-Jagan forces) and to delay independence until the anti-Jagan forces could be strengthened."

The note continued: "Through the Central Intelligence Agency, the United States provided Forbes Burnham's and Peter D'Aguiar's political parties, which were in opposition to Jagan, with both money and campaign expertise as they prepared to contest the December 1964 parliamentary elections. The U.S. Government's covert funding and technical expertise were designed to play a decisive role in the registration of voters likely to vote against Jagan. Burnham's and D'Aguiar's supporters were registered in large numbers, helping to elect an anti-Jagan coalition. Special Group/303 Committee–approved funds again were used between July 1963 and April 1964 in connection with the 1964 general strike in British Guiana. When Jagan's and Burnham's supporters clashed in labor strife in the sugar plantations that year, the United States joined with the British Government in urging Burnham not to retaliate with violence, but rather to commit to a mediated end to the conflict. At the same time, the United States provided training to certain of the anti-Jagan forces to enable them to defend themselves if attacked and to boost their morale.

"Following the general strike, 303 Committee–approved funds were used to support the election of a coalition of Burnham's People's National Congress and D'Aguiar's United Force. After Burnham was elected Premier in December 1963, the U.S. Government, again through the CIA, continued to provide substantial funds to both Burnham and D'Aguiar and their parties. In 1967 and 1968, 303 Committee–approved funds were used to help the Burnham and D'Aguiar coalition contest and win the December 1968 general elections. When the U.S. Government learned that Burnham was going to use fraudulent absentee ballots to continue in power in the 1968 elections, it advised him against such a course of action, but did not try to stop him."

192 *"the most dangerous area in the world"*: Memorandum of conversation, June 30, 1963, Birch Grove, England, "Subject: British Guiana." Participants included President Kennedy, Dean Rusk, Ambassador David Bruce, McGeorge Bundy, Prime Minister Harold Macmillan, Lord Home, and Sir David Ormsby-Gore. FRUS, Vol. XII.

193 *"all about the dirty tricks"*: Naftali, Zelikow, and May, *The Presidential Recordings.* Later that day, the president read aloud from the doctrine paper, a classic of geostrategic gobbledygook: *In the interests of U.S. national security seek to replace local leadership with indigenous leaders who are more amenable and sympathetic to the need for eliminating the breeding areas for dissension . . . seeking to insure that modernization of the local society evolves in directions which will afford a congenial world environment for fruitful international cooperation and for our way of life.* "That's a lot of crap," Kennedy said scornfully. " 'For our way of life.' "

193 *On August 21, Robert Kennedy asked McCone*: RFK argued for a "Remember the Maine" incident—a staged attack on Guantánamo—at this meeting and continued to advocate it during the missile crisis. McCone memo, August 21, 1962, in "CIA Documents on the Cuban Missile Crisis,"

CIA/CSI, 1992; McCone memo on McCone-JFK meeting, August 23, 1962, FRUS, Vol. X, document 385.

193 *"How are we doing with that set-up on the Baldwin business?"*: Naftali, Zelikow, and May, *The Presidential Recordings*. J. Edgar Hoover's FBI went to interrogate Baldwin and to tap his home telephone. Baldwin was a graduate of the naval academy who had resigned his commission in 1927, worked as a military analyst for *The New York Times* since 1937, won the Pulitzer Prize for his dispatches from Guadalcanal and the western Pacific in 1943, and was a dependably pro-military voice in the pages of the paper. His sources at the Pentagon were first-rate. After his visit from the FBI, the shaken Timesman told a colleague in a conversation taped by the bureau on the night of July 30: "I think the real answer to this is Bobby Kennedy and the President himself, but Bobby Kennedy particularly putting pressure on Hoover." A transcript of that conversation was on the attorney general's desk the next day. The president's foreign intelligence advisory board met with John Kennedy the following afternoon and told him that Baldwin's work was a grave danger to the United States. "We would suggest," said James Killian, the author of the 1954 "surprise attack" report under Eisenhower, "that the Director of Central Intelligence be encouraged to develop an expert group that would be available at all times to follow up on security leaks . . . a team available to him operating under his direction." Clark Clifford, a member of the board and a drafter of the CIA's charter in the National Security Act of 1947, when he served as Harry Truman's White House counsel, urged President Kennedy to create "a full-time group that is working on it all the time" at the CIA. "They can find out who are Hanson Baldwin's contacts," Clifford said. "When he goes over to the Pentagon, who does he see? Nobody knows now. The FBI doesn't know. But I think it would be mighy interesting." Clifford's many friends in the Washington establishment would have been appalled at this skulduggery. Congressional hearings in 1975 laid responsibility for the taps solely on Attorney General Kennedy and the FBI—not President Kennedy and the CIA.

194 *"I would be only too happy"*: McCone to Kennedy, August 17, 1962, declassified August 20, 2003, CIA/CREST.

194 *"an understandable reluctance"*: McCone, "Memorandum for: The President/The White House," February 28, 1963, JFKL.

194–95 *"Put it in the box and nail it shut"* and *"universal repugnance"*: "CIA Documents on the Cuban Missile Crisis," CIA/CSI, 1992.

195 *"who wants to start a war?"*: "IDEALIST Operations over Cuba," September 10, 1962, CIA/CREST.

195 *The photo gap*: The whys and wherefores of the "photo gap" are in Max Holland, "The 'Photo Gap' That Delayed Discovery of Missiles in Cuba," *Studies in Intelligence*, Vol. 49, No. 4, 2005, CIA/CSI.

195 *"I never knew his name"*: Halpern in James G. Blight and Peter Kornbluh
     (eds.), *Politics of Illusion: The Bay of Pigs Invasion Reexamined* (Boulder, CO:
     Lynne Rienner, 1998).

196 *"a considerable discussion (with some heat)"*: "CIA Documents on the Cuban
     Missile Crisis," CIA/CSI, 1992.

196 *"'Massive activity'"*: "Minutes of Meeting of the Special Group (Aug-
     mented) on Operation Mongoose, 4 October 1962," declassified February
     19, 2004, CIA/CREST; McCone memo, October 4, 1962, FRUS, Vol. X.

196 *"The near-total intelligence surprise"*: The report survives in a 2001 declassi-
     fied excerpt in an editorial note in FRUS, 1961–1963, Vol. XXV, docu-
     ment 107, and a 1992 version in "CIA Documents on the Cuban Missile
     Crisis," CIA/CSI, 1992, pp. 361–371.

197 *"Those things we've been worrying about."*: McGeorge Bundy, *Danger and
     Survival* (New York: Random House, 1988), pp. 395–396.

198 *"Damn it to all hell and back"*: Richard Helms with William Hood, *A Look
     over My Shoulder: A Life in the Central Intelligence Agency* (New York: Ran-
     dom House, 2003), p. 208.

198 *"we had also fooled ourselves"*: Robert Kennedy, *Thirteen Days* (New York:
     Norton, 1969), p. 27.

Chapter Nineteen

199 *"The president flicked on his tape recorder"*: Until 2003 the question of what
     was really on the White House tapes was still a hot dispute. After four
     decades, what really happened, and who said what to whom, has been
     settled by a reliable transcript, the result of more than twenty years of la-
     bor by the John F. Kennedy Presidential Library's historian, Sheldon
     Stern.
        Conventional wisdom contends that the crucible of the Cuban missile
     crisis transformed John and Robert Kennedy, making a brilliant leader
     out of a callow commander in chief, converting young Bobby from hawk
     to dove, and changing the White House from a Harvard seminar into a
     temple of wisdom. It is in part a myth, founded on an inaccurate and fal-
     sified historical record. President Kennedy fed favored journalists with
     poetic but palpably untrue stories. Robert Kennedy's posthumously pub-
     lished book on the crisis contains inventions and made-up dialogue, re-
     peated by otherwise reliable historians and the loyal circle of Kennedy
     acolytes.
        We now know that the Kennedys distorted the historical record and
     concealed how the crisis was resolved. And we now can see that where
     they plotted a path out of the crisis, they were as often as not following
     a course charted by John McCone. See Sheldon Stern, *Averting "The Final*

Failure": John F. Kennedy and the Secret Cuban Missile Crisis Meetings (Stanford, CA: Stanford University Press, 2003). This chapter relies on Stern's transcriptions and McCone's declassified memos, except where noted.

200 *Thinking of the Mongoose missions*: Carter, "16 October (Tuesday)/(Acting DCI)," declassified February 19, 2004, CIA/CREST; "Mongoose Meeting with the Attorney General," October 16, 1962; "CIA Documents on the Cuban Missile Crisis," CIA/CSI, 1992; Aleksandr Fursenko and Timothy Naftali, *One Hell of a Gamble* (New York: Norton, 1997), pp. 227–228.

202 *The six single-spaced pages of notes*: McCone, "Memorandum for Discussion Today," CIA/CREST; untitled McCone memo; and "Talking Paper for Principals," all dated October 17, 1962, declassified March 5, 2003.

203 *"opinions had obviously switched"*: Presidential recordings, October 19–22, JFKL.

203 *"the course which I had recommended"*: McCone memos, October 19–22, 1962, CIA/CREST. A formal meeting of the National Security Council was held in the Oval Room of the Executive Mansion at 2:30 p.m. on Saturday, October 20. The meeting was not taped, but Cline's briefing notes and handwritten scribbles survive, as does the formal record of the NSC's note taker, Bromley Smith. Cline's notes are in "CIA Documents on the Cuban Missile Crisis," CIA/CSI, 1992.

207 *"there was no such deal ever made"*: McCone oral history, April 21, 1988, Institute of International Studies, University of California at Berkeley.

207 *"he's a real bastard, that John McCone"*: This snarl was caught on tape on March 4, 1963, presidential recordings, JFKL. It was first reported by the historian Max Holland, author of *The Kennedy Assassination Tapes* (New York: Knopf, 2004), and recounted in his monograph "The 'Photo Gap' That Delayed Discovery of Missiles in Cuba," *Studies in Intelligence*, Vol. 49, No. 4, 2005, CIA/CSI.

207 *McCone had tried to put a leash on Mongoose*: McCone's actions are reflected in the tapes of the 10 a.m. meeting on October 26, his memos, and the FRUS record of the meeting. The tape transcript is fragmentary. On October 30, "Mr. McCone stated that all MONGOOSE operations must be held in abeyance until this week of negotiations is over." Marshall Carter, memorandum for the record, October 30, 1962, declassified November 4, 2003, CIA/CREST. Covert operations planned and conducted against Cuba during and after the missile crisis are detailed in FRUS, Vol. XI, documents 271, 311, 313, and 318–315.

208 *the final mission to kill Fidel Castro*: The plot is outlined in the 1967 CIA inspector general's report to Helms, declassified in 1993. J. S. Earman, Inspector General, "Subject: Report on Plots to Assassinate Fidel Castro, 23 May 1967," CIA. Quotes and citations in the following paragraphs are drawn from the report.

John McCone never found out about the last plot as it unfolded. But he came close. On August 15, 1962, a reporter for the *Chicago Sun-Times* telephoned CIA headquarters, asking about connections between the notorious Mafia chieftain Sam Giancana, the CIA, and the anti-Castro Cubans. The word went up to McCone, who asked Helms if this could possibly be true. In response, Helms handed over a three-page single-spaced memo from the CIA's chief of security, Sheffield Edwards. It recorded that RFK had been briefed on May 14, 1962, about "a sensitive CIA operation" conducted against Fidel Castro between August 1960 and May 1961, involving "certain gambling interests" represented by "one John Rosselli of Los Angeles" and one "Sam Giancana of Chicago." The attorney general knew those names very well. The memo never mentioned assassination, but its meaning was clear. Helms handed it to McCone with his own covering note: "I assume you are aware of the nature of the operation discussed in the attachment." McCone became intensely aware in the four minutes it took to read it. He was furious beyond words.

That may be why Helms never troubled to tell him about the new assassination plot that FitzGerald was leading—or about who was in charge of the plotting. In 1975, Helms told Henry Kissinger that Bobby Kennedy had "personally managed" more than one assassination attempt against Fidel Castro. Kissinger and Ford, memorandum of conversation, January 4, 1975, GRFL.

Chapter Twenty

210 *"We must bear a good deal of responsibility for it"*: JFK Tapes, November 4, 1963, JFKL. The recording, worth hearing, is available online at http://www.whitehousetapes.org/clips/1963_1104_jfk_vietnam_mem oir.html.

210 *"I was part and parcel of the whole conspiracy"*: Conein's 1975 testimony to Senate investigators was declassified in September 1998. All quotations in this chapter from him are taken from that transcript. Born in Paris in 1919, Conein was sent to Kansas City to live with an aunt, a French war bride, in 1924. He raced to enlist in the French Army when World War II erupted in 1939. When France fell in 1940, he made his way to the United States and wound up in the OSS. In 1944, based in Algiers, he was dropped into occupied France to rendezvous with the Resistance. With France liberated, the OSS sent him to southern China to join a French-Vietnamese commando team assigned to attack a Japanese port in northern Vietnam. He formed an attachment to Vietnam. The affair ended badly for both.

Conein awaits his biographer. Stanley Karnow, the historian and author of *Vietnam: A History* (New York: Viking, 1983), spent seventy hours
interviewing him, but abandoned the project after deciding his subject
was beginning to resemble Somerset Maugham's fictional spy Ashenden,
a man so consumed by espionage that he cannot sort out his cover stories from the story of his life. "He was out of his time," Karnow said. "He
was the swashbuckling soldier of fortune—the guy who has ceased to exist except in fiction. A marvelous storyteller. Whether the stories were
true or not was beside the point. They were almost always almost entirely true."

The author wrote Conein's obituary, "Lucien Conein, 79, Legendary
Cold War Spy," *The New York Times*, June 7, 1998.

211 *"do what you can to save South Vietnam"*: Rufus Phillips oral history, FAOH.

211 *"a flashpoint"*: John Gunther Dean oral history, FAOH.

211 *a new Lao government*: The decision to try to buy a new government was
made after Allen Dulles warned President Eisenhower that "we had a good
deal to fear in the 1959 general elections" in Laos, and the president replied
"that it would be a serious matter if any country such as Laos went Communist by the legal vote of its people." NSC minutes, May 29, 1958, DDEL.
The CIA's own analysts reported: "The Communist resumption of guerrilla
warfare in Laos was primarily a reaction to a stronger anti-Communist
posture by the Laotian government and to recent US initiatives in support
of Laos." Special National Intelligence Estimate 68-2-59, "The Situation in
Laos," September 18, 1959, declassified May 2001, CIA/CREST.

211 *"The suitcase contained money"*: John Gunther Dean oral history, FAOH.

212 *a roulette wheel*: James interview with author.

212 *"That was the real go-ahead"*: William Lair oral history, Vietnam Archive
Oral History Project, Texas Tech University, interview conducted by Steve
Maxner, December 11, 2001. Used with the kind permission of Mr.
Maxner and the archive.

212 *double its tribal forces in Laos and "make every possible effort to launch guerrilla
operations in North Vietnam"*: The latter order is in the Pentagon Papers,
United States–Vietnam Relations, 1945–1967, Vol. 2 (Washington, DC: U.S.
Government Printing Office, 1972), p. 18. The former is in a Special
Group memo reprinted in FRUS, Vol. XXVIII: "The genesis of this program stems from high level U.S. Government approval in late 1960 and
early 1961 [for] CIA [to] enlist tribal support to fight communism. The
main effort in this program has been development of the Meo, the largest
non-Lao ethnic group in Laos. . . . As authorized by the Special Group in
June 1963, this program has expanded to a present force of approximately 19,000 armed Meo guerrillas (23,000 authorized) engaged in village defense and guerrilla activities against the Pathet Lao."

213 *"the ignorance and the arrogance"*: Richard L. Holm, "Recollections of a Case
Officer in Laos, 1962 to 1964," *Studies in Intelligence*, Vol. 47, No. 1, 2003,
CIA/CSI.

213 *"the activisits were all for a war in Laos"*: There was a great debate inside CIA
headquarters about the wisdom of a war in Laos. "The Agency was very
badly split," said Robert Amory, Jr., the deputy director of intelligence
from 1953 to 1962. "The activists were all for a war in Laos. They thought
that was a great place to have a war. . . . Fitzgerald was very strong for
it." Amory was not, and he soon resigned, but not before he helped draft
President Kennedy's first major national television address, on the subject of Laos, on March 23, 1961. The president could not or would not
pronounce the nation's name correctly; he thought no one would care
for a country called "Louse." He said LAY-os was threatened by communist forces within and without, including combat specialists from North
Vietnam. "Its own safety runs with the safety of us all," he told the nation. "In real neutrality, observed by all. All we want in Laos is peace,
not war."

213 *The Americans sent to Vietnam had an equally profound ignorance of the country's history and culture*: Ronald H. Spector, *Advice and Support: The Early
Years of the United States Army in Vietnam, 1941–1960*, rev. ed. (New York:
Free Press, 1985), pp. x, xi. "Added to this propensity to try to make
something out of nothing was an American ignorance of Vietnamese history and society so massive and all-encompassing that two decades of
federally funded fellowships, crash language programs, television spe-
cials, and campus teach-ins made hardly a dent," Spector wrote. "Before
the United States sets out to make something out of nothing in some
other corner of the globe, American leaders might consider the historical
and social factors involved."

213 *"They had everything they wanted"*: Neher oral history, FAOH.

213 *Project Tiger*: The author described the fate of the CIA's Vietnamese agents
in "Once Commandos for U.S., Vietnamese Are Now Barred," *The New
York Times*, April 14, 1995. Hanoi's double-crossing of the CIA from 1961
to 1963 is definitively detailed in Richard H. Schultz, Jr., *The Secret War
Against Hanoi: Kennedy's and Johnson's Use of Spies, Saboteurs, and Covert
Warriors in North Vietnam* (New York: HarperCollins, 1999). Schultz, director of international security studies at the Fletcher School of Law and
Diplomacy, conducted extensive oral history interviews and reviewed de-
classified documents for the book.

214 *"We harvested a lot of lies"*: Barbour oral history, FAOH.

214 *In October 1961, President Kennedy sent*: The sprawl of the CIA's paramilitary
forces in the region at the time was impressive, as detailed by General
Lansdale in a report to the White House. In Vietnam, CIA officers com-

manded 340 South Vietnamese soldiers of the First Observation Group, created by the agency in 1956 and trained to kill Vietcong infiltrators in the south, the north, and Laos. From Taiwan, Civil Air Transport, the CIA airline, flew hundreds of missions a year in Laos and Vietnam; the Chinese Nationalist army and the CIA trained hundreds of Vietnamese to serve as paramilitary officers. In Thailand, Bill Lair's own paramilitary forces stood at 550 trained Thai officers. At Fort McKinley outside Manila, the CIA ran a sprawling school for Filipino soldiers to fight communism throughout Asia. Hundreds more trainees from all across the region were being sent to the CIA base on the island of Saipan.

214 *"the sending to Vietnam of some U.S. military forces"*: That secret was very deep indeed. The author obtained a unique copy of Taylor's full and uncensored report to the president from the CIA's archives in September 2005. It was the personal copy of Deputy Director of Central Intelligence Charles Pearre Cabell. Cabell had highlighted the sentence and written in the margins of his copy, *To CIA readers: This concept must be kept very secure. CPC.*

215 *"Nobody liked Diem"*: Robert F. Kennedy oral history, JFKL, collected in Edwin O. Guthman and Jeffrey Shulman (eds.), *Robert Kennedy, in His Own Words: The Unpublished Recollections of the Kennedy Years* (New York: Bantam, 1988), p. 396.

216 *"Diem himself cannot be preserved"*: Telegram from the Department of State to the embassy in Vietnam, Washington, August 24, 1963, 9:36 p.m., FRUS, Vol. III.

216 *"I should not have given my consent to it"*: JFK Tapes, November 4, 1963, JFKL.

216 *the president had ordered Diem ousted*: On Saturday evening, August 23, 1963, when JFK decided to topple Diem, the news from Vietnam was grim. South Vietnamese commandos trained by the CIA were killing Buddhist protestors, the president's daily brief from the CIA that morning noted, and "Nhu told a U.S. source yesterday that the generals recommended the imposition of martial law. [Nhu] denied this amounted to a coup, but warned it could become one if Diem vacillated or compromised on the Buddhist issue." FRUS, 1961–1963, Vol. III, document 271. If Kennedy read this, he would have been encouraged to approve the Hilsman cable authorizing a move against Diem. The history of the Hilsman cable has been well established by declassified State Department records in the FRUS Vietnam series. McCone told Dwight Eisenhower that the president's casual approval of the uncoordinated cable was "one of the government's greatest errors" to date—a high standard. The former president was furious. Where was the National Security Council? What was the State Department doing running coups? McCone replied that

Kennedy was surrounded by "liberals in his government who want to reform every country" in the world. Well, Eisenhower shot back, who appointed those damned liberals? The old general "expressed much concern over the future of the United States." McCone memo, "Conference with Former President Eisenhower," September 19, 1963, DDEL.

216 *Helms handed the assignment to Bill Colby, the new chief of the CIA's Far East division*: It is a terrible irony that Colby—who in a 1982 oral history for the LBJ Library said that "the overthrow of Diem was the worst mistake we made"—may well have planted a seed for it in an August 16, 1963, memo to Helms, Roger Hilsman at State, and Michael Forrestal at NSC. It weighed the chances for a "successful coup d'etat" and noted that "assassination may be an integral part of projected coups or may be done in hope that something better will somehow emerge from the resulting chaotic situation."

216 *"songs they may sing"*: Colby cited in Harold Ford, *CIA and the Vietnam Policymakers*, 1996, CIA/CSI, available at http://www.cia.gov/csi/books/vietnam/epis1.hmtl. Ford was for many years a senior CIA analyst on Vietnam.

216 *At the White House, Helms listened*: Helms was at the White House meeting at noon on August 29, 1963, with the president, McNamara, and Rusk, among a dozen other top officials. The note taker recorded that Ambassador Lodge had already instructed the CIA's Rufus Phillips "to tell the Vietnamese generals that the U.S. Ambassador is behind the CIA approach." The message to the generals was that the CIA, the embassy, and the White House spoke with one voice. "The President asked whether anyone had any reservations about the course of action we were following," and Rusk and McNamara did. The president then decided that "Ambassador Lodge is to have authority over all overt and covert operations" in Vietnam. A personal, eyes-only cable went out to Lodge reserving presidential command over those covert operations. Memorandum of conference with the president, August 29, 1963, National Security file, JFKL. Lodge's job was to make sure that the American hand would not show. "I received my instructions from Ambassador Lodge," Conein testified. "If they were cabled instructions, he had a very good habit of not reading something. He would fold a piece of paper and what pertained to you for instructions, he would let you read that, and that alone, so you didn't know who was sending it or where it came from. . . . 'Those are the instructions, do you understand them?' 'Yes, sir.' 'All right, go carry them out.'" On the president's desire for secrecy, see Bundy to Lodge, October 5, 1963, FRUS, Vol. IV.

216 *"CIA has more money; bigger houses than diplomats; bigger salaries; more weapons; more modern equipment"*: The clash between Lodge and Richard-

son is poignantly recorded in John H. Richardson, *My Father the Spy: A Family History of the CIA, the Cold War, and the Sixties* (New York: Harper-Collins, 2005).

217 *Lodge decided he wanted a new station chief*: Specifically, he wanted General Ed Lansdale, the ugly American. Absolutely not, said McCone, who had "no confidence in him at all. They could replace Richardson if Lodge wants it but not someone from the outside." Memorandum of telephone conversation between the secretary of state and the director of central intelligence, September 17, 1963, FRUS, 1961–1963, Vol. IV, document 120.

217 *"exposed him, and gave his name publicly to the newspapers"*: RFK oral history, JFKL; Guthman and Shulman, *Robert Kennedy, in His Own Words,* p. 398. The burning of a station chief by an ambassador was unprecedented in the history of the CIA. McCone sent a four-page briefing paper to President Kennedy the day before the president had a scheduled press conference on October 9, 1963, defending the CIA against the fury Lodge's leaks had set in motion. "You will undoubtedly be asked about CIA's role in Vietnam," McCone wrote. "The criticism which has found its way into hundreds of news articles and editorials is seriously eroding the spirit of this organization which I have now spent two years trying to rekindle." The president hewed closely to McCone's briefing in his answers to the press.

217 *"We were fortunate"*: Tran Van Don, *Our Endless War* (San Francisco: Presidio, 1978), pp. 96–99.

217 *"against the assassination plot," "supporting assassination,"* and *if I were the manager of a baseball team*: Church Committee, *Alleged Assassination Plots Involving Foreign Leaders,* Interim Report, U.S. Senate, 94th Congress, 1st Session, 1975.

218 *"a complete lack of intelligence," "exceedingly dangerous,"* and *"absolute disaster for the United States"*: McCone memos, "Special Group 5412 Meeting," October 18, 1963, and "Discussion with the President—October 21," CIA/CREST. See also Ford, *CIA and the Vietnam Policymakers.*

218 *"We should not thwart a coup"*: Lodge to Bundy and McCone, October 25, 1963, FRUS, 1961–1963, Vol. IV, document 216. By then it was too late. On October 29, McCone, Helms, and Colby arrived at the White House for a 4:20 p.m. meeting with the president, his brother, and the entire national-security team. Colby presented a detailed military map showing that Diem's strength and the coup leaders' forces were evenly divided. So were the president's men. The State Department was in favor, the military and McCone opposed. But the White House had set in motion a force it could not stop.

218 *"money and weapons"*: Don, *Our Endless War,* pp. 96–99.

218 *"Diem looked at me quizzically and said, 'Is there going to be a coup against me?' "*: Phillips oral history, FAOH.

219 *The coup struck on November 1*: Conein's account here comes from his declassified Church Committee testimony; the cable traffic is reproduced in
FRUS. Conein said that Nhu had arranged with the military commander
of the Saigon military district to stage a fake Vietcong uprising in Saigon.
The plan included the assassination of key American officials. Nhu then
planned to send troops from the commander's contingent to put down
the fake revolt and save Vietnam. But the commander told the coup plotters about Nhu's plans. As Conein put it, the rebel generals "double
bumped" Nhu: when the real coup began, Nhu thought it was his fake
coup. According to the Church Committee, Conein passed three million
piasters ($42,000) to an aide of General Don's late on the morning of No-
vember 1 to procure food for the coup forces and to pay death benefits
for those killed during the coup. Conein said in his testimony the sum he
took from his house was five million piasters, or about $70,000. Colby
said it was $65,000.

221 *the president leaped to his feet and "rushed from the room with a look of shock
and dismay"*: General Maxwell D. Taylor, *Swords and Plowshares: A Memoir*
(New York: Da Capo, 1990), p. 301. The White House–Saigon cables cited
in this passage are reprinted in full in FRUS, Vol. IV.

221 *"'Hey, boss, we did a good job, didn't we?'"*: Rosenthal oral history, FAOH.

Chapter Twenty-one

In 1975, the Senate Select Committee to Study Governmental Operations with
Respect to Intelligence Activities (hereinafter the "Church Committee") convened under the chairmanship of Senator Frank Church. Its investigators demanded and received depositions taken in secret, and later took limited public
testimony. The work of lasting value was in the secret files.

This chapter is based in part on recently declassified testimony delivered by senior CIA officers—among them Richard Helms, John Whitten (identified by the
alias "John Scelso"), and James J. Angleton. They gave secret depositions to the
Church Committee in 1976 and to a follow-up investigation by the House Select
Committee on Assassinations in 1978 (hereinafter "HSCA"). Helms, McCone, Angleton, and others also testified before the Rockefeller Commission created by
President Ford in 1975. The release of these transcripts twenty and twenty-five
years after the fact sheds new light on what the CIA was thinking after the assassination, on its own investigation of the killing, and on its failure to fully inform
the Warren Commission.

The depositions were declassified between 1998 and 2004 under the JFK Assassination Records Collection Act passed by Congress in 1992. Many have been
published on a CD-ROM as *Assassination Transcripts of the Church Committee*, available online at http://www.history-matters.com. The work of the CIA's John Whit-

ten investigating the Kennedy assassination for the agency was located at the JFK Library by the journalist Jefferson Morley in his research for a forthcoming biography of the Mexico City station chief Win Scott. He graciously shared copies with the author in 2006. That work is hereinafter cited as "Whitten report."

222 *"I'm sure glad the Secret Service didn't catch us"*: Richard Helms with William Hood, *A Look over My Shoulder: A Life in the Central Intelligence Agency* (New York: Random House, 2003), pp. 227–229.

222 *"What raced through my mind"*: LBJ, telephone conversation with Bill Moyers, December 26, 1966, LBJL. Many of Lyndon Johnson's White House tapes related to the Kennedy assassination have been collected, edited, annotated, and published by Max Holland in *The Kennedy Assassination Tapes* (New York: Knopf, 2004). Citations from that work are hereinafter "LBJ Tapes/Holland."

223 *"Tragic death of President Kennedy"*: Helms, *A Look over My Shoulder,* p. 229.

223 *"Mexico had the biggest and most active telephone intercept operations in the whole world"*: Whitten deposition, 1978.

224 *"CIA had no sources"*: Whitten report, undated but December 1963, CIA/ JFKL.

224 *he was enraged*: McCone's 11:30 p.m. meeting on November 22, 1963, included Deputy Director Carter, Richard Helms, and the agency's chief administrative officer, Red White, who recorded in his office diary that McCone had taken General Carter and " 'wire-brushed' him thoroughly, had expressed himself as being most dissatisfied with the way the Agency was being managed." L. K. White diary, November 23, 1963, CIA/CREST.

225 *"the most bitter feelings"*: Whitten gave his professional biography and described his run-ins with Angleton in both his 1976 and 1978 depositions; the quotation is from the latter.

225 *"His having been to the Cuban and Soviet embassies"*: Helms deposition, August 9, 1978, House Special Committee on Assassinations. Top Secret, declassified May 1, 2001.

225 *McCone . . . broke the news of the Cuban connection*: McCone memo, November 24, 1963, CIA/CREST; LBJ and Eisenhower conversation, August 27, 1965, LBJ Tapes/Holland.

225 *"this assassin"*: LBJ to Weisl, November 23, 1963, LBJ Tapes/Holland.

226 *He had talked face-to-face*: The innocent explanation was that Soviet intelligence officers in Mexico City were filling their cover roles as visa officers by day, just as CIA officers did in embassies worldwide. In a memoir, the Soviet intelligence officer Oleg Nechiporenko said he first overheard and then witnessed Oswald pleading for a visa in his barely passable Russian. He appeared to want to go to Cuba to save both himself and Fidel Castro from the forces of American intelligence: "Oswald was extremely agitated

and clearly nervous, especially whenever he mentioned the FBI, but he suddenly became hysterical, began to sob, and through his tears cried, '*I am afraid . . . they'll kill me. Let me in!*' Repeating over and over that he was being persecuted and that he was being followed even here in Mexico, he stuck his right hand into the left pocket of his jacket and pulled out a revolver, saying, '*See? This is what I must now carry to protect my life.'* " Nechiporenko, *Passport to Assassination: The Never-Before-Told Story of Lee Harvey Oswald by the KGB Colonel Who Knew Him* (Secaucus, NJ: Birch Lane, 1993).

226 *The station sent headquarters a list*: The sequence of events, first raising the question of whether Cubela might be a double agent, is reconstructed in "The Investigation of the Assassination of President John F. Kennedy: The Performance of the Intelligence Agencies," Church Committee staff report, 1975, declassified in 2000.

227 *Dulles immediately called James Angleton*: Angleton deposition, 1978, HSCA.

227 *"Helms realized that disclosing the assassination plots would reflect very poorly on the Agency"*: Whitten testimony, 1976.

227 *"We were treading very lightly"*: Helms testimony, August 1978, HSCA.

228 *"gross incompetency"* and *"a direct admission"*: Hoover and DeLoach cited in "The Investigation of the Assassination of President John F. Kennedy." This secret Senate staff report, declassified in 2000, twenty-five years after it was conducted, found that the evidence "tends to impeach the process by which the intelligence community provided information to the Warren Commission." It concluded: "There is doubt as to whether these agencies can ever be relied upon to investigate their own operations and their own performance in critical situations."

229 *"Dozens of people were claiming that they had seen Oswald here, there, and everywhere"*: Whitten testimony, 1976.

229 *"We would have seen it more sharply"*: This and all other quotations from Angleton in this chapter are from his deposition before the HSCA, October 5, 1978, declassified 1998.

231 *"I'd like to talk to you"*: Mark told of his encounter with Nosenko, a previously unpublished account, in a State Department oral history, FAOH.

231 *Much was lost in translation*: For example, Nosenko said an army sergeant at the American embassy in Moscow whom he identified as a spy for the KGB worked as "a code machine repairman." This later came out in English as "a mechanic," as in garage mechanic. When Nosenko tried to correct the record, he was accused of changing his story.

232 *"a great deal had gone wrong on his watch"*: A formal acknowledgment of that fact finally appeared in 2006. See "The Angleton Era in CIA," in *A Counterintelligence Reader*, Vol. 3, Chap. 2, pp. 109–115, available online at http://www.ncix.gov/history/index.html.

233 *the CIA threw Nosenko into solitary confinement*: The case was chronicled years later by two senior CIA officers: Richards J. Heuer, Jr., "Nosenko: Five Paths to Judgment," *Studies in Intelligence,* Fall 1987, CIA/CSI; and John Limond Hart, *The CIA's Russians* (Annapolis, MD: Naval Institute Press, 2002), pp. 128–160.

234 *"I recognized we couldn't keep him in durance vile"*: Helms interview, *Studies in Intelligence,* December 1993, CIA/CSI.

234 *seven major studies of the case*: In 1976, the CIA's John Limond Hart was called out of retirement to re-investigate the Nosenko case. Hart had uncovered the deceptions of his predecessor as the chief of station in Seoul, Al Haney, nearly a quarter century before. He had gone on to a distinguished career—chief of station in Saigon, chief of foreign intelligence collection in China and Cuba, and chief of operations for Western Europe. He had known Angleton since 1948, when they served in Rome together—when the CIA won the Italian elections, the cold war was new, and Angleton still sane. The two men sat down for a four-hour interview on the case of Yuri Nosenko in 1976. When Hart read the transcript the next day, the words made no sense at all. "Perhaps because of his legendary thirst," Hart wrote, "Angleton's muddled mind by then had become a grab bag of haphazard minutiae, much of it totally irrelevant." Hart pronounced the Nosenko case "an abomination," the worst thing he had ever encountered in a lifetime of intelligence work. Hart, *The CIA's Russians.*

Chapter Twenty-Two

236 *"a goddamn bunch of thugs"*: LBJ to Senator Eugene McCarthy, February 1, 1966, available online at http://www.whitehousetapes.org/clips/1966_0201_lbj_mccarthy_vietnam.html. LBJ expressed his "divine retribution" theory—"that because President Kennedy had been in a sense responsible for Diem's demise, he in turn was assassinated himself," as Richard Helms remembered—at a December 19, 1963, meeting with McCone, Helms, and Desmond FitzGerald. LBJ repeated this to Hubert Humphrey, who would be his vice president; Ralph Duggan, a White House aide; and Pierre Salinger, a Kennedy press secretary.

236 *"The Attorney General intended to stay on"*: McCone memo, "Discussion with the President, 13 December—9:30 a.m.," declassified October 2002, CIA/CREST. McCone's memo continued: "I explained to the President that I had told Bobby he could not bring back the intimacy of the relationship with the President which he had had with his brother because that was a blood relationship, not an official relationship. A type of relationship which is seldom found between brothers and never found be-

tween officials, either in business or government." It was not found between the new president and his attorney general. Bobby could not stand
to be in the White House with Johnson. "He's mean, bitter, vicious—
an animal in many ways," he said a few months later, in the April 1964
oral history, for the Kennedy Library.

236 *"change the image of the CIA'"*: McCone memos, December 28, 1963; January 13, 1964; and February 20, 1964. The president was worried about
his own image. He was discomfited by the publication of *The Invisible Government*, the first serious best seller examining the CIA and its relationship with the White House. It revealed the existence of the Special
Group, the committee of top CIA, State, Pentagon, and White House men
who approved covert action—and it made clear that presidents ultimately controlled those secret missions. The chairman of the Special
Group, national security adviser McGeorge Bundy, thought it might be
best to change its name. After rejecting suggestions from his staff—
among them "the Invisible Group"—he issued National Security Action
Memorandum 303, changing the name to the 303 Committee.

The committee's declassified records show that the CIA undertook 163
major covert operations, slightly fewer than five each month, under President Kennedy. Under President Johnson, 142 new major covert operations were launched through February 1967, slightly fewer than four
each month. The members' deliberations often were pro forma. In the
course of a few spring days in 1964, they approved a shipment of arms
for the military coup that overthrew the government of Brazil—"we
don't want to watch Brazil dribble down the drain while we stand
around waiting for the next election"—and sent an extra $1.25 million
to swing the presidential ballot in Chile—"no problem, since we could get
more if needed." President Johnson rarely sought the details of such decisions, though they had the imprimatur of his office.

237 *"extremely worried"*: McCone memo, "DCI Briefing of CIA Subcommittees
of Senate Armed Services and Senate Appropriations Committees, Friday, 10 January 1964," declassified December 15, 2004, CIA/CREST;
Harold Ford, *CIA and the Vietnam Policymakers*, 1996, CIA/CSI, available
online at http://www.cia.gov/csi/books/vietnam/epis1.html.

237 *"The President should be informed that this is not the greatest thing since peanut
butter"*: McCone, Helms, and Lyman Kirkpatrick cited in William Colby,
memorandum for the record, "Meeting on North Vietnam," January 9,
1964, CIA/CREST.

238 *"highly dissatisfied"*: McCone memos, April 22 and 29, 1964, and October
22, 1964, CIA/CREST; the latter also appears in FRUS, Vol. XXXIII, document 219. It is worth quoting, for it shows that President Johnson and
John McCone had never had a substantial conversation about the CIA:

"On 22 October I prepared to depart with Mrs. McCone to attend the funeral of Herbert Hoover, Sr. I was called by the White House and advised that the President requested specifically that we accompany him. . . . While traveling with the President I was able to discuss a number of matters with him. The principal items were: *The President stated that he did not know too much about CIA's organization.* . . . I emphasized the objectivity of the organization, the fact it had no parochial 'axe to grind' in any field most particularly those relating to foreign policy and defense policy. The Agency looked upon its responsibility as that of collecting intelligence by every possible means and evaluating our own intelligence and that gathered by all other Community members carefully and objectively. *The President asked the size of the organization.* I told him our budget was about [*deleted*] and said we had about [*deleted*] employees. He asked about the future outlook. I said that I thought the organization was pretty well shaking down, the five-year forecast indicated no increases in personnel and the increases in the budget were minimal and attributable largely to the wages and salary increases and other escalations. I said this resulted from very careful management and that we hope to 'hold the line' unless new tasks were assigned to the Agency. This would necessitate additional people and money. *The President asked what part of our budget went for operational activities such as political action, paramilitary, etc.,* and I said about [*deleted*]. *This was the first opportunity I have had to discuss the Agency with the President.* I thought he was interested and impressed." McCone memo, "Discussion with the President—22 October 1964," emphasis added.

McCone tried to make the president pay attention to the fact that the fate of nations could turn on a successful trick of espionage. He had a couple of stories to tell, the best of which was this: a young station chief by the name of Clair George, posted in Bamako, Mali, one of the world's most obscure capitals, got a tip from a member of the host government in 1964. The African official said he had heard from a diplomat at the Chinese embassy that Beijing would conduct its first nuclear test in a matter of weeks. The report went straight to CIA headquarters. An early spy satellite looked down on the preparations at the test site in China. McCone personally took charge of the analysis. "We knew what they were doing," he recalled in an oral history for the LBJ Library. "Hard intelligence."

McCone told the White House and American allies that the Chinese would test a nuclear weapon within thirty to sixty days: "And on the thirty-first day they exploded the bomb. They made a prophet out of me." This intelligence coup began with news from nowhere—the capital of Mali. After that, Clair George was a made man. Twenty years later he became chief of the clandestine service. But McCone had far too few such success stories.

239 *the new Defense Intelligence Agency*: The DIA was "a perfect example of how not to create a government agency," said Admiral Bobby Ray Inman, who served as its vice director in the mid-1970s before running the NSA and serving, briefly, as deputy director of central intelligence. Bobby R. Inman, "Managing Intelligence for Effective Use," Center for Information Policy Research, Harvard University, December 1980.

239 *"take NRO and shove it"*: Transcript of telephone conversation between Director of Central Intelligence McCone and the assistant secretary of defense, February 13, 1964, FRUS, Vol. XXXIII, declassified 2004.

240 *a highly detailed confession*: Robert J. Hanyok, "Skunks, Bogies, Silent Hounds, and the Flying Fish: The Gulf of Tonkin Mystery, 2–4 August 1964," *Cryptologic Quarterly*, Vol. 19, No. 4/Vol. 20, No. 1, Winter 2000/Spring 2001, declassified November 2005. The quarterly is an official and highly classified NSA publication.

241 *the American destroyers sent a flash message that they were under attack*: Eight hours later, President Johnson asked McCone: "Do they want a war by attacking our ships in the middle of the Gulf of Tonkin?" McCone answered: "No. The North Vietnamese are reacting defensively to our attacks on their off-shore islands. They are responding out of pride."

242 *"McNamara had taken over raw SIGINT"*: Ray Cline oral history, LBJL.

243 *"shooting at flying fish"*: Hanyok, "Skunks, Bogies, Silent Hounds, and the Flying Fish."

Chapter Twenty-Three

244 *"Vietnam was my nightmare"*: Richard Helms with William Hood, *A Look over My Shoulder: A Life in the Central Intelligence Agency* (New York: Random House, 2003), pp. 309–311.

244 *"our ignorance—or innocence"*: Helms oral history, September 16, 1981, LBJL.

245 *"'Coward! Traitor! Weakling!'"*: LBJ quoted in Doris Kearns, *Lyndon Johnson and the American Dream* (New York: Harper and Row, 1976), pp. 251–252.

245 *"Counterinsurgency became an almost ridiculous battle cry"*: Amory oral history, JFKL.

245 *"What we needed . . . were people who could shoot guns"*: Robert F. Kennedy oral history, May 14, 1964, JFKL, collected in Edwin O. Guthman and Jeffrey Shulman (eds.), *Robert Kennedy, in His Own Words: The Unpublished Recollections of the Kennedy Years* (New York: Bantam, 1988), p. 310. President Kennedy established the Special Group (Counterinsurgency) on January 18, 1962, under National Security Action Memorandum 124.

RFK led it—despite McCone's warning that it would be "an embarrass-ment for Bobby if it became known the Attorney General was running dirty tricks in favor of the counterinsurgency committee"—and created a great grab bag of worldwide programs in its name.

245 *"Our Counterinsurgency Experiment and Its Implications"*: De Silva to Colby, undated, forwarded from Colby to McCone via Helms ("Subject: Saigon Station Experiment in Counterinsurgency"), November 16, 1964; with Marshall Carter's covering memo ("McCone's War"), declassified May 29, 2003, CIA/CREST.

246 *"if South Vietnam fell"*: "DCI Briefing for CIA Subcommittee of House Ap-propriations Committee, December 5, 1963," declassified March 15, 2004, CIA/CREST.

246 *"VC may be the wave of the future"*: McCone cited in Harold Ford, *CIA and the Vietnam Policymakers*, 1996, CIA/CSI, available online at http://www.cia.gov/csi/books/vietnam/epis1.html.

246 *"the Vietcong use of terror"*: Peer de Silva, *Sub Rosa: The CIA and the Uses of Intelligence* (New York: Times Books, 1978), pp. 220–254.

247 *The corruption of intelligence*: George W. Allen, *None So Blind: A Personal Ac-count of the Intelligence Failure in Vietnam* (Chicago: Ivan R. Dee, 2001), pp. 188–194.

247 *"My world turned to glue"*: De Silva, *Sub Rosa*, p. 256.

247 *"There must be somebody out there that's got enough brains"*: LBJ Tapes, March 30, 1965, 9:12 a.m., LBJL.

248 *"increasing pressure to stop the bombing"* and *"mired down in combat in the jun-gle"*: McCone memos, April 2 and 20, 1965, LBJL. See also Ford, *CIA and the Vietnam Policymakers*.

248 *"Let me tell you about these intelligence guys"*: Robert M. Gates, *From the Shadows: The Ultimate Insider's Story of Five Presidents and How They Won the Cold War* (New York: Simon and Schuster, 1996), p. 566. The source of this story was Richard Helms. Helms remembered it vividly as Johnson's statement to John McCloy at a dinner in the White House residence. It certainly sounds like LBJ.

Chapter Twenty-Four

249 *"light the fuse"*: LBJ Tapes/Holland, April 2, 1965.

249 *"close up the place and give it to the Indians"*: Carter, memorandum for the record, April 2, 1965, CIA, FRUS, 1964–1968, Vol. XXXIII, declassified 2004.

249 *"Now, I need you," Lyndon Johnson said*: Transcript of telephone conversa-tion between President Johnson and Admiral Raborn, April 6, 1965, 4:26 p.m., FRUS, Vol. XXXIII, declassified 2004, LBJL.

250　*"Our CIA says"*: LBJ Tapes, April 30, 1965, 10:50 a.m. and 11:30 a.m.

251　*"You don't think CIA can document it?"*: LBJ Tapes, April 30, 1965, 5:05 p.m.

251　*"It was tragic"*: Ray Cline, *Secrets, Spies, and Scholars: Blueprint of the Essential CIA* (Washington, DC: Acropolis, 1976), pp. 211–212.

251　*"Poor old Raborn"*: James Hanrahan, "An Interview with Former CIA Executive Director Lawrence K. 'Red' White," *Studies in Intelligence*, Vol. 43, No. 1, Winter 1999/2000, CIA/CSI.

252　*"If you ever decide to get rid of him, you just put that fellow Helms in there"*: Transcript of telephone conversation between the president and Russell, 8 p.m., September 14, 1965, FRUS, Vol. XXXIII, declassified 2004, LBJL.

252　*"You think that we can really beat the Vietcong out there?"*: LBJ Tapes, July 2, 1965.

253　*"as invisible as possible"*: William Lair oral history, Vietnam Archive Oral History Project, Texas Tech University, interview conducted by Steve Maxner, December 11, 2001. Used with the kind permission of Mr. Maxner and the archive.

254　*"We saw some of our young guys killed"*: Lilley oral history, FAOH.

255　*Colby was disheartened*: Colby to Helms, August 16, 1966, FRUS, 1964–1968, Vol. XXVIII. The memo describes Colby's impressions during his October 1965 tour.

256　*"No one was talking theory here"*: The Shackley account is from his posthumous memoir, written with Richard A. Finney, *Spymaster: My Life in the CIA* (Dulles, VA: Potomac, 2005).

257　*"an exemplary success story"*: Memorandum from the Central Intelligence Agency to the 303 Committee, September 8, 1966, FRUS, 1964–1968, Vol. XXVIII, document 248.

257　*Wild Bill Donovan*: Donovan began his stint as ambassador by reviving the disastrous Li Mi operation. The defeated Chinese Nationalist forces had settled into the Golden Triangle, in the hills of eastern Burma, the northern borderlands of Thailand, and the western edge of Laos. They had become an aggressive occupying force running an international opium trade. Donovan saw them as freedom fighters, and he plunged into their cause, "providing supplies while denying publicly that there was any U.S. involvement," said Kempton B. Jenkins, then a State Department political officer in Bangkok. A sham evacuation of the Li Mi forces, overseen by Donovan, looked impressive—CIA pilots flew 1,925 men and boys out of the Golden Triangle to Taiwan—but thousands of men remained. Instead of fighting communists, they set about cornering the opium market, building refineries to make morphine, and shipping the drugs down to Bangkok. Jenkins provides a detailed look at Donovan's liaisons with the Thai police and military. Jenkins oral history, FAOH. See also Frank C. Darling, *Thailand and the United States* (Washington, DC: Public Affairs,

1965), for a look at the beginnings of CIA involvement in the region after the Korean war. The expanding power of the CIA's Laos station in the 1950s is well described in the FAOH oral histories of John Gunther Dean, L. Michael Rives, and Christian A. Chapman, all of whom served at the American embassy there.

257 *"Money was no object"*: Thomas oral history, FAOH.

258 *"financing of a political party, electoral support for this party, and support for selected candidates for parliament from the party"* . . . *to continue "the leadership and control of the present ruling group" and "to ensure that the party created is successful in winning a comfortable and commanding majority in elections"*: These goals are set out in the CIA's memorandum prepared for the 303 Committee, September 28, 1965, and 303 Committee minutes, October 8, 1965. FRUS, Vol. XXVII.

258 *The CIA had warned*: On March 5, 1965, in a discussion of ongoing covert action in Indonesia, a senior CIA officer told the 303 Committee that "the loss of a nation of 105 million to the 'Communist camp' would make a victory in Vietnam of little meaning." 303 Committee minutes, March 5, 1965. A separate CIA memorandum for the 303 Committee, dated February 23, 1965, lays out the developing covert-action program in Indonesia: "Since the summer of 1964, [*deleted, but probably the Indonesia station and/or Colby's Far East division*] has worked with the Department of State in formulating concepts and developing an operational program of political action in Indonesia. . . . The main thrust of this program is designed to exploit factionalism within the PKI itself, to emphasize traditional Indonesian distrust of Mainland China and to portray the PKI as an instrument of Red Chinese imperialism. Specific types of activity envisaged include covert liaison with and support to existing anti-Communist groups. . . . [Ongoing covert programs include] political action within existing Indonesian organizations and institutions [and] covert training of selected personnel and civilians, who will be placed in key positions. . . . [Among the goals is to] cultivate potential leaders within Indonesia for the purpose of ensuring an orderly non-Communist succession upon Sukarno's death or removal from office." The 303 Committee records are in FRUS, Vol. XXVI.

259 *"I recruited and ran Adam Malik"*: McAvoy interview with author. The documentation on the CIA's role in Indonesia, including the December 2, 1965, cable from Green to Bundy detailing a CIA payment to Adam Malik, is in FRUS, 1964–1968, Vol. XXVI, pp. 338–380. The volume was officially suppressed by the CIA and withdrawn from circulation—but not before some copies were printed, bound, and shipped. The National Security Archive posted the relevant pages in July 2001. The author's interview with McAvoy took place by telephone from McAvoy's home in

Hawaii. McAvoy's crucial role as a CIA officer in Indonesia was confirmed by three of his contemporaries at the agency.

259 *"in a clandestine setting"*: Green oral history, FAOH.

260 *"It was certainly not a death list"*: Martens oral history, FAOH.

261 *Ambassador Green later told Vice President Hubert H. Humphrey . . . that "300,000 to 400,000 people were slain"*: Memorandum of conversation, February 17, 1967; LBJ Oval Office meeting with Adam Malik, memorandum of conversation, September 27, 1966; both in FRUS, 1964–1968, Vol. XXVI.

261 *"I think we would up that estimate to perhaps close to 500,000 people"*: Green testimony, Senate Foreign Relations Committee, January 30, 1967, declassified March 2007.

262 *"We didn't create the waves"*: Green oral history, FAOH.

263 *"deeply troubled about the leadership problem in CIA"*: Bundy to LBJ, "Subject: The CIA," citing a conversation with Clifford, January 26, 1966.

263 *a long list of his accomplishments*: Raborn to Moyers, February 14, 1966.

263 "totally oblivious": LBJ to Bundy, February 22, 1966, LBJ Tapes, All cited in FRUS, Vol. XXXIII, and declassified in 2004.

263 *The committee got back to work in May*: NSC memo to LBJ, March 24, 1966; undated memo for the deputy director of central intelligence, "The 303 Committee, Senior Interdepartmental Group and the Interdepartmental Regional Groups"; "Coordination and Policy Approval of Covert Operations," February 23, 1967, CIA. All cited in FRUS, Vol. XXXIII, and declassified in 2004. The 1967 document on covert action is a uniquely detailed record. It listed major covert actions to date, showing the refinement of executive control over the CIA:

    a. Projects approved by DCI on internal authority:
    (1949–1952)—81—Truman Administration
    b. Projects approved by DCI in coordination with Operations Coordination Board or Psychological Strategy Board:
    (1953–1954)—66—Eisenhower Administration
    c. Projects approved or reconfirmed by Operations Coordination Board, the Special Group or 303 Committee:
    Eisenhower Administration—104
    Kennedy Administration—163
    Johnson Administration—142

Chapter Twenty-five

265 *"a circus rider"*: Richard Helms with William Hood, *A Look over My Shoulder: A Life in the Central Intelligence Agency* (New York: Random House, 2003), p. 311.

266 *"We knew then . . . that we could not win the war"*: Gates, *From the Shadows: The Ultimate Insider's Story of Five Presidents and How They Won the Cold War* (New York: Simon and Schuster, 1996), pp. 20–22.

266 *"This Agency is going flat out"* and *"the war is by no means over"*: Memorandum by the chief of the Far East Division, Central Intelligence Agency, July 25, 1967, FRUS, Vol. V.

267 *"Stop the buildup"*: George W. Allen, *None So Blind: A Personal Account of the Intelligence Failure in Vietnam* (Chicago: Ivan R. Dee, 2001), pp. 213–219. Allen wrote that the aim of the administration was to use manufactured intelligence for "opinion manipulation and political persuasion, with the aim of altering perceptions to make them coincide with certain notions, whether those notions were supportable by evidence or not." The practices he identified—the falsification of secret intelligence to control public perception and to manufacture political support—may sound familiar to many Americans today. Of course, there were built-in biases in the agency's reporting from Saigon, and these did not go unnoticed. In the summer of 1967, the question was whether Thieu or Ky would be South Vietnam's next president. The ultimate choice lay with the Vietnamese military command. The CIA maintained that the commanders would choose Ky. State Department officers in Saigon, including John Negroponte, the future czar of American intelligence, were certain it would be Thieu. "John told me later that the last report from the CIA—still predicting Ky—was filed just at the time that Ambassador Lodge was called to a meeting with the military command at which he was told that its candidate would be Thieu," recalled the State Department's Robert Oakley. "CIA had had a very close relationship with Ky for a long time; so they had a bias in his favor which undoubtedly colored their reporting." Oakley oral history, FAOH.

267 *On September 19, McNamara telephoned the president*: LBJ Tapes, September 19, 1966, transcribed in FRUS, Vol. IV.

268 *"You guys simply have to back off," Komer told Carver*: Komer's comments and the correspondence between Helms and Carver are in a full set of declassified cables between CIA headquarters and the Saigon station covering the order of battle controversy as it happened in September 1967, CIA/CREST.

268 *"We believe that Communist progress"*: NIE 53-63, cited in Harold P. Ford, "Why CIA Analysts Were So Doubtful About Vietnam," *Studies in Intelligence*, 1997, CIA/CSI.

269 *"The compelling proposition"*: John Huizenga, "Implications of an Unfavorable Outcome in Vietnam," September 11, 1967, CIA/CREST, with Helms's covering memo, declassified in 2004. Huizenga was chief of the CIA's Office of National Estimates staff, and later the director of the office.

Chapter Twenty-six

270   *"over CIA involvement"*: "Problem of Exposé of CIA Clandestine Youth and
      Student Activities," undated but February 1967, CIA/FOIA.
270   *"LBJ left me the responsibility of pulling the Agency's scorched chestnuts out of the
      fire"*: Richard Helms with William Hood, *A Look over My Shoulder: A Life in
      the Central Intelligence Agency* (New York: Random House, 2003), p. 345. A
      May 19, 1966, memo from Helms to Moyers at the White House detail-
      ing the personal and professional lives of *Ramparts* editors and reporters
      was declassified on November 13, 2006. Such reporting was arguably
      outside the CIA's charter.
271   *Since 1961, Secretary of State Rusk had been warning*: Rusk had asked the Spe-
      cial Group to address the following problems in a December 9, 1961,
      memo: "I. CIA now provides certain support to private organizations of an
      educational or philanthropic nature. 2. These covert funds become the
      subject of common gossip, or knowledge, both here and abroad. 3. Covert
      funds draw suspicion upon the organizations concerned and, indeed, may
      bar them from entry into certain countries. 4. Covert funds scare away
      funds from other sources which do not wish to become involved with CIA-
      type activities or purposes. 5. In most cases, there is no need to conceal that
      funds are being provided by the U.S. Government. 6. Every effort should
      be made to move from covert to overt support. . . . 7. What can be done
      about this in connection with such organizations as (a) Asia Foundation,
      (b) African student activities and (c) possibly others?" FRUS, Vol. XXV.
         The 303 Committee, meeting on June 21, 1968, to address the Asia
      Foundation problem, noted that "no one can accurately predict what, if
      any, federal monies will be allocated" to replace the CIA's subsidy. Nev-
      ertheless, "if there were deep sighs for the good old days of straight covert
      funding, they were not audible due to the hum of the air conditioner in
      the White House Situation Room." FRUS, Vol. X.
271   *"We lack adequate detail"*: Memo from the Deputy Director of the Bureau
      of Intelligence and Research to the Deputy Undersecretary of State for
      Political Affairs, February 15, 1967, FRUS, Vol. XXXIII, declassified 2004.
272   *an hour-long off-the-record conversation*: Pearson's papers are at the LBJ Li-
      brary. His work appeared in more than six hundred American newspapers
      with a combined circulation of fifty million readers. Lyndon Johnson had
      a pew in the church of his heart roped off for Pearson, who had publicly
      supported his run for the Democratic nomination for president in 1960.
272   *"This story going around about the CIA"*: LBJ Tapes/Holland, February 20,
      1967.
273   *"an irreducible minimum"*: Thomas Hughes, draft revision of NSC 5412,
      dated April 17, 1967, and discussed May 5, 1967, FRUS, Vol. XXXIII.

274 *"ability to keep former employees quiet"*: Russell cited in "Briefing by the Director of CIA Subcommittees of the Senate Armed Services and Appropriations," May 23, 1967, declassified March 4, 2001, CIA/CREST.

274 *what to do with Harvey*: James Hanrahan, "An Interview with Former CIA Executive Director Lawrence K. 'Red' White," *Studies in Intelligence,* Vol. 43, No. 1, Winter 1999/2000, CIA/CSI.

274 *"his extreme bitterness toward the Agency"*: Osborn to Earman, memorandum for the record, October 4, 1967, CIA/FOIA.

275 *"Angleton by the mid-1960s"*: Robert M. Hathaway and Russell Jack Smith, "Richard Helms as Director of Central Intelligence," 1993, CIA/CSI, declassified February 2007.

276 *"a man of loose and disjointed thinking"*: John L. Hart, "The Monster Plot: Counterintelligence in the Case of Yuri Ivanovich Nosenko," December 1976, CIA/CSI.

276 *"Loyal Agency employees had come under suspicion"*: Hathaway and Smith, "Richard Helms as Director of Central Intelligence," p. 124.

276 *"we are deluding ourselves"* and *"paralysis of our Soviet effort"*: McCoy memos to Helms cited in Hathaway and Smith, "Richard Helms as Director of Central Intelligence," p. 108.

276 *"one scrap of supportive evidence"*: Kingsley oral history interview, June 14, 1984, CIA, cited in Hathaway and Smith, "Richard Helms as Director of Central Intelligence," p. 123.

276 *"Jim was a man obsessed"*: Taylor interview by Hart, in "The Monster Plot," CIA/CSI.

277 *"The subsequent accuracy of this prediction"*: Hathaway and Smith, "Richard Helms as Director of Central Intelligence, p. 127.

277 *"intelligence had a role in his life"*: Helms oral history interview, April 21, 1982, cited in Hathaway and Smith, "Richard Helms as Director of Central Intelligence," p. 143. The CIA history provides a fascinating footnote to the aftermath of the Six-Day War of 1967: "James Angleton found himself increasingly disturbed by the prospect of an endless cycle of war and more war in the Middle East. With this in mind he composed what those who saw it remember as an eloquent plea for some dramatic move to break through this destructive pattern. In a blind memo [to Helms, Angleton proposed] an anti-Soviet alliance consisting of Israel and some of the conservative Arab states such as Jordan and Saudi Arabia. The whole thing depended on urgency, Angleton continued; the longer Israel occupied the territories captured from the Arabs, the less willing Tel Aviv would be to give them up. [A deleted section of the history evidently discusses the crypto-diplomatic role played by Angleton and the Near East division chief James Critchfield in trying to create this alliance.] At this point the American State Department got wind of the scheme and vetoed any further U.S. role in the proceedings.

Without the Americans as intermediaries, the arrangement crumbled. In the embittered views of Angleton and Critchfield, an opportunity of possibly historic proportions had been allowed to slip away." Ibid., pp. 146–147.

278 *an excruciatingly sensitive operation . . . code-named Buttercup*: The Buttercup operation is described at length in FRUS, Vols. IV and V.

278 *The CIA had created and run the local Communist Party*: This heretofore unknown operation was described by Tom Polgar in an interview with the author.

278 *The program, code-named Globe*: The Globe operation was described in interviews with CIA officers, including Gerry Gossens.

279 *"You have to get the infrastructure"*: Helms testimony, President's Commission on CIA Activities (Rockefeller Commission), pp. 2497–2499.

279 *"There have been charges that it is morally wrong"*: Albert R. Haney, "Observations and Suggestions Concerning the Overseas Internal Security Program," June 14, 1957, NSC Staff Papers, pp. 11–12, DDEL.

279 *"You can get into Gestapo-type tactics"*: Amory oral history, JFKL.

280 *"Castro was the catalyst"*: Polgar interview with author.

280 *military juntas were good for the United States*: Memorandum for the director, "The Political Role of the Military in Latin America," Office of National Estimates, April 30, 1968, LBJL. This was a formal twenty-nine-page statement by the chairman of the ONE, Abbot Smith, giving a tour of the region's eight most recently established military dictatorships, six of which were deemed good for American interests.

281 *"Mobutu gave me a house"*: Gossens interview with author.

281 *In a classic battle of the cold war*: The capture of the CIA base chief, David Grinwis, is described in an unpublished interview with Grinwis at the Hoover Institute at Stanford University. Grinwis, the American consul Mike Hoyt, and two CIA communicators were held for 114 days before Belgian paratroops freed them. The battle between Che's Cubans and the CIA's Cubans is best told in Piero Gleijeses, *Conflicting Missions: Havana, Washington, and Africa, 1959–1976* (Chapel Hill: University of North Carolina Press, 2002), pp. 137–159.

281 *A right-wing general, Rene Barrientos, had seized power*: The details of the CIA's covert actions in support of Barrientos from 1962 to 1966 are in FRUS, Vol. XXXI, documents 147–180, declassified 2004.

282 *"This can't be Che Guevara"*: Henderson oral history, FAOH.

282 *"I am managing to keep him alive"*: Rodriguez's reporting from Bolivia is reproduced verbatim in two memos that Helms delivered to the White House on October 11 and 13, 1967, declassified in 2004 and reprinted in FRUS, Vol. XXXI, documents 171 and 172.

283 *"Can you send fingerprints?" . . . "I can send fingers"*: Polgar interview with author.

283 *"Once again CIA operations"*: UAR desk to Lucius D. Battle, March 16, 1967, FRUS, Vol. XVIII.

283 *"He had been on the U.S. payroll"*: Battle oral history, FAOH.

284 *"You will be criticized"*: Humphrey speech quoted in Helms transcript, *Studies in Intelligence*, September 1993.

284 *"Review all projects which are politically sensitive"*: Memorandum from the Deputy Director of Plans of the Central Intelligence Agency (Karamessines) to all staff chiefs and division chiefs, September 30, 1967, declassified 2004, FRUS, Vol. XXXIII.

Chapter Twenty-seven

285 *"I'm quite aware of that"*: Richard Helms with William Hood, *A Look over My Shoulder: A Life in the Central Intelligence Agency* (New York: Random House, 2003), p. 280.

286 *"The Subcommittee is very much interested in the operations of various militant organizations in this country"*: McClellan letter to Helms, October 25, 1967, declassified 2004, CIA/CREST.

286 *"A Negro training camp"*: Karamessines memo to White House, October 31, 1967, declassified 2004, CIA/CREST.

287 *"I'm not going to let the Communists take this government"*: "Luncheon Meeting with Secretaries Rusk and McNamara, Walt Rostow, CIA Director Richard Helms," November 4, 1967, LBJL.

287 *"any direction other than their own"*: "International Connections of U.S. Peace Groups" and Helms cover letter to the president, November 15, 1967, declassified April 2001, CIA/CREST.

287 *next to no intelligence on the enemy's intent*: On February 16, 1968, Helms met with the President's Foreign Intelligence Advisory Board. He said American intelligence on the Tet offensive had failed first and foremost "because of the lack of penetration of the Vietcong." FRUS, Vol. VI.

288 *"Westmoreland doesn't know who the enemy is"*: "Notes of the President's Luncheon Meeting with Foreign Policy Advisors," February 20, 1968, FRUS, Vol. VI. Though some historians and memoirists have given the CIA analyst George Carver great credit for changing LBJ's mind about the war in the weeks and days before his decision to stand down, the CIA's leading Vietnam historian, Harold Ford, wrote that the influence of Carver and the CIA "was clearly less than that of many other forces above and beyond the inputs of CIA's intelligence: the shock of the Tet offensive itself; the sharply rising tide of antiwar sentiment among the Congress and the public; the candid, very grim post-Tet assessments given by JCS Chairman Earle Wheeler, Paul Nitze, and Paul Warnke; and the sudden defections of Clark Clifford and most of the other 'Wise Men'

who had previously backed Johnson's war effort. Nonetheless, to these causes of the President's change of heart must be added the late-March assessments given him by State and CIA officers."

PART FOUR
Chapter Twenty-eight

291 *he would have created a new organization outside the CIA*: Richard M. Nixon, *Six Crises* (New York: Doubleday, 1962), p. 454. Nixon wrote that he stated his intention to JFK in 1960.

291 *Nixon and Helms met for their first long talk*: Recorded in "Notes of Meeting, Johnson City, Texas," August 10, 1968, 12:25 p.m. FRUS, Vol. VI. Helms met Nixon for the first time in November 1956, when he and Allen Dulles briefed the vice president on the crushed Hungarian revolution. In his posthumous memoir, Helms omits the LBJ Ranch session described here, which was evidently their second face-to-face encounter.

292 *"What do you think about Helms?"*: Telephone conversation between President Johnson and President-elect Nixon, November 8, 1968, 9:23 p.m., LBJ Tapes, FRUS, Vol. VII.

292 *"Richard Nixon never trusted anybody"*: Helms interview with Stanley I. Kutler, July 14, 1988, Wisconsin Historical Archives, box 15, folder 16, cited with the kind permission of Professor Kutler.

293 *"I haven't the slightest doubt . . . that Nixon's carping affected Kissinger"*: Helms quoted in John L. Helgerson, "CIA Briefings of Presidential Candidates," May 1996, CIA/CSI.

293 *"Both were incurably covert"*: Thomas L. Hughes, "Why Kissinger Must Choose Between Nixon and the Country," *The New York Times,* December 30, 1973.

293 *"make it very clear to the Director"*: Report of the Covert Operations Study Group, December 1, 1968, CIA/CREST. The study dovetailed in part with the final report of the President's Foreign Intelligence Advisory Board to LBJ in December 1968. The board called the results of American espionage "inadequate." It urged "an intensification of efforts to obtain significant intelligence on priority targets through clandestine agent collection operations." It strongly recommended that the 303 Committee review "all approved covert programs in order to evaluate progress being made, and in appropriate instances, cancel unproductive projects." FRUS, Vol. X, document 222.

295 *"Dr. Kissinger—Information Request"*: The one-paragraph memo turned up in the files of Red White, who in 1969 held the post of deputy director of

central intelligence for support—the agency's chief administrator. Declassified May 15, 2003, CIA/CREST.

296 *"I don't mean to say that they are lying"*: Memo from [*deleted*] to Helms, June 18, 1969, FRUS, 1969–1972, Vol. II, document 191, declassified December 21, 2006.

296 *"Useless"* . . . *"A superficial mindless recitation"*: Kissinger to Nixon, "Subject: NIE 11–8–69, 'Soviet Strategic Attack Forces,' " with covering memo from Helms annotated by Nixon on December 8, 1969, FRUS, 1969–1972, Vol. II, document 198.

296 *"Whose side is the Agency on?"*: Helms, *A Look over My Shoulder: A Life in the Central Intelligence Agency* (New York: Random House, 2003), pp. 382–388.

297 *Helms always had believed that gadgets were no replacement for spies*: Even the best electronic-eavesdropping intercepts were not intelligence. In 1968, the CIA and the NSA had a program code-named Guppy, which intercepted the mobile phone lines of the Russian leadership in Moscow. In September 1968, on the eve of the invasion of Czechoslovakia, the head of the Warsaw Pact telephoned the Soviet leader Leonid Brezhnev from the Moscow airport. The CIA heard the call. "The problem was they were no fools and spoke in a word code—you know, 'the moon is red,' or some silly phrase—and we didn't have the faintest idea whether that meant the invasion was on or off," said a State Department intelligence officer, David Fischer. Fischer oral history, FAOH.

297 *the Strategic Arms Limitation Treaty talks then under way in Helsinki*: The KGB resident in Helsinki and the CIA station chief had agreed that neither side would try to penetrate the other's delegation. "The consequences of getting caught would certainly outweigh any intelligence that could be collected," said the State Department's David Fischer. "As far as I know, both sides honored that agreement. Lord knows there were enough opportunities to entrap some poor American delegate with a buxom Finnish blonde." Fischer oral history, FAOH.

297 *Soviet strategic nuclear forces*: In 1979, the CIA's Howard Stoertz, Jr., then the national intelligence officer for strategic programs, reported "a series of gross overestimates in the late 1950's and early 1960's and a series of gross underestimates in the middle and late 1960's" in the CIA's analysis of Soviet strategic forces. Stoertz, Memorandum for Director, National Foreign Assessment Center, declassified July 2006. In March 2001, the director of central intelligence, George J. Tenet, said, "Every National Intelligence Estimate written on the subject from 1974 to 1986 . . . overestimated the rate at which Moscow would modernize its strategic forces." Tenet remarks, Conference on CIA's Analysis of the Soviet Union, Princeton University.

297 *"The President called Henry Kissinger and me into the Oval Office"*: Helms, memorandum for the record, "Talk with President Nixon," March 25, 1970, FRUS, January 1969–October 1970, Vol. XII, document 147, declassified December 19, 2006. In a May 13, 1970, follow-up on proposed covert action against Moscow, Helms laid out a five-point plan:

- Sino-Soviet tensions. The Sino-Soviet border conflict and the worldwide struggle for control of Communist parties make the Soviets highly susceptible [*one line of source text not declassified*].
- Soviet involvement in the Middle East. Because the Soviet presence in the Middle East entails many volatile factors, there will be opportunities for inducing strain between the Arabs and the Soviets.
- Soviet relations with East Europe. The steady growth of nationalism in East Europe in the face of Soviet military intervention and economic exploitation makes this area a fertile ground for [*less than one line of source text not declassified*] operations to heighten tensions between the USSR and its vassal states.
- Soviet/Cuban relations. Castro's well-founded suspicion regarding Soviet maneuvers to dominate political and economic life in Cuba, possibly affecting Castro's own future leadership, creates a situation that invites [*less than one line of source text not declassified*] manipulation.
- Soviet domestic dissidence and economic stagnation. By fostering unrest among the Soviet intelligentsia it may be possible to create pressures inducing the Kremlin to curtail its foreign involvements in order to concentrate on critical domestic situations.

298 *"facing the threat of a Communist Party or popular front election victory"*: Helms, "Tensions in the Soviet Union and Eastern Europe: Challenge and Opportunity," undated but early April 1970, FRUS, January 1969–1970, Vol. XII, document 149.

298 *Guy Mollet of France*: Wells Stabler, who served as chief of the political section at the American embassy in Paris from 1960 to 1965, said, "Guy Mollet [and other French leaders of the Fourth Republic] had what you might call a fiduciary relationship with the United States and they indeed received some financial support from the US government. I would go to visit Guy Mollet and we would have a nice chat. The telephone would then ring and he would look up and smile at me and say, 'Well, one of your colleagues is here to see me.' We would have this revolving door act between myself and someone of the CIA station in Paris. . . . I found it quite frankly a rather embarrassing situation." Stabler oral history, FAOH.

298 *at least $65 million*: The program begun in 1948, as detailed in Chapter 3, had cost at least $65 million, according to a 1976 report by the newly

formed House Intelligence Committee. The minutes for the 303 Committee meeting of June 25, 1965, state: "The Italian proposal was generally
viewed as a 'necessary evil' and approved with the following proviso: Mr.
[McGeorge] Bundy, deploring the chronic failure of the Italian democratic political parties to utilize their own bootstraps, used the term 'annual shame.' "

On August 4, 1965, Bundy sent the following memo to President
Johnson: "Over the years the U.S. has assisted the democratic Italian political parties and trade unions at a very high rate. Over the period
1955–1965, the total amount of assistance is just under [*deleted*]. In recent years we have been cutting this assistance back, primarily because
the professionals closely related to the operation have concluded that we
have not been getting our full money's worth and what the Italian political parties need is not so much U.S. money as energetic administrative
leadership. President Kennedy had a personal feeling that political subsidies at this level were excessive. . . . Meanwhile, by separate and somewhat unusual channels, [*deleted*] have let us know that they would like a
lot more money. . . . It remains true that the anti-Communist battle in
Italy is one of politics and resources; but simple handouts and intelli-
gently applied resources are two entirely different things." The 303 Committee minutes and the Bundy memo are in FRUS, Vol. XII, declassified
April 2001.

299 *"financial resources, political resources, friends, the ability to blackmail"*: Fina
oral history, FAOH.

299 *"that cold-eyed fellow"*: Robert Barbour oral history, FAOH. Barbour's predecessor, Samuel Gammon, said, "Graham would pull the wings off flies
with relish if it were necessary as a power operation." These were men
who admired Martin.

299 *shadowy and strange*: Michael E. C. Ely oral history, FAOH.

299 *"slippery as a cold basket of eels"*: Ambassador James Cowles Hart Bonbright
oral history, FAOH.

299 *Martin had converted Marshall Plan funds*: Benson E. L. Timmons, III, oral
history, HSTL. Timmons was a deputy chief of the Marshall Plan mission
in Paris.

299 *"I have great personal confidence in Graham Martin"*: Nixon to Kissinger, February 14, 1969, FRUS, Vol. II, document 298.

299 *Talenti went to see*: According to Richard Gardner, the American ambassador to Italy from 1977 to 1981; Gardner remarks, Carnegie Council, January 19, 2006. See also Gardner's memoir, *Mission Italy: On the Front Lines
of the Cold War* (Lanham, MD: Rowman & Littlefield, 2005). In 1981, Talenti joined the Reagan White House staff as an unpaid political adviser.
He became part of a now-forgotten influence-peddling case known as the

Wedtech scandal, which eventually led to the resignation of the attorney general of the United States, Ed Meese.

299 *"he was just the man"*: Wells Stabler oral history, FAOH, and interview with author.

300 *Nixon and Kissinger focused the CIA*: Selected 303 Committee minutes covering the first eighteen months of the Nixon administration were declassified in April 2006. The CIA's covert support for Thieu's National Alliance for Social Revolution began in September 1968, when the 303 Committee authorized the first allotment of $725,000 in cash. Half of that sum was handed to Thieu in increments from September 1968 to March 1969. Records cited: Memorandum for the 303 Committee, August 29, 1968, FRUS, January–August 1968, Vol. VI; Kissinger to Nixon, "Covert Support for the Lien Minh (National Alliance for Social Revolution)," March 27, 1969; Kissinger to Nixon; "Operations Against Barracks and Storage Facilities in Dien Bien Phu in North Vietnam," July 18, 1969; Kissinger to Nixon, "Operations to Undermine Enemy Morale in Vietnam," December 9, 1969; memorandum for the 303 Committee, December 11, 1969; and "Minutes of the Meeting of the 303 Committee, 23 December 1969," in FRUS, January 1969–July 1970, Vol. VI, documents 47, 98, 156, 157, and 165.

301 *"the President wondered"*: Memorandum for the record, "Subject: Discussion with the President on Tibet," February 4, 1960, CIA/CREST.

301 *the agency requested $2.5 million more to support Tibet's insurgents*: FRUS, Vol. XVII, 1969–1976, documents 273–280, citing 303 Committee meeting of September 30, 1969, and 40 Committee meeting of March 31, 1971. (The 303 Committee was renamed the 40 Committee in February 1970.)

302 *"The CIA had no hand in it?"*: Kissinger-Chou memorandum of conversation, FRUS, Vol. XVII, 1969–1976, document 162, declassified September 2006

302 *The CIA was out of business in China for years to come*: Not *entirely*. A year after Nixon went to China, the CIA's Jim Lilley—born in China, twenty years an American spy in Asia—proposed that he join the soon-to-open United States Liaison Office in Beijing. It was to be the first American diplomatic mission since Mao took power close to a quarter century before.

Lilley got the go-ahead, and he served two years as the first station chief in Beijing, latterly under George H. W. Bush. This was prior to Bush's becoming director of central intelligence in 1976. Lilley's status as a CIA officer was openly declared to the Chinese communist government, and it was accepted on one condition: no spying. Lilley could recruit no espionage agents and run no covert operations—or else.

Lilley filed away a coded list of future targets of opportunity for the day that the CIA might open a real station in Beijing. But he was stymied until Bush arrived. The gregarious crypto-diplomat took Lilley under his wing, brought him to receptions to meet top Chinese officials, and introduced him to the rest of the diplomatic corps. Bush said: "I want you to be part of my job," Lilley recalled. "I want to work with you and make you part of the team." Lilley thus made friends with the future leaders of the United States and China. Bush and Lilley latched on to Vice Premier Deng Xiaoping, who would emerge as the head of the regime that took power after Mao's death. (Deng used to say it doesn't matter if a cat is black or white, so long as it catches mice. He would have made a good station chief.) Deng, Bush, and Lilley started working together. The new friends agreed in principle to collect military, strategic, and technological intelligence against the Soviet Union when the time was ripe. Bush and Lilley returned to China as private citizens and convinced Deng to open up China to American oil companies. The intelligence deal was consummated in full in 1989, after President Bush made Jim Lilley the American ambassador to China.

303 *The CIA's bagman was Pote Sarasin*: The Lotus records, declassified in December 2006, are in FRUS, Vol. XX, documents 2, 120, and 129. Document 2—memorandum of conversation, "Subject: Lotus," Bangkok, January 16, 1969—sets the scene.

303 *"democracy doesn't work"* and *"There should be no change"*: FRUS, Vol. XX, documents 142 and 143 (Ambassador Len Unger's report on the coup and Kissinger's analysis of the coup for Nixon, November 17, 1971).

304 *"Get the CIA jerks"*: Transcript of telephone conversation between President Nixon and Henry Kissinger, April 17, 1970, FRUS, Vol. VI, January 1969–July 1970.

304 *"Get the money to Lon Nol"*: Nixon to Kissinger, April 20, 1970, FRUS, Vol. VI, January 1969–July 1970.

304 *"CIA had described the flow of materials through Sihanoukville"*: "Record of President's Meeting with the Foreign Intelligence Advisory Board," July 18, 1970, FRUS, January 1969–July 1970, Vol. VI, declassified April 2006.

304 *"$6 billion per year on intelligence"*: Ibid.

305 *"people lying to him about intelligence"*: "Record of President's Meeting with the Foreign Intelligence Advisory Board," July 18, 1970, FRUS, 1969–1972, Vol. II, declassified December 2006. Here we see an example of the futility of official secrecy. The record was declassified twice in two different ways. The first revealed the intelligence budget as of 1970—$6 billion. The second concealed it on the grounds of national security—but reveals more of Nixon's critique than the first. The author applauds the inconsistency of government censors in this instance.

Chapter Twenty-nine

306 *Few Latin American nations paid more than lip service to the ideals of democracy*:
     One was Costa Rica, whose democracy was established in 1949 by José
     Figueres Ferrer, known as "Don Pepe." He had just been re-elected pres-
     ident for the third time in 1970. He was married to an American, he
     spoke excellent English, and on occasion over the years he had accepted
     money from the CIA, a fact he freely acknowledged later in his life.
         "I was conspiring against the Latin American dictatorships and wanted
     help from the United States," he told *The New York Times*. "I was a good
     friend of Allen Dulles." The agency thought it had bought Figueres. It had
     only rented him.
         In early 1970, the American ambassador was a career diplomat named
     Clarence Boonstra and the newly arriving CIA station chief was a hard-
     drinking, sixty-year-old Cuba hand named Earl Williamson. "Earl had
     worked with me in Cuba years before," Ambassador Boonstra said in an
     oral history. "When he was proposed as station chief, I had objected un-
     less Williamson would work under my orders and would not do what he
     was noted for, disrupting things with unnecessary covert action—monkey
     business." Then Nixon nominated a new ambassador, Walter Ploeser, a
     defeated Republican congressman and a major political fund-raiser. Sud-
     denly the red threat loomed. "For some time Costa Rica had been plan-
     ning to permit the Soviet Union to establish an embassy," Ambassador
     Boonstra said. "That's what Costa Rica stood for, democracy and openness
     to everyone."
         The new envoy and his station chief were under the misimpression
     that there was "a great communist scheme establishing Costa Rica as a
     central point for subversion in the hemisphere," Ambassador Boonstra
     said. "And they began all types of actions, carrying on a crusade." They
     worked to subvert the newly reinstalled president of Costa Rica, but they
     failed miserably. The station chief, deep into a drinking bout with his
     Costa Rican friends, proclaimed that Don Pepe's days in power were
     dwindling. Word got back to the president quickly. He publicly de-
     nounced a plot to overthrow him, publicly identified the CIA station
     chief, publicly declared him persona non grata, and very publicly ex-
     pelled him from the country.
         The "monkey business" of CIA station chiefs like Earl Williamson was
     hardly covert action. "There is throughout Latin America a growing sen-
     sitivity . . . to allegations of CIA intervention in Latin affairs," wrote a
     State Department intelligence analyst in March 1970. "The sensitivity is
     especially acute in Chile."
         If the agency delivered money, guns, and intelligence into the hands

of coup plotters throughout the cold war, so did the Soviets. If the agency mounted covert operations that led to the death, imprisonment, and torture of innocent civilians, the enemy did it too. American cash bought elections all over the world, and the Kremlin had its own black bags. But America's backyard was tough terrain for Moscow. "Latin America is a sphere of special U.S. interests," the KGB chief and future Soviet leader Yuri Andropov wrote during the Nixon administration. "We must remember this. Our policy in Latin America must be cautious." Andropov quoted in Christopher Andrew and Vasili Mitrokhin, *The World Was Going Our Way: The KGB and the Battle for the Third World* (New York: Basic Books, 2005), p. 77.

306 *One of the few was Chile, where the CIA saw a red threat rising*: Unless otherwise noted, citations and quotations about the operation in this chapter are taken from a collection of CIA records declassified between 1999 and 2003, available online at http://foia.state.gov/SearchColls/CIA.asp. See also Peter Kornbluh, *The Pinochet File: A Declassified Dossier on Atrocity and Accountability* (New York: New Press, 2004).

306 *a political-warfare program*: The CIA's files give the flavor of part of the covert campaign to swing the 1964 election. In a July 21, 1964, memo to the 303 Committee, the CIA proposed an additional $500,000 to defeat Allende. The money would permit Eduardo Frei Montalva, the Christian Democrat, to "maintain the pace and rhythm of his campaign effort"— and allow the CIA to meet any "last minute contingencies." On July 23, 1964, the 303 Committee approved the proposal. In a memo to McGeorge Bundy, the CIA's Peter Jessup said, "We can't afford to lose this one, so I don't think there should be any economy shaving in this instance. We assume the Commies are pouring in dough, we have no proofs. They must assume we are pouring in dough; they have no proofs. Let's pour it on and in." Secretary of State Rusk briefed LBJ on the Chilean election at an NSC meeting on September 1: "It looked as if a victory for the non-Communist forces in Chile would come up in the election 4 September, partly as a result of the good work of CIA; and this development would be a triumph for democracy and a blow to Communism in Latin America." With $300,000 allocated for the defeat of Allende in 1970, the CIA was probably outspending the KGB two-to-one in Chile. Soviet intelligence archives suggest that Allende got at least $50,000 from Moscow and $100,000 in Soviet funds laundered through the Chilean Communist Party. The trouble with Allende, in the Kremlin's eyes, was that he was a bourgeois socialist, a parlor pink, not a real communist.

307 *senior representatives of the Vatican*: The relationship between the CIA and the Holy See has been profound since 1947, but it remains deeply ob-

scured. The singular "Report on CIA Chilean Task Force Activities, 15 September to 3 November 1970," slipped out and illuminated this small facet.

307 *"posters were printed, news stories planted"*: Richard Helms with William Hood, *A Look over My Shoulder: A Life in the Central Intelligence Agency* (New York: Random House, 2003), p. 400. Helms in his memoir calls Chile (before 1970) "a small democratic country." An old joke in British journalism (before 1970) proposed that the world's most boring headline would be: "Small Earthquake in Chile, Not Many Dead."

307 *"I had never seen such dreadful propaganda"*: Edward M. Korry remarks, Centro de Estudios Publicos, Santiago, Chile, October 16, 1996. Published in *Estudios Publicos*, Spring 1998.

308 *"Kendall went to Nixon"*: Helms interview with Stanley I. Kutler, July 14, 1988, Wisconsin Historical Archives, box 15, folder 16, cited with the kind permission of Professor Kutler.

309 *" Mr. Helms, he said, "you already have your Vietnam"*: Polgar interview with author.

310 *Track One was political warfare*: And it was supplemented by hundreds of thousands of dollars from the American multinational ITT, which had vast holdings in Chile. The money was delivered with the guidance of the CIA and at the suggestion of a member of ITT's board of directors—John McCone.

310 *"Anyone who had lived in Chile"*: Phillips testimony, Church Committee, July 13, 1975, declassified 1994.

313 *"flavor their final assessments"*: Haig to Kissinger, December 7, 1970, FRUS, 1969–1976, Vol. II, document 220.

313 *"the key left-wing dominated slots under Helms"*: Nixon to Kissinger, November 30, 1970 [Haig cited in footnote], FRUS, 1969–1976, Vol. II, document 216, declassified December 21, 2006.

313 *"a major overhauling"*: Haig to Kissinger, December 7, 1970, FRUS, 1969–1976, Vol. II, document 220.

313 *"Nixon railed against the CIA"*: Shultz oral history in Gerald S. Strober and Deborah Hart Strober, *Nixon: An Oral History of His Presidency* (New York: HarperCollins, 1994), p. 83. This book is an invaluable resource, as is the Strobers' oral history of the Reagan administration.

313 *"A meat-ax approach could be disastrous"*: K. Wayne Smith to Kissinger, "Presidential Meeting with OMB on Intelligence Budget," December 21, 1970, FRUS, Vol. II, document 221. Nixon continued to press for deep cuts and radical changes at the agency. "I want a real shakeup in CIA, not just symbolism," he told Kissinger on January 21, 1971, in a written note. FRUS, Vol. II, document 224.

314 *He had made his reputation at the Nixon White House*: Schlesinger was one of

a quartet of men who rose to power by slashing the government at Nixon's bidding:

- Caspar Weinberger, Schlesinger's boss at the budget office, went after the welfare state under Nixon. A decade later he doubled the Pentagon's spending as Ronald Reagan's defense secretary.
- Donald Rumsfeld whacked at the war on poverty for Nixon at the Office of Economic Opportunity. In 1975, he succeeded Schlesinger at the Pentagon, becoming the youngest secretary of defense in history.
- Dick Cheney, a budget-cutting congressman in his day, succeeded Rumsfeld as President Ford's White House chief of staff, then succeeded Weinberger as secretary of defense in 1989. He is at this writing the vice president of the United States and the viceroy of secret government operations.
- Rumsfeld returned as secretary of defense under the second Bush administration—the oldest secretary of defense in history, presiding over an establishment that spent half a trillion dollars a year.

Thus ran the path to power for the four Nixon men who led the Pentagon for twenty-two of the thirty-three years from 1973 to 2006. All four came to share the president's contempt for the Central Intelligence Agency.

314 *ending the Vietnam War on American terms*: A typical Nixon review of the CIA's performance in that role followed his command for a worldwide propaganda campaign in support of the renewed bombing of North Vietnam. The agency's "performance in the psychological warfare field is nothing short of disgraceful," Nixon wrote in a memo to Kissinger and Haig on May 19, 1972. "It produced not much more than a mouse. Or to put it more honestly, it produced a rat. . . . I do not simply blame Helms and the CIA. After all, they do not support my policies."

314 *"There is no evidence that the intelligence community"*: James R. Schlesinger, "A Review of the Intelligence Community," Top Secret, March 10, 1971, declassified with deletions in 1998, CIA/NARA. The report stressed ideas that were central to the abolition of the office of the director of central intelligence after 9/11: the DCI presided over warring republics, not a confederation of states. His authority over the empire of intelligence beyond the CIA was nonexistent. Schlesinger suggested the creation of a new office: a director of national intelligence, with real authority over all the tribes and fiefs. The time was not ripe for open debate about the CIA. It would be thirty-three years before the idea was embraced and enacted.

314 *"the most controversial gutfight"*: Haig to Kissinger, with attachment from Kissinger and Shultz to Nixon, "Review of the Intelligence Community,"

March 27, 1971, FRUS, Vol. II, document 229. The fight led to the creation of a National Security Council Intelligence Committee—led, of course, by Kissinger—that was supposed to take over the management of American intelligence. The committee met for the first time on December 3, 1971. It did not reconvene in 1971 or 1972.

314 *The president directly ordered Helms to hand over control*: Memorandum by President Nixon, "Organization and Management of the U.S. Foreign Intelligence Community," November 5, 1971, FRUS, Vol. II, document 242. Helms forced Deputy Director Cushman out for two reasons. First, to protect the agency from Richard Nixon; second, because of the untoward support Cushman had given to the CIA veteran and soon-to-be-incarcerated Watergate plumber E. Howard Hunt. Helms sent a frosty note to Nixon on December 3, 1971, the day that the aforementioned NSC Intelligence Committee convened. "I attach hereto a copy of the kind of delegation of authority to the Deputy Director of Central Intelligence which would seem to be in keeping with your directive," it said. "When General Cushman's replacement is sufficiently indoctrinated, I will sign such a paper for him." That replacement, General Vernon Walters, entered on duty six months later—May 2, 1972. The issue soon was overtaken by events set in motion by Howard Hunt and the Watergate affair.

315 *"The CIA isn't worth a damn"*: Nixon comments at July 23, 1971, White House budget meeting, cited in *The Haldeman Diaries: Inside the Nixon White House, The Complete Multimedia Edition*, CD-ROM, Sony Electronic Publishing, 1994, entry for July 25, 1971. Nixon kept up the pressure for a purge over the next year. "One department which particularly needs a housecleaning is the CIA," he wrote to Haldeman on May 18, 1972. "The problem in the CIA is muscle-bound bureaucracy which has completely paralyzed its brain and the other is the fact that its personnel, just like the personnel in State, is primarily Ivy League and the Georgetown set rather than the type of people that we get into the services and the FBI. I want a study made immediately as to how many people in CIA could be removed by Presidential action. . . . I want action begun immediately, through [budget director Caspar] Weinberger, for a reduction in force of all positions in the CIA in the executive groups of 50 percent. This reduction in force should be accomplished by the end of the year so that we can then move to get in some better people. Of course, the reduction in force should be accomplished solely on the ground of its being necessary for budget reasons, but you will both know the real reason and I want some action to deal with the problem."

316 *"placing stop and go buttons on the machinery"*: Phillips testimony, Church Committee.

Chapter Thirty

318 *Nixon . . . bugged the White House*: Between February 16, 1971, and July
     12, 1973, President Nixon secretly recorded more than 3,700 hours of his
     meetings and conversations with voice-activated hidden microphones at
     the White House and Camp David. He made the decision, in part, to pre-
     serve a record to protect him against the inevitable memoirs of Henry
     Kissinger.

     Nixon blamed Kissinger for the decision to wiretap White House aides
     to stop press leaks. "Henry ordered the whole goddamn thing," the pres-
     ident told his press secretary, Ronald L. Ziegler, on May 14, 1973. "He or-
     dered it all, believe you me. He was the one who was in my office
     jumping up and down about, 'This and that got out.' I said, all right, in-
     vestigate the sons of bitches," the president said, his voice rising to a
     shout. "And he read every one of those taps. He reveled in it, he grov-
     eled in it, he wallowed in it."

318 *trying to stop leaks to the press*: Of course, no president was above a little
     leaking when it suited him, as the following conversation shows. The
     topic of the "Helms report" was India's prime minister, Indira Gandhi,
     whom Nixon referred to as "that bitch," and whose leadership was the
     subject of a top secret study Helms had delivered to the White House:

> Nixon: Incidentally, that Helms report—give me a copy of that. I'm
> going to put it out to the press. Put the whole goddamn thing
> out. . . . I want that report of Helms put into the hands of a
> columnist who will print the whole thing. Now I want you to get
> it out. . . . Now that's the way they play it. That's the way we got
> to play it. You don't agree?
> Kissinger: Yes, I agree. . . .
> Nixon: Just be sure to get it yards away from the White House.
> Kissinger: Right. I'll get that done today.

     Transcript of conversation, December 6, 1971, 6:14–6:38 p.m., FRUS,
     1969–1972, Vol. E-7, declassified June 2005.

318 *"a unique character"*: Sam Hart oral history, FAOH.

319 *"He described the mission as national security"*: Barker oral history in Gerald
     S. Strober and Deborah Hart Strober, *Nixon, An Oral History of His Presi-
     dency* (New York: HarperCollins, 1994), p. 217.

319 *"he was in fact doing some things for the President"*: The conversation was
     recorded at CIA headquarters; the tape was later obtained by the Water-
     gate Special Prosecution Force, and the transcript is in the National
     Archives.

319–20 *"an operation which the CIA knew nothing about"*: Walters oral history in

Strober and Strober, *Nixon: An Oral History*, p. 60. Walters, who spoke nine languages, had served as a staff assistant to President Eisenhower and an interpreter for Ike, Vice President Nixon, and senior State Department and Defense Department officials in the 1950s. He had been the army attaché and liaison to the CIA in Italy from 1960 to 1962 and in Brazil, where he helped foment a military coup, from 1962 to 1967. As defense attaché in France from 1967 to 1972, he was instrumental in the negotiations before and during the Paris peace talks. Nixon had been an admirer ever since Walters helped save him from an angry mob during a trip to Caracas in 1958.

320 *"Dick, are you still up?"*: Richard Helms with William Hood, *A Look over My Shoulder: A Life in the Central Intelligence Agency* (New York: Random House, 2003), pp. 3–5.

321 *"We are going to catch a lot of hell"*: Colby quoted in Strober and Strober, *Nixon: An Oral History*, p. 312.

321 *"We could get money anyplace in the world"*: Helms interview with Stanley I. Kutler, July 14, 1988, Wisconsin Historical Archives, box 15, folder 16, cited with the kind permission of Professor Kutler. In this interview, Helms recounted a conversation illustrating how close his new deputy director came to cooperating with the demand for hush money. Before his third and final meeting with Dean at the White House, Vernon Walters turned to Helms and said, "Look, suppose I give in. The worst that can happen is that I get fired, or I have to resign." Walters had no understanding of the situation, no grasp of the fact that the agency was in the utmost danger. "He had been around for six weeks. He didn't know what was going on," Helms said. "He probably didn't even know that the Agency had unvouchered funds."

Helms's biographer, Thomas Powers, wrote at the end of the 1970s that "the CIA's role in Watergate is going to be a subject of debate for the rest of time." Watergate's leading chronicler, Stanley Kutler, wrote at the start of the 1990s that the agency's role "seems destined to remain shadowy." The record now is far clearer. The employment of six former CIA men in the Watergate break-in was part of the Nixon administration's habit of running clandestine operations out of the White House. Nixon tried to use the CIA to contain the FBI. He succeeded, very briefly. Helms and Walters complied with the president's order to go along with the cover-up for sixteen days at most. The cover-up would have worked if Helms had risked all. It failed because he valued the CIA more than he valued Richard Nixon.

322 *Kissinger proposed replacing Helms with James Schlesinger*: FRUS, Vol. II, document 284, editorial note.

322 *"Very good idea"*: November 10, 1972, entry in *The Haldeman Diaries: Inside*

the Nixon White House, The Complete Multimedia Edition, CD-ROM, Sony Electronic Publishing, 1994.

322 *"to ruin the Foreign Service"*: White House Tapes, conversation between Nixon and Kissinger, Oval Office, November 13, 1972, National Archives.

322 *"to tear up the Department"*: November 21, 1972, entry in *The Haldeman Diaries.*

323 *"Look, Mr. President"*: Helms interview with Kutler.

323 *"a CIA conspiracy to remove you from office?"*: Transcript of Nixon interview with Frank Gannon, Walter J. Brown Media Archives, University of Georgia, available online at http://www.libs.uga.edu/media/collections/nixon. Gannon interviewed Nixon for nine days in 1983; full transcripts were published in 2002.

323 *"one that really had R.N. tattooed on him"*: Helms interview with Kutler.

323 *"They've got 40,000 people over there reading newspapers"*: John L. Helgerson, *Getting to Know the President: CIA Briefings of Presidential Candidates, 1952–1992* (Washington, DC: Center for the Study of Intelligence, CIA, 1995). Nixon had more than doubled the actual personnel at headquarters.

323 *"Schlesinger must be the man in charge"*: White House Tapes, Oval Office, December 27, 1972. In this taped memo, Nixon emphasized "the need to improve *quality* as well as reduce *quantity* of top intelligence people in the CIA itself. The CIA, like the State Department, is basically a liberal establishment bureaucracy. I want the personnel there cut in at least half—no, at least by thirty-five to forty percent—and I want a definite improvement insofar as attitudes of those in CIA with regard to our foreign policy."

324 *"There wasn't a dry eye in the house"*: Halpern oral history in Ralph E. Weber, ed., *Spymasters: Ten CIA Officers in Their Own Words* (Wilmington, DE: Scholarly Resources, 1999), p. 128.

Chapter Thirty-one

325 *"to change the concept of a 'secret service' "*: William Colby, *Honorable Men: My Life in the CIA* (New York: Simon and Schuster, 1978). My portrayal of this passage in the history of the CIA is influenced by interviews with Bill Colby conducted in person and by telephone between 1988 and the week before his death in 1996.

326 *the enemy had breached the CIA's defenses*: There were, we now know, some low-level penetrations of the CIA at the time. An analyst named Larry Wu-tai Chin had been spying for China for twenty years undetected. The best evidence we have today suggests that none of the moles were Soviet. But in Angleton's view, absence of evidence was not evidence of absence.

327 *"the central intelligence agency—small 'c,' small 'i,' small 'a' "*: Schlesinger quoted in Douglas F. Garthoff, "Directors of Central Intelligence as Leaders of the U.S. Intelligence Community, 1946–2005," 2006, CIA/CSI.

327 *one of the most dangerous decisions a director of central intelligence had ever made*: Schlesinger says today that he did not mean for people to take his order to tell all literally, and that it had never occurred to him that anyone would actually comply. But it is inconceivable that the officers of the CIA would ignore a legal order from a director.

328 *The CIA's exceedingly vague charter*: The legal basis for the agency to conduct covert action depended on lawful direction from the National Security Council, a clear understanding between the president and the director of central intelligence, and a modicum of oversight from Congress. That tripartite relationship was entirely dysfunctional in 1973. The powers of the national security adviser—a purely administrative position that had no basis in law or statute—were by then whatever he could get away with in secret.

329 *Colby locked them up*: He did confide in the four members of Congress to whom he had to report, the chairmen of the Senate and House subcommittees who handled the CIA's budget. He had nothing to fear from them. The Senate subcommittee had convened exactly once since the fall of 1970.

329 *"We did not cover ourselves with glory"*: Colby statement, House Select Committee on Intelligence, August 4, 1975. The CIA had reported "no military or political indicators of Egyptian intentions or preparation to resume hostilities with Israel."

329 *"But there will be no war"*: Cited in Mary O. McCarthy, "The Mission to Warn: Disaster Looms," *Defense Intelligence Journal*, Vol. 7, No. 2, 1998. At the time of publication, McCarthy was senior director for intelligence programs on the National Security Council Staff; from 1994 to 1996, she was national intelligence officer for warning.

Chapter Thirty-two

330 *Pappas had delivered $549,000 in cash to the 1968 Nixon campaign*: The following statement was placed in the *Congressional Record* in 1993 by Representative Don Edwards, a member of the House Judiciary Committee that approved articles of impeachment against President Nixon: "The Greek dictatorship, through its intelligence agency, KYP, (which had been founded and subsequently subsidized by the CIA), transferred three cash payments totalling $549,000 to the Nixon campaign fund in 1968. The conduit was Thomas Pappas, a prominent Greek-American businessman with close links to the CIA, the colonels, and the Nixon campaign."

330 *"I am aware of what you're doing"*: Nixon White House tapes, March 7,
     1973, declassified and transcribed in 1998, National Archives. Nixon told
     his secretary, Rose Mary Woods, to make sure there would be no record
     of the Pappas visit. "I don't want to have anything indicating that I was
     thanking him for raising money for the Watergate defendants," he said.
     To this day, no one knows why the White House sent burglars to the Wa-
     tergate. The team might well have been looking for proof that the chief
     of the Democratic National Committee, Larry O'Brien, had evidence
     about the Nixon-Pappas connection—which he did. Pappas was instru-
     mental in the selection of Vice President Spiro Agnew as Nixon's running
     mate in 1968, and he had personally contributed at least $100,000 to
     Nixon's 1972 re-election campaign. In exchange for the latter donation,
     Pappas wanted Ambassador Henry Tasca to remain in Greece. Tasca was
     perhaps the only American outside the inner Nixon circle who knew that
     Pappas had been the courier for Nixon campaign funds from the Greek
     junta. Pappas never was charged in the Watergate scandal: congressional
     investigations of the Greek connection were quashed on national-
     security grounds. He died at his Palm Beach, Florida, estate in 1988.

330 *"These colonels had been plotting for years and years"*: Keeley oral history,
     FAOH.

330 *seven successive station chiefs*: They included Al Ulmer, John Richardson,
     and Tom Karamessines, chief of the clandestine service under Richard
     Helms, who first came to Athens in 1947. Throughout the 1950s, Allen
     Dulles personally tended to the king and queen of Greece and their
     palace guard while his station chiefs bought the services of Greek soldiers
     and spies. "We were running Greece," said Herbert Daniel Brewster, an
     American diplomat who devoted his career to the country from the early
     1950s onward. "It was full control."

330 *"the Central Intelligence Agency"*: Anschutz oral history, FAOH.

331 *"The only time I saw Helms really angry"*: Lehman oral history interview,
     "Mr. Current Intelligence," *Studies in Intelligence*, Summer 2000, CIA/CSI.

331 *"the CIA would explode in anger"*: Blood oral history, FAOH.

331 *"The CIA station chief"*: Kennedy oral history, FAOH.

332 *"a major asset in Athens"*: Boyatt oral history, FAOH.

332 *"I went up to Athens"*: Crawford oral history, FAOH. The Greek colonels
     had reasons for hating Archbishop Makarios. Crawford explained that
     Makarios had "aided a young man, a mainland Greek, who subsequently
     tried to assassinate the prime minister of Greece. Makarios had given him
     safe haven, the use of the Cyprus diplomatic pouch, and a fake passport
     to enable him to get back into Greece after a year of clandestine planning
     in Cyprus."

334 *"the terrible price"*: Kubisch oral history, FAOH.

Chapter Thirty-three

335   *"concerning the use of classified material"*: Ford in National Security Council
      meeting minutes, October 7, 1974, GRFL.
335   *"We don't have the tools we need"*: Schlesinger in ibid.
336   *"everything the President knew"*: Colby quoted in John L. Helgerson, *Getting
      to Know the President: CIA Briefings of Presidential Candidates, 1952–1992*,
      CIA/CSI.
336   *"It is inconceivable"*: Angleton testimony, Church Committee hearings,
      September 23, 1975.
337   *"Ford asked me to come into the White House"*: Silberman oral history, FAOH.
338   *"Mr. Helms may have committed perjury"*: Helms had been torn between
      truth and secrecy. Testifying before Congress before his posting as the
      American ambassador to Iran in 1973, he had lied about what the CIA
      had and had not done to overthrow the elected government of Chile.
      During his four years as an ambassador, he had been ordered back to
      Washington continually by congressional committees, criminal investiga-
      tors, and the high councils of the White House. Humiliated but defiant,
      Helms stood before a federal judge in Washington on November 4, 1977,
      and received a two-year suspended sentence and a $2,000 fine in lieu of
      an eight-count felony indictment. He accepted a misdemeanor charge of
      failing to testify fully to Congress—a white lie, a sin of omission. Helms
      had argued that he had sworn a higher oath as director to protect the na-
      tion's secrets. The Carter administration had weighed the prosecution
      and decided to let it proceed. The court said the dictates of the Constitu-
      tion and the laws of the United States were stronger than the power of
      secrecy.
338   *"the CIA would be destroyed"*: Memorandum of conversation, January 3,
      1975, GRFL.
338   *"Frankly, we are in a mess"*: Memorandum of conversation, January 4,
      1975, GRFL. Notes from this meeting were declassified in December
      2002:

> Ford: Colby has gone to Silberman not only with his report but
>   numerous other allegations.
> Rockefeller: At your request?
> Ford: Without my knowledge . . .
> [Dr. Kissinger described the "horrors" book.]
> Ford: We are concerned that the CIA would be destroyed. . . . And
>   Helms thinks Colby shafted him; Helms made it clear if there
>   were any dead cats to be thrown out he would throw some of
>   his own.

Kissinger: And Colby has taken to Justice the question of possible
    perjury by Helms.
Rockefeller: This raises real questions on his judgment.
Ford: We debated this and decided we could not move him out
    now.

338 *The CIA "made a mistake"*: Gerald R. Ford oral history, July 8, 2003,
JFKL.
339 *"the investigation of the CIA"*: Memorandum of conversation, February 21,
1975, GRFL.
339 *"Within the CIA there is bitter dissension"*: Memorandum of conversation,
March 28, 1975, GRFL.

Chapter Thirty-four

340 *"Let me get a grasp on the situation"*: Minutes of the Washington Special Actions Group, April 2, 1975, declassified September 7, 2004. Days after this
conversation, Cambodia fell. The American ambassador, John Gunther
Dean, and the CIA station chief, David Whipple, had a better grasp on the
situation surrounding them than their colleagues in Saigon. "The CIA
had a good idea of the makeup and leadership of the Khmer Rouge,"
Dean recounted. "David Whipple . . . gave us documentation of some of
the barbarous acts being committed by the Khmer Rouge before April
1975." Dean oral history, FAOH.
341 *Polgar awoke to the sound of rockets*: Polgar interview with author. When he
took over in January 1972 from Ted Shackley, Polgar commanded 550
CIA officers, 200 of them covert operators. His instructions from Nixon
and Kissinger remained constant after the Paris Peace Accords of 1973
were signed: "Continue the war by other means to preserve a non-
communist Vietnam." Polgar had witnessed firsthand some of the diplomacy for which Henry Kissinger had been awarded the Nobel Peace
Prize. The grand strategist had negotiated terms of a peace accord and a
cease-fire with North Vietnam weeks before the 1972 American presidential election—without the approval of the president of South Vietnam, the corrupt Nguyen Van Thieu. In Saigon, at a dinner attended by
Kissinger, the American ambassador Ellsworth Bunker, and Kissinger's
aide John Negroponte, Kissinger had personally instructed Polgar to "put
pressure on Thieu" through CIA assets among the South Vietnamese military. Polgar replied that Kissinger's order made no sense; that was not
how things worked in Saigon anymore. It made even less sense after
Kissinger leaked the story of his secret negotiations to a favorite reporter
at *Newsweek*. The reporter filed his story by cable from Saigon, and South

Vietnam's intelligence service intercepted it and gave copies to both President Thieu and Tom Polgar. The station chief showed it to Kissinger, who replied: "This has the unpleasant smell of truth."

The CIA station's budget stayed at an even $30 million a year as the American military presence dwindled in 1973 and 1974. Polgar ran intelligence-gathering operations, not paramilitary missions. CIA interrogators grilled captured communist troops and suspected spies. CIA analysts combed through piles of reports from the field. CIA branch chiefs in each of South Vietnam's four military sectors coordinated hundreds of American and South Vietnamese officers. And the enemy marched on.

The CIA kept trying to locate an enemy field headquarters—the Bamboo Pentagon was what the American military called it—but there was nothing out in the jungle but tents and tunnels and a determined foe. After the fall of Richard Nixon in August 1974, Congress revolted against the war and began cutting hundreds of millions of dollars out of the effort to keep the South Vietnamese military afloat. By March 1975, North Vietnamese troops were wiping out South Vietnamese divisions and advancing on Saigon. The failure to create a coherent plan for the evacuation of Saigon led to the death or the imprisonment of thousands of Vietnamese who had worked for the United States. Ambassador Martin returned to Washington and became a special assistant to Henry Kissinger.

344 *"imperative that the evacuation proceed without delay"*: Arnold oral history, recorded by Gayle L. Morrison. Morrison, an ethnographer, spent nine years recording first-person eyewitness accounts of Hmong and Americans who remembered the fall of Long Tieng. Her extraordinary book is *Sky Is Falling: An Oral History of the CIA's Evacuation of the Hmong from Laos* (Jefferson, NC: McFarland, 1999). My reconstruction relies on her work, including her oral histories of General Aderholt and Captain Knotts.

345 *forced a political arrangement*: Richard L. Holm, "No Drums, No Bugles: Recollections of a Case Officer in Laos, 1962–1965," *Studies in Intelligence,* Vol. 47, No. 1, Spring 2003, CIA/CSI.

Chapter Thirty-five

347 *"Bury Bush"* . . . *"a graveyard for politics"* . . . *"the total end of any political future"*: George Bush, *All the Best, George Bush: My Life in Letters and Other Writings* (New York: Scribner, 1999), pp. 195–196, 239–240; Herbert S. Parmet, *George Bush: The Life of a Lone Star Yankee* (New York: Scribner, 1999), pp. 189–194.

347 *"This is the most interesting job I've ever had"*: Bush, *All the Best*, p. 255.

347 *Bush ran headlong into Secretary of Defense Rumsfeld*: Douglas F. Garthoff,

"Directors of Central Intelligence as Leaders of the U.S. Intelligence Community, 1946–2005," 2006, CIA/CSI.

347 *Rumsfeld was "paranoid"*: Carver oral history interview, May 13, 1982, CIA/CSI.

348 *"a turbulent and troublesome period"*: George Bush letter to the president, June 1, 1976, declassified August 9, 2001, CIA.

349 *"We had been forced out of Vietnam"*: Frank G. Wisner, Jr., oral history, FAOH. He recounted at the outset, "I grew up in World War II and have vivid memories of a father going to war. . . . As a child I had met General Marshall, Allen Dulles, and had known many Secretaries of State and Defense in passing as a little boy. . . . I have very, very strong memories of the end of the war, the emergence of the post-War period, the onset of the Cold War itself, sharp reflections born of the time. . . . My father was for a number of years the head of the clandestine services of CIA. I remember the outbreak of the Korean War, its passage, the crisis in Washington during the McCarthy years, the emergence of NATO, and the Suez War. I was in England at school and felt almost as if I were on the battlefront. . . . When I arrived in Washington at the beginning of the Kennedy Administration to join the Foreign Service, I had in a very real sense already lived a life of foreign affairs."

349 *Bush prepared to meet the governor of Georgia*: The Bush-Carter briefings are detailed in CREST documents and in John L. Helgerson, *Getting to Know the President: CIA Briefings of Presidential Candidates, 1952–1992*, CIA/CSI.

351 *the Church Committee, the Senate panel that investigated the CIA*: The committee went down blind alleys trying to investigate the "alleged assassination plots" without coming to grips with the fact that presidents had authorized them. Its lasting contributions were a highly competent history of the CIA and the transcripts of the depositions it took, most of which were not declassified until after the end of the cold war. The House committee dissolved into rancor; a final draft of its report was leaked but never formally published. The first real attempt at congressional oversight was not a success. "When we got through with it, what did it amount to but a media circus?" John Horton, a forty-year veteran of the CIA and a very open-minded man, said of the Church Committee in 1987. "Who did the CIA ever assassinate? Nobody, as far as I can tell. But you would have thought that was all we were up to."

351 *"Bush wanted to be kept on"*: Helgerson, *Getting to Know the President*.

351 *he revealed a handful of ongoing operations*: George Bush, "Subject: Meeting in Plains, Georgia, 19 November 1976," CIA/FOIA. Bush told Carter about "warrantless electronic surveillance" of American citizens, the CIA's contacts with the Palestine Liberation Organization, and the unresolved case of Nicholas Shadrin, a Soviet defector working for the CIA—

or perhaps a double agent—who had been murdered in Vienna eleven months before. There was another aspect to the CIA's operations in Vienna that Bush did not mention. After the December 1975 murder of Richard Welch in Athens, Bill Colby, in one of his last acts as director, had ordered that direct talks be held in secret between the CIA and Soviet intelligence officers in Vienna. He wanted to know if Moscow had had a hand in the killing, which would have been a violation of the unwritten rules of the cold war. He also wanted to talk for the sake of talking. The two sides had never had an official channel of communication at the highest levels. Each found the conversation useful. The line stayed open for the rest of the cold war.

351 *"howling right-wingers"*: Lehman oral history interview, "Mr. Current Intelligence," *Studies in Intelligence,* Summer 2000, CIA/CSI.

352 *"Let her fly!!"*: Bush notation, George Carver memo, May 26, 1976, CIA/CREST.

352 *the agency put Team B's findings to the test*: Raymond L. Garthoff, "Estimating Soviet Military Intentions and Capabilities," Gerald K. Haines and Robert E. Leggett (eds.), *Watching the Bear: Essays on CIA's Analysis of the Soviet Union,* CIA/CSI.

353 *In retrospect, you see*: Robert M. Hathaway and Russell Jack Smith, "Richard Helms as Director of Central Intelligence," 1993, CIA/CSI, declassified February 2007.

353 *"the greatness that is CIA"*: Bush address, CIA headquarters, January 19, 1977.

Chapter Thirty-six

357 *Carter . . . wound up signing almost as many covert-action orders as Nixon and Ford*: While no precise number has been declassified, "the Carter administration . . . availed itself frequently of covert-action programs," said Carter's deputy director of central intelligence, Frank Carlucci. Carlucci oral history, FAOH.

357 *"I had a brother who had worked for CIA undercover"*: Sorensen interview with author. His brother Thomas Sorensen worked for the CIA during the 1950s. Thomas served as the number-three man at the United States Information Agency under JFK and Edward R. Murrow; he was the USIA's liaison with Richard Helms, merging news and propaganda, while Ted wrote speeches at the Kennedy White House.

358 *"President Carter called me in"*: Turner interview with author.

358 *"I was in charge of human intelligence collection"*: Holdridge oral history, FAOH.

360 *"he sought to overthrow their system"*: Robert M. Gates, *From the Shadows: The*

Ultimate Insider's Story of Five Presidents and How They Won the Cold War
(New York: Simon and Schuster, 1996), p. 95.

360 *a long hard look*: Brzezinski said, "Colonel Kuklinski volunteered to collaborate with the U.S., emphasizing that he would like to collaborate
with the U.S. military as a Polish officer. He was very instrumental in
providing the United States with a much better understanding than it
theretofore had regarding the war plans of the Warsaw Pact, the Soviet
plans for a sudden massive onslaught against Western Europe—including,
incidentally, a little-known plan to use nuclear weapons from day one of
the attack on Western Europe. I'll give you one specific example. On day
two of the attack on Western Europe the Soviet war plans provided for
the use of forty tactical nuclear weapons against Hamburg alone, in West
Germany. So this was an extremely important contribution to filling major gaps in our understanding of Soviet war planning. And to the extent
that the agency was the channel that provided the communication link
with him, it was a success for the agency even though Colonel Kuklinski
was himself never in a strict sense a CIA agent. He volunteered. He operated on his own. He didn't actually receive instructions." Brzezinski interview with author.

360 *"By God"*: Smith interview with author. Drafted out of Dartmouth at the
start of the Korean War and trained in the Russian language by the army,
Smith had focused on the Soviet target in the CIA stations in Prague,
Berlin, and Beirut throughout the late 1950s and the 1960s. He had personally recruited and run six Eastern Europeans and trained hundreds of
young CIA officers on the basics of spying in cold-war capitals without
getting caught. By 1975, when Angleton was forced into retirement,
Smith and his colleagues started recruiting their first Soviets.

His biggest recruitment was Sergei Federenko, a diplomat assigned to
arms control issues at the United Nations secretariat in New York. An engineer by training and a member of the Soviet elite by birth, Federenko
was young and ambitious. He liked to drink. He had a beautiful wife and
a girlfriend on the side in the suburbs north of New York.

"Now, I'm a con man," Smith said. "That's my nature and my training.
You don't 'recruit' a Soviet. The Soviet has to recruit himself. It's like when
you set your cap for a female. Each of you has to find something in the
other that's attractive. It is in many respects a seduction. . . . So I recruited
the guy. And—guess what? He had been educated as a scientist and he had
worked on Soviet rocketry."

Federenko provided a who's who of the Soviet delegation at the
United Nations in New York, including a rundown of the names and
foibles of the KGB officers posing as diplomats. For his stellar work,
Smith was promoted to chief of a CIA division focused on counterterror-

ism. But when it came to selecting a case officer to handle Federenko in New York, the CIA had very few to choose from. The ranks of fluent Russian speakers in the Soviet/Eastern European division of the clandestine service were very thin. Headquarters selected a thirty-four-year-old alcoholic who became a traitor to the CIA. In 1954, he had been a boy floating down the Irrawaddy River in Burma with his father when he found out that the old man worked for the agency. He had been a file clerk at the CIA for five years in the 1960s while he tried to finish a college degree. He had finally become a member of the clandestine service in 1967. He was married to a CIA officer and, in every sense, married to the CIA. His name was Aldrich Ames.

361 *"The possibilities are there to change this from a black-white conflict into a red-white conflict"*: "Subject: South Africa and Rhodesia," Special Coordination Committee Meeting, February 8, 1977, and National Security Council meeting minutes, March 3, 1977, JCL.

362 *"nobody wanted to pay attention to Africa"*: Carlucci oral history, FAOH.

362 *Gerry Gossens, a station chief*: Gossens interview with author. Born in Texas and reared in Beirut, Gossens joined the CIA in 1960 and worked through the Middle East under deep cover as an Evinrude outboard-motor salesman before joining the Africa division. Hundreds of young and ambitious CIA men—and a few women—scrambled for advantage against Soviet, Chinese, and East German spies in Africa throughout the '60s and '70s. "We were young people willing to go to hellholes," Gossens said. "We were espionage-oriented well before the rest of the Agency came around. Our branch chief used to say: 'Give me $25,000 and I can rent any African president.' But that was not what we were in business to do. We were in business to conduct espionage. And Africa was still a place that was so fluid you were in on history being made. You could start an operation by accident. You go with the Ambassador to see the President. A member of the President's staff says, 'You know, I have a broken Pentax camera. I can't get spare parts.' You do him a favor. You wind up looking at the Presidential archives."

363 *"My greatest single crisis"*: Wisner oral history, FAOH.

363 *"I asked my station chief if it were true"*: Eagleburger oral history, FAOH.

364 *"one of their basic skills"*: Stansfield Turner, *Burn Before Reading: Presidents, CIA Directors, and Secret Intelligence* (New York: Hyperion, 2005), p. 187.

364 *"They're a unique culture"*: McMahon interview with author.

364 *"Talk about apoplexy—they went bonkers"*: McMahon interview with author.

365 *"In spite of its current (and worsening) morale"*: Memorandum for Zbigniew Brzezinski, "Subject: Covert Action Possibilities in Selected [*Deleted*] Areas," February 5, 1979, NSC, JCL. There was, however, one other covert operation that started under Carter and bore fruit fifteen years later. It

was aimed at uncovering the connections between cocaine traffickers and the government of Colombia. In 1977, "the CIA station chief came to me with a plan for CIA involvement in anti-narcotics work," said Robert W. Drexler, then the deputy chief of mission at the American embassy in Bogota. "This was not to be made known to the DEA. So I approved it, and we started it. It was, in essence, a fine operation in which we used a very small number of trusted Colombian law enforcement officials, who we could monitor closely so as to ensure that they weren't being turned against us or corrupted, or that we would see it when they were; and in which we collected intelligence on the contacts between the drug traffickers and high-level Colombian officials. The idea was to pass this on in Washington. The program worked very well. The intelligence it gathered was horrifying, because it detailed the rapid spread of corruption." In 1994 and 1995, this operation climaxed with a CIA-backed takedown of one of the major Colombian cocaine rings, the Cali cartel, achieved in conjunction with the DEA.

365 *the CIA failed to warn the president of the United States*: Though almost all the records of the failure to warn of the Soviet invasion of Afghanistan remain classified, Douglas MacEachin, the deputy director of intelligence from 1993 to 1995, published an appraisal of the CIA's performance in 2002, basing his work on the secret record as well as his own first-hand experience as one of the agency's best Soviet analysts. Douglas MacEachin, "Predicting the Soviet Invasion of Afghanistan: The Intelligence Community's Record," Center for the Study of Intelligence, 2002, CIA/CSI. My account of the failure relies in large part on his work, as well as interviews with Brzezinski and Gates.

366 *"the deteriorating situation"*: Gates, *From the Shadows*, p. 132. Though Gates does not say so, this passage evidently appeared in the president's daily brief.

366 *"CIA does not see this as a crash buildup"*: "Subject: Iran," Special Coordination Committee, December 17, 1979, National Security Archive collection.

367 *"The pace of Soviet deployments"*: The December 19, 1979, report to the president is cited in *The Soviet Invasion of Afghanistan*, a classified CIA history cited in MacEachin's "Predicting the Soviet Invasion."

367 *"a spectator sport"*: MacEachin, "Predicting the Soviet Invasion."

Chapter Thirty-seven

368 *"a virtual dictatorship"*: Nixon to Haig and Ambassador Douglas MacArthur II, April 8, 1971, FRUS 1969–1976, Vol. E-4, Documents on Iran and Iraq, declassified September 12, 2006.

368 *"to confirm that the Shah was our puppet"*: Precht oral history, FAOH. In September 1979 Precht was in a Washington hospital awaiting surgery: "Before going into the operating room, I looked over and there was another person lying there, waiting his turn. It was Loy Henderson, who had been Ambassador in 1953 when Mossadegh was overthrown. I thought, 'present at the creation and present at the destruction.' After I was able to walk around, I went to his room. . . . I asked him what [the Shah] was like in his time in Iran. He said, 'He didn't count. He was insignificant. He was a weak person. And yet, we had to deal with him.' So, he confirmed what I had suspected—that the Shah had been inflated by the power that had come to Iran with the jump in oil income plus the adulation of Nixon and Kissinger and other foreign leaders."

368 *"an island of stability"*: The phrase President Carter used had an Iranian provenance. Kissinger told Nixon in an October 1969 memo that the shah "is genuinely committed to the West and feels the good job he is doing in Iran—'an island of stability,' he calls it—is an important service to the Free World." Kissinger to Nixon, October 21, 1968, FRUS, 1969–1976, Vol. E-4, declassified September 12, 2006.

369 *Howard Hart's view from the streets*: Hart remarks, Miller Center of Public Affairs, University of Virginia, September 7, 2005.

369 *"very, very sensitive classified conversations"*: Laingen oral history, FAOH.

370 *"We paid for it"*: Laingen oral history, FAOH.

370 *"We were just plain asleep"*: Turner, *Burn Before Reading: Presidents, CIA Directors, and Secret Intelligence* (New York: Hyperion, 2005), p. 180.

370 *"We haven't a clue as a nation"*: Hart remarks, Miller Center, September 7, 2005. Greg Miller, "In from the Cold, to a Cold Shoulder," *Los Angeles Times*, May 19, 2005.

371 *"I knew little about Iran"*: William J. Daugherty, "A First Tour Like No Other," *Studies in Intelligence*, Spring 1998, CIA/CSI.

371 *"Don't worry about another embassy attack"*: William J. Daugherty, *In the Shadow of the Ayatollah: A CIA Hostage in Iran* (Annapolis, MD: Naval Institute Press, 2001), p. 3.

371 *"Blank the Shah!"*: Jimmy Carter interview, Jimmy Carter Oral History Project, Miller Center, November 29, 1982.

372 *"ignorant of the local culture and language"*: Daugherty, "A First Tour Like No Other."

372 *the brainchild of the CIA's Tony Mendez*: Mendez interview with author; Tim Weiner, "Master Creator of Ghosts Is Honored by C.I.A.," *The New York Times*, September 19, 1997. See also Antonio J. Mendez, "A Classic Case of Deception," *Studies in Intelligence*, Winter 1999–2000, CIA/CSI.

373 *"The effort relied very heavily on the CIA"*: Quainton oral history, FAOH.

374 *"an unsmiling cadaver"*: Daugherty, "A First Tour Like No Other."

374 *"an act of vengeance"*: Kenneth M. Pollack, *The Persian Puzzle: The Conflict Between Iran and America* (New York: Random House, 2004), pp. 128–180.

Chapter Thirty-eight

375–76 *"His view of how you fight a war"*: Gates interview with author.

376 *"I don't think he meant to say 'scrap the Constitution' "*: Webster interview with author.

376 *"not qualified to be the head of the CIA"*: Ford oral history in Deborah Hart Strober and Gerald S. Strober, *Reagan: The Man and His Presidency* (Boston: Houghton Mifflin, 1998), p. 72.

376 *"Casey was an inappropriate choice"*: Bush quoted in John Helgerson, "CIA Briefings of Presidential Candidates," May 1996, CIA/CSI. Two other views of the man and the job: Laurence Silberman—the federal judge who led the 2005 investigation of the CIA's work on weapons of mass destruction in Iraq—was co-chair of Reagan's foreign policy group in 1980. "I truthfully would have agreed to be CIA director, which was being discussed," Silberman said. "But Casey . . . had a greater claim, although I thought it unwise to put a campaign chairman in that job." Lawrence Eagleburger, who served as secretary of state under President Bush in 1992, put it more directly: "Either you do away with the clandestine side of the CIA, which I would not like to see happen, or you simply have to be very, very careful about the kind of person you make CIA director, and that means you don't appoint Bill Casey." FAOH interviews.

377 *"Who was going to be in charge of foreign policy?"*: Poindexter oral history in Strober and Strober, *Reagan: The Man and His Presidency*, p. 111.

377 *"It was a hare-brained idea"*: George P. Shultz, *Turmoil and Triumph: My Years as Secretary of State* (New York: Scribner, 1993), pp. 294–297.

377 *"a hog on ice"*: Ibid., p. 84.

377 *"a freelance buccaneer"*: Inman interview with author.

378 *"he did not want to be the traditional Director of Central Intelligence"*: Inman testimony, Nomination of Robert M. Gates to Be Director of Central Intelligence, U.S. Senate, Select Committee on Intelligence, 102nd Congress, 1st Session, September 20, 1991, Vol. I, p. 926.

378 *"a blindered fraternity"*: Robert M. Gates, *From the Shadows: The Ultimate Insider's Story of Five Presidents and How They Won the Cold War* (New York: Simon and Schuster, 1996), p. 209.

378 *"I didn't have that fire in the belly"*: McMahon interview with author. When McMahon was assigned to shake up the analysts at the directorate of intelligence, he found that the entire structure needed reshaping. "If I wanted to know what was going on in a country, I had to ask three different offices," McMahon said. "There was an office for military intel-

ligence, an office for economic intelligence, an office for political intelligence. So if I said, 'What's going on in Mexico?' I had input from three different offices, and I had to do the integration and come up with the analysis."

378 *"CIA is slowly turning into the Department of Agriculture"*: Gates, *From the Shadows*, pp. 223–224.

379 *"close-minded, smug, arrogant" . . . "flat out wrong" . . . "pretending to be experts"*: Nomination of Robert M. Gates, 1991, Vol. III, pp. 7–23.

379 *"Working for Casey was a trial for everybody"*: Lehman oral history interview, "Mr. Current Intelligence," *Studies in Intelligence,* Summer 2000, CIA/CSI.

379 *"The CIA's intelligence"*: Shultz interview with author. In the summer of 1982, Secretary of State Shultz set up a weekly lunch with Bill Casey. After the better part of a year, Casey and Shultz, who had been friendly for a decade, discovered that they could not stand one another. "He had too much of an agenda," Shultz said. "It's a mistake for the CIA to have an agenda. They're supposed to produce intelligence. If they have an agenda, the intelligence can get slanted." From 1985 to 1987, Deputy Secretary of State John Whitehead and the CIA's Bob Gates carried on these meetings. Whitehead was appalled at "how little help I got from the CIA in knowing what was going on in countries where we had interests and where there were problems. . . . The analyses were shallow, contained very little of what I would call hard information, and often were incorrect. . . . I thought that the organization itself somehow had deteriorated, so that the information that it was receiving and the system of gathering information was not very productive anymore." Whitehead oral history, FAOH. Gaping holes were growing in the agency's map of the globe. "The principal worry I have at this point has to do with the adequacy of our intelligence effort . . . all over the world," Admiral Inman said, presciently, just before joining Casey at CIA headquarters in 1981. "We lack a data base on the areas of the world which were overlooked in the 1960's, when we were focused totally on Southeast Asia. There wasn't a lot of worry about countries in Central America, the Caribbean, Latin America, Africa. I believe the odds are very high that in this decade we will face a lot of challenges in those areas." Bobby R. Inman, "Managing Intelligence for Effective Use," Center for Information Policy Research, Harvard University, December 1980.

379 *"Sometime in the dark of night"*: Clair George testimony, Nomination of Robert M. Gates, 1991, Vol. II, p. 96.

380 *a calculated ruse*: The American ambassador to Nicaragua from 1982 to 1984, Anthony Quainton, knew the operation was a sham. "The White House had given up on the prospects of any dialogue. Egged on by Bill Casey of the CIA, it believed that the only way to solve the problem was to get the San-

dinistas out. The means for doing that was an elaborate covert action program. At first, it was presented to the Congress in an extremely disingenuous way. The administration argued that harassment would make life uncomfortable for the Sandinistas, would keep them from consolidating their power, and would bring them to the negotiating table. They would see that there were unacceptable costs to their economy if they did not negotiate. The CIA argued that this was the only way to persuade them to change their policies. As with other covert operations elsewhere in the world, it didn't seem to have the promised immediate effect." Quainton oral history, FAOH.

380 *"raised hell with Casey"*: Gates, *From the Shadows*, pp. 242–248.
380 *"'figure out what to do about Central America'"*: Clarridge interview for the CNN Cold War series, 1998. National Security Archive transcript available online at http://www2.gwu.edu/~nsarchiv/coldwar/interviews/episode 18/clarridge1.html. "The Latin American division had always been an isolated division within the Agency; it was almost like a little barony," Clarridge said in another oral history. "So the main thing was to carry the division within me. After a couple of weeks I went back up and told Casey, 'This is what we ought to do: Why don't we take the war to Nicaragua . . . ?' This was exactly what Casey wanted to hear." Strober and Strober, *Reagan: The Man and His Presidency*, p. 165.
381 *"The secret war began"* and *"The CIA had a planning process of their own"*: Quainton oral history, FAOH. In the Reagan years, ambassadors very rarely spoke up in public when the CIA created foreign-policy snafus. In one of many examples of the public-relations disasters of the war in Central America, the CIA quietly offered the State Department a public-relations bonanza. The agency had debriefed a nineteen-year-old Nicaraguan captured in El Salvador. He said he had been trained in insurrection by Cuban soldiers in Ethiopia. He had a great story to tell. Was State interested in presenting him to the public in Washington? At the CIA's behest, the State Department organized a private briefing for four trusted reporters. A press spokesman escorted the reporters into a little room and then brought in the captured Nicaraguan, who said, in so many words: "I've been tortured by the CIA. They tried to force me to say that I was sent into El Salvador. I'm a patriotic Nicaraguan. I've never been to Ethiopia." The CIA had been stung by a slick teenager.

The agency's unique "planning process" almost ended the careers of Senator Gary Hart and Senator William Cohen, the latter a future secretary of defense. They came close to being killed on a fact-finding mission in Nicaragua when a CIA plane that had just unleashed two five-hundred-pound bombs crashed into the VIP lounge at Managua's international airport. "This created a very negative attitude in those two senators about the quality of the covert operations of the CIA," Ambassador Quainton said.

381 *The secret war did not stay secret*: The CIA could not have won that war, whether or not Congress had approved it. "We never had the ability to build back the paramilitary capability that we needed to conduct a war in Nicaragua," said John McMahon. "The agency was not prepared—in personnel particularly—to fight a war or train others to fight a war." McMahon interview with author.

382 *"yuppie spies"*: Duane R. Clarridge with Digby Diehl, *A Spy for All Seasons: My Life in the CIA* (New York: Scribner, 1997), pp. 303–318.

382 *Congress strongly supported a bigger, better, stronger, smarter CIA*: The Senate had confirmed Casey 95–0 and the Congress gave him hundreds of millions of dollars in new funds at the end of 1981. "They wanted us to have a worldwide clandestine capability so we could provide intelligence on intentions and warning," said John McMahon. "They wanted us to have a good covert-action infrastructure. Now the beauty of having a good clandestine operation is that often the individual that you have recruited to provide you intelligence of what's going on in their government is also influential—and you can use him as a covert-action asset. If he's the foreign minister, you can subtly influence that country to support a UN vote or to say good things about the United States. So our covert-action capability began to come back very strongly." McMahon interview with author.

382 *"guilty of contempt of Congress from the day he was sworn in"*: Gates, *From the Shadows*, p. 213.

382 *"I hope that will hold the bastards!"*: Barry Goldwater of Arizona, the defeated Republican candidate for president in 1964, was the chairman of the Senate intelligence committee from 1981 to 1984. Casey was so stingy with the truth that Goldwater demanded chaperones from the State Department to accompany him to the witness table to serve as custodians of fact. One of those chaperones, Ambassador Dennis Kux, heard Casey muttering this line as he left the hearing room. Kux oral history, FAOH.

382 *"specifically evasive"*: Fiers testimony, Joint Hearings, Iran-Contra Investigation, Washington, D.C., 1988.

382 " *'I caught him lying to me' "*: Inman interview in Stansfield Turner, *Burn Before Reading: Presidents, CIA Directors, and Secret Intelligence* (New York: Hyperion, 2005), pp. 196–201.

382 *"If Congress would not finance the CIA's operations in Central America"*: In 1984, when Congress cut off funds for the CIA's *contras*, the war stalled, and elections were held. The CIA provided money and propaganda for Arturo Cruz, Sr., a former ambassador to the United States and the legit-

imate leader of the political opposition to the Sandinistas. But the Sandinistas' leader, Daniel Ortega, trounced him two-to-one. At this writing,
Ortega has been re-elected and Nicaragua remains one of the poorest and
most benighted nations in the Western Hemisphere. "The war was unnecessary, inhuman, and unwise," Cruz said after Reagan and Casey
were dead and departed. "We have to say that we all make tremendous
mistakes."

382 *Despite Casey's open disdain*: Kux oral history, FAOH.

383 *"The CIA was deeply involved"*: Norland oral history, FAOH.

383 *The official foreign policy of the United States*: "We would like to see a peaceful resolution of Chadian factional fighting," a November 17, 1981, State
Department briefing paper said. It was hard to see how the CIA's arming
one faction to the teeth promoted that goal. "Libyan Threat to Sudan,"
Department of State, declassified July 30, 2002.

383 *"'Fuck the Congress'"*: Blakemore oral history, FAOH.

384 *"What the hell did we give Stinger missiles to Chad for?"*: Richard Bogosian oral
history, FAOH. Bogosian, the American ambassador to Sudan during the
1991 Gulf War, witnessed Baker's query. The answer, said James K.
Bishop, the principal State Department officer for military and intelligence affairs in Africa, was that Habré was "the enemy of our enemy. . . .
We didn't know his full history until later." Bishop oral history, FAOH.
"Our intelligence on the parts of Africa which were of principal concern
to us was not good" throughout the 1980s, Bishop said. "Intelligence from
human sources was not particularly good throughout Africa. Intelligence
assets were principally employed against the 'main enemy'—the Soviets—
in cat-and-mouse recruitment games of dubious national interest."

384 *The CIA's biggest gunrunning mission*: A few Americans—very few—foresaw
the Soviet invasion. "I remember writing reports for Brzezinski as early
as August 1979 saying that the level of Soviet military advisory personnel in Afghanistan at the time portended some kind of major military involvement there," said William Odom, then the senior White House
military aide, in an interview with the author (Odom would later be a
three-star general who ran the National Security Agency under President
Reagan). "Now, as for the exact timing and the exact day that it happened, that's another issue. It did come as a surprise to the world and to
a lot of people in the Carter administration." The Soviet invasion of
Afghanistan began during Christmas week of 1979, and the CIA gave the
president of the United States next to no warning. Carter, helpless to free
the Americans trapped in Iran, approved a plan to help the Afghans
fighting against the brutal Soviet invasion. In January 1980 he ordered
the CIA to ship Soviet-bloc weapons out of the arms stockpiles of American allies into Pakistan. The Pakistani intelligence service would trans-

ship them to a handful of Afghan rebel leaders. "Two days after the Soviet invasion of Afghanistan I gave a memo to the President of the United
States which, if I recall correctly, started with the words, 'We now have
the opportunity to give the Soviet Union its Vietnam,' " Brzezinski said
in an interview with the author. "And it then went on to argue that this
was an act of aggression that posed a threat to the stability of that region,
and potentially to our position even in the Persian Gulf, and that we
should do what we can to bog the Soviets down by aiding the mujahedin.
And the President approved that. A quiet coalition was created involving
us, the Pakistanis, the Saudis, the Chinese, the Egyptians, the British to
provide support. And the purpose of that was essentially in keeping with
the first words of that memo to the President." Howard Hart's remarks
are from his speech at the Miller Center of Public Affairs, University of
Virginia, September 7, 2005.

385 *"you always have to think of the endgame"*: McMahon interview with author.
385 *"the growing desperation of the men in the Kremlin"*: Gates, *From the Shadows*,
p. 258. What was really happening in Moscow? Casey wanted to deliver
intelligence on the players at the Politburo, on the Soviet people, on Soviet minorities and dissidents, on day-to-day existence inside the evil empire. But when the CIA could not provide it through espionage, he clung
to his preconceptions. Ambassador Warren Zimmerman was the deputy
chief of mission at the American embassy in Moscow from 1981 to 1984,
and for those four years Casey and the CIA junked his unvarnished reporting of a collapsing Soviet empire. When he arrived, Zimmerman recounted, the Soviet leader, Leonid Brezhnev, "was in his dotage, he was
slurring his words, he was falling asleep, he was getting drunk." When
Brezhnev died, the nation was led briefly by Yuri Andropov, the chief of
Soviet intelligence, who was dying, too, and then by Konstantin Cher-
nenko, another leader at death's door. The Politburo, the decision-
making machine in Moscow, was "an absolutely paralyzed, ineffective
political apparatus" led by "a bunch of 70- and 80-year-olds, some of
whom had never been out of the Soviet Union," Zimmerman said. "Their
view of the United States was entirely stereotyped, based on what they
read in their horrible newspapers and magazines." They had "only the
most rudimentary knowledge and understanding of the United States."
The American understanding of what was going on in the Soviet Union
was not much better. Geriatric generals and corrupt old-guard Communist Party apparatchiks doddered through their last days, the Soviet economy crumbled under the costs of sustaining a world-class military,
harvests rotted in the fields for want of fuel to truck the food from farms
to markets—and few of these facts entered the collective consciousness
of the CIA. Nor did the agency grasp the calculus of the balance of terror.

Every single national intelligence estimate on Soviet strategic forces sent to the White House from 1974 to 1986 would overstate the rate at which Moscow was modernizing its nuclear firepower.

The peak of the unseen nuclear crisis of 1982 and 1983 came when Reagan announced that the United States would build a missile defense system—"Star Wars"—that would strike and destroy Soviet nuclear weapons in midair. America did not have—and twenty-five years later still does not have—the technology that Reagan envisioned. The Reagan administration bolstered the Strategic Defense Initiative with a rigorous counterpropaganda campaign, to convince the Soviets that "Star Wars" was based on real science and to blunt world criticism of the visionary plan. The information-warfare program gave the Soviets shivers. "They were genuinely scared," Zimmerman said. "They assumed, funnily enough, that we could build it. As it turned out, we faked our tests, and they believed it." In turn, the Soviets faked their own strength—in political lies to their people, in the public pronouncements of the Politburo— and the CIA believed it. Zimmerman oral history, FAOH.

The agency's line on Soviet nuclear weaponry and weapons research was at the time enhanced by an operation run by Jim Olson, later the CIA's counterintelligence chief. During the Carter administration, as Olson recounted, the new Keyhole photoreconnaissance satellites looked down as the Soviets dug a trench alongside a highway outside Moscow and laid telecommunications cables in it. The line ran to a nuclear-weapons research and development center outside Moscow. Manhole covers marked the line. Olson went to Moscow after elaborate training on an underground mock-up, shook off his KGB surveillance team, put on a disguise, opened a manhole, went underground, and tapped the line. The take ran for almost five years—and then the tapes went blank. James M. Olson, *Fair Play: The Moral Dilemmas of Spying* (Washington, D.C.: Potomac, 2006), pp. 9–11.

385 *the Farewell dossier*: Gus W. Weiss, "The Farewell Dossier," *Studies in Intelligence*, Vol. 39, No. 5, 1996, CSA/CSI. Weiss was the National Security Council staffer who devised key elements of the plan of attack.

386 *"It was a brilliant plan"*: Richard Allen, Miller Center of Public Affairs, University of Virginia, Ronald Reagan Oral History Project, May 28, 2002.

Chapter Thirty-nine

388 *"After a couple of jelly beans, the President dozed off"*: Quainton oral history, FAOH.

388 *"the Soviets were secretly directing the dirty work of the world's worst terrorists"*: After the cold war, evidence emerged of direct Soviet support for Wadi

Haddad, a renegade Palestinian terrorist who died in 1978. Haig's charge remains unproven.

388–89 *Ali Hassan Salameh, chief of intelligence for the Palestine Liberation Organization*: On March 2, 1973—the day Bill Colby took over the CIA's clandestine service—the PLO, which had burst into Americans' consciousness six months before by murdering eleven Israeli athletes at the Munich Olympics, kidnapped the American ambassador to the Sudan and his second-in-command. The Americans were seized at a reception at the Saudi embassy in Khartoum, the capital of Sudan. The attack was a consequence of a coup against the prime minister of the Sudan, whose paid relationship with the CIA had just been exposed. "Putting the prime minister on our payroll was just an invitation for trouble and totally unnecessary," said the State Department's Robert Oakley, Reagan's counterterrorism coordinator. "By putting him on the CIA payroll we corrupted him politically and made him extremely vulnerable." The kidnappers in Khartoum demanded that the United States free the convicted murderer of Bobby Kennedy, a Palestinian named Sirhan Sirhan. President Nixon, responding off the top of his head to a reporter's question that day, said the United States would not negotiate with terrorists. The Palestinians, on orders from Yasser Arafat, murdered the two American diplomats in cold blood.

The CIA could not respond because the U.S. government had no policy to guide it. The PLO had been in action for nine years, financed chiefly by the government of Saudi Arabia and the emirs of Kuwait. The fixation at the CIA and throughout the U.S. government with the idea of state-sponsored terrorism continued after the cold war. It made it much harder, twenty years later, for Americans to understand the rise of a rich Saudi who had lived in the Sudan, a self-anointed prince named Osama bin Laden—not a state-sponsored terrorist, but a terrorist who sponsored a state.

The first stirrings of a Middle East peace process after the 1973 Yom Kippur war led the CIA into a new and uncharted territory. In secret, Deputy Director of Central Intelligence Vernon Walters flew to Morocco to meet Ali Hassan Salameh. The meeting was initiated by Yasser Arafat; he was sending a signal that he wanted to be treated as a national leader, not a stateless terrorist. He wanted the PLO to negotiate for the West Bank after the Yom Kippur war. He wanted to establish a Palestinian National Authority. He was trying to establish himself as the moderate voice of Palestinian aspirations. Walters remembered: "Kissinger said, 'I can't send anyone else, because that would be negotiation, and the American Jewish community would go crazy. But you are an intelligence contact.' I said, 'Dr. Kissinger, I'm deputy director of the CIA. I'm probably number six or seven on their hit list.' He replied: 'I'm number one. That's why you're going.' " The meeting bore fruit. The CIA opened up a channel of high-level communications with the PLO. After Salameh returned from Morocco to his base in Lebanon and made contact with the CIA station in Beirut, the PLO intelligence chief began to meet on a regular basis with the CIA's Bob Ames. Walters oral history, FAOH.

Not everybody believed the information that the CIA was buying in Beirut. "They were prisoners of their lousy reports," said Talcott Seelye, who arrived as the American ambassador in Lebanon after his predecessor, Francis Meloy, was murdered while attempting to present his diplomatic credentials in 1976. The Salameh channel lasted for five years, until he was assassinated by Israeli intelligence in 1978. It represented a high-water mark in the CIA's understanding of the roots of rage in the Arab world, a glimmer of insight into who the Palestinians were and what they wanted—the sole and signal triumph of Bill Colby's time as director of central intelligence. Seelye oral history; FAOH; Colby interview with author.

389 *His case officer was Bob Ames*: Ames was "uniquely talented," Bob Gates said in an interview with the author. "I always considered my greatest recruit in my whole life at the agency was recruiting Bob Ames out of the clandestine service to be the head of the CIA analytical office working on the Middle East. And ironically after all of his years in the agency, working in the Middle East in dangerous operations, putting his life on the line, he was in Beirut as chief of the analytical office, visiting the embassy, when he was killed. So he was working for me when he was killed, not the clandestine service. I have often thought that if Bob Ames had lived, the United States might not have intervened in Lebanon and the course of history there might have been changed somewhat."

389 *"the wave of the future"*: Timothy Naftali, *Blind Spot: The Secret History of American Counterterrorism* (New York: Basic, 2005), p. 85.

390 *"the Agency people were busy"*: Dillon oral history, FAOH.

391 *"He was exhilarated to be back"*: Susan M. Morgan, "Beirut Diary," *Studies in Intelligence*, Summer 1983, CIA/CSI. Morgan's recently declassified firsthand account conclusively contradicts several published versions of the Beirut embassy bombing, notably that of the CIA's Bob Baer, who describes Ames's hand being recovered hundreds of yards out in the harbor of Beirut.

391 *"leaving us with too little intelligence"*: Lewis oral history, FAOH.

392 *"Our intelligence about Grenada was lousy"*: Clarridge interview for the CNN Cold War Series, 1998, National Security Archive transcript available online at http://www2.gwu.edu/~nsarchiv/coldwar/interviews/episode-18/ clarridge1.html.

392 *"The CIA had a plan to form a government"*: Gillespie oral history, FAOH.

Chapter Forty

394 *"There was a presidential finding signed by Ronald Reagan"*: Wells interview with author.

395 *"To save his own ass"*: O'Neill oral history, FAOH.

396 *"The Reagan Administration took a covert operation"*: Korn interview with author and oral history, FAOH.

397 *"Casey's recommendation to kidnap Mughniyah"*: Oakley oral history, FAOH.

398 *"Reagan was preoccupied with the fate of the hostages and could not understand why CIA could not locate and rescue them"*: Robert M. Gates, *From the Shadows: The Ultimate Insider's Story of Five Presidents and How They Won the Cold War* (New York: Simon and Schuster, 1996), p. 397.

398 *"the Agency had to reach outside itself"*: McMahon interview with author.

399 *"the mines has got to be the solution!"*: Clarridge interview for the CNN Cold War Series, 1998, National Security Archive transcript available online at http://www2.gwu.edu/~nsarchiv/coldwar/interviews/episode-18/clarridge1.html. The late Senator Daniel Patrick Moynihan, then the ranking Democrat on the intelligence committee, described the CIA's defamation of Senator Goldwater in an interview with the author. In 1984, while cutting off funds for the *contras*, Congress approved a CIA covert operation to spend more than $2 million to ensure the election of the Christian Democrat Jose Napoleon Duarte as president of El Salvador, while blunting the candidacy of the death-squad leader Roberto d'Aubuisson.

400 *"He was running a great risk"*: Gates, *From the Shadows*, p. 315.

Chapter Forty-one

401 *"It could be a breakthrough"*: Ronald Reagan, *An American Life* (New York: Simon and Schuster, 1990), pp. 501–502. Unless otherwise noted, the facts, figures, and quotations concerning the Iran-*contra* affair in this chapter are taken from the records of the joint congressional committee and the final report of the independent counsel team that investigated the fiasco.

403 *"We received a draft secret executive order telling us to go knock off terrorists in pre-emptive strikes"*: McMahon interview with author.

406 *"North's rationale"*: Kelly oral history, FAOH.

406 *"the CIA was corrupted"*: Wilcox oral history, FAOH.

407 *"get that plane the hell out of Costa Rica!"*: CIA interview with Joseph Fernandez, CIA Office of the Inspector General, January 24, 1987.

407 *"The intelligence we passed to them"*: Oakley oral history, FAOH.

407–08 *"The person who managed this whole affair was Casey"*: Sofaer oral history in Deborah Hart Strober and Gerald S. Strober, *Reagan: The Man and His Presidency* (Boston: Houghton Mifflin, 1998), p. 500.

409 *"The meeting was an unmitigated disaster"*: James McCullough, "Personal Reflections on Bill Casey's Last Month at CIA," *Studies in Intelligence*, Summer 1995, commentary by David Gries, CIA/CSI.

410 *"No scandal and a good many solid successes"*: Casey's remarkable talking points are cited in Douglas F. Garthoff, "Directors of Central Intelligence as Leaders of the U.S. Intelligence Community, 1946–2005," 2006, CIA/CSI. These words are part of the strong body of circumstantial evidence suggesting that Casey's brain tumor sparked otherwise inexplicable conduct during his last eighteen months as director of central intelligence. His divorce from reality in those days was exemplified by his romance with Renamo, the Mozambique National Resistance Movement. Renamo was a black guerrilla army created by the white racists of South Africa and Rhodesia and the most vicious rebel force afoot in the region. Trained, armed, and financed by BOSS, the South African intelligence service, Renamo used tactics including "the cutting off of ears, the severing of limbs and breasts, and general mutilation," said Ambassador Chas W. Freeman, Jr., who oversaw African affairs under President Reagan. "This mutilation became the norm, and perhaps half a million people perished." Renamo was "reminiscent of the Khmer Rouge in Cambodia," said James Bishop, the principal State Department officer for African political and military affairs, "vicious and excessive in its use of terrorism."

Casey told President Reagan that Renamo deserved the CIA's support as freedom fighters in the global war on communism. His tactics included the "cooking of intelligence to magnify the impact of Renamo," said Ambassador Freeman. Barred from direct support to the rebels, Casey took another tack. In 1986, after a ten-year ban, Congress took his word and revived covert military aid to the CIA's favored armies in Angola, including Stinger missiles, antitank weapons, and tons of automatic weapons. The agency had been backing one Angolan faction or another off and on for thirty years. The renewal of the Angola program opened an arms pipeline from the agency that ran through South Africa and depended on the apartheid regime's support. The most powerful American diplomats involved in the region strongly suspected that Casey opened up a back channel of lethal aid to the renegades of Renamo. "Casey, who was prone to follow his own foreign policy, indeed did become, to some extent, involved with Renamo, against the declared policy, and indeed the strongly held internal policy of the administration," Ambassador Freeman said.

"Casey set out to destroy our diplomacy" in southern Africa, said Frank G. Wisner, Jr. "And he almost succeeded." FAOH interviews.

410 *"Bill Casey had a lot to answer for"*: McCullough, "Personal Reflections."

411 *"a job no one else seemed to want"*: Robert M. Gates, *From the Shadows: The Ultimate Story of Five Presidents and How They Won the Cold War* (New York: Simon and Schuster, 1996), p. 414. Gates had to go to Capitol Hill to answer for his nomination. "How do you like the job so far?" a newspaper photographer asked. Gates replied with the twangy title of a country-and-western hit: "Take This Job and Shove it." An open microphone caught him. Everyone knew the next line of the song: "I ain't working here no more."

411 *"It quickly became clear that he was too close"*: Webster interview with author.

412 *"The clandestine service is the heart and soul of the agency"*: Gates interview with author.

Chapter Forty-two

413 *"It took me months to get a clear understanding"*: Webster interview with author.

414 *"No one else can understand it"*: Thompson interview with author.

414 *"We probably could have overcome Webster's ego"*: Duane R. Clarridge with Digby Diehl, *A Spy for All Seasons: My Life in the CIA* (New York: Scribner, 1997), p. 371.

414 *"A point Dick Helms made"*: Webster interview with author.

415 *"Congress doesn't believe you"*: Webster interview with author.

415 *Clarridge briefly considered fighting back*: Clarridge, *A Spy for All Seasons*, pp. 381–386.

416 *"American intelligence was generous with him," Gorbachev remarked*: Politburo minutes, September 28, 1986, Cold War International History Project, Woodrow Wilson Center.

417 *"an exercise, nothing more"*: Webster interview with author.

417 *Florentino Aspillaga Lombard*: It is hard to overstate how devastating was the realization that Castro's intelligence service had outsmarted the CIA for twenty straight years. Nor was Aspillaga's 1987 defection the end of it. On September 21, 2001, the FBI arrested Ana Belen Montes, the senior Cuba analyst for the Defense Intelligence Agency, who confessed six months later that she had been spying for Cuba since 1985. Hundreds of spies from Cuba's Direccion General de Inteligencia, the DGI, have lived and worked in the United States ever since the Bay of Pigs, according to former members of the Cuban service who have defected. They operate as diplomats and cab drivers, dealers of guns and drugs and information. The Cuban intelligence service, which reports to Defense Minister Raul Castro, Fidel's brother, has infiltrated Cuban exile groups and U.S. government agencies with notable success. Take the case of José Rafael Fer-

nández Brenes, who jumped ship from a Cuban merchant vessel in 1988. Embraced by American intelligence, he helped set up and run TV Marti, the U.S. government–financed station that beamed anti-Castro information and propaganda at Cuba, from 1988 to 1991. The Cuban government jammed TV Marti's signal the moment it went on the air in March 1990—thanks to the data supplied by Fernández Brenes. Then there was Francisco Avila Azcuy, who ran operations for Alpha 66, one of the most violent anti-Castro exile groups, all the while reporting secretly to the FBI—and Cuban intelligence. Avila planned a 1981 raid on Cuba, telling both the FBI and the DGI all about it. His information helped convict seven members of Alpha 66 for violating the Neutrality Act by planning an attack on a foreign nation from U.S. soil. Tim Weiner, "Castro's Moles Dig Deep, Not Just into Exiles," *The New York Times,* March 1, 1996.

419 *"they actually did something right"*: Lilley interview with author.

419 *a brilliant plot against the Abu Nidal Organization*: Tom Twetten interview with author. The best summary of the operation is Timothy Naftali, *Blind Spot: The Secret History of American Counterterrorism* (New York: Basic, 2005), pp. 196–198.

420 *half-baked insurgency*: John H. Kelly oral history, FAOH. Kelly became assistant secretary of state for Near Eastern Affairs in June 1989.

420 *grudge match*: In a May 1, 1987, letter to President Reagan, Son Sann, the president of the Khmer People's National Liberation Front, the intended recipient of the CIA's aid, warned against "improved US-Vietnam relations" and cautioned Reagan against "moderation" toward "the main Soviet proxy in Southeast Asia." Son Sann's letter and Powell's memo to Reagan warning against a resurgent Khmer Rouge were both declassified May 28, 1999.

420 *"One by one we killed them"*: Howard Hart remarks, Miller Center of Public Affairs, University of Virginia, September 7, 2005.

421 *"we don't have any plan"*: Twetten interview with author.

421 *"drastically reduce our assistance to the real radicals"*: Oakley oral history, FAOH.

Chapter Forty-three

423 *"Casey saw him as a protégé"*: Davis oral history, FAOH.

423 *"The CIA, who had dealt with him for so long"*: Pastorino oral history, FAOH.

424 *"As a former deputy director of the CIA"*: Dachi oral history, FAOH.

424 *The CIA's Don Winters testified*: Trial transcripts of *United States v. Manuel Noriega.*

425 *"Saddam Hussein was known to be a brutal dictator"*: Wilcox oral history, FAOH.

426 *"The arrested agents were tortured to death"*: Giraldi interview, Balkananaly sis.com, July 30, 2006. The author interviewed Giraldi in 1994 and 1995. Leaving aside the human tragedy of the agents' deaths, the CIA's reporting and analysis on Iran was consistently off the mark during this period. In the summer of 1987, during the final agonies of the Iran-Iraq War, Iran was harassing Kuwaiti oil tankers at sea. The ships then were placed under the American flag and protected by navy warships. The CIA assessed the situation in the Persian Gulf and strongly advised an end to the reflagging operation. The question went to the national security adviser, Frank Carlucci, the former deputy director of central intelligence. "The Agency produced a report which essentially said no military confrontation with Iran would work," Carlucci said. "The Iranians provoked us and we sank half their Navy in twenty-four hours. They went back and put their ships in the harbor, so we were able to sail with impunity in the Gulf. The CIA was wrong." Carlucci oral history, FAOH.

426 *"Is Iraq Bluffing?"*: Richard L. Russell, "CIA's Strategic Intelligence in Iraq," *Political Science Quarterly,* Summer 2002. Russell served for seventeen years as a political-military analyst at CIA.

426 *"I did sound the warning bell"*: Charles Allen remarks, "Intelligence: Cult, Craft, or Business?" Program on Information Resources Policy, Harvard University, April 6, 2000.

426 *King Hussein of Jordan told the president*: Memorandum of telephone conversation, with King Hussein, July 31, 1990, GHWBL.

427 *"there wasn't much intelligence"*: James A. Baker III with Thomas M. DeFrank, *The Politics of Diplomacy: Revolution, War and Peace, 1989–1992* (New York: Putnam, 1995), p. 7.

427 *"an unfortunately quite typical pattern"*: Freeman oral history, FAOH. On January 10, 1991, the CIA warned the White House and the Pentagon that "Saddam Hussein almost certainly will unleash a major terrorist campaign against Western—particularly U.S.—interests. Multiple, simultaneous attacks are likely to occur in several geographic regions—possibly including the United States—in an effort to capture maximum publicity and sow widespread panic." There was never any evidence that Iraqi intelligence cells had penetrated the United States, but the CIA and the FBI did track at least three groups of Iraqi military officers in the Middle East and Asia and captured them in the days immediately before the American attack on Iraq. CIA, "Terrorism Review," January 10, 1991, CIA/FOIA.

429 *" 'CIA hadn't a clue' "*: Clarke interview, *Frontline,* "The Dark Side," January 23, 2006, edited transcript available online at http://www.pbs.org/wgbh/pages/frontline/darkside/interviews/clarke.html.

429 *"a tidal wave of history"*: Robert M. Gates, *From the Shadows: The Ultimate In-*

sider's Story of Five Presidents and How They Won the Cold War (New York: Simon and Schuster, 1996), p. 449. Gates oversaw a National Security Council staff under Bush filled with experts who disdained the work of the analysts Gates had led at the CIA. Ambassador Robert D. Blackwill was the NSC staff man for Soviet and European affairs in 1989 and 1990. "The Agency was still putting out gobs of analytic products that I never read," he said. "During the two years I did not read a single [National Intelligence] Estimate. Not one. And except for Gates, I do not know of anyone at the NSC who did." Blackwill quoted in Jack Davis, "A Policymaker's Perspective on Intelligence Analysis," *Studies in Intelligence,* Vol. 38, No. 5, 1995, CIA/CSI.

429 *"the basic elements of Soviet defense policy":* NIE 11–3/8–88, "Soviet Forces and Capabilities for Strategic Nuclear Conflict Through the Late 1990s," December 1, 1988, CIA/CSI.

429 *"people would have been calling for my head":* MacEachin cited in Kirsten Lundberg, "CIA and the Fall of the Soviet Empire: The Politics of 'Getting It Right,'" Case Study C16-94-1251.0, Harvard University, 1994, pp. 30–31.

430 *"He'd never once been there":* Palmer oral history, FAOH.

430 *"They talked about the Soviet Union":* Crowe oral history, FAOH.

430 *"What are we going to do when the Wall comes down?":* Walters quoted in David Fischer oral history, FAOH.

430 *"there were no Soviet spies":* If there was ever a time for the CIA to press hard to understand why those spies had died, it was during the collapse of the Soviet Union, in 1990 and 1991. "When I was [first] nominated to be director in 1987 I had lunch with Dick Helms," Bob Gates told me. "And I remember Helms wagging his finger at me at the lunch in the Director's dining room, it was just the two of us, we were all by ourselves, and him telling me, *never go home at night without wondering where the mole is.*" In 1992, in the last months of Bob Gates's short turn as director of central intelligence, the case began to be resolved. Aldrich Ames was arrested in February 1994. Gates interview with author.

431 *"It was easy, once upon a time, for the CIA to be unique":* Bearden interview with author.

431 *"The ultimate tragedy is spiritual":* Giraldi interview with author.

431 *"this was rapidly evolving into a very bad situation":* Arnold Donahue, "Perspectives on U.S. Intelligence," Program on Information Resources, Harvard University, April 1998.

432 *"Sitting alone in the vice president's office was surrealistic":* Michael J. Sulick, "As the USSR Collapsed: A CIA Officer in Lithuania," *Studies in Intelligence,* Vol. 50, No. 2, 2006, CIA/CSI.

433 *"Adjust or die":* Gates note and announcement to CIA employees cited in Douglas F. Garthoff, "Directors of Central Intelligence as Leaders of the U.S.

Intelligence Community, 1946–2005," 2006, CIA/CSI. Garthoff worked at CIA from 1972 to 1999, serving many years as an analyst of Soviet affairs under Gates.

433   *"We have lost"*: Richard Kerr, "The Evolution of the U.S. Intelligence System in the Post-Soviet Era," Program on Information Resources, Harvard University, Spring 1992.

434   *"19-year-olds on two-year rotations"*: MacEachin cited in Robert Steele, "Private Enterprise Intelligence: Its Potential Contribution to National Security," paper delivered at conference on Intelligence Analysis and Assessment, Ottawa, Canada, October 22–29, 1994. Steele is a CIA veteran who champions open-source analysis.

434   *"Tensions rising as budget pinches"*: Gates note cited in Garthoff, "Directors of Central Intelligence."

Chapter Forty-four

439   *"immense democratic and entrepreneurial opportunity"*: Anthony Lake, "From Containment to Enlargment," Johns Hopkins University School of Advanced International Studies, September 21, 1993.

440   *he would be the next director of central intelligence*: Bill Clinton charmed most of the CIA briefers, who came to Little Rock, holed up in $38.50-a-night motel rooms at the Comfort Inn by the airport, and drove out to the governor's mansion to school him. But they were never quite sure how much he was really taking in. John L. Helgerson. *Getting to Know the President: CIA Briefings of Presidential Candidates, 1952–1992*, CIA/CSI.

440   *"Admiral, I didn't know"* and *"I didn't have a bad relationship"*: Woolsey remarks, Council on Foreign Relations, May 12, 2004; Woolsey interview with author.

440   *"nobody's seen the president"*: Twetten interview with author.

441   *dozens of covert-action proposals during his first two years in office*: While the precise number remains classified, "the Clinton administration requested a remarkable number of covert action proposals to deal with the increasingly troublesome array of problems it faced in the early 1990s, only to conclude that covert action could not save the United States from overt military intervention," in the words of John MacGaffin, the number-two man in the clandestine service under Clinton and the author's downstairs neighbor after he left the CIA. By the way, MacGaffin never leaked. See his "Spies, Counterspies, and Covert Action," in Jennifer E. Sims and Burton Gerber (eds.) *Transforming U.S. Intelligence* (Washington, DC: Georgetown University Press, 2005), pp. 79–95.

441   *"No harsher test was there than Somalia"*: Wisner oral history, FAOH.

442   *"the intelligence failure in Somalia"*: Crowe oral history, FAOH. Before the ad-

miral took over the President's Foreign Intelligence Advisory Board, he had to tell President Clinton what it was: "Early in the Administration, the President and I talked about what I would like to do," Crowe recalled. "I said, 'PFIAB,' and he said, 'What's PFIAB?' So I had to tell him what it was."

442 *Not long after dawn on January 25*: The events of January 25, 1993, are reconstructed from a report that Nick Starr filed for the CIA's in-house newsletter and from court records. Four and a half years later, the killer, Mir Amal Kansi, was arrested in Pakistan in a rendition operation coordinated by the CIA and backed by a $2 million reward. He said the murders were an act of vengeance for American foreign policy in the Middle East. The state of Virginia convicted him of murder and put him to death by lethal injection.

443 *"a member of the Central Intelligence Agency in Khartoum"*: O'Neill oral history, FAOH.

444 *"But the CIA eventually concluded"*: Intelligence memorandum, "Iraq: Baghdad Attempts to Assassinate Former President Bush," CIA Counterterrorist Center, July 12, 1993, CIA/FOIA.

444 *"proportionate to the attack on President Bush"*: Tim Weiner, "Attack Is Aimed at the Heart of Iraq's Spy Network," *The New York Times*, June 27, 1993.

444 *"Saddam tries to assassinate"*: Woolsey remarks, Restoration Weekend, Palm Beach, Florida, November 16, 2002.

445 *Many of its leaders had been on the CIA's payroll for years*: Tim Weiner with Steve Engelberg and Howard French, "CIA Formed Haitian Unit Later Tied to Narcotics Trade," *The New York Times*, November 14, 1993. A brief portrait of one of the CIA's men in Haiti, taken from that article: Among the military officers who took the agency's cash and led the Haitian intelligence service was Colonel Ernst Prudhomme, a member of the anti-Aristide junta that seized power in Haiti. On November 2, 1989, while he held the title of chief of national security and received the CIA's largesse, he led a brutal interrogation of Evans Paul, the mayor of Haiti's capital, Port-au-Prince. The interrogation left the mayor with five broken ribs and internal injuries. "Prudhomme himself never touched me," Paul said. "He played the role of the intellectual, the man who searched carefully for contradictions in your account—the man who seemed to give direction to the whole enterprise. He wanted to present me to the world as a terrorist. . . . He seemed to have so much information about my life, all the way from my childhood. It was if he had been following me step by step."

445 *"the Thomas Jefferson of Haiti"*: Woolsey remarks, Council on Foreign Relations, May 12, 2004.

445 *a CIA study saying half a million people might die*: Tim Weiner, "Critics Say U.S. Ignored C.I.A. Warnings of Genocide in Rwanda," *The New York Times*, March 26, 1998. It was hard to see what the CIA could have done

to prevent the slaughter even if the White House had the will, for it had
no one stationed in Rwanda. "The CIA was not very helpful in terms of
internal African politics. Never had been," said Clinton's ambassador in
Rwanda, Robert E. Gribbin III, a professional diplomat with long service
on the continent. "They weren't particularly interested in it."

445 *The president's response to Rwanda*: That response came in a major foreign
policy order called Presidential Decision Directive 25. Dated May 3, 1994,
and still largely classified, it aimed to make the United Nations take the
lead in peacekeeping operations.

446 *"Frankenstein's creature"*: James Monnier Simon, Jr., "Managing Domestic, Military, and Foreign Policy Requirements: Correcting Frankenstein's
Blunder," in Sims and Gerber, *Transforming U.S. Intelligence,* pp. 149–161.

Chapter Forty-five

449 *"I know what the Soviet Union is really all about"*: Ames interview with author.

449 *"Their names were given to the Soviet intelligence service"*: Hitz interview with
author.

451 *"You have to wonder whether the CIA has become no different from any other bureaucracy"*: Glickman interview with author.

451 *"I would disembowel the CIA"*: Odom interview with author.

451 *"The place just needs a total overhaul"*: Specter interview with author.

452 *"What does it all mean now?"*: Aspin interview with author.

452 *"Our goal is to sell intelligence"*: Snider quoted in Loch K. Johnson, "The
Aspin-Brown Intelligence Inquiry: Behind the Closed Doors of a Blue
Ribbon Commission," *Studies in Intelligence,* Fall 2004, CIA/CSI.

453 *"Counterterrorism received little attention"*: Johnson, "The Aspin-Brown Intelligence Inquiry."

453 *"inadequote numbers of people on the front line"*: Hitz interview with the author.

Chapter Forty-six

454 *"The president asked me whether I was interested in being the director of central
intelligence"*: Deutch interview with author.

455 *"Plagued by poor leadership, the Agency is adrift"*: John A. Gentry, "A Framework for Reform of the U.S. Intelligence Community," available online
at http://www.fas.org/irp/gentry/. Gentry had been a CIA analyst for
twelve years.

456 *"seeing it as nothing but trouble"*: Helms interview with author.

457 *Eight thousand people were dead, and the agency had missed it*: Stephen

Engelberg and Tim Weiner with Raymond Bonner and Jane Perlez, "Srebrenica: The Days of Slaughter," *The New York Times,* October 29, 1995.

457 *the CIA's Paris station had run an elaborate operation*: Tim Weiner, "C.I.A. Confirms Blunders During Economic Spying on France," *The New York Times,* March 13, 1996.

458 *The division was a world apart at the CIA*: Tim Weiner, "More Is Told About C.I.A. in Guatemala," *The New York Times,* April 25, 1995.

459 *"The CIA station in Guatemala was about twice the size it needed to be"*: Stroock interview with author.

459 *"The chief of station came into my office"*: McAfee interview with author.

461 *"Let me explain life to you"*: Tenet interview with author.

461 *"Dick Clarke came to me and said, 'They're going to blow you up' "*: Lake interview with author.

463 *the agency conspired with an Iraqi exile named Ayad Alawi*: In May 2004, a year into the American occupation of Iraq, the United States propelled Alawi into the post of prime minister. Despite his articulateness and ambition, he was not a political success. The near-universal knowledge of his long-standing ties to the CIA was not counted in his favor.

463 *an old and troubled romance*: In the summer of 1972, the agency delivered a $5.38 million package of aid and arms personally approved by Nixon and Kissinger "to assist . . . the Iraqi Kurds in their resistance against the Ba'athi Iraqi regime," in Kissinger's words. Kissinger then sold the Kurds down the river two years later, abandoning American support for their cause in order to pacify the shah of Iran, who had grown fearful of an independent Kurdish state. Kissinger memo, undated but on or about July 31, 1971, in FRUS, 1969–1972. Vol. E-4, document 322, declassified September 2006.

463 *"The Saddam case was an interesting case"*: Lowenthal interview with author.

464 *"It would have been a great challenge"*: Lake interview with author.

464 *"a dancing bear in a political circus"*: Lake interview with author.

464 *"It is impossible to overstate the turbulence"*: Hitz interview with author.

464 *Its ability to collect and analyze secrets was falling apart*: A strong encryption program called PGP, for Pretty Good Privacy, had been available for free on the World Wide Web since the end of the cold war. On March 20, 1997, the deputy director of the National Security Agency, William Crowell, told Congress: "If all the personal computers in the world—260 million computers—were put to work on a single PGP-encrypted message, it would still take an estimated 12 million times the age of the universe, on average, to break a single message." How was American intelligence going to unscramble that? Crowell testimony, House Judiciary Subcommittee on Courts and Intellectual Property, March 20, 1997.

464–65 *"great successes are rare and failure is routine"*: "IC21: The Intelligence Community in the 21st Century," Staff Study, House Permanent Select Committee on Intelligence, 1996.

465 *The careers of three years' worth of CIA trainees were blighted*: Completion of
the CIA's training course was no guarantee of success when stationed
overseas. Jim Olson, who served as chief of station in Moscow, Vienna,
and Mexico City, told the story of a bright young couple who reported to
him as newly minted case officers. She was a lawyer, he was an engineer.
"I had high hopes for them," he recounted. But after less than a week,
they told him that they had ethical qualms about recruiting agents "under false pretenses. They said they simply could not bring themselves to
mislead and manipulate innocent people that way." Of course, that is
what CIA officers overseas do for a living. The couple could not be sal-
vaged. They quit, and wound up driving a long-haul tractor trailer in tandem. Olson was "very curious why their moral reservations had not
turned up in training." It turned out that they had indeed expressed their
fears, but their instructors told them not to worry—that "everything
would be fine once they got to their first assignment." Everything was
not fine. Olson, *Fair Play: The Moral Dilemmas of Spying* (Washington, DC:
Potomac, 2006), pp. 251–252. A 2003 graduate of the CIA's training
school., T. J. Waters, has reported similar misfeasance by his instructors.
There seems to be a problem down on the Farm. T. J. Waters, *Class 11: Inside the Largest Spy Class in CIA History* (New York: Dutton, 2006).

465 *"depth, breadth, and expertise"*: Report of House Permanent Select Committee on Intelligence, Representative Porter J. Goss, Chairman, June
18, 1997.

466 *"From the vantage point of 2001 . . . intelligence failure is inevitable"*: Russ Travers, "The Coming Intelligence Failure," *Studies in Intelligence*, 1997,
CIA/CSI. Travers wrote: "Failure may be of the traditional variety: we fail
to predict the fall of a friendly government; we do not provide sufficient
warning of a surprise attack against one of our allies or interests; we are
completely surprised by a state-sponsored terrorist attack; or we fail to detect an unexpected country acquiring a weapon of mass destruction. Or it
may take a more nontraditional form: we overstate numerous threats
leading to tens of billions of dollars of unnecessary expenditures; database
errors lead to a politically unacceptable number of casualties in a peace-
enforcement operation; or an operation does not go well. . . . In the end,
we may not suffer a Pearl Harbor, but simply succumb to a series of mistakes that raises questions about an intelligence budget that dwarfs the
entire defense budget of most countries. The Community will try to explain the failure(s) away, and it will legitimately point to extenuating circumstances. But we are going to begin making more and bigger mistakes

more often. It is only a matter of time before the results rise to the level of acknowledged intelligence failure. . . . The reasons will be simple: we have gotten away from basics—the collection and unbiased analysis of facts."

Chapter Forty-seven

467   *"We were nearly bankrupt"*: Tenet testimony, 9/11 Commission, April 14, 2004; Tenet remarks, Kutztown University, April 27, 2005. Tenet testified that he inherited a CIA "whose dollars were declining and whose expertise was ebbing. . . . The infrastructure to recruit, train, and sustain officers for our clandestine service—the nation's human intelligence capability—was in disarray. . . . Our information systems were becoming obsolescent during the greatest information technology change in our lifetimes."

467   *the fifty greatest*: The list of the CIA's "Trailblazers" included Robert Ames, lost in the Beirut embassy bombing of 1983; Dick Bissell, progenitor of the U-2 and the Bay of Pigs; Jamie Critchfield, who had run the Gehlen organization; Allen Dulles, the Great White Case Officer; Richard Lehman, whose briefings Dulles had judged by their heft; Art Lundahl, the photointerpreter in the Cuban missile crisis; Tony Mendez, the master of disguise; and, of course, Frank Wisner, the avatar of covert action.

467   *"The only remaining superpower"*: Helms interview with author.

467   *"The trust that was reposed in the CIA has faded"*: Schlesinger interview with author.

468   *"Intelligence isn't just something for the cold war"*: Goss interview with author.

468   *"a very disturbing event"*: Charles Allen remarks, "Intelligence: Cult, Craft, or Business?" Program on Information Resources Policy, Harvard University, April 6, 2000.

468   *"The likelihood of a cataclysmic warning failure is growing"*: Mary O. McCarthy, "The Mission to Warn: Disaster Looms," *Defense Intelligence Journal*, Vol. 7, No. 2, 1998.

469   *Tenet decided to cancel the operation*: The blow-by-blow is in the 9/11 Commission report.

469   *"We will need much better intelligence on this facility"*: McCarthy quoted in 9/11 Commission report.

470   *"It was a mistake"*: Petterson oral history, FAOH.

470   *"The decision to target al Shifa"*: Carney interview with author. I covered the Nairobi bombings and the al Shifa aftermath for *The New York Times;* interviews for the latter story included senior CIA, NSC, State, and Defense officials. They were conducted on background and sadly must re-

main there, but two were with members of the "Small Group," the highest national-security circle, whose six members included the national security adviser and the director of central intelligence. Clinton's sexual dalliances with an intern had just become public, and the officials I interviewed were not quite sure what they believed anymore. But they put up a good show.

470 *"a catastrophic systemic intelligence failure"*: Cited in "Counterterrorism Intelligence Capabilities and Performance Prior to 9/11," House intelligence committee hearing, September 5, 2002. The sense that something terrible was about to happen was unbearable for some members of the intelligence community. Three weeks after that September 11, 1998, warning, John Millis, a veteran clandestine service officer who was the staff director for chairman Porter Goss at the House intelligence committee, gave a speech to CIA retirees. Millis said the agency was drowning in meaningless data, short on brainpower, approaching collapse. "People used to come to us and brag that CIA is the 911 of the government," he mused. "Well, if you're dialing 911, intelligence has already lost." Millis blew his head off with a shotgun in a seedy motel outside Washington on June 4, 2000.

470 *"in ten years we won't be relevant"*: Tenet interview with author.

471 *"to use deception, to use manipulation, to use, frankly, dishonesty"*: Smith interview with author.

471 *"people that are a little different"*: Gates interview with author.

473 *gung-ho became go slow*: Gary Schroen's accounts of the misfires against bin Laden are in his 9/11 Commission testimony. He summed it up years later: "We didn't do enough. We didn't penetrate bin Laden's inner circle; we still haven't. So, yeah, there was a failure." Schroen interview, *Frontline*, "The Dark Side," January 20, 2006, edited transcript available online at http://www.pbs.org/wgbh/pages/frontline/darkside/interviews/schroen.html.

473 *"the United States had the capability to remove Osama bin Laden"*: MacGaffin, "Spies, Counterspies, and Covert Action," in Jennifer E. Sims and Burton Gerber (eds.), *Transforming U.S. Intelligence* (Washington, DC: Georgetown University Press, 2005).

473 *The Afghans kept tracking bin Laden's travels*: The pursuit of bin Laden and the hesitation of the CIA, the Pentagon, and the White House are detailed in the 9/11 Commission report.

474 *"The bombing of the Chinese embassy"*: Vice Admiral Thomas R. Wilson, Harvard Seminar on Intelligence, Command, and Control, Program on Information Resources Policy, November 2001.

475 *"You Americans are crazy"*: 9/11 Commission report, "Intelligence Policy," Staff Statement No. 7.

475 *"The threat could not be more real"*: Tenet cited in 9/11 Commission report.

475 *"a lot of money"*: Clarke testimony in 9/11 Commission report.

476 *Al Qaeda was the obvious suspect*: The pre- and post-election briefings of George Bush by the CIA and Bill Clinton are in the 9/11 Commission report. The bombing of the USS *Cole* brought an unusually vehement attack from John Lehman, the secretary of the navy during the Reagan administration. He raged at "the obscene failure of intelligence" in the attack in an opinion article published in the *Washington Post* three days afterward. "But of course, no one could be surprised by intelligence failure. In 14 years of government service in three administrations I observed many historic crises, and in every one the consolidated product of the intelligence bureaucracy either failed to provide warning, as in Kuwait, or was grossly wrong in its assessment. . . . But nothing is ever done. *Cole* is the latest victim of a $30 billion jobs program that takes the most wondrous products of space and electronic technology and turns them into useless mush."

Chapter Forty-eight

477 *"why a foreseeable disaster went unforeseen"*: James Monnier Simon, Jr., Seminar on Intelligence, Command, and Control, Program of Information Resources Policy, Harvard University, July 2001.

178 *"cut off from the realities of the outside world by their antiquated information technologies"*: I had heard tales of how bad the CIA's work stations and information technologies were, but I never fully understood them until Bruce Berkowitz, a former CIA officer and a highly respected consultant to the agency, published the hard facts in *Studies in Intelligence* in 2003. "Analysts know far less about new information technology and services than do their counterparts in the private sector and other government organizations," he wrote after spending a year at the agency as a CIA scholar in residence. "On average, they seem about five years or more behind. Many analysts seem unaware of data that are available on the Internet and from other non-CIA sources." He said the message from CIA managers was: "that technology is a threat, not a benefit; that the CIA does not put a high priority on analysts using IT easily or creatively; and, worst of all, that data outside the CIA's own network are secondary to the intelligence mission." Bruce Berkowitz, "Failing to Keep Up with the Information Revolution," *Studies in Intelligence*, Vol. 47, No. 1, 2003, CIA/CSI.

479 *"When these attacks occur, as they likely will"*: Clarke e-mail cited in 9/11 Commission report.

480 *"Either al Qaeda is a threat worth acting against or it is not"*: Clark cited in 9/11 Commission report.

480 *"One hopes they won't be fatal"*: Garrett Jones, "Working with the CIA," *Parameters* (U.S. Army War College Quarterly), Vol. 31, No. 4, Winter 2001–2002. Among the fatal consequences of 9/11, little noticed in the civilian world, was this: by blind chance, the plane that struck the Pentagon killed most if not all of the naval intelligence staff of the Defense Intelligence Agency.

481 *"the dark side"*: Speaking from Camp David on *Meet the Press* on Sunday, September 16, 2001, Cheney said, "We also have to work, though, sort of the dark side, if you will. We've got to spend time in the shadows in the intelligence world. A lot of what needs to be done here will have to be done quietly, without any discussion, using sources and methods that are available to our intelligence agencies, if we're going to be successful."

481 *President Bush issued a fourteen-page top secret directive to Tenet and the CIA*: On January 10, 2007, the existence of the directive was acknowledged in a court filing by the CIA. The secret order authorized the CIA "to detain terrorists" and "to set up detention facilities outside the United States." Declaration of Marilyn A. Dorn, *ACLU v. Department of Defense.*

482 *"What would it have? Well, a thumbprint"*: James M. Simon, Jr., "Analysis, Analysts, and Their Role in Government and Intelligence," Harvard seminar, Program on Information Resources Policy, July 2003.

483 *"I could not not do this"*: Hayden testimony, Senate intelligence committee, May 18, 2006. At this writing, Hayden is running the CIA. He has been articulate about how close to the edge of the law he is willing to go. "We're going to live on the edge," he has said. "My spikes will have chalk on them."

485 *"Not everyone arrested was a terrorist"*: Tenet remarks, Nixon Center Distinguished Service Award Banquet, December 11, 2002. The agency acknowledged in December 2006 that it had been holding fourteen "high-value" prisoners in its secret jails and was transferring them to Guantánamo.

Chapter Forty-nine

486 *He based that statement on the confessions of a single source*: "Postwar Findings," Senate intelligence committee, September 8, 2006.

487 *"It was the wrong thing to do"*: Tenet testimony, July 26, 2006, cited in "Postwar Findings," September 8, 2006.

487 *"We did not have many Iraqi sources"*: James L. Pavitt remarks, Foreign Policy Association, June 21, 2004. The best source the CIA had was provided by the French intelligence service, which had cultivated Naji Sabri, Iraq's foreign minister, as its agent. Sabri said that Saddam did not have an active nuclear or biological weapons program. Evidently his reporting was rejected. Sabri was the man to whom Tenet referred in a February 5,

2004, speech, when he said the CIA had had "a source who had direct access to Saddam and his inner circle." The CIA had almost no ability to analyze accurately what little intelligence it had. Its experts were few and far between, and they were supported by scores of rookies. After 9/11, "analysts unfamiliar with terrorism, al-Qaida, or Southwest Asia were scrambling to get up to speed on their new assignments," noted the CIA veteran Bruce Berkowitz. "Months later, people were still rearranging furniture, remodeling offices, and rewiring computers." Berkowitz, "Failing to Keep Up with the Information Revolution," *Studies in Intelligence*, Vol. 47, No. 1, 2003, CIA/CSI.

488 *"If we are not believed, we have no purpose"*: Richard Helms, "Intelligence in American Society," *Studies in Intelligence*, Vol. 11, No. 3, Summer 1967, CIA/CSI. The article was adapted from a speech Helms gave to the Council on Foreign Relations on April 17, 1967.

489 *"Ultimately, I think, the Iraqis were right"*: Duelfer remarks, Miller Center of Public Affairs, University of Virginia, April 22, 2005.

489 *"We were bereft of any human intelligence"*: David Kay, "Weapons of Mass Destruction: Lessons Learned and Unlearned," *Miller Center Report*, Vol. 20, No. 1, Spring/Summer 2004.

491 *Tenet looked him in the eye*: Colonel Larry Wilkerson, Colin Powell's top military assistant, was there when it happened. "I can still hear George Tenet telling me, and telling my boss in the bowels of the CIA" that the intelligence was rock solid, said Colonel Wilkerson. "I sat in the room looking into his eyes, as did the Secretary of State, and heard it with the firmness that only George could give it. . . . George Tenet assuring Colin Powell that the information he was presenting at the U.N. was ironclad, only to have that same individual call the Secretary on more than one occasion in the ensuing months after the presentation and tell him that central pillars of his presentation were indeed false." Wilkerson remarks, New American Foundation, October 19, 2005; Wilkerson interview, *Frontline*, "The Dark Side," December 13, 2005, edited transcript available online at http://www.pbs.org/wgbh/pages/frontline/darkside/interviews/wilkerson.html.

491 *"I think we did get Saddam Hussein"*: *Off Target: The Conduct of the War and Civilian Casualties in Iraq*, Human Rights Watch, December 2003. The report concluded: "The intelligence for 50 strikes aimed at 55 members of the Iraqi leadership was perfect: not one leader was killed but dozens of civilians died."

491 *The agency had predicted that thousands of Iraqi soldiers and their commanders would surrender*: That was the last word on the eve of the ground attack, said army major general James Thurman, the overall operations director for the invasion. "We were told that by the CIA," said General Thurman.

"And that isn't what happened. We had to fight our way through every town." Thurman quoted in Thomas Ricks, *Fiasco: The American Military Adventure in Iraq* (New York: Penguin, 2006), p. 118.

492 *Major General Abed Hamed Mowhoush, who . . . had turned himself in voluntarily to American forces*: *Command's Responsibility: Detainee Deaths in U.S. Custody in Iraq and Afghanistan*, Human Rights First, February 22, 2006.

492 *"the cause celebre for jihadists"*: declassified excerpt in "Trends in Global Terrorism: Implications for the United States," April 2006, CIA.

493 *"Every Army of liberation"*: Lieutenant General David H. Petraeus, "Learning Counterinsurgency: Observations from Soldiering in Iraq," *Military Review*, January–February 2006. The article is posted in the U.S. Army Professional Writing Collection, available online at http://www.army.mil/professionalwriting/volumes/volume4/april_2006/.

493 *"As Iraq transitions from tyranny to self-determination"*: Pavitt remarks, Foreign Policy Association, June 21, 2004.

493 *too many hours drinking at the Babylon bar*: Lindsay Moran, who quit the clandestine service in 2003 and based her statement on reports from friends and colleagues at the Baghdad station, said: "The climate there is such that you simply cannot conduct standard case officer operations. A male colleague has described it to me as a kind of relentless overage frat party in Baghdad; that is, the case officers, without being able to conduct operations, are just sort of forced to stay on the compound and party." Moran remarks, "U.S. Intelligence Reform and the WMD Commission Report," American Enterprise Institute, May 4, 2005.

493–94 *"They had grave, grave difficulty finding a competent individual"*: Crandall oral history, Association for Diplomatic Studies and Training, Iraq Experience Project, September 20, 2004.

494 *"misinformed, misleading, and just plain wrong"*: Tenet statement, CIA Office of Public Affairs, August 11, 2003.

494 *it no longer mattered much to the White House*: By 2004, it was clear that intelligence analysis was not relied on in making even the most significant national security decisions, wrote Paul Pillar, the national intelligence officer for the Middle East from 2000 to 2005. "What is most remarkable about prewar U.S. intelligence is not that it got things wrong and misled policymakers; it is that it played so small a role in one of the most important U.S. policy decisions in recent decades." Paul Pillar, "Unheeded Intelligence," *Foreign Affairs*, March/April 2006.

494 *"just guessing"*: Bush news conference, September 21, 2004. The president dismissed pessimistic reports from the Baghdad station chief as defeatist drivel.

494 *"We're at war"*: Silberman remarks, "U.S. Intelligence Reform and the WMD Commission Report," American Enterprise Institute, May 4, 2005.

495 *"even more misleading"*: Commission on the Intelligence Capabilities of the United States Regarding Weapons of Mass Destruction, March 31, 2005.

496 *"Those were the two dumbest words I ever said"*: Tenet remarks, Kutztown University, April 27, 2005.

496 *"the meteor strikes on the dinosaurs"*: Richard Kerr, Thomas Wolfe, Rebecca Donegan, and Aris Pappas, "Collection and Analysis on Iraq: Issues for the US Intelligence Community," *Studies in Intelligence,* Vol. 49, No. 3, 2005, CIA/CSI.

496 *"We didn't get the job done"*: Tenet remarks, Kutztown University, April 27, 2005.

496–97 *"We think intelligence is important to win wars"*: Kay, "Weapons of Mass Destruction."

Chapter Fifty

498 *In his farewell at CIA headquarters*: Tenet remarks, CIA Office of Public Affairs, July 8, 2004. Unlike Tenet, Nixon in his own farewell speech had the good grace to quote the full passage about the man in the arena, "whose face is marred by dust and sweat and blood, who strives valiantly, who errs and comes short again and again because there is not effort without error and shortcoming, but who does actually strive to do the deed, who knows the great enthusiasms, the great devotions, who spends himself in a worthy cause, who at the best knows in the end the triumphs of high achievements and who at the worst, if he fails, at least fails while daring greatly."

498 *a painful personal memoir*: George Tenet with Bill Harlow, *At the Center of the Storm: My Years at the CIA* (New York: HarperCollins, 2007). The cited passages are on pages 110 and 232. Tenet did himself no favors by opening the book with a dramatic story about confronting the neoconservative mandarin Richard Perle outside the West Wing of the White House on September 12, 2001, and Perle saying: "Iraq has to pay a price for what happened yesterday." Perle was in France on that day; the quotation was at best a howling error. Tenet's owning up to the CIA's mistakes was admirable as far as it went. But he called himself "a member of a Greek chorus" and "a prop on the set" at Colin Powell's United Nations speech—every passage of which he had defended. He tried to explain away "slam dunk," but he could not. Tenet's book was attacked upon publication from right, left, and center. Among its few defenders were six senior officers who had served Tenet. They wrote an open letter calling him a man with "the courage to acknowledge errors that were made and accept the responsibility that belongs to him and the intelligence community he led."

499 *"I couldn't get a job with CIA today"*: Goss told an interviewer, on camera, in
     a clip transcribed and posted by the leftist filmmaker Michael Moore. "I
     was in CIA from approximately the late 50's to approximately the early
     70's. And it's true I was a case officer, clandestine service officer, and yes, I
     do understand the core mission of the business. I couldn't get a job with
     CIA today. I am not qualified. I don't have the language skills. I, you know,
     my language skills were romance languages and stuff. We're looking for
     Arabists today. I don't have the cultural background probably. And I cer-
     tainly don't have the technical skills."

499 *"a stilted bureaucracy incapable of even the slightest bit of success"*: Goss printed
     statement, House Permanent Select Committee on Intelligence, June 21,
     2004.

499 *"it will take us another five years of work to have the kind of clandestine service
     our country needs"*: Tenet statement for the record, 9/11 Commission, April
     14, 2004.

500 *"We haven't done strategic intelligence for so long"*: Ford interview with au-
     thor.

501 *"It is an organization that thrives through deception"*: Hamre interview with
     author.

501 *"Can CIA meet the ongoing threat?"* Hart remarks, Miller Center of Public
     Affairs, University of Virginia, December 3, 2004.

502 *"We can't get qualified people"*: Smith quoted in *CIA Support Functions: Orga-
     nization and Accomplishments of the DDA-DDS Group, 1953–1956*, Vol. 2,
     Chap. 3, p. 128, Director of Central Intelligence Historical Services, de-
     classified March 6, 2001, CIA/CREST.

502 *"I don't want to give aid and comfort to the enemy by telling you how bad I think
     the problem is"*: Goss testimony, Senate intelligence committee, September
     14, 2004.

502 *"I never in my wildest dreams expected I'd be back here"*: Goss transcript, CIA
     Office of Public Affairs, September 24, 2004, declassified July 2005.

502 *He would not wear two hats, like his predecessors. He would wear five*: Within a
     few months, Goss, who preferred not to work a five-day week, was com-
     plaining that he was exhausted: "The jobs I'm being asked to do, the five
     hats I wear, are too much for this mortal," he said in remarks at the
     Ronald Reagan Presidential Library on March 2, 2005.

502 *He forced almost every one of the CIA's most senior officers out the door*: Goss
     sacked the number-two man, Deputy Director of Central Intelligence
     John McLaughlin; the number-three man, Executive Director Buzzy
     Krongard; the chief and the deputy chief of the clandestine service,
     Stephen Kappes and Michael Sulick; the chief of intelligence analysis,
     Jami Miscik; the chief of the counterterrorist center, Robert Grenier; and
     the barons who ran operations in Europe, the Near East, and Asia. In

all, Goss got rid of three dozen of the CIA's top people in a matter of months.

504 *John D. Negroponte*: Born in London in 1939, the son of a Greek shipping magnate, Negroponte had gone to Yale with Goss but gravitated toward the State Department instead of the CIA. After a tour in Saigon, he landed on Henry Kissinger's National Security Council staff, in charge of the Vietnam portfolio. He had been President Reagan's ambassador to Honduras, where he worked closely with the CIA and the brutal Honduran military. Negroponte served for nineteen months as director of national intelligence before stepping down to take the number-two post at the State Department. He left little visible progress behind.

505 *"That sent seismic shudders through the intelligence community"*: Joan A. Dempsey, "The Limitations of Recent Intelligence Reforms," Harvard seminar, Program on Information Resources Policy, February 23, 2006. "We're fighting the last war," Dempsey said. The men and women of American intelligence "spin a lot of wheels trying to deliver on what is expected of them, but in my opinion they just don't have the capabilities surrounding them that really allow them to succeed."

505 *"nobody had any idea of who was doing what where"*: Fingar interview with author.

506 *"And we do not live in the best of worlds"*: *Commission on the Intelligence Capabilities of the United States Regarding Weapons of Mass Destruction*, March 31, 2005.

506 *"the burial ceremony"*: Goss interview with Mark K. Matthews, *Orlando Sentinel*, September 8, 2006.

508 *"the Ethic's Guy"*: *U.S. v. Kyle Dustin Foggo*, United States District Court, San Diego, February 13, 2007.

509 *"The distrust of the Americans increased"*: *U.S. vs. David Passaro*, United States District Court, Raleigh, North Carolina, February 13, 2007.

509 *Arar, who had been seized by the CIA*: In 2003, during the months of Arar's ordeal, President Bush noted in passing that Syria's rulers had left "a legacy of torture" to its people.

514 *"The only remaining superpower"*: Helms interview with author.

INDEX

Muslim Brotherhood, 138
Myers, Dee Dee, 440

Nagy, Imre, 130
Narcotics trade, 421
NASA, 159–60
Nasser, Gamel Abdel, 127, 283
Nasution, Gen., 149, 150
National Committee for a Free
    Europe, 36, 117
National Counterterrorism Center,
    512
National Reconnaissance Office
    (NRO), 239
National Security Act of 1947, 24, 25
National Security Agency (NSA), 186,
    239, 286, 318, 367, 483
  creation of, 51
  Gulf of Tonkin incident, 240,
    241–43
National Security Council (NSC), 24,
    25, 26, 29, 37, 74, 336, 442, 481
National Security Planning Group,
    376–77
National Student Association, 270
Naval Security Group, 240
Nazis used for anti-Soviet activities,
    39, 41–43
Negroponte, John D., 491, 504, 506,
    511
Neher, Leonardo, 213
Nelson, Bill, 348
New York Times, 318, 467, 481
Ngo Dinh Diem, 145, 210, 211, 215,
    217, 218, 219–21, 273
Ngo Dinh Nhu, 214, 219, 220–21
Nguyen Cao Ky, 252, 287–88
Nguyen Van Thieu, 252, 287–88, 301
Nicaragua, 94, 280, 377
  contra insurgency, 380–81, 398–400,
    401, 404, 405, 406–7, 420
  mining of ports by CIA, 399
Nicholson, Harold J., 465
9/11 Commission, 500–1, 504, 511

Nixon, Richard M., xi, 22, 74, 79,
    120, 364, 412, 498
  Bay of Pigs operation, 160, 164
  Cambodia, 304–5
  Castro elimination operations, 157
  Chile coup of 1973, 308, 309, 313,
    315
  China-U.S. rapprochement, 301
  CIA anti-Nixon plot, belief in, 323
  cold war strategy, 297–98
  Covert Operations Study Group
    report, 293–94
  creation of CIA, 40
  disdain for CIA, 291, 292–93
  domestic surveillance by CIA, 318,
    319
  funding for CIA, 313
  Greece, 330
  Guatemala coup of 1954, 103
  Helms and, 291–92
  Helms's firing and Schlesinger's
    appointment as director of
    central intelligence, 322–24
  hostage-taking by terrorists, 394
  Indonesia coup attempt of 1958,
    142, 143, 146
  Italy, 299
  Laos War, 301
  Pentagon Papers, 318, 319
  politicization of CIA estimates, 352
  presidential election of 1960, 165,
    291
  reform/restructuring of CIA, 314–15
  resignation as president, 333
  shah of Iran and, 368
  Soviet Union, 296, 297
  "spontaneous manifestations of
    discontent" in communist
    nations, U.S. promotion of,
    125–26
  Thailand, 303
  Vietnam War, 304–5
  Watergate affair, 321–22, 328, 330
Noel, Jim, 155
Noriega, Gen. Manuel, 351, 423–25
Norland, Don, 383

Venezuela, 193, 222, 280, 458
Vetrov, Col. Vladimir, 385
Viaux, Gen. Roberto, 310–11,
    312–13
Vietnam coup of 1963, 273
  assassination of Diem, 210, 217,
    218, 220–21
  execution of, 219–21
  John Kennedy assassination and, 236
  planning of, 215–18
  political situation prior to, 214–15
  Richardson's removal from, 216–17
Vietnam War, xi, 210–11, 514
  antiwar movement in United States,
    285–87, 295, 336
  Cambodian front, 304–5
  CIA's intelligence on, 244, 247
  CIA's internal divisions regarding,
    265
  CIA's reports for U.S. officials, 238,
    266–67
  commando missions into North
    Vietnam, 211, 213–14, 237–38,
    240
  domino theory and, 246, 267
  Gulf of Tonkin incident, 239–43
  Johnson's fears regarding, 244–45
  order of battle estimates, 267–68
  peace initiatives, 278
  Pentagon Papers, 267, 318–19
  Phoenix program, 340, 481
  political instability in South
    Vietnam, 252
  Strategic Hamlets program, 214
  suppression and falsification of
    reporting on, 267–69
  terrorism used in, 246, 247
  Tet offensive, 287–88
  U.S. counterinsurgency program,
    245–46
  U.S. defeat, predictions of, 248, 269,
    287–88
  U.S. evacuation in 1975, 340–43
  U.S. military escalation in 1965,
    247–48
  See also Laos War

Vinson, Carl, 40
Voice of Liberation, 99, 102

Wali, Abdul, 509
Walker, William, 186
Waller, John, 90
Walters, Gen. Vernon, 189, 319–20,
    321, 327, 328, 335, 395–96, 398,
    424, 430
Ward, Phil, 371
Ward, Terry, 460
Warner, John, 506
Warren, Earl, 227, 234
Warren, Ray, 315
Warren Commission, 226–30, 233–34,
    338
Warriors of Islam, 86
Watergate affair, 320–22, 327, 328,
    329, 330
Weapons of mass destruction, Iraq's
    possession of, 427, 428–29,
    486–91, 492, 494–95, 496
Webster, William, 421, 422, 423, 424,
    506
  appointment as director of central
    intelligence, 411–12
  on Casey, 376
  CIA internal rebellion against,
    413–14
  on Clair George, 415
  Gulf War of 1991, 426
  Helms and, 414
  Iran-contra operation, 413
  Soviet penetration of CIA, 416–17
Weinberger, Caspar W., 376–77, 405
Weir, Benjamin, 396, 402
Weisband, William Wolf, 51
Weisl, Edwin, 225
Welch, Richard, 334
Wells, Timothy, 394–96
Western Enterprises, 59–60
Westmoreland, Gen. William, 267–68,
    287, 288
Whelan, Thomas, 94

PHOTOGRAPHY CREDITS